Special Edition

USING
MICROSOFT
FRONTPAGE 97

by Dennis Jones and Neil Randall

Special Edition Using Microsoft FrontPage 97

Library of Congress Catalog No.: 96-71440

ISBN: 0-7897-1036-6

99 98 97 6 5 4 3 2 1

Interpretation of the printing code: the rightmost double-digit number is the year of the book's printing; the rightmost single-digit number, the number of the book's printing. For example, a printing code of 95-1 shows that the first printing of the book occurred in 1995.

Screen reproductions in this book were created using Collage Plus from Inner Media, Inc., Hollis, NH.

Credits

About the Authors

Neil Randall is the author or co-author of several books about the Internet, including *Teach Yourself the Internet, The World Wide Web Unleashed,* and Que's *Special Edition Using Microsoft FrontPage.* In addition, he has written about the Internet and multimedia software in magazines such as *PC/Computing, PC Magazine, The Net, Internet World, I*Way, CD-ROM Today,* and *Windows.* In his real life, he's a professor at the University of Waterloo in Canada, where he forces unsuspecting English students to develop HTML designs in his courses. (Chapters 1-3, 14, 25-29, 31, 40)

Dennis Jones is a freelance technical writer, software trainer, and novelist. He also teaches creative writing at the University of Waterloo. He lives in Waterloo, Canada. (Chapters 3-10, 12, 19-22 and Appendix A)

Matthew Brown is a Webmaster by trade, and currently works for National Knowledge Networks, Inc., a regional ISP located in Dallas, Texas. When he's not busy writing or editing books for Que, Matthew enjoys listening to a variety of music, playing Network Quake, and collecting supermodel autographs. Matthew lives in Addison, Texas with his fiancée Caroline, their two darling cats Ramses and Cleo, and one crazy teddy bear named 'Bastian. (Chapters 30, 39)

Conrad Carlberg is the president of network Control Systems, Inc., a firm that provides statistical forecasting software and services to telecommunications firms. He is a Microsoft MVP for Office applications. He lives near Denver, Colorado. (Chapters 35-38)

Elizabeth Powell Crowe has been writing and editing for 20 years. She is the author for *Genealogy Online, Information for Sale,* with John Evrett, and *The Electronic Traveller.* Elizabeth is also a contributing editor to *Computer Currents,* for which she regularly writes the columns: The Net Surfer and Internet Basics. She lives in Huntsville, Alabama with her husband and two children. (Chapter 11)

David Karlins hosts Dave's Unauthorized FrontPage Support Web at **http://infomatique.iol.ie:8080/dave.** He is a FrontPage Web designer and consultant and the author of several books on FrontPage, graphic design, and the Internet. (Chapters 15-18)

Robert Niles is a systems administrator and Web programmer for InCommand Inc., a company located in Yakima, Washington that specializes in Internet and Intranet applications.

Robert loves all things Internet, especially the Web, and CGI in particular. He has been online since 1983, exploring the very nature of the online world. In 1984 he entered the military service as a communications specialist, taking a one year intensive course at the Presidio of Monterey as a Czech linguist. After completing military service, he returned to his home in the Yakim Valley.

Robert specializes in the UNIX environment, Perl, and SQL. Previously, he was a contributing author to Que's *Special Edition Using CGI*.

Robert lives in Selah, Washington (Apple Country) with his wife, Kimberly; his son, Michael; and his daughter, Shaela. You can find him on the Web at **http://www.sehal.net/** or via e-mail at **rniles@imtired.selah.net**. (Chapters 41-42)

James R. O'Donnell, Jr., Ph.D., was born on October 17, 1963, (you may forward birthday greetings to **odonnj@rpi.edu**), in Pittsburgh, Pennsylvania. After a number of unproductive years, he began his studies in electrical engineering at Rensselaer Polytechnic Institute.

Jim's first experience with a "personal" computer was in high school with a Southwest Technical Products computer using a paper tape storage device, quickly graduating up to a TRS-80 Model II. When he isn't writing or researching for Que or talking on IRC (Nick: JOD), Jim likes to run, row, play hockey, collect comic books and PEZ dispensers, and play the Best Board Game Ever, Cosmic Encounter. (Chapters 19-22)

Bernie Roehl is a software developer based at the University of Waterloo in Ontario, Canada. He is probably best known in VR circles for REND386 and AVRIL, free software packages that are still in widespread use by hobbyists. REND386 recently won the 1995 Meckler award for outstanding software achievement. He is also the author of two books on VR, *Virtual Reality Creations* and *Playing God: Creating Virtual Worlds*.

He is currently the product reviewer for VR Special Report and a regular columnist for *VR News*, as well as having had articles appear in *Real Time Graphics* and *CyberEdge Journal*. He is also very active on the www-vrml e-mail list. (Chapter 23)

Patrice-Anne Rutledge is a computer consultant and author based in the San Francisco area. She writes frequently on a variety of topics including technology, business, and travel and is the author or co-author of nine computer books including *Building Integrated Office Applications* and *Special Edition Using Microsoft Office for Windows 97*, published by Que. As both an independent consultant and member of the IS team for leading technology firms, Patrice has been involved in many aspects of computing including software development, systems analysis, the Internet, and multimedia. (Chapter 13)

Ryan Sutter is a consultant for APG-USA working out of Bloomington, Minnesota. He has been in love with computers ever since his first encounter with a Commodore VIC20, but his favorite things in the world are his wife, Tabithah, and son, Sydney. He loves receiving e-mail. He can be reached at **rockboy@tmf.net.** (Chapters 32-34)

Dedicated to Celine Latulipe, Carrie Pascal and Stephanie Wunder
—N.R.

Acknowledgments

I would like to thank everyone at Vermeer Technologies, whose foresight in creating FrontPage led to some very good things for them and now, obviously, some good things for me as well. In particular, thanks to Ed Cuoco for his assistance in the early days of FrontPage and to Rich Schwerin of *PC/Computing* magazine for giving me the assignment of reviewing it in the first place.

The people behind the publishing deserve thanks for any book (without them, it wouldn't happen in a lot of ways), but a particular thanks here to Philip Wescott for seeing that FrontPage was a hot prospect and should have an instant book about it. Of course, "instant" in the computer book business really means instant (nothing recollected in tranquility here), but eventually sleep will kick in.

My most extensive thanks, though, goes to Dennis Jones, whose skills I now wish I'd tapped months ago. Of all my books, this one was by far the least headache-inducing, and Dennis's professionalism was the most significant cause of that. He took charge of several details while I was busy drowing in administrivia of other kinds, and without his enormous effort the book wouldn't have been done on time or nearly as well.

And thanks, as always, to Michelle and Catherine for not making me feel like an absentee scum, and to Heather for, once again, understanding how days, nights, and weekends all blend together when a project like this is underway.—N.R.

I wish to thank my co-author, Neil Randall, for the cooperation and assistance I received from him in unravelling some of the more knotty sections of FrontPage. My work would have been much harder if it had not been for Neil's expertise and his good-natured willingness to share it with me.

I would also like to thank Ben Pocock for his skilled help in writing the sections of FrontPage's use of forms, form templates, form handlers, and for the research he did into the mechanics of Web pages. And as always, I thank my wife Sandra, who kept our household (and me) going while I worked on this book.—D.J.

We'd Like to Hear from You!

As part of our continuing effort to produce books of the highest possible quality, Que would like to hear your comments. To stay competitive, we *really* want you, as a computer book reader and user, to let us know what you like or dislike most about this book or other Que products.

You can mail comments, ideas, or suggestions for improving future editions to the address below, or send us a fax at (317) 581-4663. For the online inclined, Macmillan Computer Publishing has a forum on CompuServe (type **GO QUEBOOKS** at any prompt) through which our staff and authors are available for questions and comments. The address of our Internet site is **http://www.mcp.com** (World Wide Web).

In addition to exploring our forum, please feel free to contact me personally to discuss your opinions of this book. I'm **bmilstead@que.mcp.com** on the Internet.

Thanks in advance—your comments will help us to continue publishing the best books available on computer topics in today's market.

Benjamin Milstead
Product Development Specialist
Que Corporation
201 W. 103rd Street
Indianapolis, Indiana 46290
USA

N O T E Although we cannot provide general technical support, we're happy to help you resolve problems you encounter that are related to our books, disks, or other products. If you need such assistance, please contact our Tech Support department at 800-545-5914, ext. 3833. ■

To order other Que or Macmillan Computer Publishing books or products, please call our Customer Service department at 800-835-3202, ext. 666.

Contents at a Glance

Table of Contents

V   Integrating Active Content Into Your Web Site

19   Using ActiveX Controls   401

Introduction

A very few years ago, the Internet was almost exclusively the territory of scholars and researchers, and as late as 1990 the World Wide Web did not even exist. It still might not, except that Tim Berners-Lee and his team at the European Organization for Nuclear Research (CERN), based in Geneva, decided to design and release a hypertext system that would allow easier communication among researchers in high-energy physics. The software was written specifically for the Internet and was released in 1991.

Not long after that, the Internet itself was thrown open to public use. First thousands, then tens of thousands, and now millions of people have discovered the Net and the World Wide Web. These systems have caught the public imagination to such a degree that Hollywood thrillers (of varying accuracy) are basing their plotlines on the use and misuse of both.

But even outside fiction, the Web and the Net are indeed imagination catchers. Internet Service Providers, those small-to-large companies who for a modest fee will connect corporations and individuals to the Internet and the World Wide Web, have proliferated, and thousands of people and businesses are signing up every day. They all want to "establish a presence on the

Web," which means, basically, setting up a "Web site" on a host computer, assuming that it provides Internet services. These sites, which are really mini-webs linked to each other through the Internet, are what make up the World Wide Web itself.

Putting together a site hasn't been as easy as one would think, though. Until very recently, setting one up required not only an Internet connection, but some pretty specialized knowledge about how Webs are built and maintained, and the ability to create the pages of the Web site using a language called Hypertext Markup Language (HTML). Not everyone who wanted a Web site had that knowledge and ability, or the time or desire to acquire them.

This is where Microsoft FrontPage 97 steps into the breach. FrontPage is an integrated site development environment, including a Web creation and maintenance package called FrontPage Explorer, a near-WYSIWYG (what-you-see-is-what-you-get) Web page editor called FrontPage Editor, and a fully functioning Personal Web Server that turns a PC into a Web host machine. With FrontPage, you can create a complete Web site on your PC and link your PC to the World Wide Web and the Internet. Better yet, you don't have to know HTML, because FrontPage Editor works like a word processor. You make your page look the way you want it, and the software puts the HTML code together for you.

From the moment it was first released by its original producers, Vermeer Technologies, FrontPage 1.0 garnered an unusual degree of critical praise. Everyone who wrote about it had good things to say about it, and as it made its way into circulation its users quickly agreed with the strong assessments. The package was so well received that software giant Microsoft, realizing that its Internet efforts lacked a Web design package, bought out the program, the technology, and indeed the complete company. One hundred thirty million dollars later, Vermeer Technologies was on its way to Redmond, Washington, to join Bill Gates and company and develop the package from there.

For version 1.1, Microsoft revised the FrontPage interface, but touched up the program itself in only minor ways. What the company did do, however, was to make the beta versions of the package available as free downloads from its Web site. Users were able to work with the full product for a limited period of time, and over 400,000 took the company up on its offer. On release, the package sold well, and work had already begun on a much pumped-up version 2.0.

At the same time, Microsoft placed FrontPage within the Microsoft Office family of applications, thereby announcing to the world that it was intended for anyone in business who wanted to build a Web site. Even though it was not planned as part of the Microsoft Office Suite itself (Word, Excel, PowerPoint, and Access) but rather a member of the family to be purchased separately, FrontPage was no longer a specialty product, but part of the Office mainstream. And as a member of the Office family, FrontPage had to adopt Office's numbering system as well, so when the upcoming main product was named Office 97, FrontPage 2.0 became FrontPage 97. Which is where we are today.

The challenge for the FrontPage 97 design team was to keep up with the explosive growth of technologies that has come to the World Wide Web over the past year. Version 1.1 let you produce reasonably advanced pages, but the advancements went only as far as the inclusion of frames, tables, and programmable forms. What the package didn't include were those features that professional designers now demand: Java, JavaScript, VBScript (Visual Basic Script), ActiveX, Netscape plug-ins, and perhaps most importantly, database integration. You could include these things in your FrontPage documents, but you had to put them there manually by writing the code elsewhere and copying it into FrontPage. That was okay, but not very helpful.

FrontPage 97 goes a long way towards filling those holes. You can now design JavaScripts and VBScripts right inside special FP dialog boxes. You can't do any actual designing of Java applets or Netscape plug-ins, but you can import them with their own specialized dialogs. Linking to databases begins with a newly designed wizard. And support for ActiveX is exemplary, with the imported ActiveX controls displayed in the FP documents as they'll appear on the Web. The result? A much more complete package, and one that gives you nearly everything you can do with Web pages. A few things remain unsupported—style sheets and the newest Netscape extensions stand out here—but these are browser-specific at this point anyway. They'll appear, undoubtedly, in the next FrontPage version.

Microsoft FrontPage 97 is a powerful suite of software, and *Special Edition Using Microsoft FrontPage 97* gives you all the information you need to use its power to your best advantage. ■

How to Use This Book

This book has been written to do four things:

- ■ Make it easy for you to use FrontPage Explorer to create, maintain, and develop your Web site with the maximum of efficiency and the minimum of difficulty.
- ■ Show you how to use FrontPage Editor to design, create, and maintain Web pages that people will both enjoy and find useful.
- ■ Give you the technical elements of Web design beyond FrontPage 97, including the coding and details necessary for HTML, Java, scripting, and database integration.
- ■ Help you understand the technicalities of the World Wide Web and the Internet, and how you can best design your site to take advantage of the technology as it is now, and as it will become.

Given this, what's the best way for you to approach the book?

You may already be knowledgeable about Web site design and construction. If so, you may want to skim the first chapters of this book, and concentrate on the sections that deal with FrontPage Editor, since that's the tool you'll likely spend most of your time using. Later, when you're using FrontPage in earnest, you'll find that FrontPage Explorer (covered in detail in Part VI, "Building and Managing a Web Site") has many features that will make your life as a Webmaster a lot easier.

If you're new to site setup but know a lot about HTML, reverse the preceding process, and work on FrontPage Explorer first. Knowing how FrontPage Explorer handles Web construction will help you when you turn to creating pages with FrontPage Editor. (And with the Editor, you'll be in for a treat. You may never have to worry about tags again.)

Finally, if you're already an experienced Webmaster, browse Parts I, II, and V to learn how to use FrontPage 97 and how it can make your job easier, then use the Table of Contents to identify areas of immediate interest to you. Be sure to check out the advanced features of FrontPage, as well as the chapters devoted to technical coding, and the appendices as well, which you can keep beside you as you design your site.

Eventually, though, you'll want to delve into all of the material on FrontPage Editor, FrontPage Explorer, and the Personal Web Server because together they provide a seamless, powerful environment that can handle all but the most exotic of your site construction needs.

How This Book Is Organized

Special Edition Using Microsoft FrontPage 97 covers all the features and functions of the integrated environment. It has eleven major parts, each of which is summarized briefly below.

The organizing principle is to introduce you to the FrontPage Suite, then demonstrate the features of the WYSIWYG FrontPage Editor. After that, chapters cover Web elements specific to the two major browsers, Microsoft Internet Explorer and Netscape Navigator. Next, you are introduced to the powerful new Image Composer software included with the FrontPage 97 Bonus Pack. Then an entire section is given over to the details of providing active content in your sites, such as Java, ActiveX, scripting, database integration, and VRML.

With all the Web coding issues taken care of, the book shifts to Web site management and creation. Included here is a major section on all the features of FrontPage Explorer, the powerful heart of the FrontPage 97 package, including wizards and templates, Web management and security, and FrontPage's capabilities for building and maintaining intranets. For advanced Webmasters, FrontPage 97's Software Development Kit (SDK) is covered in detail, with information about creating your own templates, wizards, and interface elements.

The next two parts cover FrontPage 97's integration with Microsoft Office, both Office 95 and the upcoming Office 97, and using FrontPage with other popular Web servers. Then the book details methods of integration with databases, an increasingly important component of advanced Web design. Finally, comprehensive appendices cover HTML, Java, JavaScript, VBScript, and VRML.

Part I: Understanding the FrontPage Integrated Environment

Chapter 1, "Getting Started," introduces the various parts of the integrated environment, and explains how you install FrontPage.

Chapter 2, "Looking Over Microsoft FrontPage," outlines each part of the FrontPage 97 package in greater detail, including FrontPage Explorer, FrontPage Editor, and the Microsoft Personal Web Server.

Chapter 3, "Essential Tools for Webmasters," orients you to some of FrontPage 97's advanced capabilities. These include the powerful WebBots and the new and equally powerful Image Composer graphics program. Also covered are FrontPage 97's built-in tools for linking to databases and incorporating ActiveX, Java, JavaScript, and VBScript, as well as the ways in which FrontPage 97 integrates with Microsoft Office 95 and 97.

Part II: Creating Your Web Pages with FrontPage Editor

Chapter 4, "Introducing FrontPage Editor," brings you up to speed on page creation, saving, and retrieval, using either FrontPage Editor and FrontPage Explorer in concert, or FrontPage Editor as a stand-alone application. It also shows you the ways you can adapt the editor display to your preferences.

Chapter 5, "Developing the Basic Page: Text, Lists, and Hyperlinks," gives you the basics of good page design, the fundamentals of HTML structure, and three fundamental elements of a Web page—text, lists, and hyperlinks.

Chapter 6, "Enhancing Pages with Graphics and Multimedia," offers detailed instruction on images and image layout, colors and backgrounds, graphical hyperlinks, and imagemaps.

Chapter 7, "Creating Tables," explores FrontPage 97's easy-to-use but sophisticated system for creating and editing one of the Webmaster's most important tools, HTML tables.

Chapter 8, "Enhancing Web Sites with FrontPage Frames," teaches you about designing for a "framed" site, about using frames with links and images, and how to create framed environments with FrontPage Editor's frame templates.

Chapter 9, "Creating Pages with FrontPage Editor Templates," steps you through FrontPage's supplied templates, which speed up the creation of pages such as bibliographies, glossaries, directories, and publicity instruments, for example, press releases.

Chapter 10, "Using WebBots, Wizards, and Interactive Page Templates," explains what Bots are and how to use them. You also learn all about forms, about getting information from people who visit your site, about forms security, and about the FrontPage templates that help you make your pages interactive.

Chapter 11, "Working Directly with HTML," looks at ways you can modify HTML code directly and how you can import data from other applications such as word processors, spreadsheets, and presentation packages.

Part III: Designing for WWW Browsers

Part III introduces you to the issues of designing Web sites for the two major Web browsers, Netscape Navigator, and Microsoft Internet Explorer.

Chapter 12, "Integrating HTML Style Sheets," shows you the details behind the creation of style sheets, one of the most important recent developments in the Web design universe. Style sheets are supported by Internet Explorer 3.0, and support is promised for future versions of Netscape Navigator.

Chapter 13, "Designing for the Netscape Family of Browsers," introduces the extensions that only Netscape Navigator displays, including page formatting with the multicolumn element.

Chapter 14, "FrontPage on the Net," introduces the resources for FrontPage Web authors that exist on the Internet itself.

Part IV: Creating and Adapting Graphics with Microsoft Image Composer

Part IV examines the wealth of features in Microsoft Image Composer, the graphics program included with the FrontPage 97 Bonus Pack.

Chapter 15, "Getting Started with Image Composer," introduces the various elements of new graphics package.

Chapter 16, "Working with Sprites," demonstrates the way in which the program revolves around the concept of the graphical "sprite."

Chapter 17, "Using Effects for Maximum Impact," outlines the wide variety of tools available in Image Composer for producing special graphical effects.

Chapter 18, "Tailoring Your Images for FrontPage Documents," examines the techniques for making your Image Composer creations suitable for import into an effective FrontPage Web document.

Part V: Integrating Active Content Into Your Web Site

Part V introduces you to FrontPage 97's expanded capabilities for including a variety of active content in your Web designs.

Chapter 19, "Using ActiveX Controls," shows how to implement FrontPage 97's close integration with the ActiveX programmable controls to give your sites even more features.

Chapter 20, "Scripting with VBScript and JScript," examines the sophisticated features in FrontPage 97 that lets you import existing scripts and create them from scratch.

Chapter 21, "JavaScript," demonstrates the techniques and procedures for writing applets using the JavaScript language.

Chapter 22, "Inserting Java Applets and Browser Plug-Ins," shows the procedures for including Java applets and applications, as well as files designed for Web plug-ins, in your FrontPage documents.

Chapter 23, "VRML and Java," explains the details behind writing code for Java applications and three-dimensional Virtual Reality Modeling Language components.

Part VI: Building and Managing a Web Site

Part VI examines the features of FrontPage Explorer, the program in the FrontPage Suite that lets you create, maintain, and manage entire sites.

Chapter 24, "Building a Web," covers web creation in detail and introduces the FrontPage wizards that help you set up specialized types of webs.

Chapter 25, "FrontPage's Templates and Wizards," steps you through using wizards and templates to set up normal and empty Webs and to create the more complex Discussion Webs, Customer Support Webs, Project Webs, and Personal Webs.

Chapter 26, "Working with an Existing Web," deals with FrontPage Explorer's different views of a web, along with the features offered by its menus, and demonstrates how to import existing directories into FrontPage to create a Web.

Chapter 27, "Configuring Your Webs," shows you how to administer a Web by setting Web parameters, permissions, passwords, and proxy servers and by configuring editors.

Chapter 28, "Managing a Web," covers managing hardware, software, and people and using the To Do List to keep your site maintenance up to date, and demonstrates how to use FrontPage 97's advanced maintenance features such as global spell, global search and replace, and hyperlink updating.

Chapter 29, "Serving Your Web to the World with the Personal Web Server," examines the details of the Personal Web Server included in the FrontPage 97 package, and examines the Publishing Web Wizard and other Web publishing features.

Chapter 30, "Setting Up an Intranet with FrontPage," introduces the features contained within FrontPage 97 that let you establish the main elements of a company intranet.

Chapter 31, "The Microsoft Personal Web Server," explores the details of the small but powerful Web server provided with the FrontPage Bonus Pack.

Part VII: The FrontPage SDK

Part VII introduces you to the FrontPage 97 Software Developer's Kit, a powerful document that shows you how fully to customize FrontPage to your needs.

Chapter 32, "Extending and Customizing FrontPage with the SDK," examines the features of the SDK and demonstrates how to create custom menus.

Chapter 33, "Creating Templates," details the procedures in the SDK for developing your own templates.

Chapter 34, "Creating Wizards," outlines the SDK's procedures for designing specialty wizards and WebBots.

Part VIII: Integrating FrontPage and Microsoft Office

Part VIII provides an examination of the increasing degree of integration between FrontPage 97 and Microsoft Office, especially the new Office 97.

Chapter 35, "FrontPage and Microsoft Office 97," looks at the ways in which FrontPage 97 and Microsoft Office 97 work hand in hand to let you create advanced Web sites.

Chapter 36, "Using Internet Assistant for PowerPoint," demonstrates how to use Microsoft's Internet Assistant add-on for the graphics presentation component of Office, Microsoft PowerPoint.

Chapter 37, "Using Internet Assistant for Excel and Word," shows how to use Microsoft Internet Assistant for both Word and Excel, as well as how to use them together for text and table integration.

Chapter 38, "Using Internet Assistants for Word, Access, and Schedule+ with FrontPage," demonstrates how to use the HTML assistants for the remaining components of Microsoft Office.

Part IX: Using Other Servers with FrontPage

Part IX demonstrates the issues involved with publishing FrontPage-created sites on Web servers beyond the Personal Web Server.

Chapter 39, "Using FrontPage with Microsoft Internet Information Server," looks at the details of the highly regarded IIS and the details behind using FrontPage 97 with this server.

Chapter 40, "Using Non-Microsoft Servers," shows how to publish FrontPage documents to servers running O'Reilly WebSite, Netscape FastTrack, and other popular Web server software.

Part X: Advanced Database Connectivity

Part X gives you the details behind building database connectivity into your Web sites, beyond the capabilities of FrontPage 97 itself.

Chapter 41, "Custom Database Query Scripts," looks at the details of producing scripts to request information from large databases maintained by your organization.

Chapter 42, "Database Tools," explores the tools available to Webmasters who must integrate their organization's databases with their Web or intranet sites.

Part XI: Appendixes

The appendixes offer references for coding HTML documents and their components.

Appendix A, "HTML 2.0 and 3.2 Quick Reference."

Appendix B, "VBScript and JScript Command Reference."

Appendix C, "JavaScript Command Reference."

Special Features in This Book

Que has a long track record of providing the most comprehensive resource books for users and developers of computer hardware and software. This volume includes many features to make your learning faster, more efficient, and easier.

Chapter Roadmaps

Each chapter begins with a Roadmap, which is a bulleted list of the chapter's key topics. With each topic is a brief description of what's covered. This will help you understand where you're going before you start.

Tips

These are to help you use the software more effectively or to maneuver you around problems or limitations.

 To avoid typing a long URL, you can use Edit, Copy to copy the URL from your browser's Location box, and then paste it into the place you need it by pressing Ctrl+V.

Notes

Notes provide information that is generally useful but not specifically needed for what you're doing at the moment. Some are like extended tips.

> **N O T E** FrontPage Editor makes it convenient to move among pages. It keeps a history list of the pages you've displayed, and you can choose Tools, Forward or Tools, Back to get around. ■

Cautions

These tell you to beware of a dangerous act or situation. In some cases, ignoring a caution could cause you very significant problems, so don't disregard them!

> **CAUTION**
>
> Once you've changed the Quality setting and saved the image, you can't change that setting again, even if you delete the image and reinsert it from the saved page. So if you're experimenting, keep a backup!

Troubleshooting

Even the best-designed software has dark corners you'd rather not find yourself in. Troubleshooting information gives you a flashlight to dispel the darkness, in the form of advice about how to solve a problem or avoid it in the first place. They're in Q&A form.

TROUBLESHOOTING

I want to use an image as a bookmark, and I can't find a way to do it. Is there one? No, there isn't. This is because an HTML page doesn't actually contain the image data but rather a "pointer" to the file where the image is stored. HTML doesn't let you define such a pointer as a named anchor, which is what a bookmark actually is. To get around this, use some text near the image (the caption, if there is one) as the bookmark.

Book Cross-References

In a package as tightly integrated as FrontPage, many operations are related to features that appear elsewhere in the book. Book cross-references, like the one next to this paragraph, direct you to the related material.

▶ **See** "Wizards: What They Are and How They Work," **p. 776**

On the Web

These sections serve the same purpose as book cross-references but direct you to an Internet resource by giving you its URL.

ON THE WEB

http://www.europe.ibm.com/go/uk/about.html   Visit the IBM Europe page site for an office directory example.

Hotkeys

Hotkeys are indicated by an underlined letter, just as they appear in FrontPage's menus and dialog boxes. For example, the hotkey to open the Insert menu is I. To use it, press the Alt key and then press I. The Insert menu appears.

Shortcut Key Combinations

Shortcut key combinations in this book are shown as the key names joined with plus signs (+). For example, Ctrl+N means: "Hold down the Ctrl key, and while holding it down, press the N key." This combination opens a new page in FrontPage Editor.

Menu Commands

Everywhere in this book, you'll see instructions like

Choose Edit, Bookmark.

This means "Open the Edit menu, and select Bookmark." This particular example opens the Bookmark dialog box.

The instruction "Mark the Set Color check box" means you can either click in the check box to put a check in it or press the C key, which does the same thing.

What's on the CD-ROM

On the CD

Because Microsoft FrontPage is so new, no third-party add-ons appeared as this book was being written. However, you may want to explore other Web page authoring tools and utilities in conjunction with using FrontPage. The CD-ROM includes browsers, HTML editors (for both Windows 3.1 and Windows 95), graphics programs, Winsock FTP clients, and specialty software for audio, video, forms creation, imagemap manipulation, and search engine interfacing.

Understanding the FrontPage Integrated Environment

Getting Started

Welcome to *Special Edition Using Microsoft FrontPage 97*.
FrontPage 97 is an extremely hot software package,
mainly because the thing it's designed to do—create
Web sites from start to finish—is an extremely hot
activity these days. This chapter introduces you to both
the software and the book you're holding in your
hands, and near the end it will tell you the ins and outs
of installing the program. ■

■ **What FrontPage 97 Is
All About**

Why Web designers feel they've
found a piece of paradise, and why
you should consider it for yourself.

■ **How This Book Will Help You
Learn FrontPage 97**

The structure of *Special Edition
Using FrontPage* makes it easy
to learn the ins and outs of the
package.

■ **Where FrontPage 97 Came
From**

A short history of the FrontPage
package, and a good lesson in
making tons of money off the
Internet.

■ **The Parts of FrontPage 97**

What are the various parts of the
FrontPage package? What do they
all do? How do they fit together?

■ **Installing FrontPage 97 and
the Bonus Pack Programs**

You've bought it, you want to use it,
so you need to get it installed.

What FrontPage Is All About

Microsoft FrontPage 97 lets you design and administer World Wide Web sites. Not just Web *pages*, which any number of excellent programs let you do, but entire Web *sites*, collections of linked pages. In fact, once you've acquired FrontPage, there's nothing standing between you and putting your site live on the Web.

FrontPage 97 contains the following three major components:

- FrontPage Explorer lets you create Web sites from scratch and even gives you wizards and templates to take you from no site at all to a site with a solid basis in only a few minutes. If you already have a Web site, Explorer gives you a visual view of it and lets you carry it further.

- FrontPage Editor allows you to create individual pages or to edit those you've created earlier in a near-WYSIWYG (what-you-see-is-what-you-get) editing environment.

- FrontPage Personal Web Server lets you test all aspects of your Web pages, and it even allows you to serve your Web site to the Internet.

In addition, FrontPage 97 ships with a group of programs called the Bonus Pack. Included here are three additional programs to help make your life as a Webmaster easier and more complete:

- Microsoft Personal Web Server expands considerably on the capabilities of the FrontPage Personal Web Server, going so far as to let you serve live webs that aren't designed to attract multitudes of visitors.

- Microsoft Image Composer gives you the tools you need to design and develop graphics specifically for use on the Web, whether or not you're an accomplished graphic artist.

- Web Publishing Wizard helps you place your webs on computers with powerful Web server software, even if those servers do not support FrontPage 97's special features.

Put all these components together, and you have what amounts to a comprehensive Web site publishing environment. To make your Web site complete, you'll want to mount it on a computer that's connected to the Internet over a fast connection 24 hours a day, but even with a lowly modem you can serve up a part-time site to get started.

What's New in FrontPage 97

FrontPage 1.1 was an immediate hit on its release in mid-1996, but it lacked some very important features. FrontPage 97 represents a major enhancement to the package, partly because of added programs, partly because of new features, and partly because of a general interface improvement.

- Microsoft Personal Web Server—A more powerful server with advanced features such as FTP serving, logging, and an interface greatly improved over FrontPage Personal Web Server.

- Microsoft Image Composer—Offers easy yet powerful image manipulation, based on *sprite* technology in which you merge many small images into one.

- Web Publishing Wizard—Step-through assistance for uploading webs to servers that do not support FrontPage extensions.

- Visual Basic and JavaScript—Scripting language built right into the FrontPage environment.

- ActiveX Controls—Easy importing of ActiveX controls, which appear in the FrontPage Editor window as they'll appear on your site.

- Java and Plug-In Imports—Easy importing of Java applets and Netscape plug-in files.

- Import Wizard—Step-through assistance for bringing existing Webs into the FrontPage environment.

- Preview in Browser—See your page in the browser of your choice at the resolution of your choice without leaving FrontPage.

- Enhanced HTML Support—Background sounds, background images, marquees, and other enhancements to advanced HTML options.

- Database Connectivity—DB Wizard makes connecting to databases far easier than before.

- SSL Support—Secure Sockets Layer support for connecting to remote sites for uploading or editing.

- Explorer Simplification—FrontPage Explorer now features two views instead of three; one of them lets you work directly with directories and files.

- Improved Interfaces—Superior toolbars and more intuitive menus make your tasks easier.

- Extended Drag-and-Drop Capabilities—Drag files into FrontPage, drag hyperlinks into pages, drag MS Office objects into and out of FrontPage, and many other options.

- Disk-Based Webs—If you don't want to use a Web server, you can build webs solely on your hard drive.
- For a complete list of enhancements, see **http://www.microsoft.com/frontpage/ brochure/whatsnew.htm**

So What Doesn't FrontPage 97 Do?

FrontPage has a great deal to offer, and new versions will continue to add more, but it doesn't have all things you might need for a complete authoring system, especially if you want an advanced multimedia site. Primarily missing in action are tools for creating Java applets, although FrontPage *does* let you easily include these applets if you already have them available. You'll also want tools such as sound and video capture programs and editors, high-end graphics software if you're a graphic artist, and specialized development tools for advanced creations such as Macromedia Shockwave pages or Virtual Reality Modeling Language (VRML) pages. In all cases, FrontPage 97 contains features that let you incorporate these items quite easily, but you need to create them elsewhere.

But "almost" is more than good enough for the vast majority of Web builders. As a collection, FrontPage's tools are closer to Web authoring nirvana than anything yet seen, particularly on the Windows 95 and NT environments, and they can be supplemented with any other authoring program you want.

Making the Best Use of This Book

Special Edition Using Microsoft FrontPage 97 is designed as a tool to help you get the most out of the FrontPage package. The first thing that has to be said (and as authors we shudder to say it) is that you don't have to read the whole thing. Nor must you read it from start to finish. It's split up into sections that help you play off your existing strengths and your existing knowledge of Web building packages.

If you're already familiar with Web page editors (HTML editors), for instance, you might want to skim through Part II, "Creating Your Web Pages With FrontPage Editor," load up FrontPage Editor, and experiment with it for a while, then hunker down with this book and work through Part VI, "Building and Managing a Web Site," which deals primarily with FrontPage Explorer—create and view a few full webs as you go along. Part VI also covers FrontPage's two Web servers, the server administration tools, and configuration issues, so these will also be of interest to complete your Web environment.

On the other hand, if you're coming at FrontPage from the standpoint of a beginning Web builder, working through the book part by part is the best approach. As you discover new features and capabilities, experiment with them until you're comfortable using them; then continue on and learn even more. And don't worry if you don't know CGI from FBI; FrontPage stands very nicely between you and the unsavory side of Web design (although not between you and the unsavory side of law enforcement, so don't get too carried away). The point is that FrontPage works as a beginner's package as well as a veteran's package, with something to offer everyone.

Where FrontPage Came From

Whatever you might think of Microsoft Corporation, there's no question that the company's greatest talent lies in recognizing excellent technology and then adapting it to its own needs. Windows itself provides an example, with most of its features coming from Apple's Macintosh operating system, which in turn saw its origins in a graphical interface developed by Xerox's Palo Alto Research Center. Microsoft Excel took the best features of Lotus 1-2-3 and made them dance in Windows, and the list goes on. The point is that Microsoft knows what's good, and it's even better when it get its excellence from outside.

Such is the case with FrontPage. The program was introduced in mid-1995 by Vermeer Technologies of Cambridge, Massachusetts, and it was immediately lauded by reviewers in computer magazines. Microsoft obviously agreed, because on January 16, 1996, the company bought not only FrontPage, but Vermeer Technologies itself, for a reported $130 million. Luckily, you don't have to pay nearly as much for a copy of the software. On April 8, 1996, Microsoft announced that the finished program would be available for $149 (way down from the original $695), and even less for owners of Microsoft Office. As a member of the immensely popular Microsoft Office suite, FrontPage stands a chance of becoming the most widespread Web creation system ever made, and with it in place, we should begin to see a wider variety of Web sites.

But FrontPage really came from the Web itself, because the entire purpose of the World Wide Web is to offer a multimedia interface for the global distribution of documents. FrontPage lets you create for precisely this interface, and it lets you easily distribute your own information in a graphically well-designed format. FrontPage makes easy the formerly difficult and complex task of merging the creation of Web documents with the publishing of those documents on the Internet, and therein lies its most important strength. The Web was initially supposed to be a medium in which practically anyone could publish, and FrontPage offers that possibility once more.

The Parts of FrontPage 97

FrontPage consists of several major parts, all of which fit together to make a complete Web site publishing package. The integration of the programs is covered in the next chapter, and the following short descriptions serve only as a means for getting you started thinking about the package's many possibilities.

FrontPage Explorer

The heart of the entire FrontPage package, Explorer is designed to let you see the web you have created. Explorer provides two main views of your web. The Hyperlink view lets you see the hierarchical relationships and links among pages, and resembles the outliner in a word processor. It also gives you a clear graphical picture of how pages in your web are linked together and also how they link to Web documents outside your site. The second view, Folder view, shows you technical details about each of the files and folders in your web.

Together, the two views let you see how your web is constructed and, in the process, help you determine what else needs to be done to perfect that web. Broken links are shown clearly, and links can be updated to automatically change references. In addition, Explorer automatically creates and maintains a To Do List of tasks still to be completed, and you can assign these tasks to anyone on your team of coworkers.

Most importantly, Explorer lets you create webs. You can build webs that are entirely empty, into which you must insert all your documents from scratch, but more importantly, Explorer's wizards and templates will build entire webs and set them in place. Once they exist, your task is to customize them and add to them, but having something to start with always makes the overall task easier.

Finally, Explorer lets you set options for your webs to help you manage them. You can determine who will have access to the Web sites at various levels—everyone from administrators to Web authors and even end users. If you want to restrict access to your webs to people within your own company, you can do so. If you want users to register before entering your site, you can do that as well. And if you want coworkers to be able to author pages in the web but not change the administrative options, it's as easy as a few entries in a dialog box.

FrontPage Editor

There's no lack of good packages out there that let you author Web documents. Typically they're called HTML editors because Web pages are written primarily in *Hypertext Markup Language* (HTML), but in the case of Microsoft FrontPage you really don't have

Part

I

Ch

1

to know HTML to generate some first-rate pages. Like your word processor, which doesn't show you the formatting codes unless you specifically ask to see them, FrontPage Editor operates on the principle that you want to see the results of your design decisions rather than the codes and tags necessary for their implementation. In other words, FrontPage Editor is a WYSIWYG program, and while it's not the first such program to hit the market, it's one of the most complete to date.

FrontPage Editor supports advanced HTML features such as tables, forms, and frames. It also lets you set the color and formatting of your pages through a series of dialog boxes, thereby making it easier to standardize the way your web looks to others. In the case of forms and frames, in fact, it goes a step further, offering wizards to help you build these relatively complex elements. And it goes yet another step further, offering automation tools called *WebBots*.

If you've ever tried to get a form on your web actually to do anything, you know how difficult it can be. Designing the form itself is relatively easy; programming the scripts to allow it to interact with the server so that clicking the Submit button sends the data somewhere useful is another matter entirely. The Bots in FrontPage's forms remove much of this difficulty, and removes also the need to learn the interface scripting process known as CGI. You can't do all complex CGI-like interactions with these Bots, at least not in the early versions, but FrontPage makes it possible for even Web authoring novices to offer full interaction in their Web sites.

However, simply authoring Web pages isn't enough for FrontPage; instead, the package integrates Editor with Explorer to make web planning and HTML authoring a relatively seamless activity.

FrontPage Personal Web Server

If you want to host your own Web site, you need a piece of software called *Web server - software*. This software, when on a computer that's connected to the Internet, lets you make your Web site accessible to users on the World Wide Web. To be effective, a Web server machine should be connected to the Internet 24 hours per day at a much higher speed than even the fastest modem allows, but if you want, you can use the Personal Web Server to offer even part-time connections at slower speeds.

But this isn't really the main function of the Personal Web Server. Instead, it's designed a way for you to test your Webs as you develop them. Once you've created some pages, you'll want to see what they look like in your favorite Web browser (Netscape, Internet Explorer, Mosaic, and so on). To do so, all you need do is start the Personal Web Server, set it for "local" mode, and then load your browser and see if everything works. As long as you're connected to the Internet at the time, you can test internal and external links alike, and you can ensure that your Web pages look exactly as you want them to.

Microsoft Personal Web Server

FrontPage Web Server has its limitations, so the FrontPage 97 package includes the Microsoft Personal Web Server as well. Essentially, Microsoft PWS is a "lite" version of the company's ultra-powerful Internet Information Server (IIS), which works only on the expensive Windows NT Server platform. The "lite" version, therefore, gives you some of the capabilities of IIS without the cost. In fact, with Microsoft PWS you can actually host a live Web site, as long as you don't plan on offering a site that invites hundreds of thousands of visitors each week.

Server Extensions

The most important concession made by the FrontPage package is that people will want to use its Web creation tools but not necessarily its included server. In fact, there's no way a professional Web server site would be willing to change from its well-established server software, so the only way to make FrontPage widely useful was to include support for existing servers. FrontPage does this through *server extensions*, which install files and directories into the existing server software to let the server work with all of FrontPage's features.

Getting data from forms is just one example (albeit an important one) of what the extensions accomplish. As explained briefly earlier, FrontPage takes the programming sting out of making forms return the data that users provide. But because FrontPage does this in a nonstandard way (in fact, almost all servers handle this differently), something has to tell the server software what the FrontPage form is trying to do. That something, in fact, is the server extension. Essentially, the server extensions add functionality to the server software to allow it to work with FrontPage as well as with the software it already supports.

FrontPage offers server extensions for many of the most popular servers. Some of these are included in the package, while others are downloadable from the FrontPage Web site at **http://www.microsoft.com/frontpage**.

Microsoft Image Composer

Whether you're a graphic artist or artistically challenged, Microsoft Image Composer will suit many of your needs. The principle for this program isn't to create graphics from scratch, but rather to edit graphics files to suit the way you want them to look on your Web site. You can merge multiple "sprites" (individual images) into one more complex image, then alter each of the component sprites, or the entire image, by clicking filters, warps, and various art effects. You can add text, change color patterns, and perform a wide range of other edits as well. And you can save your finished image as a Web-standard JPEG or GIF file for incorporation into your FrontPage documents.

Web Publishing Wizard

FrontPage's server extensions let you create webs with advanced programming features, but not all servers support these extensions. If you're publishing your web on one of these servers, the Web Publishing Wizard steps you through the process. Your web won't be able to do fancy things like connect to databases and return forms results, but your hyperlinks will be correct and the site will work.

Installing FrontPage 97

As of this writing, FrontPage was available for Microsoft Windows 95 and NT. Other versions are in development, but you can rest assured that the 32-bit Windows version will remain the primary development environments (this is a Microsoft product, after all). Examples you see throughout this book are from the Windows version, including this section on installation.

> **CAUTION**
>
> FrontPage is a 32-bit application and as such will run only on 32-bit Windows platforms—namely Windows 95 or Windows NT. You cannot install it on a computer running earlier versions (that is, 16-bit versions) of Windows.

If you've downloaded a beta version of the program, it arrives as an executable, self–extracting file. Run the file and then look for the install or setup utility common to your operating system. In Windows 95 and NT, of course, this is the SETUP.EXE file. Run that utility, and the installation will be more or less automated.

If you have the Bonus Pack CD-ROM, simply put it in the CD-ROM drive, close the door, and the Installation screen will appear. You have several installation choices here: you can install FrontPage 97 itself, Microsoft Image Composer, Microsoft Web Server, Internet Explorer, or the Web Publishing Wizard. To get started, click the program you want to install. Note that this works only if your Auto Insert Notification is enabled in the CD-ROM Devices area through the System icon in Control Panel.

Once the installation process begins, you must choose a typical installation or custom installation. Typical installation includes all three of FrontPage's components: the client software (FrontPage itself), the Personal Web Server, and the server extensions.

Through custom installation, you can elect to exclude any of these and/or install the Microsoft Personal Web Server (in which case you won't need to install it from the CD-ROM's installation screen). If you ran the installation program before and chose not to install portions, you can do so this time around. Normally, on first receiving the product, you should install the entire set of features.

Like all programs, FrontPage offers to install itself into a default directory, which you can change if you want. It also needs a separate directory for the Personal Web Server and for any webs you create. This is given a default location as well, and your next step is to confirm or change that directory. Next you'll be asked for the folder or program group in which to place the FrontPage icons, and you'll get a screen showing all the directories you've decided on. If you're using a server other than FrontPage Personal Web Server, such as the Netscape FastTrack Server, the Microsoft Internet Information Server, O'Reilly's WebSite Server, or in fact the Microsoft Personal Web Server, FrontPage knows enough to use the directories already established for these Webs as a place to find and store files.

At this point, FrontPage takes itself through the rest of the installation. When it's finished, you'll be asked if you want to start FrontPage Explorer. Since you'll want to spend the next few weeks of your life learning how to use the full suite of capabilities in this package, why not say yes and get started. When FrontPage Explorer has loaded, find the Microsoft FrontPage folder and load the Personal Web Server as well. Now go back to Explorer, choose File, New Web and start your web creation career (if you want, you can jump straight to Chapter 24," Building a Web," to get going).

If You Already Have a Web Server Running

You're not forced to use the two Web servers that ship with FrontPage. If any one of a number of popular Web server packages is already running on your computer, FrontPage will detect it during installation and automatically install the server extensions. FrontPage offers extensions for the most popular servers for UNIX and Windows but by no means for all available servers. If you're not sure, use the Personal Web Server because FrontPage installs extensions for it right out of the box.

Installing Microsoft Personal Web Server, Image Composer, Web Publishing Wizard, and Internet Explorer

To install any of these packages, click their icons on the CD-ROM installation screen. If you chose to install Microsoft PWS along with FrontPage itself, there's no need to do so again here. And except for Image Composer, you don't really have any installation choices. For Image Composer, you'll have to decide how many multimedia files you want to include with the installation, and keep careful watch on the disk space you're taking up. A full installation of Image Composer consumes nearly 400 megabytes of disk space. Yes, 400 *megabytes*, almost half a gigabyte.

From Here...

At this point, you have FrontPage installed and running. Obviously, though, that's only the very beginning. FrontPage is a rich program, and as with all rich programs, entirely mastering it takes both time and effort. Your introduction to the package continues in the next chapter, and then it's on to the actual production of Web sites and pages in Parts II and III. From here, then, you can look forward to the following:

- Chapter 2, "Looking Over Microsoft FrontPage," takes you through the ways in which the various programs interact.
- Part II, "Creating Your Web Pages with FrontPage Editor," is where you'll discover the WYSIWYG power and features of the package's HTML editor.
- Part VI, "Building and Managing A Web Site," works through the details of Web site creation and management in FrontPage Explorer.

Looking Over Microsoft FrontPage

FrontPage 97 is an integrated package, combining a powerful World Wide Web page editor, the sophisticated site management system of FrontPage Explorer, and a fast Web server. With these are FrontPage's "WebBots," which relieve you of writing CGI scripts for interactive processes. Using these tools, you can establish your own webs, create extremely sophisticated pages for them, and offer your Web site to millions of viewers and readers. ■

Starting a New Web with FrontPage Explorer

Choose from a number of Web templates and wizards, and get a brand new Web, ripe for expansion.

Opening an Existing Web Page with FrontPage Editor

FrontPage Explorer is your Web manager, but the Editor is where you'll expend most of your creative energies in a robust, full-featured, near-WYSIWYG environment.

Using a WebBot for a Simple Timestamp Application

Make your site interactive without writing CGI scripts through the use of WebBots—a unique FrontPage benefit.

Presenting Your Web Site to the World, Using the Personal Web Server

Get a glimpse of the Personal Web Server, which turns your PC into a real, fully functional Web server.

Explorer, Editor, and the Server Extensions: Working Together

Before getting started in designing your first-class Web sites, it's useful to consider how the three primary parts of the FrontPage package—Explorer, Editor, and the server extensions—function together.

(It's also useful to keep in mind a couple possible bits of confusion that Microsoft might have tried to avoid. First, FrontPage Explorer is *not* the same as Windows Explorer, and it would have been nice if the FrontPage tool had been called something like FrontPage WebViewer or something like that. Second, while Windows 95 refers to *folders*, and MS-DOS and earlier versions of Windows refers to *directories*, FrontPage uses the two names pretty much interchangeably. In this book, *folder* and *directory* mean the same thing, and they're given the name used by each particular portion of FrontPage itself.)

FrontPage Editor lets you create HTML documents, otherwise known as World Wide Web pages. It's a near-WYSIWYG (what you see is what you get) system, which means that, for the most part, what you see in the Explorer windows is what you'll see in your Web browser when you retrieve that page. Not all HTML code displays precisely as it will look on the Web, however, which is why this book refers to it as *near*-WYSIWYG. The point, though, is that authoring Web pages in FrontPage Editor is relatively easy and extremely pleasing, because as you create the page you see almost exactly what it's going to look like to the people who visit your Web sites.

Despite the importance of FrontPage Editor, however, the true core of Microsoft FrontPage is FrontPage Explorer. Explorer lets you create webs, delete webs, import files into webs, and manage your web sites at all levels. Explorer gives you a graphical view of your webs, letting you see how the various pages are linked together, and it offers tools to update links as they change with the growth of the web. With Explorer, in other words, you build and manage *webs*, while with Editor you author and edit *pages*.

The relationship between these two main tools is a rich one. On a simple functional level, you can double-click an icon in Explorer, and that page will (usually) open for editing inside Editor. More significantly, though, Editor offers a powerful feature known as WebBots, and these tie directly in with Explorer. WebBots spare you the difficulty and drudgery of programming your World Wide Web pages; they let you create forms that produce usable data, in addition to such items as counters that display the number of visitors to your site, information fields that update whenever the page is loaded, and many other similar types of features. In order to actually work, WebBots are tied to the functions of Explorer, and the additional functions of the FrontPage server extensions.

Which brings us to the third major feature of FrontPage: server extensions. Web sites can be accessed by visitors only if they're "served" by Web *server* software. FrontPage Explorer works hand in hand with special software that tells the server how to respond to pages produced by FrontPage.

All of these features are covered in the book you're now holding. What's important to keep in mind for now is that the three major parts of FrontPage operate hand in hand. You can use Editor without Explorer, but many of Editor's most important features won't work. Similarly, you can use Explorer with a different editor, but the entire WebBot system won't exist for you. And without the server extensions, you can't use either with any useful effect.

Using Explorer to Start Your Web

You're probably itching to find out what it's actually like to create your own web, so let's begin. This will be just a quick run-through to get you used to Explorer's behavior, because you'll learn about web creation in detail in the next few chapters.

Go to the Win95 Start button, go to Programs, and select Microsoft FrontPage. After a short pause, you'll see the Explorer screen.

Choose File, New, FrontPage Web, from the Explorer menu bar. You immediately see a dialog box with a list of web templates and wizards.

- The Normal Web creates a web with a single blank page, which will be the Web site's home page.

- The Corporate Presence Wizard walks you through the process of creating an organization-style web.

- The Customer Support Web provides you with a framework for developing customer support services.

- The Discussion Web is excellent for setting up a discussion site; creating one from scratch is a time-consuming business.

- The Empty Web is just that; it creates a web structure without even one page in it. You use this if you've already prepared a home page, and need an empty web to install it into.

- The Learning FrontPage Web is a brief but useful tutorial web for the software package.

- The Personal Web sets up a single home page for you, with a selection of possible hyperlink destinations you can delete or customize as you like.

- The Project Web establishes a web you can use to manage and track a project.

▶ These are covered in much more detail in Chapter 25, "FrontPage's Templates and Wizards."

For your test run, select Normal Web, and choose OK. The next dialog box asks you to specify which Web server to install the web on; accept the installation default. Then type a name for the web into the Web Name box. This name has to obey the naming conventions of the server; FrontPage Web names can't, for example, include spaces. Also, the name is case-sensitive; to the server, "MyWeb" is not the same as "myweb." Keep this in mind when you're trying to access your Web site through your Internet Service Provider (ISP).

As soon as you choose OK, FrontPage Explorer starts generating the web. But before it completes the task, it asks you, as the Web administrator, for your username and password. Type in the ones you established when you installed FrontPage, and choose OK. Explorer finishes creating the web, and opens it for you in the Explorer workspace. At the same time, it automatically starts the Personal Web Server.

And that, believe it or not, is all there is to it! You have a brand new web ready for expansion.

Explorer very conveniently gives you two views of your web. The Hyperlink view, which appears by default, shows an outline-like hierarchy in the left pane, and a graphical view of the web in the right pane. The right pane shows icons for each page, image, or World Wide Web URL, with lines showing the links among them.

▶ **See** Chapter 26, "Working with an Existing Web," **p. 649**

▶ **See** Chapter 28, "Managing a Web," **p. 689**

The second view available in FrontPage Explorer is the Folder view. This shows a view of your web much like the directory and file appearance of Windows Explorer, and functions in much the same way. In the Folder view, you have file-level control of your web, something you'll want as your web grows more complex.

You can switch between these views by choosing View/Hyperlink View, or View/Folder View, or by clicking the View buttons in Explorer's toolbar. These views are extremely useful for managing your web's structure, and for moving pages into FrontPage Editor for editing.

Using FrontPage Editor to Create Your Pages

While FrontPage Explorer is the manager for your web, the Editor is where you'll expend most of your creative energies. FrontPage Editor is a very robust, full-featured Web page editor, with numerous extensions beyond the HTML 2.0 and 3.2 standards, including frames, tables, marquees, fonts, and many other features. It is a primarily WYSIWYG environment, a rarity among HTML editors to date. With it, you can follow links from one page to another even while editing them, which in effect turns FrontPage Editor into a mini-browser. Furthermore, you can load World Wide Web pages into FrontPage Editor to study the HTML code that makes such pages work.

FrontPage Editor resembles a word processor in many ways, if a very specialized one. You can open several pages at the same time and switch between them; cut, copy, and paste page elements; do spell checks; and format character appearance and size. FrontPage Editor also supports tables, just as Word and WordPerfect do, though its table formatting options are somewhat limited because of the restrictions of HTML. Insertion of graphics also resembles word processor methods. Linking is simply another option on the Edit menu.

For a first look at FrontPage Editor, start it up by choosing Tools, Show FrontPage Editor. After a moment the Editor screen appears (see Figure 2.1).

Part

I

Ch

2

FIGURE 2.1

FrontPage Editor is open here, along with the dialog box for adding hyperlinks to the page.

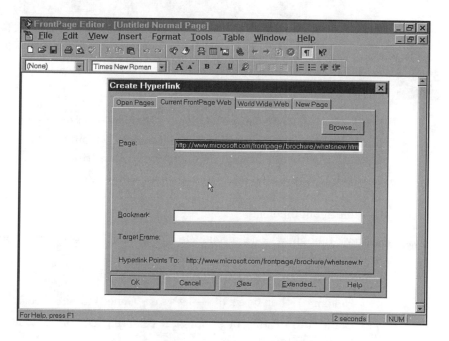

Now get the home page of your new web into FrontPage Editor's workspace, so you can have a look at it. Choose File, Open from Web. The Open File dialog box appears, withtwo tabs. One lets you load pages from the Current FrontPage Web, the other lets you load pages from some Other Location. The only Web page showing in the current web is the Home Page, with the filename DEFAULT.HTM. This is the home page (see Figure 2.2).

FIGURE 2.2

The Open Web dialog box lists all pages in whatever web is open in FrontPage Explorer.

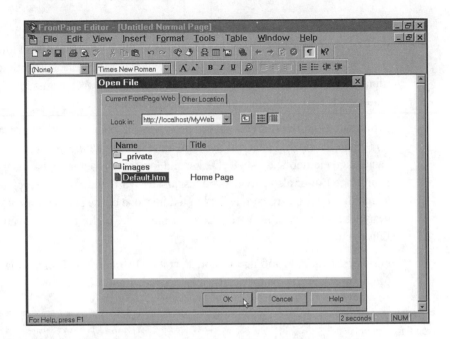

TIP You can also drag a page icon from Explorer's Link or Summary view to the Editor's title bar, and the page will open automatically in the Editor.

Double-click on Home Page. FrontPage Editor will open (it might take a few seconds) with a blank workspace. The page has no content yet, but you know you have the right page because the title bar of the Editor window says "Home Page." From here you begin the development of your page, adding images, text, hyperlinks, tables, imagemaps, forms, tables of contents—the list goes on and on, and by the end of this book you'll be knowledgeable about them all.

Just now, though, why not try out a few items to show how easy FrontPage Editor is to use. Try the following:

1. Click the down arrow beside the Style box on the far left of the toolbar. Select Heading 1, then type a title—let's say: "Gone With the Web."

2. Center this heading by clicking the centering icon on the toolbar. Then press Enter to move to the next line.

3. Now let's add a graphic below the heading. Select Image from the Insert menu, or the Image button on the toolbar, then click the Clip Art tab. Click the down arrow beside Category and choose Lines. You'll see Figure 2.3.

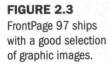

FIGURE 2.3

FrontPage 97 ships with a good selection of graphic images.

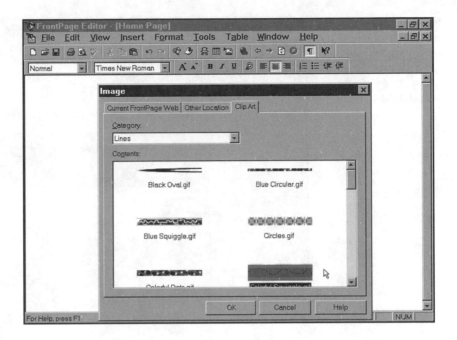

Part

I

Ch

2

4. Click the "colorful squiggle" and then OK. The squiggle appears below the title. Now click the squiggle, grab the resize buttons, and widen the image to the left and right.

5. Now make the page background gray. In fact, we'll give it a background image. Right-click a blank part of the page and choose Page Properties. Click the Background tab, and then the Clip Art tab on the Select Background Image dialog. Find Gray Marble, then click OK. Click OK again, and you have a background texture.

6. To add a table, click Table/Insert Table, select 3 rows and 5 columns, select Center alignment, a border size of 3, and specify the width as 75 percent. Then click OK, and the table appears, ready for data.

7. At this point, simply experiment with everything you want on your page, even if you don't intend to keep any of it. Try a marquee (Insert/Marquee), then a Hyperlink (Insert/Hyperlink). Continue until your page is cluttered with all sorts of options, then save the page to the Web by choosing File/Save.

8. Finally, see what your page looks like by selecting File/Preview in Browser. The file will automatically be saved in the Web, and FrontPage will ask you if you want to copy the image to a folder in the Web (say yes). You'll see the dialog box shown in Figure 2.4, and you can choose whatever browser you have installed and the resolution at which you wish to view your page. Select a resolution different from the one you're currently running, click Preview, and watch what happens.

FIGURE 2.4
You can preview your web in any browser you have installed, and at any screen resolution you wish.

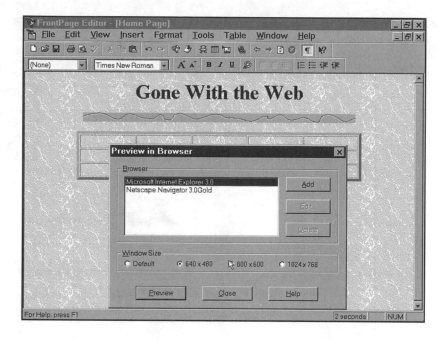

▶ **See** Chapter 5, "Developing the Basic Page: Text, Lists, and Hyperlinks," **p. 65**

Using the Personal Web Server to Offer Your Web to the World

You'll learn much more about this in Part VI of *Special Edition Using Microsoft FrontPage 97*, but here's a thumbnail of it. The Personal Web Server turns your PC into a real, fully functional Web server. If your PC is online to the Internet, and the Personal Web Server is running, the webs you've stored on your machine are accessible to anyone with the server's current IP address, a PPP line, and a Web browser. There's nothing else you need at this basic level.

This means that if you want to, you can dispense with installing your Web on your Internet Service Provider's server, and run your Web site from your desktop. All you need to do is to set yourself up with a 24-hour modem connection, and there you are. If you're really serious, you'll need to register your site to get a permanent IP address, because your site's dynamic IP address, as set by your ISP, will change whenever you log off the ISP connection and log back on again. But that's really all there is to it.

In fact, FrontPage 97 ships with two Web servers, not just one. The second, Microsoft Personal Web Server, cleverly named to be as confusing as possible when compared with FrontPage Personal Web Server, has more features and more power than the server built directly into FrontPage. But if you're using the server software only to test your web on your PC, there's no reason to install it. FrontPage PWS is just fine.

The FrontPage PWS is sufficient for testing your webs, and even for establishing a low-traffic site, but the Microsoft PWS is more powerful because of its ability to serve more connections simultaneously, and its ability to allow more active content in your Web pages than the FrontPage PWS can handle. But if you want a public Web site with lots of daily traffic and advanced interactivity features, you'll need a more powerful server such as Netscape's FastTrack or Enterprise Server, or Microsoft's Internet Information Server.

Part

I

Ch

2

From Here...

You're off to a good start. You've installed FrontPage successfully, set up your administrator's username and password, and had a taste of both FrontPage Explorer and Editor.

- Chapter 3, "Essential Tools for Webmasters," introduces you to some of the advanced interactivity features of FrontPage web creation.
- Chapter 4, "Introducing FrontPage Editor," explores the features and capabilities of the easy-to-use FrontPage Editor program.
- Chapter 5, "Developing the Basic Page: Text, Lists, and Hyperlinks," gets you started on your Web page design.
- The remainder of Part II, which examines the advanced features of FrontPage Editor.

## CHAPTER 3

Essential Tools for Webmasters

Using WebBots

Make your site interactive without writing CGI scripts.

Do-It-Yourself Graphics

Assemble, edit, and create your own images with Image Composer.

Use ActiveX Controls, Scripts, and Applets

Put active content on your pages with ActiveX components, Visual Basic and JavaScripts, and Java applets.

Even in the brief time FrontPage has been around, the needs of Webmasters and page designers for a greater variety of tools have grown. FrontPage 97 addresses most if not all of these needs, with features that even a year ago were rare on the Web and often difficult to use. Not only does it include the sophisticated site management tool of FrontPage Explorer, a superb Web page editor, and a Personal Web Server, it now provides facilities for adding active content to your pages, and creating and processing your own graphics. Better yet, the WebBot technology introduced with version 1.1 and continued in FrontPage 97 relieves you of writing CGI scripts for interactive processes. In this chapter we take a brief overview of what have now become essentials. ■

Understanding WebBots

WebBots are unique to FrontPage. They're very, very important because they relieve you of having to write CGI scripts to make your site interactive. Without CGI scripts, or WebBots to fill in for them, people can visit your site but they can't interact with it through forms, searches, discussions, or registrations. Much of the appeal of the World Wide Web is in this interactivity, and if your site doesn't have it, you're missing a lot. Until now, though, getting your pages to be interactive was a headache, because not everyone can (or wants to) write CGI scripts. Moreover, incorrectly written custom scripts can behave so badly that ISP administrators often won't allow them to be installed on their server. With FrontPage, all that has changed.

So what's a Bot? It's really no more than a chunk of programming that you embed in your page to carry out the operation you want, and FrontPage comes with several of them. Some are designed for interactive applications; others are more modest, merely inserting useful bits of information into your page. Let's have a quick look at one, so they won't be so mysterious.

Click anywhere on a document in the FrontPage Editor workspace. Then choose Insert, WebBot Component. The Insert WebBot dialog box opens, with a list of the available Bots (there are more of them than are listed; some do their work invisibly, and you never get close to them). Select Timestamp, and choose OK. You'll get a dialog box; don't worry about changing its entries, just choose OK again. The dialog box vanishes, and suddenly the current date appears at the cursor position.

Well, okay, that's nice. But you could have typed the date in yourself, so why bother with the Bot?

The answer is: This date is automated. The Bot tracks the last date the page was edited and displays that. People like to know when a Web page was last changed, and this Bot will tell them, so you don't have to remember to change the "Last edited date" every time you modify a page. That's one of the things Bots can do for you: streamline the operation of your Web site.

Incidentally, if you put the cursor on top of this date, it will turn into a little robot. That's the "Bot cursor," and it tells you if there's a Bot at this place in your page (sometimes you can't tell just by looking).

This is a minor example, but some Bots, like the Discussion Bot, are very powerful. They and FrontPage Editor together will relieve you of almost every programming chore; in fact, you could set up and run a Web site with FrontPage and never write a line of HTML code. With Bots, you can do the following:

- Comment your pages so you can see the comments, while visitors to your site won't.

- Make custom confirmation pages to reply to people who send you information.

- Add nonstandard HTML code to your pages without using a text editor.

- Include the content of another page in the current page (very handy for standardizing page headers across a site).

- Make an image or a page appear in your site for a specified length of time (advertisers take note).

- Allow a visitor to search your site for key words or phrases (if your site is a reference or research site, this will be important).

- Substitute your own page variables for standard ones.

- Set up a dynamic table of contents that will change automatically as your site changes (this is a major one for harried Webmasters!)

- Add a timestamp to your page, as you did just now.

Those are Bots; for more information on them, see Chapter 10, "Using WebBots, Wizards, and Interactive Page Templates."

Part

I

Ch

3

Creating and Customizing Graphics

Images are integral to Web pages. For what you might call "utility images" such as lines, buttons, and icons, you can search around on the Web and likely find something that suits your needs. However, most people want to personalize their site, and off-the-shelf graphics don't really contribute to this. So FrontPage 97 obligingly offers Image Composer to let you alter existing images, and create new ones.

Image Composer: A Very Brief Overview

Image Composer is a powerful graphics package, but you can learn the essentials pretty quickly. The typical installation gives you the application itself, of course, plus a tutorial and online help. A full installation adds to these basics a set of fonts, plus 231 M (yes, megabytes) of photo samples, and 18 M of Web art samples. These samples can be used as components to build custom graphics, rather like clip art.

Getting Acquainted with Image Composer

You may have been reluctant to install the full 250 megabytes of art samples, depending on how much disk space you have. So for this quick look at the application, we'll assume you installed the tutorial, and use the images that come with it. They're TIF files, but once you've completed your work, you can save the results as a GIF or JPEG to use in your web. (Actually, FrontPage Editor will automatically convert to GIF for you unless you instruct it differently.)

To get started, do the following:

1. Start Image Composer by selecting Show Image Editor from either FrontPage Explorer or FrontPage Editor.

2. The Arrange box automatically starts too; close it for now.

3. Select Insert, From File. Assuming a default installation, go to C:\Program Files\Microsoft Image_Composer\Tutorial. You'll see four TIF files listed; we'll be using the flowers files.

4. Double-click DAISY.TIF. The image of the daisy appears in the workspace (see Figure 3.1).

FIGURE 3.1

Image Composer's workspace with an image loaded and ready for editing.

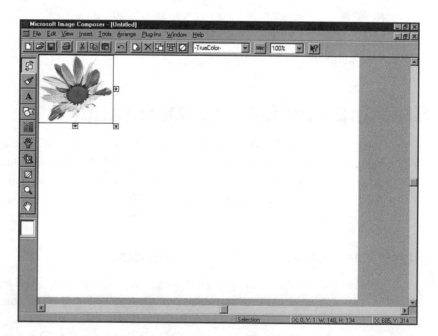

5. Move the daisy away from the left edge of your screen by positioning the cursor over the image until you see a four-arrow pointer, then drag to the right.

6. Enlarge the daisy while maintaining its original proportions by holding down the shift key, then grabbing the arrow at the bottom right of the image and dragging down and to the right. Release the mouse button, and the image will resize.

7. Now load another component into your image. Choose Insert, From File, and choose HIBISCUS.TIF. Drag the hibiscus over the daisy, then click outside the image area. You'll now have two components, combined into one image.

8. Reorient the daisy part of the image by clicking it, then dragging the rotation handle at the top right of the box. Put the petal-less side of the flower at the top left of the box (see Figure 3.2).

FIGURE 3.2
You can reorient components that are part of a complete image by dragging their rotation handles.

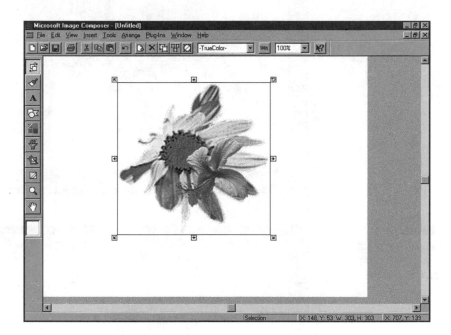

9. Now we'll add a third component. Choose Insert, From File, and choose TULIP.TIF. Move it on top of both the other images, at the petal-less edge of the daisy. Right-click the tulip and choose Send to Back. This will place it behind both of the other flowers. Click away from the flowers, and you'll see your three-part image (see Figure 3.3).

10. Now we'll sharpen the entire image. First, select all three flowers by holding down the Control key and clicking each of them in succession (you can select them all by using Ctrl+A, too). Next, click the Warps and Filters icon in the Effects toolbar on the left side of the screen. Select Filters, then Sharpen, and click Apply. You'll now have a sharper image.

11. At this point, we'll give the whole image a different look. Select all the flowers, then click the Art Effects icon on the Effects toolbar. Choose Paint, then Fresco. Click the Apply button and watch your bouquet change to a frescoed image (see Figure 3.4).

FIGURE 3.3

You can layer image components in any order you like.

FIGURE 3.4

You can apply different visual effects with a few clicks of the mouse.

When you're done, save the image as a GIF or JPG file, then import it into FrontPage Editor on the page of your choice.

Using ActiveX, Scripts, and Applets

FrontPage Editor 97 makes it easy to add ActiveX components, Visual Basic Scripts, and JavaScripts to your pages. Applets are of course more complex, because you (or somebody) has to write the Java code for the applet, and compile it so it can be used. However, the basic procedure is the same in each case.

Adding an ActiveX Control

Part

I

Ch

3

ActiveX Controls combine the convenience of Java applets with the permanence and functionality of Netscape Navigator plug-ins. Like Java applets, ActiveX Controls can be automatically downloaded to your system if they are either not currently installed or if the installed version is not the most recent. Like plug-ins, ActiveX Controls remain available to your Web browser continuously once they are installed.

These controls, formerly known as OLE Controls or OCXs, build on Microsoft's highly successful Object Linking and Embedding (OLE) standard to provide a common framework for extending the capability of its Web browser. But ActiveX Controls are more than just a simple Web browser plug-in or add-in. Because of the nature of ActiveX Controls, not only can they be used to extend the functionality of Microsoft's Web browser, but they also can be used by any programming language or application that supports the OLE standard.

To insert an ActiveX Control do the following:

1. Start FrontPage Editor, and load a document into the workspace.

2. Choose Insert, Other Components, ActiveX Control. When the dialog box appears, click the button at the right of the Pick a Control box to get the drop-down list of controls on your system. Note that FrontPage 97 comes with a selection of controls already installed for you (see Figure 3.5).

3. Choose the control you want, then choose the Properties button. You now use the properties dialog boxes to customize the control to suit your purposes.

ActiveX Controls can be complicated to use; they all require parameters of one kind or another. For a detailed examination of setting parameter values, refer to Chapter 19, "Using ActiveX Controls."

FIGURE 3.5
You can choose from among controls installed on your system.

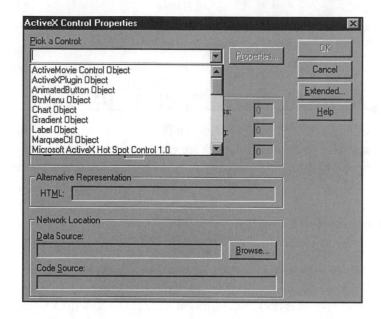

Adding Scripts

Microsoft has introduced its own scripting language, Visual Basic Script (VBScript), which is based on the Visual Basic and Visual Basic for Applications languages. Just as those two languages made it much easier to create applications for Windows and within the Microsoft Office suite, respectively, VBScript was designed as a language for easily adding interactivity and dynamic content to Web pages.

The JavaScript language, which was first introduced by Netscape in its Web browser, Netscape Navigator 2, gives Web authors another way to add interactivity and intelligence to their Web pages. JavaScript code is included as part of the HTML document and requires no additional compilation or development tools other than a compatible Web browser. While FrontPage Editor on its own is an extremely capable page editor, its capabilities are enormously extended by adding scripts.

FrontPage Editor lets you insert either Visual Basic Scripts or JavaScripts into your page by choosing the Insert, Script command. When you do this, you get the Script dialog box (see Figure 3.6).

FIGURE 3.6
Use the Script dialog box to add in-line programming to your pages.

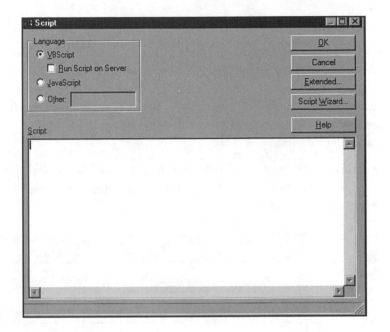

Within the Language section of this dialog box you have several options, as follows:

- VBScript—Mark this option button if you want to write your script in Visual Basic Script. When your script is completed and you close the dialog box, FrontPage inserts the Visual Basic Script icon on the page to indicate that a Visual Basic Script has been placed at that point.

- Run Script on Server—This option is currently unavailable.

- JavaScript—Mark this button if you want to write your script in JavaScript. As with VBScript, when your script is completed and you close the dialog box, FrontPage inserts the JavaScript icon to indicate that a JavaScript has been placed at that point.

- Other—This option is for scripting languages that may be developed in the future.

After selecting the language you want, click in the Script dialog box, type your code, and choose OK when finished.

You may prefer to use the Script Wizard to write your scripts. This is a point-and-click method of creating code; for more information refer to Chapter 20, "Scripting with VBScript and JScript."

Adding Applets

Applets are specialized Java programs especially designed for executing within Internet Web pages. To run a Java applet, you need a Java-enabled Web browser such as Netscape Navigator or Microsoft's Internet Explorer. These and other Web browsers are all capable of handling standard HTML, recognizing applet tags within an HTML Web page, and downloading and executing the specified Java program (or programs) in the context of a Java virtual machine.

Assuming you've created and compiled an applet and it's installed at an appropriate location in your web, you use the Insert, Other Components, Java Applet command to open the Java Applet Properties dialog box (see Figure 3.7).

FIGURE 3.7

To add an applet to a page and configure it quickly, use the Applet Properties dialog box.

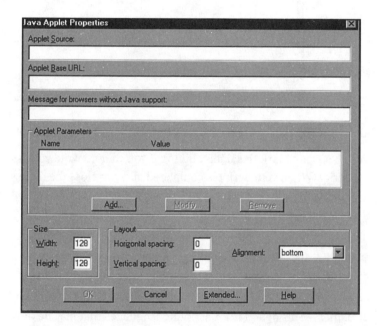

The Applet Source is the name of the source file; this will almost always have a .CLASS extension. The Base URL is the URL of the folder containing this file. You will have to add any parameter names and values required by the applet. For more detailed information on using applets, refer to Chapter 22, "Inserting Java Applets and Browser Plug-Ins."

Adding Netscape Plug-Ins

Starting with version 1 of Navigator, Netscape provided ways to enhance its browser with "helper applications" that support data formats beyond the built-in graphics and HTML. Then, with Netscape Navigator Version 2, Navigator began supporting "plug-ins," another way to extend the range of data types that can be presented on or with a Web page.

FrontPage Editor's plug-in insertion command generates the <EMBED> tag, which is recognized by both Navigator and Internet Explorer. Essentially, the <EMBED> tag is a type of link; objects specified by it are automatically downloaded and displayed when the document is displayed. To insert a plug-in, choose Insert, Other Components, Plug-In to open the Plug-In Properties dialog box (see Figure 3.8).

FIGURE 3.8
Use the Plug-In Properties dialog box to embed objects in a Web page so that plug-in-supporting browsers can use them.

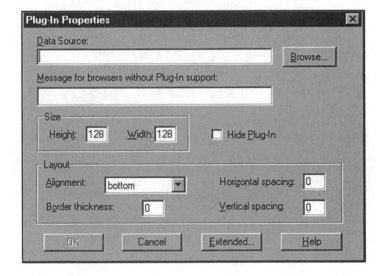

Into the Data Source box, type the name of the file you want embedded. The MIME type of the embedded file tells a user's browser what plug-in to use; if it's Netscape Navigator, and it doesn't have the right plug-in, it will offer to download one for the user.

From Here...

You're off to a good start. You've installed FrontPage successfully, and had a look at WebBots and Image Composer. Now you have many other places you can go, among them:

- Part II, "Creating Your Web Pages with FrontPage Editor," covers the nuts and bolts of page design and creation, including chapters on text and hyperlinks, graphics and multimedia, tables, frames, and templates.

- Part IV, "Creating and Adapting Graphics with Microsoft Image Composer," shows you the methods you use to make and modify your own graphics.

- Part V, "Integrating Active Content Into Your Web Site," explores the exciting new software technologies of ActiveX, VBScript and JavaScript, Java applets, and the Virtual Reality Modeling Language.

- Part VI, "Building and Managing a Web Site," shows you how to integrate the pages you create into a sophisticated, well-organized Web site that will be the envy of your neighbors in cyberspace.

Creating Your Web Pages with FrontPage Editor

## CHAPTER 4

Introducing FrontPage Editor

FrontPage Editor 97 is a very powerful Web page editor, so powerful that you'll seldom need to work directly with HTML text files. FrontPage Editor's interface and behavior resemble those of a word processor, and you'll find many advantages both in this resemblance and in FrontPage Editor's close integration with FrontPage Explorer. Furthermore, and very importantly, FrontPage Editor includes WebBots, dynamic objects you can insert into a page to produce elements like timestamps, confirmation fields, and searches. This all-in-one approach, combining FrontPage Explorer's overall view of a Web site, FrontPage Editor's near-WYSIWYG interface, several multimedia tools, and WebBots to replace programming, helps you build an attention-getting and functional site with a minimum of time and difficulty. ■

FrontPage Editor 97 Enhancements and New Features

The new version of FrontPage brings you multimedia, better font resources, direct HTML editing, and much more.

Page Creation

Create, save, and retrieve pages while using FrontPage Editor and FrontPage Explorer together.

Workspace Customizing

Change the FrontPage Editor screen display.

Previewing in Browsers

Use this new command to see exactly what your pages will look like—without connecting to the Internet.

What's New in FrontPage Editor 97?

The entire FrontPage 97 package contains very significant enhancements and improvements to FrontPage version 1.1. FrontPage Editor 97 has shared in this major upgrade, and if you've used the earlier version, here are the major differences you'll notice.

- Support for the `<font face=>` tag, allowing TrueType fonts to be used almost anywhere in a Web document.
- A Preview in Browser command, which uses the browsers on your host machine to display your pages, without being connected to the Internet.
- Direct HTML source editing from within FrontPage Editor.
- Support for inclusion of background sound with the `<bgsound>` tag.
- Support for in-line video, using the AVI file format.
- Scrolling marquee text.
- Database connectivity.
- Ability to insert JavaScripts, VBScripts, Java applets, ActiveX components, and Netscape plug-ins into a page.
- A clip art image gallery.
- A thesaurus.
- "Drag-and-drop everywhere." Extensive drag-and-drop support.

The interface has also been streamlined and rationalized, and the look and feel of it is very close to that of Microsoft Office. All in all, it's an enormous leap toward making Web page editing easy (and perhaps even fun).

Using FrontPage Editor with FrontPage Explorer

Although FrontPage Editor is capable of running in stand-alone mode, this isn't recommended. Many of its features depend on it being used concurrently with Explorer and the Personal Web Server, and running FrontPage Editor by itself will remove its more advanced functionality. Furthermore, using the two applications side-by-side lets you keep an eye on links among pages and within pages, lets you access image and page files with little fuss, and gives you an overall view of your web as it grows from a single page to a full-scale Web site.

After you start Explorer, you open a web by choosing File, Open FrontPage Web, and choosing the List Webs button. Then you select the web you want from the list box, and choose OK. (It may be necessary to supply a user name and password.) An example of what you might see in the earliest stages of Web construction appears in Figure 4.1.

N O T E If you installed and are using FrontPage file and folder defaults, the webs you create are automatically stored in the C:\FrontPage Webs\Content folder. Click that folder in Windows Explorer, and you'll see folders with the names of your webs beside them. ■

FIGURE 4.1

Explorer's Folder View of a Web site is modeled closely on Windows 95's file display.

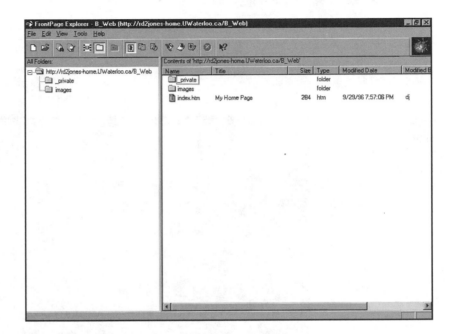

N O T E The New and Open buttons on the Explorer toolbar are for creating and opening webs only. They have nothing to do with creating or opening pages in the web. In Figure 4.1, note that the page title of the home page is My Home Page, while the page file name is INDEX.HTM. Don't confuse the page title and the page file name; the file name is a regular file in the directory structure and must be treated as one. The page title is simply a label for the page. In fact, you can have identical page titles in the same web, though you should avoid this. It's confusing for your audience and likely for you—in the former case, a visitor will see the same page title for different pages, and in the latter you'll have to remember that identical page titles refer to different pages. ■

CAUTION

The INDEX.HTM file, which is automatically created when you create a web with FrontPage Explorer, acts as the default entry point for that web. If you delete or rename INDEX.HTM, browsers will display only a file index of the pages of the web, and your visitors won't see the home page unless they can figure out which file it is.

Part

II

Ch

4

Creating a New Page with FrontPage Editor

You can't create pages with FrontPage Explorer, only with FrontPage Editor. To create a new page, use the following steps:

1. From the Explorer menu bar, choose Tools, Show FrontPage Editor or click the FrontPage Editor button on the Explorer toolbar. The FrontPage Editor starts (see Figure 4.2).

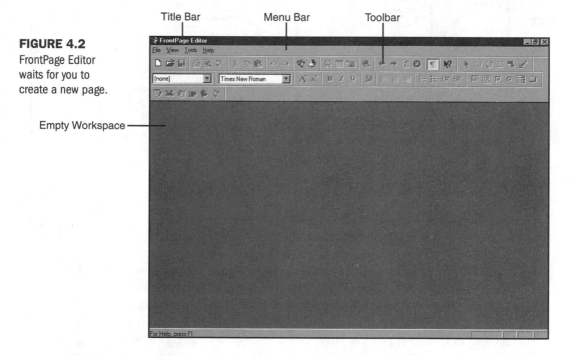

FIGURE 4.2
FrontPage Editor waits for you to create a new page.

NOTE If your FrontPage Editor screen doesn't look like the one in Figure 4.2, see "Changing the FrontPage Editor Screen Display" later in this chapter. ■

2. After Editor starts, choose File, New. The New Page dialog box appears (see Figure 4.3).

NOTE If you click the New button on the toolbar, FrontPage Editor automatically opens a blank Normal Page showing the New Page dialog box. ■

3. Select the Page Template or wizard you want.

4. Choose OK.

FIGURE 4.3

You can create pages using any one of several templates, or you can use a Page Wizard to automate the page creation process.

If you select a Normal Page, you immediately return to FrontPage Editor with a blank Normal Page opened for you. If you make another choice, you can either create a specialized page from the template you selected or generate the page with the wizard you picked.

Creating a Page from a Template   If you select a Page Template, you simply use it as a pattern for laying out the page you want. As soon as you've made even a few additions to it, though, you should save it to avoid losing your work. To do this, choose File, Save or choose the Save button on the toolbar. The Save As dialog box appears (see Figure 4.4).

FIGURE 4.4

Use the Save As dialog box to save your new page with a descriptive page title and a suitable file name.

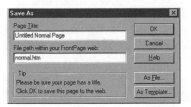

To finish setting up the new page, use the following steps:

1. Type a page title into the text box provided. It can be as long as you like, but don't make it too long; 60 characters is the practical maximum.

2. FrontPage Editor constructs a file name for the page, using nonblank characters from the Page Title box, and shows this name in the Page URL text box. Choose OK to accept this file name.

   Or you can type a different file name in the Page URL text box, and choose OK. If you don't give the file name an .HTM extension, FrontPage Editor supplies one.

CAUTION

The file extension for a Web page file should almost always be .HTM or .HTML; if you give it another extension, browsers may not properly display that page. There are a few exceptions, though—one is Error! Bookmark not defined., which is a combination search engine page.

Part

II

Ch

4

The page is saved to the current, or active, web. You can see the page title you just gave it by looking in the title bar. FrontPage Editor's behavior is different here from a word processor; the page title, not the page file name, appears in the title bar. If you click the FrontPage Explorer button on the toolbar, the Explorer views show you the new page you added (see Figure 4.5).

FIGURE 4.5

Explorer shows your new page's icon and title in the right pane of the Folder View.

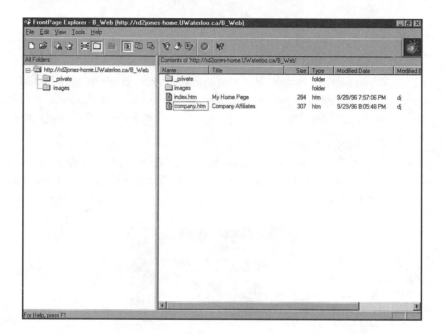

You could, of course, have accepted the default page title, which FrontPage Editor displays for you. But it's not very informative, and the page title is what your audience sees in the title bar when they're browsing your Web. People like to know what to expect in a page, so use your page titles to give them an idea of what they're looking at.

Generating a Page from a Wizard If you select a wizard in the New Page dialog box, Editor walks you through the process of creating the page, and it works in the following way:

1. In the wizard's opening dialog box, click Next. The Page URL text box, common to all wizards, appears.

2. In the Page URL text box, type a suitable file name for this page.

CAUTION

Don't accept the default file name that FrontPage Editor puts in the Page URL text box. For one thing, it's not very descriptive, and if you later create another page of the same type, you'll have to give the new page a different file name anyway. It's better to give your page files descriptive names right from the start.

3. Enter a title for the page in the Page Title text box.

4. Click Next. Continue through the Wizard's dialog boxes until the Wizard tells you it has enough information to create the page (see Figure 4.6).

5. Click Finish.

The Wizard generates the page and displays it ready for editing.

FIGURE 4.6
The Wizard tells you when it's ready to create the page for you.

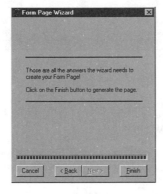

Part

II

Ch

4

 If you think you've made a mistake or want to check your work, you can always go back to a wizard's previous dialog box by choosing the Back button. If you want the wizard to do only part of the work, click the Finish button when it's done as much as you want it to.

Saving Your Wizard-Generated Page   To save your wizard-generated page, choose File, Save or click the Save button on the Editor toolbar. The Save As dialog box appears. However, you've already given the page a title and a file name when the wizard started. So you can just choose OK to accept these, and save the page to the active web. (You can change them if you want to, though.)

Editor saves the new page to the web. To verify this, make the FrontPage Explorer active (see Figure 4.7).

FIGURE 4.7

Saving a new page automatically updates FrontPage Explorer's display.

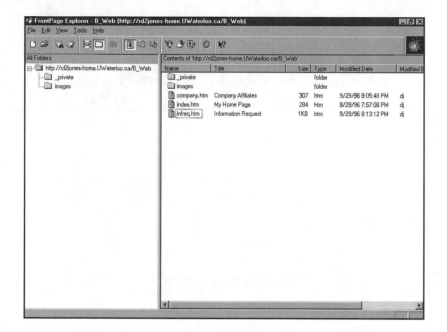

Editing an Existing Page

Start FrontPage Explorer and open the web that contains the page you want to edit. To load and edit the page, use the following steps:

1. From the Explorer menu bar, choose Tools, Show FrontPage Editor or click the FrontPage Editor button on the Explorer toolbar.

2. After the Editor starts, choose File, Open or click the Open button on the Editor toolbar.

3. From the Current FrontPage Web dialog box, select the title of the page you want to edit (see Figure 4.8).

4. Choose OK. The selected page appears in the Editor's workspace.

 If Editor isn't already running, you can double-click the icon of the page you want to edit in the right pane of either the Folder View or the Hyperlink View of FrontPage Explorer. This starts Editor and automatically loads the page you double-clicked. Alternatively, right-click the page you want to edit and choose Open from the shortcut menu that appears.

 You can also open a page in FrontPage Editor by dragging its icon from any Explorer pane to FrontPage Editor's title bar. But don't drag the icon into Editor's workspace if there's a page already there. This creates a hyperlink between the page already in Editor and the page whose icon you're dragging.

FIGURE 4.8
The Current FrontPage Web dialog box displays the page titles and file names of the pages that belong to the open web.

Retitling or Renaming a Page

As your web becomes large and elaborate, you'll likely run into situations where you need to change a page's title or URL (or file name). This is pretty straightforward.

To change the page title, use the following steps:

1. Load the page into FrontPage Editor, using whatever method you prefer.
2. Edit the page, if desired.
3. Choose File, Page Properties. The Page Properties dialog box appears (see Figure 4.9).

Part
II

Ch
4

FIGURE 4.9
You can change or edit a page title in the Page Properties dialog box.

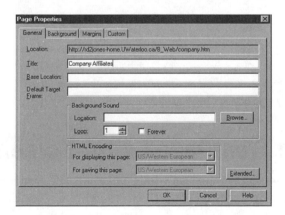

4. Choose the General sheet tab if it isn't already chosen. Then type the title you want into the Title text box.
5. Choose OK.

The new page title appears in FrontPage Editor's title bar.

N O T E Changing the page title doesn't affect the file name or the URL in any way. The file name and URL stay as they are until you change them to something else. ■

You can also give the page a different file name. To do so, use the following steps:

1. Choose File, Save As. The Save As dialog box appears.
2. Type the file name you want in the Page URL text box. If you don't type in the .HTM extension, FrontPage Editor supplies it for you.
3. Choose OK.

To see the effect of this, make FrontPage Explorer the active window, with Folder View selected. In the right-hand pane, your page is present under its new title and with its new file name. However, the original page, the one you began with, is still present. If you want to delete it, use the following steps:

1. In Explorer (in any pane that shows page icons), click the name or icon of the file to select it.
2. Choose Edit, Delete. The Confirm Delete dialog box appears.
3. Choose Yes. The file is deleted, and the Explorer screen is updated.

CAUTION

When deleting a page, be careful not to accidentally use the Delete FrontPage Web command in Explorer's File menu. Once you delete a web, it's gone for good!

N O T E If you create a default page (that is, you accept the file name and page title supplied by FrontPage Editor) and then try to create a second page of the same type without renaming the first, Explorer queries you about your action. The query lets you either overwrite the first page with the second or cancel the action entirely. Of course, you can have identical file names as long as they're in different webs or folders. ■

Changing the FrontPage Editor Screen Display

FrontPage Editor doesn't allow extensive customization of its display, though you can re-arrange the toolbars by simply dragging them around. You're restricted to turning on or off the following elements:

- Toolbars: standard, format, image, forms, advanced
- Status Bar
- Format Marks: hard line returns, bookmarks, and form outlines

FIGURE 4.10
Use the View menu to choose the screen elements to be displayed.

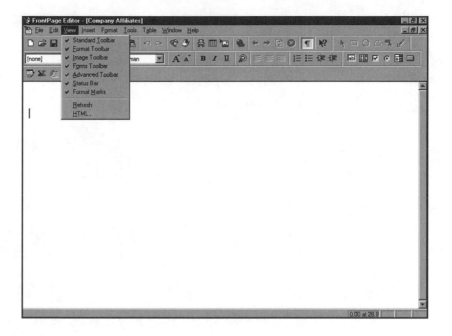

You can hide or show all these from the View menu (see Figure 4.10).

To hide or show individual screen elements, use the following steps:

1. Choose View from the FrontPage Editor menu bar.
2. Click the name of the toolbar you want to hide or show.
3. Turn the status bar on or off by clicking Status Bar on the menu.
4. Turn hard line returns, bookmarks, and form outlines on or off by clicking Format Marks on the menu.

Directly Editing HTML

The final choice on the View menu, HTML, lets you edit the HTML code of a page from within FrontPage Editor. Selecting this opens the View or Edit HTML workspace (see Figure 4.11).

This is a major improvement over FrontPage 1.1, because using other editors on a page generated by FrontPage Editor sometimes gave unpredictable results. Small tweaks to the code now become easy, and pasting in code snippets is simple.

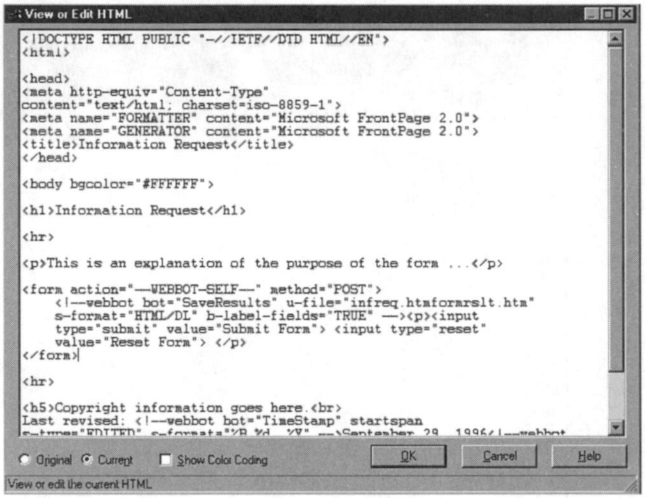

FIGURE 4.11
With FrontPage Editor
97, you can work
directly with the active
page's HTML code.

CAUTION

You may find some unpredictable behavior if you try to add unsupported code using this technique. There's no problem with supported code (assuming no syntax errors) but for unsupported HTML it's much safer to use the HTML Markup command. In fact, if you add unrecognized code in the View window, FrontPage encloses the code in a HTML Markup component when you exit the window, anyway. Note that the direct editing procedure and the HTML Markup command do not flag errors in the code —errors are accepted, with possibly lethal results.

▶ **See** Chapter 11, "Working Directly with HTML," **p. 257**

Previewing Your Work in a Browser

FrontPage Editor 97 makes page editing enormously more convenient by giving you the Preview in Browser command. This allows you to see very quickly how your page is going to appear in any browser you have installed in your host machine. Better yet, you don't have to be connected to the Internet to use the Preview in Browser command.

When FrontPage 97 installs, it searches for the browsers in your system and ties them into FrontPage Editor. You'll see this when you use the command for the first time. To do so, make the page you want to look at the active one, and choose File, Preview in Browser to open the Preview in Browser dialog box (see Figure 4.12).

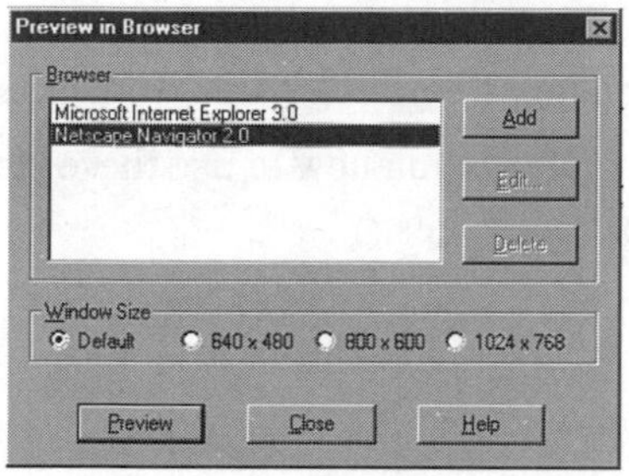

FIGURE 4.12

It's easy to assess your work in any browser you have on your system.

You can set the window size to simulate what your visitors will see in different screen resolutions. (Default uses the current resolution of your display.) Do so, then select the desired browser, and choose Preview. The browser starts and loads the page for you to view. When you've seen as much as you like, close the browser to return to FrontPage Editor.

Updating your system when you add or remove browsers is done with the Add, Edit, and Delete buttons. These take you to dialog boxes where you can make the following adjustments.

- Add: Click Add to open the Add Browser dialog box where you can add another browser to the list of available ones.

- Edit: Select a browser, then click Edit to open the Edit Browser dialog box where you can change information about a browser you have added. You cannot edit information about a browser that FrontPage automatically detects and adds to the Preview in Browser dialog box during installation.

- Delete: Select a browser, then click Delete to remove it. However, you cannot remove a Web browser. FrontPage automatically detects and adds it to the Preview in Browser dialog box during installation.

From Here...

We've now covered the options that FrontPage Explorer and FrontPage Editor give you for creating and managing pages. Now it's time to move on to the creative stuff. That can get complicated too, but it's worth it.

- Chapter 5, "Developing the Basic Page: Text, Lists, and Hyperlinks," describes the basics of good page design and starts you out making a basic page with text entry and layout, lists, and hyperlinks.

Part

II

Ch

4

■ Chapter 6, "Enhancing Pages with Graphics and Multimedia," takes you further into page design with image handling, color usage, image maps, sound, and in-line video.

■ Chapter 7, "Creating Tables," shows you how to use these structures to organize and compress the content of your pages.

## CHAPTER 5

Developing the Basic Page: Text, Lists, and Hyperlinks

FrontPage's value lies in its all-in-one approach to Web site construction, page creation, and site maintenance. You should carry this sense of integration with you as you use FrontPage Editor to compose and link pages; that is, you should keep in mind that the particular page you're working on doesn't stand in isolation. It should fit seamlessly into the larger pattern of your site. This chapter deals with what makes a good page and with the essentials of using FrontPage Editor to compose and link pages. ■

Page Design

Design your pages to please your visitors, keep them around, and make them want to come back.

Text Entry

Add headings, text, and font variety to your page.

Layout

Format and lay out text effectively.

Lists

Use lists, including bulleted lists, numbered lists, and glossary lists.

Decorative elements

Use text and background colors.

Hyperlinks

Understand hyperlinks and install them on your page.

Thinking Through Your Page Design

Compared to writing HTML code with a text editor, making a page with FrontPage Editor is easy. You can drop in a few headers, some paragraphs of text, three or four images (and maybe an image map), a list, a form, a table, and as many hyperlinks as you please, all in a very short time. Now you've got a home page. Then you do another page, and another, and soon you've got a wonderful Web site ready for the world to visit. Don't you?

Well, maybe. But bad design is the nemesis of many, many, Web pages, and you risk producing an unattractive page if you don't know and follow a few commonsense guidelines. Most important, you have to think about your visitors, and how they're likely to experience your site.

Planning for Your Visitors

If you've spent any time browsing the Web, you've already encountered plenty of sites you won't revisit because the first page you went to had one or more of the following problems:

- Took too long to load
- Had no clear purpose
- Was poorly laid out or badly written
- Had obscure navigational tools
- Didn't link to other sites as it said it would
- Had no useful information

Obviously you don't want people to have that experience with your work. But how do you make sure they don't? The short answer is to put yourself in your visitors' shoes and think like the audience you want to have. Any author, in print, multimedia, or Web has to do this or risk failure.

For illustration, consider your own experience. When you open a new book or magazine or see an unknown Web page appearing in your browser, what's in the back of your mind? You may be barely aware of it, but it's always there, and it's: "What's in this for me?" You want something from this page: information, entertainment, aesthetic pleasure, or intellectual stimulation, depending on your tastes and the needs of the moment. If you sense in the first minute or two that you're not going to get it, you very quickly go elsewhere. And so will your viewers, if they get that feeling from the first Web page they see on your site.

Keeping Your Visitors Around for More

This danger of losing the audience on the first page is something all professional authors worry about. The tool they use to prevent it is called "the hook," and they try very hard to find the best hook for whatever it is they're producing. The idea of the hook is simple: it goes at the very beginning of a work, and it's carefully designed to seize the reader's attention. More than that, it's designed to make the reader want to go on paying attention, to read the rest of this page, and the next, and the next. And as an author of Web pages, you're going to want to keep your audience's attention; otherwise, why are you bothering to make the pages at all? So put yourself in the mind of the person who's seeing your site for the first time, and ask: "What's here for me?" If the honest answer is: "Not much," you need to rethink your approach. You need a better hook, one that will make your viewer want to look around the rest of your site. But how do you make one?

Avoiding the Extremes   The first temptation is to pull out all the stops on the technology. That's a considerable temptation because it's gotten a lot simpler to produce decorative marvels on a Web page, and it's fun. The trouble is that it's likely more fun for the page designer to do than it is for her audience to experience. It's true that a visually spectacular page will keep a viewer's interest for a while (assuming he waits for it to download, which he may not), but if there's nothing to it but spectacle, it's a failure as a page (see Figure 5.1).

FIGURE 5.1
Avoid the errors here: a large image that downloads slowly, clumsy layout, uninformative page titling, and an unidentified arrow icon that might (or might not) be a navigation button.

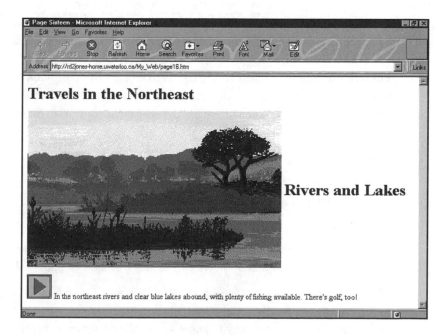

At the other extreme, a page crammed with solid text, scrolling on and on without whitespace or other elements to relieve the eye, is almost as bad. You may feel that the important information you give is enough of a hook. But even if the information the reader wants is there, will she stick around to find it? Her browser controls are in easy reach, and she may decide to go elsewhere for what she's after (see Figure 5.2).

FIGURE 5.2

Filling screen after screen with solid print is hard on your reader's eyes.

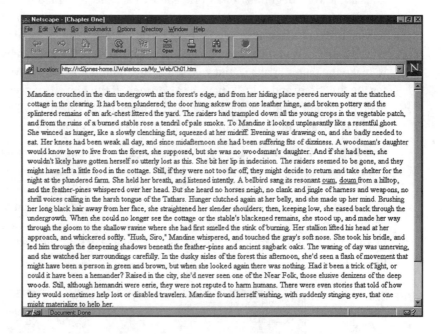

Finding a Balance   When you're trying to identify the best hook for your site, ask yourself this: What does my viewer want, and how do I show her, in a hurry, that she's going to find it? Reversing our earlier list of reasons for not staying on a Web site, we get the following:

- The first page appears quickly.
- Its purpose is immediately and clearly identified.
- It's well laid out, and well written.
- Its links accurately suggest what the viewer will find if she uses them.
- Its links behave as advertised when the viewer does use them.
- It supplies the content the viewer expects, or a quick path to that content.

That's a page that's a successful hook for a Web site. Following these guidelines will go a long, long way toward making all your pages, and therefore your entire site, both pleasing and useful. In short, your key to success is really a balance of presentation and content. An example of such balance appears in Figure 5.3.

FIGURE 5.3
This home page integrates images, text, and navigation buttons to make an attractive and functional whole.

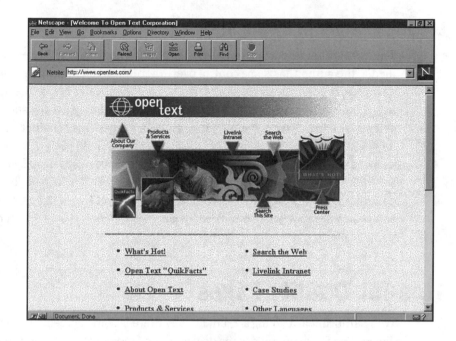

But you can produce a very efficient and useful page even without using much in the way of images and graphical controls. This is a good approach if your intended audience uses a wide range of browsers, including text-only ones like LYNX. The example in Figure 5.4 is almost entirely text, but its content is balanced by a presentation that directs the user quickly and efficiently to the resources.

Part

II

Ch

5

FIGURE 5.4
This text-based page is laid out clearly and economically. It also includes a version you can download for printing, a thoughtful touch on the part of its designer.

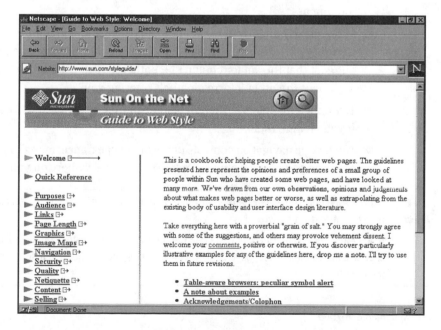

Letting Visitors in by the Side Door

There's another important fact about Web authoring you need to keep in mind. With other media, the author has some control over where the audience is going to start. People read novels from page one; moviegoers try to reach the theater before the opening credits roll; magazine readers may flip through the magazine, but they usually start reading an article at its beginning. With a Web site, though, your readers may enter at any page, depending on what link sent them there. This means that you should design every page with the same care you lavished on your home page. And since people usually like to have a look at the home page (it helps them get oriented), it's a good idea to include a go-to-home-page control on all your pages. This is especially true if you have a large or complex site or one whose organization isn't obvious when a person enters it at some point other than the home page.

Tips for Quality Pages

Web authoring is a young art, but already there is some agreement about its basic principles. The following guidelines deal with the fundamentals of text layout and hyperlink design.

- With a text-heavy page, use lots of whitespace.
- Avoid very long pages that require endless scrolling.
- Give your page a title that helps the user figure out where she is and what she's looking at.
- Write clearly and pay close attention to spelling and grammar. Nothing undermines a page's authority as much as confusing language and bad spelling. Even typos suggest that the author couldn't be bothered to check his work, and what does that say about the other information he's offering you?
- Keep the link colors at their defaults. Your users are used to them and will resent it if you change them.
- Keep your navigation controls uniform in appearance; for example, a go-to-home-page button should look the same everywhere on your site.

 TIP **http://www.sun.com/styleguide**, Sun Microsystem's Web site, offers useful general advice on page layout and writing style.

http://info.med.yale.edu/caim, the Yale Center for Advanced Instructional Media, gives extensive information about page design, with a leaning toward the production of scholarly documents.

Testing

The importance of testing can't be emphasized too much. Your pages may look flawless in your favorite browser, but how do they look in another kind of browser? Different browsers modify the general appearance of a page, and all recent versions can be user-configured to make drastic changes to the display. Furthermore, text-only browsers don't display images at all. While you can't allow for every possible variation, comprehensive testing ensures that most people can use your site. Just as important, it tells you that your pages are behaving properly, before anybody else sees them. Here are some ways of getting things right the first time:

- Test each page with the default settings of Netscape and Microsoft Internet Explorer, which are now the dominant browsers. In addition, test using the lowest common denominator of display, which is 640 × 480 in 16 colors, on a 14" monitor.

- Vary the browsers' configurations to see if this drastically changes your pages' appearance.

- Put in alternate text for images and graphical navigation controls. Remember that many people run their browsers with images turned off to download pages faster.

- Speaking of speed, always test your page's downloading time through your ISP connection. Simply opening the page in your browser as a local file will be far faster than any real-world situation, and won't tell you what you need to know. Assume that your viewers will be using a 14.4kps modem, and plan your page around that.

- Get user feedback during testing. Like any author, you're too close to your material to catch every flaw.

- Print your pages and inspect them. Hard copy often reveals problems with the writing, in a way that a screen image (for some mysterious reason) doesn't.

- Remember that long, complicated pages are harder to maintain than short, simple ones.

- After making even a minor change to your page, test it thoroughly.

- When everything is working perfectly, test it again.

Part
II

Ch
5

Creating a Page Based on the Normal Template

Now that we've had a look at some basic design principles, we'll spend the rest of this chapter exploring how to place text and hyperlinks on a clean page. The page we'll start with is the home page of a Normal web, which you'll generate with Explorer. You've learned to do this earlier, but we'll review it briefly here. To create a Normal web, use the following steps:

1. Start FrontPage Explorer. Choose File, New, FrontPage Web, and when the New FrontPage Web dialog box appears, select Normal Web.

2. When the Normal Web Template dialog box appears, leave the defaults in place and type the name of your Web into the Name of New FrontPage Web box.

3. Choose OK.

FrontPage Explorer generates the Web, and the Home Page icon (a house) appears in Hyperlink View's left pane. The icon title defaults to "Home Page" but you'll change that shortly. However, you should never change the file name of the home page, which is INDEX.HTM (visible in the right pane in Folder View) if you are using the FrontPage Personal Web Server. This is because INDEX.HTM is the file that browsers automatically search for when they're looking for a Web home page. (Some Web servers need a different default, though; check the server requirements to determine this).

With the new Web open, start FrontPage Editor. The quickest way to do this, and at the same time load the page you want, is to double-click the page icon in Hyperlink View's right pane, or its Name entry in Folder View's right pane. Whichever you do, FrontPage Editor appears with the chosen page in the editing window (see Figure 5.5). Now you're ready to start.

N O T E FrontPage Editor makes it convenient to move among pages you've opened. Choose Window, and the lower section of the menu will show the currently open documents. Click the one you want to display it. To flip rapidly between the last page and the next page, you can use the Forward and Back buttons on the Standard Toolbar. ■

Web pages, as you know, can be very elaborate. However, all you need to keep in mind just now is that the bulk of every page is made up of combinations of the following three basic elements:

- Text
- Hyperlinks
- Images

There's also active content, of course, like JavaScript, ActiveX, and so on. These aren't basic in the sense that they're required for a pleasing, functional page, so they will be dealt with in later chapters.

Change Style box   Decrease Text Size

FIGURE 5.5
FrontPage Editor
retrieves the
blank home
page, ready for
you to start
composing, with
the default title
Normal Page in
the title bar.

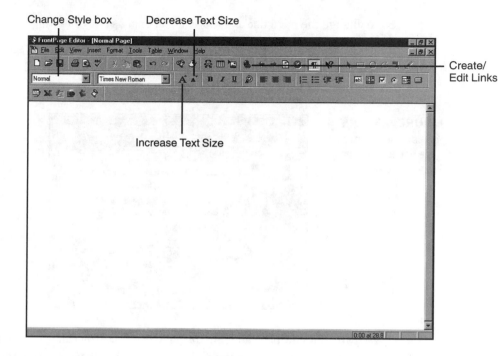

Create/
Edit Links

Increase Text Size

▶ **See** Chapter 19, "Using ActiveX Controls," **p. 401**
▶ **See** Chapter 20, "Scripting with VBScript and JScript," **p. 443**
▶ **See** Chapter 21, "JavaScript," **p. 495**
▶ **See** Chapter 22, "Inserting Java Applets and Browser Plug-Ins," **p. 539**

Part

II

Ch

5

Giving Your Page a Title that Works

Even before you start adding content to your page, you should give it a meaningful title (if
you want to modify the title later, you can always do so). You ought to put some thought
into this because a person new to your page will usually read its title for hints about where
he is and what he's looking at. The default title of Home Page just won't help him much. In
fact, there are two more reasons for taking pains with your title. First, it's what your
visitor's browser will record in its Bookmark list (Netscape) or Favorites folder (Internet
Explorer) if he marks the page; an informative title will jog his memory later about the
nature of your site. Second, Internet search programs like WAIS read the title for indexing
and retrieval purposes, and presumably you want your site to show up in their lists.

So to change the page title to a more useful one, use the following steps:

1. Choose File, Page Properties or right-click in the workspace and choose Page Properties from the shortcut menu. The Page Properties dialog box appears (see Figure 5.6).

FIGURE 5.6
You can change your page title in the Page Properties dialog box.

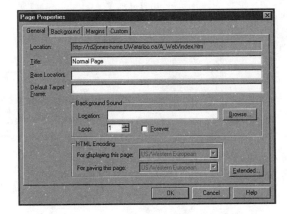

2. Type the new page title into the Title text box. You can use any characters you want. The title can also be any length, but remember that your visitors may be using a lower screen resolution than you are. A width of 60 characters is about the practical maximum.

3. Choose OK.

Your new page title appears in the FrontPage Editor title bar.

TIP Remember that your home page isn't the only one in your site that needs a functional title. Every page should have such a guidepost for its viewers. A title like "Page 31" or "Section 17" isn't much use in keeping a viewer oriented.

Previewing Your Edited Page

Now that you've made a change to the page, you may want to see what it's going to look like in a browser. To do this, it's most efficient to use FrontPage Editor's Preview in Browser command. (When you installed FrontPage, the setup program looked for the browsers you have on your machine, so you can select which one you want to use for previewing.) To preview your page:

1. Choose File, Preview in Browser. The Preview in Browser dialog box appears (see Figure 5.7).

FIGURE 5.7
You use the Preview in Browser dialog box for fast and easy previewing of a page you're working on.

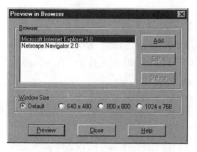

2. In the Browser list box, click the name of the browser you want to use.

3. Mark the option button for the resolution you want. "Default" uses the current resolution of your display.

4. Choose Preview. The selected browser loads and displays the page currently active in FrontPage Editor.

5. When you've checked your work, close the browser to return to FrontPage Editor.

 A convenient feature of this preview command is that you don't have to save the page before viewing it. FrontPage automatically saves the page and updates the Explorer display when you click the Preview button.

 If you make a mistake, you can choose Edit, Undo to undo your last action.

TROUBLESHOOTING

I edited a page, then previewed it, and everything was fine. To save time, I didn't close the previewing browser. Then I did another edit, and switched back to the browser. It didn't show the new edit even when I clicked the Refresh or Reload buttons. Why not? The previewing browser retrieves the page from the file it's stored in, not from the FrontPage Editor workspace. If you want to keep the previewing browser running, you have to save the page each time you want to preview it, then use the browser's Reload or Refresh buttons to display the new version of the page.

Part
II

Ch
5

Adding Basic Text to a Page

You can use several different methods to put text onto your page. The simplest kinds of text are headings and Normal text.

Using the Format Menu to Add Headings

You use headings to mark off major divisions and subdivisions of meaning within a page. FrontPage Editor offers the six levels of headings that are standard with HTML. To place one on a page, use the following steps:

1. Type the heading text at the place you want it. Do not press Enter when you're done.

2. Choose Format, Paragraph. The Paragraph Properties dialog box appears (see Figure 5.8).

FIGURE 5.8
FrontPage Editor offers multiple levels of headings.

3. Select Heading 1, then choose OK. The text changes to the largest heading style. Press the Enter key to put the insertion point on the next line.

4. To look at the other heading styles, follow steps 1 through 3 above, each time selecting a different heading type from the Paragraph Properties list box. Figure 5.9 shows the full range.

FIGURE 5.9
FrontPage Editor supplies very large (1) to very small headings (6).

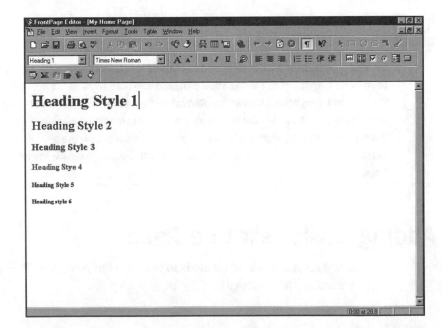

Removing a Heading and its Style   To delete a heading, use the following steps:

1. Select the heading you want to delete.

2. Press the Delete key or choose Edit, Clear.

3. The heading text disappears.

The line containing the insertion point will still retain the heading style. To remove this, choose Format, Paragraph. Then select Normal from the list box, and choose OK. The style of the line returns to Normal (default) style.

The heading style, unlike some of the other styles in FrontPage Editor, is not retained after you press the Enter key. When you press Enter at the end of a heading-style line, the style of the next line returns to Normal.

Applying Paragraph Styles with the Change Style Box   A faster and more convenient way to change heading levels is with the Change Style drop-down list box, which lets you choose from all the heading levels and text styles available. (If you've used styles in Microsoft Word, the technique is immediately familiar.) To see the styles, click the arrow button at the right of the Change Style drop-down list box (see Figure 5.10).

FIGURE 5.10
You can apply styles easily by selecting from the list in the Change Styles box.

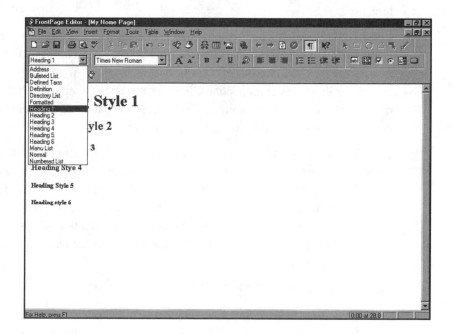

Part

II

Ch

5

To use this method to change a paragraph style, use the following steps:

1. Select the paragraph you want to modify by placing the insertion point anywhere inside it.

2. Click the arrow button at the right of the Change Style drop-down list box. The list of styles appears.

3. Click the style you want. All the text of the paragraph takes on the new appearance.

As you've already guessed, this method works for all styles, not just for headings. In some cases you might want to compose most of the text of your page in the Normal style (the default) and then use the Change Style drop-down list box to modify sections of it.

 TIP Don't overuse the larger heading styles on a single screen. If you do, a visitor to your site may feel as if she's being shouted at. Think of headings as signaling divisions and subdivisions of content, rather than as a method of emphasis.

Adding Paragraphs of Normal Text

In FrontPage Editor, you produce most text with the Normal style, which at default is set to the Times New Roman font. A new feature of FrontPage 97 is that you aren't limited to Times New Roman for Normal text—you can change fonts with the Format, Font command. The available fonts are whatever TrueType fonts you have installed on your system.

Before using different fonts, though, be aware that only recent browsers (MS Internet Explorer 3.0 and Netscape 3.0) that support the <font face = > and </font> tags will display the font you choose. In older browsers, it will show up as Times New Roman, at default, or in whatever proportional font option the browser's user has selected. Still, the more recent browsers are gaining wide acceptance, and you may feel that using this font flexibility now is preferable to updating your site later.

If you've used other Web authoring tools, you likely already suspect that FrontPage Editor's Normal style produces what the others call paragraphs. This is absolutely correct. Unfortunately, there is an ongoing debate over exactly what "paragraph" means in Web authoring, and in fact FrontPage Editor's Paragraph Format dialog box distinguishes four styles (or "formats") of paragraphs: Normal, Formatted, Address, and Heading. We'll look at the behavior of the Normal style paragraph first, leaving its font at the default of Times New Roman.

To write your text, use the following steps:

1. Place the cursor where you want the text to begin.

2. If the Change Style box says (none), you must use this box to select the style. Click the button at the right of the box, and select Normal from the drop-down list.

3. Alternatively, if the Change Style Box says something other than (none) or Normal, choose F<u>o</u>rmat, <u>P</u>aragraph, then select Normal from the list box and choose OK. Normal appears in the Change Style box.

3. Start typing. When you reach the end of a paragraph, press Enter, as you usually do. This starts a new paragraph, still in the Normal style. Go on typing until you've said what you want to.

You can see an example of Normal text in Figure 5.11. Both FrontPage Editor and browsers automatically insert a blank line before the start of each paragraph. You can't change this behavior, but there's a method for closing up the whitespace between paragraphs, which we'll look at later, in the section "Using Line Breaks to Control Text Formatting." Also, in the Normal style, the first line of a paragraph can't be indented—the Tab key doesn't do anything.

FIGURE 5.11
You use the Normal style to generate paragraphs of ordinary text.

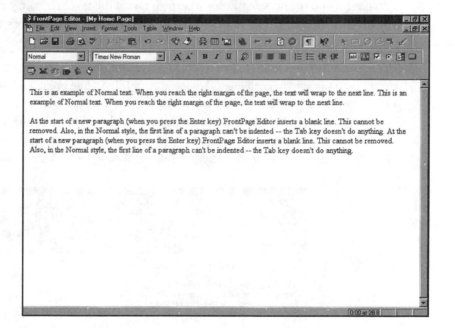

But what if you want extra whitespace between paragraphs, over and above the automatically inserted blank line? Well, if you've used other Web page editors, you'll know that you can't put in blank lines merely by pressing the Enter key. The whitespace shows up in the editing window just fine, but browsers ignore it.

But with FrontPage Editor, the blank lines you get by pressing the Enter key do appear in recent browsers. FrontPage Editor achieves this by inserting an   (an escape sequence) whenever you press the Enter key. Browsers that recognize this escape sequence (including Netscape 2.0 and 3.0, NCSA Mosaic 2.1, and Microsoft Internet Explorer 2.0 and 3.0) don't "crunch" the whitespace; they let it show up. You'll find this word processor-like feature to be a great improvement over earlier Web page editors, which demand that you insert a line break element to generate whitespace between paragraphs.

 TIP   Sometimes you need a nonbreaking space to force two words or a word and a number to stay together on one line (January 17, for example). Use Shift+Spacebar to insert such a space.

Using Line Breaks to Control Text Formatting   It's convenient that FrontPage Editor has simplified using whitespace between paragraphs, but what about the opposite problem? That is, if you need short lines of text all kept together (quoting poetry, for example) how do you keep FrontPage Editor from putting blank lines between these one-line paragraphs? If you try pressing Enter where you want the text to break, you'll always get a blank line. The solution is to insert line breaks. The line break orders a browser to jump to the very next line of its window and then deal with whatever comes after the break.

The procedure is simple: to keep short lines of text together, you press Shift+Enter when you reach the end of each line. This inserts an HTML line break tag into the text stream, which orders a browser not to leave a blank line before the start of the next line of text (see Figure 5.12). If you've turned on Format Marks (either with the View menu, or the Show/Hide Format Marks toolbar button), you'll see a line break symbol in the FrontPage Editor workspace. These symbols, of course, don't show up in a browser.

FIGURE 5.12
You use line breaks to arrange text in short lines.

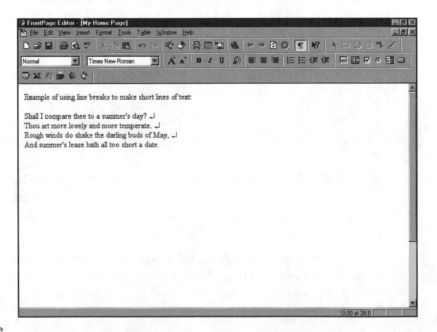

These line breaks don't define the end of a paragraph, by the way. Changing the paragraph style affects all the text between the end of the previous paragraph and the start of the next, and completely ignores the presence of the line breaks.

NOTE Choosing Insert, Break provides specialized line breaks as well as the basic one you get with Shift+Enter. These special breaks are dealt with in the "Using Line Break Properties with Images" section in Chapter 6, "Enhancing Pages with Graphics and Multimedia." ■

Enlarging and Shrinking Normal Text   Sometimes you need to increase or decrease the size of text within a paragraph for emphasis or design purposes. You can't do this with a heading; because headings are styles, they affect all of a paragraph, not just part of it. The way around this problem is to use the Increase and Decrease Text Size buttons on the Formatting toolbar (see Figure 5.13). First select the text whose size you want to change, and then click whichever button is appropriate. You can keep clicking until the text is close to the size you want—"close to," because the point size of the type isn't fully adjustable, as it is in a word processor. The sizes available, in terms of points, are 8, 10, 12, 14, 18, 24, and 36.

FIGURE 5.13
Enlarging or shrinking text is simple with the Increase and Decrease Text size buttons.

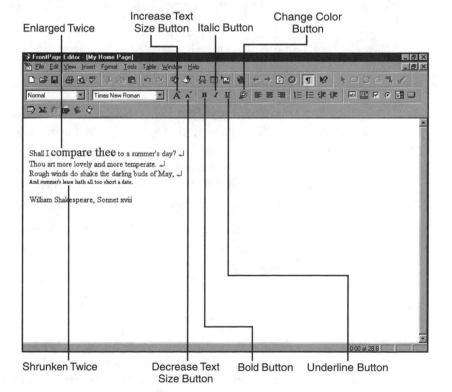

Part
II

Ch
5

The size of "Normal" text is always 12 points. The previous seven point sizes correspond to the seven HTML-defined type sizes.

Adding Character Formatting   The physical appearance of words on a page gives your readers clues about what those words are for, and how important they are relative to everything else. (All your words are important, but some are more important than others, right?) Italics are for emphasis, but also for book titles and certain kinds of citations. Headings signal blocks of related information. Bold is another emphasis, but subtly different from italic. Typewriter font gives another effect. In Web publishing (as in paper publishing) you won't go wrong if you stick to normal typographical conventions, especially the one that says "don't overdo it." If half your page displays in italic and half in bold, your reader can't tell the difference between what's important and what's really important.

With FrontPage Editor you can apply all these character formats and change the text color simply by selecting and clicking. Figure 5.13 shows the buttons you use to apply these effects, using normal word processing practices. Select the text you want to modify, then click the appropriate button to apply the effect. If you're starting new text, click the button, type the new text, and click the button again when you want to turn the effect off. The effects can be "layered"; that is, you can have text that is bold, italic, underlined, and in color.

Usage of bold, underline, and italic in page design are pretty conventional and easy to grasp. Color usage, however, is a more complex matter, and we'll consider it at more length later in this chapter, in the section "Changing Background and Text Colors."

Choosing Fonts with the Change Font Box   Using different fonts can add enormously to the impact of a page. Fonts do have what you might call (no pun intended) "character"; that is, they suggest a certain mood to the reader. Ornate fonts (TrueType Algerian would be an example) suggest a different atmosphere from the formal air that surrounds a traditional font like Bookman Old Style. Combinations of fonts lend both variety and pacing to the flow of the text on your page.

A common mistake of fledgling typographers, however, is to become overexcited at the vast range of fonts available, and change them at the least opportunity. This usually leads to a visual mess. Instead of doing this, start by figuring out the "mood" of the page, or of your site as a whole. Is it to be "traditionally" businesslike? High-technology? Whimsical? Highly personal? Artistic? Counterculture? Of course, the nature of the audience you hope to attract will help define the mood you want to create.

When you've got that worked out, look for fonts that reflect this mood. Then experiment with them on the page, seeing if they work together or cause visual chaos. You'll likely end up with a small selection of fonts: a couple for titles and/or main headings, one for body text, and one or two others for specialized purposes, which will depend on the nature of your site. Properly selected, this range of fonts will contribute to giving your page (and site) a feeling of unity and focus. This in turn adds conviction to what you want to say. When in doubt, go for fewer fonts, not more.

The simplest way to change fonts is with the Change Font list box (see Figure 5.14).

FIGURE 5.14

Use the Change Fonts box to select different fonts.

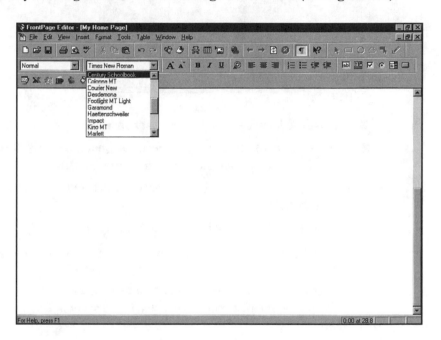

To switch to a new font for new text, simply click the button at the right end of the Change Font box, and select the font you want from the drop-down list. Whatever you type from then on will be in the new font until you either change it or place the insertion point within text of a different font.

To change the font of existing text, select the text to be modified, then choose the new font from the Change Font box. The selected text will change accordingly.

Using the Font Dialog Box   The previous methods are useful shortcuts. However, you can also control your fonts and add additional effects with the Font dialog box. Choose Format, Font to open it. Figure 5.15 shows what it looks like.

This dialog box has two sheet tabs: Special Styles, and Font, but for now we'll consider just the Font sheet. With it, you can do the following:

- Select the font name from the Font list box.
- Use the Font Style list box to apply regular, bold, italic, and bold italic character styles.

Part
II

Ch
5

FIGURE 5.15
With the Font dialog box you can not only change fonts and their sizes, but add effects such as strikethrough.

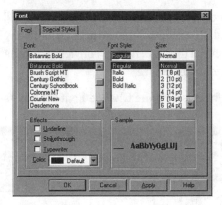

- Choose the font size from the Size list box.
- Use the Effects section to apply effects for Underline, Strikethrough, and Typewriter (which is actually monospaced Courier font).
- Use the Color drop-down list to apply color to a font or to generate a custom color for the font.
- See what the font will look like in the Sample box.

To make the font look as you want it, simply select from among the various options, and choose OK. Selected text will take on these characteristics, or you can start typing new text with them. Generating custom colors for text is quite simple, but we'll reserve discussion of how you do it for later in this chapter, in the section "Changing Background and Text Colors."

Getting Rid of Character Formatting   If you've been experimenting with character formatting on a large section of text and have messed it up so thoroughly that you want to start all over again, you can easily do so. Select the offending text and choose Format, Remove Formatting. Character size, font, color, and attributes (such as bold) will all revert to the default of Times New Roman, size 3 (12 point), regular typeface, color black.

Using FrontPage Editor's Other Paragraph Styles

So far in this chapter, you've looked at FrontPage Editor's Heading and Normal styles, which produce the page elements that formal HTML calls the heading and the paragraph. On top of that, FrontPage Editor's Paragraph Properties dialog box gives you two other styles: *formatted* and *address*.

N O T E   Because Web publishing is such a new phenomenon, some of its terminology hasn't yet settled down to a standard. FrontPage Editor uses its own vocabulary for certain elements of HTML to make the interface software feel more like a word processor. This shows especially in FrontPage Editor's use of "styles" of text, and you may find it easier to think in terms of styles rather than HTML references such as "preformatted text" or "blockquote." For consistency with the software, we'll stick with FrontPage Editor's word processor model and will refer most of the time to "styles." ■

Using the Formatted Style with New Text   Why would you need the Formatted style? Well, you may need to write text that must have tabbing or strings of spaces embedded in it. The Normal style doesn't allow this, but the Formatted style does. You can also use character attributes, such as bold or italic, as well as most other HTML elements, such as links.

However, when it comes to breaking off a line, the Formatted style behaves just as the Normal style does. That is, if you use the Enter key to break a line while you're typing text, you'll get a blank line before the start of the next Formatted paragraph. To break a line without having this happen, use a line break (press Shift+Enter).

A typical use of the Formatted style is with material that needs several levels of indent or with text that needs various short lines indented (see Figure 5.16).

FIGURE 5.16
The Formatted style preserves your program code indenting and lets you indent the first lines of paragraphs.

```
main()
{
int   x=0;
        while (x < 1)
        {
              printf("Hello, World!"\n);
              x++;
        }// endwhile
}//  end main

        This is an indent at the first line of a paragraph.  As you can see, the next line
moves out to the left margin.
```

Part

II

Ch

5

To write new text using the Formatted style, use the following steps:

1. Place the cursor where you want the new text to begin.

2. Choose Format, Paragraph, and choose Formatted from the drop-down list in the Paragraph Properties dialog box (or simply use the Change Styles box to select the Formatted style).

3. The Change Styles box shows you're in Formatted style. Now type the text you want, using tabs or strings of spaces as you need them. Remember to use Shift+Enter to keep lines together.

As you can see from Figure 5.16, the default Formatted style does have one drawback, although it's an aesthetic rather than a functional one. Most browsers, until very recently, displayed Formatted text in a monospaced font like Courier, which is rather ugly, and that's the default font FrontPage Editor uses. With FrontPage 97's support of font face tags, however, you're no longer limited to Courier. Simply choose the Formatted style, then select the font you want to use. You'll find that the Formatted style's convenience of tabs and strings of spaces is still available, even though you're not using Courier. Browsers that don't support the font face tags will still show the text in Courier, of course.

TROUBLESHOOTING

I wanted to change from Normal to Formatted style when I was partway through a paragraph. When I used the Paragraph Properties dialog box to do this, the whole paragraph changed to Formatted style. The same thing happened when I tried using the Change Styles box. What's going on? Changing a paragraph style isn't the same as changing character style (for example, selecting Bold or a font). Character style changes affect only selected text or whatever characters you type after the change. However, when you select a paragraph style (the selection method makes no difference) the style is always applied to the entire paragraph. In short, you can't change paragraph styles partway through a paragraph.

Importing Existing Text Using the Formatted Style   Another use for the Formatted style is to make sure that imported ASCII text retains its indenting and any padding it does with spaces. (Of course, if the text starts out in another format, you'll have to convert it to an ASCII text file first. If you do this, be sure to save it as text with line breaks.)

To insert an existing text file into your page, position the cursor where you want the text to start, and use the following steps:

1. Choose Insert, File. The Select a File dialog box appears.

2. Use the dialog box to find and select the file you want to insert, and then choose Open. The Convert Text dialog box appears (see Figure 5.17), giving you four options.

FIGURE 5.17
You can insert a file as either Formatted or Normal text, with options for paragraphing.

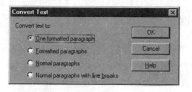

3. Mark the option button that corresponds to the Formatted result you want. (Depending on the format of the source file, you may want to experiment with the various choices.) Choose OK.

FrontPage Editor inserts the file into the page, preserving space padding, line breaks, and tabs.

Using the Address Style   This is a simple style used to put the author's address on the page. Browsers usually display it in italics. To insert it, choose Format, Paragraph, and choose Address from the list box. Alternatively, type your address, make sure the cursor is within the text, and select Address from the Change Styles box.

TIP   In additon to using Insert, File, you can drag-and-drop the text file into the FrontPage Editor. "Drag-and-Drop everywhere" is a new feature of FrontPage 97.

Part
II

Ch
5

Laying Out Text Effectively

Just getting words onto the page isn't enough. Good text layout affects a page's attractiveness and readability. FrontPage Editor has several tools to help you enhance the appearance of your pages: horizontal lines, centering, block indentation, and special character formatting.

NOTE   If you've made a complicated edit that didn't work out, and you want to discard the changes before you go on, you can use FrontPage Editor's Refresh command. Choose View, Refresh (or click the Refresh button on the toolbar) and FrontPage Editor reloads the file as it was before the edit. You'll be asked if you want to save the changes you did make; assuming you don't, answer No. FrontPage's multi-level undo feature also allows you to undo the Past 30 actions. Just click the Undo toolbar button. ■

Using Horizontal Lines

Paragraphs are units of meaning, and a new paragraph signals the reader that a new unit has begun. However, sometimes you want to announce a more significant shift of emphasis or subject, and for this the horizontal line is effective. It's often used with headings, especially to set off the "headline" of a page or to begin a major section within the page. It is also a design element, in that it adds visual interest, or relief from long blocks of text.

You place a line on a page by choosing Insert, Horizontal Line. The resulting default line, which all graphics-capable browsers display, is a shadowed line that stretches the width of the browser window. Incidentally, it forces a blank line above and below it, so you can't get text to snuggle up close to it.

N O T E If you want position text right next to a line, you have to use a graphic line, which you insert as an image. ▪

You can vary the line's appearance somewhat by adjusting its properties. These variations are actually Netscape extensions which FrontPage Editor supports, though not all browsers display them. To modify a line's appearance, click the line and choose Edit, Horizontal Line Properties; alternatively, right-click the line and choose Horizontal Line Properties from the shortcut menu. You can then change the line's displayed width, align it, adjust its weight by changing its height in pixels, change it to a solid, unshaded line, or give it a color (see Figure 5.18). You can see various line styles in Figure 5.19.

FIGURE 5.18
You use the Horizontal Line Properties dialog box to modify the appearance of a line.

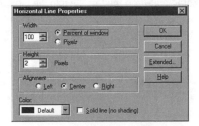

T I P A well-designed page isn't littered with lines. Use them only when they serve a purpose (organizational or decorative). Also, it's better to determine the line width in percent, not in pixels. That way its width will appear to a visitor as you designed it, independent of the screen resolution she's using.

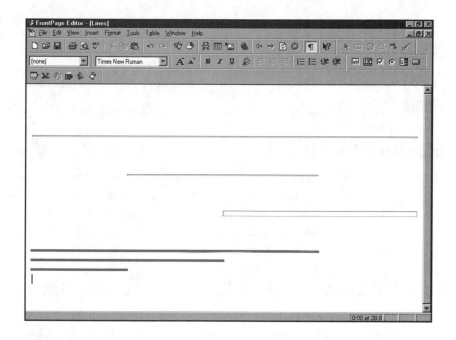

Aligning Text Horizontally

You'll often want headings or other text to be somewhere other than at the left margin. To
do so, use the following steps:

1. Click anywhere in the text you want to align.

2. Choose Format, Paragraph. The Paragraph Properties dialog box appears.

3. Click the arrow button at the right of the Paragraph Alignment drop-down list box.
   The alignment options list appears (see Figure 5.20).

4. Select the alignment you want, and choose OK.

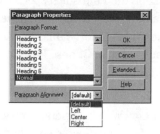

Part
II

Ch
5

N O T E The Left alignment and the Default alignment both put text against the left margin. There is no functional difference between them. ■

 T I P A quick way to align text is to use the Align Left, Center, and Align Right buttons on the formatting toolbar.

Indenting Blocks of Text

In print documents, a chunk of text is sometimes set off from its surroundings by indenting its left margin. You often see this in long quotations. To get this result, you place the cursor in the desired paragraph and click the Increase Indent button on the formatting toolbar. The indent increases each time you click the button. To decrease it, click the Decrease Indent button on the toolbar.

Applying Special Styles with the Font Dialog Box

When we worked with the Font dialog box earlier, we noticed a second sheet called Special Styles. These character styles represent the HTML approach to character formatting, which distinguishes between logical and physical styles.

The distinction can initially be confusing, but what it boils down to is this: If a browser sees the HTML tags for italic or bold characters (physical styles), it puts italic or bold on the screen, no matter how the browser preferences are set. But if it sees the emphasis or strong HTML tags (logical styles), it checks its preference settings to see how its user wants emphasized or strong text to appear. The default for the browser usually displays this text as italic and bold, respectively. However, if the user changed her "emphasized" preference setting to 14-point Caslon, the browser dutifully displays Caslon instead of italic. In short, logical styles are flexible at the browser end and physical ones aren't.

In the Font dialog box, the Font Style box on the Font sheet specifies only logical styles. So do the toolbar buttons for these character styles. If you want physical styles for bold or italic, you have to use the Special Styles sheet to force this condition. This sheet also provides logical styles such as Citation and Sample. Choose Format, Font, and click the Special Styles tab to see the sheet (see Figure 5.21).

As usual, you can apply these styles by selecting text then choosing the style you want. Tables 5.1 and 5.2 give more detail about how Web browsers display them. For most of your page creation work, you'll likely use the Font sheet to specify the look of your text.

FIGURE 5.21
You use the Special Styles sheet to apply HTML physical styles for certain types of character formatting.

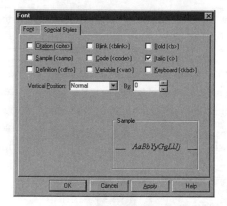

Table 5.1 Physical Character Styles in FrontPage Editor

Style	Effect
Bold	Forces browser to display bold
Italic	Forces browser to display italic
Underlined	Forces underlining
Typewriter font	Forces monospaced font, default Courier

Table 5.2 Logical Character Styles in FrontPage Editor

Style	Effect
Strong	Bold unless changed by browser options
Emphasis	Italic unless changed by browser options
Strike-through	Strike-through characters
Citation	Italic for citing references
Sample	Output sample (resembles typewriter font)
Definition	Italic for definitions
Blink	Blinks text
Code	HTML code (resembles typewriter font)
Variable	Usually italic for defining a variable
Keyboard	Indicates user-supplied text (resembles typewriter font)

Part
II

Ch
5

T I P To quickly format some characters, select the text, right-click it to open the shortcut menu, and click Font Properties to make the Font dialog box appear.

If you need superscripts or subscripts, you will find these also in the Special Styles sheet. To apply the formatting to selected or new text, click the arrow button at the right of the Vertical Position box, and select from Superscript or Subscript. The By box lets you specify how much the affected text is offset from the text baseline (see Figure 5.22). Note that the number in this box will be negative if you're using a subscript.

FIGURE 5.22
You can make text into superscript or subscript.

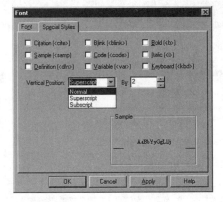

Using Symbols

From time to time, you need characters that don't appear on the keyboard, for example, the copyright or trademark symbols. To insert such a character, place the cursor where you want the symbol to appear and choose Insert, Symbol. The Symbol dialog box appears (see Figure 5.23). Click the character you want (a larger representation of it appears beside the Insert button), choose Insert, and then choose Close. Clicking the Insert button twice will insert the character twice, and so on.

FIGURE 5.23
When you need specialized symbols, you'll find them in the Symbol dialog box.

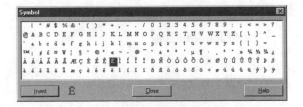

Setting Page Margins

At the time of writing (late 1996), margins show up only in Internet Explorer 3.0. You set them by choosing File, Page Properties, and going to the Margins sheet in the Page Properties dialog box. Mark the check box for the margin you want (left or top), and type a value into the size box. The units are in pixels.

Using Lists to Present Your Content

We agreed earlier that the content and presentation of your pages should be in balance. That is, all the elements in a well-designed page support and reinforce each other so that the whole is greater than the sum of its parts. (This goes for a well-designed Web site, too.)

Lists are excellent for helping you achieve this synergy in your pages because they are good at integrating presentation and content. They're very adaptable, too, because you can combine different kinds of lists to deal with different kinds of information. It's because of this flexibility that lists are everywhere in everyday life, from the humble loaf-of-bread-and-quart-of milk version to the fantastically complicated checklists that govern the mission of interplanetary probes. In fact, lists are probably the oldest written documents of civilization; 45 centuries ago, scribes were already recording how many bushels of barley the local farmers owed to the king in taxes.

We don't use clay tablets nowadays, but our electronic pages do contain lists by the dozens. They not only organize things for our visitors, they also help us organize our thinking as we put them together. What makes lists even more useful is that you can put hyperlinks, styles, and character formatting into them. You're not limited to a fixed font and type size, for instance. And you can nest lists of one kind inside lists of another.

The trouble with coding lists in HTML is that the work is so picky; one tag out of place in a nested list and terrible things happen to your page. Fortunately, FrontPage Editor relieves us of this picky stuff so that we can concentrate on what the list says, rather than how it's put together. And we have a full range of listing tools at our disposal, from bulleted to definition.

Making a Bulleted List

You use a bulleted list for items that need no particular order, although there's sometimes an implied grading of importance within it. (Formally, these are called unordered lists.)

Bulleted lists can summarize important points in an argument or emphasize key items of information. They're the most common list type on the World Wide Web, partly because they're visually attractive, and partly because they're good for so many different things.

To make a simple bulleted list, put the cursor where you want the list to start and use the following steps:

1. Choose Format, Bullets and Numbering. The List Properties dialog box appears (see Figure 5.24) with four page icons, three of which offer various bullet styles.

FIGURE 5.24
With the List Properties dialog box you choose between Numbered and Bulleted lists.

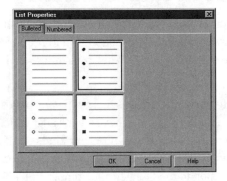

2. Click the page icon with the bullet style you want (or choose the nonbulleted page icon to turn off bullets).

3. Choose OK. The dialog box vanishes, and a bullet appears on the page.

4. Start typing your list, pressing Enter at the end of each item.

5. When you've finished, press Enter twice to stop inserting bulleted items.

6. If you need to insert an item into the list, position the insertion point immediately to the right of the preceding item, press Enter, and type the new item (see Figure 5.25).

 T I P   A fast way to start a list (of any kind) is to use the Change Style drop-down list box. It contains all the types of lists that FrontPage Editor supports. Alternatively, click the Bulleted List button or the Numbered List button to start a list of that type.

Deleting a List or a List Item   To delete the whole list, select it and press the Delete key, or choose Edit, Clear. After deletion, one bullet will remain; to get rid of it, press the Backspace key.

To delete an item in a list, select it and press the Delete key or choose Edit, Clear. This removes the text. Then press the Delete key again. This removes the bullet.

FIGURE 5.25
A bulleted list which is about to have a new item inserted after the third entry.

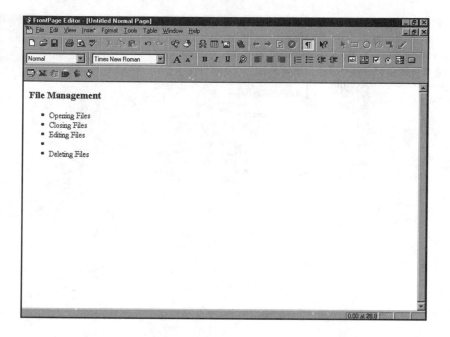

Making Bulleted Sublists Within Bulleted Lists You use sublists (called nested lists) to arrange less important points or headings under more important ones. If you've used the outlining tools in applications like WordPerfect, Word, or PowerPoint, this principle will be familiar to you. It's a powerful method of organizing information. To start a nested list under a superior list, use the following steps:

1. Place the cursor at the end of the line under which the nested list will appear. This can be within an existing list or at the end of the last item of an existing list.

2. Press the Enter key to make a new bullet, but don't type anything.

3. Click the Increase Indent button twice. Then click the Bulleted List button. The bullet of the nested list appears; this bullet will have a different style from those in the superior list.

3. Type the items of the nested list.

4. To end it, press Enter to get a bullet without any text. Then press the Delete key. The insertion point will return to the superior list.

5. If the superior list isn't complete, go on entering data until it is. Then press Enter twice to end the list.

You can see a nested list with three levels in Figure 5.26. Incidentally, you can create more levels for a list than you're ever likely to need.

Part

II

Ch

5

FIGURE 5.26

You use nested lists to arrange less important points or headings under more important ones.

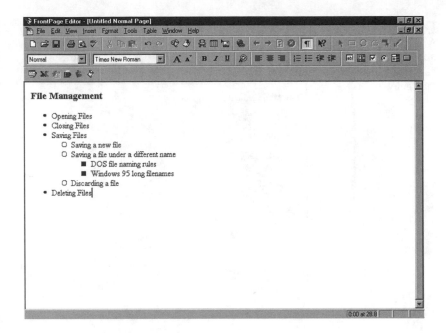

 TIP It's easy to "promote" a list item to the superior list above it. Place the insertion point inside the item, and click the Decrease Indent button twice. Similarly, to "demote" an item to the list below it, place the insertion point inside the item, and click the Increase Indent button twice.

Changing the Bullet Styles   While FrontPage Editor has supplied you with the three most popular bullet styles, you can change the usage of these styles within nested lists. For example, you might want all the bullets in the lists of Figure 5.26 to be round, solid ones. To make such changes, do the following:

1. Place the insertion point inside the nested list whose bullets you want to change.

2. Choose Format, Bullets and Numbering. The List Properties dialog box appears. Note that it now has an extra sheet, called Style (we won't use it for the moment, however).

3. Click the Bulleted tab, then click the style of bullet you want.

4. Choose OK. The nested list immediately acquires the new bullet style.

This works for the topmost list, as well, not just for the nested lists below it.

Adding Paragraph Styles and Character Formatting   You can vary a list's paragraph style and character format. In Figure 5.27, some text is in bold, and line breaks have been used to separate the items of the topmost list. Additionally, the third-level nested list contains a hyperlink.

FIGURE 5.27
You can use character formatting, line breaks, and hyperlinks inside lists.

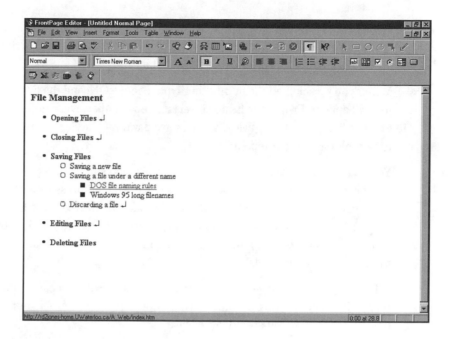

Making a Numbered List

These are somewhat less common on the Web than bulleted lists. They're used for tables of contents, for establishing a rank order from highest to lowest, for a set of instructions, or for any data where relative importance needs to be shown. Because of the numbering, they're formally called ordered lists.

You make a numbered list just as you make a bulleted list: Choose Format, Bullets and Numbering, and click the Numbered sheet tab. Here you have several different numbering styles which you can arrange into whatever hierarchy you see fit (see Figure 5.28).

FIGURE 5.28
The Numbered list sheet gives you five numbering styles and the "unnumbered" option.

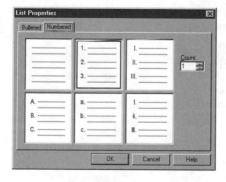

Part

II

Ch

5

Usually your list will start at 1, at a, and so on. However, if it must start at a higher number, adjust the number in the Count box accordingly. If you put 2 in the box, for example, and choose the a,b,c type list, the list will start at b.

When you've selected the numbering type, choose OK, and the first item of the numbered list will appear. FrontPage Editor inserts a new number every time you press Enter. To end the list, press Enter twice. You can use paragraph styles, character formatting, and hyperlinks within numbered lists.

You start a numbered nested list the same way you start a bulleted nested list. Place the cursor at the end of the item before the nested list, and press Enter to get a new number. Then click the Increase Indent button twice, and the nested list will start. Complete it, press Enter once to get a blank entry, then click the Decrease Indent button twice. The insertion point returns to the superior list. FrontPage Editor adjusts all numbering to match the additions or deletions.

When you try this out, you'll notice that FrontPage Editor doesn't automatically supply a hierarchy of numbering formats. If your superior list uses Arabic numerals, so will your nested list, unless you specify otherwise.

You change the style of the nested list numbering using the following steps:

1. Place the insertion point inside the nested list, then choose Format, Bullets and Numbering.
2. Click the Numbered sheet tab.
3. Click the page icon that shows the style you want.
4. Choose OK. The nested list takes up the new style.

You can see an example of an ordered, nested list in Figure 5.29.

To delete the list or parts of it, or to promote or demote list items, use the methods we applied earlier to bulleted lists. (See above, "Deleting a List or a List Item" and "Making Bulleted Sublists Within Bulleted Lists.")

FIGURE 5.29
You can put ordered lists inside numbered lists.

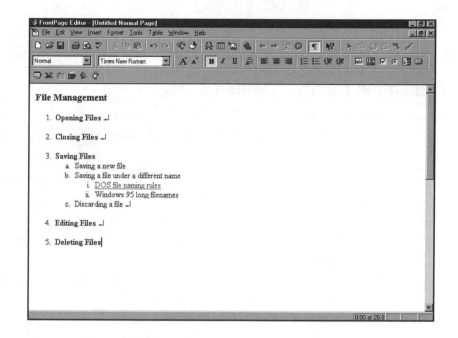

Changing the Style of an Existing List

You may put a bulleted list together, then decide it would be more useful as a numbered one. To make this change, do the following:

1. Place the insertion point somewhere inside the list, then choose Format, Bullets and Numbering. The List Properties dialog box appears, with the Style sheet fully visible (see Figure 5.30).

Part

II

Ch

5

FIGURE 5.30
Changing the list format is easy with the Style Sheet.

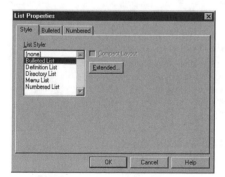

2. From the List Style list box, click the type of list you want.

3. Choose OK. The list immediately takes on the new style.

Combining List Types Within a List

You can mix types of lists to fine-tune your presentation of content. For example, you can include a nested list of numbered instructions inside a bulleted list (see Figure 5.31). To do this:

1. Place the insertion point at the end of the line before the new nested list. Then press Enter, but don't type anything.

2. Click the Increase Indent button twice.

3. Choose Format, Bullets and Numbering to open the List Properties dialog box and reveal the Style sheet.

4. From the List Style box on the Style sheet, select the type of list you want (numbered, in this example) and choose OK.

5. The new list format appears. Type the list. When finished, press the Enter key to make a blank item, but don't type anything.

6. Click the Decrease Indent button twice. The list symbol for the superior list appears.

FIGURE 5.31
You can use mixed lists to put different types of information together.

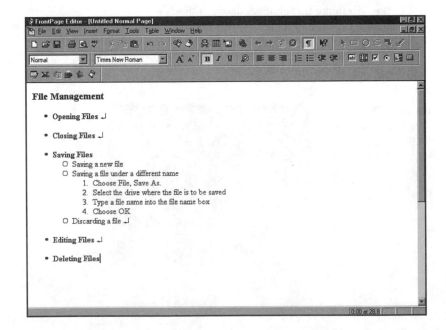

Using the List Buttons or Change Style Box to Modify Existing Lists

You can use either the Numbered List or the Bulleted List button to manipulate existing lists. To change a list or nested list from one type to another, place the insertion point anywhere in it, and click the appropriate button. Only that list changes; lists subordinate or superior to it aren't affected. If you want to change the formatting of the bullets or numbers, choose Format, Bullets and Numbering to display the List Properties dialog box, and make your changes from there.

Alternatively, place the insertion point inside the list, and choose the new list type from the drop-down list in the Change Styles box.

Modifying the Properties of One Item in a List

You won't want to do this often, but here's what you do if you want to (for example) mix numbers and letters inside a numbered list:

1. Right-click on the item or items whose list property you want to change. The shortcut menu appears.

2. Click List Item Properties. The List Properties dialog box appears.

3. Click the page icon of the new format you want, then choose OK. The item gets its new property, but the other items in the list are unaffected. Note that you can't mix bullets and numbers.

 TIP To get to the List Properties dialog box in a hurry, right-click inside the list and then click List Properties to make the dialog box appears.

Removing a List Format

If you decide your list should be ordinary text, you can get rid of the list style by selecting the entire list and clicking the Decrease Indent button. If you have nested lists, they won't be affected until you click the Decrease Indent button for each of them.

Making Directory or Menu Lists

The appearance of both directory and menu list types depends on the tags the browser supports. If you make either list in FrontPage Editor, they looked exactly like bulleted lists. Netscape 2.0 and 3.0, and Mosaic also show them as bulleted lists. Internet Explorer 2.0, however, displays them as indented lists without bullets, while Internet Explorer 3.0 shows them as bulleted lists.

Part

II

Ch

5

A browser that does support directory lists shows the entries evenly spaced across the screen. Few browsers support the directory tag, so if you want the effect, use a table. The menu list, in browsers that support this option, shows a list without bullets, and nested lists are simply indented. You're unlikely ever to need the menu list or the directory list.

▶ **See** Chapter 7, "Creating Tables," **p. 157**

Definition Lists

Also called glossary lists, definition list are a useful reference format. You can see a typical example of a definition list in Figure 5.32.

FIGURE 5.32

Definition lists provide structured lists made up of terms and their definitions.

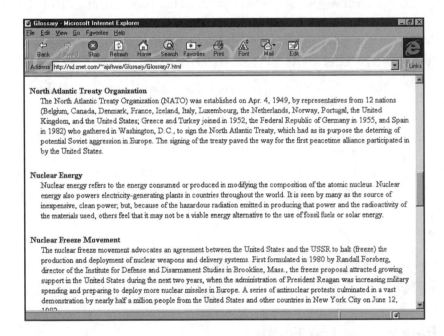

A definition list is a collection of entries, and each entry is made up of a term and its definition. Naturally, this structure isn't only for formal definitions; you can use it for anything that needs a short heading term and one or more indented paragraphs of information beneath this. For the sake of appearance, the term should be short enough to fit on one line of a browser display, but the definition text can be as long as you like. To start a new definition list, use the following steps:

1. From the Change Style box, select Defined Term.

2. Type the term to be defined, and press Enter. The insertion point automatically indents.

3. Type the definition, and press Enter.

4. Note that the Change Style box says "Defined Term" again. Repeat steps 2 and 3 until you're finished, then press Enter three times to end the list.

Definition lists are that simple. You can embed other lists inside definition lists, and vice versa. Definition lists can contain hyperlinks and whatever character formatting you want.

NOTE Converting lists to and from definition lists causes more problems than it solves. When you convert a list to a definition list, what you get is a list made completely of definitions, so you have to add the terms by hand. If you go from a definition list to a bulleted or numbered list, both terms and definitions convert to first-level bullets or numbers. ■

CAUTION

Don't use the heading styles inside lists. This style forces line breaks and can leave your list looking very fragmented. If you want to emphasize parts of a list, use character formatting.

Using Text Colors and Background Colors on Your Page

Both content and presentation are important in Web pages, just as they are in any form of communication. However, content is what most people are after, and you should remember this when you're adding colors to a page. If most of the content of the page is in the text (and often it will be), you shouldn't allow that text to be obscured by even the most stunning visual effects. White text in normal size on a black ground, for example, is excruciatingly hard to read; if you want this combination, be prepared to allocate space to a large font or heading style. Some color combinations, like orange and green, or purple and yellow, seem to vibrate, and will instantly detract from whatever your words are trying to say. So be careful when selecting background colors and text colors.

Don't bother using color depths over 8-bit (256 colors) either. Most people's systems are set up for 256 colors at most, and the extra bandwidth needed to transmit more than this is simply wasted.

And of course, remember to test with different browsers and resolutions.

Part
II

Ch
5

Changing the Background and Text Colors

Both these changes can be made at once from the same dialog box, so we'll consider them together. To change either color, use the following steps:

1. Choose File, Page Properties. When the Page Properties dialog box appears, click the Background tab to bring that sheet to the front.

2. Mark the Specify Background and Colors option button.

3. Click the button at the right of the Background drop-down list box. A drop-down list of available colors appears (see Figure 5.33).

FIGURE 5.33

Use the Background sheet of the Page Properties dialog box to modify the background color or text color of your pages.

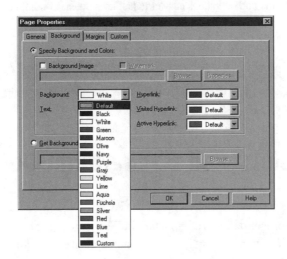

4. Click the color you want. If you now click OK, the dialog box will vanish, and your page background will immediately assume that color.

5. To set the text color, click the button at the right of the Text drop-down list box. The same color list appears. Select the color you want, then click OK.

All new text and existing text not already colored with character formatting or the Text Color button will take on the color you selected in step 5.

Defining Custom Colors

If the range of colors available from the drop-down list isn't enough, you can mix your own hue using the Custom color selection at the bottom of the list. Follow steps 1 to 3 previously shown, but instead of clicking a color, click the Custom rectangle at the bottom of the list. The Color dialog box appears (see Figure 5.34).

FIGURE 5.34
The Color dialog box lets you either pick from predefined colors or define your own.

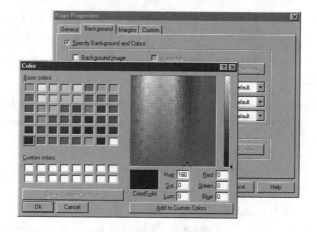

You create a new color in one of the following three ways:

1. Drag the mouse pointer over the large colored rectangle on the right of the dialog box. You'll see the color in the Color/Solid box change to show what color it is you've got. You change the color's luminance by dragging the black triangle that's next to the vertical bar beside the color box.

2. Adjust the numbers in the boxes for Red, Green, and Blue.

3. Adjust the numbers in the boxes for Hue, Saturation, and Luminance.

When you've adjusted the color, back out of the dialog boxes by choosing OK until they're all closed. The page background will have the color you chose.

This doesn't save your custom color, however. If you want to save it to a custom palette, click the Add to Custom Colors button in the Color dialog box before you leave this box.

> **CAUTION**
>
> Custom colors may look great in your 256-color or higher display, but they won't appear to the same effect (or at all) on a 16-color system. Using them is more likely a waste of time than an enhancement.

Changing the Color of Part of Your Text

Picking a new text color by the method described above creates a global change to the page. You may sometimes want to change the hue of selected parts of the text, while leaving the rest of it alone. First select the text to be changed, and then do the following:

1. Choose Format, Font, to open the Font dialog box.

Part
II

Ch
5

2. On the Font sheet, click the arrow button at the right of the Color box. A drop-down list of colors appears (it's the same list as the one you saw in the procedures above).

3. Click the color you want. The dialog box closes, and the selected text takes on the new color.

Naturally, you can create new text in the new color by following the previous steps and typing the text. You can also make custom colors by clicking the Custom choice to open the Color dialog box, and then using the procedures described earlier.

Finally, the Text Color button on the toolbar opens the Color dialog box, and you can specify colors from there.

The best way to understand the effects of these changes is to experiment and see the results through the eyes of your visitors. What will the person using a 16-color, 640×480 display make of your ingeniously coordinated color scheme? Or if she's got a 256-color display, does she really want to read three screens of yellow text on a black background? Or worse, red on purple?

> **CAUTION**
>
> The Background sheet of the Page Properties dialog box is also where you change the default link colors to custom colors. You should think very hard about this before you do it. How would you react to a map that used blue for the land and green for the water, just because the cartographer decided it looked better that way?

N O T E Many applications, including browsers, have a built-in set of colors, called a color table (or palette), that they use for screen display. If a downloaded page contains a color that isn't in the browser's table, the browser either substitutes a similar color or dithers multiple colors from its table to get as close as it can. If you make up a custom color, it may not appear in a browser as it does in FrontPage Editor. Test your work, as always. ■

Making Colors Consistent Across Pages

You may want to get a consistent "look" across your site or part of it, and it's a little inconvenient to define the background color and text color for each page as you create it. To get around this, first set up a model page with the color combination you want. Then, for each new or existing page that is to have that combination, open the Page Properties dialog box and go to the Background sheet. Mark the option button called Get Background and Colors from Page, then type the file name of the model page into the text box (or use the Browse button to locate the page). Choose OK, and the color combination is applied to the current page.

Using the Text Editing Tools

Just as word processors do, FrontPage Editor provides commands for spell-checking, finding and replacing words or strings of words, and a Thesaurus. None of these tools is a substitute for careful proofreading and competent writing, but they help.

Spell-Checking Your Work

FrontPage 97 uses the same spelling engine as Office (added words are also available for all of FrontPage and Office). Choose Tools, Spelling (or click the Check Spelling button on the toolbar) and the Spelling dialogue box appears. The first possible error is already showing in the Not in Dictionary box (see Figure 5.35).

FIGURE 5.35
Using the spell-checker to find suspected errors.

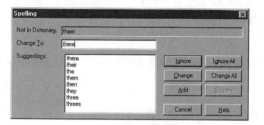

You can accept the suggested change that appears in the Change To box, or select a different change from the Suggestions list box, or type your own correction into the Change To box. Whichever you do, choose the Change button when you're ready to make the change. You can also do one of the following:

■ Choose Ignore to bypass the word, or Ignore All to bypass this and all later occurrences of it (you do this if the word is correct, but you don't want to add it to the spell-checker's custom dictionary).

■ Choose Change All to change this and all other occurrences of the word.

■ Choose Add to add the new word to the custom dictionary. If you do this, it won't get flagged as an error in this or any other document.

■ Choose Suggest to get other spelling suggestions from the dictionary. This choice isn't available unless you select a word from the Suggestions list box.

Choosing the Change, Change All, Ignore, or Ignore All buttons immediately takes you to the next possible error, until the page has been checked completely.

Using Find and Replace

These related commands work just as they do in a word processor. To find occurrences of a string of text, choose Edit, Find. The Find dialog box appears (see Figure 5.36).

FIGURE 5.36
You can search for occurrences of a word with the Find dialog box.

The search direction can be specified by marking the option buttons, and you can make the search case-sensitive by marking the Match case check box. Depending on what you're looking for, you may want to mark the Match whole Word Only check box, as well; if you don't, the command will find all occurrences of the text pattern even if it's embedded inside a word.

To search and replace a word or text string, choose Edit, Replace to open the Replace dialog box (see Figure 5.37).

FIGURE 5.37
The Replace command is handy for selective or global replacement of a text string.

Type the search string into the Find What box, and the replacement text into the Replace With box. Here you should consider carefully whether you need to mark the Match whole Word Only check box. If it's unchecked, and you replace "led" with "brought" (for example) you'll discover that "filed" becomes "fibrought" after the replacement. This may be amusing, but is counterproductive. If it happens, choose Edit, Undo immediately to cancel the changes.

You can automatically replace all occurrences of the search string by choosing Replace All. To replace selectively, choose Find Next, and if you want to replace, choose the Replace button. If you don't want the replacement, choose Find Next again to go on to the next occurrence of the search string until you're finished with the document.

Using the Thesaurus

Mark Twain said that "the difference between the right word and the almost-right word is the difference between a lightning bolt and a lightning bug." If you're staring at the almost-right word and can't think of the right one, try using FrontPage Editor's Thesaurus to find it.

First, position the insertion point immediately before the word that's giving you trouble. Then do the following:

1. Choose Tools, Thesaurus to open the Thesaurus dialog box (see Figure 5.38).

FIGURE 5.38
Use the Thesaurus when you're having trouble finding the exact word for what you want to say.

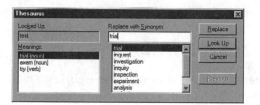

2. The Replace with Synonym box suggests a word as the replacement. If you like it, choose Replace. The dialog box closes, and the original word is automatically replaced with the new one.

3. If the suggested word isn't right, select a better one from the right-hand list box, and choose Replace.

4. If that list box doesn't show you what you want, select a similar meaning from the Meanings list box. More words appear in the right-hand list box. Select one of these, and choose Replace.

5. Still not satisfied? Select any word from either list box, and choose Look Up. Yet more words appear in the list boxes. (To go back to the previous list, choose Previous.)

6. Keep doing this until you find the word you're after, and choose Replace.

You can also use the Thesaurus to find antonyms, the opposite of synonyms. The word "Antonym" sometimes appears at the bottom of the list in the Meanings list box; select this to get a list of opposites.

There are two problems with using the Thesaurus. The first, minor one, is that it's easy to become so fascinated with words that you just keep wandering among them—harmless, though, and perhaps good for your vocabulary. The second, more serious problem has to do with style; you don't want to become infected with the disorder known as "thesaurusitis." You know you've contracted the disease when you start replacing words like "image" with "simulacrum" and "help" with "succor." The effect is often pretentious and may also obscure your meaning. When it comes to style, simple is usually best.

Previewing and Printing Your Pages

Printing your pages is a good idea, because language errors seem to stand out better on paper than they do on a screen. Hard copy also gives you another perspective on your page design. You can preview a page before sending it to your printer by choosing File, Print Preview. You print by choosing File, Print or by clicking the Print button on the toolbar.

Understanding Hyperlinks

Without hyperlinks there would be no World Wide Web, just a multitude of isolated pages like unknown islands in an uncharted sea. It's not for nothing that people speak of "navigating" the Web; it really is like a vast and ever-expanding collection of islands, and the hyperlinks are like the trade and communications routes that bind them together across the electronic deeps.

Less poetically, *hyperlink* generally refers to the highlighted words (or specially defined images) that you click in a Web page to access a different resource on the Web or the Internet. Tucked away behind this highlight or image is a string of HTML code that gives your browser the URL for the new location and directs the browser to jump to that location. FrontPage Editor generates this code automatically when you tell it to set up a hyperlink.

Using Hyperlinks Effectively

Most of your hyperlinks will made up of words rather than images. When you're choosing which words to use for the link, think about them from your readers' point of view. It helps if the link itself suggests what happens if you follow it. An ambiguous link, which a reader must follow to discover whether he really wants to go there, is a potential waste of time. An ambiguous link says "Click here for HTML 3.2"; a clear one says "HTML 3.2 Command Reference." You can make the purpose of a link even clearer by wording the surrounding text to give it a context.

Also, hyperlinks by their very nature stand out from their background. They drag the reader's eye toward them, and if they're not well chosen, or there are too many of them, their presence can overpower the meaning of the surrounding text. You should also avoid links that are so short that they're meaningless ("back") or are very long, like a full sentence. Additionally, you should not change the default link colors. People expect the defaults, so they can easily tell what links they've visited. If you fool around with the link colors, they'll have to adjust to a different standard, and they won't like it.

If your page is longer than a couple of screens, you should consider repeating the navigation links at suitable points. This is so that the reader doesn't have to scroll all the way back to the top of the document to get at the links. Figure 5.39 shows textual navigation controls repeated at the bottom of a home page, along with corresponding graphical controls.

FIGURE 5.39
Navigating from the bottom of this home page is easy because it repeats the navigation controls that appear at the top.

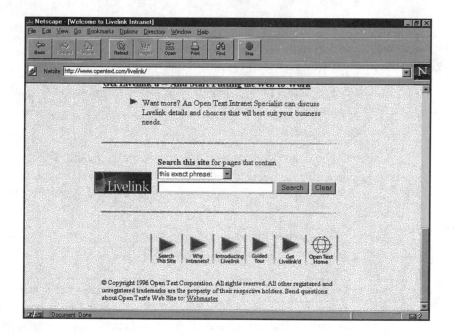

 TIP Avoid using the "back" and "forward" labels for navigation links. Depending on how a person reached your site, clicking such buttons may not take her where she thinks it will.

Setting Up a Hyperlink

The simplest use of a hyperlink is to take your visitor to the top of another page in your Web site. To set this up, open two pages in FrontPage Editor, one to be the hyperlink page and the other to be the destination page. Make the hyperlink page the active one. Then do the following:

1. In the active page, select some text to be the hyperlink.
2. Choose Edit, Link or click the Create/Edit Link Button on the toolbar. The Create Hyperlink dialog box appears, as in Figure 5.40.

Part
II

Ch
5

FIGURE 5.40
You use the Create
Link dialog box to
select the destination
for a hyperlink.

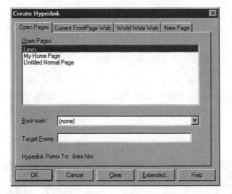

3. If the Open Pages sheet isn't showing, click its tab. Its list box displays all the pages currently open in FrontPage Editor. Select the desired destination page by clicking its name.

4. Choose OK.

The dialog box closes, and you've now set up the hyperlink. The text you used as the hyperlink is now highlighted and underlined with the default link color. To test it, choose Tools, Follow Hyperlink. The destination page should appear in the FrontPage Editor workspace.

You can also check the link by using the File, Preview in Browser command; remember to make the hyperlink page the active one before you do this.

 The numbered procedure above is also a convenient way to make a "return to top of current page" navigational control. When you've selected the hyperlink text for the control, go to the Create Link dialog box, select the name of the currently active page, and choose OK. In other words, the page is linked to itself.

 If you put the cursor over a hyperlink but don't click it, the URL of the destination appears in the status bar. This is handy for identifying the link destination without actually having to go there.

Deleting Hyperlinks

There are two situations where you may want to delete a hyperlink: first, if you decide the link isn't worthwhile; and second, if its destination has vanished. To do this, click anywhere in the link text. Then choose Edit, Unlink. The link is deleted. Saving the file updates the Explorer display.

Another way to delete a link is to click in it, then click the Create or Edit Hyperlink button. When the Edit Hyperlink dialog box appears, choose Clear, then OK.

Extending the Reach of Your Hyperlinks

As stated earlier, hyperlinks are the key element of the Web and its most powerful tool. From any location in your currently open Web, you can link to one of the following:

- The top of any page in the open Web (as we did above)
- A specified location in any page in the open Web ("bookmarking")
- A page in another Web on the same host machine
- A resource anywhere in the Web or the Internet (pages at other Web sites, FTP sites, Gopher sites, and so on)

Hyperlinks and bookmarks give you tremendous flexibility in structuring your Web. For instance, you could keep a table of contents on a single page, and set up links to other pages that hold the information itself. In general, hyperlinks make it unnecessary to produce monster pages. This has at least two advantages: shorter pages are easier to maintain, and it's easier to keep navigational aids handy for the reader. Also, most readers start to lose their orientation if they have to keep scrolling through screen after screen of information.

Linking to Bookmarks on Currently Open Pages   As with all links, you need two things in order to create a link to a bookmark on an open page: the hyperlink itself, and its destination. In this case, our destination is a specific place on the current page, or on a different but open page. Since it models itself on a word processor, FrontPage Editor refers to this destination as a *bookmark*, which is a common tool in major Windows word processors. This makes sense, since we're working with pages, anyway.

You can link to a bookmark from any page in your web, and you can establish bookmarks in any page that you have permission to modify. The formal term for a bookmark is *"named anchor."*

N O T E   The term "bookmark" is also used in Netscape to mean an entry in a quick-access list of Web or Internet sites. FrontPage Editor uses "bookmark" differently, to mean a page location rather than a site address.

To set up the bookmark, which is the destination of the link, use the following steps:

1. Select an appropriate word or phrase anywhere in the destination page to be the bookmark (you can't choose an image to be a bookmark, by the way).

Part

II

Ch

5

2. Choose Edit, Bookmark. The Bookmark dialog box appears (see Figure 5.41).

FIGURE 5.41

Use the Bookmark dialog box to define the destination of a hyperlink.

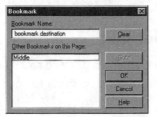

3. The selected text shows up in the Bookmark Name text box. You can accept this or type something else.

4. Choose OK. A dashed underline appears under the bookmarked text (this underlining does not appear in a browser).

 T I P   To clear a bookmark, click anywhere in the marked text, and choose Edit, Bookmark, Clear. The Bookmark vanishes.

With the bookmark defined, you next set up the hyperlink itself. First make the origin page active and then use the following steps:

1. Select the text you want to make into the hyperlink.

2. Choose Edit, Hyperlink or click the Create or Edit Link button on the toolbar. The Create Hyperlink dialog box appears.

3. If the Open Pages sheet isn't the active one, click the Open Pages tab to make it so.

4. In the Open Pages sheet, select the name of the page that has the destination bookmark.

5. In the Bookmark box, use the arrow button to display the Bookmark list for that page (see Figure 5.42).

6. Select the bookmark you assigned to the destination point. When you do, its name appears in the Bookmark text box.

7. Choose OK.

The hyperlink text is now highlighted and underlined with the default link color. Now open the origin page with the Preview in Browser command, and test the link. The destination page should appear with the bookmark at the top of the browser window.

FIGURE 5.42

You can choose among a page's bookmarks by using the Bookmark list in the Open Pages list box.

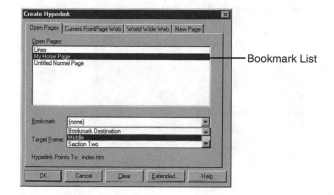

Bookmark List

 T I P When you put the cursor on top of a link, FrontPage Editor's status bar displays the name of the bookmark that is the link destination (if the destination is a bookmark, of course). In the status bar, the bookmark name is preceded by a pound sign (#). This is the HTML code that indicates a named anchor.

TROUBLESHOOTING

I want to use an image as a bookmark, and I can't find a way to do it. Is there one? No, there isn't. This is because an HTML page doesn't actually contain the image data, but rather a "pointer" to the file where the image is stored. HTML doesn't let you define such a pointer as a named anchor, which is what a bookmark actually is. To get around this, use some text near the image (the caption, if there is one) as the bookmark.

Linking to Closed Pages   This is really more of a shortcut than a feature. It simply lets you make a link within the currently open Web without bothering to open the destination page. To do so, take the following steps:

1. Select the text or image for the link and then choose Edit, Hyperlink.

2. When the Create Hyperlink dialog box appears, click the Current FrontPage Web tab (see Figure 5.43).

3. Use the Browse button to insert the destination page name into the Page box, or type in the name. You can type in a bookmark, if one has been defined (and if you can remember it). Then choose OK to establish the link.

FIGURE 5.43
Use the Current
FrontPage Web sheet
for quick linking to
another page.

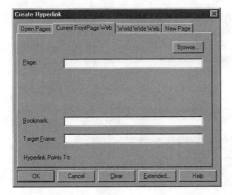

Linking to a New Page FrontPage Editor allows you to create a new page and make a hyperlink to it at the same time. It's a time-saver. To do so, select the image or text for the link, and open the Edit Hyperlink dialog box. Then use the following steps:

1. Click the New Page tab to select that sheet, if it isn't already selected (see Figure 5.44).

FIGURE 5.44
Save time by using the
New Page tab to both
link to and create a
new page.

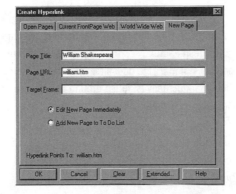

2. The Page Title text box displays the text selected for the link. (If you select an image, the text box is empty.) Modify the content of the text box, if necessary, to make the title for the new page.

3. In the Page URL box, type the file name you want for the page.

4. Mark the Edit New Page Immediately option button. (If you decide to work on the page later, you can click Add New Page to To Do List, instead).

5. Choose OK. The New Page dialog box appears.

6. Set up the new page using the New Page dialog box.

When you complete the page setup, the new page appears in FrontPage Editor's workspace, ready for editing and with the link already established.

Linking to the World Wide Web   It's now that you'll get a real sense of the power of hyperlinks. Local hyperlinks are useful things, but connecting your pages to the Web puts vast resources at your disposal. Remember, though, that it's your visitors who count here. They'll use the resources you've selected, so you've got a lot of responsibility to them.

Links to the Web are set up through the World Wide Web sheet in the Create Hyperlink dialog box (see Figure 5.45). The Hyperlink Type box lets you select which protocol the link uses, and the URL box is where you put the address of the resource. When you've filled it in, choose OK.

FIGURE 5.45

Use the World Wide Web tab to connect your pages to the resources of the Web and the Internet.

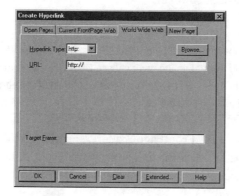

It's that simple. To test the link, open your Internet connection, and use the Preview in Browser command.

If you don't know the URL, there's a fast way to beat the problem. First make sure your PC is connected to the Internet, then do the following:

1. Place the insertion point in the URL box. Then choose Browse. This automatically opens Internet Explorer 3.0 (or your registered default browser), which tells you to "Find the page you want to link to in the browser, then switch back to FrontPage."

2. Go to the site you want to link to. When it loads, keep Internet Explorer open.

3. Switch back to FrontPage Editor. The URL of the location appears in the URL box.

4. Close Internet Explorer, then choose OK.

Test the link with the Preview in Browser command, if you wish.

Your links to the World Wide Web work in the same way as the links within your own Web. If a visitor to your page clicks a link that references a page somewhere else in the

Web, she'll go there. If she clicks a link to an image file that resides on another server, her browser displays that image in a window all by itself.

Linking with Drag and Drop   A really quick way to set up a link to a current page is to go to the right-hand pane of either Hyperlink View or Folder View in FrontPage Explorer. Find the page or image in Explorer that you want linked to the current page and drag it into FrontPage Editor's workspace. Put the link cursor where you want the link to be, and when you release the mouse button, the page title of the linked page appears in the workspace as the hyperlink. You can edit the link text, if you like.

Furthermore, if Explorer shows a link to another Web site, the icon for that can be dragged onto the current page. The link text is the remote site's URL, but it can be edited. This method is very simple and powerful.

 Another fast way to make a link is to choose Insert, Hyperlink from the FrontPage Editor menu bar, but without selecting any text for the link before you do this. Then, in the Create Hyperlink dialog box, choose the page you want to link to, then choose OK. FrontPage Editor automatically inserts a new text hyperlink onto the current page. In addition, you can drag-and-drop links from your Web browser, both to a window and to the task bar.

Testing and Editing Links   Like FrontPage Explorer, FrontPage Editor has a Follow Hyperlink command. To use it, click the link and choose Tools, Follow Hyperlink. If the link is to current page, the page scrolls to that location. If it's to another page, the other page is opened.

If the link references a page on another server, FrontPage Editor tries to find that page and open it. In this case, if nothing happens for a long time, it may be because the server isn't responding. If you suspect this has happened, click the Stop button on the toolbar to end the linking attempt. Then it's time to figure out what went wrong and fix it. Often it's a typographical error in the URL, sometimes it's a problem at the server end.

If the linkage does succeed, the page appears in the FrontPage Editor workspace, not in a browser window. You can save it with the File, Save As command, and it will be stored in your current Web. This is very useful if you want to investigate the page's HTML or other structures in it, such as tables.

Editing a link is simplicity itself. Click anywhere in the link text and choose Edit, Hyperlink. The Edit Hyperlink dialog box appears, but the four sheets in it are exactly the same as those in the Create Link dialog box. Make any changes you want, and choose OK.

Keeping Your Visitors out of Dead Ends   The Web is a place people like to move around in. Well-chosen navigational links laid out in a useful way give your Web pages a professional gleam. (And trying to keep visitors at your site by making it hard for them to leave is, well, counterproductive).

A major error to avoid is leaving your visitor in a dead end, which is a page he can't leave without using his browser's Back button. As an example, suppose a visitor turns up at your site, but the link he used to get there brings him to a page that isn't your home page. Suppose also that you didn't bother to establish a link from this page back to your home page or to any other location in your site. So when he's finished viewing this page, he's stuck. He can only go back to the site he came from, and it's not your site. Thus he won't get a chance to see what else you have to offer him. For this reason alone, you should have a link at least to your home page in every page on your site.

Accessing Other Internet Resources   You noticed that the World Wide Web sheet gave you several communications protocols other than HTTP, which is the Web transfer protocol. This is because the Web, big as it is, is only part of the Internet. FrontPage Editor makes it easy to connect to these other resources, such as the following:

- FTP sites—File Transfer Protocol (FTP) is the communication standard for copying files from one place to another on the Internet and on the Web. You make an FTP link just as you make a Web link: insert the URL of the site into the URL box of the World Wide Web sheet, and choose OK. When the link executes, your user usually has to log onto the FTP site with the username "anonymous" and use his e-mail address as a password. Then he can get the file. You can make life much easier for him by specifying the exact path to the file, so he won't need to spend time wandering around an unfamiliar directory structure.

- Gopher sites—These are collections of text-based menus that let you look for classes of information stored around the Internet. Again, you set up a link to a Gopher server by using the World Wide Web sheet in the Create Link dialog box.

- Mailto—A mailto link simply gives your visitors a chance to send you mail easily. You select the `mailto` protocol and add your e-mail address to it in the URL box. When a visitor clicks this link, she gets a screen where she can type a message to you and then send it.

- WAIS—This is the Wide Area Information Server, an data retrieval system that searches indexed databases.

- News—This protocol lets you link to a newsgroup; if your visitor clicks it, that's where she'll end up.

- Telnet—With this, you let readers get to an interactive service on a remote machine. From the user's point of view, he is actually logged into that machine, and can input commands.

■ File—This one's very simple. It tells the link to display a file that is stored on the local disk. Insert the file's path name into the URL box and choose OK.

You can type any URL right into Frontpage Editor, and FrontPage automatically turns it into a hyperlink. Thus, if you type "http://www.microsoft.com" or "www.microsoft.com," FrontPage Editor turns it into a hyperlink automatically. The same is true for "file:," "news:," "ftp:," "telnet:," and "mailto:." You can even type in any email address ("your address@domain.com") and it will automatically turn into a "mailto:" link.

From Here...

We've covered an enormous amount of material in this chapter, and you've already acquired many of the tools you need to create good Web pages. But there's much more. Look to the following chapters for further ways to enhance your site:

■ Chapter 6, "Enhancing Pages with Graphics and Multimedia," where you learn to use images and image maps, get the most from graphics file formats, lay out text and images effectively, and use sound and in-line video.

■ Chapter 7, "Creating Tables," which shows you the best ways to use tables to organize and present information.

■ Chapter 8, "Enhancing Web Sites with FrontPage Frames," where you find out how to design for a "framed" site, how to use frames with links and images, and how to create framed environments with FrontPage 97's frame templates.

## CHAPTER 6

Enhancing Pages with Graphics and Multimedia

Many books and some magazines give the reader long blocks of unbroken text to cope with. This works fine on the printed page, but dense text doesn't look all that good on computer monitors. Even the best screen resolutions come nowhere near the clarity of print on paper, and studies have shown that people read more slowly from a screen than they do from a page of a book. As a result, most people dislike slogging through screens crammed with words. If that's all your Web site offers them, they'll get tired and eyesore and go elsewhere. You need images (and perhaps sound) to prevent them from leaving, and in this chapter we'll carry out a thorough exploration of how you use FrontPage Editor to add graphical and multimedia content to your Web pages. ■

Using Images Well

Design your pages to get the most out of graphics.

Image Basics

Place images on pages, use nonlocal images, and delete images.

Images and Text

Position text and images coherently, and use floating images, alternative text, and backgrounds.

Images as Hyperlinks

Use images to link inside and outside your site, create navigational tools, and use thumbnails.

Image File Formats

Convert GIF and JPEG image file formats, use interlacing, and make transparent GIFs.

Multimedia

Use sound, inline video, and video clips to give your pages life.

Getting the Most Out of Images

Images add visual interest, provide information, amplify the meaning of text, break text into manageable chunks, and (very important) give your site character. They're a resource no Web page author should willingly do without.

However, getting the best results from them takes some thought. If you have an artist's eye, you're already ahead of the game. If you're not trained in design, though, all is by no means lost. However, before you start throwing pictures at a page, ask yourself the following questions:

- What purpose should the image or images serve?
- What content will best suit this purpose?
- How big are the images (that is, how long to download)?
- How many should there be?
- How well do they relate to the text (if there is text) and to each other?
- Where do they look best on the page?

Working out these answers will help you avoid building pages that are a hodgepodge of unrelated elements. Once you've decided what images to use, keep the following in mind as you choose or create them:

- Don't use a background image that makes your text and graphics hard to see.
- Don't use huge graphics that take forever to download. If you want to make such an image available, put in a thumbnail with a link to the larger image. The largest single image you should consider is 25K, unless there's a very, very good reason to go bigger. Keep the total size of all graphics on a page to 30K or less.
- Speaking of size, be careful about using really wide graphics. If your visitor is running his or her browser at less than full screen, the hardware supports only VGA (640×480) resolution, the image may be lopped off at the side. Keep the image width to less than five or six inches, and test out your results.
- When designing imagemaps, be sure the clickable areas are easily identifiable.
- Don't overuse "special effects" such as blinking text, fades, dissolves, and crawls. After the novelty wears off, many people are irritated by a page that flashes, squirms, and slithers. In particular, if you want somebody to concentrate on the meaning of a section of text, don't distract them with something bouncing around right next to it.

Understanding Image Basics

Graphics inserted into a Web page are called *inline images*. The two most common graphic file formats for Web publications are GIF (Graphics Interchange Format), and JPEG (Joint Photographic Experts Group). All graphics-capable browsers support these two formats, and display them without fuss. However, several other formats exist, examples being TIFF, PCX, and BMP. More recent versions of the Netscape and Mosaic browsers handle these as well, by calling up helper applications, which are programs designed to display images stored in these formats.

Which format, GIF or JPEG, should you use in your pages? Well, each has its strengths. The advantage of GIF is that it's the bread-and-butter format for the Web, at least for the time being. Browsers decompress it quickly, so it's reasonably brisk about showing up on your visitor's screen. It's the format of choice for line art; that is, art without continuous shading of tones—photographs, for instance. It provides up to 256 colors and can simulate more by dithering. You can go in the other direction, since a useful characteristic of GIFs is that you can use image editors to reduce the number of different colors in them. This reduces the file size. Then again, you can simply reduce the size of the image with a graphics editor; this is a possibility with JPEGs, too.

GIF image files do tend to be larger than equivalent JPEG ones, so what you gain in fast GIF decompression you lose (somewhat) in having to store bigger files on your site. On the other hand, JPEG files, while they're smaller, decompress more slowly than GIF files. Their advantage over GIFs is that they support up to 16.7 million colors, so that cont-inuous-tone images reproduce better on the screen. However, there's no point in using actual High Color or True Color images on a Web page; few people use these color depths on their systems, so the extra quality is wasted.

With JPEG images you can also adjust the compression level (in FrontPage Editor this is referred to as quality) to reduce the size of a graphic. If you do this, inspect the results, since the higher the compression, the more the image will be degraded. You have to find the right balance of size and quality.

Part

II

Ch

6

N O T E For best results, you should scale the compression of a JPEG graphic using a native graphics program (such as Lview or Image Composer) rather than FrontPage Editor's Quality command. ■

Some images, especially of icons and buttons, are available on the Internet for free use. However, to individualize your Web site, you'll likely want unique graphics. Original artwork can be produced either with graphics packages, such as the Image Composer software included with FrontPage 97, or by more traditional means like paint or photography (if you're not an artist or a photographer, you may want to enlist the skills of someone who is). Photographs and artwork must be scanned to make the required graphics files, which you can then insert into your pages.

▶ **See** Part IV, "Creating and Adapting Graphics with Microsoft Image Composer," **p.315**

Putting an Image onto a Page

FrontPage at its default settings stores your Web in an appropriately named folder inside the C:\FrontPage Webs\Content folder. Within your Web's folder are several more folders, and one of these is the images folder. This is the most convenient place to keep the graphics for your Web, since having all your images in one place also makes it easier to stay organized.

N O T E   When you reference a graphic that is stored outside the current web, and then save the page that displays the graphic, FrontPage Editor will ask if you want to copy that graphic to the current web. If you say yes, the graphic ends up in the web's root directory, not in the images folder. To copy the graphic to the images folder, you must supply the relative path name for that folder. ■

Once you've added a graphic to the images folder, use the following steps to insert it into your page:

1. Place the cursor where you want the image to appear.

2. Choose Insert, Image. The Image dialog box appears with three sheet tabs. Select the Current FrontPage Web tab, then double-click the images folder icon to make the list of image files appear (see Figure 6.1).

FIGURE 6.1
Using the Image dialog box to select an image from the Current FrontPage Web sheet.

3. Select the image file you want by clicking its name in the list.

4. Choose OK. FrontPage Editor inserts the image into the page (see Figure 6.2).

FIGURE 6.2

The image you've selected appears at the cursor position.

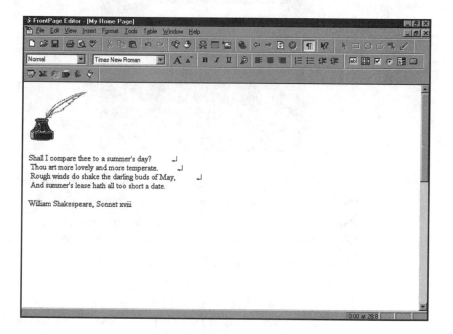

 TIP If you want to edit an image that's already on a page, double-click the image. This opens Image Composer.

Deleting an Image

Oops! You didn't want that image there. To get rid of it, first click it (you know it's selected when the sizing handles appear on its borders). Then choose Edit, Clear or press the Delete key. The image vanishes. Alternatively, you can right-click the image and choose Cut.

Using Images Not in the Current Web

Sometimes the image file you want isn't in the images folder of the Web you're working on. FrontPage Editor gives you a quick way to import images from somewhere else. Place the cursor where you want the image, and use the following steps:

1. Choose Insert, Image so that the Image dialog box appears. Then choose the Other Location sheet (see Figure 6.3).

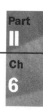

Part

II

Ch

6

FIGURE 6.3

You can retrieve images from folders elsewhere on your system, or from remote locations.

2. To insert an image stored elsewhere on your system, use the Browse button to open the next dialog box, which is a standard Windows 95 file-opening dialog box.

3. Find and select the name of the image file you want, then choose Open. All dialog boxes close, and the image appears on your page at the cursor position.

4. Choose File, Save. The Save Image to FrontPage Web dialog box appears (see Figure 6.4).

5. To save the new image to the root folder of the current Web, simply choose Yes. To save it to the web's images folder, type images/ (with a forward slash) into the Save as URL box, right ahead of the file name, to make the proper path. If you've inserted more than one graphic and want them all saved to the web's root folder, choose Yes to All.

FIGURE 6.4

Use the Save Image to FrontPage Web dialog box to add a graphic to your Web automatically.

If you now check Explorer's Folder View and click the images folder (or the root folder, depending on the path name you saved with), you'll see that the graphic has been added to your Web.

You can also access images at other sites, both in webs on your local host and on the World Wide Web. To do this, you mark the From Location option button on the Other Location sheet, and type the URL of the remote image into the text box. When you choose OK, FrontPage Editor establishes a link to the image and preserves the link when you save the page. If you then look at Explorer's Hyperlink View, with the Hyperlinks to Images option turned on, you'll see an icon for that remote image (you may need to choose FrontPage Explorer's View, Refresh command to update the display).

TIP Many URLs are long and complicated, and typing them is prone to errors. To get around such typing, first use the Preview in Browser command to view the page or image to which you want link. Then select the page URL that appears in the browser's Location or Address text box (this text box's name varies with the browser) and copy it to the Windows Clipboard, using the browser's Edit, Copy command or Ctrl+C. Then switch to the FrontPage Editor window at the location you need the URL, and use Ctrl+V to paste the URL into the appropriate text box.

CAUTION

The danger in referencing another site is that it may become inaccessible, may vanish entirely, or its Webmaster may delete the image. If it's at all possible, make your images safe by downloading them to your host machine. However, remember that copyright law applies to the Internet and the Web; many images are for free use, but not all. Don't use the latter without permission from the owner.

Adding a Clip Art Image

New with FrontPage 97 is the access to Microsoft Office clip art that it provides; if you don't have MS Office, FrontPage 97 does include six categories of clip art of its own: backgrounds, bullets, buttons, headers, lines, and miscellaneous. To use them, do the following:

1. Choose Insert, Image to open the Image dialog box. Choose the Clip Art sheet and click the button at the right end of the Categories box to open the drop-down list (see Figure 6.5).

2. Select the category you want. FrontPage Editor shows you previews of the clip art in that category in the Content box.

3. Scroll through the previews until you find the one you want. Click it to select, then choose OK. The graphic is inserted into your page.

You're not stuck with the supplied clip art, though. You can customize the collection by adding or removing GIF or JPEG images from the clip art category folders. You can also add or remove category folders, and all these modifications will show up in the Clip Art sheet of FrontPage Editor. The category folders in a default installation are located in:

C:\Program Files\Microsoft Office\Clipart (if you installed Office 97)
or
C:\Program Files\Microsoft FrontPage\Clipart (if you did not install Office 97)

Part
II

Ch
6

FIGURE 6.5
Choose from a
selection of clip art
to enliven a page.

Inserting a New Image

If you're a Webmaster (or even if you aren't) who enjoys creating new images on-the-fly. As before, choose Insert, Image, but this time choose the New sheet (see Figure 6.6). Then do the following:

If you're a Webmaster who enjoys creating new images on-the-fly (or even if you aren't), you can use the "Tools/Show Image Editor" menu command to create a graphic from scratch.

FrontPage Editor will launch Image Composer and you can simply cut-and-paste, using the clipboard, to get a newly created image into FP Editor.

About Netscape's Image Size Extensions

Netscape's width and height extensions tell a browser how much page space to reserve for an image, and browsers that support the extensions can then fill in the surrounding text before the image downloads. Thus, your reader can see and click a text link, if he or she wants to, without waiting for a slow graphic to appear. You don't have to worry about putting in these width and height values yourself, because FrontPage Editor automatically inserts them into the generated HTML code when you place an image on a page.

Coordinating Images and Text

If you've experimented with simple pages by putting blocks of text with an image, you have noticed that the text lines up with the image's bottom edge. Sometimes this is what you want, but it's typographically limiting—you need more than that to lay out a good-looking page. What about centering images, putting them at the right margin, and getting multiple lines of text to flow down an image's side? FrontPage Editor lets you do all these things.

Positioning Text Around an Image

As you observed previously, if you add Normal text beside an image or insert an image into an existing line of Normal text, the text lines up with the image's bottom edge. If you don't want this effect, you can change it. To do so, use the following steps:

1. Select the image by clicking it.

2. From the FrontPage Editor menu, choose Edit, Image Properties. The Image Properties dialog box appears.

3. Choose the Appearance tab. In the Layout area, click the arrow button at the right of the Alignment box (see Figure 6.6).

FIGURE 6.6
You change text position relative to an image by choosing from the Alignment options.

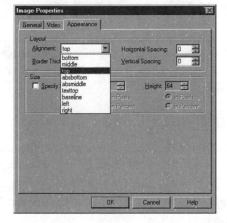

4. Depending on which alignment you want, click bottom, middle, or top.

5. Choose OK. The text moves to the appropriate position beside the image (see Figure 6.7).

Part
II

Ch
6

FIGURE 6.7

FrontPage Editor lets you align text with the bottom, middle, or top of an image.

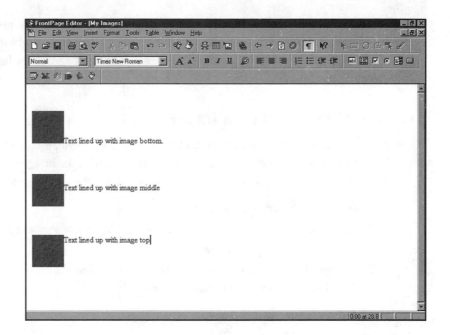

TIP You can get to the Image Properties dialog box quickly by right-clicking the image whose properties you want to change, and choosing Image Properties from the shortcut menu.

Aligning and "Floating" Images

Centering or right-aligning an image is simple. You select the image and then choose Format, Paragraph. When you reach the Paragraph Properties dialog box, open the Paragraph Alignment drop-down list box and pick the alignment you want. When you choose OK, the image is repositioned. An even faster method is to click the Align Left, Center, or Align Right buttons on the toolbar.

Often you'll want to wrap text around an image. FrontPage Editor supports two Netscape extensions that let you "float" an image so that this happens. To make an image float against the left or right margin so that existing or future text wraps around it, use the following steps:

1. Select the image.

2. Choose Edit, Image Properties to open the Image Properties dialog box. Choose the Appearance sheet tab.

3. Click the arrow button beside the Alignment drop-down list box to open the list of alignment options (see Figure 6.6).

4. Select the Left or Right option.

5. Choose OK. The image moves to the appropriate margin, and any text present flows around it (see Figure 6.8).

FIGURE 6.8
Text wraps around an image in a browser that supports the align extensions.

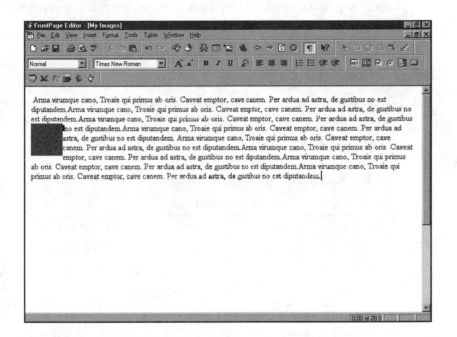

 TIP The Image Properties dialog box has an Edit button. Click this to start Image Composer and automatically load the selected image.

Deleting a Floating Image

If you carefully inspect the text near the image, you'll see a small black rectangle the height of the text line. (Depending on how you assembled the text and image, the rectangle may not be adjacent to the image but embedded in the text nearby.) Be careful not to delete this black marker; if you do, the image will be deleted as well. The marker doesn't show up in a browser.

TROUBLESHOOTING

I used the Right alignment option from Paragraph Format dialog box to position an image at the right margin, but my text isn't wrapping around it. What's wrong? You may understandably think that the Left and Right alignment options in the Paragraph Properties dialog box are the same as the Left and Right alignment options in the Image Properties dialog box. They aren't,

Part
II

Ch
6

although they use exactly the same wording. The difference is that the paragraph alignments don't allow text wrapping; they merely position the image. Incidentally, don't apply mixed Image Properties alignments and Paragraph Format alignments to the same image. A graphic with a Right paragraph alignment and a Right Image Properties alignment may behave unpredictably. There's no practical reason to mix the alignment types, anyway.

Using Other Netscape Alignments

You have four other Netscape extended commands for lining up text and images. All are accessible from the Alignment drop-down list box in the Image Properties dialog box. Table 6.1 describes what they do.

Table 6.1 Netscape *align* Extensions	
Option	**Effect**
Texttop	Aligns tallest text with image top
Absmiddle	Aligns text bottom with middle of image
Absbottom	Aligns text bottom with bottom of image
Baseline	Same as Absbottom

These extensions actually make little discernible difference in a browser display (even in Netscape's display).

Using Line Breaks with Images

So far, we've found out how to align a single line of text at the top, middle, or bottom of an image. We also know how to make text flow around an image that floats against the right or left margin. But how do you put just a few lines next to an image, for instance, if you want a two-line caption beside a graphic that's several lines high?

This effect is an important typographical tool, and fortunately it's supported by FrontPage Editor. You adjust the text layout by inserting special types of line breaks.

Let's say you start out with a page that looks like the one in Figure 6.9. The image captioning looks very awkward; you want both lines of text beside the image, not broken up as they are.

FIGURE 6.9
An image sits against the left margin, with a caption positioned using the default Image Property alignment of Bottom.

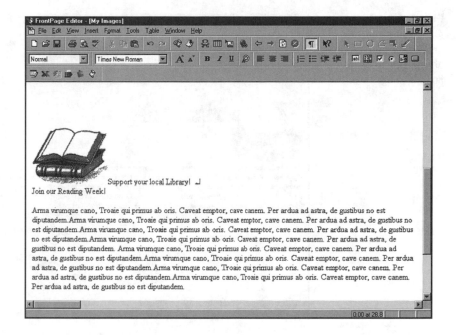

To get the desired layout, first change the image properties of the graphic to a left or right floating alignment. Then do the following:

1. Place the cursor where you want the special line break to occur.

2. Choose Insert, Break. The Break Properties dialog box appears (see Figure 6.10).

FIGURE 6.10
Specialized line breaks give you more control of the relationship between images and text.

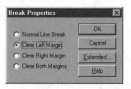

3. Depending on where your image is, choose Clear Left Margin or Clear Right Margin. If you're using a left-floating image and a right-floating image opposite each other, choose Clear Both Margins. (In the example, the text is wrapped around a left-floating image. The break will go after "Join our Reading Week.")

4. Choose OK.

The text following the special line break moves down until it's past the bottom of the image, and then slides over to the appropriate margin (see Figure 6.11). If you have images of unequal size opposite each other, the Clear Both Margins option moves the text down to clear the bottom edges of both images.

FIGURE 6.11

A specialized line break forces the text after it to drop below a floating image.

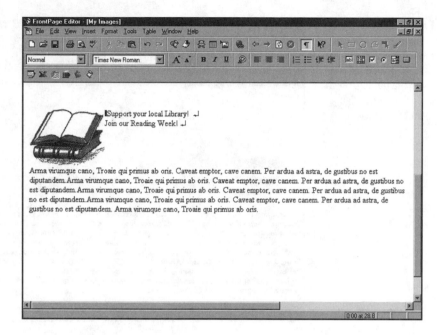

Spacing Between Text and Image

You know that whitespace is an important component of any page, and you may dislike the way text gets crowded close to your images. Fortunately, you can adjust the text-to-image spacing with the Horizontal Spacing and Vertical Spacing boxes in the Appearance sheet of the Image Properties dialog box. The values you fill in here determine the spacing; a typical value of 5 in each results with what is shown in Figure 6.12.

Adjusting Image Size

Also on the Appearance sheet, you can mark the Specify Size check box to let you set the width and height of the graphic in pixels or percent. Fiddling with this can give weird results, especially if the image is a floating one. The adjustments don't affect the size of the image file, either; you'll still need a graphics editor to do that. It's likely most useful for making minor adjustments to balance the relationship of image and text.

FIGURE 6.12

Adding whitespace around an image keeps it from seeming crowded by surrounding text. Here, the image is also a floating one, so that the text wraps around it.

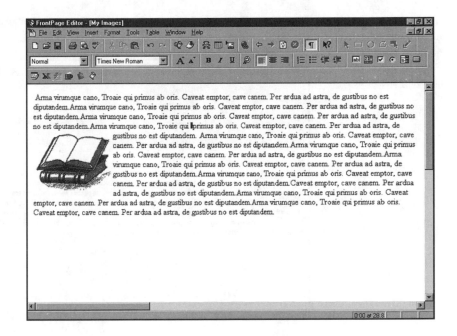

Adding Borders to an Image

You might want a visible boundary around a graphic, although such boundaries aren't used a lot. When they are, they're often understood to indicate a clickable image. If you want one, there's not much variety; you're stuck with a simple black-line rectangle. You can vary its line thickness, but that's all. To add a border, go to the Appearance sheet of the Image Properties dialog box, and type a nonzero value into the Border Thickness box.

Providing Alternative Text

This is important. You have to tell people who are running their browsers with images turned off or who are using a text-only browser that there's an image on the page. Even if they have images turned off, they might like to see your graphic, but they have to know it's there.

You add alternative text by using the General sheet of the Image Properties dialog box. In the Alternative Representations section, use the Text box to type the word or phrase that stands in for the graphic, then choose OK. (Remember to test the results!) Don't, by the way, try to give an elaborate description of the picture. A few well-chosen words are plenty. Figure 6.13 shows what alternative text looks like.

Part
II

Ch
6

FIGURE 6.13
Tell your readers about the presence and nature of a graphic by including alternative text.

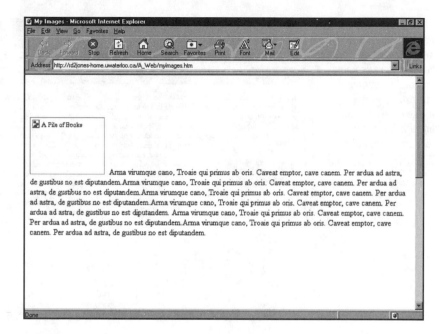

Adding a Background Image Using a File

Background images, as distinct from background colors, are actual graphics that sit behind your text and your foreground images. You use them to add texture, color, site identification, or other visual effects to your pages. Aesthetics and legibility are important here; remember, a background is just that. You shouldn't let it get above itself and have ambitions of becoming the foreground. If it distracts from your content or diffuses the impact of your foreground images, it's trying too hard.

FrontPage Editor lets you use any graphics file as a background (it doesn't have to be a GIF). A few banks of appropriate images are available on the Web, and you can download them for your own use. If you have Office 97 installed on your system, you can use its clip art, and there's also the clip art that ships with FrontPage 97.

 Two such image resources are

Randy's Icon and Image Bazaar:

http://www.iconbazaar.com/backgr/

Bill's Background Library:

http://cameo.softwarelabs.com/billsite/bkground/designio.htm

CAUTION

If you draw on a Web or Internet resource (other than simply linking to it), find out whether the site wants an acknowledgment that it supplied the resource. Copyright laws apply on the Internet, just as they do elsewhere. Besides, acknowledging someone else's contribution to your work is good manners. Incidentally, I'd be very wary of using obviously copyrighted images, such as cartoon figures.

Once you've obtained the image, you can make it into your background. FrontPage Editor does this by treating the image like a tile and laying enough identical tiles to cover everything in sight. To put in the image, use the following steps:

1. Choose File, Page Properties to open the Page Properties dialog box. Click the Background sheet tab and mark the Background Image check box.

2. Click the Browse button. The Select Background Image dialog box appears.

3. Since the dialog box is identical to the Image dialog box (except for its title) you already know how to use it. Select the name of the background file, and return to the Background sheet by choosing OK or Open, depending on context.

4. The image gets tiled across the page to produce your background (see Figure 6.14).

FIGURE 6.14

This dark background is striking with the white heading, but the white text may be almost impossible to read on some browsers and monitors.

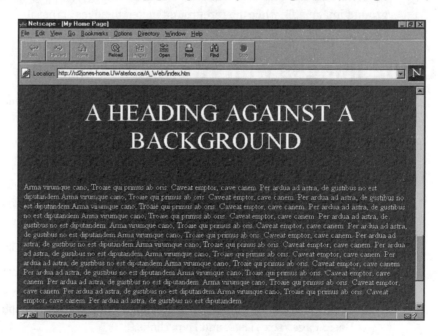

Part

II

Ch

6

A real time-saver is using the Get Background and Colors from Page check box in the Background sheet of the Page Properties dialog box. This copies all the color choices and the background image from another page into the current one. It's very handy for keeping your pages' appearances consistent.

Remember that using a background image from another site puts your page's appearance at someone else's mercy. If the site's URL changes or its Webmaster deletes the image file, you'll lose your background. You're better off downloading the image and storing it locally.

 When you use a background image, also set the page's background color so that it's close to the predominant hue of the image. Why? So that a browser running with images turned off (which will include background images) displays your page with something like its intended appearance.

Using Watermarked Background Images

Your background images will scroll in a browser, along with the foreground objects and text. Marking the Watermark check box on the Background sheet will keep the background image still, while the foreground material moves across it.

Using Images with Hyperlinks

With FrontPage Editor, image-based hyperlinks are just as easy to make as text-based ones. Such images are frequently used as navigation controls within a site, as well as serving as links to remote locations.

Creating Image-Based Hyperlinks

This is simplicity itself. If you know how to make a text hyperlink, you already know how to construct one from an image. Do the following:

1. Insert the image into the page, using any of the methods you learned earlier.
2. Select the image by clicking it. Then choose Edit, Hyperlink to open the Create Hyperlink dialog box.
3. Set up the link with any of the procedures you learned in Chapter 5, "Developing the Basic Page: Text, Lists, and Hyperlinks."

That's all there is to it! To edit the link, select the image and choose Edit, Hyperlink.

▶ **See** "Setting Up a Hyperlink," **p. 111**

Making Navigational Controls

The Web is a place people like to move around in. Well-chosen navigational tools laid out in a useful way give your Web pages a professional gleam. (Trying to keep visitors at your site by making it hard for them to leave is, well, counterproductive.) Buttons are the most common navigation symbols, and there are dozens of places on the Web that offer these simple images for free-use downloading. Put them into your page in an organized way, link them to their destinations, and they'll tie your site together so that it'll be a pleasure to visit.

Be consistent with button usage, though; a button that has function X on one page shouldn't have function Y on another. Always provide alternative text for them, in case your visitor has images turned off or is using a text browser. Consider putting a visible text label with each button. It makes life easier for your visitors, and they'll like you for it.

Using Imagemaps to Make Graphical Hyperlinks

Creating an imagemap by hand-coding it in HTML can be a real headache. FrontPage's ability to help you make imagemaps and link them easily is one of its most powerful features. The image maps it creates, by the way, are client-side. That is, the information about the map structure is embedded in the Web page that's downloaded to the browser client; the information does not reside on the server.

What is an *imagemap*? Functionally, it's a graphic that has hotspots in it; when a viewer clicks a hotspot, he or she's automatically sent to another location on the Web or in the current site. To put it another way, imagemaps are graphics with embedded hyperlinks. A good example is Yahoo's Yahooligans page, at **http://www.yahooligans.com/** (see Figure 6.15).

Since you're creating a Web site with its own character and needs, you're likely going to have to create or assemble the major imagemap graphics yourself. Before you start, though, think about what the graphic should look like, and especially remember that hotspots don't stand out as such in a browser window. This means you have to be careful to let people know where the hotspots are and what will happen if they're clicked.

Part
II

Ch
6

The first thing to do, then, is design the graphic so that it has obvious "clickable" areas. Often the best way to do this is to make those hotspot regions look like buttons, as the example in Figure 6.15 does. Another thing to consider is whether the links' destination is made clear by the hotspot. If it isn't, you should consider adding text to describe what will happen if someone follows the link. Alternatively, modify the image itself to make its destination clearer. Try hard to see the imagemap as if you were coming across it for the first time, and try even harder to imagine how it can be misunderstood. (A corollary to Murphy's Law says that if something can be misunderstood, it will be.)

FIGURE 6.15
An image with clearly defined clickable regions (as here, with the round buttons in the heading image) is a good way to approach imagemap design.

Clickable regions—

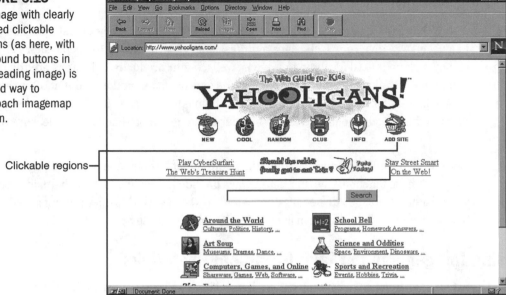

Another thing: Don't jam too many hotspot links into one image. Small hotspots, a few pixels across, are hard for users to point to, and an image with a dozen clickable regions starts to be confusing.

Finally, set up text links that duplicate the imagemap's hotspot destinations. This is for people who are running their browsers with images turned off.

> **CAUTION**
>
> If your Internet Service Provider (ISP) doesn't have the FrontPage server extensions installed on the server, your imagemaps probably will not work properly when you copy your web from your PC to the server. If that happens, go to FrontPage Explorer's Web Settings dialog box in the Tools menu. The Advanced tab gives some alternate imagemap styles; try Netscape. If this also gives problems or you're concerned about browsers that don't support Netscape-like behavior, contact your ISP administrator to discuss using the CERN or NCSA styles.

Creating an Imagemap   To make an imagemap, you need an image. It can be in any file format, though you should remember that GIF or JPEG are the formats recognized by all browsers, without the need for plug-ins or helpers. Begin by inserting the image into the page, select it, and use the following steps:

1. Decide whether you want the hotspot to be a rectangle, a circle, or a polygon. From the Image toolbar, select the appropriate drawing tool (see Figure 6.16).

N O T E   If you can't see the Image toolbar, choose View, Image toolbar to toggle it on. When it appears in the toolbar area, drag it to the place you want it. ■

FIGURE 6.16
The Image toolbar gives you different ways to shape a hotspot. Here, it's been dragged to the workspace as a floating toolbar.

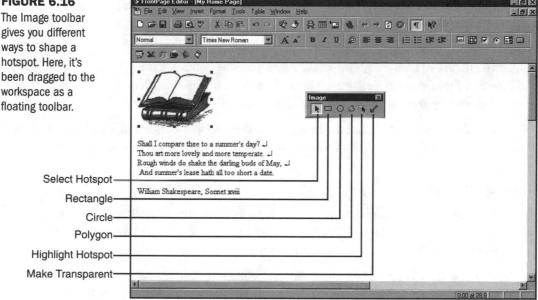

2. Put the cursor on the image. The cursor changes to a crayon.

3. Hold down the left mouse button and drag to get the outline you want. Then release the mouse button (the black rectangles on the outline are sizing handles). The Create Link dialog box appears (see Figure 6.17).

4. Establish the link using the Open Page, New Page, Current Web, or World Wide Web tab.

FIGURE 6.17
You use the Create Link dialog box to link imagemap hotspots to Web resources.

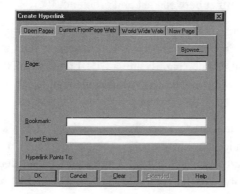

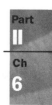

Part
II

Ch
6

Believe it or not, that's all you need to do. If you want to edit the link, select the image, click the hotspot, and then choose Edit, Link.

 TIP A quick way to edit an imagemap link is to right-click the hotspot and select Image Hotspot Properties from the shortcut menu.

The nature of imagemaps is to have more than one hotspot in the graphic. To get them neatly fitted, you can resize each hotspot by dragging its sizing handles, or you can move it around by putting the mouse pointer on its border and dragging it.

Deleting a Hotspot   Click the image so that the hotspot borders appear. Then click the hotspot you want to get rid of, and either press the Delete key or choose Edit, Clear.

Linking to Images

You now know how to link to pages, bookmarks, and remote locations—but how do you link to an image? In fact, it's pretty straightforward. Select the text, image, or hotspot you want for the link, and choose Edit, Hyperlink.

Now use the Create or Edit Hyperlink dialog boxes to find the name of the image to which you want to link. Complete the link, then choose OK. When the link is clicked in a browser, the browser window clears, and the image is then downloaded and displayed in that window. That is, the image isn't fitted into or overlaid on the page from which it was called.

Using Thumbnails

By now you may be somewhat paranoid about keeping your visitors waiting around for graphics to download. Yet, attractive images are a lot of the appeal of a good Web site. How do you resolve this conflict between art and efficiency?

In two words: use thumbnails. You make a thumbnail by using a graphics editor (Image Composer will do the job very effectively) to resize the image, then save this smaller image to a new file. The results can be significant: a GIF that is 340×500 pixels in 256 colors reduces from a file size of 168K to one of 31K. It downloads (all other things being equal) in less than a fifth of the time the original took.

Once you have this thumbnail image, insert it into your page and link it to the larger version. Then your visitor can look at it and decide whether he wants to view the big picture, so to speak. This is good audience psychology: you've let the user decide the matter, and he or she won't feel that you've forced a finger-drumming wait if he or she chooses to download the original. If you have a lot of images, you can put a whole gallery of thumbnails onto a page, and let your visitors wander among them at will.

The thumbnail should be kept in the images/folder. If its large version is also there, you simply link to it using the previously described procedure in "Linking to Images." If the large version is at another location, you use the World Wide Web sheet and supply the other location's URL.

Making the Most of Image File Formats

Web images are almost all JPEG or GIF files, with the balance at the moment tending heavily toward the GIF format. You can manipulate these formats, to a limited degree, with the tools FrontPage Editor gives you (see Figure 6.18). You do this to control image quality and influence download speed.

FIGURE 6.18
Modify image file behavior by using the options in the General sheet of the Image Properties dialog box.

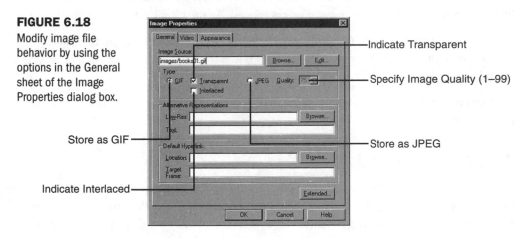

Converting Image File Formats

When you insert an image, FrontPage Editor checks to see if it's GIF or JPEG. If it is neither GIF nor JPEG, and it is 256 colors or less, FrontPage Editor automatically converts it to GIF. If it is more than 256 colors, FrontPage Editor converts it to JPEG.

If you want to store a file in the other format, you mark the appropriate check box for GIF or JPEG. Then, when you save the page, the image is converted. If you go from GIF to JPEG, you also get a chance to adjust the quality of the stored JPEG image by typing a number from 1 to 99 into the Quality box (75 is the default). With the best quality (99), you get the lowest file compression and slowest downloading; with the lowest quality (1), you get the highest file compression and the fastest downloading. There's no free lunch, is there?

CAUTION

Once you've set the Quality and saved the image, you can't change that setting again, even if you delete the image and reinsert it from the saved page. If you're experimenting, keep a backup!

 People sometimes link to images on other servers so they won't have to store a lot of large images on their own web host. If your Internet Service Provider limits the disk space you can use for your web, this may be the only thing you can do to get the image resources you want.

Using Interlaced GIFs for Speed

A browser that supports interlaced images (GIF only) builds up such an image in four passes, with the picture becoming clearer with each pass. On the first pass, the text and links of the page are also displayed, so that the viewer can start reading (or clicking a link) without waiting for the image to be completed. Again, it's all in the interests of speed.

You can create an interlaced GIF from a non-interlaced one by marking the Interlaced check box in the Image Properties dialog box. When the page is saved, the image is stored as an interlaced GIF.

If you want to produce your own interlaced GIFs, Image Composer saves its GIF files in this format.

Using Low Res for Speed

Another tool in your speed-up kit is the Low Res (low resolution) option. To employ this, first use a graphics program to make a lower-resolution version of the original, and then save that graphic to your images folder. This version should be smaller than the original; a common trick to achieve this is to change it to black and white.

When you want to use the Low Res option, use the following steps:

1. Select the original, full-resolution image and go to the General sheet of the Image Properties dialog box.
2. In the Low-Res box in the Alternative Representations section, insert the name of the low-resolution image (the Browse button is handy here).
3. Choose OK.

Now when someone goes to the page, the browser loads the low-resolution image and the page text first; only after that does the browser go back and display the high-resolution version of the image. This speeds things up. Notice that you don't have to do any linking here, as you do with the thumbnail technique. The HTML generated by FrontPage Editor takes care of everything for you.

Making Transparent Images

You want to give your pages a unified and harmonious appearance, and you achieve this through your choice of images, text, and layout. You can add to this sense of unity by using transparent GIF images (only GIFs support this option; it doesn't work with JPEGs). A transparent image lets the page background appear through parts of the graphic, as though the picture were painted on acetate instead of paper. This embeds the image into its surroundings and gives a sense of integration. You can see the difference in effect in Figure 6.19.

FIGURE 6.19

The upper, transparent GIF is better harmonized with its surroundings than the one below it, which is opaque.

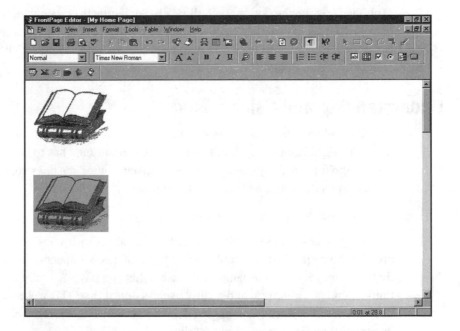

If you feel that a graphic looks better if a particular color in it is transparent, you can get this effect with the Make Transparent tool from the Image toolbar. To make a particular color invisible, use the following steps:

1. Select the graphic and click the Make Transparent button.
2. Put the cursor (it looks like the eraser end of a pencil) on the color you want to do away with, and click. All instances of that color in the graphic become transparent.

When you first look at the image properties for some graphics, the Transparent check box is grayed out because the graphic contains no transparent colors. To establish a transparent color, use the Make Transparent tool, from the Image toolbar.

Conversely, you may want to make a transparent graphic into an opaque one. To achieve this effect, select the image and then go to the General sheet of the Image Properties dialog box. Clear the Transparent check box in the Type section. Choose OK, and the graphic will be rendered opaque. You can't check the box again, though, to bring back the transparency. To do that, you have to use the Make Transparent tool, as described above.

Multimedia

Multimedia is moving swiftly onto the Web. Such effects certainly increase page appeal, but they're time-consuming to download, and active content like JavaScript presents security questions. Keep these factors in mind when you're deciding which, if any, special effects to add to a page.

Understanding and Using Sound

Imagine a bleary-eyed Web page artist, at 3 a.m., looking for ideas out there on the Web while her significant other slumbers in the next room (and has to be up at 6 a.m. to go to work). She finds a likely site, and enters it. Instants after she does so, a shattering trumpet fanfare splits the night: and it loops, three times.

You can imagine the rest for yourself.

Sound does have its drawbacks, particularly (as above) when its inclusion is badly considered by the page creator. If you're going to use it, keep it under control, and remember that not everyone has the same audio tastes that you have. Actually, a lot of people still think sound is a gimmick, and a fairly useless one at that. This will change when the Web becomes a full-powered information delivery system with short downloads and solid, informative audio content—but that time isn't yet here.

That said, a bit of well-chosen and unobtrusive sound can indeed enhance your page, at least for people who have recent browsers that handle audio. (Not everybody has a sound card installed, either, though that's changing fast.) Probably the best design advice is not to make the sound clip too loud and don't loop it and loop it and loop it—unless it really is a very soft, unobtrusive background noise.

From the technical point of view, the worst problem with sound is that even a few seconds' worth of audio takes a significant time to download; a minute or two of it, depending on the file format and quality, can produce downloads in the multi-megabyte range. As a rule of thumb, keep audio clips short enough to make files sizes of 20k or less. Some audio file types do allow compression, which helps, although there's always the no-free-lunch factor—the higher the compression, the smaller the file, the poorer the quality. These compression formats are as follows:

- AIFF-C (6:1 compression)—The acronym stands for Apple Audio Interchange File Format, and the C indicates the extended version that supports compression (plain AIFF doesn't). The format produces stereo sound at high fidelity, and is usually found on Macintosh platforms. The DOS/Windows file extension is .AIF, which doesn't actually distinguish these files from the uncompressed version of the format, AIFF.

- MPEG (up to 20:1 compression)—This format, which is the international standard for both video and audio compression, was designed by the Moving Pictures Expert Group, hence MPEG. It provides stereo sound at high quality, and the files can be quite smaller than equivalent ones in uncompressed formats. The DOS/Windows file extensions are usually .MPG or .MP2.

The uncompressed formats are:

- AIFF—It's essentially the same as AIFF-C (see above) except it lacks the compression. For DOS/Windows, the extension is also .AIF.

- AU—This is from Sun Microsystems, and is very common on the Web. It's as good as telephone quality, which makes it a reasonable choice for sound bites that are mostly speech. The DOS/Windows extension is .AU.

- SND—This is a plain-vanilla sound format, supporting both stereo and mono. The DOS/Windows extension is .SND.

- WAV—This is a Microsoft format, and another common one. It's useful for both stereo and mono, and the quality is good. The DOS/Windows file extension is .WAV.

- MIDI—This Musical Instruments Digital Interface isn't actually a file format; instead, it's a file of instructions that is sent to an electronic sound synthesizer to tell it what to play and how to play it. The computer receiving the file must have a MIDI player for the sound to be heard. MIDI files do, however, allow complex sounds to be stored in relatively small files. The DOS/Windows file extension is .MID.

Adding Background Audio to Your Page   Background audio is a sound file that plays automatically when someone downloads a page, assuming the person's browser supports the feature. Adding background sound is fairly simple even in HTML, but FrontPage Editor makes the task even easier. Do the following:

Part

II

Ch

6

1. Choose File, Page Properties. The Page Properties dialog box appears.

2. Choose the General tab, then click the Browse button to open the Background Sound dialog box (see Figure 6.20).

3. If the sound file is in the current web, use the Current FrontPage Web sheet to select the file. Otherwise, use the Other Location sheet.

4. When the file is selected, choose OK to return to the General sheet of the Page Properties dialog box.

5. To make the sound repeat, type the number of repetitions into the Loop box; to keep it going, mark the Forever check box (and remember that forever is a long time).

6. Choose OK. The background audio is now inserted into the page. An inconvenience of the way FrontPage Editor handles this is that there's no indication in the editor workspace that a background sound is embedded in the page.

FIGURE 6.20

Add a background sound by specifying the file name in the Current FrontPage Web sheet or the Other Location sheet.

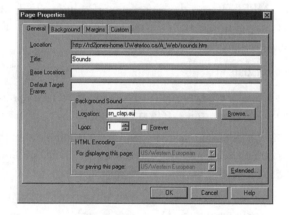

You can also use the Insert, Background sound command to place audio on a page. This choice doesn't give you the looping options, however.

N O T E The <LOOPDELAY> attribute, which sets a delay between repeats of the sound file, is not directly implemented in FrontPage Editor. Attempting to add it with the View HTML feature doesn't work, since the attribute gets stripped out when you leave the View HTML workspace. What you must do, if you want the delay, is use the Insert, HTML Markup command to manually add all the code for the background sound. For example:

```
<BGSOUND SRC = "SOUND.WAV" LOOP = 10 LOOPDELAY=30>
```

can be typed into the HTML Markup text box. When you click OK, the code is inserted into the page (with the help of a WebBot). ■

Now test the page in Internet Explorer 2.0 or 3.0, which support the HTML BGSOUND tag (that's what FrontPage Editor uses to insert this type of audio). Netscape 3.0 requires Java applets to play background sound.

Removing Background Audio   To get rid of audio in the background, simply open the General sheet of the Page Properties dialog box, and delete the file name from the Location box in the Background Sound section. Choose OK, and the audio is gone.

Linking to a Sound File   Set this up as you would any other link, with the target of the link being the desired sound file. When a visitor clicks the link, assuming his or her browser has the plug-in or helper application that plays the file format, he or she will hear the playback of the file (see Figure 6.21). Internet Explorer, as noted above, supports the BGSOUND tag, so it doesn't need plug-ins or helpers.

FIGURE 6.21
Netscape's WAV player plays back a sound file when the link is clicked.

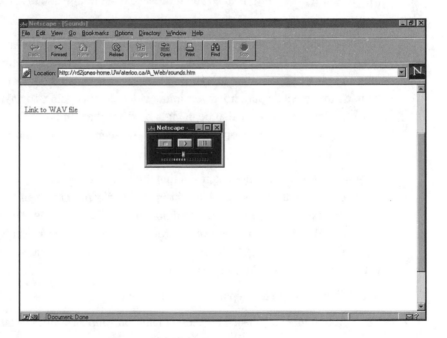

Part

II

Ch

6

Understanding and Using Video

The basic principle of adding video clips to a page is the same as adding audio clips. Video comes in files of various formats, but they all have one thing in common: they're big. Even with heavy compression, and in a small playback window, a minute of video requires megabytes of data. When linking to such a file, you should be sure to indicate how big it is, so people can decide for themselves whether they want to wait for it to download.

The major video formats on the Web now are MPEG Levels 1 and 2, and Apple's Quicktime. Hot on their heels is Microsoft's AVI (also known as Video for Windows), which is making steady inroads into the domain. All these offer video compression, the highest ratio being that of the two MPEG formats, which offer good results at ratios of even 20:1.

Whatever scheme is used, though, all video must play back at 30 images (or frames) per second for full-motion effects. The larger the images, the more processing power is required of the playback machine, the more storage space the file requires, and the longer the download time. Because of this, full-screen video is (to say the least) uncommon on the Web. If you're selecting videos, or making your own, remember that smaller is faster in every respect. It's a matter of the inverse-square law—an image at 320×240 pixels (which is still pretty big) is one-fourth the size of an image at 640×480.

Using Inline Video　We owe this development to Microsoft, and at the time of writing (late 1996) only Internet Explorer 3.0 supports this method of displaying AVI video clips. It's an alternative to the much more common method of having visitors play back a clip using the plug-in application installed in their browsers. All the factors of file size and playback image size apply, however; inline video doesn't gain you anything in these respects. The viewer must also be using a browser that supports the method. How quickly Netscape will embrace the option remains to be seen, so for the moment the effect is available only to users of Internet Explorer 3.0.

The engaging part of inline images is that, once downloaded, they can be made to stay quietly on a page until wanted. They sit up and perform only when called upon, which makes them easier to live with than infinite-loop GIF animations. There are a few sources of AVI files on the Web for you to download and experiment with; one such is **http://www.acm.uiuc.edu/rml/Mpeg/**. Despite its name, the site has several video file types in addition to MPEG.

To install an AVI clip into a page, do the following:

1. Choose Insert, Video. The Video dialog box appears with the familiar two sheets, Current FrontPage Web, and Other Location.

2. Use either sheet to find the video file you want, select it, and choose OK or Open, depending on where you found the file.

3. FrontPage Editor inserts a marker into the page to show where the clip will appear. This marker is the same size and proportions as the clip image will be.

4. Use the Preview in Browser command to test the clip in Internet Explorer. (If it's a new file, you'll be asked if you want to save it to the current web; answer Yes.)

5. As soon as the browser opens, the playback will begin and run until it ends. To restart, click anywhere in the picture; to stop or restart part of the way through, also click in the picture.

You can control the clip's behavior using the Image Properties dialog box. To do this, select the placeholder by clicking it, then choose Edit, Image Properties. When the Image Properties dialog box opens, choose the Video tab (see Figure 6.22).

FIGURE 6.22
You can adjust characteristics of the video playback such as looping and display of controls.

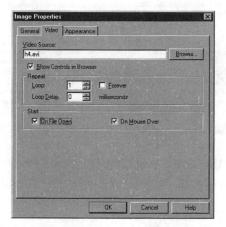

These controls allow you to browse for another video file (more about this later), and also allow more viewer control of the clip, as follows:

- Show Controls in Browser puts a set of simple playback controls on-screen with the clip.
- Loop and Forever determine how many times the playback of the clip repeats.
- Loop Delay determines the time interval between repeated playbacks.
- On File Open tells the browser to start playing as soon as the clip file loads.
- On Mouse Over, if checked when On File Open is unchecked, will halt playback except when the mouse pointer is on top of the image.
- On Mouse Over and On File Open, if both checked, will cause the playback to run to completion as soon as the file loads, and then wait until the mouse pointer is on top of it before it runs again.

When the viewer sees the video clip in his or her browser, and the Show Controls in Browser checkbox is marked, the clip has simple stop-go controls available with it (see Figure 6.23).

Part
II

Ch
6

FIGURE 6.23
Microsoft Internet
Explorer is playing an
inline AVI file. The
browser controls are
turned on.

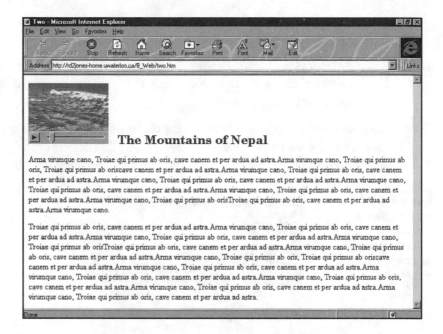

InLine Video with Browsers that Don't Support It   This is all very well, you may say, for
people who are using Internet Explorer. But if you previewed the video-equipped page in
Netscape, you'll have noted that there's an ugly blank rectangle where the clip resides.
How do you deal with this?

The answer is that you put a plain graphic in to provide for browsers that don't handle
in-line images. To do this, return to the Image Properties dialog box, and select the General sheet (see Figure 6.24).

FIGURE 6.24
Use the Image
Properties dialog box
to insert a substitute
for a video clip.

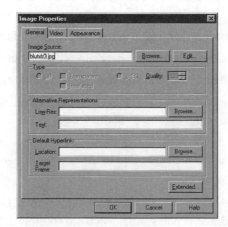

Use the Browse button to locate a GIF or JPEG file to use as the substitute. Then choose OK. From now on, non–Internet Explorer browsers will display the graphic instead of the empty box, while IE browsers will automatically play the clip.

 The most efficient way to set up a clip is to insert the graphic placeholder first, then use the Video sheet of the Image Properties dialog box to place the associated video clip on the page. You don't actually need the Insert, Video command at all.

Linking to a Video Clip.   That's one problem solved. What about people using non-Internet Explorer browsers who want to see the clip? The answer here is to give them a link so that their browsers' plug-ins can play it for them. This assumes they know about the clip; your substitute graphic should tell them that it's available.

You might think it efficient to make the substitute image itself into the link. This seems a good idea at first, but it has a major pitfall: IE-equipped users who click the clip to stop or start it will not only do that, they'll activate the link! This will give them a second playback of the clip in an AVI player window. Good as the clip may be, this is probably too much of a good thing.

Accordingly, make the link from some nearby text or a clearly labeled graphic. Any file you use for inline video should be reasonably fast to load, but it's polite to indicate the file size with the link, anyway.

Finally, you can include non-inline clips in your pages by setting up a link to them so they can be played back in a browser. As mentioned earlier, non-AVI clips have to be displayed that way, since only AVI can be used for inline video.

Designing for Animated GIFs   Recently, animated GIFs have proliferated on the Web. While they can add vivacity to a page—some are attractively whimsical—they can also distract from the content. There's been some heated debate over their use, and a few basic principles are emerging, as follows:

- Don't overuse them. One per screen is enough, if not more than enough.
- Text is almost always where the information is. Keep a balance between moving images and static words, and remember that motion always draws the attention.
- Because of the previous point, don't place animations too close to highly important text.
- Consider running the animation sequence once or twice, and then stopping it.
- Don't flash; change the animation slowly.
- When a design decision is in doubt, go for simplicity rather than complication.

Making an Animated GIF   An animated GIF works on the essential principle of any animation: a series of slightly differing images that, when viewed in quick succession, give the impression of movement. You need two basic tools to make them. First is a graphics program (Image Composer or Paintshop Pro, for example) to create the animation frames. The other required application is a "blending" application, such as GIF Construction Set, or Image Composer's plug-in for animating GIFs, available from Microsoft's web site, to blend the frames into the final image, which you then insert onto your page. The more complicated the animation, the larger the size of the resulting file.

You can find out more about the GIF Construction Set at

http://www.mindworkshop.com/alchemy/

Making these little creatures is more complex than their appearance suggests, and producing good ones is a lot of work. Still, they're fun, and a clever one properly used can catch a new visitor's attention in a way that little else can.

Scrolling Text with a Marquee

Marquees are those boxes that have text moving through them. Opinions vary on their best use; some people keep the text moving, other prefer to slide it into view, then leave it static. Your own design sense will be your best guide here.

To insert a marquee, first choose Insert, Marquee to open the Marquee Properties dialog box (see Figure 6.25).

FIGURE 6.25

Make scrolling text look the way you want with the Marquee Properties options.

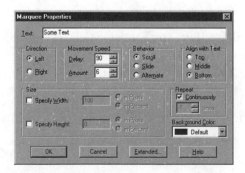

Use the Text box to type the text you want to scroll. The marquee properties are adjusted as follows:

- The Left and Right option buttons determine the direction of scroll.
- Amount sets the speed of the scroll. Delay is an adjustment that essentially makes the scroll move smoothly or in slight increments.

- Slide moves the text onto the screen and stops it.
- Alternate scrolls the text onto the screen, then bounces it back and forth.
- If there's text beside the marquee, the Align with Text option buttons place it at the middle, the top, or the bottom of the marquee height.
- The Width of the marquee can be set as a percentage of the page or as pixels.
- The repetitions of the marquee movement are set with the Repeat section.
- The Background Color determines the color of the marquee box in which the text appears. Default keeps the box the same color as the page, so the text appears to float across the page surface.

You can align the marquee on the page using the alignment buttons on the toolbar. You can't use the Format, Font command to change the marquee font, unfortunately; however, you can modify its style by first selecting the marquee box and then choosing a style from the Change Style box.

To make changes to the marquee properties later, right-click the marquee and select Marquee Properties from the shortcut menu.

From Here...

In the last two chapters we covered the essentials of text, hyperlinks, and graphics. Now we can move on to new territory, which includes tools for page and site organization, and customizing "boilerplate" pages for your own purposes. We'll do all this in:

Chapter 7, "Creating Tables," which shows you how to design, set up, and modify tables to enhance the organization of your pages.

Chapter 8, "Enhancing Web Sites with FrontPage Frames," which guides you through the complexities of setting up a "framed" site, and shows you how to use frames with graphics, hyperlinks, and frame templates.

Chapter 9, "Creating Pages with FrontPage Editor Templates," where you explore the templates supplied with FrontPage, and learn how to use them to create your own customized bibliographies, glossaries, directories, and other page formats.

Creating Tables

Tables are a powerful method of presenting page content in an accessible and understandable way. They're especially useful in the World Wide Web environment because of the limitations of our hardware. Most of us peer at relatively small screens, and a screen's resolution is much less than that of a printed page. Any tool that helps us compress information into small, organized areas is a very useful one, and tables fill this specification perfectly. ■

Table Setup

Create the basic table framework to organize your information.

Table Editing

Modify row and column structure and cell layout.

Cell Editing

Format your cell content effectively with alignment and varying cell widths.

Decorative Elements

Use cell and table background colors and images.

Using Tables for Better Content Organization

Like lists, tables are common in our lives, especially in business and science. In Web pages, they can contain text and images, just as printed tables do. You can use them to arrange text in parallel columns or to set an explanatory block of text beside the image that resides in the adjacent cell. You can insert lists into cells, and you can even insert tables into other tables. All this gives you tremendous flexibility in arranging data and images (see Figure 7.1).

FIGURE 7.1

An image is in the left cell of the table's top row and a bulleted list in the right. Table borders are shown for clarity; they're optional.

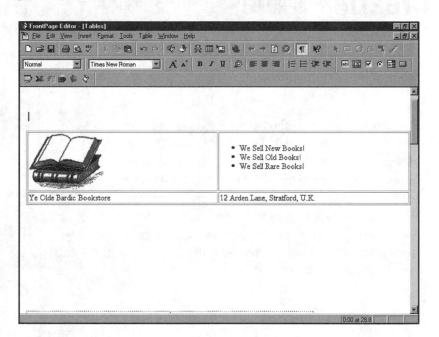

Tables can also contain hyperlinks to other resources, which gives them a whole new dimension. For example, you can make a table containing thumbnails of images and link these to the larger versions.

In another example, each entry in a periodic table of the elements can be linked to a re-source that gives detailed information about that element. You can also insert forms or a WebBot into a cell, which makes a table almost an interactive tool in itself.

You can see this in Figure 7.2, where the bulleted hyperlinks are actually contained inside the cells of a two-column table. (In this example, the cell and table boundaries don't show.)

FIGURE 7.2

A table set up as a bulleted table of contents. The cell contents are hyperlinks.

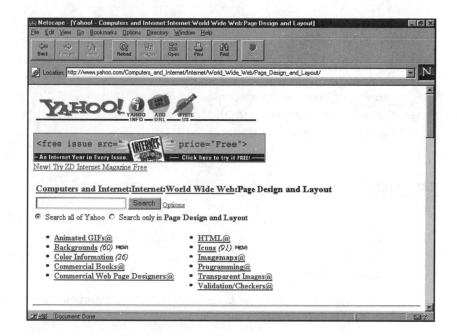

To understand better how tables work, you can save a page containing one to a file, then manipulate the table properties to see what happens. In Figure 7.3, a page has been saved as a file, so that the properties of the tables in it can be modified and experimented with. Each table in the figure contains hyperlinks, some as bulleted lists, others as simple text links. (The larger, bulleted-list table is partly hidden behind the dialog box.)

FIGURE 7.3

It's helpful to modify the table properties of a Web example to see how things work. Here, the cell borders of two tables have been made visible by setting the Border Size (in the foreground Table Properties dialog box) to 3 pixels.

Part

II

Ch

7

Tables are supported by all the major graphical browsers (Netscape 2.0 and 3.0, Internet Explorer 2.0 and 3.0, and Mosaic 2.1), so feel free to include them in your pages. Different browsers treat visible cell borders differently, though, so you should check to see what the borders look like in each browser before you settle on a design. Equally important, remember that many people cruise the Web at 640×480 resolution; if you create tables that take advantage of the width of a 1024×768 display, your visitors using a lower resolution may not see what you envisioned.

Setting up a Table

FrontPage Editor gives you a lot of options for table appearance, but don't begin a complicated table by plunging right into FrontPage Editor. Begin by planning it, if only by roughing it out on paper, to organize the data and its presentation. You'll save yourself a lot of time and revision.

Once you've worked out the table's content and structure, use the following steps:

1. Choose Table, Insert Table. The Insert Table dialog box appears, as shown in Figure 7.4.

FIGURE 7.4

Set up a table and specify size and layout parameters in the Insert Table dialog box.

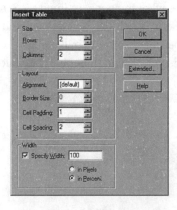

2. In the Rows and Columns text boxes, specify the number of rows and columns.

3. In the Alignment list drop-down list box, specify whether you want the table against the left margin, centered, or against the right margin.

4. In the Border Size text box, specify how many pixels thick the cell and table borders are to be. A value of zero specifies no borders.

5. In the Cell Padding text box, specify how many pixels of space you want between the cell contents and the inside edge of the cell boundary.

6. In the Cell Spacing text box, specify how many pixels of space you want between cells.

7. In the Specify Width text box, specify how wide you want the table to be, either in pixels or as a percentage of the browser window.

8. When you are done, choose OK. The table appears. If you chose a Border Size of zero, the cells are outlined in dotted lines (see Figure 7.5). These dotted cell boundaries don't appear in a browser. (You can make the dotted lines disappear by clicking on the "Show/Hide ¶" toolbar button.)

FIGURE 7.5
Two empty tables: the upper table has a border size of zero and a width of 75%; the lower table has a border width of 2 and a width of 50%.

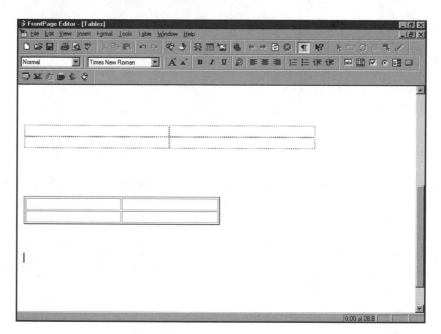

Actually putting content into a cell is straightforward. Click in the cell and, if it's text you want, just start typing. The text wraps when it reaches the cell margin, pushing the bottom of the whole row down so that you can kccp going. To insert images, other tables, lists, or any other page element, click in the cell and use the appropriate menus to insert the component. The cells resize to suit the content. To get the cursor "out" of any table, simply use Ctrl-Enter in a table's upper-left cell.

Using the Table Menu

Now that we have a table, you can get a better look at the Table menu (except for Insert Table, its entries were grayed out when you last saw them). Click anywhere in the table, and choose Table to make the menu appear (see Figure 7.6).

Part
II

Ch
7

FIGURE 7.6
Use the Table menu for manipulating and selecting parts of a table.

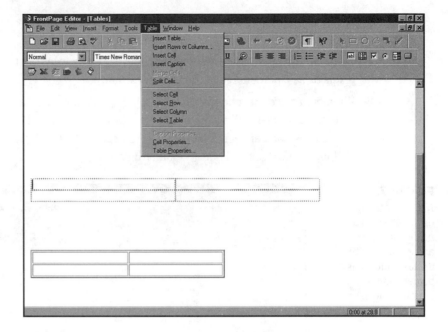

Many of the operations you perform on table elements require you to select those elements. You can use the menu to select cells, rows, and columns, or the entire table. Of course, you also can drag across table elements to select them.

You can also select a row or a column by placing the cursor on the table border to the left of that row or above that column. When the cursor changes to a small black arrow, click once to select the row or column.

Modifying the Properties of an Existing Table

As you work on a table, you may discover that you need to change some of its characteristics. To do this, click anywhere in the table, and choose Table, Table Properties. The Table Properties dialog box appears, as shown in Figure 7.7.

The Table Properties dialog box duplicates part of the Insert Table dialog box. You can modify the table layout and the width of the table using the same procedures. You can also apply colors to the table; we look at this procedure a little later, in the section "Adding Colors and Backgrounds to Tables and Cells."

To get to the Table Properties dialog box quickly, right-click anywhere in the table and select Table Properties from the shortcut menu.

FIGURE 7.7
Change the settings for an existing table with the Table Properties dialog box.

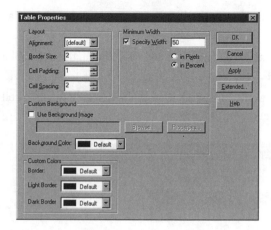

Deleting a Table or Parts of a Table

One of the things you most need to know when you're experimenting is how to delete an experiment gone wrong. To get rid of a table entirely, click anywhere in it. Then choose Table, Select Table and press the Delete key. Another way is to double-click in the left margin to select the entire table and then either press the Delete key or choose Edit, Clear.

You remove columns or rows by the same method: select and then delete, and they vanish as though they had never been. However, if you delete a cell (distinct from deleting its content), all the cells to its right slide over to fill the empty space, and a gap is left at the right side of the table (see Figure 7.8; borders in the example are turned on to make this easier to see).

Adding Rows or Columns

Even with the best planning, you sometimes discover a class of information you didn't allow for, and you need a new row or column for it. To add either one, select the existing row or column that will be adjacent to the new one. Then choose Table, Insert Rows or Columns. The Insert Rows or Columns dialog box appears, as shown in Figure 7.9. Fill in the data for the number of rows or columns to insert and where they should go relative to the selection you made. Then choose OK.

Inserting a Cell

If you deleted a cell and decide you want its real estate back, you can insert a new cell by using Table, Insert Cell. Where the new cell appears is governed by the following:

Part
II

Ch
7

■ If the cursor is in an empty cell, the new cell is added immediately to the left of the current cell.

■ If the cursor is at the left end of any data in a cell, the new cell is added to the left of the current cell.

■ If the cursor is at the right end of any data in a cell, the new cell is added to the right of the current cell.

FIGURE 7.8
Deleting a cell leaves a blank area in the table, as the cells to its right move into the space left by the deleted cell.

Space caused by deleted center cell of row

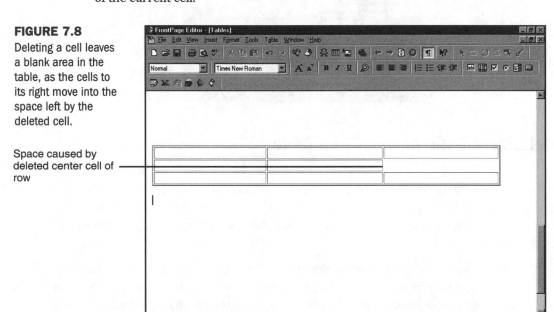

Adding and Formatting a Caption

To add a caption, first click inside the table. Then choose Table, Insert Caption, and the insertion point moves to the line immediately above the table's first row. Simply type the caption; it centers itself automatically.

FIGURE 7.9
Use the Insert Rows or Columns dialog box to add data space to your tables.

You have some flexibility with its placement and appearance. To adjust them, click anywhere in the caption and choose Table, Caption Properties to open the Caption Properties dialog box (see Figure 7.10). Mark the appropriate option button to place the caption above or below the table. For lateral placement click the Left Align, Center, or Right Align buttons on the toolbar.

FIGURE 7.10
Captions can go above or below a table.

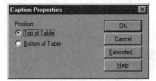

To change the caption font, simply select the text and choose Format, Font to make the changes with the Font dialog box. You can also use the character formatting buttons on the toolbar for bold, italic, underline, or color.

To delete a caption, select it, then press the Delete key twice.

Inserting a Table into an Existing Table

You can get an interesting and powerful effect by putting a table inside a cell of another table. To do this, click the cell where you want the subtable to appear, and choose Table, Insert Table. Set up the subtable properties as you like, and then choose OK. You can see an example of a table in another table's cell in Figure 7.11.

FIGURE 7.11
Placing a table within the cell of another table gives a "subdivided" effect. Both tables have captions.

Splitting and Merging Cells

A perfectly regular grid of cells may not exactly match the way your data needs to be laid out. To change the cell patterns so that they serve your purposes better, you can split or merge them. To split a cell, click in it, and then choose T<u>a</u>ble, <u>S</u>plit Cells. The Split Cells dialog box appears, as shown in Figure 7.12.

FIGURE 7.12

You can change a table's cell subdivisions by splitting cells.

Now you have a choice of dividing the cell into columns or rows. Set up whichever you want, and choose OK. Splitting the cells leaves the data intact in the left cell (row split) or the upper cell (column split). In Figure 7.13, you can see a table with both row-split and column-split cells.

FIGURE 7.13

The top right cell has been split into two rows and the bottom left cell into three columns.

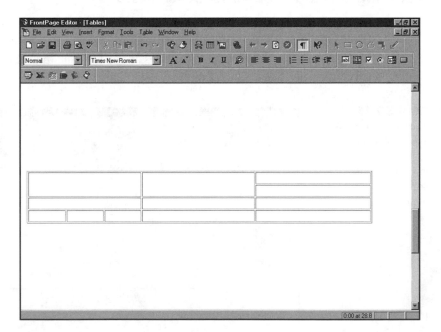

To put cells together, select them, and then choose T<u>a</u>ble, <u>M</u>erge Cells. The data will be intact in the resulting cell, though you may have to do some reformatting.

Modifying the Table's Appearance

A plain-vanilla table is good at organizing content, but we need to think about presentation, too. Using column and row headers, captions, color, and suitable alignment of cell content will make your tables pleasing to the eye.

Adding Headers

Most tables have column headers to denote the kind of data in each column; many tables also have row headers. An example would be a sales report with product names as row headers, and sales for each quarter as column headers. You often want to emphasize such headers, and one way is to select the text and use character formatting. Here's a second method, though, which is to change the cell properties. To do this, select the cell or cells you want as header cells, and then choose Table, Cell Properties to display the Cell Properties dialog box (see Figure 7.14). Mark the Header Cell check box and then choose OK.

 TIP To reach the Cell Properties dialog box quickly, select the cell and press Alt+Enter.

FIGURE 7.14
The Cell Properties dialog box lets you make a cell into a header cell.

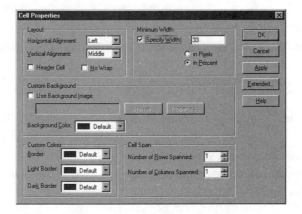

The text in the selected cell is rendered in bold. If you want to remove the header formatting, reopen the Cell Properties dialog box and deselect the Header Cell check box.

Aligning the Content of a Cell

Depending on your cell content, you may want it positioned in different places. An image, for example, usually looks better if it's centered within the cell borders. You get these effects as well by using the Cell Properties dialog box. In the Layout section, you can

Part
II
Ch
7

specify horizontal and vertical text alignment with the drop-down list boxes. Figure 7.15 shows an image with the Horizontal Alignment set to "Center" and Vertical Alignment set to "Middle."

FIGURE 7.15
Centering images and text in cells improves their appearance.

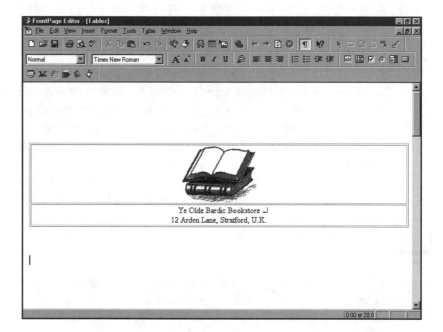

Using No Wrap

The No Wrap check-box, if marked, prevents word wrap from being applied to the contents of a cell. However, even with the box checked, and while you are in FrontPage Editor, a long line of text will continue to wrap within the cell. That is, the "no wrap" effect does not actually appear until you view the page in a browser. This can have profound effects on a table's layout, so be sure to check your work in a browser if you do use the No Wrap option.

Specifying Minimum Cell Width

The Cell Properties dialog box gives yet another way to proportion cells, or in this case, full columns. As usual, you should keep the "minimum width" units set to percent, not pixels, to allow for different resolutions your viewers may be using.

A three-column table will have the default minimum cell widths set at 33%, that is, the cells take up at least 33% of the total table width each (to be precise, 33%, 33%, and 34%, from left to right). Changing these percentages lets you can adjust the width of a whole column, independent of other columns, as shown in Figure 7.16. Getting the cell width percentages coordinated with the table width percentage can be tricky, and will take some experimentation and some browser previewing.

FIGURE 7.16
You create columns of differing widths using Minimum Width cell settings.

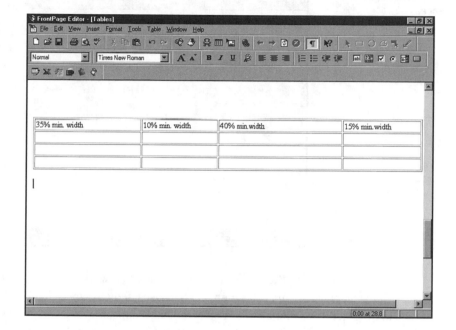

Making Cells Span Rows and Columns

Another way of modifying your table's grid is to make a cell bigger or smaller. This is called spanning, and you change a cell's span by first selecting a cell and then using the Cell Properties dialog box. In the Cell Span section, enter the number of rows or columns you want the cell to stretch across, and choose OK. The ultimate effect of this can be very similar to merging or splitting cells. Where it's different is that when you span a cell, the cells it spans across are "pushed" down or sideways, as if you had inserted cells. You can delete these extra cells, of course. In the example in Figure 7.17, the large center cell was produced by setting its span at 2 rows and 2 columns. The cells that were pushed out to the right and downward by this were then deleted.

Adding Colors and Backgrounds to Tables and Cells

Both the Table Properties dialog box and the Cell Properties dialog box have sections where you can specify background colors, images, and border colors. As these sections are identical in both cases, we consider them together.

Part
II

Ch
7

FIGURE 7.17
Using cell spanning
lets you customize
your table's appear-
ance.

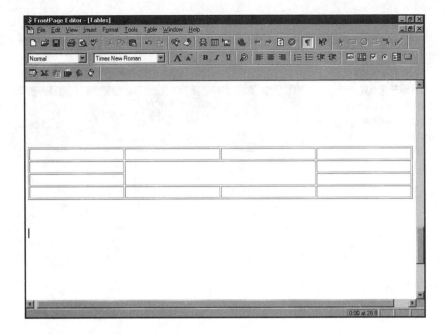

Figure 7.18 shows the Table Properties dialog box with the Color list for the Background
Color displayed. This list is identical to those used elsewhere in FrontPage Editor, including the ability to mix a custom color, and also appears when you go to set the border color
parameters in the Custom Colors sections of these two dialog boxes.

FIGURE 7.18
The color list lets you
pick colors for table or
cell backgrounds, and
table or cell borders.

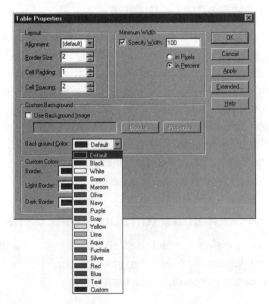

The major difference is that using the Table Properties dialog box sets the colors for the entire selected table, while using the Cell Properties dialog box sets the colors for the selected cell only.

Entire tables or selected cells can have a background image, which you choose by marking the Use Background Image check box and inputting the file name of the desired image in the text box. The procedure is identical to the one you learned in Chapter 6, "Enhancing Pages with Graphics and Multimedia."

Finally, a word about design: Don't make the backgrounds of your tables too busy or their colors garish and distracting. The table is a means to an end, not an end in itself—the information it organizes is what's important.

Inserting Page Elements into a Table

Adding text to a table is simple—you merely click in the cell and start typing. All of FrontPage Editor's text formatting tools are at your disposal, so go ahead and use them.

As for images, links, and multimedia components, you add these to a table cell by clicking in the cell and going on just as if the new element were standing by itself on the page. The fact that it's in a table makes no difference at all. Don't make your table too busy, though.

As we discussed at the beginning of this chapter, tables are a powerful organizational tool. In Figure 7.19, you can see a page that puts a series of elaborately equipped tables to good use.

FIGURE 7.19
The tables on this page put a lot of information into well-organized spaces.

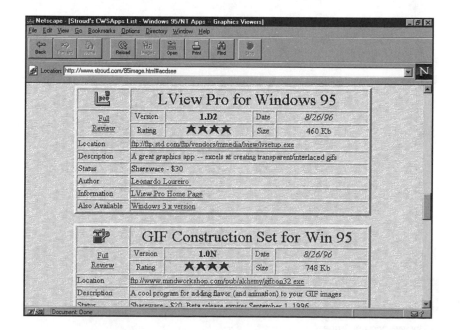

Included in each table are graphics, a graphical hyperlink in the top left corner, text hyperlinks, and variously sized cells and columns. The author has also used different fonts to suggest different types of information, but hasn't gone overboard with them. Not used are table cell colors or backgrounds, which in this case is good—there's a lot of information here, and adding such decorative elements (because the page already has a background image) would have been too much.

From Here...

In this chapter we've explored the way FrontPage 97 helps you arrange and present your information using tables. With these, and with everything else we've covered so far, you can build a well-organized, efficient, and visually attractive Web site. But we haven't finished yet.

- Chapter 8, "Enhancing Web Sites with FrontPage Frames," is where you find out about designing a "framed" site, about using frames with links and images, and how to create ready-made framed environments with frame templates.

- Chapter 9, "Creating Pages with FrontPage Editor Templates," shows you how you can use these organizational and presentation tools to generate real-world documents like tables of contents, data sheets, schedules, and directories.

- Chapter 10, "Using WebBots, Wizards, and Interactive Page Templates," shows you how to use that other great organizational tool, the fill-in form.

## CHAPTER 8

Enhancing Web Sites with FrontPage Frames

Frames were originally developed by Netscape, and their use in Web sites is expanding steadily. Simply put, *framing* is a method of placing two or more windows on the screen and giving the viewer individual control of none, some, or all of them. Frames can even contain other frames, and the page within a frame can reference other pages independently of the rest of the display. This gives a Web designer great flexibility in choosing how to organize and present information, whether it's text, graphics, or active content.

To see what this means, look at the example in Figure 8.1. The fixed frame at the top of the screen contains navigation controls, while the leftmost frame contains a scrollable menu. The pages referenced by the menu items appear in the largest frame. ■

Strategies for frame design

Though frames are potentially very useful to your pages, poorly constructed frame design can turn users away faster than a 500k graphic on your main page.

The Frames Wizard

The Wizard detours you around any need to use HTML for your frames; you will never need to write a line of HTML code.

Linking Among Frames

Interframe linking demands a well-organized site, because a badly designed one will be confusing to set up and very difficult to maintain.

Using Frames with Images and Imagemaps

These graphical links are just as easy to make as text links, and can provide useful visual aids to navigation.

Putting Framesets Inside Frames

You can build a complex display this way, but be careful to test the results—they might look very strange!

Using the FrontPage Frame Templates

Templates are a fast and efficient way to create framed sites.

FIGURE 8.1

Frames allow different pages to appear and behave independently in the browser screen.

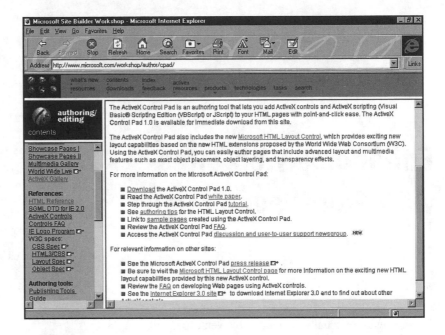

Why Use Frames?

To put it somewhat formally: Use frames if you want your user's browser window to display both static and dynamic elements. A *static element* remains visible no matter what your user does; the *dynamic element* changes according to his input. In Figure 8.1, the menu frame is static and the scrollable window is dynamic.

One great advantage of the frame environment is the way it can keep your visitor oriented. The static part keeps a "map" of the site (or part of it) in front of him, and the dynamic elements show different parts of the site, on command. So he doesn't have to scroll up or down, for example, to find the hyperlink that returns him to the home page or to another major section of the site. The links are always there, right in front of him. Or you can present an image within one frame and give your visitor several screens' worth of information about it in an adjacent frame. While she scrolls within the information frame, the image remains visible at all times. The only way to do this without frames would be to repeat the image for each screenful of data, which is obviously a waste of space, time, and energy.

So frames are potentially very useful to the designer of Web pages. However, many people use early browsers that don't support frames, and still other people simply don't like them. As a good Webmaster, you should provide for such visitors by giving them the option of exploring a nonframe version of your site. Doing this can substantially increase the work of creating a site, so you must decide for yourself whether frames are worth the extra effort.

Designing for the Framed Environment

Just as with tables, handmade frame creation with HTML coding is a picky business. FrontPage Editor, recognizing this, gives you its Frames Wizard to make your work easier. This Wizard works with *framesets*, which is what FrontPage Editor calls a group of frames that appears together in a browser display. You don't actually insert framesets into a page; a frameset acts like a scaffolding to relate pages to each other. Framesets can be created or edited only with the Frames Wizard.

Even before you start up the Wizard, though, you need to think about how (or even if) you're going to use the frame environment. Keep the following in mind:

- Use frames only if you need them, not just because they're decorative (and they're only decorative for people who have browsers with frame support).

- Don't crowd a page with frames. This obviously reduces their sizes. In particular, a viewer shouldn't have to scroll to see all of an image. The practical maximum is three frames.

- Use static frames sparingly. Use them for navigational tools, or table of contents information, or for site identification such as a logo. Static frames are like the instrument panel of a car, which drivers indeed need to refer to—but drivers spend most of their time looking through windshields.

- Commit most of the screen area to dynamic frames, where information can be retrieved and displayed.

- Don't develop your frame layout for monitors with screens bigger than 15 inches. Most people—and many businesses—don't use the larger screens yet, especially in the consumer market. Even a 15" monitor has about 20% more viewing area than a 14". In fact, you'd be wise to assume your visitor has a 14" monitor, running at 640x480 resolution, in 16 colors, and plan accordingly.

Using the Frames Wizard

When you're ready to make up your frameset, start FrontPage Editor and choose File, New. The New Page dialog box appears. Select the Frames Wizard and click OK. The Frames Wizard–Choose Technique dialog box appears (see Figure 8.2).

FIGURE 8.2

Begin a frameset by starting the Frames Wizard.

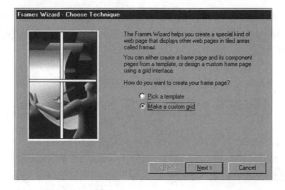

CAUTION

At the time of writing, there was an oddity in the behavior of the Frames Wizard. If you run FrontPage Editor as a stand-alone and complete a frameset using the Wizard, FrontPage Explorer will open as soon as you choose Finish. However, there is an error message (which may be buried behind the Explorer window) that says you don't have a Web open. You haven't actually lost your work; close the error dialog box, open or create a Web, and choose Finish again. The frameset will be saved.

Here you can choose to create the frame layout from an existing template, or you can set up one of your own by picking the Make a Custom Grid option. We'll take the custom route to begin with, because that will give you the best insight into how frames really work. Click Next, and the Edit Frameset Grid dialog box appears (see Figure 8.3).

FIGURE 8.3

The Frames Wizard–Edit Frameset Grid lets you customize the number and proportions of your frames.

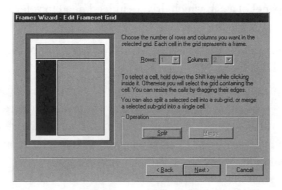

You can manipulate the frame layout by selecting the various frames in the grid and changing their Rows, Columns, Split, and Merge settings. You can also adjust the sizes of the frames by putting the cursor on a frame boundary and dragging the boundary. Once you have the right number of suitably proportioned frames, click Next. The Edit Frame Attributes dialog box appears (see Figure 8.4).

FIGURE 8.4

You use the Frames Wizard–Edit Frame Attributes dialog box to specify what page loads into a frame, and where the links in a frameset display their destination pages.

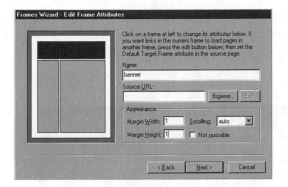

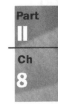

This dialog box is where we decide on the main business: What's displayed in a frame and how the links in that frame behave. To complete the basic specifications for the frameset, follow these steps:

1. Select a frame by clicking in it. In the Name box, type a name for the frame. (This is simply a label for the frame, so you can reference it. It doesn't affect what's displayed in the frame.)

2. In the Source URL box, type the URL of the page the frame will display. It's usually easier to use the Browse button to open the Choose Source URL box (see Figure 8.5).

FIGURE 8.5

The Choose Source URL dialog box enables you to choose from an HTML Page tab, from an Image tab, and from the Any Type tab. Any Type lists all the page and image URLs in the current Web.

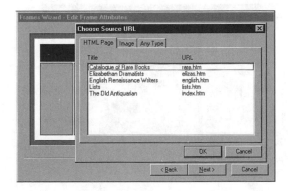

3. Select the URL you want from one of the sheets and click OK, which returns you to the Edit Frame Attributes dialog box. Ignore the Edit button for the moment; we'll cover its function later.

4. You can adjust the Margin Width and Margin Height, which control the separation of the frames in a browser.

5. If you want the frame size to be *fixed* (which means the user can't resize it by dragging the frame border), select Not Resizable.

6. If you want to disable scrolling for a frame (the viewer won't be able to scroll the page in it, no matter how long the page) change the Scrolling list box to No.

7. Repeat steps 1 through 6 for each frame of the frameset. Then click Next, and the Choose Alternate Content dialog box appears (see Figure 8.6).

FIGURE 8.6

It's a good idea to provide alternate pages for nonframe browsers. The Frames Wizard–Choose Alternate Content dialog box is where you do this.

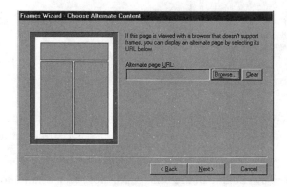

8. If you want people to see your site even if their browsers don't support frames, use the Browse option to insert the URL of your home page, or appropriate alternative page, into the Alternate Page URL box. Then click Next. The Save Page dialog box appears (see Figure 8.7).

FIGURE 8.7

Save the new frameset to your Web from the Save Page dialog box.

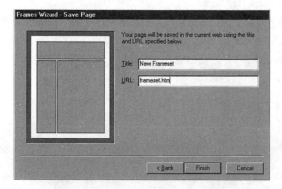

9. Give the frameset a suitable page Title and URL (remember the importance of meaningful page titles) and click Finish.

You've now created a frameset. In the Open File dialog box, this set will appear just as an ordinary page appears. However, if you open it, you automatically get the Frames Wizard. This is how you set up an editing session for a frameset.

FrontPage Editor isn't WYSIWYG enough to show you what the framed environment will look like. Furthermore, because you can't open the frameset as a page in FrontPage

Editor, you have to start a frame-supporting browser and access the frameset page from that environment in order to check your work.

An example of a framed environment, created by the method described immediately above, appears in Figure 8.8.

The frames contain the pages you specified when you put their page URLs into the Wizard. If a user later clicks a link, that link's destination page is displayed in the frame in place of the specified pages.

FIGURE 8.8
A three-frame page created with the Frames Wizard. The three navigation buttons in the top frame are hyperlinked bulleted lists inside a table.

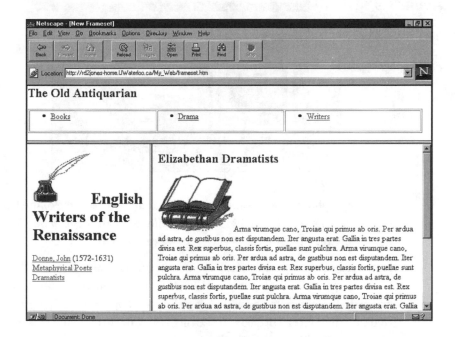

CAUTION

If your link loads the destination page into the same frame as the origin page, it's extremely important to avoid a dead end at the destination. If the user can't find her way out of a frame, its contents will sit there until she moves to another site entirely. That's a constant reminder to her that you designed your site carelessly. Make sure you add a link to such a page to keep it from becoming a dead end.

How do you create a static frame, one whose contents will stay put when you use one of its links? (If you don't do that, your navigation buttons and site logo will disappear as soon as your visitor clicks a link.)

The next section covers this.

Making a Link Display its Destination in a Different Frame

Remember the names you gave to the various frames in the Wizard's Edit Frame Attributes dialog box? You use these names to specify a target frame for the hyperlink. You *don't* specify the target frame by using the URL of a document. The target is the name of a frame in a frameset; it's never a page title or page file name.

This can be confusing, so let's look at a specific example (see Figure 8.9).

FIGURE 8.9

Frame names, not URLs, are used to specify the frame in which a page appears.

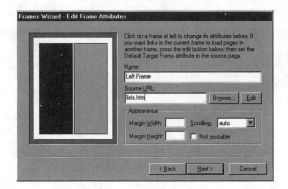

This figure shows a very simple set of two frames. The name of the left frame is Left Frame; the name of the right is Right Frame. You can see only one frame name at a time, depending on which frame is selected; we've selected the left.

Now, let's suppose you want all the links in the left frame to force their destination pages to show up only in the right frame. In other words, the left frame is going to be the static frame. In the example, the actual page that will appear in the left frame is LISTS.HTM (look in the Source URL box to see this). So when everything is working, the LISTS.HTM page will stick like glue to the left frame. When we click one of its links, the destination page will appear in the right frame.

To set this up, take the following steps:

1. Click the Edit button. The source page, LISTS.HTM, appears in the FrontPage Editor workspace.

2. Now we need to change its page properties, so choose File, Page Properties. The Page Properties dialog box for LISTS.HTM appears (see Figure 8.10).

3. Type **Right Frame** into the Default Target Frame box. This label is case-sensitive, so type it exactly as it appears in the Name box in the Wizard's Edit Frame

Attributes dialog box. This target frame is the frame in which the link's destination page will display.

4. Click OK. Then save the page.

FIGURE 8.10

Use the Page Properties dialog box to specify a target frame.

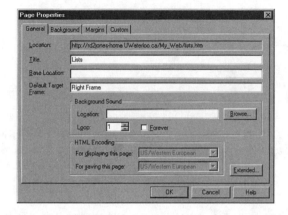

CAUTION

If you get the Default Target Frame name wrong in the Page Properties dialog box, FrontPage won't warn you. You'll learn about your mistake when testing. When you click a link in the source page, you'll get the destination page showing up full-page in a new browser window. There's no harm done, however, except to your pride. Go back and edit page properties to fix the problem.

After you've saved your work, finish setting up the frameset. When you test the frameset in your browser, clicking a link in the left frame should affect only the display in the right frame.

This is the method you use to set up a static frame in the frameset. When the frameset is called and used by a visitor to your site, it works as follows:

1. The pages specified in the Edit Frame Attributes dialog box are loaded into the appropriate frames in the browser window.

2. The user clicks a link in the page displayed in the static frame (for convenience, we'll call this the "static page").

3. When the link executes, the software checks the properties of the static page. It discovers the name of a Default Target Frame (you typed in this frame name, remember?)

4. The browser displays the destination page in the named Default Target Frame, which of course shouldn't be the static frame.

It comes down To this: to create a static frame, specify a target frame in the page properties of the page that displays in the static frame. Once you've done this, the content of the static frame is fixed (see the following Caution). Only the display in the target frame will change as links are clicked.

N O T E   This can be worded as a general principle: If a Default Target Frame is specified for a page, every link on that page will display its destination in the target frame only. ■

CAUTION

You can overwrite a static frame's content in two ways. If another page's Default Target Frame specifies the static frame, that will do it. So will specifying the static frame as the target frame of a hyperlink. Of course, you may encounter situations where you actually do want to overwrite the content of the static frame.

N O T E   You don't have to use the Frames Wizard to add or edit a Default Target Frame entry. You need only to open the Page Properties dialog box for the page and make the changes there. The Wizard's Edit button is actually just a shortcut. Always make sure you type the frame name correctly, and remember to save the page before testing it. ■

Using Target Frames and Text Links in the Current Web

So far, we've specified which page shows up where by using the Page Properties dialog box. But you can also specify the display frame of a page by creating or editing the link that calls it. To do this, select some text for the link and choose Edit, Link. (Or set up to edit an existing link; the procedure is identical for both new and existing links.) Assuming you're working with the current Web, click either the Open Pages or Current FrontPage Web tab when the Create Link or Edit Link dialog box appears (see Figure 8.11).

To set up the target frame, do the following:

1. From the Open Pages or Current FrontPage Web sheet, select the destination page for the link, and type the target frame name into the Target Frame box.

2. Click OK.

3. Save the page before testing it. On testing, the destination page should appear in the frame specified by the link's Target Frame entry.

FIGURE 8.11
You can specify target frames in the Target Frame box.

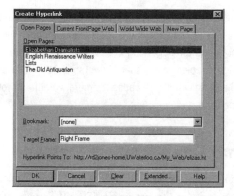

There are also four special target types you can use. Typing one of these into the Target Frame box of the Create or Edit Hyperlink dialog boxes will have the following effects:

- Underscore blank—the page the link points to loads into a new browser window.

- Underscore self—the page the link points to overwrites the page where the calling link resides, but the frame layout in the browser window is not disturbed.

- Underscore parent—the page the link points to overwrites the page where the calling link resides and resets the browser window (for example, to avoid loading a framed page into the current frame).

- Underscore top—the page the link points to loads at the top level. Essentially, this resets the browser window.

Using Target Frames and Text Links with World Wide Web URLs

This task is the same as setting up a target frame for the current Web, only you use the World Wide Web sheet. The Web site's page will show up in the frame you specify. Remember, however, that it will have less room for display and it may look cramped.

Using Target Frames when Linking to a New Page

Again, no surprises here—on the New Page sheet, type the name of the frame where the link will force the new page to display.

Using Target Frames and Bookmarks

Bookmarks and frames don't really have a lot to do with each other, although you can specify both when creating or editing a link. The destination page simply scrolls to the bookmark when it displays in the named frame.

NOTE You may be wondering why you have two ways of deciding in what frame a destination page displays. After all, if you can specify the target frame for each link, why do you need the Default Target Frame option in the Page Properties dialog box? The answer is: convenience. This Page Properties option enables you to specify the target frames for all links on that page, so you don't have to set them individually. Because it's merely a default, you override it when you specify the target frame for a particular link. ■

Coping with Browsers that Don't Support Frames

This is going to be a common situation for a while. If you haven't specified an alternative page, calling your frameset results in the message "This Web page uses frames, but your browser doesn't support them" appearing in the browser display (the message is built into the called frameset). With no alternative page, your visitor has to leave your site. The best way for you to deal with this (apart from not using frames) is to supply an alternative. You can do this when you create or edit the frameset. When your visitor links to the frameset, she is moved to the unframed alternate you specified, and she can go on from there.

> **CAUTION**
>
> If you design a site that uses frames, you might confuse users who don't have frame browsers because they won't see things the way you intended. Give them a duplicate set of navigation tools on each page, designed to load the pages in a non-framed state.

NOTE You can use the <NOFRAMES> tag to tell a visitor he's accessing a framed site. Use a syntax like the following:

```
<FRAMESET>
<NOFRAMES>You need a frames-supporting browser to view frames!</NOFRAMES>
</FRAMESET>
```

The tag indicates content viewable only by browsers that do not support frames. Browsers that support frames will not display content between the beginning and ending NOFRAMES tags. You can create a page that is compatible with both types of browser by using NOFRAMES. ■

Should I Set up My Home Page as a Frameset?

There's little point in it, unless you're determined to force people with frame-capable browsers to view frames from the moment they reach your home page. There's even less point when you consider that many people simply don't like frames. You should give your visitors a choice. Let them click a control (prominently labeled!) that takes them to the framed environment, if that's what they want and if it's appropriate for their software.

> **N O T E** If you're really determined, though, you can set up a framed home page by creating an empty Web and then creating a frameset for it. Give this frameset the file name INDEX.HTM, and that's your "framed" home page. ■

Using Target Frames with Images and Imagemaps

Setting up image-based links to use target frames is very similar to the procedure for establishing text links. Choose Edit, Link, and use the Open Pages tab, the Current Web tab, the World Wide Web tab, or the New Page tab to enter the frame name in the Target Frame box.

▶ **See** "Developing the Basic Page: Text, Lists, and Hyperlinks," **p. 65**

▶ **See** "Enhancing Pages with Graphics and Multimedia," **p.121**

Likewise, drawing a hotspot (the portion of an image that will act as the link) on an image brings up the Create Link dialog box, and you use the Open Pages tab, the Current Web tab, the World Wide Web tab, or the New Page tab to enter the frame name in the Target Frame box.

Using Image Properties with Frames

If you open the Image Properties dialog box for an image, you find a Default Hyperlink section down at the bottom. Use its Location box (with the Browse button, if appropriate) to set a default destination for the image's hyperlink. Use the Target Frame box to specify the frame where the destination page will appear (see Figure 8.12).

> **N O T E** Are you wondering why you'd use Image Properties to set a default destination and target frame for an image's hyperlink, when you can get the same result by specifying both when you establish a link? The answer: You'd do this when the image has hotspots, to set a default if the user clicks an area not covered by the hotspot. ■

Putting Forms into Frames

You can instruct a form to send its results to a frame. You do this with the Form Properties dialog box, where you type the name of the target frame into the Target Frame box, and click OK.

FIGURE 8.12
The Default Hyperlink
area is where you
specify the Location
and Target Frame of an
image's link.

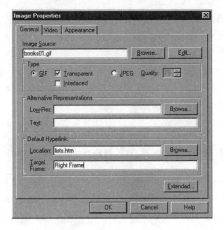

Putting Framesets Inside Frames

This is getting rather exotic, but you can put framesets inside frames. First, create the
frameset that you want contained in another, existing frameset. Then follow these steps:

1. Choose File, Open, and select the name of the container frameset. The Frames
   Wizard opens.

2. Click Next to move to the Edit Frame Attributes dialog box.

3. Select the frame where you want the contained frameset to appear.

4. Click the Browse button to open the Choose Source URL dialog box. Then choose
   the contained frameset from the list and click OK.

5. Click Next until the Finish button appears, then click it.

When you test the container frame in your browser, the contained frame will appear in the
target frame you chose for it (see Figure 8.13). Be sure to test these frame subsets very
thoroughly, because they can give unattractive results if another page tries to occupy their
frame.

Floating Frames

While FrontPage Editor doesn't support it yet, there is an alternate way to create com-
pound documents; you can place frames in your HTML document using the IFRAME
element. Called "floating frames," this design technique allows you to insert HTML documents into your document in the same way you insert images using the IMG element.
This means you can use the ALIGN= attribute just as you do with IMG to align the frame
with the surrounding text. The following example aligns a frame at the left margin and
wraps subsequent text around the right side of the frame:

FIGURE 8.13
You can put a frame subset into a container frameset. Here, the three frames in the bottom left of the screen belong to a second frameset.

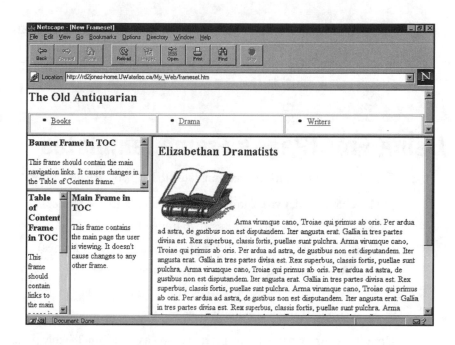

```
<IFRAME SRC="xx.htm" ALIGN=LEFT>
</IFRAME> Here's some text to the right of a frame.
<BR CLEAR=LEFT>Here's some text beneath the frame.
```

The IFRAME syntax may not be compatible with all browsers. In that case, you can use a FRAME element within the IFRAME tags to provide an alternative presentation. For example:

```
<IFRAME SRC="xx.htm" ALIGN=LEFT>FRAME SRC="xx.htm"
<IFRAME>
```

In the previous example, the text of xx.htm will display in a floating frame in either an IFRAME or non–IFRAME-compatible browser. Remember that you set the attributes of IFRAME and FRAME independently. For example, if you want to specify position or size, you include those attributes in both the IFRAME tag and the FRAME tag.

Deleting a Frameset

You can delete a frameset with FrontPage Explorer. The frameset appears in the Explorer display just as a page would; you simply select it and choose Edit, Delete. However, if you delete a frameset, you must also remove all frame target entries in Page Properties and in links that referenced the deleted frameset. If you don't, browsers will become confused about where they're supposed to be looking and will give unpredictable results.

N O T E The pages produced by the Frames Wizard templates (discussed next) are independent of the frameset. In other words, deleting the frameset does not remove the pages it referenced. You have to delete these manually, if needed, by selecting each one in FrontPage Explorer and choosing Edit, Delete. ■

Using FrontPage's Frame Templates

FrontPage Editor supplies six templates to help you create different framesets.

- A bannered, two-column Table of Contents (three frames)
- A document with footnotes (two frames)
- A Table of Contents with two navigation bars (four frames)
- A top-down, three-level hierarchy (three frames)
- A nested, three-level hierarchy (three frames)
- A simple Table of Contents (two frames)

Creating your own custom framesets is so easy that you'll likely prefer that approach if you use frames to any extent. However, the templates can be useful, so let's take a look at them.

Creating a Bannered Table of Contents

To do this, take the following steps:

1. Choose File, New, and select the Frames Wizard.
2. When the Choose Technique dialog box appears, select the Pick a Template button and click Next.
3. When the template list appears, select the first template and click Next. You will see the layout of the frameset at the left of the Pick Template Layout dialog box (see Figure 8.14).
4. Continue stepping through the Wizard. When you reach the Save Page dialog box, type a meaningful page title and URL into the appropriate boxes.
5. Choose Finish. In the examples, for consistency, we'll use the default page titles and file names that the Wizard supplies.

After the Wizard creates the template, you can find out exactly what it did by taking a look at FrontPage Explorer. In the example shown in Figure 8.15, the Web contained only a home page before the Wizard was run. Things have changed!

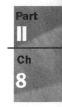

II

Ch

8

FIGURE 8.14
The Banner with Nested Table of Contents layout tells you the frame names: Banner, Contents, and Main.

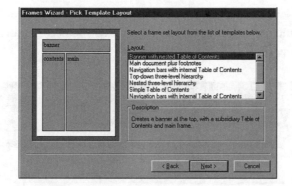

FIGURE 8.15
Use FrontPage Explorer to identify the frameset and the pages the Wizard template created for you.

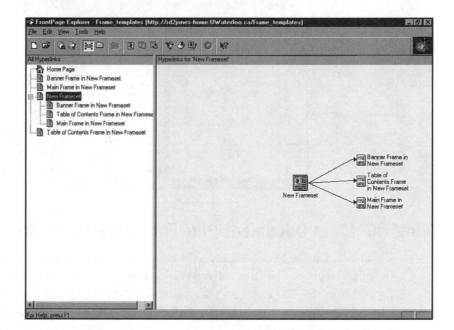

We now have the frameset itself (New Frameset) and three ordinary pages: one for the banner content, one for the Table of Contents, and one (Main Frame in New Frameset) for a single content page that will be referenced by the Table of Contents (TOC). In a real site, naturally, there could be many of these content pages, possibly one for each TOC entry. Here, the Wizard created one content page for you, because each frame of a frameset must have an URL associated with it when the frameset is generated. In a real-world application, of course, you'd want to change the page titles and perhaps the file names to ones that are more meaningful to your particular Web.

To put the frameset into service, use FrontPage Editor to add the content to the banner and TOC pages and create as many content pages as you need. Figure 8.16 shows an example of how the results look in a browser.

FIGURE 8.16

Your visitors can use the Table of Contents frame to see other pages without losing the Table of Contents itself.

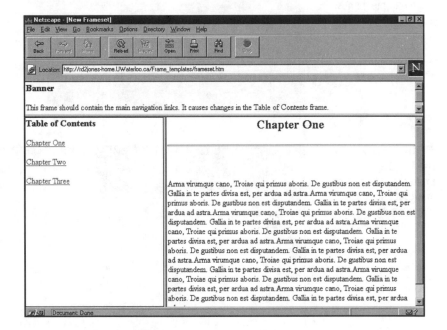

Using the Main Document Plus Footnotes Template

To do this, choose File, New, and select the Frames Wizard. Accept the Pick a Template default, and choose Next. In the next dialog box, select the Main Document Plus Footnotes Template. This creates a main page with a scrolling footnote frame below it. Step through the Wizard until the frameset is complete and saved, then inspect it in FrontPage Explorer (see Figure 8.17).

In the main document page (named Main Frame in New Frameset), all links reference the lower frame (named Footnotes). You can verify this by inspecting the page properties of the main page; its Default Target Frame is set to the frame name Footnotes.

In a browser, the main document's footnotes will scroll in a separate frame. The virtue of this for your visitor is that it's much more convenient than flipping back and forth through a single page—or linking to another full-screen page—every time she wants to read a footnote. She just clicks a footnote entry in the main document, and the note appears at the bottom of the screen. To implement this application, put all the footnotes on one page, bookmark each one, and link all the bookmarks from the appropriate places in the main document.

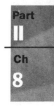

FIGURE 8.17

Explorer's views of the frameset of the document/footnote structure.

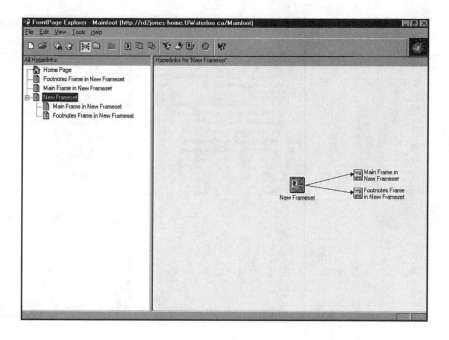

N O T E   As you know, the traditional footnote indicator is a superscript number. You can get these by going to FrontPage Editor's Font dialog box, choosing the Special Styles sheet, and using the Vertical Position box. However, a footnote superscript in a printed document is really just a link to the bottom of the page. Since the reader can already see a Web link, do you really need superscripts in a Web page to indicate a footnote? Probably not. Moreover, using superscripts in FrontPage Editor makes line spacing slightly uneven. ■

Using the Navigation Bar/Internal Table of Contents Template

This template gives you static frames at the top and bottom of the page. It's a good starting point for a complex, framed environment that requires extensive navigational tools. Alternatively, one static frame could be a site identification area and the other could be the navigation control panel. Your imagination can certainly fill in other possibilities.

Two more frames lie between these two static areas; the left is suggested as a TOC, the right as the main data display area. Again, you can use your imagination to work out other uses for the arrangement. Whatever you decide, use the previous procedure for creating the frameset. When it's finished, it shows up in Explorer like the example shown in Figure 8.18.

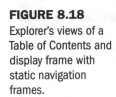

FIGURE 8.18
Explorer's views of a Table of Contents and display frame with static navigation frames.

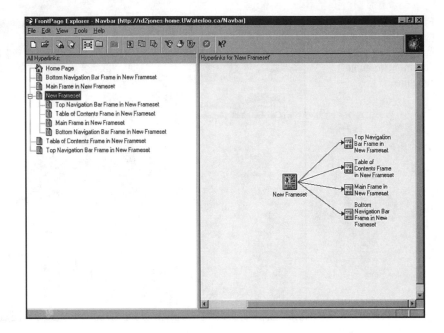

This is a more complex frameset than we've looked at so far. The links in the two static frames (top and bottom) make their destination pages appear in the left frame (the TOC frame, at default), and the links in the TOC frame make their destination pages appear in the right frame (the main frame). Links in the main frame—unless you set them otherwise—make their targets replace the current page in that frame.

You can change all this, as you know. For example, you can reset the page properties of the page in the top static frame to make its target document appear in the bottom frame (then, however, the bottom frame wouldn't be static). And so on. With a frameset as potentially complicated as this one, you'd need to do some careful page and data organization. You would also need even more careful testing if you decided to modify the targets of the various frames.

Using the Top-Down, Three-Level, Hierarchy Template

Use the top-down, three-level hierarchy template for all or part of a site whose page and data organization is, as the name suggests, hierarchical in nature.

The frameset establishes the hierarchy as follows:

- The default target of the top frame is the middle frame.
- The default target of the middle frame is the bottom frame.
- The bottom frame's default target is itself.

So you'd use this scheme to go from broad categories to more precisely distinguished ones to fine detail. Depending on how much information you had for each entry, you would use either full pages or bookmark entries within pages. An example of a hierarchical information structure is shown in Figure 8.19.

FIGURE 8.19
A hierarchical frame structure gives a cascade effect—in this case, from general information to more specific to quite detailed.

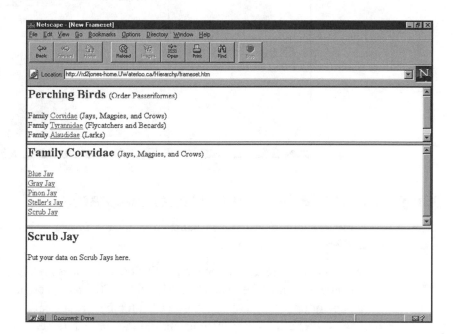

Using the Nested, Three-Level, Hierarchy Template

The nested, three-level hierarchy template is similar in approach to the previous frameset, but the hierarchy works from left to top-right and then down.

In practice, the links in the left frame display their destination pages in the top-right frame; those in the top-right frame display their destination pages in the bottom-right frame. In Figure 8.20, you can see a nested version of the pages that appeared earlier in the top-down hierarchy. The visual characteristics of your page content (such as large or small images, number of images, quantity of text) will influence which frame layout you choose.

FIGURE 8.20

A nested hierarchy gives a different effect from a vertically organized one.

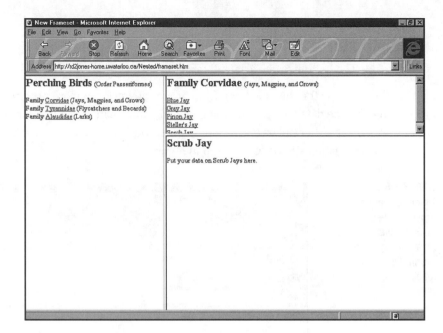

Using the Simple Table of Contents Template

This is the least complex of the six supplied templates, providing just a frame for a TOC and another for the data display.

It's easy to put it to use. Set up the information page or pages first, with or without bookmarks as needed, enter the requisite entries in the TOC page, and link them to the information page or pages. Figure 8.21 shows a fresh bibliography page—created with FrontPage Editor's Bibliography template—in the content frame.

FIGURE 8.21
This simple Table of Contents frame is linked to a page of bibliographical entries.

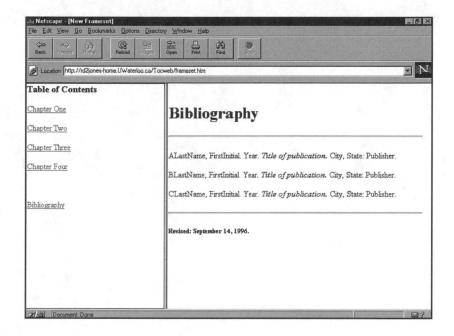

From Here...

In this chapter you learned the somewhat complicated craft of making and managing frames. Frames are still finding their way into the World Wide Web, of course, so we'll all be watching to see whether they fulfill their early promise of a more adaptable and flexible interface. While we're waiting to find out, let's explore the following:

- Chapter 9, "Creating Pages with FrontPage Editor Templates," which steps you through FrontPage 97's supplied templates. These templates speed up the creation of pages like bibliographies, glossaries, directories, and publicity instruments such as press releases.

- Chapter 10, "Using WebBots, Wizards, and Interactive Page Templates," which explains what Bots are and how to use them. You will also learn about forms, and about the specialized templates that will help you make your pages interactive.

- Chapter 11, "Working Directly with HTML," shows you how to tweak your code with FrontPage Editor's View HTML environment, and with the HTML Markup tool.

Creating Pages with FrontPage Editor Templates

You've already found out from your travels in the World Wide Web that certain page styles and formats are repeated from site to site. These guest books, bibliographies, glossaries, hotlists, and the like are so common that a standardized approach to making them isn't only possible, but desirable. That's because using a standard format saves you time and energy; you don't have to keep reinventing the wheel. These standardized formats are the basis of FrontPage Editor templates.

Each template provides a mock-up for the layout and overall appearance of the completed page. You can either insert your own data into the appropriate areas and leave it at that, or, using the methods you've already learned, customize the page as much or as little as you like. Although FrontPage's templates aren't suited to every Web project, they can help you get started, and even get you past the dreaded Web author's block. Furthermore, you can create and save your own templates to speed up the process of developing a site that has many similar pages. ■

Reference Documents

Reference documents are critical to researchers. FrontPage provides excellent templates for bibliographies, glossaries, and directories.

Web-Specific Pages

Many documents are peculiar to the needs of the Web. Among themes are pages for hotlists, hyperdocuments, and FAQs.

Publicity Instruments

The Web is more and more a place for commerce these days, and the content reflects it. Some examples of business-oriented pages are data sheets, What's New pages, product descriptions, and seminar schedules.

Custom Templates

When you need an often-used, standardized page layout, create your own. FrontPage Editor makes it a straightforward operation.

Creating a Bibliography

In the world of research, bibliographies are taken very seriously indeed. They not only give credit to the sources you used, but also allow other people to refer easily to these sources. On the World Wide Web, bibliographies are fairly static documents, and usually imitate their paper-based counterparts. A bibliography has a strict format (which one depends on the discipline), so FrontPage provides a template that conforms to a widely accepted style.

 T I P   FrontPage's bibliographic format represents only one of many permissible styles. You may need to refer to a reference manual such as the MLA (Modern Languages Association) Handbook for more complex formats.

You start any template-based page in the same way. Because of this, we'll go through it just once and not mention it again. Choose File, New, and select the template you want from the list box; in this case, Bibliography. Choose OK, and the template immediately opens in FrontPage Editor's workspace (see Figure 9.1). To help you further, the template includes instructions for use in the form of a Comment, which is the purple text. As you remember, comments don't show up in browsers, so you don't have to remove this one unless you want to.

FIGURE 9.1
This bibliography template can be customized according to your particular needs.

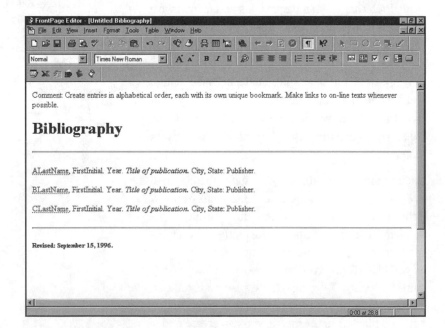

If you've ever struggled with bibliographic formatting, you'll appreciate the help the template gives you. You have A, B, and C before LastName to indicate that all entries must appear in alphabetic format from A to Z down the page. From this point, all you have to do is replace the LastName, initial, title, city, state, and publisher with those that correspond to your particular references. Remember to retain the punctuation and italicization the template has set up for you.

You not only get the formatting, you get bookmarks: ALastName, BLastName, and CLastName have the dotted underlines that signal these link targets. Once you link to them from the original document page, your reader can inspect your reference materials with next to no effort.

When the page is complete, save it. Remember (and remember with all the templates) to use the Page Properties dialog box to give the page a meaningful title, and make sure you change its file name to something other than the default.

You can see a real-world example of a bibliography in Figure 9.2.

Part

II

Ch

9

FIGURE 9.2
This formal bibliography refers you to the documents cited in the Web site (**http://info.med.yale.edu/caim/stylemanual/M_Literature.html**).

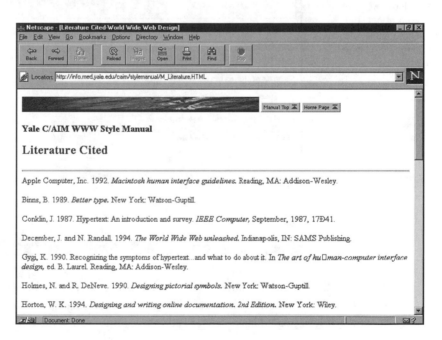

NOTE Though not all of the real-world examples in this chapter have been prepared with FrontPage, they show you design approaches that can easily be reproduced with FrontPage's editing tools. ■

The author compiling this bibliography did not use hyperlinks to other documents, because these were exclusively print references. However, hyperlinking in bibliographies will become more common as more and more resources are put online. Note, however, that the citation style closely follows that of the FrontPage Editor template.

Creating a Press Release

With more and more corporations and businesses addressing audiences via the World Wide Web, a growing spate of press releases was inevitable. If you need to add yours to the flood, here's how to do it with FrontPage Editor's Press Release template. Start by opening the template in FrontPage Editor's workspace (see Figure 9.3).

FIGURE 9.3
With the Press Release template, you can tell the world of the Web about your new product, service, or technical achievement.

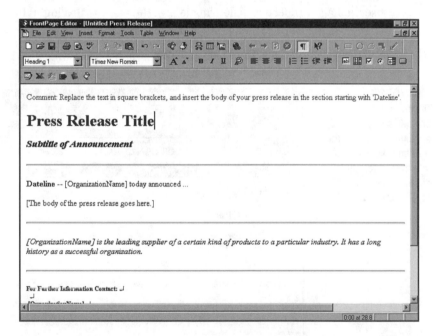

Edit the title and subtitle lines, and use the Replace command to substitute your own text for [OrganizationName]. Then put the text of your release under the dateline. If you have a company logo, you'll likely want to add that at the head of the document.

Looking over the template will show you where you need to do further customization, such as in the address block at the bottom. (Notice that this block isn't styled as Normal text, but as Heading 5 style.) If you have a suitable background image for your announcement, add that, using the Page Properties dialog box. Get rid of that dull gray default background, at least, but don't choose a color or pattern that makes the text hard to read. Then save the page. A sample of a press release is shown in Figure 9.4.

FIGURE 9.4
This straightforward press release is directed to a technical audience (**http:// www.rockwell.com:80/ rockwell/ pr960910.html**).

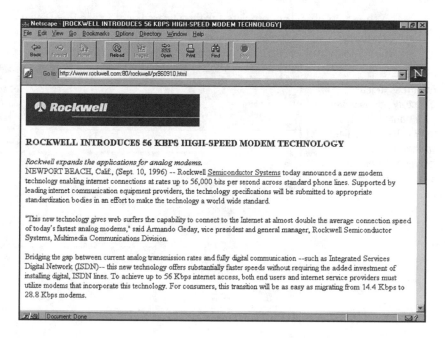

The example's design parallels that of the FrontPage Editor template, with the addition of a company logo at the page head. Then comes the press release title, an italicized subtitle, the dateline, and the body text. At the bottom of the document (out of sight, in the example) are navigation controls and a link to the person who deals with customers for the product.

Given the number of press releases floating around the Web, it was inevitable that FrontPage Editor would pay some attention to getting them organized.

Creating a Directory of Press Releases

If you've ever browsed through an efficient corporate archive, you've likely come across a directory of press releases. The good ones extend beyond the limits of paper-based documentation and use hyperlinks to create a dynamic, organized collection.

Press release directories have become so common on the World Wide Web that users have developed an accepted format for their presentation. Most begin with a large, bold-face title followed by a short menu that divides press releases according to the year, month, or exact date of issue. This makes it a lot easier for a visitor to find what he or she is looking for.

When you open the template for the Directory of Press Releases, you see the screen in Figure 9.5.

FIGURE 9.5

The Press Release Directory title is set up as a bookmark (notice the dashed underline) so that it's easily referenced from other pages in your Web.

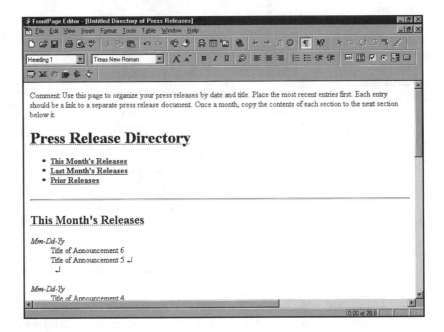

The template suggests that you organize all listings by date and title, dividing your page into three main sections: This Month's Releases, Last Month's Releases, and Prior Releases. These divisions represent the standard for directories that order by date, but you can increase or decrease the number of divisions by adding to or deleting from the internal links listed below the main title. These links target bookmarks on the same page, and the titles of the individual releases are listed below the bookmarks.

Don't put the press releases themselves into this page, though, no matter how short they are. If you do this, the page will get bigger and bigger as the number of releases grows, and the bigger the page gets, the slower it downloads. Instead, link the release titles to other pages, and put the text of the releases there. This will speed up response time, and the shorter pages will make the whole structure easier to maintain.

Unless your organization regularly issues a vast number of press releases, arranging your directory by month is probably the most effective method; but don't neglect directory maintenance. At the end of each month, remember to copy the contents of This Month's Releases to Last Month's Releases and delete any items that have become stale.

In the example shown in Figure 9.6, you can see a simple version of such a directory. The company logo appears first, followed by navigation buttons. Then come the dates and titles of the releases, with the dates serving as links to the pages where the releases themselves are stored. By linking to other pages, the person maintaining the directory keeps the main page from becoming too large and difficult to update.

FIGURE 9.6
This simple press release directory links the main page to the releases themselves (**http:// www.alliedsignal.com/ news/index.html**).

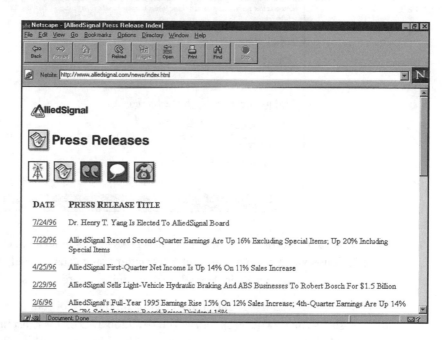

Creating an Employee Directory

A lot of organizations have homes on the Web, and for these FrontPage offers an Employee Directory template. This template provides plenty of scope for customization—it demands it, actually, because of its nature. This will be obvious as soon as you open the template (see Figure 9.7).

There's a spot for your organization's logo, followed by the main title, and then a series of alphabetized hyperlinks. (If you're wondering whether FrontPage Editor has a sorting command, no, unfortunately, it doesn't.) Each of these links is an employee name, and targets a bookmark farther down the page. Each bookmark is with an employee entry. When you look at one of these bookmarks, you'll see an image placeholder. This can be deleted or replaced by a photograph of the employee. The purple text with the employee entry is a comment, and in this case, simply represents text that should be replaced. To do this, click the purple text. It will turn black to show that it's selected. Type whatever you want to automatically replace it.

FIGURE 9.7
The Employee Directory template will need more customization than any other FrontPage template.

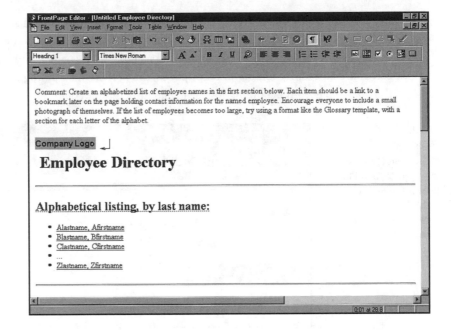

You'll have to customize the bookmarks and links in this template, obviously, since the supplied ones won't point to the right places after you've customized. Notice that the employee entries also have their Web addresses, and a mail-to address.

Deciding whether to use staff photos depends on the size of your staff. Having a lot of images slows the download speed, as you're all too aware. A way around this, for a large staff, would be to have all the as on a page, with their photos, all the Bs on another page, with theirs, and so on. The names still appear in the directory, but they're linked to the appropriate page, and to a bookmark within that page.

Creating an Office Directory

This isn't actually a directory for an office, it's a directory of offices. The template assumes you're a far-flung organization, with offices around the world. You may not be global, but if you have more than one office (even if it's only two), this template's for you. You can see what it looks like in Figure 9.8.

FIGURE 9.8

The Office Directory helps you set up a list of locations where you have representation or business facilities.

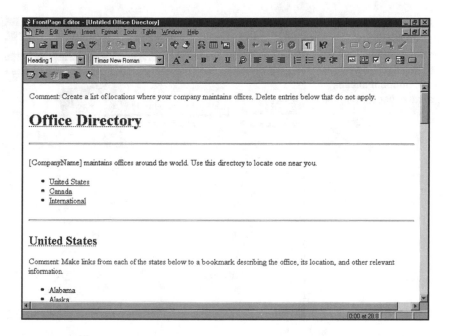

The main heading, Office Directory, is bookmarked. This assumes you'll reach it from another page, probably your organization's home page. The next section suggests a geographical arrangement for the directory, in this case by country; adapt it as necessary.

Each geographical location in that section is linked to another section, where you establish yet more links. These take the reader to the office information itself. The template offers a sample formatting for the actual office entry—in the example, for Massachusetts. This entry includes a mail-to address and the URL of that office's home page. A nice touch is the Directions entry. You'd link this to a page that tells the reader how to reach the place. You could even include an appropriately scaled map on that page, formatted so the reader could print it out and take it with him.

TIP Another nice touch to add, though the template doesn't mention it, would be a link to an Employee Directory page for that particular office. Visitors will not only know how to reach the place from your Directions entry, but they'll also know who's going to be there when they arrive.

In the example in Figure 9.9, the company logo appears first, followed by a list of the offices in the region. Clicking a link takes the user to detailed directions for reaching the office, with a map and telephone numbers. At the end of the list there is a link to a personnel recruiting office, which diverts job-seekers from contacting the individual offices directly—an efficient touch.

FIGURE 9.9
This page from IBM
provides a directory for
its UK offices (**http://
www.europe.ibm.com/
go/uk/about.html**).

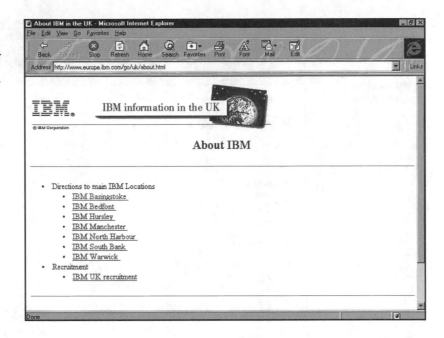

Creating a Frequently Asked Questions (FAQ) Page

With so many people browsing through the tangles of the World Wide Web, the number of questions posed to Webmasters increases by the minute. FAQ lists target the most frequently repeated of these questions and provides thorough answers. So many answers are needed that FAQ lists now accompany almost every newsgroup and mailing list on the Net and the Web. To help you set up one of your own, FrontPage offers you a template. Open it, and you get the screen shown in Figure 9.10.

The FAQ template resembles the Employee Directory template, providing users with an introductory area from which they can access all major sections of the FAQ page. The Table of Contents hyperlinks work like the This Month, Last Month, and Previous Month divisions in the Press Release Directory, giving readers suitable points of entry to information areas of the site.

FIGURE 9.10

With the FAQ template you get a Table of Contents menu, ready for customization.

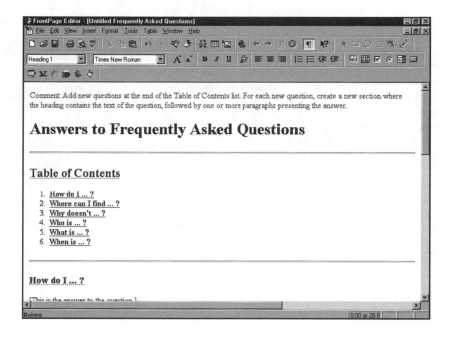

If you plan on only a few questions and responses, the FrontPage Editor template will be adequate. However, if your FAQ page is extensive, you should consider setting up separate pages for each class of questions and linking to bookmarks in them. As usual, this is to enhance response speed.

You can see an example of a large FAQ site in Figure 9.11. It offers a header area from which you can access mirror sites in several languages, and from which you can download the FAQ answers in several file formats. The Contents entries are links to bookmarks farther down the page. These bookmarked areas in turn each have Tables of Contents, and each entry in these subtables is a link to a page where you find the answers to the question. These pages have further hyperlinks to places where you can get even more information on the subject.

 TIP When wording the responses to your FAQs, remember that you may be addressing a newcomer to the Internet, or at least a newcomer to your site. Avoid highly technical answers that could confuse people, or worse, encourage more questions.

FIGURE 9.11
This site classifies questions into specialized areas for more efficient access to information (**http:// www.boutell.com/ faq/#intro**).

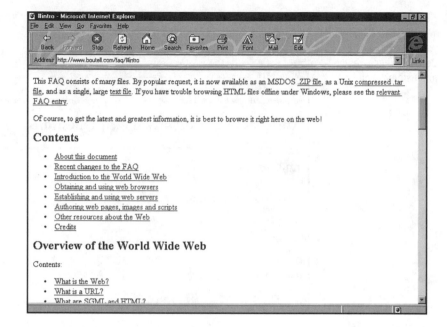

Glossary of Terms

Because the World Wide Web has grown so fast, many of its users are novices. This means that the need for definitions and explanatory terms has increased dramatically, and this is where glossaries come in. You can see FrontPage's Glossary of Terms template in Figure 9.12.

You insert new entries in alphabetical order within the appropriate sections of the page. Notice that the words to be defined use the Defined Term style, to force the next line to indent; they also have the Bold character formatting.

Each letter in the alphabet line is linked to the corresponding section of the glossary. For example, clicking D transports a searcher to the D section of the page (you'd already figured that out, hadn't you?). For longer, more complex glossaries, the alphabetized

FIGURE 9.12

FrontPage's Glossary of Terms functions much like a dictionary.

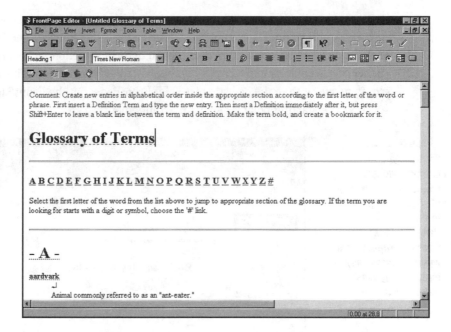

menu at the top of the page could link to separate pages of defined terms. And you can include a # sign (or whatever symbol you like) to represent an Other section, where you put terms that begin with numbers or nonalphabetic characters.

The template includes bookmarks for the individual terms. These aren't necessary for the template to function as is; they're merely there to remind you that you can link to specific terms ("aardvark," for example) from some other spot in your Web.

Because most glossary pages start small, yours may not always contain entries for each letter of the alphabet. Display all the letters anyway, and establish a section for each. Mark empty sections as "Empty," as the template does. Omitting unused letters will bother your readers; they'll think you've left them out by accident, and assume you're careless or that you're too lazy to put them in, which is worse.

In the example in Figure 9.13, the glossary has been subdivided into separate pages for A-G, H-M, and so on. On each of these four pages is the alphabet line for that page, with each letter a link to a bookmark at the head of the subsection for that letter. Within these subsections are links to the pages that explain the various terms. This is a more complex glossary layout than the one suggested by FrontPage, but the FrontPage template could serve as the starting point for such an arrangement.

FIGURE 9.13

For a large and complex glossary, you might use a structure of subdivisions like the one shown here (**http://www. washingtonpost.com/ wp-serv/business/ longterm/glossary/ indexag.htm**).

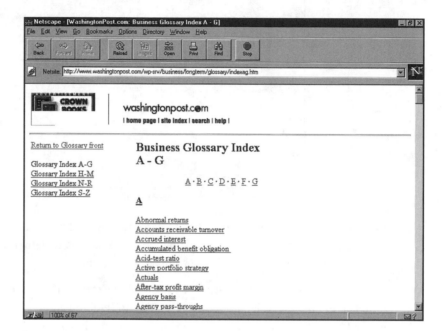

Creating a Hotlist

One of the most common lists on the Web is the hotlist. This is just Internet-speak for a list of the author's favorite sites, Web pages that (to the person making the listing, anyway) display ingenuity, creativity, excellent content, or unusual design. Although you can incorporate a hotlist into your home page, you'd likely be better off to install it on a separate World Wide Web page; these lists tend to grow.

The FrontPage Hotlist template appears in Figure 9.14.

FIGURE 9.14
FrontPage Editor's
Hotlist template
builds around
categories of site.

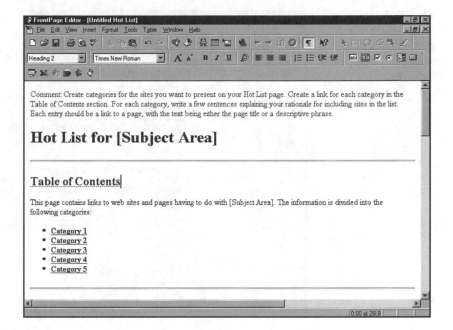

Part

II

Ch

9

The template's page title is in boldface and its layout suggests that you assign a general subject to the page. The Table of Contents section divides the subject into categories, each category being a link to a section of the page. Within these latter sections are the actual hyperlinks to the external World Wide Web sites. Notice the Back to Top internal link at the bottom of each section. These are highly desirable, especially if your hotlist is a long one. The other templates use such navigational controls, too, and so should you in your custom pages.

You can see an example of a very elaborate real-world hotlist in Figure 9.15. This has the category subdivisions suggested by the FrontPage Editor template, and some sorting options on the left. The links at the top of the page point to other directories on the host machine, and these directories contain sublists of hyperlinks to the "hot" sites themselves. It's quite complicated, and would be a vast amount of work to maintain, but it shows you the possibilities.

FIGURE 9.15
An "industrial-strength"
hotlist requires a lot of
design and mainte-
nance (**http://
www.100hot.com**/).

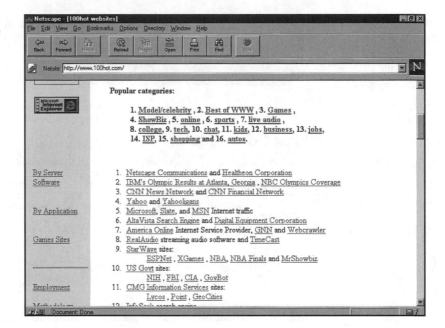

Creating a Hyperdocument Page

In FrontPage, a hyperdocument page is any page of a larger, hyperlinked document that consists of several such pages. In this sense, you could say that any Web site with more than one page is itself such a document; or even that the whole World Wide Web is one gigantic hyperdocument.

You make a hyperdocument if you have a body of information whose parts are related, but when added together are too big to go on one Web page. To get started, open the Hyperdocument Page template, as shown in Figure 9.16.

FrontPage Editor sets up this page as part of a hierarchy. The HyperDocument Name is the name of the larger document—for instance, a manual, a book, or a report. This hyperdocument should have a home page that introduces and describes the work as a whole. Create the home page first, then link it to a Table of Contents page—or, depending on the size of the document, you could put the TOC on the home page itself.

▶ **See** "Table of Contents Bot," **p. 231**

When you use the template to create an individual page, start off by replacing HyperDocument Name with the name of the larger document, and set up a link to the larger document's home page. Then, where the page template says Section Name, establish a link to the Table Of Contents (TOC) page. The template layout suggests that this TOC would have section headings, each section containing individual page titles that are linked to the appropriate page. In this case, the Section Name on the individual page should be linked, via bookmark, to the corresponding section heading in the TOC. If you don't have sections in your TOC, simply make the Section Name link into a link to the TOC page itself.

FIGURE 9.16
A hyperdocument page is linked to other documents in the same collection of information.

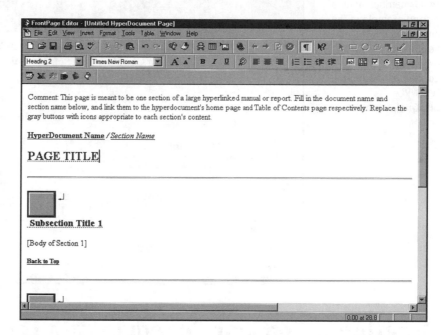

Each subsection of the page template suggests a bookmark for the subsection title. This is optional; you'd keep the bookmark only if the TOC or some other page in the hyperdocument needed to be linked to the subsections.

The gray buttons above the subsection titles suggest navigation controls. You could make them into such controls, or you could replace them (as the template suggests) with icons related to the subsection content. Alternatively, if there were a large image related to each subsection, you could replace each button with a thumbnail image linked to its parent image.

In a complicated document, it's important to give your visitor good navigational tools. This template puts a Back to Top link at the end of each subsection to achieve this.

In the example in Figure 9.17, the hyperdocument is a very large linked collection called the "Information Quality World Wide Web Virtual Library," provided by the Australian National University. The example shows the Table of Contents page; as you can see, the linkages are wide-ranging and numerous. Because of the complexity of the TOC, the author has arranged it as a table containing hyperlinks. Elsewhere on the page (not visible in the example) are links to a forum, to e-mail, to usage statistics, and to other resources including the Library of Congress.

FIGURE 9.17
This hyperdocument is a good example of the enormous power and flexibility of Web hyperlinks (**http://coombs.anu.edu.au/WWWVL-InfoQuality.html**).

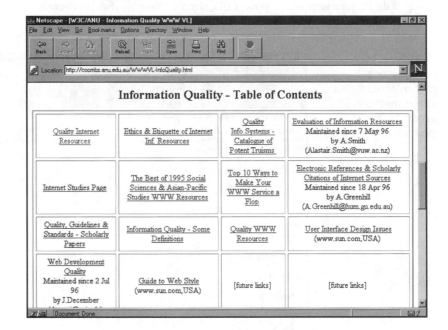

Creating a Seminar Schedule with Lecture Abstracts

These two templates, Seminar Schedule and Lecture Abstract, are designed to work together. The schedule is the master document, and it's linked to any number of other pages, each of which gives details about some kind of presentation (this doesn't have to be a lecture, obviously).

Using the pair is very straightforward. First, open the Seminar Schedule template to get the screen shown in Figure 9.18.

As usual, replace the page's heading material with text suitable to your event, and add a description of the event. Depending on the size and complexity of your conference, you then have several options for customizing the Schedule page.

FIGURE 9.18
The Seminar Schedule helps you organize the events of your conference or seminar.

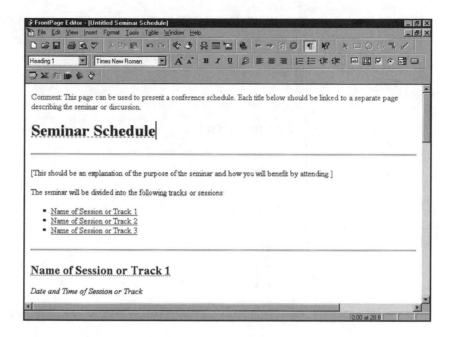

If the event has several different sessions, each with several presentations, customize the Name of Session links to take the viewer to that section. Under each session heading, insert the lecture/presentation title. Below that, add the names and personal data on each speaker, and link each of these entries to a page you prepare with the Lecture Abstract template. If each presentation has only one presenter, just link the Title of Lecture entry to the appropriate abstract page.

When you're ready to make up the lecture pages, open the Lecture Abstract template to get the page shown in Figure 9.19.

Setting up this page is mostly customization work. The only essential link is the one that takes the reader back to the Schedule page. The most difficult part will be writing the abstract, which is a boiled-down version of the key content and/or purpose of the presentation. The Bulleted List section of the page will help you here, as it will force you to identify the main emphases of the presentation. Finally, there's space for the presenter's biography, and at the very end of the page is the usual copyright area, which you can delete if you like. You may have noticed by now that the date at the end of each template is today's date. That's a WebBot at work; it's the Timestamp WebBot, and you use it to add the current date to any page.

▶ **See** "Timestamp Bot," **p. 232**

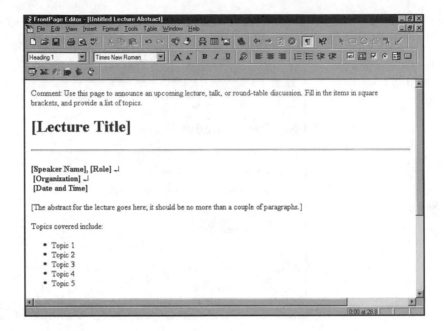

Creating a Meeting Agenda

There's not much to do in the Meeting Agenda template, except the usual customization (see Figure 9.20).

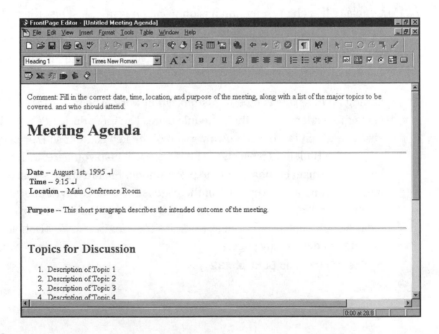

In fact, the Meeting Agenda template is closely modeled on the Lecture Abstract, with a date, time, and location section, a purpose section, and a list of topics for discussion. Naturally, you'd link to it from another document, since an agenda isn't much use if nobody can get to it. And since you'll need hard copy for the meeting itself, why not print it from FrontPage Editor?

Creating a Product Description

This template helps you define the strengths and benefits of a product you manufacture or a service you provide. When it's finished, you'll have a useful marketing tool (see Figure 9.21).

FIGURE 9.21
The Product Description template helps you write a marketing sheet for something you produce.

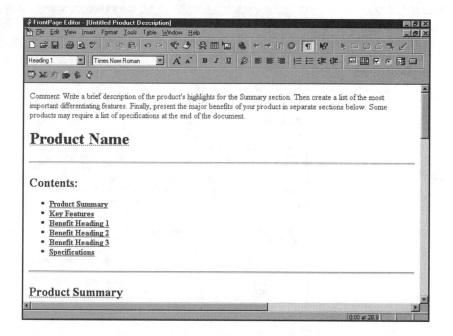

The Product name is bookmarked, so searchers can reach it from another page, possibly a catalogue of items or if it's new, from a Press Release page.

Like several other FrontPage Editor templates, this is organized as a contents section whose entries are linked to other sections of the page. Since images attract people's attention, you should consider inserting a picture of the product near the page head. If you provide a service, the image should relate to that. Whatever you do, though, make sure the picture is clear enough for the object or service to be easily identifiable. Depending on what you need to show about it, you might want to make this on-page image into a thumbnail, and link it a larger image that shows more detail.

You need a good grasp of the character and benefits of your product or service in order to customize the rest of the page to best effect. In fact, the usefulness of several FrontPage Editor templates isn't confined to layout and link structures. Several of the templates, and this one in particular, force you to think hard about what you need to communicate. Since the core of a Web page is its content, this is no small virtue.

The author of the example in Figure 9.22 has applied this technique. Beginning with the product name, he moves to a product brief (the summary) and then goes on to the machine's key features. A graphic of the equipment provides some visual interest. At the top of the page (out of sight in the example) are navigation buttons to related parts of the site. Included later in the body of the document are block diagrams and tables of specifications for the equipment.

FIGURE 9.22
This product description page furnishes complete technical specifications for a piece of hardware (**http:// www.dmo.hp.com/ cgi-bin/fe.pl/gsy/ 2a2.html**).

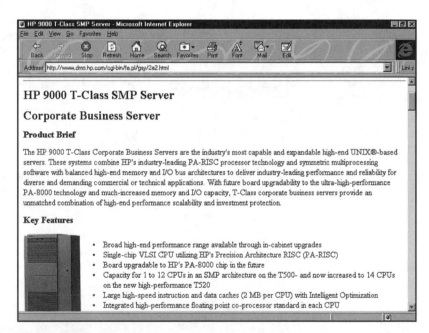

Creating a Software Data Sheet

This is a specialized product description template focused on the characteristics of computer software (see Figure 9.23).

This template has the Benefits and Features sections of the generic Product Description template, but it adds an area where you can specify hardware platform requirements and an area where you can insert pricing and availability of different configurations of the software. The page's most prominent feature is the large screenshot of the software in operation. Since software is otherwise invisible, this is one place you won't want to skimp on image size, despite the download time penalty. Make sure the image is good and clear, and experiment with different screen resolutions to get the best mix of legibility and information density into the shot.

Part

II

Ch

9

FIGURE 9.23

The Software Data Sheet template is keyed to the needs of the software industry.

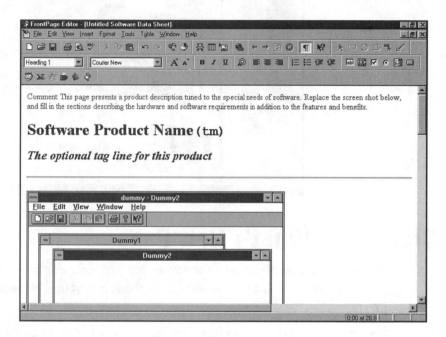

The template doesn't include linking and bookmarking for the Benefits, Features, Hardware Requirements, and Pricing sections. You may want to add such links and bookmarks, if the product is complex and the page is getting long. Just as with the Product Description page, you'll probably link to this one from a product catalogue, or if it's new, from a press release.

The example in Figure 9.24 shows the graphical element in particular. It's also a framed page, with navigation controls in the left frame, and visuals of the software interface in the main frame, and is linked from a Products page elsewhere on the site. With each visual is a hyperlink that takes the visitor to specific information about the software. The clean appearance of this page gives an immediate visual appeal.

FIGURE 9.24
This software product page relies heavily on graphics for its impact (**http://www.calgari.com**).

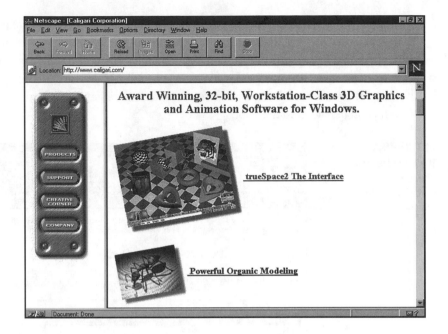

Creating a What's New Page

This template is for Webmasters or anyone who is maintaining a Web site. It provides you with a pattern for telling your visitors about changes to your site (see Figure 9.25).

It's a simple template—although if you have a complex site and make frequent changes, keeping it up to date may not be so simple. You have to do this, though, just as you must keep your site from becoming static or stale. One of the main attractions of the Web is its constant flux, and people, for better or worse, are more interested in what's new and different than in what they saw or read last month. If you're running a reference or scholarly site, being new and different isn't so important, but you still have to keep up with changes in the discipline while you maintain existing research or reference data.

This What's New information shouldn't usually go on your home page. Instead, make a prominent navigational tool, and use it to direct your visitors to the What's New page. When you update the page, check your site's links to external URLs on the Web and the Internet. Few things are as frustrating for your visitor as trying to follow an interesting-looking link from your site and discovering that the link's destination has vanished. It's your responsibility to make sure this doesn't happen.

In the example in Figure 9.26, the page designer livens up the page with some active content in the black-bordered rectangle, and goes on with hyperlinks to the additions and new features of the site. Farther down the page (out of sight in the example) are links to the What's New lists of the previous week. This site updates its What's New page every day; most sites won't require that much maintenance. The very top graphic of the page is an image map linked to other parts of the site.

FIGURE 9.25
You can let your visitors know what you've been up to with the What's New template.

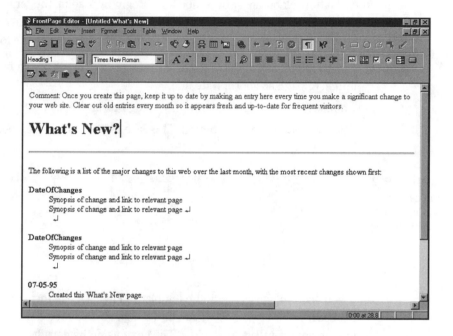

FIGURE 9.26
The Yahoo! site updates its What's New page on a daily basis (**http://www.yahoo.com/new/**).

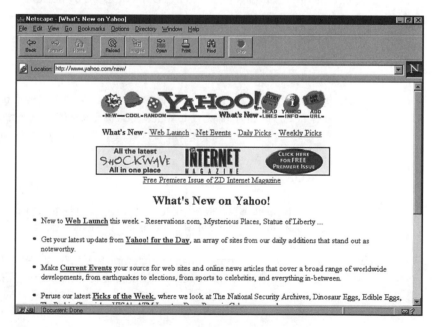

Part

II

Ch

9

Creating Custom Templates

This is basically a page editing task, though it may be a long and complicated one, depending on how elaborate your template is. Begin by loading the template that you want to make the basis for your own, or by creating a new page with a page Wizard, or simply by creating a Normal page. Once the page is in the workspace, take the following steps:

1. If you haven't already done so, use the Page Properties dialog box to give the template page an appropriate title.

2. Choose File, Save As. The Save As dialog box appears.

3. Choose the As Template button. The Save as Template dialog box appears (see Figure 9.27).

FIGURE 9.27

You can save a page layout and design as a custom template.

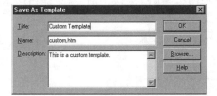

4. If you want to, you can edit the template's Page Title in the Title box. Do this if necessary, then type a file name into the Name box. You don't need to add an extension; FrontPage will add a .TEM extension by default.

5. Type a description of the template into the Description box. This will appear in the New Page dialog box when you choose the template to create a page.

> **CAUTION**
>
> The Description is required; if it isn't there, the OK button is grayed out. In any case, there is no good reason not to include it. If you insist, go to Windows Explorer, open C:\Program Files\Microsoft FrontPage\Pages, then open the appropriate template folder, and edit the .INF file therein.

6. Choose OK.

N O T E   Since a template is merely an HTML file, any page can be a template. That means you can open any page from the Web, save it, and use it as such. ■

Assuming a default installation, the custom template will be saved in the C:\Program Files\Microsoft FrontPage\Pages folder, within a subfolder bearing the name you assigned to the template. This name will have a .TEM extension. From now on, whenever you choose FrontPage Editor's File, New command, the custom template's name will appear in the list box. If you want to remove the template, both from the system and from the New Page list box, simply use Windows Explorer to go to the Pages folder, and delete the folder bearing that name.

Using the templates described in this chapter, you can create hybrid templates, too. Simply open the templates you want to use, and cut and paste the appropriate parts of them into the new template. Then save the new template as a custom one, using the procedure above. It's no more complex than cutting and pasting with a word processor.

About the Pages folder and its templates

All FrontPage Editor templates are stored in their own folders in the C:\Program Files\Microsoft FrontPage\Pages folder. When you save an HTML page as a template, its unique folder is created with the name you assigned to the template; unlike most folder names, this one has an extension, .TEM (for template, obviously). It's this extension that makes the template accessible through the New command, and if it isn't there, the template won't appear in the New Page list box. Within the folder is the template file itself, which is simply an HTML file; the template folder name must match this file's name. Also in the folder is an .inf file. This is a text file storing the name and description of the template, as well as the path names of any separate files (such as image files) required by the template file. By the way, there's no officially stated limit on the number of templates you can have. It's probably as large as your hard drive has room for.

From Here...

The page types we've explored in this chapter are useful, and you'll get a lot of mileage out of them. You can incorporate many of their features into "scratch" pages you begin with the Normal template. Yet there are still more sophisticated features you can add to the pages of your site. To find out how, see the following chapters:

- Chapter 10, "Using WebBots, Wizards, and Interactive Page Templates," discusses those funny bots and how they help make your Web interactive. You also learn about forms, and using specialized templates to make your pages interactive.

- Chapter 11, "Working Directly with HTML," which shows you how you can edit HTML directly in FrontPage Editor, and how you use the HTML Markup tool to add HTML to your pages.

- Chapter 12, "Integrating HTML Style Sheets," which shows you how to use this new technique for developing and maintaining a consistent and easily modified look for an entire site or for a set of pages.

Using WebBots, Wizards, and Interactive Page Templates

This chapter deals with one of the most important facets of the World Wide Web: its interactivity. Without this, the Web would be like channel-browsing on television; you'd get to look, but you'd never get to talk to anybody. But on the Web you can talk to your heart's content, and if you have something useful or entertaining to say, you may find that a lot of people are listening to you. ■

WebBots

These Bots relieve you of the task of writing CGI scripts.

Designing FrontPage Forms

Effective forms are organized, brief, and attractive.

Customizing Forms

Customizing lets you use fields, text, and images of your choice.

Using Templates

FrontPage templates provide a quick way to set up interactive pages.

Using the Personal Home Page Wizard

Customize your own home page by selecting options from this Wizard.

Understanding WebBots

WebBots (or *Bots*) are a key part of FrontPage because they automate certain procedures that other Web authoring tools require you to hand-code in HTML or in a scripting language such as Perl. FrontPage puts several different kinds of Bots at your disposal.

But what's a Bot? Well, simply put, a Bot represents a chunk of programming that gets embedded into the HTML code of a page when you insert the Bot. Depending on the type of Bot, the program it represents executes when one of the following happens:

- The author saves the page.
- A visitor to the site accesses the page.
- The visitor clicks an interactive portion of the page, such as the Submit button for a form.

You use some WebBots only with forms; others are what you might call "utility" Bots because they carry out useful, routine tasks that streamline page and site creation. A few are almost invisible; they execute automatically when you tell FrontPage Editor to do something, and they show up neither in FrontPage Editor nor in a browser. An example of the last type is the imagemap Bot. If you inspect the HTML code for an imagemap, you'll see the word "bot" tucked away in it. That's as close as you ever get to this particular WebBot.

You use the Insert menu to put most of the "visible" Bots into a page. We'll look at some of the simple utility Bots first, just to get acquainted with Bot behavior.

Using the Comment Bot

The Comment Bot lets you insert text that will appear only in FrontPage Editor (FrontPage Editor doesn't show it as a Bot on the menu, but it is one, nevertheless). It works much like a comment or annotation in a word processor in that it's invisible to end users. In our context, that means that when someone views the page in her Web browser, she doesn't see the comment text.

The Comment Bot is extremely useful, especially if different people are editing the same Web page and they need to leave explanations for each other. In fact, FrontPage Editor sometimes does exactly this, for your benefit. Several of its Wizards and templates have Comment Bots embedded in them to prompt you about how to use features of the page.

To insert a Comment Bot, use the following steps:

1. Position the cursor where you want the comment to appear.
2. Choose Insert, Comment. The Comment dialog box appears (see Figure 10.1).

FIGURE 10.1

Add the comment text using the Comment dialog box.

3. Enter the text you want for the comment, and choose OK. The Comment dialog box closes, and the comment appears in the FrontPage Editor workspace in purple text (assuming that you are using the defaults).

Now position the cursor on top of the comment text. The cursor becomes an arrow attached to a small, robotlike figure. This is the WebBot cursor, or Bot cursor, and it appears whenever the ordinary cursor is in a region of the workspace where there's a Bot. Even if you can't see the Bot component itself, the Bot cursor will appear to tell you it's there.

If you want to change the text of the comment, click it. This automatically selects the entire text block. Now choose Edit, WebBot Component Properties, and the Comment dialog box appears. Make your changes, and choose OK. (Or you can just double-click the bot to edit it).

 You can also right-click while the Bot cursor is visible, and choose Comment Properties from the shortcut menu.

Include Bot

The Include Bot inserts the contents of a file into a page. You use this if you have several pages in a web that need identical formatting for one or more elements, such as a standard heading at the top of each page. By using the Include Bot, you can include this heading on as many pages as you like. Furthermore, if you need to change it (inserting a new logo, for example) you can make the change in only one file, instead of editing every page where the element appears. Each page using the Include Bot is updated automatically when the included file changes.

To use the Include Bot, choose Insert, WebBot. The Insert WebBot Component dialog box appears (see Figure 10.2).

FIGURE 10.2

Use the Insert WebBot Component dialog box to choose from a selection of Bots.

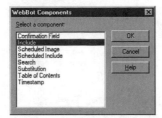

Select the Include Bot from the list box, and choose OK. The Include Bot Properties dialog box appears (see Figure 10.3).

FIGURE 10.3

Specify the included file with the Include Bot Properties dialog box.

Enter the URL of the file to be included, either by typing it or by selecting Browse to search the current web. Note that you can only enter page URLs, not image URLs.

Scheduled Image Bot

The Scheduled Image Bot inserts a graphic file from the web and displays it for a specified period of time. If the time period has not arrived or has elapsed, one of the following happens:

- A message such as `Expired Scheduled Image` appears in FrontPage Editor. When the page is viewed from a browser, nothing appears.

- A specified alternate image appears in both FrontPage Editor and Web browser.

The Scheduled Image Bot is particularly useful for advertising or displays that run only for a period of time. With the Scheduled Image Bot, you can, for example, insert a client's advertisement for a day or week and, after the time expires, replace it with a specified alternative.

To put a scheduled image into your page, select that Bot from the Insert WebBot Component dialog box. The Scheduled Image Bot Properties dialog box appears (see Figure 10.4).

FIGURE 10.4

Use the Scheduled Image Bot Properties dialog box to specify how long an image will be included on your page.

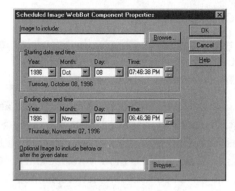

Then use the following steps:

1. Use the <u>B</u>rowse button to select an image from the web, or type in the URL of the image.

2. Specify the starting and ending date and time for the image to appear. The defaults are today's date for the starting date and one month later for the ending date.

3. Optionally, specify an image to be displayed before or after the dates given in step 2. If this field is left empty and the system date is outside the specified range, nothing shows up when a user views the page in his browser.

4. Choose OK. The image will appear on the page. If it's a new, unsaved page, you first have to save the page then reopen it or refresh it before the image actually appears; until then, only the image's file name is displayed.

A scheduled image has the following behaviors:

■ Although the image looks like a normal one, you can't select it and edit the image properties, such as borders, image type, or alignment. Attempting to open the Image Properties dialog box leads you to the WebBot Component Properties box instead. In other words, the object on the page is really a Bot, not an image.

■ If the computer's system date falls outside the range given by the start and end dates you specified, and if there is no optional image specified, the message Expired Scheduled Image appears in FrontPage Editor in place of the image. Of course, neither the image nor this message appears in a browser.

■ You can link or unlink the scheduled image or the optional image using <u>E</u>dit, Hyperlin<u>k</u> (or U<u>n</u>link) and the usual linking methods.

Using the Scheduled Include Bot

You insert the Scheduled Include Bot just as you do the Scheduled Image Bot (the dialog boxes are identical in function, so we won't show the box again). The difference here is that an HTML page file is inserted into the document.

Since you're inserting a page, you have some options for making it appear as you want it. Although you can't edit the inserted material directly (trying this just displays the Scheduled Include Bot Properties dialog box), you can, of course, edit the Bot's source page. Because of this, the Scheduled Include Bot is more versatile and configurable than the Scheduled Image Bot. You can create notices, newsletters, limited time offers, holiday pages, and in-depth advertisements, and include them as pages. You can also specify an optional page to display outside the date range specified.

N O T E   Sometimes it's better to use the Scheduled Include Bot than the Scheduled Image Bot for inserting an image. Even though it takes slightly more work to do (you have to create a HTML page and insert the image into it), inserting an image with this Bot allows you to create hotspots on the image as well as modify its properties. ▪

Using the Search Bot

When you insert a Search Bot, a simple form appears allowing a reader to search all pages in the current web or a discussion group for a string of words. When you insert a Search Bot, you get the Search Bot Properties dialog box (see Figure 10.5).

FIGURE 10.5
Use the Search Bot Properties dialog box to establish the parameters of a search.

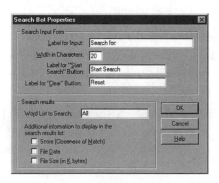

N O T E   The Search Bot searches only the current web. It isn't intended as a search engine for locations beyond that web. ▪

You can modify the Bot's properties in the following ways:

- ▪ Put your own text, such as "Search My Web For:" in the Label for Input text box.

- Set the field width for the search string.
- Customize the Clear and Start button labels.
- Specify the Word List to Search to set the search range. All searches all the pages of the current web. If you've set up a discussion group, you can enter its directory name here, and the Bot searches all entries in that discussion group directory. If you want to exclude some pages from a search, you must store these in a hidden directory.

  ▶ **See** "Using Hidden Directories with WebBots," **p. 232**

- Use the check boxes to specify whether to display the closeness of the match, the last update of a matched page, and the matched page's size in kilobytes.

When a visitor to your site submits words to search for, the Search Bot returns a list of pages on which the words appear. If your Web is complex or large, your visitors will thank you for including an easily accessible Search Bot.

Substitution Bot

The Substitution Bot inserts onto the page the value of a page configuration variable, such as the original author, the person who modified the page, the page URL, or the page description (which can be free-form text). Also listed are any page configuration variables you added in FrontPage Explorer.

To use the Bot, select it from the Insert Bot dialog box. Then open the Substitute With list box in the Substitution Bot Properties dialog box. Select the name of the variable you want, and choose OK. Its value appears on the page.

Table of Contents Bot

This Bot creates a table of contents (TOC) for your Web site. To use it, select the Bot from the Insert Bot dialog box. The Table of Contents Bot Properties dialog box appears (see Figure 10.6).

With this Bot, you can do the following:

- Select the page that is the starting point of the TOC. On execution, the Bot follows all links from this page. If you want a list of all pages on your web, assign the home page as the starting point.
- Choose the heading size for the table of contents. The TOC heading is taken from the Page Title of the starting page.
- Mark the Show Each Page Only Once check box to keep the same page from appearing over and over in the TOC. With the check box deselected, you'll get a TOC entry for the page for each link to it.

■ Mark the Show Pages with No Incoming Links check box to include all pages on the site, even orphan pages with no links to them.

■ Mark the Recompute Table of Contents When Any Other Page Is Edited check box to update the TOC every time you edit a page in the web. Large Web sites can take a long time to update, so mark this box only if you can wait. To "manually" update a table of contents, open the page containing the Table of Contents Bot and resave it.

FIGURE 10.6
Setting the Table of Contents Bot properties lets you customize this essential part of a Web.

TROUBLESHOOTING

I inserted a Table of Contents Bot, but it's not showing the TOC in the FrontPage Editor workspace—just three dummy entries. And I can't edit the dummy entries. What have I done wrong?

You haven't done anything wrong. You don't see the real TOC except in a browser. Admittedly, this makes page layout a little more difficult, since you can't see directly what the page is going to look like. The best way to deal with this is to use the Preview in Browser command to evaluate your work as you go. Remember, however, that this TOC page will inevitably be fluid because it will change as your site gains and loses pages.

Timestamp Bot

The Timestamp Bot automatically inserts the last date the page was saved or updated. It can, optionally, also include the time of either of these events.

It's a simple Bot. Use its Properties dialog box to select whether it gives the date of the last edit or the date the page was updated. An update is either the last edit or when the page's URL was regenerated because of a change in the structure of the web.

Using Hidden Directories with WebBots

Hidden directories are important to web security and WebBot behavior. Hidden-directory names are indicated by a leading underscore character.

When you create a new web, FrontPage Explorer puts the special directory _private into it. Browsers can't directly read files in this or any other hidden directory. For example, if a site visitor tries to access the location **http://www.mysite/_private/header.htm**, she will be prompted for a user name and password.

By default, FrontPage Explorer and Editor do not show files stored in hidden directories. Search Bots do not search hidden directories, and the Table of Contents Bot does not add links to pages in hidden directories. However, you can configure FrontPage Explorer to show the content of hidden directories. In the FrontPage Explorer menu bar, choose Tools, Web Settings. When the Web Settings dialog box appears, select the Advanced tab, and mark the Show Documents in Hidden Directories check box on the Advanced tab.

The _private directory is often used with the two Include Bots. For instance, you may want a standard header file for each page in the web but don't want people to be able to access that header file directly. Put it into the _private directory and call it from there with the appropriate Bot.

 TIP If you want to create a link to a file in a hidden directory, mark the Show Documents in Hidden Directories check box so that you can use Browse buttons to locate the file.

Forms: Why Bother?

I don't know who invented the first form (he or she must have been a bureaucrat, though) but they've been proliferating like weeds ever since. There's a good reason for this: they're useful. In a society like ours, which depends so heavily on the processing of information, they're essential for organizing both the way the information is gathered and how it's presented. If a census-taker merely asks a person to "tell me all about your household," she'll probably get some of the data she's after, but she'll miss at least some, and receive unwanted information. In this disorganized state, the information is almost useless. But give the same census-taker a form to guide the data collection, and life suddenly becomes much easier.

Designing Effective Forms

Since you intend your forms to gather information, you have to persuade people to fill them out. However, people dislike forms almost on principle, and if the form is badly organized, too long, and filled with irrelevant questions, nobody will touch it. The following are a few things you can do to create user-friendly forms:

■ If you can, create an enticement to complete the form. Remember how people ask "What's in this for me?" when they first enter your site? This inclination is doubled when they run into a form.

■ Keep the form short. List the form's objectives and ask only for data that meets them. Don't get sidetracked by nice-to-know items; stick to the need to know. If a form takes more than a minute or two to fill out, most people won't bother.

■ Briefly tell the reader why you want the data and how it will be used. If she understands the form in this context, she'll be more likely to fill it out correctly. But don't overburden her with an explanation; a couple of sentences should summarize your intentions adequately.

■ Ask general questions first, starting with a couple of easy ones. Then go for the details. Ask demographic questions (age, income, sex, education, occupation, and so on) last of all. Don't ask them if you don't absolutely need to, either. Too many personal questions will make the reader apprehensive about submitting the form.

■ Nobody reads forms carefully, so ask your questions as briefly and clearly as you can. If the question takes multiple sentences to ask, find a way to shorten it, and don't ask two questions at the same time. Remember that if something can be misunderstood, it will be.

■ Avoid ambiguous questions, such as "Do you find our service good?" That's brief, admittedly, but it's a badly designed query. Is the "service" your delivery speed, your customer response line, or what? What is "good"? Fast but expensive? Slow but cheap?

■ Avoid leading questions, where the wording influences the answer. They're unethical, for one thing, and they can give you results you don't want or intend. If you ask "Is our aggressive Web advertising campaign offensive?" you're almost asking for a "Yes" because a lot of people disagree with the idea of advertising on the Web, especially "aggressive" advertising.

■ Before putting the form into service, test it on some real live people and use the feedback to modify it. Even professional form and survey designers don't get it right on the first try.

Understanding World Wide Web Forms

When a visitor to your site fills out a form and clicks the Submit button, this action sends his information to a program on the Web server. The server program must exist, because without it, nothing happens; the data doesn't get saved anywhere.

When the data comes in, the server program processes it. This processing can be as simple as saving the data to a file, or as complex as sorting the data and calculating results from it before the information is sent to the intended recipient. The program also sends the respondent a confirmation that the information was received.

The software standard that controls how your visitors interact with your site is called the Common Gateway Interface (CGI). The server programs that deal with such incoming information are called CGI scripts and are written to conform to the CGI specifications. When your visitor clicks that Submit button on your form, the data she sends goes to the script, and the script processes it according to the way the script was written.

Without FrontPage, you have to write a CGI script to handle your forms and install that script on the Web server. Writing these scripts is a headache for anyone without some programming experience; worse, badly written ones can cause severe misbehavior at the server end, and many ISPs won't let you put your own scripts in their servers. Fortunately, FrontPage enormously simplifies the whole messy business. You don't have to write any CGI scripts because certain FrontPage WebBots take their place. FrontPage calls these Bots *Form Handlers*.

Part
II

Ch
10

> **CAUTION**
>
> To use forms generated by FrontPage, your Web pages must reside on a server that runs the proper FrontPage extensions. If the Web server doesn't have these extensions, it won't have the software that evaluates the submitted information, and your forms won't work. If this happens, contact your ISP administrator.

If you're already familiar with programming and compiling CGI scripts, though, you'll be happy to know that FrontPage fully supports them. However, you'll need them only when adding specialized features or when a page dependent on a CGI script is imported from another Web server.

> **CAUTION**
>
> Like writing CGI scripts, CGI security is far beyond the scope of this book. However, you should be aware that, because CGI opens the door to end user interaction (in fact, that's its purpose), there's always the possibility that an aggressive and unethical user could submit statements and codes that, in effect, could control your Web server's behavior. For more on CGI security issues, see
>
> **http://hoohoo.ncsa.uiuc.edu/cgi/security.html**
>
> and
>
> **http://www.cerf.net/~paulp/cgi-security/**

N O T E For an exhaustive treatment of CGI scripting, refer to Que's *Special Edition Using CGI.* ■

Understanding FrontPage Forms

With FrontPage forms, you can get just about any information you want from your visitors (assuming they're willing to give it). Moreover, you can instruct FrontPage to save the data in various HTML or text formats, allowing viewing and manipulation by various external software applications and macros.

Every FrontPage form has the same basic structure: at least one question, one or more fields for the reader to enter information, a Submit button to send the information to the server, and a Clear (or Reset) button to remove existing entries from the fields. Also associated with the form, at the server end, is some Bot-generated software to process the submitted data.

You can create a FrontPage form in any of three ways: with the Forms Wizard, by designing a custom form of your own, or with a template. We'll explore each of these in turn.

 TIP   Do a draft on paper before starting the form in FrontPage Editor. This forces you to organize and visualize the form; you'll create the software version with less backtracking and revision.

Creating a Form Using the Form Page Wizard

The Form Page Wizard lets you easily and quickly create many of the forms you need. The Wizard takes a lot of the drudgery out of the work, supplying you with suitable formatting and inserting the required WebBots for you.

To start the Wizard, choose File, New. The Template or Wizard dialog box appears. Choose Form Page Wizard and then choose Next to move to the second dialog box. As usual with a FrontPage Editor wizard, you must supply the Page URL and Page Title at this stage. Do so and choose Next to go on.

N O T E   You might not want the form to stand on a page by itself. To insert it into an existing page, simply copy it to the Windows Clipboard and paste it at the appropriate place. ■

Adding Questions to Your Form   The third dialog box is where you get down to business and start asking questions of your respondents (see Figure 10.7).

When you choose Add, the Wizard opens a list box where you can pick the type of input this question collects. The list is pretty comprehensive. You can see what it does by reading the Description section of the dialog box. If the Description section lists several items (that is, form fields), don't worry. You can customize the form later as much as you like.

FIGURE 10.7
Use the Form Page Wizard dialog box to specify the questions for your form. This one shows contact and ordering information.

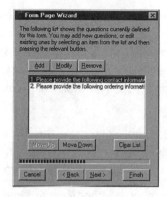

The Edit Prompt for This Question text box shows the default wording of the question. Depending on which input type you select, the prompt differs. You can edit it if you need to. When you have the prompt right, choose Next.

Specifying Fields for the Input Type   Now you get to decide which data items to collect from users (see Figure 10.8). These chunks of data are assigned to fields. From the user's viewpoint, fields are simply the text boxes on the form where she types her input. The Wizard uses terms like value, field name, and variable. For our purposes, think of the name of the variable as being the same as the field name, and the value of the variable as being the data itself. Better yet, think of the variable as a bucket with the field name painted on it, and the value as whatever someone pours into the bucket.

FIGURE 10.8
You can choose several data items and two subtypes in this section of the Form Page Wizard.

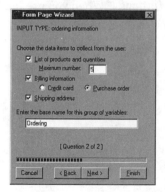

Although this dialog box is slightly different for each input type (ordering, account, and so on), it's always divided into three parts: the first section reminds you of the input type, the second section lets you choose data items, and the third section lets you specify the base name for this particular group of form variables.

Part
II

Ch
10

No matter what the input type, the second section is always set up the same way. A check box adds a field, while the option buttons and text boxes modify what the field looks like. For example, marking the Billing Information check box in Figure 10.8 tells the Wizard to insert fields for billing information. The Credit Card and Purchase Order option buttons further define what type of fields appear. If you don't want a particular data item to be asked for, clear the check box.

Usually you needn't worry about changing the contents of the Enter the Base Name for This Group of Variables text box. It's just what the Wizard uses to help organize the field structures of the form. Changing it merely changes the standard prefix of the field names.

When everything is to your satisfaction, choose either Next or Finish. If you choose Finish, FrontPage Editor immediately generates the form page. If you choose Next, you go back to the dialog box shown in Figure 10.7 so that you can add another input type to the form, edit an input, or get rid of it (be careful of the Clear List button; it removes everything).

Go through this cycle until you have all the input types you want, and return to the dialog box shown in Figure 10.7. If you have several input types, you can change the order of presentation by using the Move Up and Move Down buttons.

If you choose Finish at this point, FrontPage Editor immediately generates the form. However, there are some refinements you can add if you want to. To do this, choose Next instead of Finish.

Finishing the Form with Presentation Options   When you use the Next button to leave the dialog box shown in Figure 10.7, you find yourself looking at another dialog box in the Form Page Wizard (see Figure 10.9).

FIGURE 10.9
The Presentation
Options dialog box
gives you control of
how some elements of
your form appear.

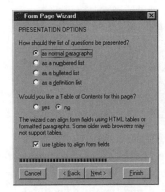

You can format your questions as one of the following:

- Normal paragraphs
- Numbered lists
- Bulleted lists
- HTML Definition lists

You can also create a table of contents for the form. Do this if your form has a lot of sections; otherwise, don't bother (and remember, if you have a form that long, you may have difficulty getting anybody to use it!).

Finally, you can automatically create tables to keep the form fields aligned. If you don't want this to happen (because browsers' handling of forms differs somewhat) clear the Use Tables to Align Form Fields check box.

When you are finished with this dialog box, you can choose Finish to generate the form immediately. However, you'll likely want to choose Next, because that's how you get to decide a very important part of the whole information-gathering process: how to save the data so that you can look at it.

Part

II

Ch

10

N O T E If you're wondering if you can edit a template-based form, you can. We'll deal with form customization a little later in this chapter. ■

Specifying Form Output Options The dialog box shown in Figure 10.10 allows you to choose how the data will be saved. You have the following three options:

- Save Results to a Web Page   This creates an HTML file in the web. Whenever a user clicks the Submit button on the form, the name/value pair of each field is added to that file. The "name" is the name of the field (such as ORDER_QTY) and the "value" is whatever data the user typed into that field on the form.
- Save Results to a Text File   This does the same as choosing Save Results to a Web Page, except that the output is in plain ASCII text. Use this if you want to import the data into another application, such as a database or spreadsheet.
- Use Custom CGI Script   This tells FrontPage that a CGI script, which you have to write, accepts the data and produces a results file.

The Enter the Base Name of the Results File text box is where you type the name of the file that stores the output (avoid using the default). Base name simply means that this is the name to which the appropriate extension is added: .HTM, .TXT, or .CGI, depending on the kind of output you asked for.

FIGURE 10.10
In this dialog box you determine the results file format.

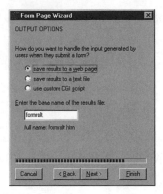

At last you can choose <u>N</u>ext, then <u>F</u>inish, and let FrontPage Editor create the form. You're not quite done, though. You'll need to edit the `This Is an Explanation...` section at the top of the form to suit your needs. You might also want to modify the form title and probably the copyright information at the bottom of the form. (Note that there's a Timestamp Bot included with the copyright data.) When you've finished, save the form page.

Getting at the Information People Send You   If you told the Wizard to save the results as a Web page, take a look at FrontPage Explorer. You'll see that you now have a "results" page. Its default Page Title is pretty cumbersome, so you should change it using the page's Page Properties dialog box.

This page stores the data sent when a user fills out the form and clicks the Submit button. All you have to do to look at the information (once somebody sends you some) is to open the results page and look at it.

If you told the Wizard to save the results as a text file, the file shows up in FrontPage Explorer. However, if you open it from Explorer, it is retrieved into whatever application handles .TXT files on your system (the default is Windows Notepad). If you chose Use Custom CGI Script, that script processes the information and stores it as the script instructs. Whatever you did to save the data, though, you now have it and can use it as needed.

Getting Started on Customized Forms

The forms that FrontPage Editor generates for you are "generic"; they're good, but they're not great. However, you can customize them extensively by editing the text, inserting images, adding or removing text boxes, and modifying the form's properties. Or you can begin from scratch and build a form from the ground up.

Before you begin, though, there's an important point about form pages. If you inspect any form, you see a dashed line surrounding it. This identifies the form boundary. If you insert a form field onto the page outside this boundary, you're actually starting a new form, so be careful.

N O T E You can customize a form created by the Form Page Wizard. Everything about customization, as described in the following paragraphs, also applies to modifying forms you've created with the Wizard. ■

Rough out your form design on paper first to get an idea of how it should look. Then open a new page, and you're ready to start. You insert and edit text and images with the standard editing and insertion tools. At this stage, creating the form is just like creating any kind of page, so go ahead and do it. But when you start adding the form fields, life is going to get a little more complicated.

So before going on to add the form fields, we need to look more closely at how the software actually handles the data returned from these fields. With the Wizard, all we had to decide was the format for the saved information or whether it should be passed to a custom CGI script. But for custom forms, we need to understand how the Save Results Bot works.

Part
II

Ch
10

Understanding the Save Results Bot

The Save Results Bot is the most common form handler used in FrontPage. This Bot takes the information submitted by a form and saves it to a file in a format you select. There are various flavors of HTML, text, and database formats.

To specify the behavior of the Save Results Bot for a particular form, right-click any field in the form, and select Form Properties from the shortcut menu. This opens the Form Properties dialog box, which allows you to set parameters for the five FrontPage form handlers.

With the Form Properties dialog box open, click the button at the right of the Form Handler list box. Select the Save Results Bot and then click the Settings...button. This opens the Settings for Saving Results of Form dialog box, which has three tabs: Results, Confirm, and Advanced.

Using the Results Tab   You use the Results tab (see Figure 10.11) as follows:

■ In the File for Results text box, enter the name of the file where the form data will be stored. Supply an absolute path name if you want to save the file outside the web but in the server (for example, C:\TEMP\RESULTS.HTM).

■ Use the File Format drop-down list box to select the format for the result file. Mark the Include Field Names in Output check box to also save the variable name and value of each field in the results file.

■ The Additional Information to Save section includes five check boxes that, when selected, provide additional information in the results file about the respondent of each submitted form.

FIGURE 10.11

Use the Results tab to configure the behavior of the Save Results Bot.

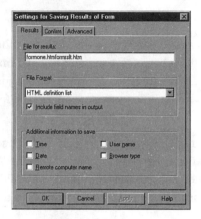

Using the Confirm Tab   In the URL of Confirmation Page text box, you can enter an optional confirmation page. A standard confirmation page is sent to the reader automatically if this text box is left blank. You optionally use the URL of Validation Failure box to send a page telling the submitter that the information submitted is invalid.

Using the Advanced Tab   You can use the Advanced tab to specify a second result file and its format (see Figure 10.12). Do this if you want the returned form data to be stored in a different format from that in the main results file, for easier processing by another application.

In the Additional Field Selection section you can specify which form fields to include in the second results file. Simply type the desired field names, separated by commas, in the order you want them to be stored. If you leave the Forms Fields to Include (Default Is All) list box blank, all fields are included in the order shown on the form in the second result file.

Using Hidden Fields   Also in the Form Properties dialog box is a provision for hidden fields. These don't show up in a browser but are sent to the form handler as a field name plus the value in that field. This is called a *name-value pair*. You create name-value pairs by choosing Add and then filling in a field name and a value for the field in the Name/Value Pair dialog box. You can modify or remove the entry once it's created.

FIGURE 10.12
Use the Advanced tab
to set up a second file
for the results
returned by a form.

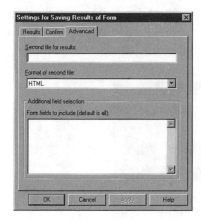

Part

II

Ch

10

Now that we've sorted all that out, we can actually go on to putting some form fields onto our page.

 N O T E The Target Frame text box deals with a framed environment. For details, see Chapter 8, "Enhancing Web Sites with FrontPage Frames." ■

Selecting Fields to Add to Your Form

To insert a field, choose Insert, Form Field, and then select the desired kind of field from the submenu that appears. The field will be inserted at the cursor position. You have seven field types, ranging from one-line text boxes to image fields. We'll explore each in turn.

T I P You can select all the form field types, except Image, from the Forms toolbar.

Adding a One-Line Text Box   The one-line text box gives you a field one line high and up to 999 characters long. You use it when a short answer is all that's needed, such as name, phone number, or e-mail address. When you select it, a text box appears on the screen inside a dotted form boundary. You can now type any text you want to label the box for its users.

 If you use the Change Style dialog box to turn on the Formatted Style within the form boundary, you can use the spacebar to pad fields and text to line them up properly. This is extremely useful for arranging text and boxes neatly. Also, you can use the Increase Indent and Decrease Indent buttons to line up blocks of fields. Finally, you can use tables inside forms to arrange your form fields.

But what about configuring the form field content? You do this by clicking the field to select it, then choosing Edit, Form Field Properties. As soon as you do, the Text Box Properties dialog box appears (see Figure 10.13).

FIGURE 10.13

Use the Text Box Properties dialog box to set up the parameters for the form field.

You set up a text box using the following steps:

1. Assign a name to the Text Box field. You do this by entering an appropriate name in the Name text box. This is the "name" part of the name/value pair associated with the field. (It has nothing to do with the prompt or question text that appears on the form itself.)

2. If you want the box to start off with specific text in it, type that text into the Initial Value text box. If you don't want an initial value, leave the text box blank.

3. To set the width of the box when it appears on the form, type a number into the Width in Characters text box.

4. If you want a password, choose the Yes option button in the Password Field section to activate the option.

Now comes a very important step: data validation. This allows you to reject spurious data at the browser or client side of the information transaction. If you do this, the server isn't burdened with validation, thereby relieving it of a lot of its data-processing load. Choose the Validate button to open the Text Box Validation dialog box (see Figure 10.14).

FIGURE 10.14

Validate your users' input before it's sent to the server.

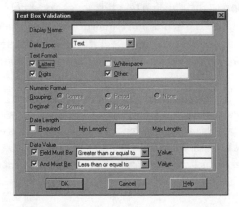

The Display Name dialog box is used to specify a name the user will see in error dialogs if the internal field name isn't the one that the user sees on the form. Make this name the same as the one the form shows for the field, and the user will know which field to correct.

The other fields here are self-explanatory; you can specify the kind of data type (no constraints, text, numeric, integer), the kinds of text allowed, the numeric format, minimum, maximum, and required data length, and the data value ranges. To get this right, you have to have a thorough understanding of the information formats you want; plan ahead, and test, test, test.

Once you've specified the validation parameters, choose OK to return to the Text Box Properties dialog box, and choose OK again to place the completed field on the form. When a user types the wrong kind of data into a field (numbers instead of text, for example) and presses the Submit button, he'll get a message asking him to make a specified correction.

Part

II

Ch

10

CAUTION

If you specify a validation failure page in the Confirm sheet of the Settings dialog box in the Forms Properties dialog box, the user doesn't see error messages if he tries to submit an incorrect form. Instead, he gets the validation failure page.

When you click a text box, sizing handles appear. You can change the size of the box, within limits, by dragging them.

Adding a Scrolling Text Box   This field lets the user type in multiple lines of text. The Scrolling Text Box Properties dialog box resembles that of the one-line text box, except that you can specify the number of lines allowed for a scrolling text box. Setting the properties for a scrolling text box is similar to setting them for a one-line text box, except that you can specify the number of lines, but no password. The validation procedure is identical.

To open a field's Properties dialog box quickly, double-click the field in the FrontPage Editor workspace.

Adding a Check Box   You use check boxes for a list of fields that can be selected or not selected (see Figure 10.15). For example, if you want to know which books on a supplied list a reader owns, she can check several fields, one, or none. You can specify the field's initial state as marked or not marked. The default value is ON, which means that if the check box's initial state is not marked, when someone does mark it, the value returned to the form handler is ON. If the box remains unmarked, a null value is returned. You use these values to figure out which fields are true or false for a given respondent.

As a check box returns only ON or null, no validation is required.

FIGURE 10.15
Use the Check Box Properties dialog box to set the returned data values.

Adding Radio Buttons   You use radio buttons instead of check boxes when the reader must give one, and only one, answer from a list. One button in a group of buttons is always selected; clicking another one selects that one instead. You have to have more than one button for the tool to be useful; a single button will always be on, which doesn't tell you much.

You use the Radio Button Properties dialog box to set up the group (see Figure 10.16). All the buttons that work together must have the same group name, which you enter in the Group Name text box. In the Value text box, type the value that the field returns when it's selected, that is, when somebody has clicked it. The Initial State can be Selected or Not Selected.

FIGURE 10.16
Radio buttons must be grouped into sets with the Radio Button Properties dialog box.

There is also a validation procedure for radio buttons; if the Data Required checkbox is marked, the user must actively check one of the radio buttons. The Display Name box serves the same purpose as with the one-line text box.

Using a Drop-Down Menu   A drop-down menu is another way to give choices to a user. The Drop-Down Menu Properties dialog box is a little more complicated than the others (see Figure 10.17).

FIGURE 10.17

You can give the user a menu by using the Drop-Down Menu field.

Set up a drop-down menu using the following steps:

1. Type a name for the menu in the Name text box.

2. Choose Add. The Add Choice dialog box appears. In the Choice text box, type the menu entry as it appears to the user.

3. If you want the form to return the value specified in the Choice text box, leave the Specify Value check box blank. If you mark it, a new, untitled box automatically opens so you can type the value that is returned instead (however, the user's menu entry will remain the same as in the Choice text box).

4. Click Selected or Not Selected to specify whether the menu entry is highlighted in the user's browser. Selected returns the value in the Choice text box; Not Selected returns a null value.

5. Choose OK to return to the Drop-Down Menu Properties dialog box. Repeat steps 2 through 4 until the menu is complete.

6. Then in the Drop-Down Menu Properties dialog box, select Yes or No to enable or disable multiple selections by the user.

7. Specify the height of the menu box. The menu behavior varies depending on the browser, so experiment.

8. Modify or rearrange the entries, if necessary, with the Modify, Move Up, and Move Down buttons.

9. Use the Validation button to go to the Validation dialog box, and set the required conditions, if any, for the data.

10. Choose OK to insert the menu field into the form.

Adding a Push Button Finally, life gets a little simpler with the Push Button Properties dialog box (see Figure 10.18). All you need do here is to assign the button a name, then type the label you want on it into the Value/Label box. Then mark the appropriate radio button to choose whether it's a Normal, Submit, or Reset button (Submit you know about; Reset clears all the form's fields). A Normal button is a generic one that does nothing until you assign a script to it. Choose OK, and the button appears on the form.

FIGURE 10.18
The Push Button Properties dialog box gives you a bit of control over the look of the Reset and Submit buttons.

Adding an Image Field   You might think that inserting an image field has the same purpose as inserting an image, but it doesn't. An image field actually does the same thing a Submit button does—no more, no less. When you insert an image field, you give it a name in its Field Properties dialog box, then edit its image properties if you like, and finally choose OK. You can't edit its link, though, because an image field cannot have a link. It's really just a fancy Submit button.

Changing the Form Properties   Changing the form's properties is the final way of customizing a form. Right-click anywhere inside the form boundaries and then select Form Properties from the shortcut menu. This opens the Form Properties dialog box, which we looked at in detail earlier.

▶ **See** "Understanding the Save Results Bot," **p. 241**

Creating a Custom Confirmation for Your Visitors

When someone visiting your site submits a form, FrontPage automatically returns to him a confirmation of what he entered. This is a bare-bones confirmation, though, and you might like something a little more decorative. You achieve this with the Confirmation Field Bot, which you use in a confirmation page you create.

To do this, first use FrontPage Editor to go to the form the visitor will use, and then double-click any field you want to confirm. Write down the field name that appears in the Name text box and click Cancel. Do this until you have a list of all the field names you're going to confirm.

Then create a new Normal page and edit it to have the look you want. At each place you want a confirmation to appear, use the following steps:

1. Choose Insert, WebBot Component. From the list box, choose the Confirmation Field Bot. The Bot Properties dialog box appears.

2. In the Name of Form Field to Confirm text box, type the name of a field from your written list and choose OK. The field name appears in your page.

3. Repeat steps 1 and 2 until you've entered all the confirmations; then save the page.

4. Go to the form you want to confirm. Right-click it, and select Form Properties. The Form Properties dialog box appears.

5. Choose the Settings button. When the Settings dialog box appears, click the Confirm tab to make the Results tab appear.

6. In the URL of Confirmation Page text box, insert the URL of the confirmation page you just created. Choose OK and then choose OK again to close the Form Properties dialog box.

7. If you want invalid input to open a validation failure page rather than to display error messages, enter the URL of the validation failure page (which you have to create) in the lower text box.

8. Save the page and test it. When you submit the form, you should see your custom confirmation (or validation failure page for invalid input) in your browser.

Understanding the Discussion Bot Form Handler

You've likely noticed that the Form Properties dialog box offers a WebBot Discussion Component as a form handler. This Bot is specifically designed to handle inputs from a discussion web, which you create using the Discussion Web Wizard in FrontPage Explorer. This is certainly the best way to set up a discussion group. However, you might want to modify some of the properties of such pages, and you do this in FrontPage Editor.

To change the look of the page, use the normal editing tools; a discussion group page is like any other except in its form handler and some of its properties. To modify the properties, right-click within any form boundary and choose Form Properties. When the Form Properties dialog box appears, choose Settings. The resulting Settings for Discussion Form Handler dialog box has two tabs: Discussion and Article.

Understanding the Discussion Tab   You use this tab to specify how the discussion web behaves in normal operation (see Figure 10.19) as follows:

■ Use the Title text box to edit the name of the discussion group. This name appears on all articles.

■ Use the Directory text box to specify the directory where FrontPage stores all the articles. This directory must be hidden.

■ Use the Table of Contents Layout section to customize the look of the TOC, which is automatically regenerated every time someone submits an article. You can modify what appears in the TOC's subject descriptions by typing field names into the Form Fields text box. You can have more than one field; just separate them with spaces. Marking the Time and Date check boxes displays the date and time of submission for each article. Marking the Remote Computer Name and User Name check boxes displays remote computer names and the usernames of the authors. Finally, you can decide if the articles appear from oldest to newest or the reverse.

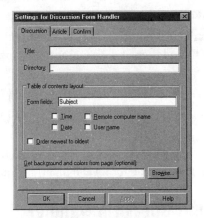

FIGURE 10.19
The Discussion tab lets you customize the group title, TOC appearance, and confirmation page.

Understanding the Article and Confirm Tabs   These are very simple. The Article tab simply establishes additional information to show up in each article. You can specify the URLs of your standard header and footer, time and date of the article's submission, and remote computer name and author name. If you want a custom confirmation or validation failure page, insert the URL of these into the appropriate boxes on the Confirm sheet.

Understanding Registration Forms

A Registration Form gives you some control over who gets into a particular web on your host. The basic procedure is this: a new user accesses a registration form stored in the root web of your site, and registers with a username and password for a particular child web of the root web. This isn't very tight security. However, it does make it unnecessary for registered users to keep entering their name into some types of form fields, because the server finds out who they are when they log on. Also, there's some assurance to others that it's really you communicating with them, and not an impostor.

Creating a Registration Form   Begin by using FrontPage Explorer to open the web for which you want to register users; when you've finished, this will be a "protected" web. After the web is open, use the following steps:

1. Choose Tools, Permissions to move to the Web Permissions dialog box.

2. Choose the Settings tab, and click the Use Unique Permissions for This Web option button. Click the Apply button, then OK.

3. In the Users tab, choose Only Registered Users Have Browse Access, then click Apply, then OK.

4. Remaining in FrontPage Explorer, open the server's root web. (All registration forms must reside in the root web to work properly, even though users are registering for a child web.)

5. With the root web still open, switch to FrontPage Editor. Choose File, New and select the User Registration template from the list box.

6. Use the instructions included with the template as a guide to modifying it. After that, change the title and heading of the page to suit the web it's for. If you want more information from the registrant, add form fields to collect it.

7. Once you have the form to your liking, right-click any form field and select Form Properties to open the Form Properties dialog box. Notice that the Form Handler is automatically set to be the Registration Bot.

8. In the Form Properties dialog box, click the Settings button. Click the Registration tab.

9. In the Registration tab's Web Name box, type the name of the protected web that the users are going to be registering for.

10. Use the Results, Confirm, and Advanced tabs, as desired, to set other parameters for the form. Choose OK.

11. Choose OK again to close the Form Properties dialog box, and save the page. The web is now set up to accept only registered users.

> **NOTE** We referred above (in step 7) to the Registration Bot's appearance in the Form Handler text box, in the Form Properties dialog box. This Bot is specifically written to handle registration forms. Don't change this setting, or the forms won't work. ■

Using the Registration Form   To register for the protected web, users have to access the root web and complete the form page for the protected web. This includes choosing a username and password. So if you have more than one protected web, you need a Registration Form for each one, and the registrants have to be able to get at these forms.

The security check is actually made at the browser level. When a user's browser contacts the URL of the page, a username and password box appears in the browser window. The user can't get into the web unless he knows both these items. Once he's in, however, all pages in that web are accessible to him, even if he leaves the web and returns. The security isn't enforced again until the browser is shut down and then restarted.

Using Templates to Create Interactive Pages

FrontPage supplies eight templates that have Bots or interactive elements installed in them. The way they use Bots and form fields gives you useful examples to follow when you're setting up the interactive parts of your site. Now that you know a lot more about how your visitors can communicate with you through your site, it's time to have a look at these types of pages. The templates are:

> **CAUTION**
>
> When you use the templates, remember to use their Form Properties to rename the files where they store their results (if applicable). Leaving the result files at their default names may cause data to be overwritten or jumbled.

■ The Guest Book template uses a scrolling text box to gather comments about a site. It sends the data with the username of the commentator to a file named GUESTLOG.HTM. This file is displayed in the lower part of the page by an Include Bot, so the visitor can see what other people had to say about the site. This page also has a Comment Bot at the top to give instructions for use, and a Timestamp Bot at the bottom. All the templates have these two Bots, so we won't bother mentioning them again.

> ▶ **See** "Using the Comment Bot," **p. 226**
> ▶ **See** "Timestamp Bot," **p. 232**

■ The Search Page template simply uses the Search Bot to find instances of a text string in the current web's public pages. The page includes two bookmarks for navigation and a section that describes how to use the query language.

> ▶ **See** "Using the Search Bot," **p. 230**

■ The Survey Form template is complex, and you'll need to customize it extensively. Its form section includes many types of form fields, and you'll learn a lot from analyzing it in detail.

■ The Table of Contents template is nothing more than a page with a Table of Contents Bot in it. Remember you don't see the real TOC unless you view the page in a browser.

■ The Employment Opportunities Page template, like the Survey, needs considerable modification before you use it. It does serve up useful examples of form fields, and it's a good example of bookmarking for navigation within a page.

■ The Feedback Form template is really an elaborated example of the Guest Book. An interesting addition is the set of four option buttons that help classify the kind of feedback being given. Inspect these buttons' properties to see how default button values are used.

■ The Confirmation Form template is a general-purpose tool for letting users know you've recorded the information they sent you. (The page header says "Feedback Confirmation," but this has nothing in particular to do with the Feedback Form.) The template uses several Confirmation Field Bots. To use it, type its name into the URL of Confirmation Page text box of the page you want confirmed.

▶ **See** "Creating a Custom Confirmation for Your Visitors,"**p. 248**

■ The Product or Event Registration template (not to be confused with the Registration Form) is a straightforward form that lets users tell you that they want to register for an event or a product. As a practical application, you could use it alongside the Seminar Schedule template to register participants for a series of presentations.

▶ **See** "Creating a Seminar Schedule with Lecture Abstracts," **p.214**

Creating Your Home Page with the Personal Home Page Wizard

You already know that a home page is the core of any Web site, offering its owner the ability to communicate his personal interests, academic pursuits, employment history, or simply his likes and dislikes, to a (potentially) global audience. Home pages are also places for experimentation, where people publicize their most recent technical or artistic projects.

However, while the content of each home page varies according to the personality and interests of its author, the style and formatting of most home pages conform to a (more or less) accepted norm. For example, most have large-font, boldface, centered titles that often incorporate the authors' names. They usually contain a few images, but the core of a home page is often a hyperlink list that leads visitors to the author's favorite Web sites or Internet resources. Also, comment forms are frequently included so that visitors can tell the site's owner what they think of it.

Since home pages have such a consistent format, FrontPage has designed a Personal Home Page Wizard that helps you build a basic home page. You select items from a list of common page elements which the Wizard turns into a "plain-vanilla" design. You then customize this to provide for the special needs of yourself and your visitors.

Getting started is easy. Since the Wizard creates the INDEX.HTM file when it saves the new home page, you should begin by using FrontPage Explorer to create an Empty Web. Then with that web open, go to FrontPage Editor.

You start the Personal Home Page Wizard by choosing File, New, and selecting Home Page Wizard from the list box. The first thing you see is the Personal Home Page Wizard dialog box, where you can pick the major categories of your home page (see Figure 10.20).

FIGURE 10.20

In this dialog box you can decide the overall "flavor" of your home page: business, personal, or a mix.

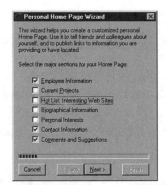

Mark the ones you want, and choose Next. The route you take from here will vary according to the categories you picked. For example, if you selected Employee Information, you get a dialog box where you can specify what information to include about each employee. You'd add exact descriptions of job functions later, during customization of the page. Later in the Wizard you can choose how to present information—in bulleted, numbered, or definition lists. The whole process is quick and easy, and with all you've learned this far, you won't have any trouble completing the page or customizing it afterward.

From Here...

In this chapter, you've learned a lot about the interactive side of the Web, the side that turns it into a vast forum for the interchange of ideas, information, and even some wisdom. It's a lot to digest, and you'll likely want to take some time for experimentation. When you're ready to go on, see the following chapters:

- Chapter 11, "Working Directly with HTML," which shows you how to edit HTML directly in FrontPage Editor, and how you use the HTML Markup tool to add HTML to your pages.

- Chapter 12, "Integrating HTML Style Sheets," which shows you how to use this new technique for developing and maintaining a consistent and easily modified look for an entire site or for a set of pages.

- Chapter 13, "Designing for the Netscape Family of Browsers," where you get details on the strengths, weaknesses, and quirks of the currently dominant Web browser.

Part
II

Ch
10

## CHAPTER 11

Working Directly with HTML

Up to now, you've dealt with FrontPage in purely automated form: telling FrontPage what you want to accomplish and letting the program do the hard part. And indeed, the point of FrontPage is to keep you from having to code HTML yourself. Still there are times when you want really fine control. FrontPage lets you do that, too. ■

HTML

What HMTL is, and why you may have to deal with it for more complex Web layouts.

Coding by Hand

How to use FrontPage Editor's HTML View to put in code by hand.

Markup Command

Certain FrontPage features can make even this go faster. How to use the HTML Markup Command.

Other Editors

You don't have to use only hand-coding: several other HTML Editors can create ASCII text from HTML code.

Importing HTML

How to bring HMTL code from other files into the FrontPage Editor.

Understanding HTML

Hypertext Markup Language (HTML)is a subset of the Standard Generalized Markup Language, a standard for typesetting. When you look at an HTML file in an editor, it is plain text. However, the ASCII includes special embedded command codes that the browser understands. The commands give you control of how your page looks, to some extent: what is bold, italic, and centered, or the size of the type.

HTML is not complex. Coding in HTML is just as easy as the old codes of early word processors; it's also just as tedious when you forget the closing code of matched pairs, such as bold and italic.

The codes to control the look of the page are always embedded in angled or pointed brackets (the symbols for less than and more than: < >). Some HTML commands are paired; others are not. The commands or codes are called *tags*.

HTML is understood by all browsers and is the reason the Web works the way it does. Even an all-text browser can understand the simplest text tags of HTML, but when you get into more complex ones, such as frames, things get a little more program-dependent.

However, you don't have to know any HTML to get started with FrontPage. The FrontPage Editor generates the HTML code for you as you build your page. If you need to fine-tune some aspects, however, you can get to the actual HTML code: You can use an ASCII editor such as Notepad or an HTML editor such at HotDog, or you can simply use FrontPage Editor. We'll look at all these options, but first let's see how you can enter direct HTML code in FrontPage Editor.

To do this, first call up the page in FrontPage Editor. FrontPage Editor shows you the page as it looks in a browser. You can look at the HTML code by using View, HTML. The View HTML window will let you choose the Generated option to look at the code that FrontPage Editor will produce when you save the active page (see Figure 11.1). You can also choose to have Editor color-code the HTML parts as opposed to the plain text (the part the Web visitor will see). That way you can easily see what part is HTML code, and what is plain text.

You can use this option to look at HTML code from an already saved file. You can also look at the HTML code that FrontPage Editor reads on a file you have been editing, by choosing the Original button. When you are through examining the code, choose Close.

You can use the View HTML window to make changes, too, which will be shown in the section "Hand-Coding in FrontPage Editor's HTML View" below.

FrontPage Editor gives you all the tools you need to create professional-quality Web pages. Indeed, you may find it does everything you need.

FIGURE 11.1

You can display the generated HTML code using the View menu. FrontPage puts in the !DOCTYPE line for the server; that line is ignored by browsers.

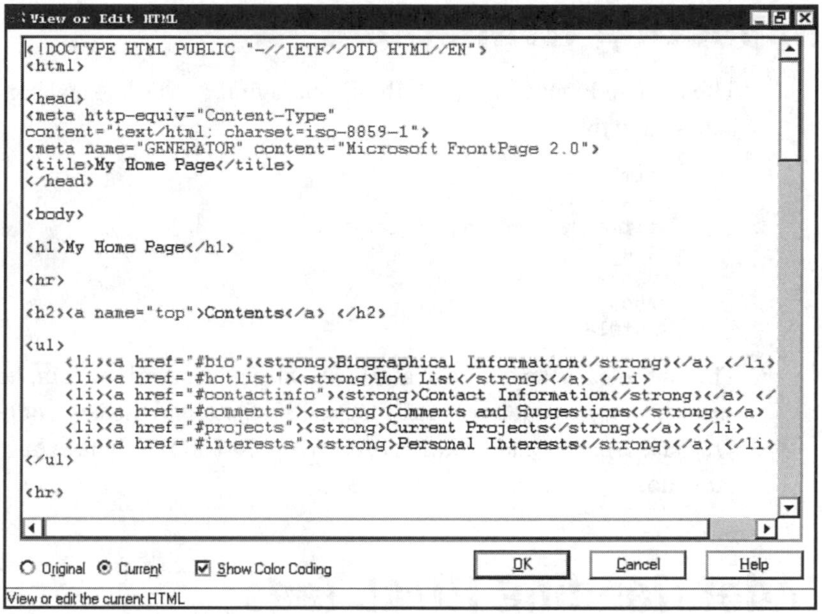

The only problem is that FrontPage Editor's HTML view is too limited and cumbersome for any but the most basic insertions and changes. The HTML Markup Bot helps here, but you may still occasionally want to do hands-on composition or editing of the source file, using either a generic text editor or a specialized HTML editor.

The main thing to remember is that the resulting file must be read and saved as plain-vanilla ASCII text. So if you are really brave, you can edit HTML code with any ASCII text editor, even Windows Notepad. Heavy-duty editing with Notepad is only for the truly stout of heart, but to fix a line or two quickly it does as well as the FrontPage Editor HTML view.

Be aware that if you edit an existing FrontPage HTML file with another editor, and there are WebBots embedded, the finished file may behave in strange ways.

Furthermore, if you create a page with a third-party editor, be sure to bring the resulting code into FrontPage Explorer with the Import command for best results. However, if your imported page has HTML code not supported by FrontPage, it may get stripped out, or the appearance of the page in FrontPage Editor may be unpredictable. Remember that the safest way to insert unsupported code is with the HTML Markup Bot, which won't change, syntax check, or strip your code.

We'll look at some alternative HTML editors in the section "Using Other HTML Editors."

Inspecting HTML Code

The code in Figure 11.1 (with the FrontPage !Doctype line and some blank lines removed) is basically this:

```
<html>
<head>
<title>My Home Page</title>
</head>
<body>
</body>
</html>
```

This is the basic structure of all HTML files no matter how complex they get. The tags `<head>`, `<body>`, and `<html>` start tagged sections, and those sections are closed with `</head>`, `</body>`, and `</html>` respectively. Not all HTML tags have to be closed, but most do.

Understanding HTML Tags

HTML pages enclose instructions to the browser in angle brackets, as mentioned above. These instructions are called tags. The tags do not show in the browser window; they simply instruct the browser how to display the text. When you insert tags, it doesn't matter whether they are capitalized or not; however, in practice, capitalizing them makes them easier to find later for additions and changes.

For most tags, you have to include a close tag. Close tags always have the forward slash before the tag name after the first angle bracket.

Every HTML page begins with the HTML tag `<html>`, and ends with the close tag `</html>`. These two tags tell the browser where the page begins and ends.

Understanding the Head/Body Structure

In between the HTML tags, every page has two sections: the head and the body. Both sections must be defined for the browser to display the page properly. The head is everything between the `<head>` and `</head>` tags; the body is anything between the `<body>` and `</body>` tags.

In the head section of Figure 11.1, you'll notice that there's a line that says, `<title>My Home Page</title>`. The browser will display the words between those title tags in the title bar of the browser's display. This is an important consideration: While the average visitor won't pay much attention to the title bar while visiting, text within the title tag is what browsers usually save with a bookmark or "Favorites." If you do title your HTML document "My Home Page," that's how it will look in a bookmark file or in a World Wide Web catalog such as Lycos. Therefore, choose your title text carefully; it's probably how you'll be recalled for future visits.

Other codes can also appear in the head section of an HTML document. For example, you could use a link tag here, to define a relationship between the document and yourself as the owner or manager of the document. Your link could look like this:

```
<LINK rev=made href="mailto:yourid@youraddress">.
```

Another tag you may want to put in the Head section is the <meta> tag. The Meta tag is a generic tag; you can use it to embed information about your document that does not fit in the other HTML tags. It's usually used to give the page keywords for indexing in catalogs. An example would be

```
<meta keywords= coffee, food, retail>
```

Everything else in the HTML document is part of the body; this is enclosed in the <body> and </body> tags.

Other Interesting Tags

There are other important tags to use in HTML. Some must be paired as the tags above are, such as:

<I> and </I> to begin and end italicized text

<B> and </B> to begin and end bold text

<BIG> and </BIG> for large type

<A HREF=xxxx> and </A> for a hypertext link to another file or a bookmark within this file

<Address> and </Address> to begin and end a formatted section for contact information

<ul> and </ul> for unnumbered lists

<dl> and </dl> for definition lists

<dt> and </dt> for defined terms in definition lists

<dd> and </dd> for the definitions in definition lists

<em> and </em> for emphasized text

<strong> and </strong> for extra emphasis

<H#> and </H#> for headlines, usually from H1 (the largest) to ' (the smallest)

Part
II

Ch
11

Others do not have to be paired, such as:

<IMG SRC=xxxxx> for placing an image

<li> for list items

<P> for a paragraph break: a line break and a blank line

 for a line break, but no blank line

<HR> for a rule between sections

These are just a very few of the tags in HTML, but they are enough to get you started.

Hand-coding in FrontPage Editor's HTML View

You're bound to run into HTML tags that are new and neat, and you'll want to include them in your FrontPage webs. If you were really brave, you could insert these tags in your page in a text editor like Notepad. But there's no need to do that with FrontPage Editor's HTML view.

The HTML view can be used as a simple text editor. Simply place your cursor at the spot you want to change, and type, cut, or paste as you need to. This is very convenient: You can copy text from one file and paste it into another using the HTML view in this way.

If you have the Show Color Coding box checked, you will notice that as soon as you put in a beginning angle bracket, everything after that changes color until you add the closing bracket. The View or Edit HTML screen helps you to be sure you haven't left off important brackets this way.

> **CAUTION**
> The View HTML window as of this writing has no search and replace, no spell-checking, nor any other of the features available to you in FrontPage Editor. It's a very limited text editor. Future editions may add these capabilities.

For example, suppose you want a section of your page to appear to the user in a non-proportional font: a set of instructions for example. Using FrontPage Editor's HTML view, you would position your cursor after the <body> tag, press return, and enter the <pre> tag. Type in your text, and end it with the </pre> tag, as in Figure 11.2. When you switch back to FrontPage Editor, you will see the results, as in Figure 11.3.

FIGURE 11.2

Using the HTML view of FrontPage Editor, you can insert tags and text yourself. This <pre> tag means that the text will show exactly as you type it, including all spaces and line breaks.

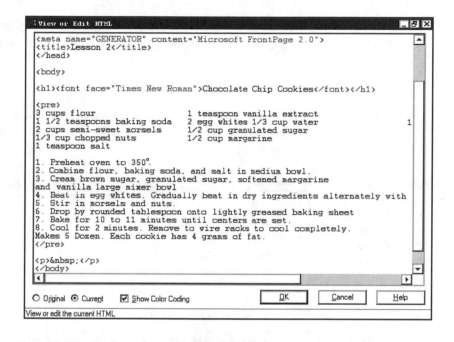

FIGURE 11.3

This is how preformatted text appears to the browser.

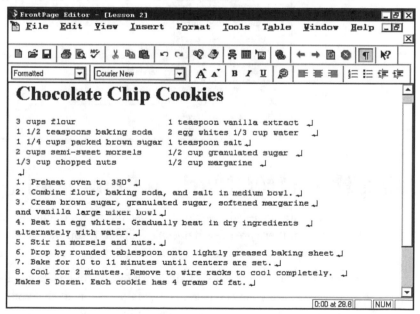

Another example of using the HTML view might be to include a background sound for Microsoft Internet Explorer users. In the HTML view, put your cursor after the `<body>` tag. Insert the tag:

```
<BGSOUND SRC="htttp://mysite/mydirectory/mmmmmm.wav">
```

where "`mmmmmm.wav`" is the name of the sound you want to play, as in Figure 11.4. Then when Microsoft Internet Explorer users see your page, the sound file will play. Netscape will ignore the `<BGSOUND>` tag.

FIGURE 11.4

You can use the View and Edit HTML window to insert a background sound for Microsoft Internet Explorer.

Using the HTML Markup Command

FrontPage Editor gives you the ability to use the most commonly employed HTML extensions, but there are a few it doesn't support. If you want to use those unsupported HTML tags in your page, you could edit them into your page using the HTML view.

But there's an easier way. The HTML Markup Command lets you insert whatever HTML code you want into your web page. For example, suppose that you need to use the Netscape columns extensions. FrontPage Editor doesn't support these columns, so you turn to the HTML Markup Command. Choose Insert, HTML Markup. The HMTL Markup Dialog Box appears.

Now write the code for the columns. When you've finished, choose OK. At the insertion point FrontPage Editor shows a small yellow icon with a <?> in it. All you have to do to get rid of the code is to delete the yellow container. If you want to modify the code, select the container and choose <u>E</u>dit, Properties or Alt + Enter. The HTML Markup dialog box with the existing code appears.

This is the best to include code that FrontPage doesn't yet support. This is because FrontPage Editor has some limited syntax checking. When you enter HTML code in the HTML View, if FrontPage doesn't understand the code, it will sometimes substitute what it thinks you meant instead. This can lead to some unpredictable results. When you enter with Markup Command, it leaves it as you typed it, regardless.

However, note that the syntax checking is limited. Sometimes FrontPage Editor doesn't catch non-standard HTML. If you see unexpected results in the finished page, suspect bad HTML that the syntax checker missed.

Using the HTML Markup Command to Insert Existing HTML

You may find some HTML code that you'd like to include in your page, but it's complicated and long, and you don't want to type it in. (An example would be some interesting HTML in a site you've visited. Be sure to ask permission of the original author first.) But if you copy the code to the Windows Clipboard and paste it into FrontPage Editor's workspace, you see only the literal code, not its output. To get around this, just use the HTML Markup Command. Paste the code into the HTML Markup dialog box and choose OK.

N O T E Though the inserted HTML may be supported by FrontPage, you still get the yellow question mark flag. This signals the presence of HTML Markup. If you want, you can use the Annotation command to document the content of these yellow flags, so you remember what you did there. ■

Although FrontPage supports most of the current HTML codes, the extensions are forever becoming more diverse and powerful. By using the HTML Markup Command, you can include all the newest features in your FrontPage web pages.

View or Edit HTML does do some basic syntax-checking. If you make a mistake or two, the View or Edit HTML will reject the errors and do its best to fix them, by adding missing close tags or replacing an unknown tag with what it assumes you wanted.

FIGURE 11.5
Unrecognized tags appear as question boxes in the Editor view. You can edit the HTML code directly by clicking on the question mark box.

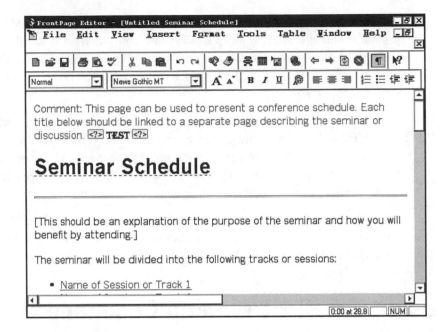

Unknown tags appear as question marks in the Editor screen, as in Figure 11.5. Clicking on the question mark will let you edit the questionable code.

Using Other HTML Editors

With the cautions given in the section "Understanding HTML" held firmly in mind, you may still want to use another HTML editor. Some are simple, others do a great deal of hand-holding. Some of the better ones are free, some cost under $50.

The more sophisticated ones verify your code for conformity to HTML standards, as well as for syntax errors such as tags missing from tag pairs. Others warn you about elements that give indigestion to common browsers. Mind you, these validation checks have nothing to do with whether a page makes sense to humans; they ensure only that it makes sense to a browser.

Some of these validation checkers are tools you can download and use yourself. Others are online on the World Wide Web; in this latter case, you send the URL of your page to the validation checker. It calls the page, checks it, and sends you back a list (a short list, we hope) of things it didn't like about the page's HTML code. A list of such checkers can be found in the note below. Now, let's look at some specific HTML editors you may want to consider.

ON THE WEB

http://www.yahoo.com/Computers_and_Internet/Software/Data_Formats/HTML/ Validation_Checkers/ is Yahoo's site that has resources for validation checking.

WebThing

WebThing is a grand 32-bit HTML editor and workshop. Its best feature is that you can import RTF files, and have WebThing's mailbox covert them to text, tables, or an outline automatically, as in Figure 11.6. WebThing has an excellent Help file. The fee for the software? Doing something optimistic and kind for the world. You can get it at **http:// www.arachnoid.com/lutusp/webthing.htm**; the file is about 2M compressed.

FIGURE 11.6
At the click of a button, an RTF file can become HTML in WebThing.

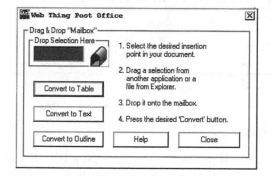

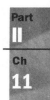

Almost Reality

Almost Reality aims to be the freeware HTML editor that supports all the HTML 3.0 code, and it has all the features of an expensive editor. Almost every tag and code in HTML has either a menu command or a button in this editor, as you can see in Figure 11.7, making everything very easy. Still in beta, the latest version is at **http://www.lm.com/~pdixon/ index.html**, and is about 2M to download.

FIGURE 11.7

Almost Reality tries to make all HTML coding point and click.

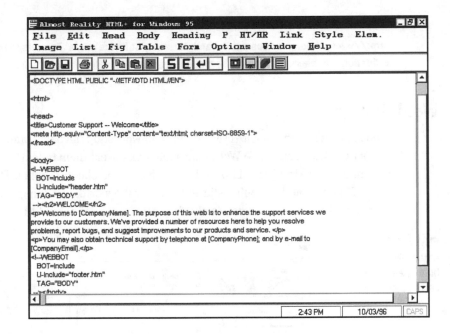

DerekWare HTML Author

Another Freeware editor, this one is notable for the New Page Editor, which makes background colors, images, and sounds incredibly easy to insert. The download file is about half a megabyte, and can be found at **http://shell.masterpiece.com/derek/**.

ReVol

A nineteen-dollar shareware editor, this one's most helpful feature is the Import Wizard. The Import Wizard helps you to import a text document and format it into HTML code, helping you to convert a spreadsheet or database file into an HTML document, If you need to convert a file listing from an FTP site, the Import Wizard can help you, as it can also read index files, the file created by some UNIX systems to list all the files in a certain directory. In fact if you need to import any text file and format it, the Import Wizard is the place to start. ReVoL Web Worker Version 1.2a, about 3M to download, is available at **http://webzone.ccacyber.com/www/jlister/revol.htm**.

HotDog

HotDog is a nice shareware HTML editor, giving you quick ways to insert lots of code. With a plethora of tools and menus (see Figure 11.8), it aims to make HTML code as painless as word processing. For thirty dollars it can make your life a lot easier; the Help file even has some cut-and-paste code for neat tricks like tables with different-sized cells. You can get the 4M download file at **http://www.sausage.com** for a thirty-day demo.

FIGURE 11.8
HotDog gives you a wide range of tools for modifying code.

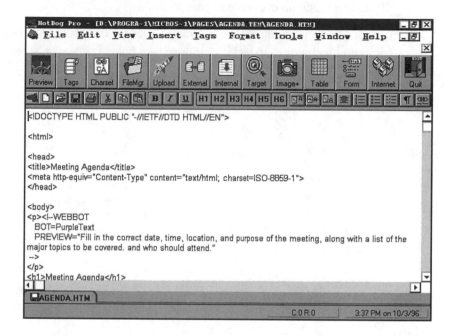

You don't really need to validate the code produced by FrontPage Editor as long as you haven't tinkered with it. The pages you make with Editor will be understood by browsers, within the limits of the extensions you used (such as frames) and whether the browser supports the extensions. However, if you've modified the code at all, it is a very good idea to run it through a validation checker to look for syntax errors, or an HTML editor that does the same.

N O T E Sometimes, even if you pass a valid page through a validator, you will get an error. The key is to be sure you have selected the correct version of HTML in the validation check. If you put HTML 3.0 code through a validation check on HTML 2.0, you'll get errors. ■

From Here...

You've absorbed a lot of information in this section, and in doing so, you've acquired many of the tools you need to create good Web pages. But there's more to a Web page than mere mechanics. To get on the Web with some measure of style and class, you need to understand some more technical aspects. Look to the following Chapters for further ways to enhance your Web:

Part
II

Ch
11

Chapter 12, "Integrating HTML Style Sheets," shows you how to have all your pages singing off the same sheet of music. With style sheets, your visitor will see your distinctive touch on every file of your Web site.

Chapter 13, "Designing for the Netscape Family of Browsers," shows you the specific tricks and techniques to make your page take full advantage of Netscape extensions.

Chapter 14, "Front Page on the Net," gives you an inside look at the things Microsoft Internet Explorer can do that no other browser can, and how you can control it.

Designing for WWW Browsers

## CHAPTER 12

Integrating HTML Style Sheets

Microsoft's Internet Explorer 3.0 is the first browser to support style sheets. However, because the tool is so useful, Netscape and Spyglass will certainly be adding the capability to future editions of their browsers. Style sheets are important, from the page designer's point of view, because they provide a shorthand for page formatting, much in the same way that styles do for the major word processors.

FrontPage Editor 97 doesn't support creation of style sheets; that is, there isn't a style sheet tool or command. However, adding style sheet functionality to your Web pages is certainly possible within FrontPage Editor, and you'll doubtless find reasons for doing so. ■

What style sheets are

Find out about these new Web tools and their syntax.

Understanding the different types of style sheets

Use inline, embedded, and linked style sheets with your pages and your site, using FrontPage Editor's editing tools.

Cascading style sheets

Understand the hierarchy of different style sheet levels.

Style Sheet Properties

Use this reference list to compose your own style sheets.

What Are Style Sheets?

A style sheet is a template you create yourself; it embeds special commands within HTML formatting tags to specify the appearance of a Web page, or pages. Style sheets provide:

■ More complex formatting capabilities, especially greater control over text appearance and placement. These formatting effects can be achieved without complex and awkward HTML workarounds.

■ More flexible and simpler control of the formatting within pages or across multiple pages of a site. You don't need to turn tags on and off to change the look of individual page elements, and the reduced number of tags makes your HTML code much easier to read and follow.

■ Fast changes to the formatting of a page or pages, by changing a few parameters in a linked style sheet. This lets you make major changes to the appearance of a whole site, without the drudgery of modifying every page the site contains.

■ Greater potential for sophisticated page design, based on a style sheet standard which most (and perhaps eventually all) browsers will be able to recognize. There will be a much lower incidence of proprietary tags, so that Web authors won't have to allow for the quirks of particular browsers when designing pages.

The implementation of style sheets in Internet Explorer 3.0 is that of the World Wide Web Consortium's working draft on the enhancement. You can access this at

http://www.w3.org/pub/WWW/TR/WD-css1.html

You can use style sheets on your Web pages without fear of blowing up non-supporting browsers; when the parameters are properly embedded within tags, a non-supporting browser simply ignores them and applies its default formatting. You can also use cascading styles sheets, which is just a way of using multiple styles to determine how your page looks. A style sheet-supporting browser follows a set hierarchy to determine which formatting elements gct displayed and which don't.

With IE 3.0, you have three different approaches to employing style sheets:

■ Linked style sheets: Your regular Web pages link to such a sheet (this is actually a file with a .css extension) which determines how they'll look. With this method, you can change the look of many pages by changing only the style sheet file.

■ Embedded style sheets: Here, you actually insert a style sheet into a particular page. Changing a parameter modifies the look of the complete page.

■ Inline styles: These modify the behavior of a single tag, a group of tags, or a block of information on a single page.

You can mix these approaches on a single page, too — using one doesn't preclude the use of others. The rules of precedence for the different style sheets are described later in this chapter, in "Understanding Cascading."

As an example of the power of these techniques, Figures 12.1 and 12.2 display the same document, styled with two different linked style sheets.

FIGURE 12.1
This page, from the Microsoft style sheet demo page, shows a document treated one way.

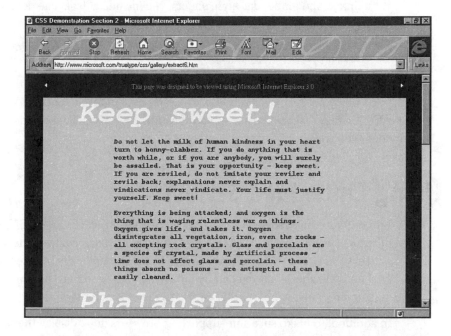

FIGURE 12.2
The same document, with an entirely different treatment.

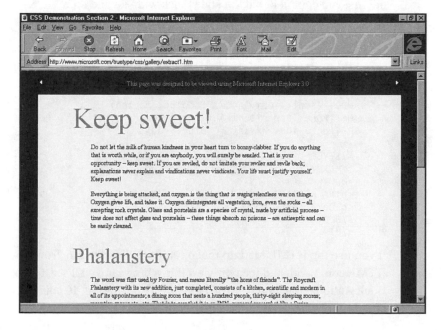

Understanding Style Sheet Syntax

With linked and embedded style sheets, you include at least one definition of the style. The style definition format is as follows:

```
<ANY HTML TAG>{property1 name: property1 value; property2 name: property 2
➥value}</ANY HTML TAG>.
```

Note that we use curly braces to set off the definition itself. Within these braces, there can be as many properties as you like. The style definitions are enclosed in the <STYLE> </STYLE> tags. Where these are placed within the HTML file depends on the kind of style sheet you're using.

Using Embedded Styles

Embedding a style sheet is straightforward. Insert a <STYLE> </STYLE> tag pair into the document between the <HEAD> tags. This styling block controls the appearance of the entire web page in which it's embedded. IE 3.0 automatically registers the MIME media type for style sheets, so you can include the TYPE="text/css" parameter within the style tags to direct non-supporting browsers to disregard the style sheet.

In addition, to make sure non-supporting browsers don't display the text of the style definitions, you comment out the style block with <!- and ->.

Here's an example of what it looks like:

```
<HTML>
<HEAD><title>Some Styles</title>
<STYLE TYPE="text/css">
<!-
BODY {font: 10pt "Arial"; color: maroon}
H1 {font: 24pt "Book Antiqua"; color: blue}
P {font: 10pt "Arial"; color: red}
->
</STYLE>
</HEAD>
<BODY>
<h1>A HEADING </h1>
<p>Some Text</p>
</BODY>
</HTML>
```

If you use the HTML Markup tool or edit this directly into FrontPage Editor with the <u>V</u>iew <u>H</u>TML command, and then preview it in a browser, you'll see a 24 point blue heading in Book Antiqua font, and the words "Some Text" in Arial, 10 point, in red. (The style sheet effects don't appear in FrontPage Editor.)

T I P You would assign styles to the <BODY> tag to set the overall appearance of your page. These effects take place globally. Then, to set individual styles for particular elements, you define these in the rest of the <STYLE> block.

N O T E FrontPage Editor exhibits a peculiarity when incorporating style sheets into the HTML of a page. Strictly speaking, the <STYLE> block should be within the <HEAD> tags. However, when you save the page, the style block is moved to sit right after the <BODY> tag. This appears to have no effect on how the sheets work. You also see Markup Bot icons on the page representing the added HTML; if you insert text or other items anywhere above these icons, the styling won't affect those items. ■

The values inside the curly braces next to the H1 define the style for all Heading 1 headings in the page; the values inside the curly braces next to the P do the same for all paragraph (normal) text in the page. You can change the global look of the page by changing the values within the curly braces. A little later in this chapter you can see a table listing all the IE 3.0-supported properties you can use in a style sheet.

Using Inline Styles

You use inline styles to set the properties of a section of a Web page, distinct from globally. To do this, you embed them within the tag itself. To set the color and attributes of a section of text, you'd use this syntax:

```
< P STYLE ="color:green;font-style:italic">
```

This text is green and in italics.

```
</P>
```

As you can figure out for yourself, the result is green, italicized text. Note that curly braces aren't used here, but quotation marks, to define the properties list.

Note also that if an inline style differs from an embedded style, or from a linked style, the inline style is used.

Sometimes you want to change the look of a large block of a page, and inserting the same properties for each tag within that block would be tedious and error-prone. For this, you use the <DIV> tag. For example:

```
<DIV STYLE = "font-size: 14pt; color: red">
. . . block of HTML code . . .
</DIV>
```

This makes a global color and font size change to all the text contained within the <DIV> tags. In other words, if you have several <P> sections and a <UL> section or two, you don't have to set inline styles for each tag. However, if you do add an inline style to one tag of that larger block, the style will override the <DIV>-defined style and apply the different appearance to the part enclosed in that tag (only).

Grouping Tags

Sometimes you want several different tags styled the same way. You can define the styles individually for each tag in the embedded style section, but there's a shortcut. If you wanted formatted and normal text to have the same look, for example, you'd write

```
P PRE {font-style: italic; color: blue}
```

and this would affect both kinds of text.

Using Linked Style Sheets

To set this up, create a file with the style definitions using the same techniques you use for embedded styles. Save the file with a .css extension, and link to it from the page that is to have that style. In practice, if you wanted all the pages in your Web to have the same style, you'd link each one to the style sheet. The syntax is as follows:

```
<HEAD>
<TITLE> Title of Page </TITLE>
<LINK REL=STYLESHEET HREF="http://www.myplace.com/mystyles.css" TYPE="text/
css">
</HEAD>
```

Internet Explorer does not yet support links to multiple style sheets, so you can have only one style sheet link per page.

Understanding Cascading

If you use several style sheets whose definitions conflict, the results are settled by "cascading." This means in practice that a page author's styles will take precedence over readers' style sheets, which in turn take precedence over the browser defaults. Within each member of this hierarchy, inline styles take precedence, followed by embedded styles, followed by linked styles. Note, however, that Internet Explorer does not yet support reader style sheets, and with this, browser linked style sheets override all embedded <STYLE> blocks.

Style Sheet Properties

The style sheet properties supported by Internet Explorer 3.0 are shown in Table 12.1.

Table 12.1	**Internet Explorer 3.0-supported properties**		
Attribute	**Description**	**Values**	**Example**
font-size	Sets text size	points (pt) inches (in) centimeters (cm)pixels (px)	{font-size:12pt}
font-family	Sets typeface	typeface name	{font-family: font family name courier}
font-weight	Sets type thickness	extra-light light demi-light medium demi-bold bold extra-bold	{font-weight: bold}
font-style	Italicizes text	normal italic	{font-style: italic}
line-height	Sets the distance between baselines	points (pt) inches (in) centimeters (cm) pixels (px) percentage (%)	{line-height: 24pt}
color	Sets color of text	color-name RGB triplet	{color: blue}
text-decoration	Underlines or highlights text	underline italic line-through none	{text-decoration: underline}
margin-left	Sets distance from left edge of page	points (pt) inches (in) centimeters (cm) pixels (px)*	{margin-left: 1in}

Part

III

Ch

12

continues

Table 12.1 Continued

Attribute	Description	Values	Example
margin-right	Sets distance from right edge of page	points (pt) inches (in) centimeters (cm) pixels (px)*	{margin-right: 1in}
margin-top	Sets distance from top edge of page	points (pt) inches (in) centimeters (cm) pixels (px)*	{margin-top: -20px}
text-align	Sets justification	left center right	{text-align: right}
text-indent	Sets distance from left margin	points (pt) inches (in) centimeters (cm) pixels (px)*	{text-indent: 0.5in}
background	Sets background images or colors	URL, color-name RGB triplet	{background: #33CC00}

The named colors you can use are:

black	silver	gray	white
maroon	red	purple	fuschia
green	lime	olive	yellow
navy	blue	teal	aqua

T I P To place an image in a style sheet, specify the URL in parentheses:

{background: URL (http://www.myplace.com/graphics/books.gif)}

N O T E Internet Explorer 3.0 interpreted the margin element incorrectly in some cases. This has been fixed in Internet Explorer 3.01. For more information on making margins appear correctly in both browser versions, go to:

http://www.microsoft.com/workshop/author/howto/css-f.htm

and click the link called "Updated Margin Usage in Style Sheets." ■

From Here...

This chapter completes most of our work on basic page design and layout. Now you have a choice of several directions:

Part IV, "Creating and Adapting Graphics with Microsoft Image Composer," is the place to go if you want detailed information on using this powerful graphics package to develop your own graphics, or customize existing ones.

Part V, "Integrating Active Content Into Your Web Site," explores the exciting new software technologies of ActiveX, VBScript and JavaScript, Java applets, and the Virtual Reality Modeling Language.

Part VI, "Building and Managing a Web Site," shows you how to integrate the pages you create into a sophisticated, well-organized Web site that will be the envy of your neighbors in cyberspace.

Part III

Ch 12

Designing for the Netscape Family of Browsers

To see and interact with your Webs, each of your readers will use a World Wide Web browser. Technically called a client, a browser is a program that displays HTML pages and, increasingly, other types of documents as well. The most famous browser is Netscape Navigator, usually abbreviated to just Netscape.

Still, Netscape isn't the only browser out there. Microsoft Internet Explorer, for example, is also a popular browser, and many others also exist. As a Web designer, you have no choice but to care about all these different packages, because some of them have quirks, or allow some proprietary codes that force you to consider how to design for the greatest number of people. As one major example, consider that, at the time of this writing, Netscape supported HTML frames; not all browsers do. If you insist on using frames and you don't provide non-frame code, not all users will find your pages usable. Similarly, not all browsers support tables, but those that don't are disappearing from view.

The Web browsers that are being developed today have ever-expanding capabilities. This is great for the Internet surfer who is willing to give up lots of hard drive space in order to have all the browsers and all the capabilities, but it makes the Web designer's job much more challenging. All browsers support the minimum HTML 2.0 specifications. Beyond that, they each branch out into different areas of technology, and each browser offers different plug-ins, add-ons, and HTML enhancements. Web designers have to decide of which of these enhancements and plug-ins they want to take advantage. This chapter focuses on Web design specific to Netscape Navigator. ■

 TIP Don't try to take advantage of every add-on and HTML enhancement around—it will make your life difficult, and your Web pages cluttered.

Viewing Your Pages in Netscape

Currently, Netscape is the most popular browser, with an estimated 50 percent market share. There are two different versions of Netscape: Netscape Navigator and Netscape Navigator Gold. The difference between the two is that Gold contains an editing feature in addition to being just a browser. For the purpose of Web design, you can consider the two versions identical. Because of Netscape's popularity, there is a huge amount of documentation and information online (at **http:\\www.netscape.com**) about designing for Netscape, both on the Netscape Web site and on other independent Web sites.

Just like Internet Explorer, Netscape Navigator supports almost everything: forms, tables, imagemaps, frames, Java, JavaScript, and a whole lot more. Netscape also uses a technology known as plug-ins. Plug-ins are basically tools developed by companies other than Netscape Communications that "plug in" to Netscape. These tools aren't launched as an external viewer, they are integrated right into Netscape, and they greatly expand the capabilities of the browser. Currently, there are nearly 100 different plug-ins available for free, and they allow a range of new possibilities from better graphics parsing to incorporating Microsoft Excel spreadsheets into HTML documents. Some of the more prominent plug-ins include Adobe's Acrobat Reader, NCompass' ActiveX, and Macromedia's Shockwave.

One of Netscape's prime advantages right now is its built-in support of Java and JavaScript. These two programming languages allow users of all different levels to create interactive content for the Web. Users all over the Internet are taking advantage of it. If you want to design fabulous Web pages that look impressive in Netscape, you may want to consider including some JavaScript, which is really easy to learn. Java is more difficult, but also worth the effort, as you can see from Silicon Graphics' Web site in Figure 13.1.

One of the most important features of Netscape is its frames support. This is extremely helpful since FrontPage lets you design your pages with frames. Frames are not yet supported in all browsers, but many Web sites are incorporating frames, because they are a great way of keeping people at your site while simultaneously letting them explore other sites. If you want to design a page with frames, you can do so while ensuring that your page still looks good in other browsers that don't support frames. Frames also allow you to keep some information static, and always on screen, without having to be constantly reloaded. This is great for company banners and navigational imagemaps. Figure 13.2 shows a great example of frame usage in Netscape.

FIGURE 13.1
At Silicon Graphics' Java-enabled site, moving the pointer over the menu results in highlighted items.

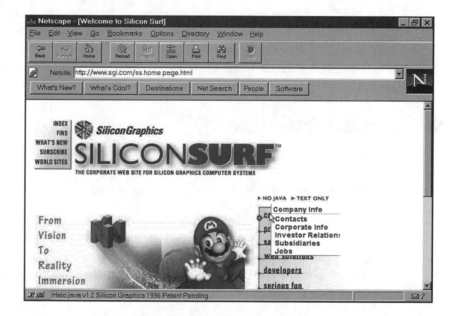

FIGURE 13.2
The Sharrow Advertising Web site has frames for a navigation bar, the date, the company name, and a main frame.

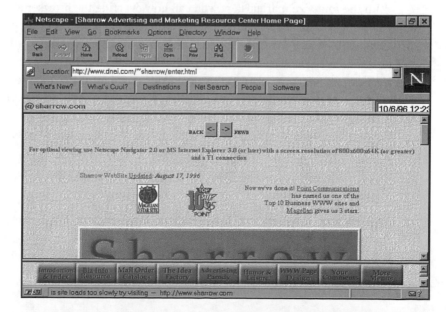

Part

III

Ch

13

Special Considerations for Netscape Browsers

ON THE WEB

Refer to Netscape's Introduction Navigator 3.0 page to learn more about incorporating the latest Netscape features in your Web site.

http://www.netscape.com/comprod/products/navigator/version_3.0/index.html

As pointed out earlier, designing for Netscape can be quite easy because of the huge amount of documentation available on the Net. It is also easy because almost anything that you've already seen on the Net can be designed to work in Netscape. Making your site Netscape-enhanced, therefore, is simple. Your only worry is what to do about all those people who view your site from a different browser.

Netscape Text Extensions

There are a few HTML extensions for text that Netscape has incorporated. These include different-sized font markup, relative font-size markup, subscript/superscript, strikeout, underline, and font face tags.

N O T E For the rest of this chapter, proprietary extensions for Netscape are shown in raw HTML code. FrontPage Editor makes using raw HTML unnecessary for the most part, but not in all cases (although eventually it should). The differences between the browsers' display capabilities become clearer when the raw HTML code is considered, hence its use in this chapter. ■

With the font-size markup tags, you can now override the browser and specify how large you want the individual sentences, words, and even characters to appear. You can also specify the `<basefont>` for the whole document, with a value of 1–7 (default is 3). The tag for `<basefont>` is `<basefont size=value>`. For changing the size of a subsection of font, the tag is `<font size=value>`, where valid values range from 1–7 and the default `<font>` size is 3. Or, if you've already specified a `<basefont>` or you want to specify your font changes with respect to the default `<basefont>` of 3, then you can use a '+' or '-' character in front of the number value to specify that it is relative to the document's `<basefont>`.

For example, you can set your document `<basefont>` to 4 with the tag `<basefont size=4>`. Then, if you want to emphasize a particular letter, word, or phrase by making its font size 6, you can use either `<font size=6>` or `<font size=+2>`.

Another way of specifying that a certain portion of text should be bigger or smaller relative to other text is to use the `<big></big>` and `<small></small>` tags. This directs the browser to make the emphasis the fonts, but allows the browser to choose how to do so.

The superscript and subscript tags are a great benefit for the scientists, engineers, and mathematicians publishing on the Web. The tags are simple:

```
<sub>I want this text subscripted</sub>
<sup>I want this text superscripted</sup>
```

Figure 13.3 shows an example of the `<big>`, `<small>`, `<sub>`, and `<sup>` tags at work in Netscape.

FIGURE 13.3

Netscape actually bolds and enlarges any text that is surrounded by the `<big></big>` tags.

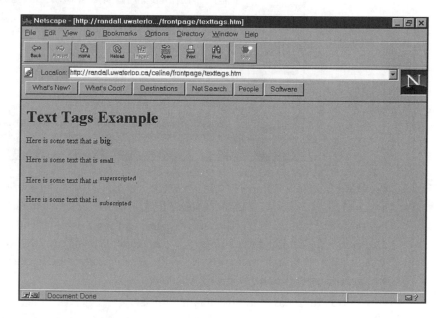

You can also strike out and underline text using the `<s>` and `<u>` tags as illustrated:

```
<s>Strikeout this text.</s>
<u>Underline this text.</u>
```

Use the `<font face>` tag to display a specific font on the user's computer. You use the `size=value` and `color="value"` attributes with this tag. You can also indicate two alternate font choices if your first choice isn't available on the user's machine. In this example, you first search for the Century Schoolbook font; if it's not available, you display the text in Palatino:

```
<FONT FACE="Century schoolbook,palatino" SIZE=-1>
```

Figure 13.4 displays an example of the `<font face>` tag:

N O T E You can do subscript and superscript simply by invoking the Format, Font, going to the Special Styles tab, and choosing Subscript or Superscript for the Vertical Position. ■

Part
III

Ch
13

FIGURE 13.4

Use the `<font face>` tag to display specific fonts on your Web pages.

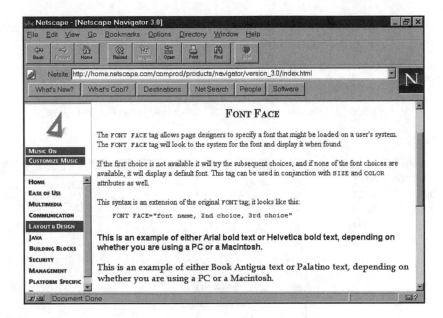

Creating Multiple Columns   Netscape 3.0 introduces the ability to create multiple columns in your Web pages, similar to those found in newspapers or newsletters. The `<multicol>` tag has three attributes: `cols=value`, `width=value`, and `gutter=value`. The `cols` attribute determines the number of columns to display, gutter sets the space between columns with a default of 10 pixels, and width sets the width between columns. You can also express this value as a per-centage, as in the following example:

```
<multicol cols=2 width=90% gutter=50>
```

Netscape's Web site includes a sample Stockwatch Investment Newsletter that illustrates the use of the `<multicol>` tag, shown in Figure 13.5.

Controlling Whitespace   Netscape 3.0 also gives you control over your pages' vertical and horizontal whitespace. You use the `<spacer>` tag to set the whitespace between words in a line, lines in a page, and margins.

This tag has several attributes—`type=value`, `size=value`, `width=value`, `height=value`, and `align=value`. You can create vertical, horizontal, or block `<spacer>` tags; these are the three values you can use with the type attribute. Some examples of the `<spacer>` tag include:

```
<spacer type=block height=1000 width=25 align=left>
<spacer type=horizontal size=100%>
```

 TIP   You can also nest the `<spacer>` tag into a table or frame as well as control it with JavaScript.

FIGURE 13.5
Create newspaper-
style columns with the
`<multicol>` tag.

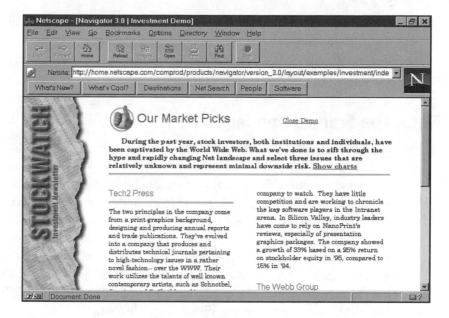

Figure 13.5, which shows the Stockwatch Investment Newsletter, also illustrates how to effectively use the `<spacer>` tag in a Web page.

Netscape Graphics Extensions

Because of the importance of graphics to the Web, Netscape and other browser developers are continually working on methods to enhance the variety for image display. Netscape has incorporated a number of HTML extension tags to allow images to be displayed in different ways.

The `<img>` tag has been expanded. Images can now be aligned in the following formats: right, left, top, middle, bottom, texttop, absmiddle, absbottom, and baseline. Right and left are floating alignments. A right-aligned image will appear in the next empty space on the right-hand edge of the browser screen and a left-aligned image will appear in the next empty space on the left-hand edge of the browser screen.

As for the rest of the alignments, here's a list of definitions:

- `align=top` Aligns the image with the top of the tallest item in the line.
- `align=texttop` Aligns with the top of the tallest text in the line.
- `align=middle` Aligns the middle of the image with the bottom of the current line.
- `align=absmiddle` Aligns the middle of the image with the middle of the current line.

Part
III

Ch
13

- `align=baseline` or `align=bottom`   Aligns the middle of the image with the bottom of the current line.

- `align=absbottom`   Aligns the bottom of the image with the bottom of the current line.

Netscape Frames and Targets

Netscape frames allow you to guide the user through your site, without constant repetition in your Web pages. You use frames basically to divide the Web page into multiple, scrollable regions, although frames may also be fixed and/or not scrollable. Each frame can be given an individual URL and an individual name. The frames can resize themselves automatically in response to a change in the size of the browser. Users can also change the size of individual frames by clicking and dragging. If a user wants to get rid of a frame completely, all he or she has to do is drag the frame divider until the frame is no longer visible. Figures 13.6 and 13.7 display two examples of using frames. The Film Festivals Server page displays a banner with a nested table of contents. The Where to Stay in the Caribbean page uses frames to display a simple banner.

FIGURE 13.6

You can include a table of contents in your Web page using frames.

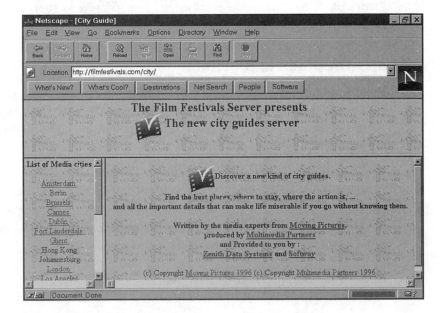

FIGURE 13.7
With frames, you can add a simple banner to your page.

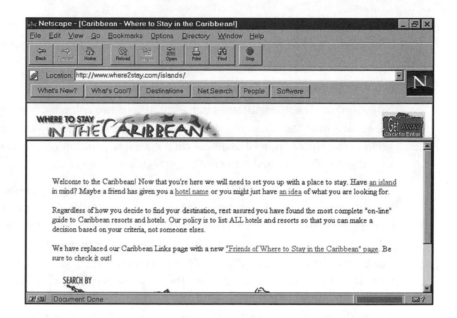

Because each individual frame can have a name, URL anchors can now have targets. This means that if you have a link in one frame, you can arrange for that location to load into one of the other visible frames when the user clicks. This is done by means of a `target` specification in the anchor, with the destination frame's name as the target value. This is how you can allow users to visit other sites, while maintaining your navigation bar or your company logo on-screen. Before showing how a target works, have a look at the basic HTML for creating frames.

In a frame document, there are no `<body></body>` tags, instead there are `<frameset></frameset>` tags. The `<frameset>` tag has two basic attributes, `rows=value` and `cols=value`. When you look at pages designed with frames, they are usually either row-oriented or column-oriented.

So the first thing to do in designing frames is to draw what you want on a piece of paper and determine whether it is column or row oriented. Frames are defined in HTML in a nested manner. If you want three horizontal frames, then you use percentages and list the relative row sizes as the values for the `rows` attribute. For example, you might have `rows=15%,70%,15%`. So, your opening `<frameset>` tag would look like this:

```
<frameset rows=15%,70%,15%>
```

Then you define what you want in your first frame by using the `<frame src=value>` tag. For example if you want the page `topframeimage.html` to be in the top frame, then use:

```
<frame src="topframeimage.html">
```

Part
III

Ch
13

Now, if you want your second row to be split into two columns, you introduce a nested `<frameset>` tag, but with a column attribute. If you want your columns to have a 40:60 ratio, then your tag would look like the following:

```
<frameset cols=40%,60%>
```

Now, you must define what goes into each of your two columns, from left to right using the `<frame src>` tag. Then you must have a closing `</frameset>>` tag for your nested `<frameset>`. Now you need to define what goes into your bottom row using the `<frame src>` tag. Finally, you end with another `</frameset>` closure tag.

When you declare what HTML page goes into a frame using the `<frame src>` tag, you can follow this with attributes about the frame. For example, you can specify whether or not the frame should be allowed to scroll with `scrolling='yes/no'` attribute. If you don't set this, then the default is for scrollbars only when they are needed. You can also specify margin widths and heights, to allow for space between the dividers and your frame's content. The attributes for doing this are the `marginheight=value` and `marginwidth=value` attributes. There is also the `name="value"` attribute with which you specify a name for your frame. (If you want to use the frame as a target for URLs, then you will need to give it a name.) Lastly, you can specify that the frames are not resizable by the user with the `noresize` attribute. All of these attributes are part of the `<frame src>` tag. An example of these in use might be:

```
<frame src="mypage.html" scrolling="yes" marginheight=5 marginwidth=5
➥name="middleframe" noresize>
```

If you want to design a page with frames, but you want to have an alternative for those people whose browsers don't support frames, there is a tag to help you. The `<noframes></noframes>` tag can be placed after the last `</frameset>` tag. It acts as a `<body></body>` tag, and you can put alternate HTML between the two. This HTML will only be rendered by browsers that don't do frames. Browsers that can handle the frames will ignore everything after the last `</frameset>` tag.

Microsoft FrontPage supports frames, and the frames wizard eases much of the developmental burden discussed here. Knowing what frames do, and how they work, can help you edit them further (and perhaps more quickly) to make them work exactly as you want them to.

In addition, Netscape 3.0 includes the ability to create borderless frames by setting the frameborder attribute to `no` on the `<frameset>` tag. This removes the borders from all frames in the frameset.

The SchwabNow! Web page, illustrated in Figure 13.8, demonstrates the use of borderless frames.

FIGURE 13.8
You can create borderless frames in Netscape 3.0.

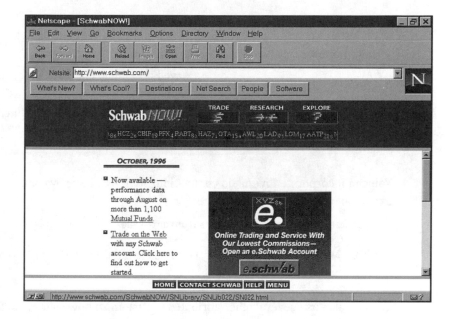

Multimedia Content

Netscape 3.0 incorporates LiveAudio, LiveVideo, QuickTime, and Live3D multimedia technology directly in the software, eliminating the need for external viewers.

Using LiveAudio   Netscape's LiveAudio feature automatically plays sound, audio, and music files in a Web page. LiveAudio supports the formats defined in Table 13.1.

ON THE WEB

Refer to Netscape's Innovators page for links to sites that incorporate the latest Netscape technology, such as LiveAudio.

http://www.netscape.com/comprod/products/navigator/version_3.0/innovators/ index.html

Table 13.1   Audio Formats

Audio Format	Description
AU	Sound format developed by Sun.
AIFF	Macintosh audio format.

continues

Part
III

Ch
13

Table 13.1   Continued

Audio Format	Description
WAV	Wave Form Audio File Format; the Microsoft Windows sound standard.
MIDI	The Musical Instrument Digital Interface, used to transmit music files created with an electronic instrument.

You can incorporate LiveAudio content into your Web page by using the <embed> tag. For example:

```
<embed src="myaudio.wav" autostart=true>
```

N O T E   All these examples can easily be invoked by clicking on the Insert Plug-In toolbar button on the Advanced Toolbar. ■

You can also use several other attributes to customize how your audio file plays on your Web page including:

- loop=[true, false, integer]
- starttime=[minutes:seconds]
- endtime=[minutes:seconds]
- volume=[0-100]
- width=[#pixels]
- align=[top, bottom, center, baseline, left, right, texttop, middle, absmiddle, absbottom]

N O T E
Use the controls attribute to determine the size and features of your audio console. The default value, console, includes play, pause, stop, and volume controls. You can also customize the control with the smallconsole, playbutton, pausebutton, stopbutton, and volume-level values. ■

ON THE WEB

A sample Web page that includes LiveAudio content is Alice's Adventures in Wonderland by Lewis Carroll.

http://www.megabrands.com/alice

Using LiveVideo   With Navigator's LiveVideo feature you can instantly view embedded AVI movies. AVI is the video file format standard for Microsoft Windows. You can click an AVI image to start and stop it and use the right mouse button to play, pause, rewind, fast forward, frame back, and frame forward.

To incorporate AVI files for LiveVideo to play, you use the <embed> tag, just as you did to embed audio files. For example, to embed the AVI file myvideo.avi in your Web page, specifying height and width pixel coordinates, the HTML code would be:

```
<embed src="myvideo.avi" height=240 width=320>
```

You can also use the autostart, loop, and align attributes—described in the previous section—to customize how your video clip plays.

The CineWorld site gives you several examples of how to incorporate video, including AVI files, in your Web pages. Figure 13.9 illustrates this site, displaying a video that takes you on a stroll down Paris' Champs Elysees. You'll find CineWorld at:

http://www.amexpub.com/cineworld/main/main_screen.html

FIGURE 13.9
When you embed AVI files in your Web page, Netscape users can view them automatically.

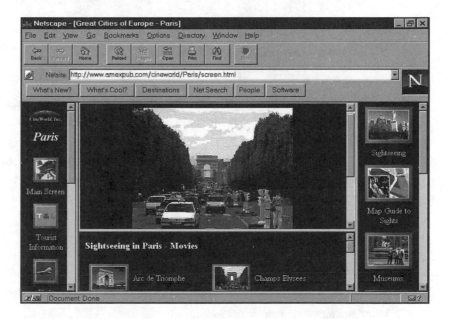

Part
III

Ch
13

Using QuickTime Netscape 3.0 enables you to automatically play QuickTime MOV files. With its Fast Start feature, you're able to run QuickTime multimedia while it's still downloading. You'll again use the <embed> tag to include MOV files on your Web page, as in the following example:

```
<embed src=myqtime.mov">
```

QuickTime also supports the width, height, autoplay, and loop attributes as well as several others.

A good example of a site that uses QuickTime is the CNN Video Vault. Figure 13.10 displays the Video Vault Web page. You'll find this page at:

http://cnn.com/video_vault/index.html

FIGURE 13.10

You can easily embed QuickTime movies.

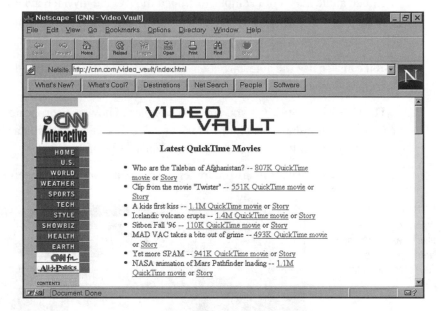

Using Live3D   Live3D is a VRML (Virtual Reality Modeling Language) viewer that lets you display VRML worlds incorporating sound, music, video, text, graphics, and animation. As a Web page designer, you can use VRML technology to create 3-D games, multiuser chats, interactive content, and unique 3-D navigational methods. Again, use the <embed> tag to embed a VRML world into your Web page:

```
<embed src="myworld.wrl">
```

ON THE WEB

To see VRML in action, look at the Planet9 Studios and Black Sun Interactive Web sites.

http://www.planet9.com

http://ww3.blacksun.com

Figure 13.11 displays a VRML world in the Planet9 Studios site. The animated effect, of course, doesn't display in this sample screen shot.

FIGURE 13.11
It's simple to incorporate VRML worlds in your Web page that users can view with Live3D.

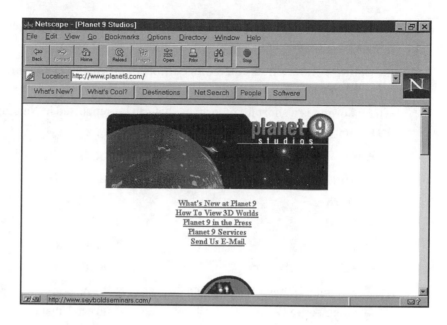

ON THE WEB

For more information on VRML, refer to The Easy VRML Tutorial page.

http://www.mwc.edu/~pclark/vrmltut.html

The Introduction to VRML page also has a lot of useful information.

http://www.netscape.com/comprod/products/navigator/live3d/intro_vrml.html

Netscape Plug-Ins

If you are designing a Web page to communicate a mass of already digital information, then designing for Netscape may be easier than designing for other browsers. This will be the case if the information you want to communicate is in one of the many forms of which Netscape plug-ins are designed to take advantage. For example, you may have some company promotional material in Adobe Acrobat form, or you may have a small table that is in Microsoft Word. These documents can be incorporated right into Web documents and seen by users who view with Netscape. This means less work for you in migrating your data between different formats.

There are nearly 100 plug-ins currently shipping, and designing with these plug-ins in mind means being aware of what all of these plug-ins do. That in itself is no easy task, but Netscape has a page that outlines what all of the plug-ins do, and includes links to the

Part
III

Ch
13

companies which have created the plug-ins, so that you can easily get more information. The page is located at

http://home.netscape.com/comprod/products/navigator/version_2.0/ plugins/index.html

The following is a short list of formats that can be supported in Netscape or can be easily formatted for Netscape using some of the plug-ins:

- Acrobat
- MPEG
- Word
- Excel
- PowerPoint
- ASAP WordPower
- Astound/Studio M documents
- Chemscape Chime
- Vector graphics
- AVI
- MIDI
- AutoCAD DWG or DXF
- Envoy documents
- CGM
- JPEG
- PNG
- TIFF
- CCITT GP4
- BMP
- WMF
- EPSF
- Sun Raster
- RGB
- PCX
- Fractal images
- WordPerfect
- QuickTime
- WAV
- AU
- AIFF
- MPEG
- Macromedia Authorware
- Macromedia Director
- Macromedia Freehand files

Of course, plug-ins don't just allow different file formats to be included in Web pages. Some of these programs let you create entirely new environments for Web exploration. For example, VRML is a new dimension in Web interaction. It allows users to control and move through 3-D interactive worlds while in a browser such as Netscape. There are a number of plug-ins devoted to allowing users to move through these VRML worlds. When you design for Netscape you can design a VRML world yourself. This means using VRML in addition to HTML.

Even though Netscape incorporates several plug-ins—such as LiveAudio, LiveVideo, QuickTime, and Live 3D—directly into Navigator, you'll probably still want to take advantage of what other plug-ins can offer. The following is a brief list of some of the most interesting plug-ins to Web page designers. You can download all of these from Netscape's plug-in page previously mentioned.

N O T E When you start downloading software from the Net, you'll begin to discover *alpha* and *beta* versions. Alpha indicates software in its early stages, often containing many unfinished features. Beta denotes software further towards completion. Eventually, beta versions become release versions: the ones you can actually buy. ■

■ **Acrobat Reader 3.0**

This beta plug-in enables you to display and print PDF (Portable Document Format) files directly in Navigator. You can create PDF files using Adobe Acrobat.

■ **ActiveX by NCompass**

Use this plug-in to embed Word, Excel, and PowerPoint documents in your Web pages. You can also use it to view other ActiveX controls, if the ActiveX `<object>` includes the appropriate `<embed>` tag.

■ **CarbonCopy/Net by Microcom**

Using this plug-in, you can remotely control another user's computer over the Net.

■ **Figleaf Inline by Carberry Technology/EBT**

The Figleaf Inline plug-in lets you embed a wide variety of graphic file types directly into your Web pages. Figleaf supports CGM, GIF, JPEG, PNG, TIFF, CCITT G4, BMP, WMF, EPSF, Sun Raster, and RGB.

■ **Shockwave for Directory by Macromedia**

You can use the Shockwave plug-in to display Shockwave animations created with Macromedia Director.

■ **PowerPoint Animation Player & Publisher by Microsoft**

This plug-in offers the ability to display animated PowerPoint presentations in Web pages.

■ **RealAudio by Progressive Networks**

The RealAudio plug-in offers live and on-demand real-time audio from your Web site.

■ **ichat Plug-in by ichat**

Ichat directly integrates a chat feature into Navigator, enabling you to build real-time chat capabilities on your Web page.

Part

III

Ch

13

T I P You can usually use the `<embed>` tag to embed a file in your Web page that's viewed or played by a plug-in.

Designing for Netscape and using plug-ins can be quite challenging. It is not the purpose of this chapter to outline how to design content for every plug-in—there are just too many. However, there is some consistency in how all of these add-on features are incorporated in HTML, and that is what will be dealt with here.

To incorporate most of the special files that can be used with Netscape plug-ins, the file can be linked into HTML as a GIF or WAV file would be. For example, if you want to link an Adobe Acrobat file into your HTML, you put the name of the .PDF file along with the folder in which it is located within an anchor:

```
<a href="/cgi-bin/byteserver3/Amber/PDFS/MyAcrobatFile.pdf">Click here to
➥view my Acrobat File</a>
```

Notice that in the previous example, the file is located in a cgi-bin/byteserver3 folder. This special type of folder will be needed for many of the plug-ins' files. This is because what makes the plug-ins files special is often the way they are delivered from the server. Optimized Adobe Acrobat files can be delivered one page at a time from the server using special software.

TROUBLESHOOTING

Does this mean my server has to have special capabilities if I want to serve up plugged-in content? Could this be why I can't get my plug-in content to work? Yes, this could very definitely be the cause. It's not an insurmountable problem, though. You simply have to make your server administrator aware of what you want to do, and then he or she can get the appropriate server plug-in installation material from the same company that provides the plug-in to Netscape users. Sometimes this plug-in delivery system is available free, in which case you'll have no problem. If it's not free, it will depend on how rich your server is. As FrontPage continues to develop, it will begin to support some selected plug-ins, but the companies producing the plug-ins will offer their own server add-ons to allow them to appear.

In the Adobe Acrobat case, you don't necessarily need a specialized server. Any non-optimized PDF file can be viewed in the Netscape window (without one-page-at-a-time display) with the Acrobat Reader and Netscape Navigator, without special capabilities on the part of the server. But page-at-a-time display requires a Web server with byteserver capability, either built-in (as with the Netscape and Open Market server products) or as a CGI script. Adobe plans to freely distribute the CGI script when it is finalized. In this case, if your server is a Netscape or Open Market server, you're already set. If not, it will simply be a matter of having your server administrator include the special CGI script.

Figure 13.12 displays an Adobe Acrobat file, a listing of computer courses from San Francisco State University's Extended Learning catalog.

FIGURE 13.12
You can embed PDF files in your Web pages that users can read with Adobe Acrobat Reader.

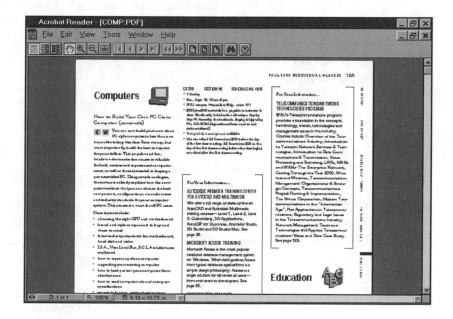

Java and JavaScript

Lately, developing anything really exciting to run on Netscape has meant developing Java and JavaScript content. Java is a full-fledged computer language, and JavaScript is a small scripting language. If you have a lot of programming experience, then you can jump right into Java and start creating some really incredible interactive content for your Web pages, in the form of applets. If you don't know much about programming, but you still want to add some interactivity to your Web pages, then you can easily learn JavaScript and start making your Web pages more interesting.

Java applications become part of an HTML document in the form of applets. An applet is a small application. Using the Java language it is possible to write large applications, but the language has a number of added features that make it ideal for portable, small applications that can be downloaded over the net. A Java Applet becomes part of a Web page in the same way that a picture becomes part of a Web page. You simply add HTML tags that define the applet.

Assume you or someone you know has created a Java Applet that makes a string of text disappear letter by letter and then reappear letter by letter. Imagine that the name of this applet is 'Peekaboo'. Anyone can include this applet in HTML and decide what string they

Part
III

Ch
13

want to have disappearing and reappearing. To embed this applet in HTML code, you need to have the applet stored on the server in a special applet directory. You also need to know how much space the applet is going to take up on a Web page. Finally, you need to know the name of the parameter through which you assign your text string. Assume the applet code is in the applet's directory, and the string you want to enter is 'Hello, World!'. Assume this will be 50 pixels high and 300 pixels wide. The HTML for including such an applet is as follows:

```
<applet codebase="applets " code=Peekaboo.class width=300 height=50>
➥<param name=text value="Hello, World!">
➥</applet>
```

The `<applet>` tag includes the codebase, which indicates the relative or absolute directory location of the applet code (in the previous example the directory is relative to the current document) and the code, which gives the applet name (which must have a `.class` extension), followed by the width and height. Most applets have parameters which allow the applet to change, without having to change any code. Every parameter in an applet has a unique name. You can assign different values to an applet parameter by using the `<param>` tag.

N O T E FrontPage 97 now allows you to insert Java applets or JavaScript directly into your page. For Java applets, you can invoke the Insert, Other Components, Java Applet menu item, or click on the Insert Applet toolbar button on the Advanced Toolbar of FP Editor. For JavaScript, you are also provided with a Script Wizard to make it very easy to create JavaScript. Just invoke the Insert, Script menu item, or click on the Insert Script toolbar button on the Advanced Toolbar of FP Editor. ■

There are many more hints and tips that could be given for including Java applets in HTML documents, but most of that information is available in Chapter 22 of this book, and online at the Netscape or Sun pages.

JavaScript can't exactly be explained quite so easily, because JavaScript is actually part of HTML, rather than a separate entity such as Java applets. I will, however, include a very simple JavaScript here to show you how it interacts with HTML. Consider the programming problem which is presented when any new language appears—to present the words "Hello, World!" in the new language. You can use JavaScript to have this phrase appear on a Web page. (I know that this can be done simply by typing them into an HTML document, but it can also be done using JavaScript.) The JavaScript would simply be:

```
<script language="Javascript">
➥document.write("Hello, World!")
➥</script>
```

In JavaScript, document.write is a built-in function, and in this case, "Hello, World!" is the parameter. For an example of JavaScript that does something which can't be done using simple HTML, consider this JavaScript:

```
<script language="Javascript">
 <!-- to hide script contents from old browsers
 function compute_square(form)
 form.square.value = square(form.number.value)
 Function square(num)
 return num * num
 //end hiding contents from old browsers -->
</script>
```

This JavaScript contains a function. Incorporating just this JavaScript into a Web page won't do anything. However, by making a call to this function from somewhere else in your HTML document, you can have yourself a little square calculator that operates right in Netscape, without going back to the server. An example of a call to the previous function might be:

```
<form>
 Enter a number:
 <input type="text" name="number" size=5 ><br>
<input type="button" value="Get Square of Value" onclick=
➡"compute_square(this.form)">
 Result:
 <input type="text" value="square" size=15>
</form>
```

This form will take the value that the user has typed into the input area, and when the user clicks, will use the number as the input for the compute_square function that is shown. The result (the square of the number) will appear in the Result box.

 TIP When you create an HTML form using FrontPage editor, you can right-click on a form field, pick Form Field Validation from the context menu, and then specify various validation rules for that form field. This causes FP Editor to automatically create JavaScript (or VBScript) to perform the form field validation automatically.

Netscape 3.0 introduces a new technology called LiveConnect which lets you "connect" JavaScript, Java applets, and Netscape plug-ins with each other. LiveConnect enables you to enhance the interactivity of your Web pages—JavaScript can call Java methods and plug-in functions; Java can call these same plug-ins as well as JavaScript functions. For example, in the LiveConnect example illustrated in Figure 13.13, JavaScript calls a Java applet that opens a navigation window in the HotWired site.

Part
III

Ch
13

FIGURE 13.13
You can use LiveConnect to create an interactive site such as HotWired.

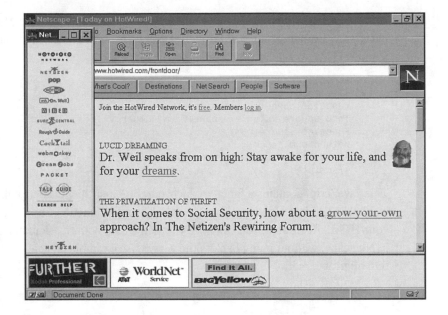

ON THE WEB

For more information on JavaScript refer to the JavaScript Authoring Guide.

http://www.netscape.com/eng/mozilla/gold/handbook/javascript/index.html

The JavaScript Resources page also has a lot of useful information.

http://www.netscape.com/comprod/products/navigator/version_2.0/script/script_info/index.html

From Here...

If you're serious about Web design, you have to make yourself continually aware of the differences among browsers. You can't be certain that all your users will view your site through Netscape Navigator. You run the risk of alienating users if you don't provide pages they can work with, and you might even need to produce specific pages for specific browsers, including pages that minimize special features entirely. Now that you know the different display features of Netscape Navigator, it's on to:

- Chapter 21, "JavaScript," which covers the use of JavaScript in FrontPage in more detail.

- Chapter 23, "VRML and Java," shows you how to create more sophisticated Web pages with the use of VRML.

■ Appendix A, "HTML 2.0 and 3.2 Quick Reference," takes you to the best HTML sites available on the Web.

■ Appendix C, "JavaScript Command Reference," covers the basics of JavaScript commands.

Part
III

Ch
13

## CHAPTER 14

FrontPage on the Net

Although we sincerely hope you won't need a great deal more information than this book provides about producing excellent Web sites with FrontPage 97, you should keep in touch with the FrontPage resources available on the Internet. Upgrades, free software, add-ons, discussion groups, and Web providers can be found very easily, and these will provide you with even more grist for your Web-designing mill. In this chapter, we'll outline some of the growing collection of resources. ■

What's on the Microsoft Web Site?

Microsoft's FrontPage area is the obvious starting place, and here you'll find information and assistance.

Web Presence Providers that Support FrontPage Extensions

You want to make full use of FrontPage 97, so why not get an account with a presence provider that supports it fully?

FrontPage Resources on the Web and the Net

Since FrontPage 97 exists to let you produce Web sites, it only makes sense that you can find information about the package on the Web itself. And since FrontPage is constantly increasing in popularity, you can rest assured that an increasing number of sites will become available in the near future, especially since the program is open-ended enough to invite input from its users. In fact, you might want to start your own FrontPage site, complete with hints, tips, pointers, technical help, and maybe even some nicely designed templates or wizards. You might even be able to make some bucks at it.

The other areas dedicated to FrontPage beginning to spring up are discussion groups on UseNet. Currently, only Microsoft itself offers FrontPage-specific newsgroups, but these, too, will begin to appear on news servers in a short while. Again, feel free to start your own such group.

If you're a FrontPage user with no access to a Web server that supports the FrontPage extensions, the Web will help you here as well. The number of Web presence providers (companies who give you a place to put your Web) that support FrontPage is growing constantly as the package becomes widely accepted among designers, and as of this writing these providers number close to a hundred. So if you need a place to put your Web, you should consider spending a few dollars a month to give yourself the opportunity.

Note that this chapter, however, is about FrontPage resources only. There is also a nearly infinite number of resources available about Web design in general, including collections of Java applets and ActiveX controls, HTML style guides, tutorials and assistants, and software to assist your Web building.

Parts of this book covered more than just FrontPage. Here's a quick list to give you somewhere to start looking for info on these other topics:

■ Gamelan (**http://www.gamelan.com**)

This is the most important place to surf if you are interested in any and all things Java. Tons of resources and lots of applets to play with.

■ Javasoft (**http://www.javasoft.com**)

This is the official Sun Java site and a good place to find breaking Java news and of course, to get your hands on the latest Java releases.

■ ActiveX.COM (**http://www.activex.com**)

A huge archive of ActiveX controls and information.

■ Microsoft's ActiveX Resource Center (**http://www.microsoft.com/activex/**)

The official ActiveX Center of the Universe, at the Redmond company's own site.

■ Yahoo!, World Wide Web Section (**http://www.yahoo.com/ Computers_and_Internet/Internet/World_Wide_Web/**)

For tons of resources on HTML, VRML, you name it, this is a great place to start your search.

FrontPage Resources on the Microsoft Web Site

Okay, so maybe the company that produces a product isn't the most unbiased when it comes to presenting it. Still, if you're looking for the latest news about your software or hardware, or the latest upgrades, patches, drivers, and so forth, it's a fact that heading for that company's Web site is the right place to go. For FrontPage users, that's certainly the case, especially since Microsoft's Web site in general is becoming much more useful to its customers. Here we'll look at what you'll find on that site as a FrontPage user.

The URL for the site is **http://www.microsoft.com/frontpage/**. This will take you to the, uh, front page of the FrontPage information, and we won't show any pictures of it here because it changes frequently. As of this writing, text links were available to the following pages:

■ The download area for FrontPage 97 (**http://www.microsoft.com/frontpage/ 97beta/**)

This link takes you to a page with a link to the actual download site, and a link to a form for ordering a CD-ROM of the software. Note that this link probably won't exist by the time you get this book, but it's important to keep visiting the page to see if new beta (that is, unfinished) versions of the product, or portions of the product, have been posted.

■ News about FrontPage (**http://www.microsoft.com/frontpage/news/**)

All the news that's fit to print about FrontPage, including the FrontPage 97 press release.

■ Listing of presence providers that support FrontPage server extensions (**http:// www.microsoft.com/frontpage/wpp/list/**)

This is the link you want if you're looking for a service provider who can give you space to launch your FrontPage site. These providers support the FrontPage extensions, which means that the WebBots will all function properly.   Most of these companies are Web-hosting providers, not ISP's, but it is still a useful list.

■ Gallery of sites created with FrontPage (**http://www.microsoft.com/frontpage/ createdwith/contest.htm**)

Part
III

Ch
14

It's always nice to see what others have done with FrontPage. Here you'll find links to sites that have been built by users of the FrontPage package. Here you'll also find a link to the "Created with FrontPage" logo program (**http://www.microsoft.com/frontpage/createdwith/default.htm**). If you participate in this program, which basically means building a site that doesn't disparage Microsoft or do anything illegal, you can get the nice blue logo that tells your visitors that you're a FrontPage user. Assuming you want them to know, that is.

In addition, graphical links were available to the following areas:

■ Learn About FrontPage (**http://www.microsoft.com/frontpage/learn.htm**)

Here you'll find the product brochure, pricing information, and an extremely valuable technical overview, worth reading by anyone planning to use the product extensively. Also here is a table showing the new features in the latest version of FrontPage, an explanation of the programs in the bonus pack, a paper on why FrontPage is so important to Web publishers (once again, maybe a tad biased), and links to FrontPage mentions in the news and to the various (positive) reviews garnered by FrontPage.

■ Work With FrontPage (**http://www.microsoft.com/frontpage/work.htm**)

This is indispensable! Click here, and you get additional links to

Authoring Resources—HTML conversion tools, background image libraries, ActiveX applications and Microsoft Office viewers, Web servers and Web utilities, and Microsoft Internet applications.

Bonus Pack Information—Details about Image Composer, Internet Explorer, Microsoft Personal Web Server, and Microsoft Publishing Wizard.

Software Developer's Kit (SDK)—The entire SDK is available here, including documentation for its use.

Web Hosting Details—Information for Web providers on how to host FrontPage webs, plus the Web Publishing Wizard.

Server Extensions—Link to the freely downloadable server extensions for all available servers.

Support Online—Here you'll find answers to common questions, plus access to the Microsoft Knowledge Base.

Other Companies Offering FrontPage Products—Companies are beginning to profit from FrontPage's success, and here you can find new Web wizards and UNIX support packages, among other features that will be added in future.

■ Randy's Tips for FrontPage users (**http://www.microsoft.com/frontpage/documents/tips/**)

A regular feature by the senior programmer of FrontPage, this link offers a series of helpful tips.

- Web Presence Providers (**http://www.microsoft.com/frontpage/wpp/**)

  A suite of information for Web hosting locations, plus a catalog of links to existing registered presence providers. We'll look at these later in this chapter.

As with anywhere else on the Web, any of these links can change or disappear at any time, of course. But it's worth checking this site once every week or so to see what's been added. And dig down into each subarea to extract the most from it. There's a substantial amount of valuable information that no FrontPage user should be without.

▶ See " FrontPage's Templates and Wizards," **page 625**

FrontPage Web Presence Providers

A growing number of presence providers are offering space on their servers to host FrontPage webs. What this means is that their servers will fully support the FrontPage extensions, so that programmable elements such as Bots for forms and database connectivity will function properly when served to the Web. Without support for the FP extensions, these features will not work at all, and must be redesigned using much more complex programming methods.

Here is a listing of several of these providers, but by no means all of them. These were taken primarily from the links on the Microsoft site, but some were found independently. Rates vary widely, but in general you can count on anywhere from $15-$300 per month. And these are the standard rates only; additional traffic and disk space will add significantly to the totals. Initial setup costs will also increase this amount. In addition, you might want to set up your own domain name, which costs anywhere from $150 to $300 extra. In general, there are rates in each provider's offerings for personal sites and varying levels of business sites.

Table 14.1 FrontPage Web Presence Providers	
Name	**URL**
FrontPage Today	**http://www.fptoday.com/**
AT&T Easy WWW	**http://www.att.com/easycommerce/easywww/ overview.html**
Act Group	**http://www.actgroup.com/FrontPage.htm**

Part

III

Ch

14

continues

Table 14.1 Continued

Name	URL
AIS Network Services	http://www.aisnetwork.net/aisnet/frontpage.html
Akorn Access	http://www.akorn.net/FrontPage/index.html
Advanced Internet Services	http://fp.sedona.net/
Web Creations	http://hook.atipa.com/mfp.html
BBN Planet	http://www.bbn.com/web_hosting/
BitShop	http://www.bitshop.com/services/frontpage.html
BizNet	http://www.bnt.com/
BlueHawk Communications	http://fp.bluehawk.com/
BuckEye Internet Services	http://www.buckeyeweb.com/fpsh.htm
CerfNet	http://cerfnet.com/frontpage/frontpage.html
Colorado Online	http://colorado.on-line.com/webhost.htm
ComCity	http://www.comcity.com/cfront.htm
SpryNet	http://www.sprynet.com/about/webhost/index.html
TCSN	http://www.tcsn.net/frontpage.htm
Coron	http://www.coron.com/frontpage.htm
Critical Mass Communications	http://www.criticalmass.com/frontpage
CRWeb	http://www.crweb.com/webhost.html
CSD Internetworks	http://www.kenton.com/fpdetails.htm
DeZines Web Hosting	http://dezines.com/fpbasic.html

From Here...

At this point, you're probably eager to get your Web site underway, then find a server where you can post it to the world. There are a couple important issues to resolve first, though, about graphics creation and building interactivity into your site. So from this point, head for the following:

- Part IV, "Creating and Adapting Graphics with Microsoft Image Composer," where you'll discover the rich resources of this excellent package.

- Part V, "Integrating Active Content into Your Web Site," which introduces you to the ins and outs of database integration and adding Java applets, ActiveX controls, Netscape plug-ins, and JavaScript and VBScript applets to your pages.

- Part VI, "Building and Managing a Web Site," which takes you through the Web creation and management features of FrontPage Explorer and its integration with servers.

Part
III

Ch
14

Creating and Adapting Graphics with Microsoft Image Composer

## CHAPTER 15

Getting Started with Image Composer

In Chapter 6, "Enhancing Pages with Graphics and Multimedia," you learned to insert graphic images on your Web site to create attractive and useful pages. And you learned to use images as site maps to help your visitors navigate your site in an intuitive way. FrontPage does include a nice selection of clip art. But in order to create really unique images, you need a graphics product powerful enough to create and edit sophisticated images, and one that integrates smoothly with FrontPage. Enter the Microsoft Image Composer—a powerful graphic design program that is bundled with the FrontPage bonus pack. ∎

Installing Microsoft Image Composer

Image Composer is included in the FrontPage 97 Bonus Pack. Make sure that Image Composer has been installed, making it easy to open image files.

Launching Image Composer from FrontPage

You can start Microsoft Image Composer directly from the FrontPage Explorer.

Navigating the Image Composer Environment

Control the Image Composer screen and sort through the tools and palettes.

Creating Sprites

Create the basic building blocks of every graphic image in Image Composer.

Sending Image Composer Files to FrontPage

Once you've edited an image, send it back to FrontPage to be included on a Web page.

Editing Clip Art in the Image Composer

In Chapter 6 you learned to insert clip art on a page. Here we get to edit that clip art using Image Composer to make it unique.

What Can Image Composer Do?

Microsoft Image Composer is powerful enough to create flashy logos, subtle background textures, expressive artistic text and a wide variety of other graphic images. Image Composer is not simply a tool for creating Web graphics. You can design images to include in printed documents, video displays, to insert in PowerPoint Presentations, or to copy into any other application.

Image Composer is, however, uniquely suited to creating Web site graphics. One powerful feature, that we will explore in the Chapter 18, is the ability to maintain relatively consistent colors regardless of what Web browser your visitors are using.

All the aesthetic considerations you explored in Chapter 6—where you learned to insert graphic images—apply at a different level when you create your own images with Image Composer. The difference is, creating your own images gives you far more power to control the look and feel of your Web site. Looking for a subtle button to place on your site that will whoosh visitors to a sophisticated art gallery? The tools are here in Image Composer. Looking for a flashy, wild logo that expresses your non-corporate image? You can do this all yourself. How much artistic talent do you need? You be the judge—but Image Composer will do its best to help you transform a scanned image, an original graphics file, or a vision in your head into an image ready to place on your Web site.

Microsoft Image Composer is bundled with the bonus pack version of FrontPage 97. It is installed from the same CD that you used to install FrontPage.

Using Microsoft Image Composer with FrontPage

Typically, you may well work on your Web site with the FrontPage Explorer and FrontPage Editor running, and Image Composer open as well. The real fun comes when you switch seamlessly back and forth between the FrontPage Editor and Image Composer, editing image content, adding graphical text, changing image color, and tweaking your graphic images so that your site has the look you want.

Once you have installed Image Composer, you can open it directly from the FrontPage Explorer. You can also open Image Composer from the FrontPage Editor by selecting Tools, Show Image Editor or by double-clicking the image. Once you open Image Composer, it is often handy to keep it open while you edit your Web page. That way you can use your Taskbar to toggle back and forth.

In this chapter, we'll explore two ways to send your edited image to a FrontPage Web—using the File option to do that, or just copying the image through the Clipboard. We'll come back to these options later in this chapter.

Installing Image Composer

If you installed Microsoft Image Composer as part of installing Microsoft FrontPage 97, it's already there, and you can skip right on ahead to the next section of this chapter. If you elected not to install Image Composer during your original FrontPage 97 setup, or if you're not sure whether or not you installed Image Composer, you can do that easily from your FrontPage 97 installation CD.

To install Image Composer, place the CD in your CD drive and select Start, Run from the Taskbar. In the Open area type **E:\Setup.exe** and click OK in the Run dialog box. See Figure 15.1.

You'll be given the option of installing Image Composer.

FIGURE 15.1
The Run dialog Box.

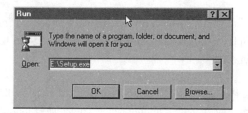

After you install Image Composer, you can open it from the Taskbar, or launch it directly from the FrontPage Explorer.

 Unless you have unlimited hard disk space, you are better off pulling clip art image files off the FrontPage 97 CD as needed.

Starting Image Composer

You can start Image composer from your Taskbar, just as you would any other application. But if you are working in FrontPage, the easiest way to start editing a graphic is to launch Image Composer directly from the FrontPage Explorer.

There are two ways to start Image Composer from the FrontPage Explorer. If you are creating a *new* graphic image for your Web site, you can start the Image Composer by clicking the button in the FrontPage Explorer toolbar. See Figure 15.2.

FIGURE 15.2
The Show Image Editor tool.

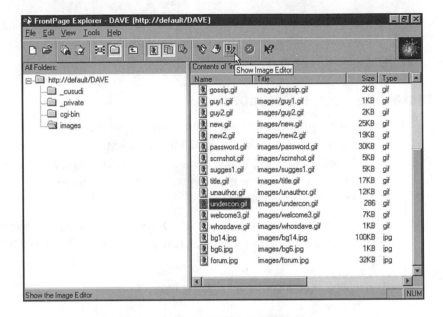

If you wish to edit a graphic image that you have already imported into your Web site (as you learned to do in Chapter 6), you can double-click that image in the FrontPage Explorer Folder view or Hyperlink view.

 TIP You should take care to close Microsoft Image Composer when you are done editing an image. Microsoft recommends against having more than three copies of Image Composer running on your computer and that's good advice. The prudent thing is to keep it to one copy running at a time.

Associating your Image Files with Image Composer

What if you have been using another program to edit images? Perhaps you're a new convert to Image Composer. That's OK, welcome to the club. If you previously configured the FrontPage Explorer to launch a different image editor when you double-click an image file, that can be changed.

Change the default image editor by selecting Tools, Options from the FrontPage Explorer menu. Click the Configure Editors tab and select the file format that you wish to associate with Image Editor (for example GIF files, or JPEG files). Use the Modify button to change the associated image editor to Image Composer. See Figure 15.3.

FIGURE 15.3
The Editor Associa-
tion dialog box.

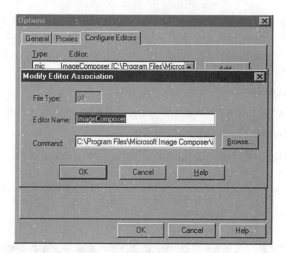

Getting Going with Image Composer

What do you need to start creating or editing an image using Image Composer? The short answer is not a thing. You can create a graphic image from scratch in Image Composer.

However, if you have an image you wish to edit, you can import an image file. Image Composer will import with any of the following file types:

- A scanned photo in TIF file format.
- A GIF image file.
- A Targa file.
- A JPEG image file.
- A bitmap file (*.bmp or *.dib).
- An Adobe Photoshop file.
- A file created in Altamira Composer.

You can open files from any of the above formats in Image Composer. If you created an image in a graphics program that is not on the list above, chances are overwhelming that your graphics program will allow you to export your image to one of those formats.

Exploring Image Composer Tools & Palettes

There's quite a bit on the Image Composer window, and the screen may look a little intimidating at first. However in no time you'll be gliding in and out of Image Composer like Van Gough with his paint and brushes.

Besides the image editing area, there are five, removable parts of the Image Composer screen:

- The Toolbar at the top of the screen.
- The Toolbox to the left of the screen.
- The Color Swatch—that colored square in the lower left corner of the screen.
- The Status bar on the bottom of the screen.
- The Palette that takes up the bottom third or so of the screen.

See Figure 15.4.

FIGURE 15.4
The Image Composer window.

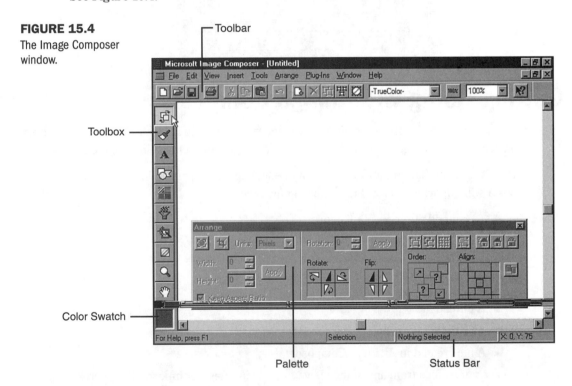

A Look at the Toolbar

Much of the Image Composer Toolbar will look familiar to users of FrontPage and other Microsoft Office applications. There are the same file management tools—New, Open, Save. The Print button looks familiar as does the Undo button.

What's new are tools that let you select and work with *Sprites*. We'll come back to what Sprites are momentarily, but for now we'll go with a quick definition: Sprites are graphic image objects that you import or create in Image Composer. See Table 15.1 below for a list of Image Composer tools.

Table 15.1   The Image Composer Toolbar

Tool	Tool Name	Description
(pic of New)	New	Creates a new Image Composer file.
(pic of Open)	Open	Allows you to open or manage existing image files.
(pic of Save)	Save	Saves the current file. If the file has been named, the file is resaved with the same name.
(pic of print)	Print	Opens the Print dialog box.
(pic of Cut)	Cut	Removes selected objects and places them in the Clipboard to be pasted.
(pic of Copy)	Copy	Copies selected objects into the Clipboard to be pasted.
(pic of Paste)	Paste	Places the contents of the Clipboard on the page.
(pic of Undo)	Undo	Undoes the last command you performed.
(pic of Ins Im File)	Insert Image File	Opens the Insert from File dialog box, allowing you to place saved graphic image files from a list of formats.
(pic of Delete)	Delete	Deletes the selected object(s) from the page.
(pic of Dup)	Duplicate	Creates a duplicate of the selected object(s), offset down and to the right of the original.
(pic of Clr All)	Select All	Selects all objects on the page.
(pic of Clr Slc)	Clear Selection	Deselects whatever objects are selected.
(pic of CF)	Color Format	Pick from a list of color formats.
(pic of Act Siz)	Actual Size	Resets an imported image back to its original size.
(pic of Zoom %)	Zoom Percent	Zoom in to make objects appear larger, or press Ctrl+click to zoom out and see more objects.
(pic of Help)	Help	Click, then point to any part of the screen for help on that feature.

The Toolbox to the Left of the Screen

The Image Composer Toolbox is where we'll find all the real goodies. Most of them won't get explored in depth until Chapters 16 and 17. But we'll take a peek at them now. See Table 15.2 for a list of Toolbox tools.

Table 15.2	The Image Composer Toolbox	
Toolbox Tool	**Tool Name**	**Description**
(pic of Arrange)	Arrange	Sizes, rotates, moves Sprites front to back, or aligns Sprites.
(pic of Paint)	Paint	Paints images with a large variety of brush stroke types.
(pic of Text)	Text	Lets you create and edit text.
(pic of Shapes)	Shapes	Draws rectangles, ovals, and polygons.
(pic of Patterns Fills)	Patterns & Fills	Fills selected Sprite(s) with colors & patterns.
(pic of Warps & Filters)	Warps & Filters	Lets you apply creative distortion to selected images.
(pic of Art Effects)	Art Effects	Fills objects with a variety of shadings.
(pic of Color Tuning)	Color Tuning	Allows you to tune highlights and shadowing.
(pic of Zoom)	Zoom	Like the Zoom List in the Toolbar, zooms in on part of the page.
(pic of Pan)	Pan	Let's you adjust the section of the page being viewed.

Selecting Fill Color

The Color Swatch—that colored square in the lower left corner of the screen—lets you select the default fill color. Once you select a color from the Color Swatch Palatte, all new shapes are rendered with that color fill.

Duck! Here Comes a Palette

One of the things that makes the Image Composer seem a little chaotic at first is that the Palettes change depending on what tool you have selected from the Toolbox.

If you truly find the Palettes maddening, you can turn them off by selecting Tools, Options and using the Tool Palettes tab in the Options dialog box to deselect the Show New Tool Palette on Change check box.

Creating Sprites

Sprites are sort of the atoms of the Image Composer Universe. The smallest object that you create. Or is there a smallest object in the universe? The analogy has its limits but think of Sprites as the basic building blocks of a file in Image Composer. Later in this chapter we'll investigate the relationship between these little (or big) Sprites and Image Composer files. But for now, we'll rest content to create a cute little Sprite and play with it for a while. To do that, we'll pick up a tool or two from the Image Composer Toolbox.

Creating & Editing Sprites with Tools in the Toolbox

To the left of the screen we have the Toolbox. The ten tools allow us to accomplish all kinds of image editing. It will take the next three chapters to try experiments with all these tools. But we can look at some of the tools right away.

As you select different tools in the Toolbox, you will notice different *palettes* appear in the lower portion of your Image Composer window. Palettes *change* depending on what Toolbox tool you are working with.

To Create a Square   The Shape tool in the Toolbox allows you to create ovals, rectangles, and other polygons. We'll explore shapes in detail in the next chapter, but let's experiment with one quickly now.

1. Click the Shapes tool in the Toolbox. The tooltip will help you find the tool.

 TIP When you select the Shapes tool in the Toolbox, the Shapes-Geometry Palette opens in the lower part of the screen.

2. Select the square looking rectangle tool in the Shapes-Geometry Palette.

3. Draw a rectangle in the drawing area (see Figure 15.5).

FIGURE 15.5
Drawing a rectangle.

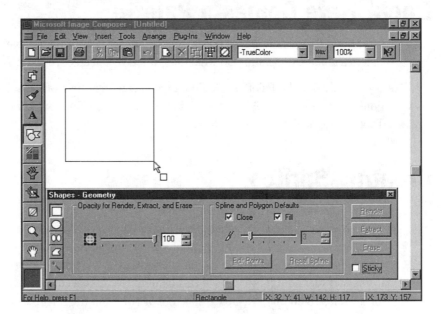

4. Click the Render button in the Shapes-Geometry Palette.

To Resize a Selected Object

1. Click the lower right handle—an arrow pointing down and to the right.

2. Click and drag *down* and *to the right* to enlarge the selected Sprite (see Figure 15.6).

To Rotate a Selected Object

1. Click the first tool in the Toolbox—the Arrange tool. The Arrange tool Palette shows the selected Sprite's location, alignment, and rotation angle.

2. Click the rotation handle—the upper right of the eight corner and side arrows. The upper right handle looks different. It is used to rotate an object (see Figure 15.7).

FIGURE 15.6
Enlarging the selected Sprite.

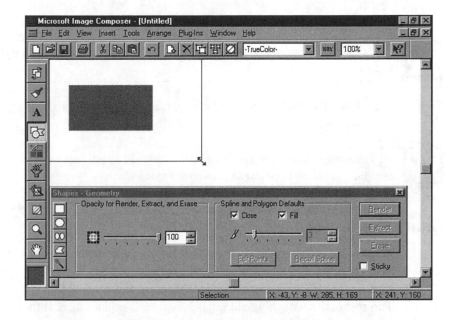

FIGURE 15.7
Rotating a Sprite.

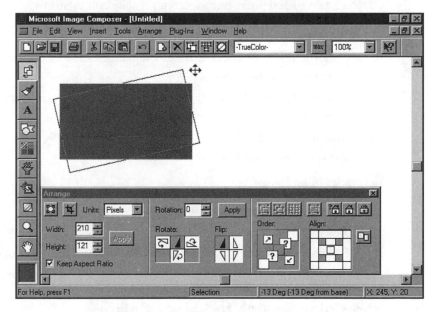

3. Drag up slightly on the rotation handle to angle the selected object.

Warps and Filters   No, warps and filters are not tools to stretch our your backbone and screen your lungs from harmful contaminants in the air. But they do let you have a lot of fun with a selected Sprite. Before we explore other components of the Image Composer environment, let's try getting a little warped and filtered.

1. Click the Warps and Filters tool in the Toolbox.

 Here's another chance to note how the Palette changes as we select a different tool from the Toolbox.

2. Click the Escher warp and click on the <u>A</u>pply button in the Warps and Filters dialog box.

 We'll do some serious filtering and warping in Chapter 17! If you want to experiment with something safe now, try adding an Edge outline to the Sprite.

Using the Toolbar

The toolbar at the top of the Image Composer screen includes tools familiar to everyone who has worked with Microsoft Office applications—buttons to open new and saved files; a button to save files; and buttons to cut, copy, and paste objects. Nothing too scary here. The rest of the tools help edit images, and we'll explore most of them in the next two chapters as we need them. But we can try a couple of them now.

To Zoom in on an Image

1. Click the Zoom Percent list in the Toolbar, and select a percentage to enlarge the *view* of your image.

2. You will often need to use the horizontal and vertical scrollbars to "find" your image once you have zoomed in or out.

3. Hold down the Ctrl key while you click with Zoom selected. Ctrl+Click zooms out, allowing you to see more, but smaller objects.

To Duplicate an Image

1. Click the Duplicate tool in the Image Composer Toolbar.

2. You can undo the duplicate image by clicking the Undo button.

3. Try duplicating the image again. And again. And again. And again…OK, Stop! That's enough (see Figure 15.8).

Using the Color Swatch to Select Colors

When you click the Color swatch, you can assign colors to any object. Identify that little square in the lower left corner of your screen. That's it.

1. Click the Color Swatch.

2. Select a color in the Color Picker Palette.

3. Lighten or darken the color hue by clicking the vertical bar next to the color palette in the Color Picker.

4. When you have selected a color, OK the Color Picker dialog box.

5. Draw another rectangle, and render it. The fill color will reflect your selection in from the Color Swatch.

FIG. 15.8
Duplicating, Again and
Again and...

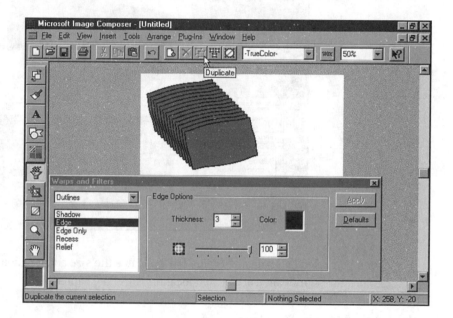

Changing Colors for a Selected Sprite

You can re-assign a new color to a selected Sprite. The Patterns and Fills tool in the Toolbox allows you to do all kinds of fun things with fills, but it can also fill a selected Sprite with the currently selected color fill.

1. Select the Sprite to which you want to assign the selected color swatch.

2. Click the Colors and Fills tool in the Toolbox.

3. Select Current Color Fill from the Patterns and Fills list, and set the Opacity Spin Box to 100 (see Figure 15.9).

Interpreting the Status Bar

The strip of information on the bottom of the screen is the Status Bar. It indicates, first of all, whether or not you have a Sprite selected. If not, the message is simply "Nothing Selected." Try clicking off your Sprite. The Status Bar still indicates pixel coordinates as you move your cursor around the screen—how many pixels up (Y axis) or to the left (X Axis) your cursor is located at.

FIGURE 15.9
Selecting a Color Fill
and Opacity.

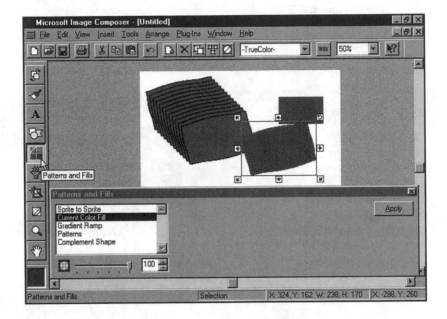

When you select a Sprite, the Status Bar indicates the size and location of that object. We'll explore the significance of size and location more in Chapter 16.

Making Palettes Go Away

As we've seen, Palettes change depending on which Toolbox tool is selected. What if you would just like a nice, clear screen to work with? You can simply close any Toolbox Palette by clicking the close button in the title bar. For our readers who like pressing keyboard keys, the F2 function key will toggle between a displayed and a disappeared Palette.

Sprites, Composition Guides, and Files

It is not necessary to save a Sprite, or a bunch of Sprites, in order to place them in a FrontPage Web. You can simply copy them into a page in the FrontPage Editor, and then save the Web page. As you save the page, the images you have copied onto the page will be saved as files in the Web Site.

In many cases, you will create images with the Image Composer, copy them onto a page, and simply close Image Composer without saving the files.

Does this mean you can never edit those images in Image Composer? Not at all. You can open an image from the FrontPage Explorer *in Microsoft Image Composer* simply by double-clicking the file in the Hyperlink or Folder view.

Why then, would anyone want to bother saving a file in Image Composer? One good reason is that you may create a file with many Sprites, not all of which you want to copy into a Web. You can save many Sprites by saving the file they are part of.

When you do save a file, you can control the size of that file by editing the size of the *Composition Guide*. The Composition Guide does not necessarily take up the entire Image Composer Workspace. Like the Sprite (or Sprites) that sit on it, the Composition Guide area can be sized.

Selecting a size for the Composition Guide area, and arranging Sprites within that area gives you control over how your image will appear on your Web site.

When a file in Image Composer is saved, *only* the Sprites that are within the Composition Guide are saved. When you select the Send to FrontPage feature in Image Composer, *only Sprites within the Composition Guide* get sent to the open FrontPage Web site.

The *entire* Composition Guide area gets sent to FrontPage when you select the Send to FrontPage feature. Sometimes that's not so helpful. It requires that your Sprite (or Sprites) be aligned just right on the Composition Guide, or the image doesn't look right on the Web site.

There are a couple of ways to resolve this problem. You can resize your Composition Guide area, and arrange your Sprite (or Sprites) within it properly. Or, the other option is to simply copy your Sprite into the FrontPage Editor via the Clipboard. Both of these options have advantages, and we'll investigate them.

CAUTION

Keep in mind that when you copy a Sprite onto a FrontPage Editor Web page, *the file is not saved anywhere until* you save the FrontPage Editor page. At that point, the image is saved, but the Image Composer file is not.

Copying Sprites

Since copying a Sprite to a Web page is the simplest way to put an image on your FrontPage Web site, let's explore that first.

You can simply select a Sprite, and use the Copy tool in the Image Composer toolbar to copy that image to the FrontPage Editor. The procedure is:

1. Right click a Sprite, or select several Sprites at once by clicking the Arrange tool in the Image Composer Toolbox and drawing a marquee around all the Sprites you wish to select.

2. Click the button in the toolbar.

3. Use the Taskbar to open or switch to an open page in the FrontPage Editor.

4. Place your insertion point on a Web page and click the Paste button in the FrontPage Editor toolbar.

5. Save the FrontPage Editor file. You will be prompted to assign a file name to your imported image.

Defining Composition Guides

You can specify the size of your Composition Guide in the Composition Properties dialog box.

You can place Sprites outside of the Composition Guide. However, if you save your file in a format other than a Microsoft Image Manager file, only Sprites inside the Composition Guide are saved. If you print your file, you have the option of printing only the Sprites inside the Composition Guide, or the entire view.

Deciding on whether or not to save your file as an Image Composer file or another format, and handling the relationship between Sprites and the Composition Guide can get a little tricky. So let's explore three examples:

■ If you created several Sprites, but were only using one in a Web site, you could save the entire file (including Sprites outside the Composition Guide) as a Microsoft Image Composer file. You could then open that file anytime you wished using Image Composer, and copy and paste *any* of the Sprites into FrontPage.

■ If you created a file with only one Sprite, and you wished to send that Sprite/file directly to FrontPage, you should resize your Composition Guide so that it matches the size of the Sprite. Save the file as either an Image Composer file or a GIF (or JPEG file). Then use the Send to FrontPage option in the file menu.

▶ **See** Chapter 6, "Enhancing Pages with Graphics and Multimedia," **p.121**

■ If you want to save a Sprite *with a separate background*, you can define the Composition Guide—and assign it a color and size, and then define the Sprite(s) on that guide—and move them around on the guide. We'll explore how to use this last, useful option shortly.

■ If you feel that this is all too complicated, no problem. Just copy your Sprites into FrontPage and don't even worry about saving files. When the day comes that this method doesn't give you enough freedom to work with files in the most efficient way, try out the other options.

To Define the Size of a Composition Guide   Composition width is defined in pixels—those tiny dots that make up a monitor viewing area. You can define a Composition Guide to be any number of pixels wide or high. The default is 640 pixels by 480. This is the size of a normal VGA monitor.

1. You can define Composition Guide size by right-clicking a blank part of the editing area, and selecting Properties from the shortcut menu.

2. Enter width and height in the Composition Properties dialog box.

To Define the Background Color of a Composition Guide

1. Right-click a blank part of the editing area.

2. Select Properties from the shortcut menu.

3. Enter up to 255 in the Red, Green, and Blue areas of the Composition Properties dialog box.

 TIP Entering 255 for all three colors produces a white background for the Composition. Entering 0 for all three colors creates a black background.

You can click the current color "box"(the preview of the current color) to display the palette.

Arranging Sprites in a Composition Guide

If you wish to put together a Sprite (or more than one) on a Composition Guide and send that to FrontPage, you need to size your Composition Guide and then arrange your Sprites on it.

You can arrange Sprites on a Composition Guide by selecting them, and dragging them onto the Composition Guide.

In Figure 15.10, the three Sprites don't quite fit in the Composition Guide. Figure 15.11 shows what happens when we select File, Send to FrontPage.

In Figure 15.12, the Composition Guide has been made wider by about 80 pixels.

FIGURE 15.10
Two and a half Sprites in the Composition Guide.

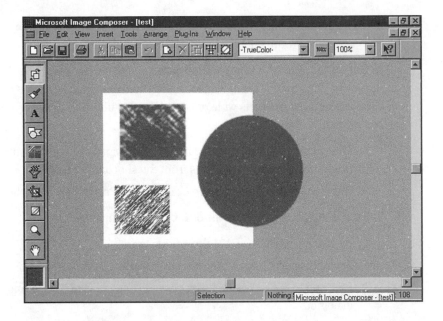

FIGURE 15.11
Composition Guide Truncating Sprites sent to FrontPage.

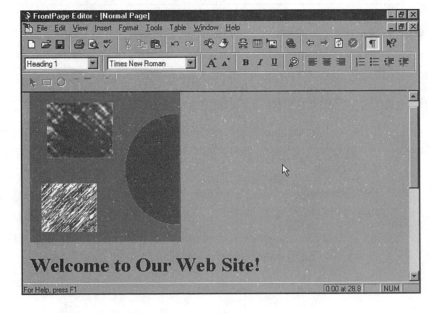

FIGURE 15.12
Composition Guide
Including Sprites sent
to FrontPage.

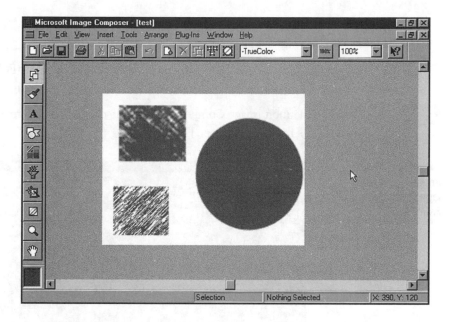

Now, when the file is sent to FrontPage, the entire Composition Guide will fit, and all three Sprites will fit in the image.

Editing Inserted Clip Art

In Chapter 6, you learned to insert clip art images onto your page. That helped jazz things up a bit. But let's face it, visitors to your Web site are going to recognize that clip art. Sometimes that's fine—familiar icons help visitors feel at home at your site and help them navigate around.

Sometimes it's appropriate to be more creative. And if your creative skills or confidence level aren't quite at the point of creating images from scratch, modifying someone else's image is a good way to add some variety and spice to your site.

To Edit Clip Art in Image Composer

Earlier you learned to insert clip art images directly onto a Web page using the FrontPage Editor. When you save your page, the inserted clip art file is saved to the Web site.

▶ **See** Chapter 6, "Enhancing Pages with Graphics and Multimedia," **p.121**

Once you have inserted a clip art image on your page, and saved the page, you can edit that clip art directly from the FrontPage Explorer. Simply switch to the FrontPage

Explorer (the Show FrontPage Explorer button in the FrontPage Editor toolbar), and then double-click the clip art image in the Folder or Hyperlink view.

As soon as you double-click the image file in the FrontPage Editor (Folder or Hyperlink view), Image Composer opens with the selected file ready for editing.

As soon as you launch Image Composer by double-clicking an image, you're there! Your graphic image is ready to edit (see Figure 15.13).

FIGURE 15.13

Image Composer launched from the FrontPage Editor.

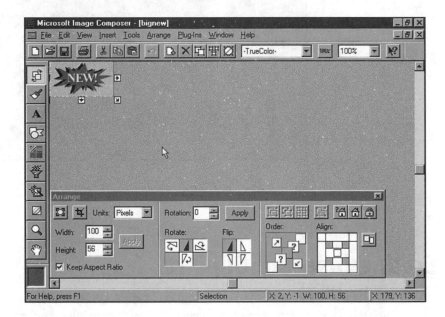

You can experiment with any of the editing features we've looked at in this chapter, and then send your image back to FrontPage. Instead of re-inserting a new graphic image, you can just select View, Refresh from the FrontPage editor menu, and the image will be updated. Figure 15.14 shows the large "New" clip art image with a little touching up in Image Composer.

FIGURE 15.14
Clipart edited in
Image Composer.

From Here...

In this chapter, we explored the Image Composer environment, and even had a little fun editing a bitmap image. We investigated different ways to take our Image Composer graphic images into FrontPage. Hopefully all this has whetted your appetite for some serious (or unserious) image creation and editing. The fun part comes next.

Look to the following chapters for further ways to create and edit graphic images:

- Chapter 16, "Working with Sprites" will give you the ability to create new graphic images using text, drawings, and imported images.

- Chapter 17, "Using Effects for Maximum Impact" will cover the wide range of image effects available using Patterns & Fills, more Warps and Filters, Art Effects, and Color Tuning.

- Chapter 18, "Tailoring your Images for FrontPage Documents" will examine different options for making your Image Composer files work well with your Web site.

## CHAPTER 16

Working with Sprites

In Chapter 15, "Getting Started with Image Composer," we began to examine Sprites. We saw that they are the basic building blocks of Image Composer graphical objects. Remember that an Image Composer file can be composed of one or many Sprites.

Microsoft Image Composer allows us to create, edit, shape, warp, align, and combine Sprites in ways that open up whole new vistas for your FrontPage Web site. Image Composer allows you to present text styles and text patterns not available from the font list in the FrontPage. Image Composer shapes, combined with arranging tools, allow you to create attractive and intuitive symbols, icons, and graphical guides for visitors to your site. In this chapter we'll explore the process of creating custom icons, special bullets, and helpful graphical clues that can make your FrontPage-created Web site comfortable and fun for your visitors. ■

Working with Graphical Text

Stretch, rotate, and warp text to create imaginative text presentations.

Drawing with Shapes

Create your own custom designs.

Painting Sprites

Touch up Sprites with brushstrokes.

Arranging Sprites

Combine shapes and text to design custom buttons, tools, and link icons.

Creating Imagemaps

Let visitors to your site navigate via an entertaining and intuitive imagemap.

Graphical Text

Microsoft Internet Explorer 3.0 supports a nice variety of fonts. In Chapter 5, "Developing the Basic Page: Text, Lists, and Hyperlinks," you learned to format text in fonts besides standard Times Roman. And, provided your visitors are using Internet Explorer 3.0, those fonts will display when your site is visited. The limitations are that not everyone is using I.E. 3.0, and that you're still constrained in what you can do with text. All the font selections in the world won't let you tilt text, stretch text, or fill text with fun gradient fills and shading. But Image Composer will. And from there, it's a simple matter to send or copy that graphical text to FrontPage.

Since this is so much fun, why not do most or all of your text in Image Composer, jazz it up to the max, and then zip it over to the FrontPage Editor? The drawbacks are that you are working with graphical image files, with all the implications for speed that were discussed in Chapter 6, "Enhancing Pages with Graphics and Multimedia," and editing text is much simpler using the word-processing power of the FrontPage Editor. So the choice is yours, but use text from Image Composer sparingly—and to good effect.

Composing Text

You can compose text in the Text Palette by clicking the Text tool in the Image Composer Toolbox. Simply type your message into the Text area of the Text Palette (see Figure 16.1).

FIGURE 16.1
The Text Palette dialog box.

Before you click the Apply button to compose the text as a Sprite, you can select text font, color, size, and even opacity.

Feel free to click the Apply button at any time. Clicking the Apply button allows you to see how your sprite will look with the selected effect. If, after you apply an effect, you don't like the way your text looks, simply click the Undo button in the toolbar.

You can select text in the Image Composer Workspace, and click the Text tool in the toolbox to change text properties.

If you wish just to get rid of your text Sprite, click it and press the Delete key.

Opacity

Opacity is technically a measure of the ratio between solid and opaque ("filled in") pixels. Opacity ranges from 100%—fully colored—to 0%. Zero percent opacity is so transparent you can't even see it! And anything below 10% will be faint indeed.

You set opacity by dragging the opacity slider between 0% and 100%. Or you can set opacity by entering a number in the Spin box.

> **TIP** An opacity setting of 100 makes your text completely opaque, or nontransparent. An opacity setting of less than 10 makes your text filmy, translucent, and light.

Font Colors

One advantage of creating graphical text in Image Composer is that you have an unlimited array of colors and fills to use. The whole spectrum of colors available from the Color Picker can be applied to text. When you compose text in the Text Palette, you can click the Color Picker (the Color Swatch in the lower left corner of the screen) to choose a color.

In Chapter 14, "FrontPage on the Net," you learned to apply colors to a selected Sprite by clicking the Color Swatch and selecting colors and hues from the Color Picker dialog box. A shortcut is to right-click the Color Swatch. Then you can click the color you want and apply it to your text (see Figure 16.2).

FIGURE 16.2
Selecting a color from the Color Swatch.

Selecting Font Type

You can choose from a list of fonts by clicking the Select Font button in the Text Palette. Click the font you wish to display, and you will see a sample of how your text will look in the Font Preview Box on the right side of the Font dialog box (see Figure 16.3).

FIGURE 16.3

The Font dialog box.

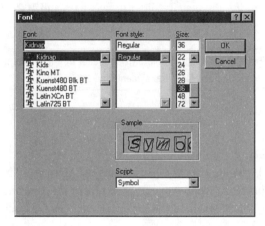

 TIP   You can also select font size in the Font dialog box. We'll explore another way to adjust font size later on in this chapter.

Editing Text

Even after you have shaped, shaded, stretched, rotated, and generally distorted text beyond recognition, you can still edit the text content easily. Simply click the text in the workspace, and then click the Text tool in the toolbox. The text will be easy to edit in the Text area of the Text Palette.

Use your cursor to place your insertion point anywhere in the text. Use delete or backspace to delete text, or type new text in at the insertion point. When you have edited your text, click the Apply button and your new text will drop right on top of the original text. You can then delete the original text and replace it with the revised text.

Sizing Text

You can select text size from the Text Palette. But you have even more flexibility to size text by using the handles on a text Sprite once you have created it.

You can compress text horizontally by dragging in on either side handle (see Figure 16.4).

FIGURE 16.4
Compressing a Text
Sprite.

You can also compress a text Sprite vertically by dragging in on the top or bottom handles.

You can stretch text by dragging *out* on any of the handles.

 TIP If you stretch text too far, you may get a warning that Image Composer can handle the Sprite more efficiently if you edit the bounding box. We'll explore resizing the Bounding box later in this chapter.

Of course, if you stretch too far, compress too much, or just plain wreck your text, there's always the Undo button in the toolbar!

Rotating Text

You can rotate a text Sprite the same way we learned to rotate Sprites in Chapter 15, "Getting Started with Image Composer,"—by clicking the rotation handle in the upper-right corner of the Sprite and pulling down (to rotate clockwise) or up (to rotate counterclockwise). Rotated text can be a helpful component in buttons and imagemaps, and just for spicing up a Web page (see Figure 16.5).

FIGURE 16.5
Rotating text.

Using Graphical Text in a FrontPage Web

The Sprites you create using the Text tool in Image Composer have the same graphical image properties as any other image. You can copy them into the FrontPage Editor or send them into a Web site (see Figure 16.6).

FIGURE 16.6
Rotated text placed in the FrontPage Editor.

▶ Refer to Chapter 15, "Getting Started with Image Composer," for copying Sprites to the FrontPage Editor or sending Composition Guides to a FrontPage Web site.

Once you copy or send your image into FrontPage, you can apply all the image-editing features you learned in Chapter 6, "Enhancing Pages with Graphics and Multimedia," including sizing, floating, and wrapping text around your new image.

Part IV
Ch
16

Working with Shapes

Image Composer allows you to create rectangles and squares, ovals and circles, straight and curved lines, freehand drawings, and objects with any number of sides. Table 16.1 lists the tools in the Shapes Palette.

Table 16.1   The Shapes Palette

Tool	Tool Name	What It Does
▢	Rectangle	Draws squares or rectangles. To draw a square, hold down the Ctrl key while you draw the rectangle.
○	Oval	Draws circles or ovals. To draw a circle, hold down the Ctrl key while you click and drag a rectangular shape that will frame the circle or oval.
⬭	Splines	Draws lines, curved lines, freehand drawings, shapes, and filled-in shapes. Hold down the Ctrl key while you draw to force straight lines.
◁	Polygon	Creates shapes with any number of sides. Click once to set a point; double-click to complete the polygon.
✦	Color Lift	Copies colors from one sprite to another.

Making Shape Tools Stick   If you are going to be drawing more than one oval, rectangle, polygon, or spline, you can select the Sticky check box in the Shapes Palette. With the Sticky check box selected, your selected shape remains the default until you pick another shape, and you can draw circles, squares, or lines repeatedly. With the Sticky check box deselected, each time you render a shape, you need to pick a Shape tool before you can begin to draw.

Working with Rectangles

In Chapter 15, "Getting Started with Image Composer," we covered the basics of creating rectangles. You can make a rectangle square by holding down the Ctrl key as you click and drag the rectangle outline.

Circles and Ovals

To draw a circle or an oval, first select the Shapes tool in the Image Composer Toolbox, and click the Oval tool in the Shapes Palette.

Once you have selected the Oval tool, click the Render button.

Splines

A spline is a line...and more. Splines can include Sprites with wavy or rounded edges. Image Composer's splines are a flexible and utilitarian tool for creating all kinds of shapes. You can set the width of a spline, edit nodal points within it, and elect to fill the spline or leave it open. Figure 16.7 shows one type of spline—a wavy line.

FIGURE 16.7
A wavy line spline.

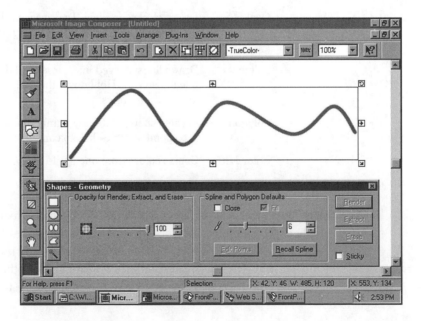

Setting the Width of a Spline   If you elect not to fill your spline, you can adjust the width of the outline by dragging the Spline Line Width Slider (say that quickly six times!). The Spline Line Width Slider is in the Spline and Polygon Defaults area of the Shapes-Geometry Palette, and becomes active only when you deselect the Fill check box. As you drag the Slider, the Spin box shows the outline width of the rectangle being set (see Figure 16.8).

FIGURE 16.8

The Geometry palette.

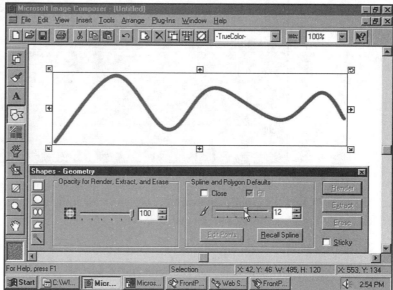

Unlike other shapes, Splines can be closed or not closed. If you deselect the Close check box in the Shapes Palette, you can draw freehand lines and curves that do not form a closed shape.

Drawing a Straight Line   Before we experiment with some of the trickier splines, explore the most basic type—a nice straight line. Straight lines can be copied into a FrontPage Editor document to create unique, customized horizontal lines.

1. Select the Spline Tool in the Shapes-Geometry Palette.
2. Click the starting point for the line.
3. Click the ending point of the line.
4. Click the Render button in the Shapes-Geometry Palette.

You can then move your line by selecting the Arrange tool in the Toolbox and dragging the middle of the Sprite to a new location. You can rotate your line by dragging clockwise or counterclockwise on the rotate handle in the Sprite (see Figure 16.9).

FIGURE 16.9

Rotating a straight line spline.

Making Waves   Sprites allow you to create smooth curves and wavy lines. Each point on the wave can then be individually edited.

To draw a wavy line, do the following:

1. Select the Spline button in the Shapes Palette.

TIP   If you are creating many examples of the same shape, or you need many attempts to create a shape, click the Sticky check box to retain a default shape.

When you are drawing a spline, your cursor takes on a special wavy icon appearance.

2. Click the starting point for your curved line.
3. Click the next nodal point in the spline.
4. Continue to click at nodal points until you have marked all the nodal points for your wavy line (see Figure 16.10).
5. Before you render the line, you can click the Edit Points button in the Spline and Polygon Defaults area of the Shapes-Geometry Palette, and edit any of the nodal points (see Figure 16.11).
6. Before you render the line, you can adjust the Spline Line Width.
7. When everything is set, click the Render button (see Figure 16.12).

FIGURE 16.10
A wavy wavy spline.

FIGURE 16.11
Editing nodal points
on a spline.

FIGURE 16.12
Smoothed out curves
on a spline.

Odd Shapes and Zigzag Lines

You can use the Polygon tool to create closed shapes of any configuration. You can also use the Polygon tool to create zigzag lines.

Drawing zigzag lines with the Polygon tool is very similar to drawing curved lines with the Spline tool. Deselect the Closed check box. Then click to place nodal points, select line width, edit points as necessary, and then render the line (see Figure 16.13).

To draw a closed shape, select the Closed check box in the Shapes Palette. Using the Polygon tool, click each nodal point of the shape.

Before you render a polygon, you can edit the points (see Figure 16.14).

Once you have edited the points and selected a line width, you can render your polygon shape (see Figure 16.15).

FIGURE 16.13
A zig-zag spline.

FIGURE 16.14
Drawing a polygon.

FIGURE 16.15
A rendered polygon.

Closed Polygons You can use the Polygon tool to draw zigzag lines by *not* selecting the Close check box in the Shapes Palette. And you can create closed shapes that are not filled in by selecting the Close check box, but *not* the Fill check box. But you can also create closed and filled polygons.

As you do, the closed areas of the shape are filled with the selected color swatch. And in the next section of this chapter you will learn to select from even more intriguing fill options.

The process of drawing a closed filled polygon is similar to creating a closed polygon without a fill. Just click the Fill check box before you render the shape.

Arranging Sprites

Once you begin to compose graphic images from more than one Sprite, you will find it necessary to arrange Sprites. Sprites can be aligned—so that a group of images is on the same horizontal or vertical plane, or even all centered together. You can also position Sprites in front of or behind each other. This technique is often used to place text on top of a shape (see Figure 16.16).

FIGURE 16.16
Placing text over a
polygon spline.

The Arrange Palette also lets you manipulate Sprite properties in other useful ways, as
follows:

Fit Sprites to a Bounding Box

Crop Sprites

Group Sprites

Size Sprites by percent

Rotate Sprites precisely

Assign a default location to a Sprite

Taken together, these features allow you to create imagemaps and navigational buttons to
which you can attach hotspot hyperlinks. The resulting imagemaps allow visitors to your
page to jump to hyperlinked bookmarks or Web pages by pointing and clicking at one
element in a larger picture.

▶ For instructions on assigning hyperlinks to images, see Chapter 6, "Enhancing Pages with
Graphics and Multimedia," page 121.

Moving Sprites Forward and Back

By arranging Sprites front and back, you can place text against a shape to create an effective navigational button.

You will find buttons to move selected Sprites in front of and behind each other in the Order area of the Arrange Palette. When you point at the buttons, tooltips will identify those buttons. Those buttons are listed in Table 16.2.

Table 16.2   Moving Sprites Forward and Backward

Ordering Tool	What It Does
Send Forward	Moves the selected Sprite one level above the other Sprites that share the same space.
Send Backward	Moves the selected Sprite one level behind other Sprites that share the same space.
To Back	Sends the selected Sprite all the way to the back of (behind) all other Sprites that share the same space.
To Front	Brings the selected Sprite all the way to the front of all other Sprites that share the same space.

Ordering Three Sprites   Let's say you have three Sprites you wish to combine into a button that will be used as a hyperlink in your FrontPage web. Those three Sprites might be an oval, a polygon, and text (see Figure 16.17).

FIGURE 16.17
Three sprites waiting to be stacked on top of each other.

You can move one Sprite on top of another simply by selecting it and dragging from the middle of the Sprite (see Figure 16.18). (We'll explore centering one Sprite over another later in this chapter).

TIP When you drag one Sprite on top of another, that Sprite is placed on top of the target Sprite.

There are times when you will drag one Sprite on top of another but you want the *target* Sprite to be on top of the pile (see Figure 16.19).

FIGURE 16.18
Placing Text on an Oval Sprite.

FIGURE 16.19
The Text Sprite needs to be moved to the top of the stack!

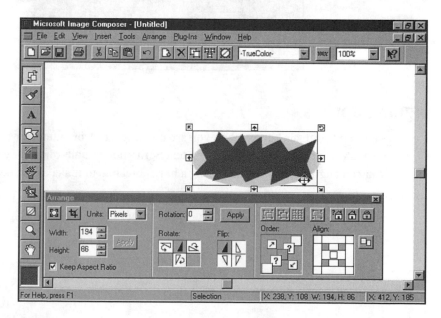

If this is the case, select the Sprite you wish to move one layer back, and click the Send Backward tool in the Order area of the Align Palette.

> **WARNING**
>
> Clicking the Send to Back button will send the selected object *all the way* to the back of the stack of Sprites.

When in doubt, experiment. You can arrange objects in any order to create an effective image (see Figure 16.20).

FIGURE 16.20

Three Sprites—layered.

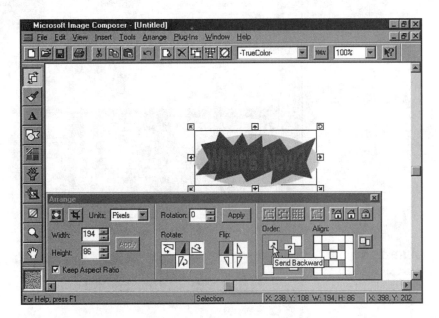

Aligning Sprites

Aligning Sprites is handy when you are creating a row of buttons or tools to let visitors navigate your site. You can center a text Sprite horizontally and vertically within a shape. You can align several buttons along a horizontal line to make a nice neat row of buttons.

The first step in aligning a group of Sprites is to select the Arrange tool from the Toolbox, and draw a marquee around all the Sprites you wish to align (see Figure 16.21).

FIGURE 16.21
Selecting three
Sprites with a
Marquee.

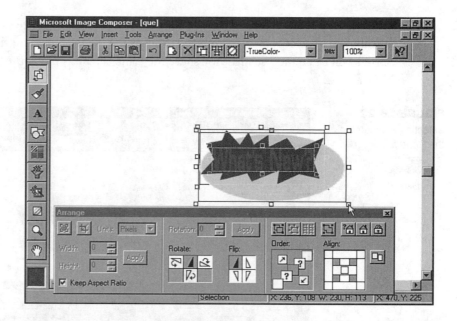

> **WARNING**
>
> Before aligning Sprites, make sure you have selected *all* the Sprites to be aligned.

You can align Sprites in the following ways:

By tops

By bottoms

By right edges

By left edges

By centers

To Align Sprites: The process of aligning Sprites is basically the same no matter what kind of alignment you wish. The two steps are:

1. Select all the Sprites to be aligned.

2. Click one of the Alignment options in the Align area of the Arrange Palette.

Centering Sprites   Centering is particularly useful for creating buttons. You can select a background and text—or more objects as well if you wish—and align their centers to create a button.

After you select all the Sprites which are to be center-aligned, Image Composer will prompt you to select one of the images to act as the "center" for centering. All other Sprites will be aligned so that they share the same center as the Sprite you select (see Figure 16.22.)

FIGURE 16.22
Selecting a center for the Sprites.

Aligning Sprites Horizontally and Vertically   You align Sprites horizontally and vertically in much the same way you center Sprites. Select all the Sprites to be aligned and click the Tops, Bottoms, Right Side, or Left Side tools in the Align area of the Arrange Palette.

Centering Sprites Horizontally and Vertically   Not only can you align centers, tops, or bottoms (or lefts and rights) of selected Sprites, you can align the centers of selected Sprites *horizontally or vertically*. The best way to explain horizontal center aligning is to show an example. Figure 16.24 below shows three buttons with their centers aligned only horizontally. This was accomplished by selecting all the Sprites, and clicking on the Horizontal Align button in the Align area of the Arrange Palette.

Grouping Sprites

Once you have arranged two or more Sprites, you can group them. Grouping Sprites allows you to move and size them together. For example, if you created a button out of three Sprites, you could group those three Sprites, then move and duplicate the button as you would a single Sprite. Most formatting features, however, cannot be applied to grouped Sprites.

After you group Sprites, you can ungroup them and edit any of the single Sprites individually. To group two or more Sprites, do the following:

1. Select the Arrange Palette.

2. Draw a marquee around the Sprites you wish to group, or hold the Shift key down and click more than one Sprite.

3. Click the Group button just above the Order area in the Arrange Palette (see Figure 16.23).

FIGURE 16.23
Grouping Sprites.

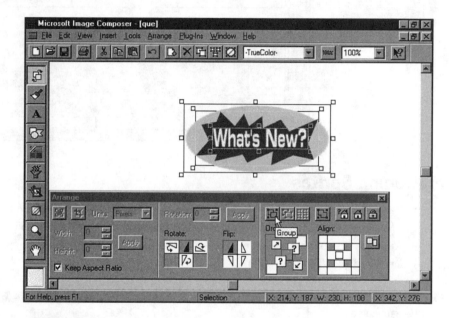

Once you have grouped Sprites, you can move the new (grouped) Sprite just as you would any other Sprite. However, if you want to edit the features of one of the Sprites, you need to ungroup first by clicking the (grouped) Sprite and clicking the Ungroup button in the Align Palette.

 One handy technique for creating a set of buttons is to group all the Sprites used in a model button, duplicate the button, then ungroup and edit the text in each button (see Figure 16.24).

FIGURE 16.24
Ungrouped Sprites—
with edited text.

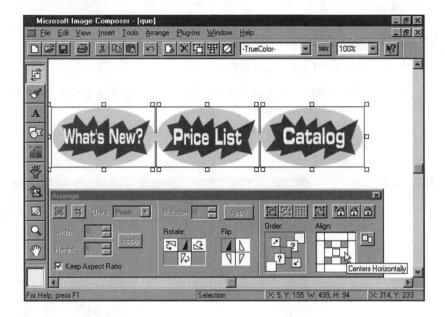

Flattening Sprites

Grouped Sprites can still be ungrouped at any time—and their individual component
Sprites edited, deleted, or moved within the group. However, grouped Sprites cannot be
edited. If you wish to edit a grouped Sprite, you can flatten it. This new Sprite can then be
resized (see Figure 16.25).

FIGURE 16.25
Buttons—grouped as
one Sprite.

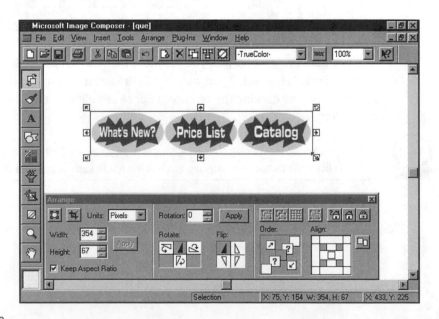

Any number of Sprites or grouped Sprites can be included in a flattened Sprite. The flattened Sprite can be edited, *but it cannot be unflattened*. So before making the plunge, be sure you want to flatten a group of Sprites permanently.

Fitting Sprites to a Bounding Box

The Fit to Bounding Box tool in the Arrange Palette crops any unnecessary pixels out of the area around your Sprite. This is a handy tool to use before copying your Sprite onto your Web page.

Cropping Sprites

You can crop any Sprite by selecting the Crop tool in the Arrange Palette, and dragging in on the special crop handle that appears. You need to click the Crop tool each time you wish to crop, because it does not stay selected.

Sizing Sprites by Percent

If you want your Sprite to fill half a visitor's Web page when she visits your site, set the size to 50%. For three-quarters of a page, set to 75%. You can set Sprite size in percent by selecting Percent from the Units list in the Arrange Palette.

To assign the percentage size, click the Sprite you wish to size and select a percent value.

Rotating Sprites Precisely

In Chapter 15, "Getting Started with Image Composer," you learned to rotate Sprites by dragging clockwise or counterclockwise on the rotation handle. If you want to assign an exact angle to a rotation, you can do that in the Rotation area of the Arrange Palette.

 TIP If you want to align an angled line or shape with angled text, select both Sprites, and assign them the same rotation angle.

You can also flip a selected Sprite or Sprites by using the Rotate and Flip buttons in the Align Palette.

Giving a Sprite a Home

If you wish to fix a set location in Composition Guide for a Sprite, click the Home button—the one that looks like a house at the right edge of the Align Palette. Once you set a home location for your Sprite, then whenever you have moved it, you can click the Return to

Home Position button to zip the Sprite back to its home. If you don't want the Sprite moved, period, no ifs ands or buts, you can click the Lock Position button.

Clicking the Lock Position button a second times toggles this feature off.

Creating Imagemaps

You can combine Sprites in a group and bring them into FrontPage to function as an imagemap. Imagemaps are becoming a standard feature on Web sites these days. And with the tools you've acquired in this chapter, you can create your own. Once the imagemap has been created in Image Composer, copy it into a page in the FrontPage Editor and assign hyperlinks to different parts of the image.

▶ Assigning hyperlinks to Image Maps is covered in Chapter 6, "Enhancing Pages with Graphics and Multimedia," page 121.

Designing your imagemap in Image Composer gives you a tremendous amount of freedom to control the content and style. Using just the tools we've covered in this chapter, you can create functional and friendly imagemaps with buttons, icons, or, if you're really artistic, drawings that will send the visitor to just where he or she wants to go (see Figure 16.26).

FIGURE 16.26

An image map created in Image Composer and copied into the FrontPage Editor.

From Here...

In this chapter, we explored a wide variety of ways you can create, edit and combine Sprites. Look to the following chapters for further ways to creatively work with graphic images:

- Chapter 17, "Using Effects for Maximum Impact," will cover the wide range of image effects available using Patterns & Fills, more Warps and Filters, Art Effects, and Color Tuning.

- Chapter 18, "Tailoring your Images for FrontPage Documents," will examine different options for making your Image Composer files work well with your Web site.

Part
IV
Ch
16

Using Effects for Maximum Impact

Microsoft Image Composer is loaded with an arsenal of fun effects that you can use to enhance your graphic images. Tasteful but creative, provocative but friendly image editing can make your site really unique and expressive.

In Chapter 16, "Working with Sprites," you explored using graphical text, and combining text with image sprites to make customized buttons. By applying the arsenal of effects that comes with Image Composer, you can also transform your text into a whole series of fun, scary, impressive, and eye-catching looks.

With the addition of special fills, your images can glow, shine, and take on 3-D effects and rainbow-like shadings. Other artistic options include altering imported photos—to give the impression that they were created using watercolor paints, charcoal, pencil, and other artistic tools. ■

Use Special Fills

Fill selected Sprites with everything from palette colors to checkerboards. Lift fills from one Sprite and place them in another.

Outlining and Enhancing Colors

Add a variety of outlines to any Sprite, including 3-D shading.

Edit Imported Photos

Enhance colors, bring pictures into focus, change tints, turn gray hair black, and change burnt toast to perfectly done.

Get Artistic

Use Art Effects like paint and charcoal to give imported photos, text, and shapes unique textures and looks.

Working with Special Patterns and Fills

You can use just about anything for a fill pattern in Image Composer. You can change the color of any Sprite. You can apply gradient fills to give your Sprite that ethereal look of fading off into the somewhere. You can place patterns inside your Sprite. You can use Complement Fills to create a "cookie-cutter effect." And you can steal a fill from one Sprite, including from an imported photo, and use it for a fill in another Sprite.

Changing Colors

After you create a Sprite and render it, you can change the fill with the Patterns and Fills tool in the Image Composer toolbox.

First, select the Sprite you wish to recolor. Then click the Color Picker in the Color Swatch and select a fill color and hue.

Once the correct fill color has been selected, click the Patterns and Fills tool in the Toolbox, and choose Current Color Fill from the list of Patterns and Fills.

Finally, click the Apply button to transfer the current color fill to the selected Sprite(s) (see Figure 17.1). If the "recoloring" masks the Sprite too much, simply click the Undo button.

FIGURE 17.1
Transfering a color fill.

Applying Gradient Ramp Fills

Gradient Ramp fills enable you to fade from one color to another. The term "ramp" is a metaphor for gradual change—like the ramp that takes you from one level of a parking garage to another. Applied to shades or colors, a ramp creates a rainbow-like series of colors that transition from the start to the finished color.

You can assign a total of four colors to a Gradient fill, and they will blend into each other. To apply a Gradient Ramp fill, do the following:

1. First select the Sprite or Sprites to receive the fill.

2. Click the Patterns and Fills tool in the Toolbox and select Gradient Ramp from the Fills list.

3. Image Composer comes with 19 preconfigured shading patterns. You can start by experimenting with them. Scroll through the list of Gradient fills in the Ramp Name list, and select one.

4. Click Apply to apply the Gradient Ramp fill to your selected Sprite(s) (see Figure 17.2).

FIGURE 17.2
Applying a Gradient Ramp.

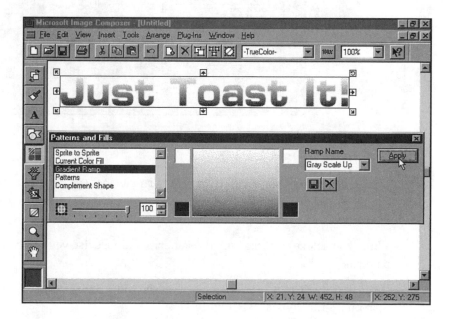

Customizing Gradient Ramps   You can create your own custom Gradient Ramp by selecting two, three, or four colors in the Pick Color swatches of the Gradient Ramp area of the Patterns and Fills Palette.

Often Gradient Ramps will use the same color on top or on one side, and a second color on the bottom or the other side. But you can mix and match up to four colors.

Experiment! Some Gradient fills work best as backgrounds; others work fine as fills for text.

One technique that is often used for effect is to place a Gradient Ramp–filled rectangle behind text (see Figure 17.3).

FIGURE 17.3
Using a Gradient Ramp-filled Sprite behind text.

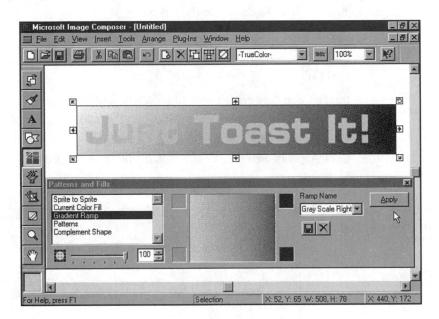

Using Pattern Fills

Image Composer comes with a set of Pattern fills that can be used in any selected Sprite. As with other fills, first select the Sprite(s) to be filled. Then access the Patterns and Fills Palette from the Toolbox.

When you select Patterns from the Patterns and Fills list, you can choose from a list of patterns.

If you apply a Stripes pattern, you can set the width and spacing of the stripes using the Spin boxes that appear (see Figure 17.4).

FIGURE 17.4
Setting stripe width
and spacing.

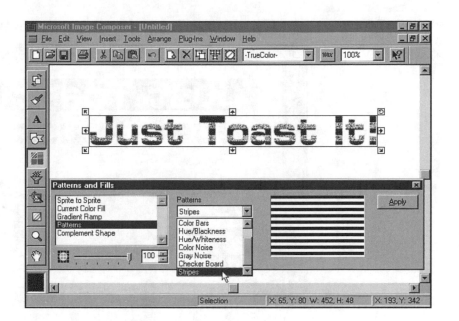

Creating Complement Shape Text

Complement Shapes look like you used your original Sprite as a cookie cutter to cut a piece out of a background.

The background assumes the fill that has been applied to the Sprite.

There are two steps to creating a Complement Shape, as follows:

1. Select the Sprite to apply the Complement fill to, and using the Patterns and Fills Palette, choose a Complement fill.

2. Pull the Complement fill off to the side, leaving the original Sprite. The result is actually two sprites—one is the original object, the second is a "negative" of the first object (see Figure 17.5).

Transferring a Fill from a Sprite

Any Sprite can provide a fill for another Sprite—even a photo. This opens up some very interesting possibilities for filling drawings, but especially for textured text.

FIGURE 17.5

A Complement Shape fill.

To fill one Sprite from another one:

1. The target Sprite must be on top of the source Sprite.

2. With the target Sprite placed on top of the source Sprite, select the target Sprite.

3. Choose the Sprite to Sprite fill from the list of Patterns and Fills.

See Figure 17.6.

TIP Make sure your target Sprite is selected when you apply the Sprite to Sprite fill.

If you want your source Sprite to fill your entire target Sprite, the source Sprite must fill the entire area behind the target Sprite, as shown in Figure 17.6 earlier.

After you apply the Sprite to Sprite fill, you will be prompted to click the source Sprite. Do so, and the fill will be transferred to the selected (target) Sprite.

After you transfer the source Sprite fill to the target, you can pull the target Sprite off the source and use the two Sprites in any combination you wish—or you can simply delete the source Sprite once you've borrowed its fill.

You can experiment with different transfer options from the Sprite Texture Type list, but you will probably find that the Transfer Full option works best to transfer a fill to a selected Sprite (see Figure 17.7).

FIGURE 17.6
Transferring a fill from Sprite to Sprite.

FIGURE 17.7
Sprite to Sprite fill transfer—"Toast" filled with toast.

Outlining, Filtering, and Enhancing Sprites

In Chapter 15, "Getting Started with Image Composer," you experimented with some of the fun features on the Warps and Filters Palette. But that was only the beginning. The

Warps and Filters Palette contains a number of hidden utilitarian goodies, including the ability to apply outlines, to filter images, and to enhance photos and other Sprites.

Outlining Sprites

Outlines can help frame an image. Combining outlines with subtle fills can produce attractive text. Outlines can also be used for shaded 3-D effects.

The Outline list in the Warps and Filters Palette has five different types of outlines (see Table 17.1).

Table 17.1	Outline Effects
Effect	**What It DOES**
Shadow	Can be adjusted to provide different angles of 3-D–style shading
Edge	Outlines images with a line using the selected color swatch
Edge Only	Creates an outline for the selected Sprite, and then clears the fill
Recess	Creates a shadow above and to the left of the selected Sprite
Relief	Creates a shadow below and to the right of the selected Sprite

Placing a Shadow   To place a shadow on a selected Sprite, select the Warps and Filters Palette and choose Outlines From the Warps and Filters Group List.

Select Shadow Offset from the Offset X and Offset Y Spin boxes. Y axis offset defines the shadow below the Sprite. X axis offset is to the right of the Sprite. Offset defines the width of the shadow.

TIP   The larger the offset values, the more shadow you will have.

You can change the color of the shadow by clicking the Color Swatch and selecting a color from the palette.

You can reduce the opacity of the shadow with the Opacity slider.

▶ **See** "Working with Sprites," **p. 339**

When you have defined the offsets and the color for the shadow, click the Apply button in the Patterns and Fills Palette (see Figure 17.8).

FIGURE 17.8

Applying a shadow.

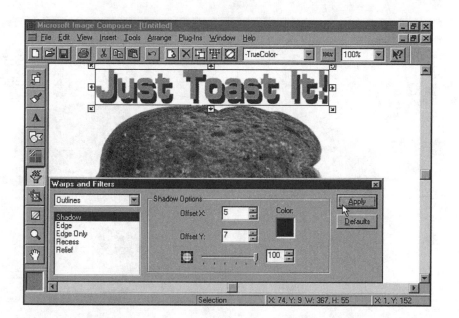

Part

IV

Ch

17

CAUTION

Each time you apply an outline, the new effect is added to the existing effects. So reapplying an outline will double the thickness of the outline.

Placing an Edge Placing an edge is similar to adding a shadow to a selected Sprite. The difference is that there is no offset—the outline is uniform all around the Sprite.

Outlines are effective in making faint images sharply defined. Often outlines are placed around light-colored or filled text for effect (see Figure 17.9).

Remember that FrontPage Editor allows you to place borders around graphic images. So if you want to place a border around an image, you can do so there. Any border you attach to a Sprite in Image Composer cannot be removed in the FrontPage Editor.

On the other hand, outlined text, as illustrated in Figure 17.9 for example, cannot be done in the FrontPage Editor. Do that in Image Composer before you copy the Sprite to FrontPage.

Placing an Edge-Only Outline Edge-only outlines work exactly like regular outlines, except that they remove all fills from the target Sprite (see Figure 17.10).

As with other outlines, you can set the thickness of the outline and the opacity.

FIGURE 17.9
Putting an edge on
your message.

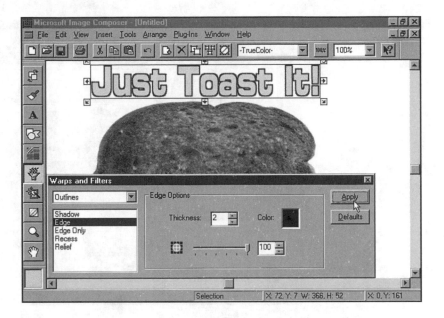

FIGURE 17.10
Text with edge only
outlining.

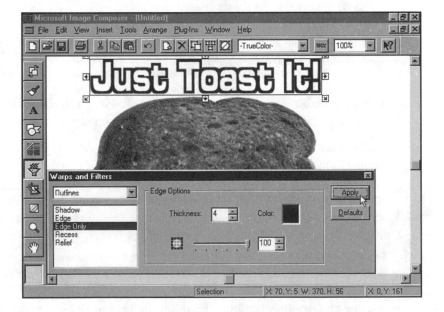

Recessing a Sprite   Recessing a Sprite is a form of applying a shadow outline. The
Recess outline is calculated to create an effect of an embedded or notched image (see
Figure 17.11).

FIGURE 17.11
Recessed text.

There are no offsets, line thickness, colors, or opacity settings for the Recess outline. They are all preset.

Placing a Sprite in Relief   Placing a Sprite in relief creates an illusion that the object is set off from the page. Relief is another form of applying a shadow outline. The Relief outline also comes with preset offsets, line thickness, colors, and opacity. Relief outlines give an edge and 3-D feel to any image. Relief outlines can often be used to good effect with imported photos (see Figure 17.12).

Filtering Sprites

Filters can be used to touch up photos for various artistic effects. Filter effects include the following:

> Blur
>
> Soften
>
> Sharpen
>
> Sharpen Lite
>
> Outline

Usually you will want to experiment with filtering effects to find one that will enhance your imported photo image.

FIGURE 17.12
Placing a Sprite in
relief.

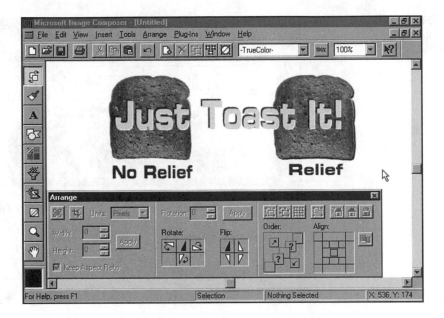

To experiment with filters, select an imported photo image and apply the filter. Filters can also be applied to text, for example to create that annoying blurry text that says "Focus Here" on T-shirts (see Figure 17.13).

FIGURE 17.13
Had your glasses
checked lately?

The higher the settings in the Horizontal and Vertical Blur Spin boxes, the blurrier your Sprite will become.

> **CAUTION**
>
> Using too much blurry text can be bad for your eyes, and can annoy your visitors. If that's your mission, use too much of it.

Color Tuning

The Color Tuning Palette enables you to adjust the colors and brightness of an imported photo as follows:

Part
IV
Ch
17

The Brightness Slider in the Color Tuning Palette lets you recolor a photo. Here's where you can perform miracles of hair coloring, change a pink house to green, or change burnt toast to golden brown.

The Contrast Slider in the Color Tuning Palette works like the contrast dial on your TV or computer monitor. You can sharpen or lighten the contrast in a selected Sprite.

Saturation changes the amount of gray in a color.

Enhancing Sprites

Not only can you turn a focused object blurry, you can actually sharpen a blurry Sprite with Image Composer. Use the Sharpen option from the Filters list in the Warps and Fills Palette to bring out-of-focus photos into better focus.

The more you apply the Sharpen or Sharpen Lite effects, the more detail is emphasized. Keep your finger ready to click the Undo button when you go too far!

Warp Transforms

Cataloging every single effect provided by Image Composer is beyond the scope of this book. Look for my next work from Que, *One Billion Effects from Image Composer,* to explore a few more effects than can be covered here. I'm joking about the book, but there is an almost unlimited combination of effects you can create by using various effects on top of each other. One effect we cannot skip is Warp Transforms. They're too much fun to miss.

Once you've tried Warp Transforms, you'll be hooked on them as well. Just remember that your Web site visitors may not find them as much fun as you do if you overuse them. Once per Web site is about the limit on these wild effects.

Waving a Flag   The Wave effect can be selected from the Warp Transforms Group in the Warps and Filters list. You can experiment with different settings in the Frequency % and Amplitude % Spin boxes. You can wave only vertically (the Y Only option button), horizontally (the X Only option button), or both. And your wave can be symmetrical or asymmetrical.

If this means anything to you trig majors, the wave effect applies a sine wave warp. When you select a higher Frequency %, you increase the number of waves within the target Sprite. When you select a higher number in the Amplitude % Spin box, you increase the height of the individual waves. In short, you need to experiment. One setting to try is to set the Amplitude to 10% or less and select a Y Only Wave Axis. This setting can be used to "wave" a rectangle (see Figure 17.14).

FIGURE 17.14
Waving a flag.

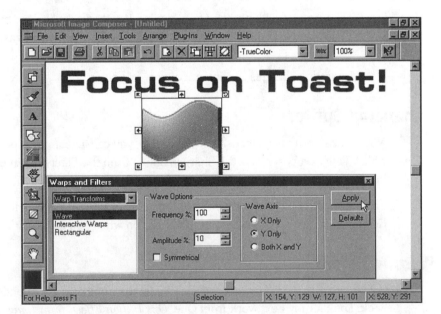

Interactive Warps

Interactive Warps are available from the Warp Transforms Group in the Warps and Filters Palette.

Interactive Warps are called "interactive" because once you select one of these effects, you tug and stretch, pull and push on parts of the selected Sprite to warp and transform it.

Each Interactive Warp works differently, and each one has an infinite number of permutations, depending on how you stretch and pull on the selected Sprite after applying a Warp. All Interactive Warps are applied in two steps, as follows:

1. Select the target Sprite, and choose one of the Interactive Warps from the Interactive Warps list in the Warps and Filters Palette.

2. Click and drag the corners or center of the marquee that appears around the Sprite. Some Interactive Warps are applied by dragging on corners of the Sprite, others by dragging on the middle (see Figure 17.15).

TIP You can tell whether the warp requires dragging on the corner or the center by the handles or grid that appears over the Sprite when you select the Warp option. If you see handles on the corners, drag on them. If you see a grid over the Sprite, drag on the spot where grid lines intersect.

Part
IV

Ch
17

FIGURE 17.15
Selecting an interactive Warp.

You can tug and pull on more than one handle in a selected Sprite (see Figure 17.16).

By liberal use of the Undo key and lots of experimentation, you can apply just the right Interactive Warp effect to enhance the message emanating from your Web site. You can also apply more than one interactive Warp effect to a Sprite (see Figure 17.17).

FIGURE 17.16
Warping text.

FIGURE 17.17
Using multiple Warps
on a Sprite.

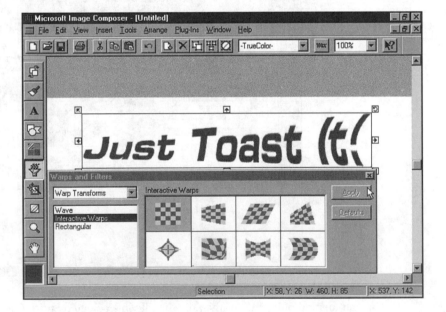

Art Effects

Art effects can be applied to any Sprite, but they are frequently used to transform imported photos into what appear to be drawings, paintings, sketches, charcoal images, and so on. A grainy black-and-white photo can become a sharply etched line drawing (see Figure 17.18).

FIGURE 17.18
Using art effects to transform a photo.

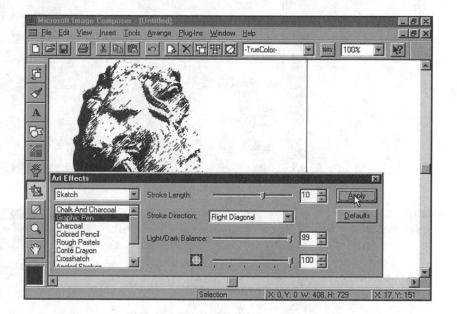

There is truly an unlimited array of Art effects available in the Art Effects Palette. You can experiment with applying them to imported photos to create various artistic effects. A color photo of a goldfish in a bowl can become an impressionist watercolor painting (see Figure 17.19).

Some Art effects can be applied to text, with interesting results. The general rule is that effects from the Exotic and Utility Group Lists can be applied to text (see Figure 17.20).

Many of the effects from the Paint, Sketch, and Graphics groups are a little too subtle to have much impact on text display. They are often best used to transform an imported photo into a simulated painting, sketch, or drawing (see Figure 17.21).

FIGURE 17.19
Photo transformed to
a watercolor painting.

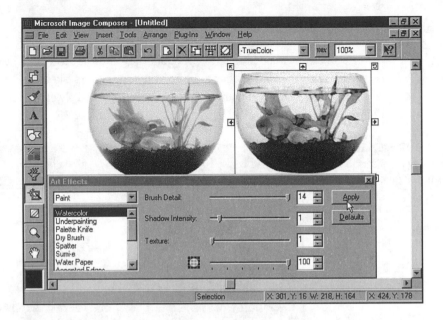

FIGURE 17.20
Text with a chrome
look.

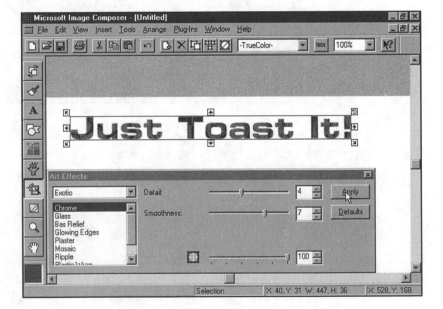

FIGURE 17.21
Photo transformed to
a pen drawing?

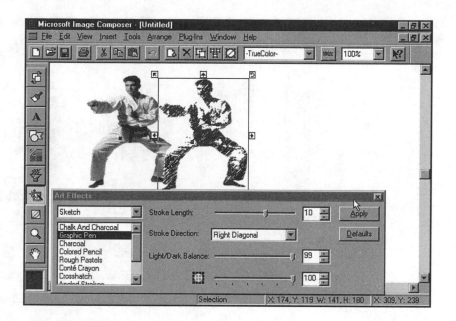

Using the Paint Palette

The Paint Palette provides you with 16 tools with which to create Paint effects. These Paint tools all differ in their effect. But the process of applying Paint effects generally takes three steps, as follows:

1. Select the Paint effect from the buttons on the left side of the Paint Palette.
2. Select a brush or effect size from the grid in the middle of the Paint Palette.
3. Select a Sprite, and apply the Paint effect by "painting" over all or part of the Sprite with the selected Paint tool.

Using the Paintbrush

The Paintbrush, along with the brush size you pick in the Size grid, can be used to "paint over" sections of the selected Sprite, using the color selected in the Color Picker swatch (see Figure 17.22).

Part
IV

Ch

17

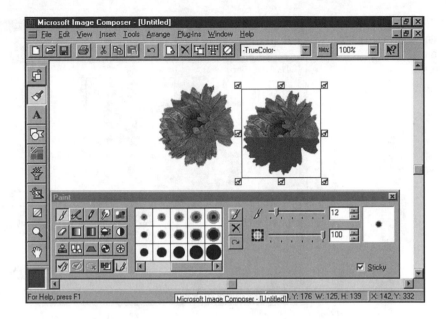

Using the Airbrush and Pencil

The Airbrush tool is similar in effect to the Paintbrush tool, but this tool applies color in a more airy, spray-painted mode.

The Pencil tool applies the selected Color Picker color in a thin line as you "draw over" a selected Sprite. It can be used to apply a very fine "paint-over" to a Sprite.

The Smear tool is not the most attractive of paint effects. Smear pretty much muddies up the coloring of the selected Sprite as you color over it. You'll find a way to use it some-day—like when you are creating a Web site for the Muddy Creek Chamber of Commerce, and the photo they give you comes out too clear (see Figure 17.23).

Erasing and Tinting Effects

When opacity is set to 100%, the Erase tool wipes out everything it paints over.

The Tint tool tints images with the selected color swatch as you click and drag over the selected Sprite. For example, select a light pink or rose color from the Color Picker, then paint over an image to give it a rosy glow.

The Colorize tool changes color to the selected swatch color as you paint over parts of the selected Sprite. By reducing the Opacity setting, you can touch up a photo. By cranking up the Opacity, you paint over the old colors.

FIGURE 17.23
Getting muddy.

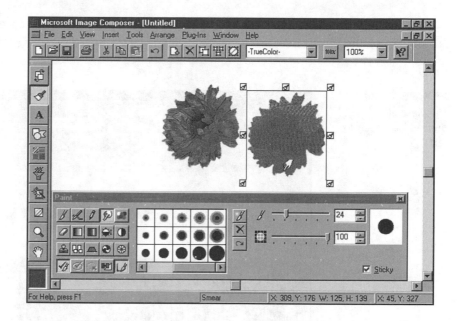

The Dodge-Burn tool is an intriguing paint effect that lightens or darkens as you paint over a Sprite. Try it. For those of you who develop and print your own photos, these effects are similar to dodging or burning a photo as you print it. Dodging can be used to reduce the exposure of a selected area of the photograph. Burning increases the exposure of the selected elements of the photo. Dodging lightens the selected area of the image. Burning darkens the areas where it is applied.

Use the Contrast tool to make an image sharper or to give it less contrast. Depending on how you set the Step Contrast Slider, this effect sharpens or blurs the contrast on a selected Sprite as you paint over it.

Transferring and Using the Rubber Stamp

The Rubber Stamp effect lets you pick up the color of a Sprite and "stamp it" on another Sprite, producing a very blurry effect.

The Transfer effect is similar to Rubber Stamp. It copies part of a Sprite onto other parts of the Sprite.

Warp Effects

Earlier in this chapter we explored adding Warp effects to selected Sprites. By combining Warp effects with a Paint tool, you can apply Warps selectively just to parts of a Sprite. Paint tools come with three Warp effects—Mesa, Vortex, and Spoke Inversion.

The Mesa effect lets you warp selected parts of a Sprite as you paint over it. Used sparingly, the Mesa effect brush can be used on text to create interesting effects (see Figure 17.24).

FIGURE 17.24
The Mesa effect—applied judiciously to text.

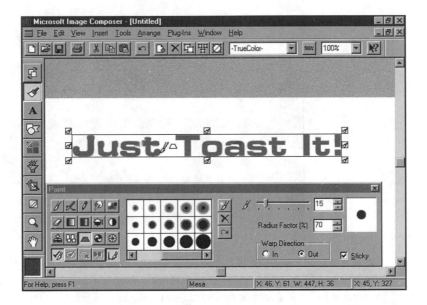

Vortex is another Warping effect that is applied to part of a Sprite. It creates a whirlpool effect to the applied Sprite, similar to if the Sprite got sucked down a drain. Start with a low percentage of warp when you experiment with this effect, and don't use it on a full stomach!

Spoke Inversion is a little too strange to describe. Perhaps a blowgun is a useful metaphor. It creates a Weblike blur on the portions of a selected Sprite that you paint it over. Use sparingly on text.

From Here...

In this chapter, we have reached into the far corners of Image Composer's ability to lend unique and creative effects to images. We used techniques that can be applied to imported photo files or Sprites created in Image Composer, including text Sprites.

Look to the following chapters for further ways to create and edit graphic images:

- Chapter 18, "Tailoring your Images for FrontPage Documents," examines different options for making your Image Composer files work well with your Web site.

Tailoring Your Images for FrontPage Documents

In the previous chapters, you explored a wide variety of tools and effects available in Microsoft Image Composer. In many cases, all that will be required to place your graphic image creations in a FrontPage 97 Web site is to copy selected sprites from Image Composer to the FrontPage Editor.

There are some additional ways to take advantage of Image Composer creations. While FrontPage 97 comes with a pleasant selection of clipart to use as background images, a really unique Web site might require a customized background. We'll explore how to do that in this chapter.

You can also achieve some additional control over the quality and speed of JPEG images by tweaking the compression in Image Composer before sending the file to FrontPage, so we'll take a look at that. Similarly, you can add transparent attributes to GIF files directly in Image Composer, even before you send the image to the FrontPage Editor. ■

Creating Custom Background Fills

Create a custom background on the fly, directly from the FrontPage Editor.

Adjusting JPEG Compression

A larger degree of image compression causes a JPEG image to resolve more quickly but decreases image quality.

Saving GIF Images with Transparent Backgrounds

You can add transparent background attributes right in Image Composer.

Using Image Composer's Sample Sprite Catalog

Image Composer includes a color format designed to make your colors look consistent regardless of what browser visitors are using to view your FrontPage Web site.

Creating Custom Background Fills

Your Web page backgrounds are a crucial part of setting the tone for your site. They exude an atmosphere like the paint on your living room walls or the music in the air when someone visits your home.

You can create customized background fills for your FrontPage Web by using the FrontPage Editor and Image Composer. In Chapter 6, "Enhancing Pages with Graphics and Multimedia," you learned to select custom background colors and fills, and you saw that FrontPage has a large set of images that can be used as attractive backgrounds.

You can also use Image Composer to create truly unique, fully customized backgrounds and fills for your Web pages. All of the fills and effects that are explored in Chapters 15, "Getting Started with Image Composer," 16, "Working with Sprites," and 17, "Using Effects for Maximum Impact," can be combined to create background fills. It is important to avoid the temptation to make your page background so flashy or distracting that it overshadows your Web site content—you may have noticed a site or two with this problem in your travels.

The following is a list of five things to avoid in backgrounds:

1. Dark colors combined with dark text fonts.
2. Distracting images that overshadow the site contents.
3. Image files so large that visitors wait too long for the page background to resolve.
4. Backgrounds that clash with your images.
5. And finally, always avoid ugly background images (get a second opinion when in doubt).

What Are Backgrounds Made Of?

The background of your Web site page is the width of a screen, and its length depends on how long your page is—it could be very, very long. When you create a background image, you do not create one large image that will be big enough to paper over the entire page. You create a small image, and from the standpoint of downloading speed, the smaller the better. This small image is then tiled—that is, little images are placed side by side and top to bottom so that they cover the entire page.

Background image files are generally in JPEG format. This is because JPEG images support far more colors than GIF files and resolve more quickly because they are compressed. The advantages of GIF files—interlacing and transparency—are not really useful for background image files since you rarely want them to be transparent, and interlacing your background would be distracting in the extreme.

▶ Refer to Chapter 6, "Enhancing Pages with Graphics and Multimedia," for a full discussion of the relative benefits of GIF and JPEG image formats.

Since backgrounds are composed of small JPEG image files, we can create them in Image Composer and send them right into an open FrontPage Web.

Launching Image Composer to Create a Custom Background

Let's say you are working in the FrontPage Editor, and the time comes to select a custom background to mesh aesthetically with your Web page. You look at the nice selection of background clip art, but there's nothing there that will really add a dynamite background. No problem, you can create a custom background image using Image Composer.

You may have noticed, back in Chapter 6, that custom background graphic image files are *tiled*—that is, rather than one super-large image file filling the entire page background, a small image file is repeated over and over, like tiles on a floor. This method produces a much smaller, more manageable, and faster image file than trying to save a huge image large enough to fill the entire background of yoru page.

Since the sample clip art background images that come with FrontPage 97 are a very nice size, my trick is to pick one, rename it, and edit it in Image Composer to create a unique, customized background. Let's do that.

1. With a Web open in the FrontPage Explorer, and a Web page open in the FrontPage Editor, right-click the page.

2. Select Page Properties from the Shortcut menu.

3. Click the Background tab in the Page Properties dialog box.

4. Select the Background Image check box (see Figure 18.1).

5. Click the Browse button.

6. Click the Clip Art tab in the Select Background Image dialog box.

7. From the Category list in the Select Background Image dialog box, select Backgrounds.

8. Select *any* background image—we're going to change the image (see Figure 18.2).

9. Click the OK button in the Select Background Image and Page Properties dialog box.

10. Save your page in the FrontPage Editor, and okay the prompt to save your new image(s).

Part
IV

Ch
18

FIGURE 18.1
Selecting a back-
ground image.

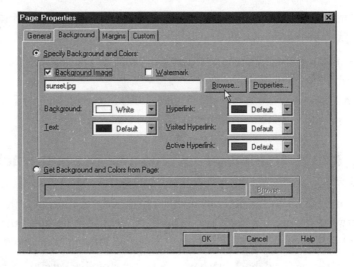

11. Switch to the FrontPage Explorer, and in Folder view, rename the background
    image with a custom name, like BK1.GIF. You will be prompted to update your links
    so that this renamed file becomes the background image for linked pages. Do that.

12. Double-click the renamed image to open that file in Image Composer.

FIGURE 18.2
Selecting a Back-
ground Image.

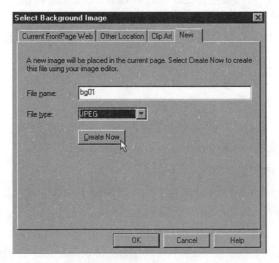

Designing a Background Image in Image Composer

When you launch Image Composer by double-clicking a renamed background image in
the FrontPage Explorer, a new file is opened in Image Composer. The file is already
named—with the name you assigned in the FrontPage Editor.

The image file opens with a single Sprite and a Composition Guide. Both the Sprite size and the Composition Guide can be adjusted, but this is a nice, small size for a background image tile.

You can edit the fill of the rectangular (square, to be precise) Sprite. Look back over the effects and fills covered in Chapters 15, 16, and 17 and experiment until you have a fill that you think will look good tiled in the background of your Web site. A good technique is to combine one fill—gradient ramps often work well—with one effect (see Figure 18.3).

FIGURE 18.3

Creating a background image tile.

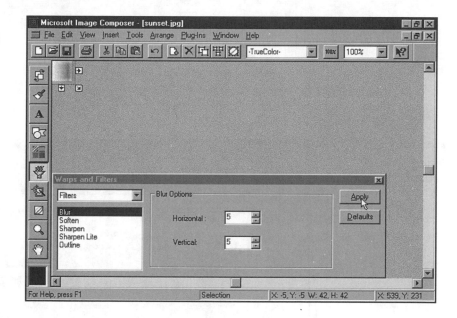

When you are satisfied with the image, select File, Send to FrontPage. Exit Image Composer, saving changes to your image file. Refresh the view in the FrontPage Editor and note the new, custom background you created (see Figure 18.4).

There's no substitute for trial and error here. See how the image looks behind your FrontPage Web page. You may want to test your background using your Web browser. That way you will know how long it takes to load the background image (see Figure 18.5).

If you don't like the image, you can reopen the file in Image Composer, double-click the background image file in the FrontPage Explorer, and send it back into Image Composer.

If you think you might want to use your background image with another Web site, you can save it in a directory (one you will remember). You can always reopen the file and send it to a new, different, open, FrontPage Web at a later date.

FIGURE 18.4
Custom background—
designed in Image
Composer.

FIGURE 18.5
Testing a custom
background image.

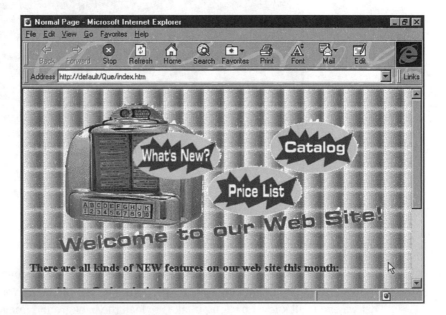

Adjusting JPEG Compression

The spectrum of JPEG compression basically runs from fast with low quality to slow with good quality. The more compression you select, the faster the image appears when a visitor comes to your site. However, a larger amount of compression generally means less quality to the picture.

Here, again, there is often no avoiding trial and error. You can try saving an imported photo with very little compression. Then send the image to FrontPage, test the site with your browser, and see if the wait is too long.

Saving a Selected Photo Sprite as a Compressed JPEG File   You can open a photo saved in TIF format and save it as a JPEG file in Image Composer. When you do that, you can select the amount of compression. Use the following steps:

1. Open an existing or new Image Composer file.
2. Select Insert, From File to insert a photo file from your disk or a CD-ROM. Image Composer comes with a nice selection of photos you can use, or you can open a scanned file or photo from a disk or CD-ROM of photos.
3. Click the photo Sprite, and select File, Save Selection As.
4. From the Save File as Type list, select JPG.
5. Select the Compression check box.
6. You should generally start with a low compression ratio—try 10% at first. Set the compression ratio by dragging the Amount slider (see Figure 18.6).
7. Enter a file name, and click Save.

FIGURE 18.6
Saving a photo in JPEG format.

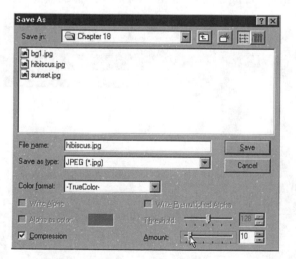

Testing Image Resolution Speed   Once you have saved a selection, you can close your current Image Composer file and open the just-saved one. This file will have the Composition Guide matched to the Sprite size.

You can let FrontPage 97 estimate the download time for your page. This is calculated and displayed on the right-side of the FrontPage Editor status bar as you work on your page.

If you want a more exact test of download time, you can test the resolution speed by saving the Web page and previewing the page in your Web browser. If the image takes too long to resolve, you can resave the file with a higher compression ratio.

Saving GIF Images with Transparent Backgrounds

In Chapter 6, you learned how to apply transparency to GIF files using the Make Transparent tool in the Image toolbar. You can also assign transparency in Image Composer and with more control over the level of transparency.

To assign transparency to an Image Composer file, you must save it in GIF format. JPEG files cannot be transparent.

Assign transparency by saving (or resaving) a file as a GIF file. Enter a file name if necessary. And click the Transparent color check box.

You can change the color that will become transparent by clicking the Transparent color Color Swatch, and selecting a color from the Palette (see Figure 18.7).

FIGURE 18.7
Selecting a transparency color.

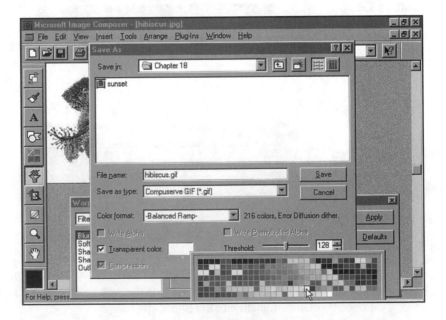

You can also regulate the degree of transparency using the Threshold Slider. Threshold determines just how transparent your image will be. Higher Threshold levels mean your image is less transparent.

Using Image Composer's Sample Sprite Catalog

Once you know how to create your own Sprites, you can appreciate and take advantage of the sample Sprite photos and other sample image files that come with Image Composer.

You can view thumbnail images of the Sprites on the Image Composer CD-ROM by selecting Help, Sample Sprites Catalog. The Index tab in the Sample Sprites Catalog dialog box shows an alphabetical list of sample Sprites. Looking for a picture of an almond? Scroll down the list and find one (see Figure 18.8).

FIGURE 18.8
Looking for a picture of an almond.

To view a sample Sprite, click the Display button in the Sample Sprites Catalog dialog box (see Figure 18.9).

You can also look for sample Sprites by category. You do this from the Contents tab of the Sample Sprites dialog box. Then select either photos or Web images by double-clicking one of those two icons (see Figure 18.10).

FIGURE 18.9
Viewing a sample
sprite.

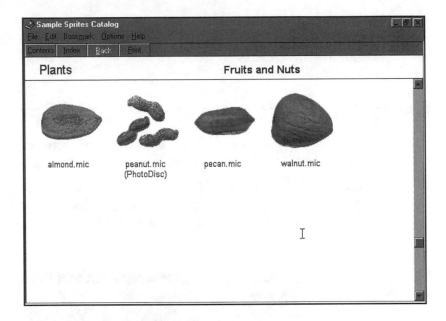

FIGURE 18.10
Looking for Sprites by
Category.

The Web images include:

- Backgrounds
- Bullets

- Buttons
- Counters
- Horizontal Rules
- Navigational Controls

From these categories, you'll find hundreds of images to spruce up your site. You may even find some that are as good as ones you make yourself!

Once you find an image you like, double-click the file in the file list to insert that image into your open Image Composer file. Of course, you can edit these images and resave them to create custom tools, buttons, and backgrounds.

 TIP Once you find the name of a sample Sprite in the catalog, you can zip to it in the Index tab and double-click to open the file.

Part
IV

Ch
18

Integrating Active Content Into Your Web Site

## CHAPTER 19

Using ActiveX Controls

With Internet Explorer 3.0, Microsoft has introduced ActiveX Technologies, a related set of technologies to "Activate the Internet." By building on its highly successful Object Linking and Embedding (OLE) standard, Microsoft has introduced a standard for adding active content to Web pages. This standard allows the capabilities of the Web browser to evolve continually, and also allows data and information from existing applications to be easily accessed.

ActiveX Controls combine the convenience of Java applets with the permanence and functionality of Netscape Navigator plug-ins. Like Java applets, ActiveX Controls can be automatically downloaded to your system either if they are not currently installed or if the installed version is not the most recent. Like plug-ins, ActiveX Controls remain available to your Web browser continuously once they are installed.

This chapter introduces you to ActiveX Controls, shows you examples of the available Controls, and demonstrates how you can install them into your pages with FrontPage Editor. ∎

Learn About Microsoft's ActiveX Controls

This chapter discusses Microsoft's ActiveX Controls and how you use them with FrontPage Editor to increase the capabilities of Internet Explorer 3.0 and other compatible applications.

Find out How ActiveX Controls Are Made Secure

Learn why it is a good idea to use only "signed" Controls and how they decrease the risk of tampering.

Find out What ActiveX Controls Mean for FrontPage Users and Programmers

Find out what the existence of ActiveX Controls means to the users and developers of World Wide Web software, information, and products.

See What ActiveX Controls Can Do in a Web Page

Find out what some of the ActiveX Controls can do.

What Are ActiveX Controls?

ActiveX Controls are more than simple Web Browser plug-ins or add-ins—because of the nature of ActiveX Controls, not only can they be used to extend the functionality of Microsoft's Web browser, but they also can be used by any programming language or application that supports the OLE standard. For example, an ActiveX Control could be written to enable Internet Explorer 3.0 automatically to search Usenet newsgroups for specific information and, at the same time, perform a similar function through integration into Microsoft Office products such as Excel or Access. Netscape Navigator plug-ins, on the other hand, can be used only in Web browsers such as Navigator and Internet Explorer 3.0.

As with Netscape Navigator's plug-ins, ActiveX Controls are dynamic code modules that exist as part of Microsoft's Application Programming Interface (API) for extending and integrating third-party software into any OLE-compliant environment. The creation of (and support for) ActiveX Controls by Microsoft is significant, primarily because it allows other developers to integrate their products seamlessly into the Web via Internet Explorer or any other OLE application, without having to launch any external helper applications.

For Internet Explorer users, ActiveX Controls support allows you to customize Internet Explorer's interaction with third-party products and industry media standards. Microsoft's ActiveX Control API also attempts to address the concerns of programmers, providing a high degree of flexibility and cross-platform support.

What ActiveX Controls Mean for End Users

For most users, integrating ActiveX Controls is transparent because they open up and become active whenever Internet Explorer 3.0 is opened. Furthermore, often you will not even see ActiveX Controls at work, because most ActiveX Controls are not activated unless you open up a Web page that initiates them. For example, after you install the Shockwave for Macromedia Director ActiveX Control, you will notice no difference in the way Internet Explorer 3.0 functions until you come across a Web page that features Shockwave.

Once an ActiveX Control is installed on your machine and initiated by a Web page, it will manifest itself in one of the following three potential forms:

- Embedded
- Full-screen
- Hidden

Embedded Controls   An embedded ActiveX Control appears as a visible, rectangular window integrated into a Web page. This window may not appear any different from a window created by a graphic, such as an embedded GIF or JPEG picture. The main difference between the previous windows supported by Internet Explorer 3.0 and those created by ActiveX Controls is that ActiveX Control windows support a much wider range of interactivity and movement, and thereby remain live instead of static.

In addition to mouse clicks, embedded ActiveX Controls also read and take note of mouse location, mouse movement, keyboard input, and input from virtually any other input device. In this way, an ActiveX Control can support the full range of user events required to produce sophisticated applications.

Full-Screen Controls   A full-screen ActiveX Control takes over the entire current Internet Explorer 3.0 window to display its own content. This is necessary when a Web page is designed to display data that is not supported by HTML. An example of this type of ActiveX Control is the VRML 2.0 ActiveX Control available from Microsoft. If you view a VRML world using Internet Explorer 3.0 with the VRML 2.0 ActiveX Control, it loads into your Web browser like any other Web page, but it retains the look and functionality of a VRML world, with three-dimensional objects that you can navigate through and around.

Hidden Controls   A hidden ActiveX Control doesn't have any visible elements, but works strictly behind the scenes to add some features to Internet Explorer 3.0 that are not otherwise available. An example of a hidden Control would be the Preloader Control, discussed later in this chapter. This ActiveX Control is used to preload a graphic, sound, or other element that will subsequently be viewed by the Internet Explorer 3.0 user. Since the element is downloaded while the user is browsing through the current Web page, appearance response time is much greater.

Regardless of which ActiveX Controls you are using and whether they are embedded, full-screen, or hidden, the rest of Internet Explorer's user interface should remain relatively constant and available. So even if you have a VRML world displayed in Internet Explorer 3.0's main window, you'll still be able to access Internet Explorer 3's menus and navigational controls.

What ActiveX Controls Mean for Programmers

For programmers, ActiveX Controls offer the possibility of creating Internet Explorer 3.0 add-on products and using development ActiveX Controls to create your own Internet-based applications. Creating a custom ActiveX Control requires much more intensive background, experience, and testing than actually using one. If you are a developer or are interested in creating an ActiveX Control, the following discussion will be useful.

The current version of the ActiveX Control Application Programming Interface (API) supports four broad areas of functionality.

ActiveX Controls can do the following:

- Draw into, receive events from, and interact with objects that are a part of the Internet Explorer 3.0 object hierarchy.
- Obtain MIME data from the network via URLs.
- Generate data for consumption by Internet Explorer 3.0, by other ActiveX Controls, or by Java applets.
- Override and implement protocol handlers.

ActiveX Controls are ideally suited to take advantage of platform-independent protocols, architectures, languages, and media types such as Java, VRML, and MPEG. While ActiveX Controls should be functionally equivalent across platforms, they should also be complementary to platform-specific protocols and architectures.

When the Internet Explorer 3.0 client is launched, it knows of any ActiveX Controls available through the Windows 95 Registry, but does not load any of them into RAM. Because of this, an ActiveX Control resides in memory only when needed, but many ActiveX Controls may be in use at one time, so you still need to be aware of memory allocation. ActiveX Controls simply reside on disk until they are needed. By having many ActiveX Controls readily available, without taking up any RAM until just before the time they are needed, the user is able to view seamlessly a tremendous amount of varied data. An ActiveX Control is deleted from RAM as soon as the user moves to another HTML page that does not require it.

Integration of ActiveX Controls with the Internet Explorer client is quite elegant and flexible, allowing the programmer to make the most of asynchronous processes and multithreaded data. ActiveX Controls may be associated with one or more MIME types, and Internet Explorer 3.0 may, in turn, create multiple instances of the same ActiveX Control.

At its most fundamental level, an ActiveX Control can access an URL and retrieve MIME data just as a standard Internet Explorer 3.0 client does. This data is streamed to the ActiveX Control as it arrives from the network, making it possible to implement viewers and other interfaces that can progressively display information. For instance, an ActiveX Control may draw a simple frame and introductory graphic or text for the user to look at while the bulk of the data is streaming off the network into Internet Explorer 3.0's existing cache. All the same bandwidth considerations adhered to by good HTML authors need to be accounted for in ActiveX Controls.

Of course, ActiveX Controls can also be file-based, requiring a complete amount of data to be downloaded first before the ActiveX Control can proceed. This type of architecture is not encouraged due to its potential user delays, but it may prove necessary for some data-intensive ActiveX Controls. If an ActiveX Control needs more data than can be supplied through a single data stream, multiple simultaneous data streams may be requested by the ActiveX Control, so long as the user's system supports this.

While an ActiveX Control is active, if data is needed by another ActiveX Control or by Internet Explorer 3.0, the ActiveX Control can generate data itself for these purposes. Thus, ActiveX Controls not only process data, they also generate it. For example, an ActiveX Control can be a data translator or filter.

ActiveX Controls are generally embedded within HTML code and accessed through the OBJECT tag.

N O T E While creating an ActiveX Control is much easier to do than, say, writing a spreadsheet application, it still requires the talents of a professional programmer. Third-party developers offer visual programming tools or BASIC environments that provide ActiveX Control templates, making the actual coding of ActiveX Controls much less tedious. However, most sophisticated ActiveX Controls are, and will be, developed in sophisticated C++ environments, requiring thousands of lines of code. ■

ON THE WEB

http://www.microsoft.com/intdev/ This site is the home of Microsoft's Internet Developer's Web site. If you are interested in learning more about creating ActiveX Controls, this Web site is a good place to start.

Part
V

Ch
19

ActiveX Control Security

ActiveX Controls are pieces of software; therefore, all of the dangers of running unknown software apply to them as much as anything you may download from the Internet. ActiveX Controls are unlike Java applets, which run in an environment designed to ensure the safety of the client and can usually cause trouble only by exploiting bugs or flaws in the Java run-time security systems. ActiveX Controls, on the other hand, can do anything on the client computer. Although this increases their potential to perform functions within your Web browser and other compatible applications, it also poses an added security risk. How do you know that a downloaded ActiveX Control won't erase your hard drive?

To address this concern, Microsoft's Internet Explorer 3.0 Web browser supports Authenticode code-signing technology. This enables vendors of ActiveX Controls and other software components to digitally *sign* these components. When they are downloaded and the digital signature is recognized, a code signature certificate, like that shown in Figure 19.1, is displayed on the screen. This certificate ensures that the software component is coming from the named source and that it hasn't been tampered with. At this point, you get to choose if you want to install the software component.

FIGURE 19.1
Authenticode technology in Microsoft's Internet Explorer 3.0 helps ensure that downloaded software components are genuine and come from a trusted source.

By default, Internet Explorer 3.0 installs in "High" security mode. In this mode, downloaded software components that are unsigned, or whose signatures can't be verified, will not be installed. In this case, an Alert box will be displayed that reads something like: "This page contains active content that is not verifiably safe to display. To protect your computer, this content will not be displayed. Choose Help to find out how you can change your safety settings so you can view potentially unsafe content." Note that in high security mode, the user doesn't even have the option of installing software components whose authenticity can't be verified.

To change the security mode of Internet Explorer 3.0, select the Security tab of the View, Options menu. Click the Safety Level button and select your desired security level. Under Medium security, you will be warned of all potential security problems, and given the option to proceed or not (see Figure 19.2).

> **CAUTION**
> You should almost never select the None security level, as this leaves your system completely unprotected from malevolent or poorly written software. Only select this level if you are certain that all of the sites you are visiting are safe.

FIGURE 19.2
Medium security level puts the burden on the user—you will be warned of potential security risks, but given the option to continue anyway.

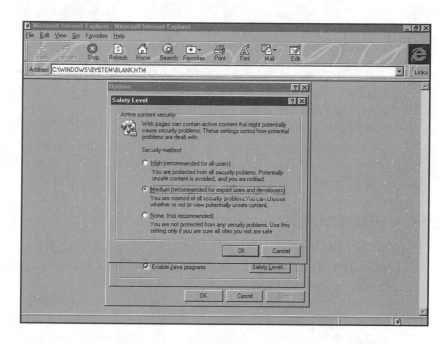

N O T E Fred McLain created the Exploder ActiveX Control to demonstrate the dangers that ActiveX Controls pose to the security unwary. This Control, if installed and executed, performs a clean shutdown of your computer and, if you have an energy-conservation BIOS, it actually turns your machine off! The Exploder ActiveX Control Web site is located at **http:// www1.halcyon.com/mclain/ActiveX/**. ■

Part
V

Ch
19

HTML Implementation of ActiveX Controls

Implementing ActiveX Controls in HTML Web pages requires the use of the HTML <OBJECT> and <PARAM> tags to include and configure each desired Control. While not too difficult, the syntax for using these Controls and determining the correct configuration parameters for each—particularly now, with the technology in its infancy—can be an intimidating task.

FrontPage Editor 97 makes the process a lot easier through its point-and-click method of Control installation. If you've used Microsoft's freeware ActiveX Control Pad, the method will be familiar, since FrontPage Editor uses a version of that software. Before we begin, however, a brief discussion of how ActiveX works in a page will be helpful.

As stated above, including ActiveX Controls in HTML documents requires use of the <OBJECT> tag to embed the Control within the page. Controls are configured through the attributes of the <OBJECT> tag, and configuration parameters set using the <PARAM> tag within the <OBJECT>...</OBJECT> container.

Using FrontPage Editor, any locally installed ActiveX Control can be placed within a Web page. Individual Label Controls can be displayed as they would appear, for instance, as will images and other elements. FrontPage Editor also allows you to configure the many options of each embedded ActiveX Control—set the <OBJECT> and <PARAM> configuration values—using a simple dialog box customized for each Control. When Control configuration is complete, the HTML code needed to implement the Control in your Web page is written into the HTML document.

The *<OBJECT>* Tag

ActiveX Controls are embedded in HTML documents through use of the HTML <OBJECT> tag; they are configured through use of the <PARAM> tag. Listing 19.1 is an example of using the ActiveX Marquee Control, embedded within an HTML Web page. The attributes of the <OBJECT> tag itself determine the ActiveX Control (or other Web object) used, as well as its size and alignment on the Web page. The <OBJECT>...</OBJECT> container tags also enclose the <PARAM> tags that are used to set the Control-specific parameters.

On its own, Netscape Navigator does not support ActiveX Controls and will ignore any Controls embedded in a Web page through the use of the <OBJECT> tag. However, with one of the Ncompass Labs plug-ins installed, Netscape Navigator also supports ActiveX Controls and will interpret embedded objects correctly.

> **N O T E** NCompass only works if <EMBED> is used within <OBJECT>. ■

ON THE WEB

http://www.ncompasslabs.com/   This site gives all the information you need and shows some examples of using Microsoft's ActiveX Technologies in Netscape Navigator through the Ncompass Labs plug-ins.

The next sections discuss each of the important attributes of the <OBJECT> tag and some of the possibilities for using the <PARAM> tags.

Listing 19.1   Marquee.htm—Example Using the ActiveX Marquee Control Object

```
<HTML>
<HEAD>
<TITLE>Marquee Example</TITLE>
</HEAD>
```

```
<BODY BGCOLOR=#FFFFFF>
<CENTER>
<HR>
<OBJECT
   ID="Marquee1"
   CLASSID="CLSID:1A4DA620-6217-11CF-BE62-0080C72EDD2D"
   CODEBASE="http://activex.microsoft.com/controls/iexplorer/marquee.ocx
   ➥#Version=4,70,0,1161"
   TYPE="application/x-oleobject"
   WIDTH=100%
   HEIGHT=100
>
<PARAM NAME="szURL" VALUE="queet.gif">


<PARAM NAME="ScrollPixelsX" VALUE="2">
<PARAM NAME="ScrollPixelsY" VALUE="2">
<PARAM NAME="ScrollStyleX" VALUE="Bounce">
<PARAM NAME="ScrollStyleY" VALUE="Bounce">
</OBJECT>
<HR>
</CENTER>
</BODY>
</HTML>
```

ID   The ID attribute of the <OBJECT> tag is used to give the ActiveX Control a name that can be used within the Web browser (or other application) environment. This is the easiest way for the parameters of the ActiveX Control to be accessed and manipulated by other elements running within the Web browser (usually VBScript or JavaScript applications). For example, in Listing 19.1, a VBScript to change the background color of the Marquee Control to red, if clicked, would look like the following:

```
Sub Marquee1_OnClick()
Marquee1.BackColor = 16711680
End Sub
```

CLASSID   The CLASSID attribute is perhaps the most intimidating looking piece of the <OBJECT> tag of an ActiveX Control. However, it is simply the identification code for the ActiveX Control being used. It is what Internet Explorer uses to load the correct ActiveX Control code module from your computer, and its value is set for each Control by the Control's author. The code for the ActiveX Marquee Control, displayed in Listing 19.1, is "CLSID:1A4DA620-6217-11CF-BE62-0080C72EDD2D".

CODEBASE   Unlike Netscape Navigator plug-ins, ActiveX Controls can be automatically downloaded and installed when Internet Explorer 3.0 (or another compatible application) encounters a document that makes use of them. The key to this feature is the CODEBASE attribute. The CODEBASE attribute defines the URL from which the ActiveX Control can be downloaded, and defines the version of the Control used. Then, when Internet Explorer attempts to render the Web page on a client machine, the CODEBASE attribute checks if

Part

V

Ch

19

each ActiveX Control embedded in the HTML document exists on that machine, and checks if it is the latest version. If a more recent version exists at the URL defined by the CODEBASE attribute, it is automatically downloaded and installed, subject to the security settings in place in the local copy of Internet Explorer being used.

 TIP   Whenever possible, only use ActiveX Controls that have been digitally signed by their vendors in your Web pages. This helps to ensure that these Controls can be downloaded and installed on your users' machines without a problem.

TYPE   The TYPE attribute defines the MIME type of the ActiveX Control. In general, this will be application/x-oleobject. For other object types embedded in an HTML document using the <OBJECT> tag, the value of this attribute will be different.

WIDTH and HEIGHT   The WIDTH and HEIGHT attributes of the <OBJECT> tag define the size of the ActiveX Control within the Web page. For hidden Controls, such as the Timer or Preloader Controls, these attributes can be kept at their default values of 0. For Controls such as the Marquee or Label Controls, these attributes need to be sized correctly for their desired appearance.

The *<PARAM>* Tags

The <PARAM> tags are used to configure the appropriate parameters of each ActiveX Control. In general, the syntax of the <PARAM> tag is as follows:

```
<PARAM NAME="ParameterName" VALUE="ParameterValue">
```

For instance, in the Marquee Control example shown in Listing 19.1, the URL of the document being placed in the marquee is given by:

```
<PARAM NAME="szURL" VALUE="queet.gif">
```

To make use of an ActiveX Control effectively, you need to know the names and possible values of all of its parameters that can be set with the <PARAM> tag. One of the benefits of using FrontPage Editor for creating Web pages that use ActiveX Controls is that the software knows what parameters are used by each Control.

Using Microsoft ActiveX Controls in FrontPage

Microsoft provides a set of ActiveX Controls with Internet Explorer 3.0 and hosts an ActiveX Gallery Web site to show them off, along with ActiveX Controls from other vendors. This Web site is located at **http://www.microsoft.com/activex/controls/**.

Many of the Microsoft-produced Controls are also included with FrontPage 97. (If they appear only as placeholders when you try them out, you'll need to download them from the above site.) The following sections demonstrate how you use FrontPage Editor to place them on your pages and describe the workings of several of these Controls.

Adding an ActiveX Control

Start off by choosing Insert, Other Components, ActiveX Control. Alternatively, click the Insert ActiveX Control button on the toolbar. The ActiveX Control Properties dialog box appears (see Figure 19.3). Then do the following:

1. Click the arrow button at the right of the Pick a Control box. The list of available Controls appears.

2. Select the Control you want. Then, in the Name box, type a name for the component. This isn't strictly necessary, but it will make it easier to figure out what each Control is doing if you look at the HTML code later.

3. If you want an alternate representation for the Control (for browsers not supporting ActiveX) type the HTML code for this alternative into the HTML box. For instance, `<img src="inkwell.jpg" width="116" height="103">` in this box will produce a JPEG image in Netscape in place of the Control.

4. Choose OK. The dialog closes, and the component appears on the page.

Part
V
Ch
19

FIGURE 19.3
You can select from the ActiveX Controls on your system with the ActiveX Properties dialog box.

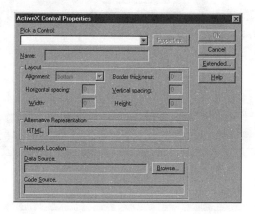

You can set the alignment, width, spacing, and border thickness of the Control in the Layout section of this dialog box. The Data Source and Code Source boxes in the Network Location section are used for the following:

■ Specifying a data file for Controls that require or optionally take information from such a file. The file formats vary from Control to Control.

■ Specifying the Code Source defines the URL from which the ActiveX Control can be downloaded and defines the version of the Control used. This is actually an alternate method of specifying the CODEBASE parameter for the Control (see the Object Tag section above for more on CODEBASE).

Setting ActiveX Control Properties

ActiveX Controls will usually have to be customized; this customization is largely a matter of editing the parameters to suit your needs.

To start an edit session for a new Control, just choose the Properties button in the ActiveX Properties dialog box after you've selected and named the Control. To edit an existing Control, double-click it to open the dialog box, and choose the Properties button. Either way, you get the two windows where you do your editing (see Figure 19.4).

FIGURE 19.4
The Edit ActiveX Control and Properties dialog boxes allow you to set the Control parameters and appearance.

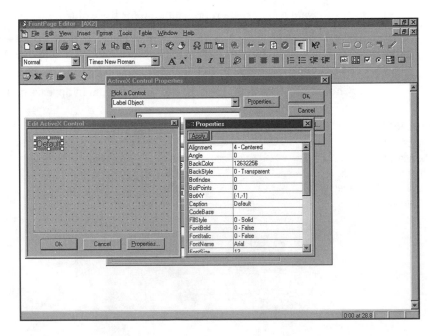

The first is the Edit ActiveX Control window, which gives a WYSIWYG (what-you-see-is-what-you-get) representation of the current configuration of the ActiveX Control. This is most evident for Controls such as the Label Control—for hidden Controls, this window merely shows the current size for which the Control is configured, which may be zero by zero.

The other window is the Properties dialog box for the specific ActiveX Control chosen. This dialog box gives you the ability to set all of the necessary parameters of the <OBJECT> and <PARAM> tags needed to configure the ActiveX Control. You don't need to know the class ID code, and you don't need to remember the specific parameter names that must be configured. FrontPage Editor Pad does all of that for you. To change a parameter in the Properties box, click the parameter in the dialog box, type in a new value in the text box (or select one from a drop-down or pop-up menu, if one appears), and click the Apply button.

N O T E It is difficult to determine the appropriate size for some Controls, such as the Animated Button Control. This difficulty exists because the Controls need to be sized to fit an animation file that FrontPage Editor isn't able to show you. Some trial and error may be necessary. ■

When you've finished entering the parameters, close the Edit ActiveX Control and Properties windows. At this point, the HTML code needed to implement the Control, using the parameters you selected, is automatically generated and placed in the HTML document.

Exploring FrontPage Editor's ActiveX Controls

The selection of ActiveX Controls that ships with FrontPage 97 (or can be downloaded from the Microsoft site) includes both general utility-type Controls and a set of form components. In the following sections, we'll look at a representative sample.

N O T E FrontPage Editor's ActiveX Control Properties list box refers to many of these Controls as "objects." Objects and Controls, in our present context, mean the same thing. ■

Animated Button Control

The ActiveX Animated Button Control creates an area of the Web page that can be used as an animated button. The Control takes an AVI animation file as one of its parameters and plays different sequences of frames in the AVI, depending on certain events. The events that the Animated Button Control can respond to include the following:

- Default event
- Mouse cursor over the Control

■ Focus on the Control

■ Left mouse button click-and-hold on the Control

Listing 19.2 shows an example of how this Control is implemented in an HTML document. The TYPE, WIDTH, and HEIGHT attributes of the <OBJECT> tag control the size and placement of the Control on the page. The <PARAM> tags for the Control determine the AVI animation to be used, along with the frame sequences to be used for each event.

Listing 19.2   HTML Code to Implement the Animated Button Control

```
<OBJECT
    ID="anbtn"
    CLASSID="clsid:0482B100-739C-11CF-A3A9-00A0C9034920"
    CODEBASE="http://activex.microsoft.com/controls/iexplorer/ieanbtn.
    ⇒ocx#version=4,70,0,1161"
    TYPE="application/x-oleobject"
    ALIGN="left"
    WIDTH=300
    HEIGHT=100
>
<PARAM NAME="url" VALUE="butani.avi">
<PARAM NAME="defaultfrstart"   VALUE="0">
<PARAM NAME="defaultfrend"     VALUE="7">
<PARAM NAME="mouseoverfrstart" VALUE="8">
<PARAM NAME="mouseoverfrend"   VALUE="15">
<PARAM NAME="focusfrstart"     VALUE="16">
<PARAM NAME="focusfrend"       VALUE="23">
<PARAM NAME="downfrstart"      VALUE="24">
<PARAM NAME="downfrend"        VALUE="34">
</OBJECT>
```

The graphic in Figure 19.5 shows the response of the Animated Button Control example (shown on the ActiveX Controls Gallery Web site) for the default event.

Microsoft's parameter descriptions for the Animated Button Control are as follows:

■ URL—The URL location of the AVI file to be used

■ DefaultFrStart—The start frame for the Default state

■ DefaultFrEnd—The end frame for the Default state

■ MouseoverFrStart—The start frame for the Mouseover state

■ MouseoverFrEnd—The end frame for the Mouseover state

■ FocusFrStart—The start frame for the Focus state

■ FocusFrEnd—The end frame for the Focus state

■ DownFrStart—The start frame for the Down state

■ DownFrEnd—The end frame for the Down state

FIGURE 19.5
The Animated Button
Control plays an
animation from a
selected AVI file.

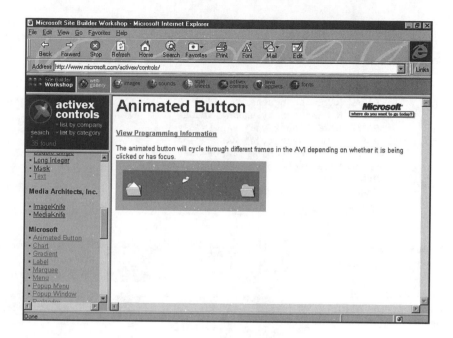

- `AboutBox`—Displays the About dialog box
- `ButtonEvent_Click`—Fired when the button is clicked
- `ButtonEvent_DblClick`—Fired when the button is double-clicked
- `ButtonEvent_Focus`—Fired when the button gets focus
- `ButtonEvent_Enter`—Fired when the mouse enters the button area
- `ButtonEvent_Leave`—Fired when the mouse leaves the button area

Chart Control

An example at the Microsoft ActiveX Gallery Web site shows one of the many kinds of charts that can be displayed using the ActiveX Chart Control (see Figure 19.6). Listing 19.3 shows an example of the way the Chart Control is embedded in an HTML document.

Listing 19.3   HTML Code to Implement the Chart Control

```
<OBJECT
  ID="chart1"
  CLASSID="clsid:FC25B780-75BE-11CF-8B01-444553540000"
  CODEBASE="http://activex.microsoft.com/controls/iexplorer/iechart.
  ➥ocx#Version=4,70,0,1161"
  TYPE="application/x-oleobject"
  WIDTH=400
```

continues

Part
V

Ch
19

Listing 19.3 Continued

```
    HEIGHT=200
>
<PARAM NAME="hgridStyle" VALUE="3">
<PARAM NAME="vgridStyle" VALUE="0">
<PARAM NAME="colorscheme" VALUE="0">
<PARAM NAME="DisplayLegend" VALUE="0">
<PARAM NAME="ChartType" VALUE="8">
<PARAM NAME="BackStyle" VALUE="1">
<PARAM NAME="BackColor" VALUE="#FFFFFF">
<PARAM NAME="ForeColor" VALUE="#0000FF">
<PARAM NAME="Scale" VALUE="100">
<PARAM NAME="url" VALUE="data.txt">
</OBJECT>
```

FIGURE 19.6

The chart shown is one
of the many possible
kinds of charts that
are possible with the
ActiveX Chart Control.

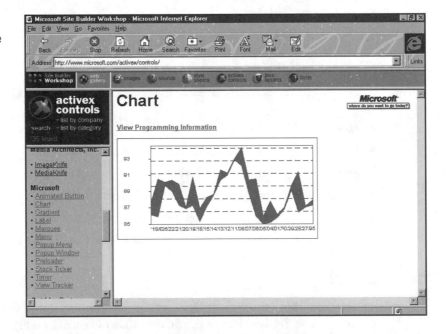

The <PARAM> tags are used to configure the Chart Control for display. The two most important parameter tags in the example shown are the NAME="url" parameter, which defines
the file containing the data to be charted, and the NAME="ChartType" parameter, which
defines the type of chart to be used. The ActiveX Chart Control supports the chart types
shown in Table 19.1 with the appropriate ChartType parameter value.

Table 19.1 ActiveX Chart Control Chart Types

ChartType Value	Type of Chart Displayed
0	Simple Pie Chart
1	Special Pie Chart
2	Simple Point Chart
3	Stacked Point Chart
4	Full Point Chart
5	Simple Line Chart
6	Stacked Line Chart
7	Full Line Chart
8	Simple Area Chart
9	Stacked Area Chart
10	Full Area Chart
11	Simple Column Chart
12	Stacked Column Chart
13	Full Column Chart
14	Simple Bar Chart
15	Stacked Bar Chart
16	Full Bar Chart
17	HLC Simple Stock Chart
18	HLC WSJ Stock Chart
19	OHLC Simple Stock Chart
20	OHLC WSJ Stock Chart

Notice that the chart type and the horizontal and vertical grid types used by the Chart Control can be changed dynamically to show the new chart immediately. You can program your Web pages that use the Chart Control with JavaScript or VBScript to allow the user to decide which type of chart he or she would like.

Microsoft's parameter descriptions for the Chart Control are as follows:

- Rows—Specifies the number of rows in the data series.
- Columns—Specifies the number of columns in the data series.

Part
V

Ch
19

- `HorizontalGrid`—Specifies horizontal grids.

- `VerticalGrid`—Specifies vertical grids.

- `RowIndex`—Specifies the row index, used along with the `DataItem` property.

- `ColumnIndex`—Specifies the column index, used along with the `DataItem` property.

- `DataItem`—Specifies a data value; entry is identified by `RowIndex` and `ColumnIndex` properties. To specify a value of 3 for row 2, column 4, set the `RowIndex` property to 2, `ColumnIndex` property to 4, and the `DataItem` property value to 3.

- `ColorScheme`—Specifies the predefined set of colors you would like to use. These colors will be used to fill regions. The possible values of this property are 0, 1, and 2.

- `BackStyle`—Determines whether the background is transparent opaque. The possible values for this property are Transparent: 0, Opaque: 1.

- `Scale`—Determines the percentage scaling factor. By default, the Control will perform 100% scaling. The value of the property should lie between 1 to 100. If the specified value is invalid, the default scaling factor will be used.

- `RowName`—Use this property along with the `RowIndex` property to specify a name for the row. This name will be used in legends and labels. On the HTML page, row names are specified using the `RowNames` `<PARAM>` tag: `<param name="RowNames" value="Nov Dec">`.

- `ColumnName`—Use this property along with `ColumnIndex` to specify a name for the column. This name will be used in legends and labels. On the HTML page, column names are specified using the `ColumnNames` `<param>` tag: `<param name="ColumnNames" value="Apple Orange Grapes">`.

- `DisplayLegend`—Use this property to view or hide the legend. This property can assume one of the following values: Show Legend: 1, Hide Legend: 0.

- `GridPlacement`—This property controls how grids are drawn. The grid lines can be drawn either over the chart (foreground) or below the chart (background). This property can assume one of the following values: Grid lines in the background: 0, Grid lines in the foreground: 1.

- Data param tags—The data param tags are used to specify the data values for the chart. To specify data values for row x, use the following syntax:
  ```
  <param name="data[x]" value="num1 num2 num3">
  ```

  Example:
  ```
  <param name="data[0]" value="37 75 100">
  <param name="data[1]" value="91 64 200">
  <param name="data[2]" value="91 64 200">
  ```

```
<param name="data[3]" value="37 75 100">
<param name="data[4]" value="91 64 200">
<param name="data[5]" value="91 64 200">
```

■ URL—This property allows you to specify a data file using a URL. The Chart Control will use the data specified in the data file to draw the chart. The format of the data file is as follows:

```
chart_type\n
number_of_rows\n
number_of_columns<\tcolumn_name_0\tcolumn_name_1\tcolumn name_2 ... >\n
<row_name_1\t>data_val_0\tdata val_1\tdata_val_2 ...data_val_n\n
<row_name_2\t>data_val_0\tdata_val_1\tdata_val_2 ...data_val_n\n
...
<row_name_m\t>data_val_0\tdata_val_1\tdata_val_2 ...data_val_m\n
```

When you're creating a data file for a chart, remember that the first line in the data file specifies the chart type, followed by a new line. (See Table 19.1 for the types of chart you can draw and their corresponding values.)

The second line in the data file specifies the number of rows in the chart, followed by a new line.

The third line specifies the number of columns followed by column names. Column names are optional. The column names show up as legends in the chart. The column name can include any alphanumeric character and space. Note that the column names should be separated only by tab characters.

Successive lines specify data values for each row. Each line starts with an optional row name followed by n numbers, where n is the number of columns. The row name can include any alphanumeric characters and space. The row name, if specified, should be followed by a tab character.

Gradient Control

The ActiveX Gradient Control provides for the creation of areas with smooth color gradients from one point in the area to another. It is a way of including multicolored boxes and lines in a Web page without requiring a separate download of an image. Also, gradients included with the Gradient Control can be easily animated with a small JavaScript or VBScript.

Listing 19.4 is an example of the ActiveX Gradient Control demonstrating a smooth transition from white to black in a rectangular box. The result is shown in Figure 19.7.

Part
V

Ch
19

Listing 19.4 HTML Example Showing the Gradient Control

```
<HTML>
<HEAD>
<TITLE>AXTEST</TITLE>
</HEAD>
<BODY BGCOLOR="#FFFFFF">
<OBJECT
     ID=IEGRAD1
CLASSID="CLSID:017C99A0-8637-11CF-A3A9-00A0C9034920"
     WIDTH=50
     HEIGHT=50
  >
  <PARAM NAME="StartColor" value="#FFFFFF">
  <PARAM NAME="EndColor" value="#000000">
  <PARAM NAME="Direction" value="4">
</OBJECT>
<H2>Using the Gradient Control</H2>
</BODY>
</HTML>
```

FIGURE 19.7

The Gradient Control allows the creation of color effects without requiring the down-loading of large image files.

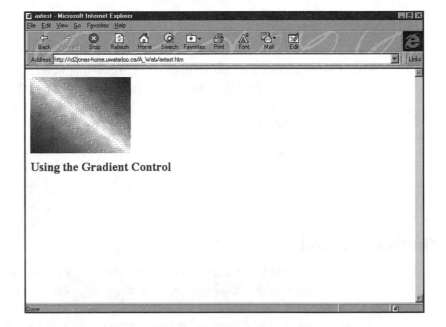

CAUTION

It should be noted at this point that the ActiveX Control technology is still pretty young, and a few of the ActiveX Controls are not 100% reliable. For instance, the Gradient Control seems to be a lot slower than it should be, and if you attempt to create a gradient that is too large (much larger than the one shown in the example), your Internet Explorer 3.0 executable is liable to hang. This is nothing to worry about, as Internet Explorer can be shut down and restarted without disturbing any of the other programs running on your machine, but it is something to keep in mind.

Microsoft's parameter descriptions for the Gradient Control are as follows:

- StartColor—The color with which the transition starts.
- EndColor—The color with which the transition ends.
- Direction—0: the color transition is in the horizontal direction; 1: the color transition is in the vertical direction; 2: the color transition is towards the center.; 3: the color transition is towards the corner; 4: the color transition is across diagonal down; 5: the color transition is across diagonal up; 6: the color transition is around the point specified in the StartPoint property; 7: the color transition is across the line joining StartPoint and EndPoint.
- StartPoint—Coordinates of the start point in the format (x,y).
- EndPoint—Coordinates of the end point in the format (x,y).
- AboutBox—Displays the About dialog box.

Label Control

The ActiveX Label Control, shown in Figure 19.8, allows text to display within a Web page using any installed font, with any style and color, and at an arbitrary angle. It is also possible to curve the line of text and animate its appearance. In the example shown in Figure 19.8 (whose code is shown in Listing 19.5), the angle of the text changes whenever the region is clicked.

Part
V

Ch
19

Listing 19.5   HTML Example Showing the Label Control

```
<HTML>
<HEAD>
<TITLE>Label Example</TITLE>
<SCRIPT LANGUAGE="VBS">
Sub Label1_Click
    Label1.Angle = (Label1.Angle + 15) mod 360
End Sub
</SCRIPT>
</HEAD>
<BODY BGCOLOR=#FFFFFF>
<CENTER>
<H1>Label Example</H1>
<HR>
```

continues

Listing 19.5   Continued

```
<OBJECT
   ID="label1"
   CLASSID="clsid:99B42120-6EC7-11CF-A6C7-00AA00A47DD2"
   CODEBASE="http://activex.microsoft.com/controls/iexplorer/ielabel.
   ➡ocx#version=4,70,0,1161"
   TYPE="application/x-oleobject"
   WIDTH=300
   HEIGHT=250
   VSPACE=0
   ALIGN=center
>
<PARAM NAME="Angle" VALUE="0">
<PARAM NAME="Alignment" VALUE="4" >
<PARAM NAME="BackStyle" VALUE="1" >
<PARAM NAME="BackColor" VALUE="#F0F000" >
<PARAM NAME="Caption" VALUE="FrontPage">
<PARAM NAME="FontName" VALUE="Arial">
<PARAM NAME="FontSize" VALUE="28">
<PARAM NAME="ForeColor" VALUE="#000000" >
<PARAM NAME="FontBold" VALUE="1" >
</OBJECT>
</CENTER>
<BR>
<HR>
This example of the ActiveX Label Control demonstrates the ability of the
Control to display text at an arbitrary position and orientation. A VBScript
changes the orientation of the text whenever the Control is clicked.
</BODY>
</HTML>
```

FIGURE 19.8

The Label Control gives the Web author the ability to place text arbitrarily on the Web page, without having to resort to graphics.

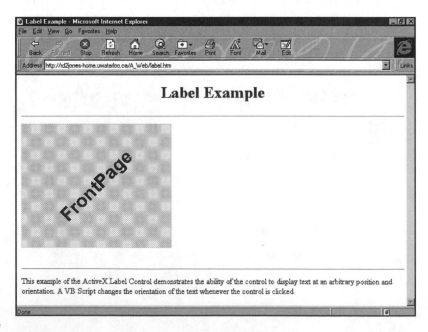

Microsoft's parameter descriptions for the Label Control are as follows:

- Caption—Specifies text to be displayed.

- Angle—Specifies angle (counterclockwise rotation) in degrees.

- Alignment—Specifies how to align text in the Control. 0: Aligned to left (horizontal) and to top (vertical); 1: Centered (horizontal) and to top (vertical); 2: Aligned to right(horizontal) and to top (vertical); 3: Aligned to left (horizontal) and Centered (vertical); 4: Centered (horizontal) and Centered (vertical); 5: Aligned to right (horizontal) and Centered (vertical); 6: Aligned to left (horizontal) and to bottom (vertical); 7: Centered (horizontal) and to bottom (vertical); 8: Aligned to right (horizontal) and to bottom (vertical).

- BackStyle—Control background. 0: Transparent; 1: Opaque.

- FontName—Name of a TrueType font.

- FontSize—Size of the font.

- FontItalic—Flag for italics

- FontBold—Flag for bold.

- FontUnderline—Flag for underline.

- FontStrikeout—Flag for strikeout.

- Mode—Which mode the text will be rendered in. 0: Normal (same as the VB Label Control); 1: Normal text with rotation; 2: apply the user-specified lines while rendering without rotation; 3: apply the user-specified lines while rendering, allow rotation.

- Param tags such as TopPoints, TopXY, BotPoints, and BotXY tags are provided to specify the two lines along which the text will be shown. Visual Basic properties such as TopPoints, TopIndex, TopXY, BotPoints, BotIndex, and BotXY are also supported.

- AboutBox—Displays the About dialog box.

- Click—When the user clicks the label.

- Change—When the label caption changes.

- DblClick—When the user double-clicks the label.

- MouseDown—When the user presses the mouse button down while the cursor is on the label.

- MouseMove—When the user moves the mouse when the cursor is on the label.

- MouseUp—When the user releases the mouse.

Part
V

Ch
19

Marquee Control

In its Internet Explorer 2.0 Web browser, Microsoft introduced the <MARQUEE> tag, which allows scrolling marquees to be easily included in a Web page. The ActiveX Marquee Control takes this concept one step further. In addition to horizontal, vertical, or diagonal scrolling of a text marquee, the ActiveX Marquee Control can also scroll images and other HTML elements. Listing 19.6 shows an example of this, which scrolls a block of text through an area that makes up about 50% of the frame. The result is shown in Figure 19.9 as it appears in the ActiveX Gallery.

Listing 19.6 HTML Example Showing the Marquee Control

```
<OBJECT
    align=CENTER
    classid="clsid:1a4da620-6217-11cf-be62-0080c72edd2d"
    width=650 height=40 BORDER=1 HSPACE=5
    id=marquee
>
<PARAM NAME="ScrollStyleX" VALUE="Circular">
<PARAM NAME="ScrollStyleY" VALUE="Circular">
<PARAM NAME="szURL" VALUE="http://www.mycompany.com">
<PARAM NAME="ScrollDelay" VALUE=100>
<PARAM NAME="LoopsX" VALUE=-1>
<PARAM NAME="LoopsY" VALUE=-1>
<PARAM NAME="ScrollPixelsX" VALUE=0>
<PARAM NAME="ScrollPixelsY" VALUE=30>
<PARAM NAME="DrawImmediately" VALUE=1>
<PARAM NAME="Whitespace" VALUE=0>
<PARAM NAME="PageFlippingOn" VALUE=1>
<PARAM NAME="Zoom" VALUE=100>
<PARAM NAME="WidthOfPage" VALUE=640>
</OBJECT>
```

N O T E There are limitations to what can be properly displayed in a scrolling marquee. Hypertext links appear to be displayed correctly; they are not active. Also, embedded objects such as in-line VRML scenes of other ActiveX Controls will not be displayed.

Also note that FrontPage Editor also supports the <MARQUEE> HTML tag to create scrolling marquees, but this tag can support only text. ■

Microsoft's parameter descriptions for the Marquee Control are as follows:

- ScrollStyleX—Sets the horizontal scroll style. Valid values are Bounce and Circular (default).

- ScrollStyleY—Sets the vertical scroll style. Valid values are Bounce and Circular (default).

FIGURE 19.9
The ActiveX Marquee Control can create scrolling marquees that move in any direction and display many different HTML elements.

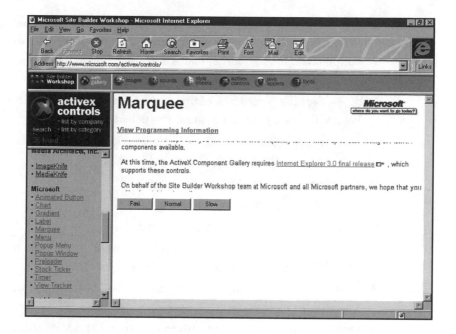

- ScrollDelay—Sets the time in milliseconds between each movement of the URL in the marquee window. Valid values are positive integers. Default is 100.

- LoopsX—Sets the number of times the image scrolls horizontally if ScrollStyleX is Circular, or sets the number of times the image bounces if ScrollStyleX is Bounce. Valid values are integers above or equal to -1. Zero indicates that a horizontal slide is to occur, -1 indicates that the image will never stop (infinite). The default is -1 (infinite).

- LoopsY—Sets the number of times the image scrolls vertically if ScrollStyleY is Circular, or sets the number of times the image bounces if ScrollStyleY is Bounce. Valid values are integers above or equal to -1. Zero indicates that a vertical slide is to occur, -1 indicates that the image will never stop (infinite). The default is -1 (infinite).

- ScrollPixelsX—Sets the number of pixels to move the URL horizontally in the marquee window each ScrollDelay milliseconds. Valid values are integers. The default is 75 pixels.

- ScrollPixelsY—Vertical counterpart of ScrollPixelX, except that the default is zero.

- szURL—Sets the URL to scroll.

- DrawImmediately—Determines whether you want to progressively render the URLs. Valid values are 1 (true) or 0 (false). The default is 1.

- Whitespace—Sets the whitespace between URLs and/or tiled images. Valid values are non-negative integers. The default is zero.

Part
V

Ch

19

■ PageFlippingOn—Determines whether the marquee will flip between multiple URLs (instead of creating one scrolling image) when the user presses the right mouse button or via the put_CurrentURL automation function. Valid values are 1 (true) or 0 (false). The default is 0.

■ Zoom—Sets the percentage of the original size you want the scrolling URLs to be. Valid values are positive integers. The default is 100.

■ WidthOfPage—Sets the width in pixels used to format the text of the URL. Valid values are positive integers. The default is 640.

■ AboutBox—Displays the About dialog box.

■ Pause—Stops the scrolling of the marquee.

■ Resume—Restarts the scrolling of the marquee.

■ HRESULT insertURL([in] int iURLtoInsertAfter, [in] BSTR bstrURL)—Inserts a new URL after the existing URL at iURLtoInsertAfter.

■ HRESULT deleteURL([in] int iURLtoDelete)—Deletes the URL at index iURLtoDelete.

■ HRESULT queryURL([in] int iURLtoGet, [out] BSTR *pbstrURL)—Gets the URL at iURLtoGet and returns it in pbstrURL.

■ HRESULT queryURLCount([out] int *pcURL)—Gets the number of URLs in the list.

■ void OnStartOfImage(void)—Issued just before the URL to be scrolled appears in the marquee window.

■ void OnEndOfImage(int HorizontalOrVertical)—Issued when the image has been completely scrolled. For example, it can be used to let VBScript change the contents of another Control after the image has stopped moving. Since the horizontal and vertical scrolling could end at different times (different loops), which one has ended is indicated by the HorizontalOrVertical value (returns "H" for horizontal, "V" for vertical).

■ OnBounce(int SideBouncedOff)—fired only in bounce mode, and the image being scrolled bounces off a side. SideBouncedOff returns the side it bounces off ("L" for left, "R" for right, "T" for top, and "B" for bottom).

■ void OnScroll(int HorizontalOrVertical)—Issued each time the Control is about to scroll the URL. HorizontalOrVertical indicates whether the horizontal or vertical scrolling is about to begin again (returns "H" for horizontal, "V" for vertical). This event is not fired for bounces or slides; nor is it fired the first time the image is scrolled.

■ void OnLMouseClick(void)—Fired when the user presses the left mouse button in the marquee window.

Menu Control

The ActiveX Menu Control enables you to create drop-down menus within a Web page. Items selected from these menus can be set up to trigger events as well as JavaScript or VBScript functions. Listing 19.7 shows example code that is used to construct two simple drop-down menus. In this example, no events are triggered by selection of the items (see Figure 19.10).

Listing 19.7   HTML Example Showing the Menu Control

```
<HTML>
<HEAD>
<TITLE>Menu Example</TITLE>
<SCRIPT Language="VBS">
<!— Hide script from incompatible browsers!
Function Timer_Timer()
    If IsObject(mnuEdit) Then
       Timer.Enabled="0"
       mnuFile.Caption="File"
       mnuFile.AddItem "New", 1
       mnuFile.AddItem "Open", 2
       mnuFile.AddItem "Save", 3
       mnuFile.AddItem "Save As...", 4
mnuEdit.Caption="Edit"
       mnuEdit.AddItem "Cut", 1
       mnuEdit.AddItem "Copy", 2
       mnuEdit.AddItem "Paste", 3
       mnuEdit.AddItem "Delete", 4
    End If
End Function
<!— —>
</SCRIPT>
</HEAD>
<BODY BGCOLOR="#FFFFFF">
<CENTER>
<H1>Menu Example</H1>
<HR>
<OBJECT
   ID="mnuFile"
   CLASSID="CLSID:52DFAE60-CEBF-11CF-A3A9-00A0C9034920"
   CODEBASE="http://activex.microsoft.com/controls/iexplorer/btnmenu.
   ➥ocx#Version=4,70,0,1161"
   TYPE="application/x-oleobject"
   WIDTH=60
   HEIGHT=30
>
</OBJECT>
<OBJECT
   ID="mnuEdit"
   CLASSID="CLSID:52DFAE60-CEBF-11CF-A3A9-00A0C9034920"
   CODEBASE="http://activex.microsoft.com/controls/iexplorer/btnmenu.
```

Part
V

Ch
19

continues

Listing 19.7 Continued

```
    ➥ocx#Version=4,70,0,1161"
    TYPE="application/x-oleobject"
    WIDTH=60
    HEIGHT=30
>
</OBJECT>
<OBJECT
    ID="timer"
    CLASSID="clsid:59CCB4A0-727D-11CF-AC36-00AA00A47DD2"
    CODEBASE="http://activex.microsoft.com/controls/iexplorer/ietimer.
    ➥ocx#version=4,70,0,1161"
    TYPE="application/x-oleobject"
    ALIGN=middle
>
<PARAM NAME="Interval" VALUE="100">
<PARAM NAME="Enabled" VALUE="True">
</OBJECT>
</CENTER>
<HR>
This example of the ActiveX Menu Control demonstrates the ability of the
Control to create and support menus within the Web browser.
</BODY>
</HTML>
```

FIGURE 19.10

Drop-down menus can be created, changed on the fly, and used to trigger scripted events, all within a Web page.

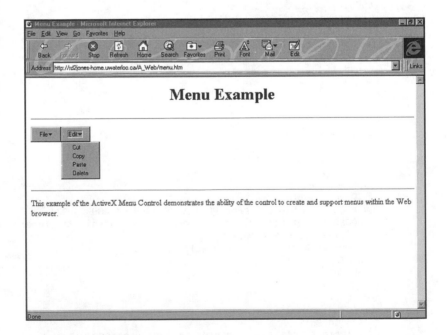

Delayed ActiveX Control Configuration Using the ActiveX Timer Control

Look through Listing 19.7 to see a curious use of the ActiveX Timer Control. At first glance, it is not obvious what the Timer Control is doing nor why it is doing it.

The Timer Control is continuously running through its count sequence, from its Interval parameter of 100 milliseconds to zero. Each time it hits zero, it triggers the `Timer_Timer()` VBScript function. This function checks to see if the `mnuEdit` object is defined, and if it is, the function sets the menu and item names for the two drop-down menus and disables the Timer Control. If the `mnuEdit` object doesn't exist, the function will do nothing and the Timer Control will continue to operate.

Why Is thls necessary? It's because the `CODEBASE` attribute of the `<OBJECT>` tag is used to allow the ActiveX Control to be automatically downloaded and installed either if it doesn't exist on the client computer or if a more recent version of it exists at the source. This means that there might be a considerable delay before the ActiveX Menu Control object becomes defined and active. If the VBScript required to configure the menu objects is run before completion of this download and installation, an error will occur because the menu objects are not yet defined.

So the Timer Control and the corresponding `Timer_Timer()` VBScript function are used to check periodically to see if the menu object has been defined. Once it is defined, the function runs to configure it, and the Timer Control is disabled.

Microsoft's parameter descriptions for the Menu Control are as follows:

- `ItemCount`—The number of menu items in the current menu (read only).
- `Caption`—The caption to be displayed.
- `Menuitem[]`—The menu item to be displayed.
- `AboutBox`—Displays the About dialog box.
- `PopUp ([in] int x, [in] int y)`—Pops up the menu. If no value is passed for X or Y position (or both), the current mouse position is used to display the pop-up menu. The x and y values are relative to the window, not to the screen.
- `Clear`—Clears off all menu items.
- `RemoveItem ([in] int index)`— Removes the specified item. If the menu item does not exist, nothing is done.
- `AddItem ([in] String, [in/optional] int index)`—Adds the passed menu item at the specified index. If no index is passed, the item is appended to the menu.
- `Select(int item)`—item indicates the menu item selected.
- `Click`—No menu items were present, and the button was clicked.

Part
V

Ch
19

Popup Menu Control

The ActiveX Popup Menu Control is similar to the Menu Control described previously, except that it displays pop-up menus rather than drop-down menus. The example in Listing 19.8 shows how VBScript is used to dynamically change the menu using the `RemoveItem()` and `AddItem()` methods of the Popup Menu Control. Figure 19.11 displays the initial configuration of the Popup Menu Control, which is triggered by clicking the Show Menu button.

Listing 19.8   popmenu.htm   HTML Example Showing the Popup Menu Control

```
<HTML>
<HEAD>
<TITLE>Popup Menu Example</TITLE>
</HEAD>
<SCRIPT Language="VBS">
Sub Iepop1_Click(ByVal x)
    Alert "Item #" & x & " SELECTED!!!"
    Call Iepop1.RemoveItem(x)
    Call Iepop1.AddItem("Item #" & x & " SELECTED!!!",x)
End Sub

Sub ShowMenu_onClick
    Call Iepop1.PopUp
End Sub
</SCRIPT>
<BODY BGCOLOR=#FFFFFF>
<CENTER>
<H1>Popup Menu Example</H1>
<HR>
<OBJECT
    ID="iepop1"
    CODEBASE="http://activex.microsoft.com/controls/iexplorer/iemenu.
    ➥ocx#Version=4,70,0,1161"
    TYPE="application/x-oleobject"
    CLASSID="clsid:7823A620-9DD9-11CF-A662-00AA00C066D2"
    WIDTH=1
    HEIGHT=1
>
<PARAM NAME="Menuitem[0]" value="One">
<PARAM NAME="Menuitem[1]" value="Two">
<PARAM NAME="Menuitem[2]" value="Three">
<PARAM NAME="Menuitem[3]" value="Four">
<PARAM NAME="Menuitem[4]" value="Five">
</OBJECT>
<INPUT TYPE="button" NAME="ShowMenu" VALUE="Show Menu" ALIGN=RIGHT>
</CENTER>
<HR>
```

```
This example of the ActiveX Popup Menu Control demonstrates the ability of
the Control to create and support pop-up menus within the Web browser.
</BODY>
</HTML>
```

FIGURE 19.11

By attaching the Popup Menu Control to the onClick() method of the Show Item HTML forms button, the menu appears whenever the button is clicked.

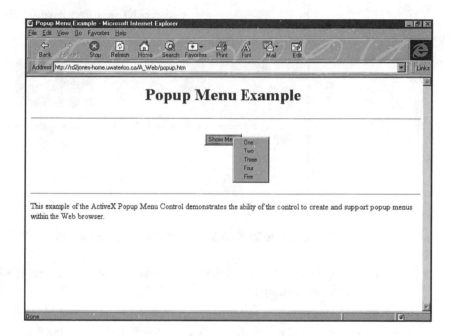

Once an item is selected from the Popup Menu Control, the Click() method of the Control is triggered via the VBScript Iepop1_Click() subroutine. This subroutine removes the selected item and replaces it with one that reflects that this menu item slot has been previously selected and displays an Alert box to display what item was picked. The next time the Popup Menu Control is the updated menu item displayed (see Figure 19.12).

Microsoft's parameter descriptions for the Popup Menu Control are as follows:

- ItemCount—The number of menu items in the current menu (read only).
- Menuitem[]—The menu item to be displayed.
- AboutBox—Displays the About dialog box.
- PopUp ([in] int x, [in] int y)—Pops up the menu. If no value is passed for X or Y position (or both), the current mouse position is used to display the pop-up menu. The x and y values are relative to the window, not to the screen.
- Clear—Clears off all menu items.

Part
V

Ch
19

FIGURE 19.12

The Popup Menu Control allows menus and menu items to be changed dynamically.

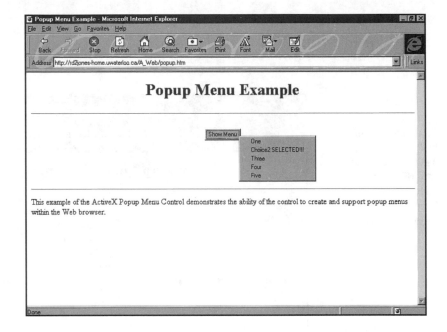

- `RemoveItem ([in] int index)`—Removes the specified item. If the menu item does not exist, nothing is done.

- `AddItem ([in] String, [in/optional] int index)`—Adds the passed menu item at the specified index. If no index is passed, the item is appended to the menu.

- `Click(int item)`—Item clicked is one of the parameters passed.

Popup Window Control

The ActiveX Popup Window Control enables you to preview Web pages—displayed in their own pop-up window. The HTML displayed is subject to the same limitations as those used with the Marquee Control—hypertext links, though displayed correctly, will not be active, and embedded objects will not appear. Listing 19.9 shows an example of using the Popup Window Control to provide a preview of a page, specifically the INDEX.HTM page of a web (see Figure 19.13). Notice that the VBScript `StrGetUrlBase()` function is used to parse the base (everything other than the document name itself) from the URL of the current document.

> **CAUTION**
>
> To try out the code in the listing, you have to access the pop-up-enabled page through a PPP connection to the Personal Web Server. Using the Preview in Browser command will make an Error 404

(can't find URL) message appear in the pop-up window when the Popup Control tries to find INDEX.HTML.

Listing 19.9   HTML Example Showing the Popup Window Control

```
<HTML>
<HEAD>
<TITLE>Popup Window Example</TITLE>
<SCRIPT Language="VBSCRIPT">
Sub Label0_MouseMove(ByVal s, ByVal b, ByVal x, ByVal y)
   PopObj.Popup strGetUrlBase & "index.htm", True
End Sub
Function StrGetUrlBase()
   Dim strBase, strSlash, idx

   strBase = Location.HRef
   If (Left(strBase,5)) = "file:" then
     strSlash = "\"
   ElseIf (Left(strBase,5)) = "http:" then
     strSlash = "/"
   Else
     strBase = ""
     strSlash = "/"
   End If

   idx = Len(strBase)
   While idx > 0 And Mid(strBase, idx, 1) <> strSlash
     idx = idx - 1
   Wend

   strBase = Left(strBase,idx)

   StrGetUrlBase = strBase
End Function
</SCRIPT>
</HEAD>
<BODY BGCOLOR=#FFFFFF>
<CENTER>
<H1>Popup Window Example</H1>
<HR>
<A ID="Link1" href="index.html">
<OBJECT
   ID="label0"
   CLASSID="clsid:99B42120-6EC7-11CF-A6C7-00AA00A47DD2"
   CODEBASE="http://activex.microsoft.com/controls/iexplorer/ielabel.
   ➥ocx#version=4,70,0,1161"
   TYPE="application/x-oleobject"
   WIDTH=400
   HEIGHT=20
   VSPACE=0
```

Part

V

Ch

19

Listing 19.9   Continued

```
    ALIGN=center
>
<PARAM NAME="Angle" VALUE="0">
<PARAM NAME="Alignment" VALUE="4" >
<PARAM NAME="BackStyle" VALUE="1" >
<PARAM NAME="BackColor" VALUE="#F0F000" >
<PARAM NAME="Caption" VALUE="Move the cursor here to preview my home page.">
<PARAM NAME="FontName" VALUE="Times New Roman">
<PARAM NAME="FontSize" VALUE="16">
<PARAM NAME="ForeColor" VALUE="#000000" >
    </OBJECT>
</A>
<OBJECT
    ID="PopObj"
    CLASSID="clsid:A23D7C20-CABA-11CF-A5D4-00AA00A47DD2"
    CODEBASE="http://activex.microsoft.com/controls/iexplorer/iepopwnd.
    ↪ocx#Version=4,70,0,1161"
    TYPE="application/x-oleobject"
    WIDTH=400
    HEIGHT=20
>
</OBJECT>
</CENTER>
<HR>
This example of the ActiveX Popup Window Control demonstrates the ability of
the Control to display Web pages in a pop-up window. In this example, the pop-up
window is attached to a MouseMove event on the displayed ActiveX Label
Control, and appears when the cursor touches the Label object.
</BODY>
</HTML>
```

Microsoft's parameter descriptions for the Popup Window Control are as follows:

- AboutBox—Displays the About dialog box.

- Popup—Brings up the pop-up window. This method accepts the following parameters:

- URL—The URL location of the page to be displayed. [This is in a sublist of Popup. DJ]

- Scale [optional]—Boolean value: [this is at the same list level as URL, immediately above. DJ]

- True—Scale the display to fit in the pop-up window.

- False—Don't scale; clip display to fit in the pop-up window.

- Dismiss—Removes the pop-up window, if one is currently being displayed.

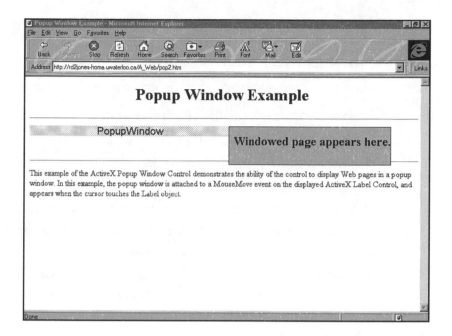

FIGURE 19.13
The Popup Window Control allows you to present previews of HTML Web pages within their own window.

Preloader Control

The ActiveX Preloader Control can be used to speed up the apparent throughput of a Web session by allowing Internet Explorer 3.0 to preload graphics, video, audio, or other HTML elements while a user is reviewing a given page.

Normally, the Web author would use the Preloader Control to quietly preload images or other HTML elements while the user is reading the current Web page. Then, when the user wants to go to the next page in the Web site, or when the user wants to view an image file, hear a sound, or watch a video clip, the Internet Explorer will already have downloaded it to the cache, and the user can view it without any further delay. Listing 19.10 shows an excerpt of how the Preloader Control is set up to download an image file into the cache.

Part
V

Ch
19

Listing 19.10   HTML Code to Implement the Preloader Control

```
<OBJECT
   ID="PreLoader"
   CLASSID="CLSID:16E349E0-702C-11CF-A3A9-00A0C9034920"
   CODEBASE="http://activex.microsoft.com/controls/iexplorer/iepreld.
   ➥ocx#Version=4,70,0,1161"
   TYPE="application/x-oleobject"
   WIDTH=1
   HEIGHT=1
 >
```

continues

Listing 19.10 Continued

```
<PARAM NAME="URL" VALUE="bigimage.gif">
<PARAM NAME="Enable" VALUE="1">
</OBJECT>
```

Microsoft's parameter descriptions for the Preloader Control are as follows:

- URL—URL to be downloaded.

- Enable—Enables (Enable=1) or disables (Enable=0) the Control.

- CacheFile—File name of the local cached file (read only).

- Bytes—The amount of data read so far in bytes (read only).

- Percentage—The amount of data read so far in percentage (read only).

- AboutBox—Displays the About dialog box.

- Complete—Fired when the download has been completed.

- Error—Fired when the download could not be completed.

Stock Ticker Control

The ActiveX Stock Ticker Control is used to display scrolling stock ticker information across a Web page. Listing 19.11 shows a typical way the Control would be coded to be included in a Web page. Figure 19.14 shows the example on the Microsoft ActiveX Controls Gallery Web site.

Listing 19.11 HTML Code to Implement the Stock Ticket Control

```
<OBJECT
   ID=iexr2
   TYPE="application/x-oleobject"
   CLASSID="clsid:0CA4A620-8E3D-11CF-A3A9-00A0C9034920"
   CODEBASE="http://activex.microsoft.com/controls/iexplorer/iestock.
   ➥ocx#Version=4,70,0,1161"
   WIDTH=300
   HEIGHT=50
>
<PARAM NAME="DataObjectName" VALUE="stocks.dat">
<PARAM NAME="DataObjectActive" VALUE="1">
<PARAM NAME="scrollwidth" VALUE="5">
<PARAM NAME="forecolor" VALUE="#ff0000">
<PARAM NAME="backcolor" VALUE="#0000ff">
<PARAM NAME="ReloadInterval" VALUE="5000">
</OBJECT>
```

The data file (STOCKS.DAT, in the listing above) used by the ActiveX Stock Ticker Control can be dynamically changed to allow the information displayed to be continuously updated. In text format, the data file will be of the form:

```
name1TABvalue1TABvalue2...CR/LF
name2TABvalue1TABvalue2...CR/LF
...
```

You can also specify an OLE object that generates data in the XRT format.

FIGURE 19.14
A Stock Ticker Control running in the Microsoft ActiveX Gallery website.

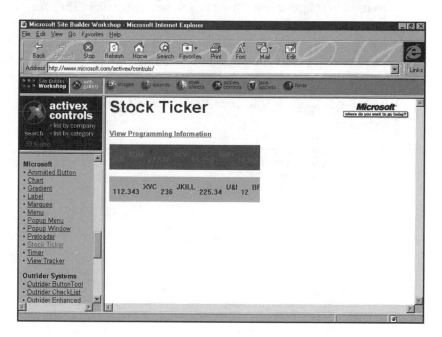

Microsoft's parameter descriptions for the Stock Ticker Control are as follows:

- DataObjectName—Name of the data source. This can be an URL or an OLE object.

- DataObjectActive—Indicates whether the data source is active. 1: active, 0: inactive. The Ticker Control displays data only when DataObjectActive is 1.

- ScrollWidth—The amount in which the display is scrolled for each redraw.

- ScrollSpeed—The intervals at which the display is scrolled.

- ReloadInterval—The interval at which the URL is reloaded periodically.

- ForeColor—Foreground color.

- BackColor—Background color.

Part
V

Ch
19

■ OffsetValues—The value (in pixels) by which the value will be offset from the name in the vertical direction.

■ AboutBox—Displays the About dialog box.

Timer Control

The following example demonstrates use of the ActiveX Timer Control. This Control can be used to trigger events based on the passage of time. The "Cool OCX" and the "Cool Controls" text strings are created by the Label Control; the former rotates and the latter changes color, each as a function of time. Listing 19.12 shows the ActiveX Timer Controls and VBScripts used to implement this example.

Listing 19.12   HTML Code to Implement the Timer Control

```
<OBJECT
   ID="timer1"
   CLASSID="clsid:59CCB4A0-727D-11CF-AC36-00AA00A47DD2"
   CODEBASE="http://activex.microsoft.com/controls/iexplorer/ietimer.
   ➥ocx#Version=4,70,0,1161"
   TYPE="application/x-oleobject"
   ALIGN=middle
>
<PARAM NAME="Interval" VALUE="200">
<PARAM NAME="Enabled" VALUE="True">
</OBJECT>

<OBJECT
   ID="timer2"
   CLASSID="clsid:59CCB4A0-727D-11CF-AC36-00AA00A47DD2"
   CODEBASE="http://activex.microsoft.com/controls/iexplorer/ietimer.
   ➥ocx#version=4,70,0,1161"
   TYPE="application/x-oleobject"
   ALIGN=middle
>
<PARAM NAME="Interval" VALUE="1000">
<PARAM NAME="Enabled" VALUE="True">
</OBJECT>

<SCRIPT LANGUAGE="VBScript">
Sub BtnToggle_OnClick
   Timer1.Enabled = Not Timer1.Enabled
   Timer2.Enabled = Not Timer2.Enabled
End Sub
Sub Timer1_timer
   Label.Angle = (Label.Angle + 5) mod 360
End Sub
Sub Timer2_Timer
   Randomize
   Cool.ForeColor = rnd() * 16777216
End Sub
</SCRIPT>
```

Microsoft's parameter descriptions for the Timer Control are as follows:

- Enabled—Enables or disables the timer. True: Enabled state; False: Disabled state.
- Interval—Interval (in milliseconds) at which the Timer event will be triggered. When this property is set to a negative value or zero, the timer will behave as in the disabled state.
- AboutBox—Displays the About dialog box
- Timer—When the timer is enabled and has a positive interval, this event is invoked at every interval.

View Tracker Control

The last example is the ActiveX View Tracker Control. This ActiveX Control has onHide and onShow events that are triggered when the place on the Web page where the Control is embedded passes out of or into view. Figures 19.15 and 19.16 show the Controls Gallery example—the implementation is shown by the code in Listing 19.13.

Listing 19.13   HTML Code to Implement the View Tracker Control

```
<OBJECT
    ID="Track1"
    CLASSID="clsid:1A771020-A28E-11CF-8510-00AA003B6C7E"
    CODEBASE="http://activex.microsoft.com/controls/iexplorer/ietrack.
➥ocx#Version=4,70,0,1161"
    WIDTH=1
    HEIGHT=1
    ALIGN="left"
>
</OBJECT>

<SCRIPT Language="VBScript">
Sub Track1_OnShow
    Alert "The View Track Control is back on the screen"
End Sub
Sub Track1_OnHide
    Alert "The View Track Control has left the screen"
End Sub
</SCRIPT>
```

Part

V

Ch

19

FIGURE 19.15
When the View Tracker Control first appears in view, or each time it reappears, its onShow event is triggered.

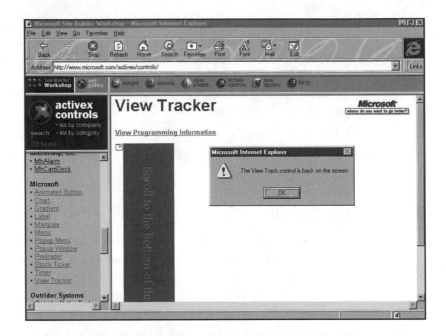

FIGURE 19.16
The View Tracker can be used to create context-sensitive menus and Web pages, whose content changes depending on what is currently displayed.

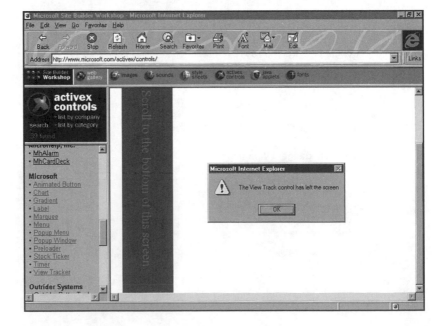

Microsoft's parameter descriptions for the View Tracker Control are as follows:

- `Image`—URL specifying an image for the Control.
- `AboutBox`—Displays the About dialog box.
- `OnShow`—Control falls within the view area.
- `OnHide`—Control scrolls off the view area.

Using the Microsoft Forms 2.0 Objects

FrontPage Editor gives you several ActiveX Controls that are oriented toward forms. These add flexibility and interactivity not readily available in the static forms components you get from the Forms Toolbar. To make these objects work together and provide the results you want, some programming will be required.

The form objects available are as follows:

- Check Box—Inserts a check box next to an independent option that you select or clear. Multiple choices with several options chosen are supported.
- Combo Box—Inserts a combination text box and list box. Users can either type in an entry or select one from a list. This box includes a scroll bar.
- Command Button—Inserts a command button that carries out an operation.
- Frame—Inserts a box in which you can group related choices. To be able to move the frame and the Controls it contains together, insert the frame before you insert the Controls.
- Image—Inserts a graphic, with options for appearance.
- Label—Inserts a label.
- List Box—Inserts a box that displays available choices. If the list is bigger than the box, the user is provided with a scroll bar.
- Option Button—Inserts an option button next to each item in a group of choices that are mutually exclusive.
- Scrollbar—Inserts a scroll bar next to a list box that contains more items than are visible.
- Spin Button—Inserts a Spin Control that lets a user increment or decrement a value.
- Tab Strip—Provides tabbed or buttoned "file folders."
- Text Box—Inserts an edit field or Edit Control that displays text typed by the user.
- Toggle Button—Inserts a toggle button that switches between two states.

Part
V

Ch
19

From Here...

You've had a look at one type of active content you can add to pages on your site. However, there are more resources than just ActiveX. For an exploration of these, go on to:

- Chapter 20, "Scripting with VBScript and JScript", where you find out about the components of the VBScript language, and how you use Visual Basic scripts to interact with Microsoft Internet Explorer.

- Chapter 21, "JavaScript," which explores JavaScript language elements and syntax, and shows how you can use this scripting language to interact with Web page elements and users.

- Chapter 22, "Inserting Java Applets and Browser Plug-Ins," where you can learn about MIME media types, Netscape plug-ins, and get an overview of the Java programming language.

## CHAPTER 20

Scripting with VBScript and JScript

In addition to Netscape's JavaScript language, there now exists for Web programmers Microsoft's own scripting language, Visual Basic Script (VBScript), which is based on the Visual Basic and Visual Basic for Applications languages. Just as these two languages made it much easier to create applications for Windows and within the Microsoft Office suite, respectively, VBScript was designed as a language for easily adding interactivity and dynamic content to Web pages. VBScript gives Web authors the ability to use Internet Explorer and other compatible Web browsers and applications to execute scripts that perform a wide variety of functions. These functions include verifying and acting on user input, customizing Java applets, interacting with and customizing ActiveX Controls and other OLE-compatible applications, and many other things. ■

Find out about Visual Basic (VB) Script

In this chapter, you'll find out about using Visual Basic Script, Microsoft's own scripting language, with FrontPage 97.

VBScript is related to Visual Basic for Applications

Find out how VBScript is related to Microsoft's Visual Basic for Applications and Visual Basic programming environments.

VBScript language components

Learn about the different components, statements, and functions of the VBScript programming language.

Use VBScript to interact with Web browsers

Learn how to use VBScript to interact with Internet Explorer through the Internet Explorer object model.

VBScript in HTML documents

See examples of VBScripts used in HTML documents to add increased interactivity, functionality, and an interface to other Web objects.

Using FrontPage Editor's Script Wizard

Add VBScript to your pages the easy way.

Using FrontPage Editor to Add Scripts to a Page

While FrontPage Editor on its own is an extremely capable page editor, its capabilities are enormously extended by adding scripts. But before getting started with investigating VBScript itself, you'll likely want to know how you persuade FrontPage Editor to insert scripts in an HTML document. It's quite simple; use the following procedure:

1. Choose Insert, Script, or click the Insert Script button on the toolbar. The Script dialog box appears (see Figure 20.1).

FIGURE 20.1
Use the Script dialog box to choose the type of script you want and to compose it.

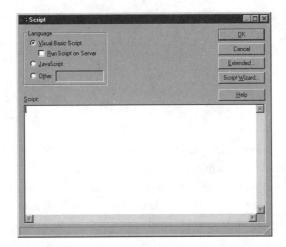

2. Mark the option button for the kind of script you want.

3. Type the code into the workspace of the dialog box and choose OK. The script will be inserted into the page.

> **N O T E** According to Microsoft, the Run Script on Server option is not available at this time (late 1996). ∎

The workspace in this dialog box is just that of a text editor, and absolutely no syntax checking is done. You don't need to include the <SCRIPT> tags; they're inserted when you choose OK to close the dialog box and add the script.

> **N O T E** You'll know there's a script in your page because a small script icon (coffee cup for Java; movie clapboard for VBScript) appears in the FrontPage Editor workspace to indicate its presence. ∎

The Script Wizard, also available through this dialog box, makes it unnecessary (much of the time) for you to type code in by hand. We will explore the use of the Script Wizard later in this chapter.

What Is VBScript?

Since Microsoft began its big push into the Internet and World Wide Web arena in December 1995, it has been pursuing the Web industry leader, Netscape, with a two-pronged approach. On the one hand, it has been adding features to its own Web browser, Internet Explorer, in order to make it more compatible with Netscape Navigator. Some of these added features include support for HTML extensions (such as frames), the ability to execute Java applets, and compatibility with the JavaScript scripting language.

The other element of Microsoft's approach is to break new ground. Not content to play catch-up with Netscape, Microsoft has introduced its own new technologies and innovations. Its biggest innovation, however, is a collection of technologies called ActiveX Technologies. Elements of ActiveX Technologies are discussed in other chapters. Another element, ActiveX Scripting, includes support for JavaScript and Microsoft's own Visual Basic Script (VBScript). ActiveX technology is now in the public domain, by the way, and has a standards committee. See Chapter 19, "Using ActiveX Controls," for more information.

Microsoft's ActiveX Scripting

However, ActiveX Scripting is more than just support for VBScript and JavaScript. Microsoft has developed a standard to allow its Web browser and other compatible applications to support arbitrary scripting engines. Vendors can develop scripting engines of their own that can be used with Internet Explorer, as long as they conform to the ActiveX Scripting standard. Microsoft discusses ActiveX Scripting in greater detail within the Internet Explorer Web site at **http://www.microsoft.com/ie/ie3/activescript.htm**, and under its Internet developer Web site at **http://www.microsoft.com/intdev/sdk/docs/olescrpt/**.

 ON THE WEB

http:// www.microsoft.com/intdev/sdk/docs/olescrpt/ This site gives you access to the specifications of Microsoft's ActiveX Scripting technologies.

The first two examples of ActiveX scripting languages are JScript, Microsoft's open implementation of the JavaScript language, and VBScript. See Chapter 21, "JavaScript," for more information.

Part

V

Ch

20

VBScript

Like JavaScript, VBScript allows you to embed commands into an HTML document. When a user of a compatible Web browser (currently only Internet Explorer, or Netscape Navigator with the ScriptActive plug-in from Ncompass Labs) downloads your page, your VBScript commands are loaded by the Web browser along with the rest of the document, and are run in response to any of a series of events. Again, like JavaScript, VBScript is an *interpreted* language; Internet Explorer interprets the VBScript commands when they are loaded and run. They do not first need to be *compiled* into executable form by the Web author who uses them.

N O T E   The NCompass plug-in cannot natively read ActiveX unless the object tag contains the appropriate *embed* information. ■

VBScript is a fast and flexible subset of Microsoft's Visual Basic and Visual Basic for Applications languages, and is designed to be easy to program in and quick in adding active content to HTML documents. The language elements are mainly those that will be familiar to anyone who has programmed in just about any language, such as If...Then...Else blocks, Do, While, and For...Next loops, and a typical assortment of operators and built-in functions. This chapter takes you to the heart of the VBScript language and show you examples of how to use it to add interaction and increased functionality on your Web pages.

N O T E   If you are acquainted with JavaScript, you will find parts of this chapter to be very familiar. That's because JavaScript and VBScript are similar languages with similar syntax, which can perform many of the same functions. If you're torn between them, check the "What Scripting Language Should You Use?" section at the end of this chapter. ■

Why Use a Scripting Language?

Although HTML provides a good deal of flexibility for Web page authors, it is static by itself; once written, HTML documents can't interact with the user other than by presenting hyperlinks. Creative use of CGI scripts (which run on Web servers) has made it possible to create more interesting and effective interactive sites, but some applications really demand programs or scripts that are executed by the client.

VBScript allows Web authors to write small scripts that execute on the users' browsers instead of on the server. For example, an application that collects data from a form and then posts it to the server can validate the data for completeness and correctness before sending it to the server. This can greatly improve the performance of the browsing session, since users don't have to send data to the server until it's been verified as correct.

Another important use of Web browser scripting languages like VBScript comes as a result of the increased functionality being introduced for Web browsers in the form of Java applets, plug-ins, ActiveX Controls, and VRML objects and worlds. Each of these things can be used to add extra functions and interactivity to a Web page. Scripting languages act as the glue that binds everything together. A Web page might use an HTML form to get some user input and then set a parameter for an ActiveX Control based on that input. Usually it's a script that will actually carry this out.

What Can VBScript Do?

VBScript provides a fairly complete set of built-in functions and commands, allowing you to perform math calculations, manipulate strings, play sounds, open new windows and new URLs, and access and verify user input to your Web forms.

Code to perform these actions can be embedded in a page and executed when the page is loaded. You can also write functions that contain code that's triggered by events you specify. For example, you can write a VBScript method that is called when the user clicks the Submit button of a form, or one that is activated when the user clicks a hyperlink on the active page.

VBScript can also set the attributes, or *properties*, of ActiveX Controls, Java applets, and other objects present in the browser. This way, you can change the behavior of plug-ins or other objects without having to rewrite them. For example, your VBScript code could automatically set the text of an ActiveX Label Control based on what time the page is viewed.

VBScript, Visual Basic, and Visual Basic for Applications

VBScript is a subset of the Visual Basic and Visual Basic for Applications languages. If you are familiar with either of these two languages, programming in VBScript will be easy. Just as Visual Basic was meant to make the creation of Windows programs easier and more accessible, and Visual Basic for Applications was meant to do the same for Microsoft Office applications, VBScript is meant to give an easy-to-learn yet powerful means for adding interactivity and increased functionality to Web pages.

How Does VBScript Look in an HTML Document?

VBScript commands are embedded in your HTML documents, just as with JavaScript and other scripting languages. Embedded VB scripts are enclosed in the HTML container tag `<SCRIPT>...</SCRIPT>`. The `<LANGUAGE>` attribute of the `<SCRIPT>` tag specifies the scripting language to use when evaluating the script. For VBScript, the scripting language is defined as `LANGUAGE="VBS"`.

VBScript resembles JavaScript and many other computer languages you may be familiar with. It bears the closest resemblance, as you might imagine, to Visual Basic and Visual Basic for Applications because it is a subset of these two languages. The following are two of the simple rules for structuring VBScripts:

■ VBScript is case-insensitive, so `function`, `Function`, and `FUNCTION` are all the same.

■ A single statement can cover multiple lines if a continuation character, a single underscore, is placed at the end of each line to be continued. Also, you can put multiple short statements on a single line by separating each from the next with a colon.

VBScript Programming Hints

You should keep a few points in mind when programming with VBScript. These hints will ease your learning process and make your HTML documents that include VBscripts more compatible with a wider range of Web browsers.

Hiding Your Scripts   Because VBScript is a new product and is currently supported only by Internet Explorer 3—though Oracle, Spyglass, NetManage, and other companies plan to license the technology for future versions of their Web browsers—you'll probably be designing pages that will be viewed by Web browsers that don't support it. To keep those browsers from misinterpreting your VBScript, wrap your scripts as follows:

```
<SCRIPT LANGUAGE="VBS">
<!-- This line opens an HTML comment
VBScript commands...
This line closes an HTML comment -->
</SCRIPT>
```

The opening `<!--` comment causes Web browsers that do not support VBScript to disregard all text they encounter, until they find a matching `-->`, so they don't display your script. Make sure that your `<SCRIPT>...</SCRIPT>` container elements are outside the comments, though; otherwise, even compatible Web browsers will ignore the script.

Comments   Including comments in your programs to explain what they do is usually good practice for most scripting languages—and VBScript is no exception. The VBScript interpreter ignores any text marked as a comment, so don't be shy about including them. Comments in VBScript are set off using the REM statement (short for remark) or by using a single quotation mark (') character. Any text following the REM or single quotation mark, until the end of the line, is ignored. To include a comment on the same line as another VBScript statement, you can use either REM or a single quotation mark. However, if you use REM, you must separate the statement from the REM with a colon. Some of the ways of including HTML and VBScript comments in a script are shown in the following script fragment:

```
<SCRIPT LANGUAGE="VBS">
<!-- This line opens an HTML comment
REM This is a VBScript comment on a line by itself.
' This is another VBScript comment
customer.name = "Jim O'Donnell"        'Inline comment
customer.address = "1757 P Street NW"  :REM Inline REM comment (note the :)
customer.zip = "20036-1303"
<!-- This line closes an HTML comment -->
</SCRIPT>
```

Elements of the VBScript Language

As a subset of Visual Basic and Visual Basic for Applications, VBScript doesn't have as much functionality. It is intended to provide a quick and simple language for enhancing Web pages and servers. This section discusses some of the building blocks of VBScript and how they are combined into VBScript programs.

VBScript Identifiers

An *identifier* is just a unique name that VBScript uses to identify a variable, method, or object in your program. As with other programming languages, VBScript imposes some rules on what names you can use. All VBScript names must start with an alphabetic character and can contain both uppercase and lowercase letters and the digits 0 through 9. They can be as long as 255 characters, though you probably don't want to go much over 32 or so.

Unlike JavaScript, which supports two different ways for you to represent values in your scripts, literals and variables, VBScript has only variables. The difference in VBScript, then, is one of usage. You can include literals—constant values—in your VBScript programs by setting a variable equal to a value and not changing it. We will continue to refer to literals and variables as distinct entities, though they are interchangeable.

Literals and variables in VBScript are all of type *variant*, which means that they can contain any type of data that VBScript supports. It is usually a good idea to use a given variable for one type and explicitly convert its value to another type as necessary. The following are some of the types of data that VBScript supports:

- Integers—These types can be one, two, or four bytes in length, depending on how big they are.
- Floating Point—VBScript supports single- and double-precision floating point numbers.

Part

V

Ch

20

- Strings—Strings can represent words, phrases, or data, and they're set off by double quotation marks.
- Booleans—Booleans have a value of either `true` or `false`.
- Objects—A VBScript variable can refer to any object within its environment.

Objects, Properties, Methods, and Events

Before you proceed further, you should take some time to review some terminology that may or may not be familiar to you. VBScript follows much the same object model followed by JavaScript, and uses many of the same terms. In VBScript, just as in JavaScript—and in any object-oriented language for that matter—an *object* is a collection of data and functions that have been grouped together. An object's data is known as its *properties*, and its functions are known as its *methods*. An *event* is a condition to which an object can respond, such as a mouse click or other user input. The VBScript programs that you write make use of properties and methods of objects, both those that you create and those objects provided by the Web browser, its plug-ins, ActiveX Controls, Java applets, and the like.

> **TIP**
> Here's a simple guideline: an object's *properties* are the information it knows, its *methods* are how it can act on that information, and *events* are what it responds to.

> **NOTE**   A very important but rather confusing thing to remember is that an object's methods are *also* properties of that object. An object's properties are the information it knows. The object certainly knows about its own methods, so those methods are properties of the object right alongside its other data. ■

Using Built-In Objects and Functions   Individual VBScript elements are objects. For example, literals and variables are objects of type *variant*, which can be used to hold data of many different types. These objects also have associated methods—ways of acting on the different data types. VBScript also allows you to access a set of useful objects that represent the Web browser, the currently displayed page, and other elements of the browsing session.

You access objects by specifying their names. For example, the active document object is named `document`. To use `document`'s properties or methods, you add a period and the name of the method or property you want. For example, `document.title` is the `title` property of the `document` object.

Using Properties   Every object has properties—even literals. To access a property, just use the object name followed by a period and the property name. To get the length of a string object named `address`, you can write the following:

```
address.length
```

You get back an integer that equals the number of characters in the string. If the object you're using has properties that can be modified, you can change them in the same way. To set the color property of a house object, just write the following:

```
house.color = "blue"
```

You can also create new properties for an object just by naming them. For example, say you define a class called customer for one of your pages. You can add new properties to the customer object as follows:

```
customer.name = "Jim O'Donnell"
customer.address = "1757 P Street NW"
customer.zip = "20036-1303"
```

Because an object's methods are just properties, you can easily add new properties to an object by writing your own function and creating a new object property using your own function name. If you want to add a Bill method to your customer object, you can write a function named BillCustomer and set the object's property as follows:

```
customer.Bill = BillCustomer;
```

To call the new method, you just write the following:

```
customer.Bill()
```

VBScript Language Elements

While VBScript is not as flexible as C++ or Visual Basic, it's quick and simple. Since it is easily embedded in your Web pages, adding interactivity or increased functionality with a VBScript is easy—a lot easier than writing a Java applet to do the same thing (though, to be fair, you can do a lot more with Java applets). This section covers some of the nuts and bolts of VBScript programming.

As VBScript is a new and evolving language, you can get up-to-the-minute information on it at the Microsoft VBScript Web site at **http://www.microsoft.com/vbscript/**.

VBScript Variables

VBScript variables are all of the type *variant*, which means that they can be used for any of the supported data types. The types of data that VBScript variables can hold are summarized in Table 20.1.

Table 20.1	**Data Types that VBScript Variables Can Contain**

Type	Description
Empty	Uninitialized and is treated as 0 or the empty string, depending on the context
Null	Intentionally contains no valid data
Boolean	`true` or `false`
Byte	Integer in the range –128 to 127
Integer	Integer in the range –32,768 to 32,767
Long	Integer in the range –2,147,483,648 to 2,147,483,647
Single	Single-precision floating point number in the range –3.402823E38 to –1.401298E-45 for negative values and 1.401298E-45 to 3.402823E38 for positive values
Double	Double-precision floating point number in the range –1.79769313486232E308 to –4.94065645841247E-324 for negative values; 4.94065645841247E-324 to 1.79769313486232E308 for positive values
Date	Number that represents a date between January 1, 100 to December 31, 9999
String	Variable-length string up to approximately 2 billion characters in length
Object	Any object
Error	Error number

Expressions

An *expression* is anything that can be evaluated to get a single value. Expressions can contain string or numeric variables, operators, and other expressions, and they can range from simple to quite complex. For example, the following is an expression that uses the assignment operator (more on operators in the next section) to assign the result 3.14159 to the variable pi:

```
pi = 3.14159
```

By contrast, the following is a more complex expression whose final value depends on the values of the two Boolean variables Quit and Complete:

```
(Quit = TRUE) And (Complete = FALSE)
```

Operators

Operators do just what their name suggests: they operate on variables or literals. The items that an operator acts on are called its *operands*. Operators come in the two following types:

- Unary—These operators require only one operand, and the operator can come before or after the operand. The Not operator, which performs the logical negation of an expression, is a good example.

- Binary—These operators need two operands. The four math operators (+ for addition, - for subtraction, x for multiplication, and \ for division) are all binary operators, as is the = assignment operator you saw earlier.

Assignment Operators *Assignment operators* take the result of an expression and assign it to a variable. One feature that VBScript has that most other programming languages do not is that you can change a variable's type on the fly. Consider the example shown in Listing 20.1.

Listing 20.1   Pi-fly.htm—VBScript Variables Can Change Type on-the-Fly

```
<HTML>
<HEAD>
<SCRIPT LANGUAGE="VBS">
<!-- Hide this script from incompatible Web browsers!
Sub TypeDemo
    Dim pi
    document.write("<HR>")
    pi = 3.14159
    document.write("pi is " & CStr(pi) & "<BR>")
    pi = FALSE
    document.write("pi is " & CStr(pi) & "<BR>")
    document.write("<HR>")
End Sub
<!-- -->
</SCRIPT>
<TITLE>Changing Pi on the Fly!</TITLE>
</HEAD>
<BODY BGCOLOR=#FFFFFF>
If your Web browser doesn't support VBScript, this is all you will see!
<SCRIPT LANGUAGE="VBS">
<!-- Hide this script from incompatible Web browsers!
TypeDemo
<!-- -->
</SCRIPT>
</BODY>
</HTML>
```

Part

V

Ch

20

This short function first prints the (correct) value of *pi*. In most other languages, though, trying to set a floating point variable to a Boolean value either generates a compiler error or a runtime error. Because VBScript variables can be any type, it happily accepts the change and prints pi's new value: `false` (see Figure 20.2).

FIGURE 20.2

Because VBScript variables are all of type *variant*, not only their value can be changed, but also their data type.

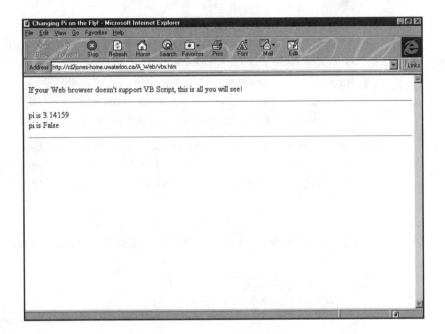

The assignment operator, =, simply assigns the value of an expression's right side to its left side. In the preceding example, the variable pi gets the floating point value 3.14159 or the Boolean value false after the expression is evaluated.

Math Operators The previous sections gave you a sneak preview of the math operators that VBScript furnishes. As you might expect, the standard four math functions (addition, subtraction, multiplication, and division) work just as they do on an ordinary calculator and use the symbols +, -, x, and \.

VBScript supplies three other math operators as follows:

- \—The backslash operator divides its first operand by its second, after first rounding floating point operands to the nearest integer, and returns the integer part of the result. For example, 19 \ 6.7 returns 2 (6.7 rounds to 7, 19 divided by 7 is a little over 2.71, the integer part of which is 2).

- Mod—This operator is similar to \ in that it divides the first operand by its second, after again rounding floating point operands to the nearest integer, and returns the integer remainder.

■ ^—This exponent operator returns the first operand raised to the power of the second. The first operand can be negative only if the second, the exponent, is an integer.

Comparison Operators   Comparing the value of two expressions to see whether one is larger, smaller, or equal to another is often necessary. VBScript supplies several comparison operators that take two operands and return `true` if the comparison is true and `false` if it's not. Table 20.2 shows the VBScript comparison operators.

Table 20.2   VBScript Comparison Operators

Operator	Read It As	Returns *true* When:
=	Equals	The two operands are equal
<>	Does not equal	The two operands are unequal
<	Less than	The left operand is less than the right operand
<=	Less than or equal to	The left operand is less than or equal to the right operand
>	Greater than	The left operand is greater than the right operand
>=	Greater than or equal to	The left operand is greater than or equal to the right operand

TIP   The comparison operators also can be used on strings; the results depend on standard lexico-graphic ordering.

Thinking of the comparison operators as questions may be helpful. When you write:

    (x >= 10)

you're really saying, "Is the value of variable x greater than or equal to `10`?" The return value answers the question, `true` or `false`.

Logical Operators   Comparison operators compare quantity or content for numeric and string expressions, but sometimes you need to test a logical value—like whether a comparison operator returns `true` or `false`. VBScript's logical operators allow you to compare expressions that return logical values. The following are VBScript's logical operators:

■ And—The And operator returns `true` if both its input expressions are true. If the first operand evaluates to `false`, And returns `false` immediately, without evaluating the second operand. Here's an example:

```
x = TRUE And TRUE        ' x is TRUE
x = TRUE And FALSE       ' x is FALSE
x = FALSE And TRUE       ' x is FALSE
x = FALSE And FALSE      ' x is FALSE
```

■ Or—This operator returns true if either of its operands is true. If the first operand is true, ¦¦ returns true without evaluating the second operand. Here's an example:

```
x = TRUE Or TRUE         ' x is TRUE
x = TRUE Or FALSE        ' x is TRUE
x = FALSE Or TRUE        ' x is TRUE
x = FALSE Or FALSE       ' x is FALSE
```

■ Not—This operator takes only one expression and it returns the opposite of that expression, so Not true returns false, and Not false returns true.

■ Xor—This operator, which stands for "exclusive or," returns true if either, but not both, of its input expressions are true, as in the following:

```
x = TRUE Xor TRUE        ' x is FALSE
x = TRUE Xor FALSE       ' x is TRUE
x = FALSE Xor TRUE       ' x is TRUE
x = FALSE Xor FALSE      ' x is FALSE
```

■ Eqv—This operator, which stands for "equivalent," returns true if its two input expressions are the same—either both true or both false. The statement x Eqv y is equivalent to Not (x Xor y).

■ Imp—This operator, which stands for "implication," returns true according to the following:

```
x = TRUE Imp TRUE        ' x is TRUE
x = FALSE Imp TRUE       ' x is TRUE
x = TRUE Imp FALSE       ' x is FALSE
x = FALSE Imp FALSE      ' x is TRUE
```

N O T E The logical implication operator Imp is the only logical operator for which the order of the operands is important. ■

Note that the And and Or operators don't evaluate the second operand if the first operand provides enough information for the operator to return a value. This process, called *short-circuit evaluation*, can be significant when the second operand is a function call.

N O T E All six of the logical operators can also operate on non Boolean expressions. In this case, the logical operations described previously are performed bitwise, on each bit of the two operands. For instance, for the two integers 19 (00010011 in binary) and 6 (00000110):

```
19 And 6 =   2 (00000010 in binary)
19 Or 6  =  23 (00010111 in binary)
Not 19   = -20 (11101100 in binary) ■
```

String Concatenation   The final VBScript operator is the string concatenation operator &. While the addition operator + can also be used to concatenate strings, using & is better because it is less ambiguous.

Controlling Your VBScripts

Sometimes the scripts that you write are very simple and execute the same way each time they are loaded—for example, a script to display a graphic animation. However, in order to write a script that will perform different functions, depending on different user inputs or other conditions, you will eventually need to add a little more sophistication to your script. VBScript provides statements and loops for controlling the execution of your programs based on a variety of inputs.

Testing Conditions   VBScript provides one control structure for making decisions—the If...Then...Else structure. To make a decision, you supply one or more expressions that evaluate to true or false; which code is executed depends on what your expressions evaluate to.

The simplest form of If...Then...Else uses only the If...Then part. If the specified condition is true, the code following the condition is executed; if not, that code is skipped. For example, in the following code fragment, the message appears only if the variable x is less than pi:

```
if (x < pi) then document.write("x is less than pi")
```

You can use any expression as the condition. Since expressions can be nested and combined with the logical operators, your tests can be pretty sophisticated. Also, using the multiple statement character, you can execute multiple commands, as in the following:

```
if ((test = TRUE) And (x > max)) then max = x : test = FALSE
```

The else clause allows you to specify a set of statements to execute when the condition is false. In the same single line form shown in the preceding line, your new line appears as follows:

```
if (x > pi) then test = TRUE else test = FALSE
```

A more versatile use of the If...Then...Else allows multiple lines and multiple actions for each case. It looks something like the following:

```
if (x > pi) then
    test = TRUE
    count = count + 1
else
    test = FALSE
    count = 0
end if
```

Part
V

Ch
20

Note that with this syntax, additional test clauses using the `elseif` statement are permitted. For instance, we could add one more clause to the previous example:

```
if (x > pi) then
    test = TRUE
    count = count + 1
elseif (x < -pi) then
    test = TRUE
    count = count - 1
else
    test = FALSE
    count = 0
end if
```

Repeating Actions   If you want to repeat an action more than once, VBScript provides a variety of constructs for doing so. The first, called a `For...Next` loop, executes a set of statements some number of times. You specify three expressions: an *initial* expression, which sets the values of any variables you need to use; a *final value*, which tells the loop how to see when it's done; and an *increment* expression, which modifies any variables that need it. Here's a simple example:

```
for count = 0 to 100 step 2
    document.write("Count is " & CStr(count) & "<BR>")
next
```

In this example, the expressions are all simple numerical values. The initial value is 0, the final value is 100, and the increment is 2. This loop executes 51 times and prints out a number each time.

The third form of loop is the `While...Wend` loop. It executes statements as long as its condition is `true`. For example, you can rewrite the first `For...Next` loop as follows:

```
count = 0
while (count <= 100)
    document.write("Count is " & CStr(count) & "<BR>")
    count = count + 2
wend
```

The last type of loop is the `Do...Loop`, which has several forms, which test the condition either at the beginning or the end. The test can either be a `Do While` or `Do Until`, and can occur at the beginning or end of the loop. If a `Do While` test is done at the beginning, the loop executes as long as the test condition is true, similar to the `While...Wend` loop. Here's an example:

```
count = 0
do while (count <= 100)
    document.write("Count is " & CStr(count) & "<BR>")
    count = count + 2
loop
```

An example of having the test at the end, as a `Do...Until`, can also yield equivalent results. In that case, the loop looks like the following:

```
count = 0
do
    document.write("Count is " & CStr(count) & "<BR>")
    count = count + 2
loop until (count = 102)
```

One other difference between these two forms is that when the test is at the end of the loop, as in the second case, the commands in the loop are executed at least once. If the test is at the beginning, that is not the case.

Which form you prefer depends on what you're doing. `For...Next` loops are useful when you want to perform an action a set number of times. `While...Wend` and `Do...Loop` loops, while they can be used for the same purpose, are best when you want to keep doing something as long as a particular condition remains `true`.

N O T E The `For...Next` and `Do...Loop` loops also have a way to exit the loop from inside—
the `End For` and `End Do` statements, respectively. Normally, these tests would be
used as part of a conditional statement, such as:

```
for i = 0 to 100
    x = UserFunc()
    document.write("x[" & CStr(i) & "] = " & CStr(x) & "<BR>")
    if (x > max) end for
next
```

Other VBScript Statements

This section provides a quick reference to some of the other VBScript statements. The following formatting is used:

- All VBScript keywords are in a monospace font.
- Words in *monospace italics* represent user-defined names or statements.
- Any portions enclosed in square brackets ([and]) are optional.
- Portions enclosed in braces ({ and }) and separated by a vertical bar (¦) represent an option, of which one must be selected.
- The word *statements...* indicates a block of one or more statements.

The *Call* statement   The `Call` statement calls a VBScript `Sub` or `Function` procedure (see below).

Part

V

Ch

20

Syntax:

```
Call MyProc([arglist])
```

or

```
MyProc [arglist]
```

Note that *arglist* is a comma-delimited list of zero or more arguments to be passed to the procedure. When the second form is used, omitting the Call statement, the parentheses around the argument list, if any, must also be omitted.

The *Dim* statement   The Dim statement is used to declare variables and also to allocate the storage necessary for them. If you specify subscripts, you can also create arrays.

Syntax:

```
Dim varname[([subscripts])][,varname[([subscripts])],...]
```

The *Function* and *Sub* Statements   The Function and Sub statements declare VBScript procedures. The difference is that a Function procedure returns a value, and a Sub procedure does not. All parameters are passed to functions *by value*—the function gets the value of the parameter but cannot change the original value in the caller.

Syntax:

```
[Static] Function funcname([arglist])
    statements...
    funcname = returnvalue
End
```

and

```
[Static] Sub subname([arglist])
    statements...
End
```

Variables can be declared with the Dim statement within a Function or Sub procedure. In this case, those variables are local to that procedure and can be referenced only within it. If the Static keyword is used when the procedure is declared, then all local variables retain their value from one procedure call to the next.

The *On Error* Statement   The On Error statement is used to enable error handling.

Syntax:

```
On Error Resume Next
```

On Error Resume Next enables execution to continue immediately after the statement that provokes the runtime error. Or, if the error occurs in a procedure call after the last executed On Error statement, execution commences immediately after that procedure call. This way, execution can continue despite a runtime error, allowing you to build an error-handling routine in-line within the procedure. The most recent On Error Resume Next statement is the one that is active, so you should execute one in each procedure in which you want to have in-line error handling.

VBScript Functions

VBScript has an assortment of intrinsic functions that you can use in your scripts. Table 20.3 shows the function that exist for performing different types of operations. (Some functions can be used for several types of operations, so they are listed multiple times in the table.)

Table 20.3   VBScript Functions

Type of Operation	Function Names
array operations	IsArray, LBound, UBound
conversions	Abs, Asc, AscB, AscW, Chr, ChrB, ChrW, Cbool, CByte, CDate, CDbl, CInt, CLng, CSng, Cstr, DateSerial, DateValue, Hex, Oct, Fix, Int, Sgn, TimeSerial, TimeValue
dates and times	Date, Time, DateSerial, DateValue, Day, Month, Weekday, Year, Hour, Minute, Second, Now, TimeSerial, TimeValue
input/output	InputBox, MsgBox
math	Atn, Cos, Sin, Tan, Exp, Log, Sqr, Randomize, Rnd
objects	IsObject
strings	Asc, AscB, AscW, Chr, ChrB, ChrW, Instr, InStrB, Len, LenB, LCase, UCase, Left, LeftB, Mid, MidB, Right, RightB, Space, StrComp, String, LTrim, RTrim, Trim
variants	IsArray, IsDate, IsEmpty, IsNull, IsNumeric, IsObject, VarType

Part
V

Ch
20

VBScript and Web Browsers

The most important things you will be doing with your VBScripts are interacting with the content and information on your Web site and, through it, with your user. You have seen earlier in this chapter a little of one particular thing VBScript can do to your Web page— use document.write() to place information on the page itself.

VBScript interacts with your Web browser through the browser's object model. Different aspects of the Web browser exist as different objects, with properties and methods that can be accessed by VBScript. For instance, `document.write()` uses the `write` method of the `document` object. Understanding this Web browser object model is crucial to using VBScript effectively. Understanding how the Web browser processes and executes your scripts is also necessary.

When Scripts Execute

When you put VBScript code in a page, the Web browser evaluates the code as soon as it's encountered. Functions, however, don't get executed when they're evaluated; they just get stored for later use. You still have to call functions explicitly to make them work. Some functions are attached to objects, such as buttons or text fields on forms, and they are called when some event happens on the button or field. You might also have functions that you want to execute during page evaluation. You can do so by putting a call to the function at the appropriate place in the page.

Where to Put Your Scripts

You can put scripts anywhere within your HTML page, as long as they're surrounded with the `<SCRIPT>...</SCRIPT>` tags. One good system is to put functions that will be executed more than once into the `<HEAD>` element of the page; this element provides a convenient storage place. Since the `<HEAD>` element is at the beginning of the file, functions and VBScript code that you put there will be evaluated before the rest of the document is loaded. Then you can execute the function at the appropriate point in your Web page by calling it, as in the following:

```
<SCRIPT language="VBS">
<!-- Hide this script from incompatible Web browsers!
myFunction()
<!-- -->
</SCRIPT>
```

Another way to execute scripts is to attach them to HTML elements that support scripts. When scripts are matched with events attached to these elements, the script is executed when the event occurs. This can be done with HTML elements, such as forms, buttons, or links. Consider Listing 20.2, which shows a very simple example of attaching a VBScript function to the `onClick` attribute of a HTML forms button (see Figure 20.3).

Listing 20.2   Button1.htm—Calling a VBScript Function with the Click of a Button

```
<HTML>
<HEAD>
<SCRIPT LANGUAGE="VBS">
```

```
<!-- Hide this script from incompatible Web browsers!
sub Pressed
    alert "Stop that!"
end sub
<!-- -->
</SCRIPT>
<TITLE>VBScripts Attached to HTML Elements</TITLE>
</HEAD>
<BODY BGCOLOR=#FFFFFF>
<FORM NAME="Form1">
<INPUT TYPE="BUTTON" NAME="Button1" VALUE="Don't Press Me!"
       onClick="Pressed">
</FORM>
</BODY>
</HTML>
```

FIGURE 20.3
VBScript functions can be attached to form fields through several different methods.

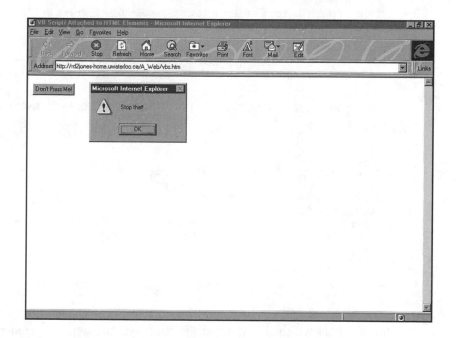

VBScript also provides you with several alternate ways to attach functions to objects and their events. The first is through the VBScript function name. To have a VBScript function execute when a given *event* occurs to an *object*, name the function `object_event`. For instance, Listing 20.3 shows an alternate way of coding Listing 20.2 using this method. Another method for simple actions is to attach the VBScript directly to the attribute of the HTML form element, as shown in Listing 20.4. All three of these listings will produce the output shown in Figure 20.3.

Part
V

Ch
20

Listing 20.3 Button2.htm—VBScript Functions Can Be Named to Be Called Automatically

```
<HTML>
<HEAD>
<SCRIPT LANGUAGE="VBS">
<!-- Hide this script from incompatible Web browsers!
sub Button1_onClick
    alert "Stop that!"
end sub
<!-- -->
</SCRIPT>
<TITLE>VBScripts Attached to HTML Elements</TITLE>
</HEAD>
<BODY BGCOLOR=#FFFFFF>
<FORM NAME="Form1">
<INPUT TYPE="BUTTON" NAME="Button1" VALUE="Don't Press Me!">
</FORM>
</BODY>
</HTML>
```

Listing 20.4 Button3.htm—Simple VBScripts Can Be Attached Right to a Form Element

```
<HTML>
<HEAD>
<TITLE>VBScripts Attached to HTML Elements</TITLE>
</HEAD>
<BODY BGCOLOR=#FFFFFF>
<FORM NAME="Form1">
    <INPUT TYPE="BUTTON" NAME="Button1" VALUE="Don't Press Me!"
        onClick="alert('I said Don\'t Press Me!')">
</FORM>
</BODY>
</HTML>
```

Sometimes, though, you have code that shouldn't be evaluated or executed until after all the page's HTML has been parsed and displayed. An example is a function to print out all the URLs referenced in a page. If this function is evaluated before all the HTML on the page has been loaded, it misses some URLs. Therefore, the call to the function should come at the page's end. The function itself can be defined anywhere in the HTML document; it is the function call that should be at the end of the page.

N O T E VBScript code to modify the actual HTML contents of a document (as opposed to merely changing the text in a form text input field, for instance) must be executed during page evaluation. ■

Web Browser Objects and Events

In addition to recognizing VBScript when it's embedded inside a `<SCRIPT>...</SCRIPT>` tag, Internet Explorer 3 and other compatible browsers will also expose some objects, along with their methods and properties, that you can then use in your programs. The Web browsers can also trigger methods you define in response to events that are triggered when the user takes certain actions in the browser (for example, when a button is clicked). The examples shown in Listings 20.2, 20.3, and 20.4 all demonstrate this—a VBScript function is executed when a Web browser *object* (the form input field named `Button1`) responds to the `onClick` *event* (triggered by the user clicking the button).

Web Browser Object Hierarchy and Scoping

Figure 20.4 shows the page on the Microsoft Web site that gives the hierarchy of objects that the Web browser provides and that are accessible to VBScript. `Window` is the topmost object in the hierarchy, and the other objects are organized underneath it, as shown. The dashed lines show where more than one object of the given type can exist. Using this hierarchy, the full reference for the value of a text field named `Text1` in an HTML form named `Form1` would be `Window.Document.Form1.Text1.Value`.

FIGURE 20.4

Objects defined by the Web browser are organized in a hierarchy and can be accessed and manipulated by VBScript.

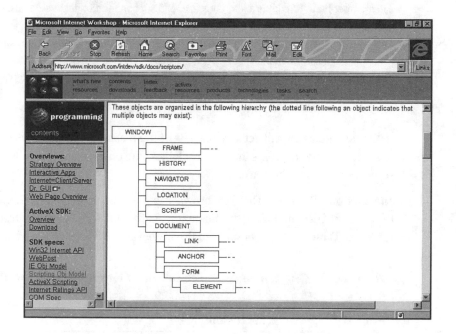

ON THE WEB

http://www.microsoft.com/intdev/sdk/docs/scriptom/   for complete specifications for
Microsoft's implementation of the Web browser object model.

However, because of the object scoping rules in VBScript, it is not necessary to specify
this full reference. Scoping refers to the range over which a variable, function, or object is
defined. For instance, a variable defined within a VBScript function is scoped only within
that function—it cannot be referenced outside of the function. VBScripts are scoped to the
current window but not to the objects below the window in the hierarchy. So, for the example above, the text field value could also be referenced as `Document.Form1.Text1.Value`.

Web Browser Object Model

Many events that happen in a browsing session aren't related to items on the page (such
as buttons or HTML text). Instead, they're related to what's happening in the browser
itself, like what page the user is viewing.

> **CAUTION**
>
> Remember that VBScript is a new language, and support for it under Internet Explorer 3 and other Web
> browsers is also very new. As a result, the specifications of the language may change, as well as the
> objects, properties, methods, and events supplied by the Web browsers. Up-to-date information about
> the language can be found through Microsoft's VBScript Web site at **http://www.microsoft.com/**
> **vbscript/**, and information about the Web browser object models can be found through the Netscape
> Navigator and Microsoft Internet Explorer Web sites.

In this section, you will get an overview of the most important browser objects, properties, methods, and events that are available—the ones you are most likely to use—and see
some examples of their use.

The _Location_ Object   The Web browser exposes an object called `Location`, which holds
the current URL, including the hostname, path, CGI script arguments, and even the
protocol. Table 20.4 shows some of the properties of the `Location` object.

Table 20.4   The _Location_ Object Contains Information on the Currently Displayed URL

Property	What It Contains
href	The entire URL, including all the subparts; for example, **http://www.msn.com/products/msprod.htm**

Property	What It Contains
protocol	The protocol field of the URL, including the first colon; for example, **http:**
host	The hostname and port number; for example, **www.msn.com:80**
hostname	The hostname; for example, **www.msn.com**
port	The port, if specified; otherwise, it's blank
pathname	The path to the actual document; for example, **products/msprod.htm**
hash	Any CGI arguments after the first # in the URL
search	Any CGI arguments after the first ? in the URL

N O T E Remember that VBScript is not case-sensitive, so for example, references to the following are all equivalent:

```
Location.HREF
location.href
location.Href
LoCaTiOn.HrEf
```

Listing 20.5 shows an example of how you access and use the Location object. First, the current values of the Location properties are displayed on the Web page (see Figure 20.5). As you can see, not all of them are defined. Additionally, when the button is clicked, the Location.Href property is set to the URL of my home page. This causes the Web browser to load that page.

Listing 20.5 Location.htm—The *Location* Object Allows You to Access and Set Information About the Current URL

```
<HTML>
<HEAD>
<SCRIPT LANGUAGE="VBS">
<!-- Hide this script from incompatible Web browsers!
sub Button1_onClick
    Location.Href = "http://www.rpi.edu/~odonnj/"
end sub
<!-- -->
</SCRIPT>
<TITLE>The Location Object</TITLE>
</HEAD>
<BODY BGCOLOR=#FFFFFF>
<SCRIPT LANGUAGE="VBS">
<!-- Hide this script from incompatible Web browsers!
document.write "Current Location information: <BR> <HR>"
document.write "Location.Href = " & Location.Href & "<BR>"
```

continues

Listing 20.5   Continued

```
document.write "Location.Protocol = " & Location.Protocol & "<BR>"
document.write "Location.Host = " & Location.Host & "<BR>"
document.write "Location.Hostname = " & Location.Hostname & "<BR>"
document.write "Location.Port = " & Location.Port & "<BR>"
document.write "Location.Pathname = " & Location.Pathname & "<BR>"
document.write "Location.Hash = " & Location.Hash & "<BR>"
document.write "Location.Search = " & Location.Search & "<BR> <HR>"
<!-- -->
</SCRIPT>
<FORM NAME="Form1">
    <INPUT TYPE="BUTTON" NAME="Button1" VALUE="Goto JOD's Home Page!">
</FORM>
</BODY>
</HTML>
```

FIGURE 20.5

Manipulating the Location object gives you another means of moving from one Web page to another.

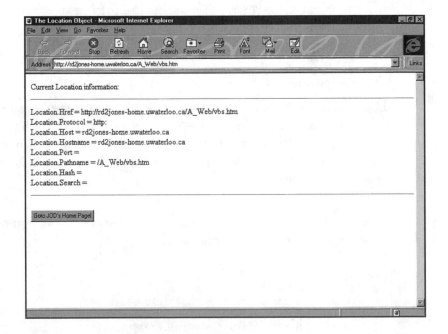

The *Document* Object   The Document object, as you might expect, exposes useful properties and methods of the active document. Location refers only to the URL of the active document, but Document refers to the document itself. Table 20.5 shows Document's properties and methods.

Table 20.5   The *Document* Object Contains Information on the Currently Loaded and Displayed HTML Page

Property	What It Contains
title	Title of the current page, or Untitled if no title exists
location	The document's address (read-only)
lastModified	The page's last-modified date
forms	Array of all the FORMs in the current page
links	Array of all the HREF anchors in the current page
anchors	Array of all the anchors in the current page
linkColor	Link color
alinkColor	Link color
vlinkColor	Visited link color
bgColor	Background color
fgColor	Foreground color

Method	What It Does
write	Writes HTML to the current page

Listing 20.6 shows a VBScript that accesses and displays some of the properties of the Document object. Notice that the Links property is an array, one for each URL link on the current Web page. Figure 20.6 shows the results of loading this Web page.

Listing 20.6   Document.htm—The *Document* Object Allows You to Access and Set Information About the Current Document

```
<HTML>
<HEAD>
<TITLE>The Document Object</TITLE>
</HEAD>
<BODY BGCOLOR=#FFFFFF>
<A HREF="http://www.rpi.edu/~odonnj/">JOD's Home Page</A>
<A HREF="http://www.rpi.edu/~odonnj/Location.htm">The Location Object</A>
<HR>
<SCRIPT LANGUAGE="VBS">
<!-- Hide this script from incompatible Web browsers!
Dim n
document.write "Current Document information: <BR> <HR>"
document.write "Document.Title = " & Document.Title & "<BR>"
```

continues

Part

V

Ch

20

Listing 20.6   Continued

```
document.write "Document.Location = " & Document.Location & "<BR>"
document.write "Document.lastModified = " & Document.lastModified & "<BR>"
for n = 0 to Document.Links.Length-1
    document.write "Document.Links(" & Cstr(n) & ").Href = " & _
        Document.Links(n).Href & "<BR>"
next
document.write "Document.linkColor = " & Document.linkColor & "<BR>"
document.write "Document.alinkColor = " & Document.alinkColor & "<BR>"
document.write "Document.vlinkColor = " & Document.vlinkColor & "<BR>"
document.write "Document.bgColor = " & Document.bgColor & "<BR>"
document.write "Document.fgColor = " & Document.fgColor & "<BR> <HR>"
<!-- -->
</SCRIPT>
</BODY>
</HTML>
```

FIGURE 20.6

Document object properties contain information about the current document displayed in the Web browser.

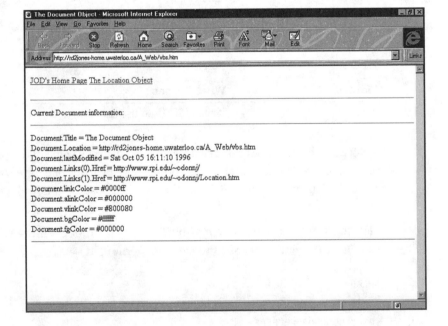

Some of the real power of the Document object, however, is realized by making use of the objects underneath it in the hierarchy, particularly the different HTML forms elements available. This is because these elements are the primary ways of interacting with the user of a Web page.

The *Form* Object

The HTML form object is the primary way for Web pages to solicit different types of input from the user. VBScript will often work along with HTML forms in order to perform its functions. The object model for HTML forms includes a wide variety of properties, methods, and events that can be used to program VBScripts.

Form **Methods and Events**   Table 20.6 shows some of the methods and events attached to HTML form objects. The methods and events can be used in VBScripts—the methods can be used to perform certain functions, and the events can be used to trigger VBScript functions. For instance, if there is a text area named Text1 as part of a form named Form1, the method Document.Form1.Text1.Focus() can be called in a VBScript to force the focus to move to that text area. On the other hand, if there is a button named Button1 in the same form, the event onClick can be used as an attribute to the <INPUT> tag to call a VBScript function when the button is clicked (an example of the different ways of doing this was shown in Listings 20.2, 20.3, and 20.4).

Table 20.6   Methods and Events that Allow You to Control the Contents and Behavior of HTML Elements

Method	What It Does
focus()	Calls to move the input focus to the specified object
blur()	Calls to move the input focus away from the specified object
select()	Calls to select the specified object
click()	Calls to click the specified object, which must be a button

Event	When It Occurs
onFocus	When the user moves the input focus to the field, either via the Tab key or a mouse click
onBlur	When the user moves the input focus out of this field
onSelect	When the user selects text in the field
onChange	Only when the field loses focus and the user has modified its text; use this function to validate data in a field
onSubmit	When the user submits the form (if the form has a Submit button)
onClick	When the button is clicked

Part
V

Ch
20

Note that focus(), blur(), select(), and click() are methods of objects; to call them, you use the name of the object you want to affect. For example, to turn off the button named Search, you type Document.Form.Search.Disable().

In addition to the methods and events, form objects have properties that can be used by VBScripts. Table 20.7 lists the properties exposed for HTML form elements.

Table 20.7 HTML *Forms* Properties that You Can Use in Your VBScript Code

Property	What It Contains
name	The value of the form's NAME attribute
method	The value of the form's METHOD attribute
action	The value of the form's ACTION attribute
elements	The elements array of the form
encoding	The value of the form's ENCODING attribute
target	Window targeted after submit for form response

Method	What It Does
submit()	Any form element can force the form to be submitted by calling the form's submit() method.

Event	When It Occurs
onSubmit()	When the form is submitted; this method can't stop the submission, though.

Properties for Objects in a Form   A good place to use VBScript is in forms, since you can write scripts that process, check, and perform calculations with the data the user enters. VBScript provides a useful set of properties and methods for text INPUT elements and buttons.

You use INPUT elements in a form to let the user enter text data; VBScript provides properties to get the objects that hold the element's contents, as well as methods for doing something when the user moves into or out of a field. Table 20.8 shows the properties and methods that are defined for text INPUT elements.

Table 20.8   Properties and Methods that Allow You to Control the Contents and Behavior of HTML *INPUT* Elements

Property	What It Contains
name	The value of the element's NAME attribute
value	The field's contents
defaultValue	The initial contents of the field; returns " " if blank.

Method	What It Does
onFocus	Called when the user moves the input focus to the field, either via the Tab key or a mouse click
onBlur	Called when the user moves the input focus out of this field
onSelect	Called when the user selects text in the field
onChange	Called only when the field loses focus and the user has modified its text; use this action to validate data in a field

Individual buttons and check boxes have properties, too; VBScript provides properties to get objects containing a button's data, as well as methods for doing something when the user selects or deselects a particular button. Table 20.9 shows some of the properties and methods that are defined for button elements.

Table 20.9   Properties and Methods that Allow You to Control the Contents and Behavior of HTML Button and Check Box Elements

Property	What It Contains
name	The value of the button's NAME attribute
value	The VALUE attribute
checked	The state of a check box
defaultChecked	The initial state of a check box

Method	What It Does
click()	Clicks a button and triggers whatever actions are attached to it

Event	When It Occurs
onClick	Called when the button is pressed.

Part

V

Ch

20

As an example of what you can do with VBScript and the objects, properties, and methods outlined, you might want to put the user's cursor into the first text field in a form automatically, instead of making the user manually click the field. If your first text field is named UserName, you can put the following in your document's script to get the behavior you want Document.Form.UserName.Focus().

An example of using VBScript with HTML forms is shown in the "VBScript Intranet Application" section below.

Example VBScript Applications

As with most programming languages, you can learn best by doing, and the easiest way to "do" is to take a look at some examples. The listings shown so far have demonstrated some of the things you can do with VBScript. Below are two more examples, giving some more practical examples of VBScript in action.

VBScript Intranet Application

Unless and until VBScript becomes more widespread on the Internet, its best applications might be intranet applications, in companies or organizations that have adopted Microsoft Internet Explorer as their standard. In order to show some of the capabilities of VBScript and the kind of applications it can be used for, I will lead you through the design of an HTML form and VBScript for submitting a timesheet.

In my organization, we are required to fill out a timesheet every other week, detailing how many hours we have worked each day on each of our projects. There are several guidelines that we have to follow when working and when filling out our timesheets: we have to account for eight hours a day of work or leave, and hours worked in excess of eight hours a day are considered overtime.

The goal of designing a Web page for the submission of a timesheet is to decrease the amount of paper flying around our office. Previously we filled out a timesheet which was initialed by our group leader and then used by the secretary to fill out a timecard. By putting the timesheet on the computer, we save a little time and paper.

Designing the HTML Form   The first step in the process is designing the HTML form for the timesheet. This is a pretty simple. We will use one form for the employee information and for the timesheet itself. The part of the form for the employee information is very straightforward, and the HTML to generate it looks like this:

```
<FORM NAME="TS" ACTION="mailto:odonnj@rpi.edu" METHOD=POST>
<TABLE BORDER>
```

```
<TR><TD ALIGN=RIGHT BGCOLOR=CYAN><B>EMPLOYEE NAME</B></TD>
    <TD BGCOLOR=YELLOW>
        <INPUT NAME="EmpName" TYPE="Text" VALUE="" SIZE=40 ></TD></TR>
<TR><TD ALIGN=RIGHT BGCOLOR=CYAN><B>ID NUMBER</B></TD>
    <TD BGCOLOR=YELLOW>
        <INPUT NAME="IDNum" TYPE="Text" VALUE="" SIZE=40 ></TD></TR>
</TABLE>
<TABLE BORDER>
```

This is used by the employees to enter their name and ID number. An HTML table is used to lay out the form, and a little color is added for appearance. We are careful to assign names to the form and to the two input fields, as they will be used by VBScript to reference those elements.

The timesheet part of the form is also pretty straightforward, although there is a lot more HTML code involved. Each line of the timesheet form requires 18 text fields, one each for the 14 days of the pay period, two for weekly totals, one for the pay period total, and one for the job order number of the project (or the numeric code for annual or sick leave). The top of this part of the form, showing the column headings and the first row of the timesheet, looks like:

```
<TR BGCOLOR=CYAN>
    <TH>Job Order Number</TH>
    <TH>SU</TH>
    <TH>MO</TH><TH>TU</TH><TH>WE</TH><TH>TH</TH><TH>FR</TH>
    <TH>SA</TH><TH>Week #1</TH>
    <TH>SU</TH>
    <TH>MO</TH><TH>TU</TH><TH>WE</TH><TH>TH</TH><TH>FR</TH>
    <TH>SA</TH><TH>Week #2</TH><TH>Pay Period</TH></TR>
<TR ALIGN=CENTER>
    <TD BGCOLOR=YELLOW><INPUT TYPE="Text" VALUE="" SIZE=16></TD>
    <TD><INPUT TYPE="Text" VALUE="" SIZE=1 onChange="Calc"></TD>
    <TD><INPUT TYPE="Text" VALUE="" SIZE=1 onChange="Calc"></TD>
    <TD><INPUT TYPE="Text" VALUE="" SIZE=1 onChange="Calc"></TD>
    <TD><INPUT TYPE="Text" VALUE="" SIZE=1 onChange="Calc"></TD>
    <TD><INPUT TYPE="Text" VALUE="" SIZE=1 onChange="Calc"></TD>
    <TD><INPUT TYPE="Text" VALUE="" SIZE=1 onChange="Calc"></TD>
    <TD><INPUT TYPE="Text" VALUE="" SIZE=1 onChange="Calc"></TD>
    <TD BGCOLOR=RED>
        <INPUT TYPE="Text" VALUE="0" SIZE=2 onChange="Calc"></TD>
    <TD><INPUT TYPE="Text" VALUE="" SIZE=1 onChange="Calc"></TD>
    <TD><INPUT TYPE="Text" VALUE="" SIZE=1 onChange="Calc"></TD>
    <TD><INPUT TYPE="Text" VALUE="" SIZE=1 onChange="Calc"></TD>
    <TD><INPUT TYPE="Text" VALUE="" SIZE=1 onChange="Calc"></TD>
    <TD><INPUT TYPE="Text" VALUE="" SIZE=1 onChange="Calc"></TD>
    <TD><INPUT TYPE="Text" VALUE="" SIZE=1 onChange="Calc"></TD>
    <TD><INPUT TYPE="Text" VALUE="" SIZE=1 onChange="Calc"></TD>
    <TD BGCOLOR=RED>
        <INPUT TYPE="Text" VALUE="0" SIZE=2 onChange="Calc"></TD>
    <TD BGCOLOR=RED>
        <INPUT TYPE="Text" VALUE="0" SIZE=2 onChange="Calc"></TD></TR>
    [etc...]
```

N O T E Don't worry, the complete listing for this VBScript application will be shown a little later. ■

You might notice a few things about the fields in this form that are different from the fields in the first form. First, the different fields are not named. If we name each field separately, the VBScript functions to process them would be very repetitive—after all, we will be doing the same operations on each row in the form. So rather than naming the fields, we make use of the Elements property of the Form object. Elements is an array of the fields in the Form object in the order they are originally defined. So, for the first row of the form shown above, the fields shown can be references with Document.Timesheet.Elements(0) through Document.Timesheet.Elements(17).

The second thing different about this form is that most of the fields set the onChange attribute of the <INPUT> tag to call the VBScript function Calc. We will discuss what this does in the next section.

So, with a total of five rows for the timesheet, and additional rows for annual leave, sick leave, and overtime, we have our HTML document for a timesheet. The resulting Web page looks like Figure 20.7. (The Submit Timesheet button and text field beside it will be explained below.)

FIGURE 20.7

Using a combination of HTML forms and tables, setting up this timesheet is simple.

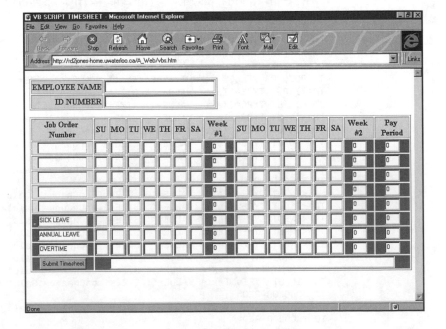

Adding VBScripts   At this point we could be done, and the employees filling out our Web page timesheet would be no worse off than when they were filling out the paper version. They could enter their name, ID number, job order number, hours worked, and total hours for the week and the pay period.

But we can use VBScript to perform some of these calculations automatically. As shown above, each form field in the Timesheet form (other than the ones for the job order number) has the VBScript function Calc attached to its onChange event. That means every time that form field changes value, Calc is called. Here is the VBScript for Calc:

```
Sub Calc
    Dim i,j,jmax,sum
    jmax = 7
    For k = 0 to 1
        For i = 0 to 6
            sum = 0
            For j = 0 to jmax-1
                If (IsNumeric(Document.TS.Elements(k*8+j*18+i+3).Value)) Then
                    sum = sum + CDbl(Document.TS.Elements(k*8+j*18+i+3).Value)
                End If
            Next
            If (sum > 8 Or (sum > 0 And (i = 0 Or i = 6))) Then
                If (i = 0 Or i = 6) Then
                    Document.TS.Elements(k*8+jmax*18+i+3).Value = sum
                Else
                    Document.TS.Elements(k*8+jmax*18+i+3).Value = sum - 8
                End If
            Else
                Document.TS.Elements(k*8+jmax*18+i+3).Value = ""
            End If
        Next
    Next
    For j = 0 to jmax
        Document.TS.Elements(j*18+10).Value = 0
        Document.TS.Elements(j*18+18).Value = 0
        For i = 0 to 6
            If (IsNumeric(Document.TS.Elements(j*18+i+3).Value)) Then
                Document.TS.Elements(j*18+10).Value = _
                    CDbl(Document.TS.Elements(j*18+10).Value) + _
                    CDbl(Document.TS.Elements(j*18+i+3).Value)
            End If
            If (IsNumeric(Document.TS.Elements(j*18+i+11).Value)) Then
                Document.TS.Elements(j*18+18).Value = _
                    CDbl(Document.TS.Elements(j*18+18).Value) + _
                    CDbl(Document.TS.Elements(j*18+i+11).Value)
            End If
        Next
        Document.TS.Elements(j*18+19).Value = _
            CDbl(Document.TS.Elements(j*18+10).Value) + _
            CDbl(Document.TS.Elements(j*18+18).Value)
```

Part
V

Ch
20

```
      Next
      Document.TS.Elements((jmax-2)*18+2).Value = "SICK LEAVE"
      Document.TS.Elements((jmax-1)*18+2).Value = "ANNUAL LEAVE"
      Document.TS.Elements(jmax*18+2).Value = "OVERTIME"
   End Sub
```

Now, this looks trickier than it really is, so we'll go through it step by step. The first two lines:

```
   Dim i,j,jmax,sum
   jmax = 7
```

set up some local variables and set jmax to the number of timesheet rows.

Next, there are two sets of nested For...Next loops to perform the calculations that we are interested in. The first set is used to add up each column of the timesheet, to see if there were any overtime hours worked—overtime defined as any hours over eight worked on a weekday or any hours worked at all on a weekend. After this number is calculated, each cell in the overtime row is set appropriately.

The next set of For...Next loops allow us to process each row in the timesheet, including the "extra" row used for overtime, and total up the hours for that row. The two lines:

```
   X.Elements(j*18+10).Value = 0
   X.Elements(j*18+18).Value = 0
```

initialize the form elements for the weekly totals to zero. The inner For...Next adds up and sets each row's totals. The section of code that does this looks like the following:

```
   If (IsNumeric(Document.TS.Elements(j*18+i+3).Value)) Then
      Document.TS.Elements(j*18+10).Value = _
         CDbl(Document.TS.Elements(j*18+10).Value) + _
         CDbl(Document.TS.Elements(j*18+i+3).Value)
   End If
   If (IsNumeric(Document.TS.Elements(j*18+i+11).Value)) Then
      Document.TS.Elements(j*18+18).Value = _
         CDbl(Document.TS.Elements(j*18+18).Value) + _
         CDbl(Document.TS.Elements(j*18+i+11).Value)
   End If
```

This code does the following:

1. Determines if there is a number entered into the field.

2. Adds the number of hours worked to the total for that row.

This is done for each week, and then the last two lines in this For...Next loop add the two weekly totals to get the total for the pay period. The last thing performed by the function is to make sure the job order number fields of the annual leave, sick leave, and overtime rows are set equal to their correct values.

With this VBScript attached to the form fields of the timesheet, completing the sheet becomes a bit easier. Weekly and pay period totals are calculated automatically each time you enter a number and move the cursor. Overtime hours will be added automatically when more than eight hours a day are worked. Obviously, the script could be made smarter—verifying that the correct number of hours per pay period are worked, for instance—but this is a good start.

Adding Memory with Cookies There's one more thing that this Web page could use, something that we do have with paper timesheets. With paper timesheets, each employee received a timesheet with his or her name, ID number, and the job order numbers of the most common projects they worked on already printed on it. One way we could do this would be to create a separate Web page for each employee. There is a better way, however, that requires only one Web page and stores the personal information on each employee's local computer. This can be done using *cookies*.

In this example, we will need seven cookies, one each for the employee name and ID number, and one each for the five job order numbers. Creating or changing a cookie is very simple and is included in the VBScript function that is called when the Submit Timesheet button is clicked:

```
Sub SubmitTS_onClick
    Document.Cookie = "EmpName=" & Document.TS.EmpName.Value & _
        ";expires=31-Dec-99 12:00:00 GMT"
    Document.Cookie = "IDNum=" & Document.TS.IDNum.Value & _
        ";expires=31-Dec-99 12:00:00 GMT"
    Document.Cookie = "JON1=" & Document.TS.Elements(2).Value & _
        ";expires=31-Dec-99 12:00:00 GMT"
    Document.Cookie = "JON2=" & Document.TS.Elements(20).Value & _
        ";expires=31-Dec-99 12:00:00 GMT"
    Document.Cookie = "JON3=" & Document.TS.Elements(38).Value & _
        ";expires=31-Dec-99 12:00:00 GMT"
    Document.Cookie = "JON4=" & Document.TS.Elements(56).Value & _
        ";expires=31-Dec-99 12:00:00 GMT"
    Document.Cookie = "JON5=" & Document.TS.Elements(74).Value & _
        ";expires=31-Dec-99 12:00:00 GMT"
    Document.TS.CookieTS.Value = Document.Cookie
    Document.TS.Submit
    MsgBox "Timesheet Submitted!"
End Sub
```

Part
V

Ch
20

This function saves each of the seven cookies, displays the cookie in the long text field at the bottom of the timesheet (this isn't necessary of course, but is helpful for this example), submits the form, and pops up a message box to tell the user that the form has been submitted (see Figure 20.8).

FIGURE 20.8
A VBScript message box is used to tell the user that the timesheet has been submitted.

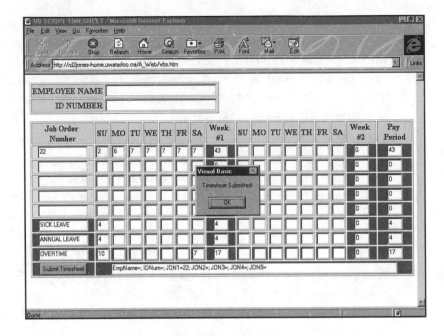

Once the cookie has been saved, whenever that Web page is loaded the cookie will be available. It is still necessary to get the information out of the cookie and into the appropriate text fields. We use a VBScript (located at the bottom of the HTML document so that it executes after the rest of the page has been loaded) to search the cookie and put the appropriate information in each of the text fields:

```
<SCRIPT LANGUAGE="VBS">
<!-- Hide this script from incompatible Web browsers!
Document.TS.EmpName.Value = GetCookie("EmpName")
Document.TS.IDNum.Value = GetCookie("IDNum")
Document.TS.Elements(2).Value = GetCookie("JON1")
Document.TS.Elements(20).Value = GetCookie("JON2")
Document.TS.Elements(38).Value = GetCookie("JON3")
Document.TS.Elements(56).Value = GetCookie("JON4")
Document.TS.Elements(74).Value = GetCookie("JON5")
Document.TS.CookieTS.Value = Document.Cookie
<!-- -->
</SCRIPT>
```

The VBScript function GetCookie is used to search the cookie for each piece of it. A document cookie is essentially a long string with each piece included as CookieName=Value, and separated from the next field by a semicolon. GetCookie uses VBScript string manipulation functions to search through the document cookie for a given piece and either returns its value, if defined, or an empty string.

```
Function GetCookie(CookieName)
    Dim Loc
    Dim NamLen
```

```
Dim ValLen
Dim LocNext
Dim Temp

NamLen = Len(CookieName)
Loc = Instr(Document.Cookie, CookieName)

If Loc = 0 Then
    GetCookie = ""
Else
    Temp = Right(Document.Cookie, Len(Document.Cookie) - Loc + 1)
    If Mid(Temp, NamLen + 1, 1) <> "=" Then
        GetCookie = ""
    Else
        LocNext = Instr(Temp, ";")
        If LocNext = 0 Then LocNext = Len(Temp) + 1
        If LocNext = (NamLen + 2) Then
            GetCookie = ""
        Else
            ValLen = LocNext - NamLen - 2
            GetCookie = Mid(Temp, NamLen + 2, ValLen)
        End If
    End If
End if
End Function
```

With this in place, the next time the Web page is loaded, the employee name, ID number, and job order numbers used on the last submitted timesheet are filled in automatically. In our example, the document cookie is also displayed in the lower text field (see Figure 20.9).

FIGURE 20.9
Using cookies allows a single Web page to serve multiple users, customizing it with their particular information.

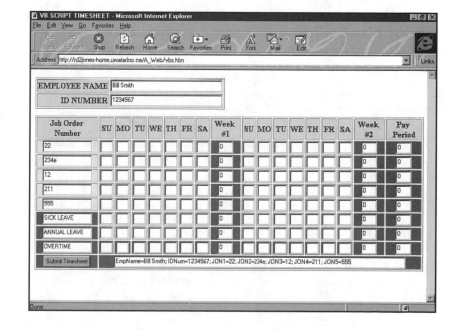

Part
V

Ch
20

The VBScript Timesheet Web Page   The complete listing for the VBScript Web page is shown in Listing 20.7. As mentioned previously, the VBScript could be made a lot smarter, and the form could be customized pretty easily to add more timesheet rows or to include a dedicated annual and/or sick leave row.

Listing 20.7   Timesheet.htm—VBScript Can Be Used to Automate Many User Input Functions

```
<HTML>
<HEAD>
<SCRIPT LANGUAGE="VBS">
<!-- Hide this script from incompatible Web browsers!
Sub Calc
    Dim i,j,jmax,sum
    jmax = 7
    For k = 0 to 1
       For i = 0 to 6
          sum = 0
          For j = 0 to jmax-1
             If (IsNumeric(Document.TS.Elements(k*8+j*18+i+3).Value)) Then
                sum = sum + CDbl(Document.TS.Elements(k*8+j*18+i+3).Value)
             End If
          Next
          If (sum > 8 Or (sum > 0 And (i = 0 Or i = 6))) Then
             If (i = 0 Or i = 6) Then
                Document.TS.Elements(k*8+jmax*18+i+3).Value = sum
             Else
                Document.TS.Elements(k*8+jmax*18+i+3).Value = sum - 8
             End If
          Else
             Document.TS.Elements(k*8+jmax*18+i+3).Value = ""
          End If
       Next
    Next
    For j = 0 to jmax
       Document.TS.Elements(j*18+10).Value = 0
       Document.TS.Elements(j^18+18).Value - 0
       For i = 0 to 6
          If (IsNumeric(Document.TS.Elements(j*18+i+3).Value)) Then
             Document.TS.Elements(j*18+10).Value = _
                CDbl(Document.TS.Elements(j*18+10).Value) + _
                CDbl(Document.TS.Elements(j*18+i+3).Value)
          End If
          If (IsNumeric(Document.TS.Elements(j*18+i+11).Value)) Then
             Document.TS.Elements(j*18+18).Value = _
                CDbl(Document.TS.Elements(j*18+18).Value) + _
                CDbl(Document.TS.Elements(j*18+i+11).Value)
          End If
       Next
       Document.TS.Elements(j*18+19).Value = _
          CDbl(Document.TS.Elements(j*18+10).Value) + _
          CDbl(Document.TS.Elements(j*18+18).Value)
```

```
            Next
            Document.TS.Elements((jmax-2)*18+2).Value = "SICK LEAVE"
            Document.TS.Elements((jmax-1)*18+2).Value = "ANNUAL LEAVE"
            Document.TS.Elements(jmax*18+2).Value = "OVERTIME"
    End Sub

    Function GetCookie(CookieName)
        Dim Loc
        Dim NamLen
        Dim ValLen
        Dim LocNext
        Dim Temp

        NamLen = Len(CookieName)
        Loc = Instr(Document.Cookie, CookieName)

        If Loc = 0 Then
            GetCookie = ""
        Else
            Temp = Right(Document.Cookie, Len(Document.Cookie) - Loc + 1)
            If Mid(Temp, NamLen + 1, 1) <> "=" Then
                GetCookie = ""
            Else
                LocNext = Instr(Temp, ";")
                If LocNext = 0 Then LocNext = Len(Temp) + 1
                If LocNext = (NamLen + 2) Then
                    GetCookie = ""
                Else
                    ValLen = LocNext - NamLen - 2
                    GetCookie = Mid(Temp, NamLen + 2, ValLen)
                End If
            End If
        End if
    End Function

    Sub SubmitTS_onClick
        Document.Cookie = "EmpName=" & Document.TS.EmpName.Value & _
            ";expires=31-Dec-99 12:00:00 GMT"
        Document.Cookie = "IDNum=" & Document.TS.IDNum.Value & _
            ";expires=31-Dec-99 12:00:00 GMT"
        Document.Cookie = "JON1=" & Document.TS.Elements(2).Value & _
            ";expires=31-Dec-99 12:00:00 GMT"
        Document.Cookie = "JON2=" & Document.TS.Elements(20).Value & _
            ";expires=31-Dec-99 12:00:00 GMT"
        Document.Cookie = "JON3=" & Document.TS.Elements(38).Value & _
            ";expires=31-Dec-99 12:00:00 GMT"
        Document.Cookie = "JON4=" & Document.TS.Elements(56).Value & _
            ";expires=31-Dec-99 12:00:00 GMT"
        Document.Cookie = "JON5=" & Document.TS.Elements(74).Value & _
            ";expires=31-Dec-99 12:00:00 GMT"
        Document.TS.CookieTS.Value = Document.Cookie
        Document.TS.Submit
        MsgBox "Timesheet Submitted!"
```

Part
V

Ch
20

continues

Listing 20.7   Continued

```
End Sub
<!-- -->
</SCRIPT>
<TITLE>VB SCRIPT TIMESHEET</TITLE>
</HEAD>
<BODY BGCOLOR=#FFFFFF>
<FORM NAME="TS" ACTION="mailto:odonnj@rpi.edu" METHOD=POST>
<TABLE BORDER>
<TR><TD ALIGN=RIGHT BGCOLOR=CYAN><B>EMPLOYEE NAME</B></TD>
    <TD BGCOLOR=YELLOW>
        <INPUT NAME="EmpName" TYPE="Text" VALUE="" SIZE=40 ></TD></TR>
<TR><TD ALIGN=RIGHT BGCOLOR=CYAN><B>ID NUMBER</B></TD>
    <TD BGCOLOR=YELLOW>
        <INPUT NAME="IDNum" TYPE="Text" VALUE="" SIZE=40 ></TD></TR>
</TABLE>
<TABLE BORDER>
<TR BGCOLOR=CYAN>
    <TH>Job Order Number</TH>
    <TH>SU</TH>
    <TH>MO</TH><TH>TU</TH><TH>WE</TH><TH>TH</TH><TH>FR</TH>
    <TH>SA</TH><TH>Week #1</TH>
    <TH>SU</TH>
    <TH>MO</TH><TH>TU</TH><TH>WE</TH><TH>TH</TH><TH>FR</TH>
    <TH>SA</TH><TH>Week #2</TH><TH>Pay Period</TH></TR>
<TR ALIGN=CENTER>
    <TD BGCOLOR=YELLOW><INPUT TYPE="Text" VALUE="" SIZE=16></TD>
    <TD><INPUT TYPE="Text" VALUE="" SIZE=1 onChange="Calc"></TD>
    <TD><INPUT TYPE="Text" VALUE="" SIZE=1 onChange="Calc"></TD>
    <TD><INPUT TYPE="Text" VALUE="" SIZE=1 onChange="Calc"></TD>
    <TD><INPUT TYPE="Text" VALUE="" SIZE=1 onChange="Calc"></TD>
    <TD><INPUT TYPE="Text" VALUE="" SIZE=1 onChange="Calc"></TD>
    <TD><INPUT TYPE="Text" VALUE="" SIZE=1 onChange="Calc"></TD>
    <TD><INPUT TYPE="Text" VALUE="" SIZE=1 onChange="Calc"></TD>
    <TD BGCOLOR=RED>
        <INPUT TYPE="Text" VALUE="0" SIZE=2 onChange="Calc"></TD>
    <TD><INPUT TYPE="Text" VALUE="" SIZE=1 onChange="Calc"></TD>
    <TD><INPUT TYPE="Text" VALUE="" SIZE=1 onChange="Calc"></TD>
    <TD><INPUT TYPE="Text" VALUE="" SIZE=1 onChange="Calc"></TD>
    <TD><INPUT TYPE="Text" VALUE="" SIZE=1 onChange="Calc"></TD>
    <TD><INPUT TYPE="Text" VALUE="" SIZE=1 onChange="Calc"></TD>
    <TD><INPUT TYPE="Text" VALUE="" SIZE=1 onChange="Calc"></TD>
    <TD><INPUT TYPE="Text" VALUE="" SIZE=1 onChange="Calc"></TD>
    <TD BGCOLOR=RED>
        <INPUT TYPE="Text" VALUE="0" SIZE=2 onChange="Calc"></TD>
    <TD BGCOLOR=RED>
        <INPUT TYPE="Text" VALUE="0" SIZE=2 onChange="Calc"></TD></TR>
<TR ALIGN=CENTER>
    <TD BGCOLOR=YELLOW><INPUT TYPE="Text" VALUE="" SIZE=16></TD>
    <TD><INPUT TYPE="Text" VALUE="" SIZE=1 onChange="Calc"></TD>
    <TD><INPUT TYPE="Text" VALUE="" SIZE=1 onChange="Calc"></TD>
```

```
        <TD><INPUT TYPE="Text" VALUE="" SIZE=1 onChange="Calc"></TD>
        <TD><INPUT TYPE="Text" VALUE="" SIZE=1 onChange="Calc"></TD>
        <TD><INPUT TYPE="Text" VALUE="" SIZE=1 onChange="Calc"></TD>
        <TD><INPUT TYPE="Text" VALUE="" SIZE=1 onChange="Calc"></TD>
        <TD><INPUT TYPE="Text" VALUE="" SIZE=1 onChange="Calc"></TD>
        <TD BGCOLOR=RED>
            <INPUT TYPE="Text" VALUE="0" SIZE=2 onChange="Calc"></TD>
        <TD><INPUT TYPE="Text" VALUE="" SIZE=1 onChange="Calc"></TD>
        <TD><INPUT TYPE="Text" VALUE="" SIZE=1 onChange="Calc"></TD>
        <TD><INPUT TYPE="Text" VALUE="" SIZE=1 onChange="Calc"></TD>
        <TD><INPUT TYPE="Text" VALUE="" SIZE=1 onChange="Calc"></TD>
        <TD><INPUT TYPE="Text" VALUE="" SIZE=1 onChange="Calc"></TD>
        <TD><INPUT TYPE="Text" VALUE="" SIZE=1 onChange="Calc"></TD>
        <TD BGCOLOR=RED>
            <INPUT TYPE="Text" VALUE="0" SIZE=2 onChange="Calc"></TD>
        <TD BGCOLOR=RED>
            <INPUT TYPE="Text" VALUE="0" SIZE=2 onChange="Calc"></TD></TR>
<TR ALIGN=CENTER>
        <TD BGCOLOR=YELLOW><INPUT TYPE="Text" VALUE="" SIZE=16></TD>
        <TD><INPUT TYPE="Text" VALUE="" SIZE=1 onChange="Calc"></TD>
        <TD><INPUT TYPE="Text" VALUE="" SIZE=1 onChange="Calc"></TD>
        <TD><INPUT TYPE="Text" VALUE="" SIZE=1 onChange="Calc"></TD>
        <TD><INPUT TYPE="Text" VALUE="" SIZE=1 onChange="Calc"></TD>
        <TD><INPUT TYPE="Text" VALUE="" SIZE=1 onChange="Calc"></TD>
        <TD><INPUT TYPE="Text" VALUE="" SIZE=1 onChange="Calc"></TD>
        <TD BGCOLOR=RED>
            <INPUT TYPE="Text" VALUE="0" SIZE=2 onChange="Calc"></TD>
        <TD><INPUT TYPE="Text" VALUE="" SIZE=1 onChange="Calc"></TD>
        <TD><INPUT TYPE="Text" VALUE="" SIZE=1 onChange="Calc"></TD>
        <TD><INPUT TYPE="Text" VALUE="" SIZE=1 onChange="Calc"></TD>
        <TD><INPUT TYPE="Text" VALUE="" SIZE=1 onChange="Calc"></TD>
        <TD><INPUT TYPE="Text" VALUE="" SIZE=1 onChange="Calc"></TD>
        <TD><INPUT TYPE="Text" VALUE="" SIZE=1 onChange="Calc"></TD>
        <TD><INPUT TYPE="Text" VALUE="" SIZE=1 onChange="Calc"></TD>
        <TD BGCOLOR=RED>
            <INPUT TYPE="Text" VALUE="0" SIZE=2 onChange="Calc"></TD>
        <TD BGCOLOR=RED>
            <INPUT TYPE="Text" VALUE="0" SIZE=2 onChange="Calc"></TD></TR>
<TR ALIGN=CENTER>
        <TD BGCOLOR=YELLOW><INPUT TYPE="Text" VALUE="" SIZE=16></TD>
        <TD><INPUT TYPE="Text" VALUE="" SIZE=1 onChange="Calc"></TD>
        <TD><INPUT TYPE="Text" VALUE="" SIZE=1 onChange="Calc"></TD>
        <TD><INPUT TYPE="Text" VALUE="" SIZE=1 onChange="Calc"></TD>
        <TD><INPUT TYPE="Text" VALUE="" SIZE=1 onChange="Calc"></TD>
        <TD><INPUT TYPE="Text" VALUE="" SIZE=1 onChange="Calc"></TD>
        <TD><INPUT TYPE="Text" VALUE="" SIZE=1 onChange="Calc"></TD>
        <TD><INPUT TYPE="Text" VALUE="" SIZE=1 onChange="Calc"></TD>
        <TD BGCOLOR=RED>
            <INPUT TYPE="Text" VALUE="0" SIZE=2 onChange="Calc"></TD>
        <TD><INPUT TYPE="Text" VALUE="" SIZE=1 onChange="Calc"></TD>
        <TD><INPUT TYPE="Text" VALUE="" SIZE=1 onChange="Calc"></TD>
```

Part
V

Ch
20

continues

Listing 20.7 Continued

```
    <TD><INPUT TYPE="Text" VALUE="" SIZE=1 onChange="Calc"></TD>
    <TD><INPUT TYPE="Text" VALUE="" SIZE=1 onChange="Calc"></TD>
    <TD><INPUT TYPE="Text" VALUE="" SIZE=1 onChange="Calc"></TD>
    <TD><INPUT TYPE="Text" VALUE="" SIZE=1 onChange="Calc"></TD>
    <TD><INPUT TYPE="Text" VALUE="" SIZE=1 onChange="Calc"></TD>
    <TD BGCOLOR=RED>
        <INPUT TYPE="Text" VALUE="0" SIZE=2 onChange="Calc"></TD>
    <TD BGCOLOR=RED>
        <INPUT TYPE="Text" VALUE="0" SIZE=2 onChange="Calc"></TD></TR>
<TR ALIGN=CENTER>
    <TD BGCOLOR=YELLOW><INPUT TYPE="Text" VALUE="" SIZE=16></TD>
    <TD><INPUT TYPE="Text" VALUE="" SIZE=1 onChange="Calc"></TD>
    <TD><INPUT TYPE="Text" VALUE="" SIZE=1 onChange="Calc"></TD>
    <TD><INPUT TYPE="Text" VALUE="" SIZE=1 onChange="Calc"></TD>
    <TD><INPUT TYPE="Text" VALUE="" SIZE=1 onChange="Calc"></TD>
    <TD><INPUT TYPE="Text" VALUE="" SIZE=1 onChange="Calc"></TD>
    <TD><INPUT TYPE="Text" VALUE="" SIZE=1 onChange="Calc"></TD>
    <TD BGCOLOR=RED>
        <INPUT TYPE="Text" VALUE="0" SIZE=2 onChange="Calc"></TD>
    <TD><INPUT TYPE="Text" VALUE="" SIZE=1 onChange="Calc"></TD>
    <TD><INPUT TYPE="Text" VALUE="" SIZE=1 onChange="Calc"></TD>
    <TD><INPUT TYPE="Text" VALUE="" SIZE=1 onChange="Calc"></TD>
    <TD><INPUT TYPE="Text" VALUE="" SIZE=1 onChange="Calc"></TD>
    <TD><INPUT TYPE="Text" VALUE="" SIZE=1 onChange="Calc"></TD>
    <TD><INPUT TYPE="Text" VALUE="" SIZE=1 onChange="Calc"></TD>
    <TD><INPUT TYPE="Text" VALUE="" SIZE=1 onChange="Calc"></TD>
    <TD BGCOLOR=RED>
        <INPUT TYPE="Text" VALUE="0" SIZE=2 onChange="Calc"></TD>
    <TD BGCOLOR=RED>
        <INPUT TYPE="Text" VALUE="0" SIZE=2 onChange="Calc"></TD></TR>
<TR ALIGN=CENTER>
    <TD BGCOLOR=RED>
        <INPUT TYPE="Text" VALUE="SICK LEAVE" SIZE=16 onChange="Calc"></TD>
    <TD><INPUT TYPE="Text" VALUE="" SIZE=1 onChange="Calc"></TD>
    <TD><INPUT TYPE="Text" VALUE="" SIZE=1 onChange="Calc"></TD>
    <TD><INPUT TYPE="Text" VALUE="" SIZE=1 onChange="Calc"></TD>
    <TD><INPUT TYPE="Text" VALUE="" SIZE=1 onChange="Calc"></TD>
    <TD><INPUT TYPE="Text" VALUE="" SIZE=1 onChange="Calc"></TD>
    <TD><INPUT TYPE="Text" VALUE="" SIZE=1 onChange="Calc"></TD>
    <TD><INPUT TYPE="Text" VALUE="" SIZE=1 onChange="Calc"></TD>
    <TD BGCOLOR=RED>
        <INPUT TYPE="Text" VALUE="0" SIZE=2 onChange="Calc"></TD>
    <TD><INPUT TYPE="Text" VALUE="" SIZE=1 onChange="Calc"></TD>
    <TD><INPUT TYPE="Text" VALUE="" SIZE=1 onChange="Calc"></TD>
    <TD><INPUT TYPE="Text" VALUE="" SIZE=1 onChange="Calc"></TD>
    <TD><INPUT TYPE="Text" VALUE="" SIZE=1 onChange="Calc"></TD>
    <TD><INPUT TYPE="Text" VALUE="" SIZE=1 onChange="Calc"></TD>
    <TD><INPUT TYPE="Text" VALUE="" SIZE=1 onChange="Calc"></TD>
    <TD><INPUT TYPE="Text" VALUE="" SIZE=1 onChange="Calc"></TD>
```

```
            <TD BGCOLOR=RED>
                <INPUT TYPE="Text" VALUE="0" SIZE=2 onChange="Calc"></TD>
            <TD BGCOLOR=RED>
                <INPUT TYPE="Text" VALUE="0" SIZE=2 onChange="Calc"></TD></TR>
    <TR ALIGN=CENTER>
            <TD BGCOLOR=RED>
                <INPUT TYPE="Text" VALUE="ANNUAL LEAVE" SIZE=16
                    onChange="Calc"></TD>
            <TD><INPUT TYPE="Text" VALUE="" SIZE=1 onChange="Calc"></TD>
            <TD><INPUT TYPE="Text" VALUE="" SIZE=1 onChange="Calc"></TD>
            <TD><INPUT TYPE="Text" VALUE="" SIZE=1 onChange="Calc"></TD>
            <TD><INPUT TYPE="Text" VALUE="" SIZE=1 onChange="Calc"></TD>
            <TD><INPUT TYPE="Text" VALUE="" SIZE=1 onChange="Calc"></TD>
            <TD><INPUT TYPE="Text" VALUE="" SIZE=1 onChange="Calc"></TD>
            <TD><INPUT TYPE="Text" VALUE="" SIZE=1 onChange="Calc"></TD>
            <TD BGCOLOR=RED>
                <INPUT TYPE="Text" VALUE="0" SIZE=2 onChange="Calc"></TD>
            <TD><INPUT TYPE="Text" VALUE="" SIZE=1 onChange="Calc"></TD>
            <TD><INPUT TYPE="Text" VALUE="" SIZE=1 onChange="Calc"></TD>
            <TD><INPUT TYPE="Text" VALUE="" SIZE=1 onChange="Calc"></TD>
            <TD><INPUT TYPE="Text" VALUE="" SIZE=1 onChange="Calc"></TD>
            <TD><INPUT TYPE="Text" VALUE="" SIZE=1 onChange="Calc"></TD>
            <TD><INPUT TYPE="Text" VALUE="" SIZE=1 onChange="Calc"></TD>
            <TD BGCOLOR=RED>
                <INPUT TYPE="Text" VALUE="0" SIZE=2 onChange="Calc"></TD>
            <TD BGCOLOR=RED>
                <INPUT TYPE="Text" VALUE="0" SIZE=2 onChange="Calc"></TD></TR>
    <TR ALIGN=CENTER BGCOLOR=RED>
            <TD><INPUT TYPE="Text" VALUE="OVERTIME" SIZE=16 onChange="Calc"></TD>
            <TD><INPUT TYPE="Text" VALUE="" SIZE=1 onChange="Calc"></TD>
            <TD><INPUT TYPE="Text" VALUE="" SIZE=1 onChange="Calc"></TD>
            <TD><INPUT TYPE="Text" VALUE="" SIZE=1 onChange="Calc"></TD>
            <TD><INPUT TYPE="Text" VALUE="" SIZE=1 onChange="Calc"></TD>
            <TD><INPUT TYPE="Text" VALUE="" SIZE=1 onChange="Calc"></TD>
            <TD><INPUT TYPE="Text" VALUE="" SIZE=1 onChange="Calc"></TD>
            <TD><INPUT TYPE="Text" VALUE="" SIZE=1 onChange="Calc"></TD>
            <TD><INPUT TYPE="Text" VALUE="0" SIZE=2 onChange="Calc"></TD>
            <TD><INPUT TYPE="Text" VALUE="" SIZE=1 onChange="Calc"></TD>
            <TD><INPUT TYPE="Text" VALUE="" SIZE=1 onChange="Calc"></TD>
            <TD><INPUT TYPE="Text" VALUE="" SIZE=1 onChange="Calc"></TD>
            <TD><INPUT TYPE="Text" VALUE="" SIZE=1 onChange="Calc"></TD>
            <TD><INPUT TYPE="Text" VALUE="" SIZE=1 onChange="Calc"></TD>
            <TD><INPUT TYPE="Text" VALUE="" SIZE=1 onChange="Calc"></TD>
            <TD><INPUT TYPE="Text" VALUE="0" SIZE=2 onChange="Calc"></TD>
            <TD><INPUT TYPE="Text" VALUE="0" SIZE=2 onChange="Calc"></TD></TR>
<!--<TR><TD BGCOLOR=CYAN COLSPAN=18> </TD></TR>-->
<TR ALIGN=CENTER>
        <TD><INPUT NAME="SubmitTS" TYPE="Button"
                VALUE="Submit Timesheet"></TD>
        <TD COLSPAN=17 BGCOLOR=RED>
            <INPUT NAME="CookieTS" TYPE="Text" SIZE="110"></TD></TR>
```

continues

Listing 20.7   Continued

```
</TABLE>
</FORM>
<SCRIPT LANGUAGE="VBS">
<!-- Hide this script from incompatible Web browsers!
Document.TS.EmpName.Value = GetCookie("EmpName")
Document.TS.IDNum.Value = GetCookie("IDNum")
Document.TS.Elements(2).Value = GetCookie("JON1")
Document.TS.Elements(20).Value = GetCookie("JON2")
Document.TS.Elements(38).Value = GetCookie("JON3")
Document.TS.Elements(56).Value = GetCookie("JON4")
Document.TS.Elements(74).Value = GetCookie("JON5")
Document.TS.CookieTS.Value = Document.Cookie
<!-- -->
</SCRIPT>
</BODY>
</HTML>
```

CAUTION

The cookie storage mechanism that is part of this Web page does not always work when the Web page is viewed locally, because cookies need to go through a Web server to be processed. Unless you are running a local server, you may need to upload the HTML document to your ISP's system and view it with the ISP's Web server to see the cookies work.

Of course, once the forms are submitted, what to do with them at the receiving end is another question—one for a different chapter. See Chapter 10, "Using WebBots, Wizards, and Interactive Page Templates," for more information.

Interacting with Objects

This is an example of using VBScript to manipulate another Web browser object—in this case the ActiveX Label Control. The Label Control allows the Web author to place text on the Web page and select the text, font, size, and an arbitrary angle of rotation. One of the exciting things about the Label Control is that it can be manipulated in real-time, producing a variety of automated or user-controlled effects.

In the following example, text is placed on the Web page using the Label Control, and form input is used to allow the user to change the text used and the angle at which it is displayed. Figure 20.10 shows the default configuration of the label, and Figure 20.11 shows it after the text and the rotation angle has been changed.

FIGURE 20.10
The ActiveX Label Control allows arbitrary text to be displayed by the Web author in the size, font, position, and orientation desired.

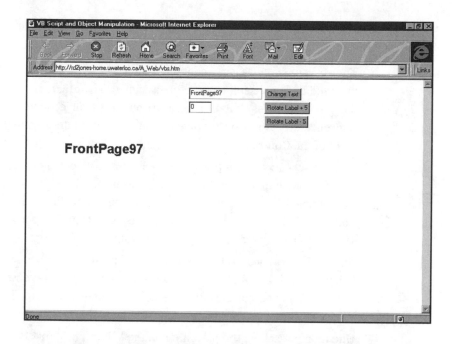

FIGURE 20.11
VBScript's ability to manipulate Web browser objects allows the label parameters to be changed dynamically.

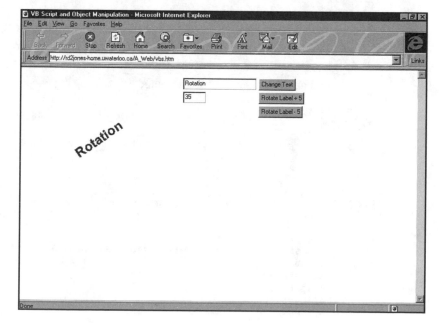

Listing 20.8 shows the code used to produce this example. The following are some things to note about the example:

- The `<OBJECT>...</OBJECT>` container tag is where the ActiveX Label Control is included and its default parameters assigned. The `classid` attribute must be included exactly as shown. The `id` attribute is the object name used by VBScript to reference the Label Control object. The other attributes define the size and placement of the Control.

- The `<PARAM>` tags within the `<OBJECT>...</OBJECT>` container allow the Web author to define attributes of the ActiveX Label Control. The `NAME`, `VALUE` pairs are unique to each ActiveX Control, and should be documented by the ActiveX Control author. For the Label Control, they define various aspects of the appearance of the label. The `NAME` is also used to manipulate the value with VBScript.

- An HTML form is used to accept input and print output for information about the Label Control. The first text area is used to set the label text, while the second text area is used to output the current label text angle. The buttons call the appropriate VBScript routine to change the label text or angle.

- One final note about the placement of the VBScripts in this HTML document: the functions are defined in the `<HEAD>` section—this is not necessary, but it is common practice, so that they will be defined before used. The last `<SCRIPT>...</SCRIPT>` section, though, which initializes the value of the form text area showing the current angle, is placed at the end of the HTML document to ensure that the object is defined and value set before it is called.

> **CAUTION**
>
> The example in Listing 20.8 requires that you have the ActiveX Label Control on your system.

Listing 20.8   Object.htm—VBScript Can Interact with Objects

```
<HTML>
<HEAD>
<OBJECT classid="clsid:99B42120-6EC7-11CF-A6C7-00AA00A47DD2"
        id=lblActiveLbl
        width=250
        height=250
        align=left
        hspace=20
        vspace=0
>
<PARAM NAME="Angle" VALUE="0">
```

```
<PARAM NAME="Alignment" VALUE="4">
<PARAM NAME="BackStyle" VALUE="0">
<PARAM NAME="Caption" VALUE="Rotation">
<PARAM NAME="FontName" VALUE="Arial">
<PARAM NAME="FontSize" VALUE="20">
<PARAM NAME="FontBold" VALUE="1">
<PARAM NAME="ForeColor" VALUE="0">
</OBJECT>
<SCRIPT LANGUAGE="VBS">
<!-- Hide this script from incompatible Web browsers
Sub cmdChangeIt_onClick
    Dim TheForm
    Set TheForm = Document.LabelControls
    lblActiveLbl.Caption = TheForm.txtNewText.Value
End Sub
Sub cmdRotateP_onClick
    Dim TheForm
    Set TheForm = Document.LabelControls
    lblActiveLbl.Angle = lblActiveLbl.Angle + 5
    Document.LabelControls.sngAngle.Value = lblActiveLbl.Angle
End Sub
Sub cmdRotateM_onClick
    Dim TheForm
    Set TheForm = Document.LabelControls
    lblActiveLbl.Angle = lblActiveLbl.Angle - 5
    Document.LabelControls.sngAngle.Value = lblActiveLbl.Angle
End Sub
<!-- -->
</SCRIPT>
<TITLE>VBScript and Object Manipulation</TITLE>
</HEAD>
<BODY BGCOLOR=#FFFFFF>
<FORM NAME="LabelControls">
<TABLE>
<TR><TD><INPUT TYPE="TEXT" NAME="txtNewText" SIZE=25></TD>
    <TD><INPUT TYPE="BUTTON" NAME="cmdChangeIt" VALUE="Change Text">
    </TD></TR>
<TR><TD><INPUT TYPE="TEXT" NAME="sngAngle" SIZE=5></TD>
    <TD><INPUT TYPE="BUTTON" NAME="cmdRotateP" VALUE="Rotate Label + 5">
    </TD></TR>
<TR><TD></TD>
    <TD><INPUT TYPE="BUTTON" NAME="cmdRotateM" VALUE="Rotate Label - 5">
    </TD></TR>
</TABLE>
</FORM>
<SCRIPT LANGUAGE="VBS">
<!-- Hide this script from incompatible Web browsers
Document.LabelControls.sngAngle.Value = lblActiveLbl.Angle
Document.LabelControls.txtNewText.Value = lblActiveLbl.Caption
<!-- -->
</SCRIPT>
</BODY>
</HTML>
```

Microsoft's JScript

With version 3 of their Internet Explorer Web browser, Microsoft has included JavaScript compatibility. However, what they have chosen to do is to create what they call JScript, which they describe as an open implementation of the JavaScript language.

Exactly what this means for Web page authors is unclear. Compatibility with the JavaScript language has been Microsoft's goal with JScript, but considering that JScript is currently a beta release of a scripting language striving for compatibility with a beta release of a different scripting language—JavaScript—there is liable to be many incompatibilities between the two. For Web authors interested in designing pages for the largest possible audience, testing JavaScript/JScript Web pages with both Netscape Navigator and Microsoft Internet Explorer seems like a good idea.

What Scripting Language Should You Use?

With a choice of scripting languages now available, the question of which to use quickly arises. JavaScript and VBScript have similar capabilities. Also, since they are both relatively new, you don't have a lot of history to rely on for making a choice. The following are a few points to consider:

- What language are you more comfortable with?—JavaScript is based on the Java and C++ languages; VBScript, on Visual Basic and Visual Basic for Applications. If you are proficient in one of these parent languages, using the scripting language that is based on it might be a good idea.

- What are you trying to do?—Both languages are object-oriented and can interact with a compatible Web browser and other objects that it may have loaded, such as Java applets or ActiveX Controls. But if you will be primarily working with Internet Explorer 3 using a feature of Microsoft's ActiveX technologies, using VBScript is probably a good idea because it is designed with that use in mind.

- Who is your target audience?—For "general-purpose" uses—like processing form inputs or providing simple interactivity—the biggest question to answer is who will be the audience for your Web pages. Though Microsoft Internet Explorer has a growing share of the Web browser market, Netscape Navigator has the lion's share. Unless your Web pages are targeted at a specific audience that will definitely be using Internet Explorer, you will probably want to use JavaScript. At least in the short term, using JavaScript will ensure you maximum compatibility.

Using FrontPage Editor's Script Wizard

Now that we've explored VBScript as you might write it into the Script dialog box, we should investigate an easier way to do Visual Basic scripting. This is where the Script Wizard comes in. You still have to know you way around VBScript, though—the Wizard assumes this. The very simple example below gives you the basis of how to use it.

N O T E The Script Wizard can be used only for JavaScript or VBScript. ▪

Let's say that for design reasons, you've decided you don't want to use a plain old hyperlink to move visitors to a different page—for example, a page where they can play back a movie. Instead, you want to use a form field button to take them there. Here's how you'd do it.

First, open the page the where you want the button. Then install the button by choosing Insert, Form Field, Push Button. When the button appears on the page, double-click it to go to the Push Button Properties dialog box. Per the default, the button name will be B1; you can leave it so.

Now, in the Value/Label box, type **Movie** for the button label. Then mark the Normal option button to make this a generic button. (A generic button does nothing until you attach a script to it, which is what we're going to do.) Then click OK, and the relabeled button appears in the FrontPage Editor workspace.

We're going to assume there's another page in the current Web site called amovie.htm, which is where the movie is played back. To connect the button to that page, start by choosing Insert, Script. When the Script dialog box opens, click the Script Wizard button and the Script Wizard dialog box appears.

The upper-left pane of the dialog box is the Select an Event pane. The Event pane provides a hierarchical view of all the objects and events that you can script. In the hierarchy, objects are listed in alphabetical order by ID name. The icons represent different types of these events and objects.

When you click an event, the Script Wizard displays that event handler in the Insert Action pane—the pane at the upper right of the dialog box. (An event handler is code that is executed when a particular event occurs.)

In this example, the event that you want is part of the Unnamed FORM Element entry. (It's unnamed because you didn't bother to name the form.) To get to that event, click the plus sign at the left of Unnamed FORM Element. Now you see an icon for B1. (B1 is the

Part
V
Ch
20

ID of the button.) At the left of this icon is also a plus sign. Click the plus sign, and an onClick event appears below B1. Click the onClick event to select it. Now the action that you choose next will be attached to the onClick event.

Now look at the Insert Action pane, at the upper right of the dialog box. This pane provides a hierarchical view of the actions and properties you can use in the event handler, as well as the global variables and procedures defined for the page.

You want to move the visitor to a different page when the button is clicked. To set this up, double-click on the Go To Page icon in the Insert Action pane. Now you see the Go To Page dialog box.

Assuming the name of our destination page is amovie.htm, type this into the Enter a Text String box, then choose OK. Now, in the lowest pane of the Script Wizard dialog box, you'll see that you have an event called Go To Page 'amovie.htm'.

To see what this looks like in VBScript, mark the Code View option button at the bottom of the dialog box. The lowest pane now displays Window.location.href = 'amovie.htm'. You can edit scripts directly in this window if you need to.

This finishes the script. Choose OK, and preview the page in a browser. When the button is clicked, the destination page appears in the browser window.

This is a very simple example, but if you already know VBScript, then with just a moderate amount of practice, you will be able to use the Script Wizard effectively.

From Here...

This rather long chapter gave you an introduction to one of the two major Web scripting languages. Now it's time to look at the other one: JavaScript. Take a look at the following chapters for more information on some of the issues touched on in this chapter:

- Chapter 21, "JavaScript" tells you about the different JavaScript language elements, how you use JavaScript to interact with page elements and users, and how you can integrate it with FrontPage.

- Chapter 22, "Inserting Java Applets and Browser Plug-Ins," covers MIME media types and Netscape plug-ins, and gives you an overview of the Java programming language.

- Chapter 23, "VRML and Java," provides an introduction to the Virtual Reality Modeling Language, and its connections to Java.

## CHAPTER 21

JavaScript

The JavaScript language, which was first introduced by Netscape in its Web browser, Netscape Navigator 2, gives Web authors another way to add interactivity and intelligence to their Web pages. JavaScript code is included as part of the HTML document and requires no additional compilation or development tools other than a compatible Web browser. In this chapter, you learn about JavaScript, get an idea of the sorts of things it can do, and learn to insert scripts into pages generated with FrontPage Editor. While FrontPage Editor on its own is an extremely capable page editor, its capabilities are enormously extended by adding scripts. ■

What is JavaScript and what can it do?

Learn about Netscape's JavaScript Web browser programming language, and how you can use it with FrontPage.

How do you program your Web pages using Javascript?

Learn about how JavaScript can be used to interact with Web page elements and users.

What does JavaScript consist of?

Find out about the different JavaScript language elements and how to use them to add functionality to your Web pages.

What do JavaScript programs look like?

Examine sample JavaScript Web browser applications to see what kinds of things JavaScript is capable of doing.

Using FrontPage Editor to Add JavaScripts to a Page

This is the same procedure described early in Chapter 20, "Scripting with VBScript." Since you may have jumped ahead to Java scripting, however, it's repeated here. Use the following procedure:

1. Choose <u>I</u>nsert, Scrip<u>t</u>, or click the Insert Script button on the toolbar. The Script dialog box appears (see Figure 21.1).

FIGURE 21.1

Use the Script dialog box to choose the type of script you want and to compose it.

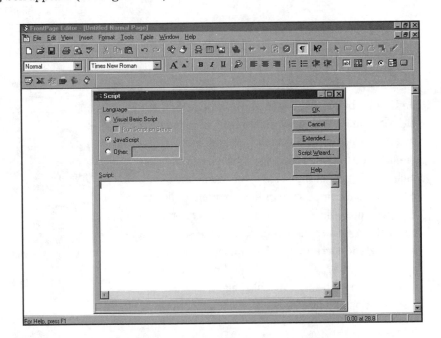

2. Mark the <u>J</u>avaScript option button.
3. Type the code into the workspace of the dialog box and choose OK. The script will be inserted into the page.

The workspace in this dialog box is just that of a text editor, and absolutely no syntax checking is done. You don't need to include the <SCRIPT> tags; they're inserted when you choose OK to close the dialog box and add the script.

The Script Wizard—also available through this dialog box—makes it unnecessary (much of the time) for you to enter code by hand. It functions with JavaScript in the same way that it does with VBScript.

▶ **See** "Using FrontPage Editor's Script Wizard," **p. 493**

N O T E You'll know there's a script in your page because a small script icon appears in the FrontPage Editor workspace where the script is located. ■

Introduction to JavaScript

JavaScript allows you to embed commands in an HTML page. When a compatible Web browser—such as Netscape Navigator 2 or higher or Internet Explorer 3—downloads the page, your JavaScript commands are loaded by the Web browser as a part of the HTML document. These commands can be triggered when the user clicks on page items, manipulates gadgets and fields in an HTML form, or moves through the page history list.

Some computer languages are *compiled*; you run your program through a compiler, which performs a one-time translation of the human-readable program into a binary code that the computer can execute. JavaScript is an *interpreted* language; the computer must evaluate the program every time it's run. You embed your JavaScript commands within an HTML page, and any browser that supports JavaScript can interpret the commands and act on them.

JavaScript is powerful and simple. If you've ever programmed in dBASE or Visual Basic, you'll find JavaScript easy to pick up.

N O T E Java offers a number of C++-like capabilities that were purposefully omitted from JavaScript. For example, you can access only the limited set of objects defined by the browser and its Java applets, and you can't extend those objects yourself. ■

Why Use a Scripting Language?

FrontPage Editor provides great flexibility to page authors, but from time to time you may want to write small scripts that execute on the users' browsers instead of on the server. For example, an application that collects data from a form and then posts it to the server can validate the data for completeness and correctness before sending it to the server. This can greatly improve the performance of the browsing session, since users don't have to send data to the server until it's been verified as correct.

Another important use of Web browser scripting languages, like JavaScript, comes as a result of the increased functionality being introduced for Web browsers in the form of Java applets, plug-ins, ActiveX Controls, and VRML objects and worlds. Each of these things can be used to add extra functions and interactivity to a Web page. Scripting languages act as the glue that binds everything together. A Web page might use an HTML form to get some user input and then set a parameter for an ActiveX Control based on that input. Usually, this will actually be carried out by a script.

Part
V

Ch
21

What Can JavaScript Do?

JavaScript provides a fairly complete set of built-in functions and commands, allowing you to perform math calculations, manipulate strings, play sounds, open up new windows and new URLs, and access and verify user input to your Web forms.

Code to perform these actions can be embedded in a page and executed when the page is loaded. You can also write functions containing code that is triggered by events you specify. For example, you can write a JavaScript method that is called when the user clicks the Submit button of a form, or one that is activated when the user clicks a hyperlink on the active page.

JavaScript can also set the attributes, or *properties*, of ActiveX Controls, Java applets, and other objects present in the browser, so you can change the behavior of plug-ins or other objects without having to rewrite them. For example, your JavaScript code could automatically set the text of an ActiveX Label Control based on what time the page is viewed.

> **CAUTION**
>
> JavaScript and VBScript are very similar, with similar syntax and capabilities. However, they are different languages and you should be careful not to mix them up when you are programming.

What Does JavaScript Look Like?

As described earlier, you use FrontPage Editor's Script dialog box to embed JavaScript commands in your pages. Doing this requires only one new HTML element: <SCRIPT> and </SCRIPT>. The <SCRIPT> element takes the attributes LANGUAGE, which specifies the scripting language to use when evaluating the script.

> **CAUTION**
>
> Don't type the <SCRIPT> and </SCRIPT> tags into the Script dialog box workspace. These tags and the LANGUAGE attribute are added automatically.

JavaScript itself resembles many other computer languages. If you're familiar with C, C++, Pascal, HyperTalk, Visual Basic, or dBASE, you'll recognize the similarities. If not, don't worry—the following are some simple rules that will help you understand how the language is structured:

- JavaScript is case-sensitive.

- JavaScript is pretty flexible about statements. A single statement can cover multiple lines, and you can put multiple short statements on a single line—just make sure to add a semicolon at the end of each statement.

- Brace (the { and } characters) group statements into blocks; a block may be the body of a function or a section of code that gets executed in a loop or as part of a conditional test.

N O T E If you're a Java, C, or C++ programmer, you might be puzzled when looking at JavaScript programs—sometimes each line ends with a semicolon, sometimes not. In JavaScript, unlike those other languages, the semicolon is not required at the end of each line. ■

JavaScript Programming Conventions

Even though JavaScript is a simple language, it's quite expressive. In this section, you will learn a small number of simple rules and conventions that will ease your learning process and speed your use of JavaScript.

Hiding Your Scripts You'll probably be designing pages that may be seen by browsers that don't support JavaScript. To keep those browsers from interpreting your JavaScript commands as HTML—and displaying them—wrap your scripts as follows:

```
<SCRIPT LANGUAGE="JavaScript">
<!-- This line opens an HTML comment
document.write("You can see this script's output, but not its source.")
<!-- This line opens and closes a comment -->
</SCRIPT>
```

The opening `<!--` comment causes Web browsers that do not support JavaScript to disregard all text they encounter until they find a matching `-->`, so they don't display your script. You do have to be careful with the `<SCRIPT>` tag, though; if you put your `<SCRIPT>` and `</SCRIPT>` block inside the comments, the Web browser will ignore them also.

Comments Including comments in your programs to explain what they do is good practice—JavaScript is no exception. The JavaScript interpreter ignores any text marked as comments, so don't be shy about including them. You can use two types of comments: single-line and multiple-line.

Single-line comments start with two slashes (`//`), and they're limited to one line. Multiple-line comments must start with `/*` on the first line and end with `*/` on the last line. Here are a few examples:

Part

V

Ch

21

```
    // this is a legal comment
/ illegal -- comments start with two slashes
/* Multiple-line comments can
   be spread across more than one line, as long as they end. */
/* illegal -- this comment doesn't have an end!
/// this comment's OK, because extra slashes are ignored //
```

CAUTION

Be careful when using multiple-line comments—remember that these comments don't nest. For instance, if you commented out a section of code in the following way, you would get an error message:

```
/* Comment out the following code
 * document.writeln(DumpURL()) /* write out URL list */
 * document.writeln("End of list.")
 */
```

The preferred way to create single-line comments to avoid this would be as follows:

```
/* Comment out the following code
 * document.writeln(DumpURL()) // write out URL list
 * document.writeln("End of list.")
 */
```

Using <NOSCRIPT>   You can improve the compatibility of your JavaScript Web pages through the use of the <NOSCRIPT>...</NOSCRIPT> HTML tags. Any HTML code that is placed between these container tags will not appear on a JavaScript-compatible Web browser but will be displayed on one that is not able to understand JavaScript. This allows you to include alternative content for users who are using Web browsers that don't understand JavaScript. At the very least, you can let them know that they are missing something, as in this example:

```
<NOSCRIPT>
<HR>If you are seeing this text, then your Web browser
   doesn't speak JavaScript!<HR>
</NOSCRIPT>
```

The JavaScript Language

JavaScript was designed to resemble Java, which in turn looks a lot like C and C++. The difference is that Java was built as a general-purpose object language, while JavaScript is intended to provide a quicker and simpler language for enhancing Web pages and servers. In this section, you learn the building blocks of JavaScript and how to combine them into legal JavaScript programs.

N O T E JavaScript was developed by the Netscape Corporation, which maintains a great set of examples and documentation. Its JavaScript Authoring Guide is available online at **http://home.netscape.com/eng/mozilla/3.0/handbook/javascript/index.html** ∎

Using Identifiers

An *identifier* is a unique name that JavaScript uses to identify a variable, method, or object in your program. As with other programming languages, JavaScript imposes some rules on what names you can use. All JavaScript names must start with a letter or the underscore character, and they can contain both upper- and lowercase letters and the digits 0 through 9.

JavaScript supports two different ways for you to represent values in your scripts: literals and variables. As their names imply, *literals* are fixed values that don't change while the script is executing, and *variables* hold data that can change at any time.

Literals and variables have several different types; the type is determined by the kind of data that the literal or variable contains. The following are some of the types supported in JavaScript:

- Integers—Integer literals are made up of a sequence of digits only; integer variables can contain any whole-number value. Octal (base 8) and hexadecimal (base 16) integers can be specified by prefixing them with a leading "0" or "0x," respectively.

- Floating-Point Numbers—The number 10 is an integer, but 10.5 is a floating-point number. Floating-point literals can be positive or negative and they can contain either positive or negative exponents (which are indicated by an *e* in the number). For example, 3.14159265 is a floating-point literal, as is 6.023e23 (6.023×10^{23} or Avogadro's number).

- Strings—Strings can represent words, phrases, or data, and they're set off by either double or single quotation marks. If you start a string with one type of quotation mark, you must close it with the same type. Special characters, such as \n and \t, can also be utilized in strings.

- Booleans—Boolean literals can have values of either TRUE or FALSE; other statements in the JavaScript language can return Boolean values.

Using Functions, Objects, and Properties

JavaScript is modeled after Java, an object-oriented language. An *object* is a collection of data and functions that has been grouped together. A *function* is a piece of code that plays a sound, calculates an equation, or sends a piece of e-mail, and so on. The object's functions are called *methods,* and its data are called its *properties.* The JavaScript programs

Part
V

Ch
21

you write will have properties and methods and will interact with objects provided by the Web browser, its plug-ins, Java applets, ActiveX Controls, and other things.

N O T E Though the terms *function* and *method* are often used interchangeably, they are not the same. A method is a function that is part of an object. For instance, writeln is one of the methods of the object document. ■

 TIP Here's a simple guideline: An object's *properties* are the information it knows; its *methods* are how it can act on that information.

Using Built-In Objects and Functions Individual JavaScript elements are *objects*. For example, string literals are string objects and they have methods that you can use to change their case, and so on. JavaScript can also use the objects that represent the Web browser in which it is executing, the currently displayed page, and other elements of the browsing session.

You access objects by specifying their names. For example, the active document object is named document. To use document's properties or methods, you add a period and the name of the method or property you want. For example, document.title is the title property of the document object, and explorer.length calls the length member of the string object named explorer. Remember, literals are objects, too.

Using Properties Every object has properties, even literals. To access a property, just use the object name followed by a period and the property name. To get the length of a string object named address, you can write the following:

```
address.length
```

You get back an integer that equals the number of characters in the string. If the object you're using has properties that can be modified, you can change them in the same way. To set the color property of a house object, just use the following line:

```
house.color = "blue"
```

You can also create new properties for an object just by naming them. For example, say you define a class called customer for one of your pages. You can add new properties to the customer object as follows:

```
customer.name = "Joe Smith"
customer.address = "123 Elm Street"
customer.zip = "90210"
```

Finally, knowing that an object's methods are just properties is important. You can easily add new properties to an object by writing your own function and creating a new object property using your own function name. If you want to add a Bill method to your customer object, you can do so by writing a function named `BillCustomer` and setting the object's property as follows:

```
customer.Bill = BillCustomer;
```

To call the new method, you use the following:

```
customer.Bill()
```

Array and Object Properties   JavaScript objects store their properties in an internal table that you can access in two ways. You've already seen the first way—just use the properties' names. The second way, *arrays*, allows you to access all of an object's properties in sequence. The following function prints out all the properties of the specified object:

```
function DumpProperties(obj, obj_name) {
    result = ""    // set the result string to blank
    for (i in obj)
        result += obj_name + "." + i + " = " + obj[i] + "\n"
    return result
}
```

So not only can you access all of the properties of the `document` object, for instance, by property name using the dot operator (for example, `document.href`), you can also use the object's property array (for example, `document[1]`, though this may not be the same property as `document.href`). JavaScript provides another method of array access that combines the two, known as *associative arrays*. An associative array associates a left- and right-side element, and the value of the right side can be used by specifying the value of the left-side as the index. Objects are set up by JavaScript as associative arrays with the property names as the left side, and their values as the right. So the `href` property of the `document` object could be accessed using `document["href"]`.

Programming with JavaScript

JavaScript has a lot to offer page authors. It's not as flexible as C or C++, but it's quick and simple. Most importantly, it's easily embedded in your Web pages so that you can maximize their impact with a little JavaScript seasoning. This section covers the gritty details of JavaScript programming, including a detailed explanation of the language's features.

Expressions

An *expression* is anything that can be evaluated to get a single value. Expressions can contain string or numeric literals, variables, operators, and other expressions, and they can range from simple to quite complex. For example, the following are expressions that use the assignment operator (more on operators in the next section) to assign numerical or string values to variables:

```
x = 7;
str = "Hello, World!";
```

By contrast, the following is a more complex expression whose final value depends on the values of the quitFlag and formComplete variables:

```
(quitFlag == TRUE) & (formComplete == FALSE)
```

Operators

Operators do just what their name suggests: They operate on variables or literals. The items that an operator acts on are called its *operands*. Operators come in the two following types:

- Unary operators—These operators require only one operand, and the operator can come before or after the operand. The − operator, which subtracts one from the operand, is a good example. Both −count and count− subtract one from the variable count.

- Binary operators—These operators need two operands. The four math operators (+ for addition, - for subtraction, * for multiplication, and / for division) are all binary operators, as is the = assignment operator you saw earlier.

Assignment Operators   *Assignment operators* take the result of an expression and assign it to a variable. JavaScript doesn't allow you to assign the result of an expression to a literal. One feature of JavaScript that is not found in most other programming languages is that you can change a variable's type on-the-fly. Consider the HTML document shown in Listing 21.1.

Listing 21.1   Var-fly.htm—JavaScript Allows You to Change the Data Type of Variables

```
<HTML>
<HEAD>
<SCRIPT LANGUAGE="JavaScript">
<!-- Hide this script from incompatible Web browsers!
function typedemo() {
   var x;
   document.writeln("<HR>");
   x = Math.PI;
   document.writeln("x is " + x + "<BR>");
   x = false;
   document.writeln("x is " + x + "<BR>");
   document.writeln("<HR>");
}
```

```
<!-- -->
</SCRIPT>
<TITLE>Changing Data Types on the Fly!</TITLE>
</HEAD>
<BODY BGCOLOR=#FFFFFF>
If your Web browser doesn't support JavaScript, this is all you will see!
<SCRIPT LANGUAGE="JavaScript">
<!-- Hide this script from incompatible Web browsers!
typedemo();
<!-- -->
</SCRIPT>
</BODY>
</HTML>
```

This short program first prints the (correct) value of pi in the variable x. In most other languages, though, trying to set a floating-point variable to a Boolean value would generate either a compiler error or a runtime error. JavaScript happily accepts the change and prints x's new value: false (see Figure 21.2).

FIGURE 21.2

Because JavaScript variables are loosely typed, not only can their value be changed, but also their data type.

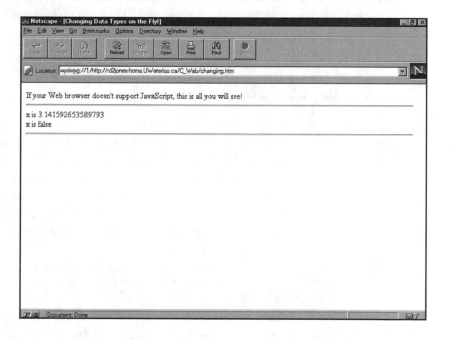

The most common assignment operator, =, simply assigns the value of an expression's right side to its left side. In the previous example, the variable x got the integer value 7 after the expression was evaluated. For convenience, JavaScript also defines some other operators that combine common math operations with assignment; they're shown in Table 21.1.

Table 21.1   Assignment Operators that Provide Shortcuts to Doing Assignments and Math Operations at the Same Time

Operator	What It Does	Two Equivalent Expressions
+=	Adds two values	x+=y and x=x+y
-=	Subtracts two values	x-=y and x=x-y
*=	Multiples two values	a*=b and a=a*b
/=	Divides two values	e/=b and e=e/b

Math Operators   The preceding sections gave you a sneak preview of the math operators that JavaScript furnishes. You can either combine math operations with assignments, as shown in Table 21.1, or use them individually. As you would expect, the standard four math functions (addition, subtraction, multiplication, and division) work just as they do on an ordinary calculator. The negation operator, -, is a unary operator that negates the sign of its operand. Another useful binary math operator is the modulus operator, %. This operator returns the remainder after the integer division of two integer numbers. For instance, in the expression:

```
x = 13%5;
```

the variable x would be given the value of 3.

JavaScript also adds two useful unary operators: -- and ++, called, respectively, the *decrement* and *increment* operators. These two operators modify the value of their operand, and they return the new value. They also share a unique property: They can be used either before or after their operand. If you put the operator after the operand, JavaScript returns the operand's value and then modifies it. If you take the opposite route and put the operator before the operand, JavaScript modifies it and returns the modified value. The following short example might help clarify this seemingly odd behavior:

```
x = 7;    // set x to 7
a = --x;  // set x to x-1, and return the new x; a = 6
b = a++;  // set b to a, so b = 6, then add 1 to a; a = 7
x++;      // add one to x; ignore the returned value
```

Comparison Operators   Comparing the value of two expressions to see whether one is larger, smaller, or equal to another is often necessary. JavaScript supplies several comparison operators that take two operands and return TRUE if the comparison is true, and FALSE if it's not. (Remember, you can use literals, variables, or expressions with operators that require expressions.) Table 21.2 shows the JavaScript comparison operators.

Table 21.2 Comparison Operators that Allow Two JavaScript Operands to Be Compared in a Variety of Ways

Operator	Read It As	Returns TRUE When
==	Equals	The two operands are equal
!=	Does not equal	The two operands are unequal
<	Less than	The left operand is less than the right operand
<=	Less than or equal to	The left operand is less than or equal to the right operand
>	Greater than	The left operand is greater than the right operand
>=	Greater than or equal to	The left operand is greater than or equal to the right operand

Thinking of the comparison operators as questions may be helpful. When you write the following:

```
(x >= 10)
```

you're really saying, "Is the value of variable x greater than or equal to 10?" The return value answers the question, TRUE or FALSE.

Logical Operators   Comparison operators compare quantity or content for numeric and string expressions, but sometimes you need to test a logical value, like whether a comparison operator returns TRUE or FALSE. JavaScript's logical operators allow you to compare expressions that return logical values. The following are JavaScript's logical operators:

- &&, read as "and"—The && operator returns TRUE if both its input expressions are TRUE. If the first operand evaluates to FALSE, && returns FALSE immediately, without evaluating the second operand. Here's an example:

```
x = TRUE && TRUE;     // x is TRUE
x = FALSE && FALSE;   // x is FALSE
x = FALSE && TRUE;    // x is FALSE
```

- ¦¦, read as "or"—This operator returns TRUE if either of its operands is TRUE. If the first operand is TRUE, ¦¦ returns TRUE without evaluating the second operand. Here's an example:

```
x = TRUE ¦¦ TRUE;     // x is TRUE
x = FALSE ¦¦ TRUE;    // x is TRUE
x = FALSE ¦¦ FALSE;   // x is FALSE
```

- !, read as "not"—This operator takes only one expression, and it returns the opposite of that expression, so !TRUE returns FALSE, and !FALSE returns TRUE.

Part
V

Ch
21

Note that the "and" and "or" operators don't evaluate the second operand if the first operand provides enough information for the operator to return a value. This process, called *short-circuit evaluation*, can be significant when the second operand is a function call. For example,

```
keepGoing = (userCancelled == FALSE) && (theForm.Submit())
```

If userCancelled is TRUE, the second operand, which submits the active form, isn't called.

String Operators   A few of the operators that were listed above can be used for string manipulation as well. All of the comparison operators can be used on strings too; the results depend on standard lexicographic ordering, but comparisons aren't case-sensitive. Additionally, the + operator can also be used to concatenate strings. The expression

```
str = "Hello, " + "World!";
```

assigns the resulting string Hello, World! to the variable str.

Controlling Your JavaScripts

Some scripts you write will be simple; they'll execute the same way every time, once per page. For example, if you add a JavaScript to play a sound when users visit your home page, it doesn't need to evaluate any conditions or do anything more than once. More sophisticated scripts might require that you take different actions under different circumstances. You might also want to repeat the execution of a block of code—perhaps by a set number of times, or as long as some condition is TRUE. JavaScript provides constructs for controlling the execution flow of your script based on conditions, as well as for repeating a sequence of operations.

Testing Conditions   JavaScript provides a single type of control statement for making decisions: the if...else statement. To make a decision, you supply an expression that evaluates to TRUE or FALSE; which code is executed depends on what your expression evaluates to.

The simplest form of if...else uses only the if part. If the specified condition is TRUE, the code following the condition is executed; if not, it's skipped. For example, in the following code fragment, the message appears only if the condition (that the lastModified.year property of the document object says it was modified before 1995) is TRUE:

```
if (document.lastModified.year < 1995)
    document.write("Danger! This is a mighty old document.")
```

You can use any expression as the condition. Since expressions can be nested and combined with the logical operators, your tests can be pretty sophisticated. For example:

```
if ((document.lastModified.year >= 1995) && (document.lastModified.month >=
   ➡10))
   document.write("This document is reasonably current.")
```

The `else` clause allows you to specify a set of statements to execute when the condition is FALSE, for instance:

```
if ((document.lastModified.year >= 1995) && (document.lastModified.month >=
   ➡10))
    document.write("This document is reasonably current.")
else
    document.write("This document is quite old.")
```

Repeating Actions   JavaScript provides two different loop constructs that you can use to repeat a set of operations. The first, called a `for` loop, executes a set of statements some number of times. You specify three expressions: an *initial* expression that sets the values of any variables you need to use, a *condition* that tells the loop how to see when it's done, and an *increment* expression that modifies any variables that need it. Here's a simple example:

```
for (count=0; count < 100; count++)
   document.write("Count is ", count);
```

This loop executes 100 times and prints out a number each time. The initial expression sets the counter, `count`, to zero. The condition tests to see whether `count` is less than 100, and the increment expression increments `count`.

You can use several statements for any of these expressions, as follows:

```
for (count=0, numFound = 0; (count < 100) && (numFound < 3); count++)
    if (someObject.found()) numFound++;
```

This loop loops either 100 times or as many times as it takes to "find" three items—the loop condition terminates when `count >= 100` or when `numFound >= 3`.

The second form of loop is the `while` loop. It executes statements as long as its condition is TRUE. For example, you can rewrite the first `for` loop in the preceding example as follows:

```
count = 0
while (count < 100) {
   if (someObject.found()) numFound++;
   document.write("Count is ", count)
}
```

Which form you use depends on what you're doing; `for` loops are useful when you want to perform an action a set number of times, and `while` loops are best when you want to keep doing something as long as a particular condition remains TRUE. Notice that by using curly braces you can include more than one command to be executed by the `while` loop (this is also true of `for` loops and `if...else` constructs).

JavaScript Reserved Words

JavaScript reserves some keywords for its own use. You cannot define your own methods or properties with the same name as any of these keywords; if you do, the JavaScript interpreter complains.

 TIP Some of these keywords are reserved for future use. JavaScript might allow you to use them, but your scripts may break in the future if you do.

JavaScript's reserved keywords are shown in Table 21.3.

Table 21.3 JavaScript Reserved Keywords that Should Not Be Used in Your JavaScripts

abstract	double	instanceof	super
boolean	else	int	switch
break	extends	interface	synchronized
byte	FALSE	long	this
case	final	native	throw
catch	finally	new	throws
char	float	null	transient
class	for	package	TRUE
const	function	private	try
continue	goto	protected	var
default	if	public	void
do	implements	return	while
import	short	with	in static

CAUTION

Because JavaScript is still being developed and refined by Netscape, the list of reserved keywords might change or grow over time. Whenever a new version of JavaScript is released, it might be a good idea to look over its new capabilities with an eye towards conflicts with your JavaScript programs.

Other JavaScript Statements

This section provides a quick reference to some of the other JavaScript commands. The commands are listed in alphabetical order—many have examples. Here's what the formatting of these entries mean:

- All JavaScript keywords are in monospaced font.

- Words in `monospace italics` represent user-defined names or statements.

- Any portions enclosed in square brackets ([and]) are optional.

- `{statements}` indicates a block of statements, which can consist of a single statement or multiple statements enclosed by curly braces.

The *break* statement   The `break` statement terminates the current `while` or `for` loop and transfers program control to the statement following the terminated loop.

Syntax

```
break
```

Example

The following function scans the list of URLs in the current document and stops when it has seen all URLs or when it finds an URL that matches the input parameter `searchName`:

```
function findURL(searchName) {
    var i = 0;
    for (i=0; i < document.links.length; i++) {
        if (document.links[i] == searchName) {
            document.writeln(document.links[i] + "<br>")
            break;
        }
    }
}
```

The *continue* statement   The `continue` statement stops executing the statements in a `while` or `for` loop, and skips to the next iteration of the loop. It doesn't stop the loop altogether, as the `break` statement does; instead, in a `while` loop, it jumps back to the condition, and in a `for` loop, it jumps to the update expression.

Syntax

```
continue
```

Example

The following function prints the odd numbers between 1 and x; it has a `continue` statement that goes to the next iteration when i is even:

```
function printOddNumbers(x) {
    var i = 0
    while (i < x) {
        i++;
        if ((i % 2) == 0) // the % operator divides & returns the remainder
            continue
        else
            document.write(i, "\n")
    }
}
```

The *for* loop   A `for` loop consists of three optional expressions, enclosed in parentheses and separated by semicolons, followed by a block of statements executed in the loop. These parts do the following:

- The starting expression, `initial_expr`, is evaluated before the loop starts. It is most often used to initialize loop counter variables, and you're free to use the `var` keyword here to declare new variables.

- A `condition` is evaluated on each pass through the loop. If the condition evaluates to TRUE, the statements in the loop body are executed. You can leave the condition out, and it always evaluates to TRUE. If you do so, make sure to use `break` in your loop when it's time to exit.

- An update expression, `update_expr`, is usually used to update or increment the counter variable or other variables used in the condition. This expression is optional; you can update variables as needed within the body of the loop if you prefer.

- A block of statements is executed as long as the condition is TRUE. This block can have one or multiple statements in it.

Syntax

```
for ([initial_expr;] [condition;] [update_expr]) {
    statements
}
```

Example

This simple `for` statement prints out the numbers from 0 to 9. It starts by declaring a loop counter variable, i, and initializing it to zero. As long as i is less than 9, the update expression increments i, and the statements in the loop body are executed.

```
for (var i = 0; i <= 9; i++) {
    document.write(i);
}
```

The *for...in* loop   The `for...in` loop is a special form of the `for` loop that iterates the variable `variable-name` over all the properties of the object named `object-name`. For each distinct property, it executes the statements in the loop body.

Syntax

```
for (var in obj) {
   statements
   }
```

Example

The following function takes as its arguments an object and the object's name. It then uses the `for...in` loop to iterate through all the object's properties, and writes them into the current Web page.

```
function dump_props(obj,obj_name) {
   for (i in obj)
      document.writeln(obj_name + "." + i + " = " + obj[i] + "<br>");
}
```

The *function* statement   The `function` statement declares a JavaScript function; the function may optionally accept one or more parameters. To return a value, the function must have a return statement that specifies the value to return. All parameters are passed to functions *by value*—the function gets the value of the parameter but cannot change the original value in the caller.

Syntax

```
function name([param] [, param] [..., param]) {
   statements
}
```

Example

```
function PageNameMatches(theString) {
   return (document.title == theString)
}
```

The *if...else* statement   The `if...else` statement is a conditional statement that executes the statements in `block1` if `condition` is TRUE. In the optional `else` clause, it executes the statements in `block2` if `condition` is FALSE. The blocks of statements can contain any JavaScript statements, including further nested `if` statements.

Syntax

```
if (condition) {
    statements
}
[else {
    statements}]
```

Part
V

Ch
21

Example

```
if (Message.IsEncrypted()) {
    Message.Decrypt(SecretKey);
}
else {
    Message.Display();
}
```

The *new* statement   The new statement is the way that new objects are created in JavaScript. For instance, if you defined the following function to create a house object:

```
function house (rms,stl,yr,garp) { // define a house object
    this.room = rms;        // number of rooms (integer)
    this.style = stl;       // style (string)
    this.yearBuilt = yr;    // year built (integer)
    this.hasGarage = garp;  // has garage? (boolean)
}
```

you could then create an instance of a house object using the new statement, as in the following:

```
var myhouse = new house(3,"Tenement",1962,false);
```

A few notes about this example: First, note that the function used to create the object doesn't actually return a value. The reason it is able to work is that it makes use of the this object, which always refers to the current object. Second, while the function defines how to create the house object, none is actually created until the function is called using the new statement.

The *return* statement   The return statement specifies the value to be returned by a function.

Syntax

```
return expression;
```

Example

The following simple function returns the square of its argument, x, where x is any number.

```
function square( x ) {
    return x * x;
}
```

The *this* statement   You use this to access methods or properties of an object within the object's methods. The this statement always refers to the current object.

Syntax

```
this.property
```

Example

If `setSize` is a method of the `document` object, then `this` refers to the specific object whose `setSize` method is called:

```
function setSize(x,y) {
    this.horizSize = x;
    this.vertSize = y;
}
```

This method sets the size for an object when called as follows:

```
document.setSize(640,480);
```

The *var* statement   The `var` statement declares a variable *varname*, optionally initializing it to have *value*. The variable name *varname* can be any JavaScript identifier, and *value* can be any legal expression (including literals).

Syntax

```
var varname [= value] [, var varname [= value] ] [..., var varname [= value]
   ➥]
```

Example

```
var num_hits = 0, var cust_no = 0;
```

The *while* statement   The `while` statement contains a condition and a block of statements. The `while` statement evaluates the condition; if *condition* is TRUE, it executes the statements in the loop body. It then reevaluates *condition* and continues to execute the statement block as long as *condition* is TRUE. When *condition* evaluates to FALSE, execution continues with the next statement following the block.

Syntax

```
while (condition) {
   statements
}
```

Example

The following simple `while` loop iterates until it finds a form in the current `document` object whose name is `"OrderForm"`, or until it runs out of forms in the document:

```
x = 0;
while ((x < document.forms[].length) && (document.forms[x].name
➥!= "OrderForm")) {
   x++
}
```

The *with* statement   The `with` statement establishes *object* as the default object for the statements in `block`. Any property references without an object are then assumed to be for *object*.

Syntax

```
with object {
    statements
}
```

Example

```
with document {
    write "Inside a with block, you don't need to specify the object.";
    bgColor = gray;
}
```

JavaScript and Web Browsers

The most important thing you will be doing with your JavaScripts is interacting with the content and information on your Web pages, and through it, with your user. JavaScript interacts with your Web browser through the browser's object model. Different aspects of the Web browser exist as different objects, with properties and methods that can be accessed by JavaScript. For instance, `document.write()` uses the `write` method of the `document` object. Understanding this Web browser object model is crucial to using JavaScript effectively. Understanding how the Web browser processes and executes your scripts is also necessary.

When Scripts Execute

When you put JavaScript code in a page, the Web browser evaluates the code as soon as it's encountered. Functions, however, don't get executed when they're evaluated; they just get stored for later use. You still have to call functions explicitly to make them work. Some functions are attached to objects, like buttons or text fields on forms, and they are called when some event happens on the button or field. You might also have functions that you want to execute during page evaluation. You can do so by putting a call to the function at the appropriate place in the page.

Where to Put Your Scripts

You can put scripts anywhere within your HTML page, as long as they're surrounded with the `<SCRIPT>...</SCRIPT>` tags. One good system is to put functions that will be executed more than once into the `<HEAD>` element of their pages; this element provides a convenient storage place. Since the `<HEAD>` element is at the beginning of the file, functions and VBScript code that you put there will be evaluated before the rest of the document is loaded. Then you can execute the function at the appropriate point in your Web page by calling it, as in the following:

```
<SCRIPT language="JavaScript">
<!-- Hide this script from incompatible Web browsers!
myFunction();
<!-- -->
</SCRIPT>
```

Another way to execute scripts is to attach them to HTML elements that support scripts. When scripts are matched with events attached to these elements, the script is executed when the event occurs. This can be done with HTML elements, such as forms, buttons, or links. Consider Listing 21.2, which shows a very simple example of attaching a JavaScript function to the onClick attribute of an HTML forms button (see Figure 21.3).

Listing 21.2   Button1.htm—Calling a JavaScript Function with the Click of a Button<HTML>

```
<HEAD>
<SCRIPT LANGUAGE="JavaScript">
<!-- Hide this script from incompatible Web browsers!
function pressed() {
    alert("I said Don't Press Me!");
}
<!-- -->
</SCRIPT>
<TITLE>JavaScripts Attached to HTML Elements</TITLE>
</HEAD>
<BODY BGCOLOR=#FFFFFF>
<FORM NAME="Form1">
    <INPUT TYPE="button" NAME="Button1" VALUE="Don't Press Me!"
        onClick="pressed()">
</FORM>
</BODY>
</HTML>
```

JavaScript also provides you with an alternate way to attach functions to objects and their events. For simple actions, you can attach the JavaScript directly to the attribute of the HTML form element, as shown in Listing 21.3. Each of these listings will produce the output shown in Figure 21.3.

Listing 21.3   Button2.htm—Simple VBScripts Can Be Attached Right to a Form Element

```
<HTML>
<HEAD>
<TITLE>JavaScripts Attached to HTML Elements</TITLE>
</HEAD>
<BODY BGCOLOR=#FFFFFF>
<FORM NAME="Form1">
    <INPUT TYPE="button" NAME="Button1" VALUE="Don't Press Me!"
        onClick="alert('I said Don\'t Press Me!')">
```

Part
V

Ch
21

continues

Listing 21.3   Continued

```
  </FORM>
  </BODY>
  </HTML>
```

FIGURE 21.3

JavaScript functions can be attached to form fields through several different methods.

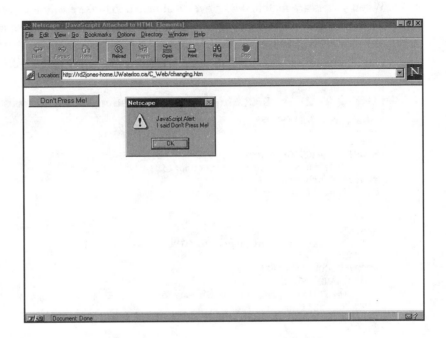

Sometimes, though, you have code that shouldn't be evaluated or executed until after all the page's HTML has been parsed and displayed. An example would be a function to print out all the URLs referenced in the page. If this function is evaluated before all the HTML on the page has been loaded, it misses some URLs, so the call to the function should come at the page's end. The function itself can be defined anywhere in the HTML document; it is the function call that should be at the end of the page.

N O T E   JavaScript code to modify the actual HTML contents of a document (as opposed to merely changing the text in a form text input field, for instance) must be executed during page evaluation. ∎

Web Browser Objects and Events

In addition to recognizing JavaScript when it's embedded inside a <SCRIPT> tag, compatible Web browsers also provide some objects (and their methods and properties) that you can use in your JavaScript programs. They can also trigger methods you define when the user takes certain actions in the browser.

Web Browser Object Hierarchy and Scoping

Figure 21.4 shows the hierarchy of objects that the Web browser provides and that are accessible to JavaScript. As shown, `window` is the topmost object in the hierarchy, and the other objects are organized underneath it as shown. Using this hierarchy, the full reference for the value of a text field named `text1` in an HTML form named `form1` would be `window.document.form1.text1.value`.

FIGURE 21.4
Objects defined by the Web browser are organized in a hierarchy and can be accessed and manipulated by JavaScript.

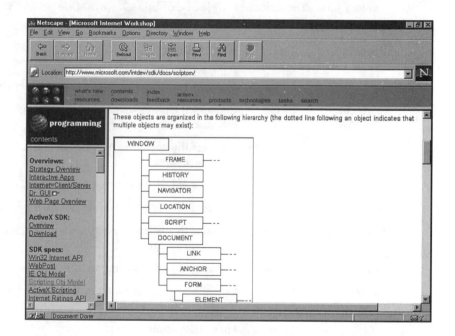

However, because of the object scoping rules in JavaScript, it is not necessary to specify this full reference. Scoping refers to the range over which a variable, function, or object is defined. For instance, a variable defined within a JavaScript function is only scoped within that function—it cannot be referenced outside of the function. JavaScripts are scoped to the current window, but not to the objects below the window in the hierarchy. So, for the example above, the text field value could also be referenced as `document.form1.text1.value`.

Part
V

Ch
21

Browser Object Model

Many events that happen in a Web browsing session aren't related to items on the page, like buttons or HTML text. Instead, they're related to what's happening in the browser itself, like what page the user is viewing.

The *location* Object   Internet Explorer 3.0 exposes an object called `location`, which holds the current URL, including the hostname, path, CGI script arguments, and even the protocol. Table 21.4 shows the properties and methods of the `location` object.

Table 21.4   The *Location* Object Contains Information on the Currently Displayed URL

Property	Type	What It Does
href	String	Contains the entire URL, including all the subparts; for example, **http://www.msn.com/products/msprod.htm**
protocol	String	Contains the protocol field of the URL, including the first colon; for example, **http:**
host	String	Contains the hostname and port number; for example, **www.msn.com:80**
hostname	String	Contains only the hostname; for example, **www.msn.com**
port	String	Contains the port, if specified; otherwise, it's blank
path	String	Contains the path to the actual document; for example, **products/msprod.htm**
hash	String	Contains any CGI arguments after the first # in the URL
search	String	Contains any CGI arguments after the first ? in the URL
toString()	Method	Returns `location.href`; you can use this function to get the entire URL easily
assign(x)	Method	Sets `location.href` to the value you specify

Listing 21.4 shows an example of how you access and use the `location` object. First, the current values of the `location` properties are displayed on the Web page (see Figure 21.5). As you can see, not all of them are defined. Additionally, when the button is clicked, the `location.href` property is set to the URL of my home page. This causes the Web browser to load that page.

FIGURE 21.5
Manipulating the `location` object gives you another means of moving from one Web page to another.

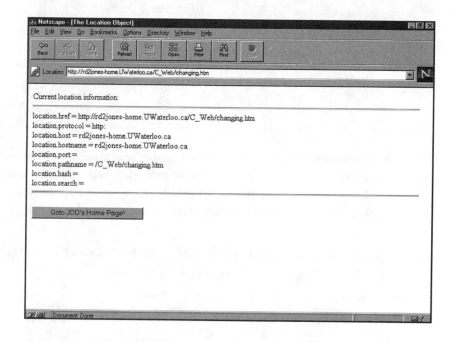

Listing 21.4   Loc-props.htm—The *Location* Object Allows You to Access and Set Information About the Current URL

```
<HTML>
<HEAD>
<SCRIPT LANGUAGE="JavaScript">
<!-- Hide this script from incompatible Web browsers!
function gohome() {
    location.href = "http://www.rpi.edu/~odonnj/";
}
<!-- -->
</SCRIPT>
<TITLE>The Location Object</TITLE>
</HEAD>
<BODY BGCOLOR=#FFFFFF>
<SCRIPT LANGUAGE="Javascript">
<!-- Hide this script from incompatible Web browsers!
document.writeln("Current location information: <BR> <HR>");
document.writeln("location.href = " + location.href + "<BR>");
document.writeln("location.protocol = " + location.protocol + "<BR>");
document.writeln("location.host = " + location.host + "<BR>");
document.writeln("location.hostname = " + location.hostname + "<BR>");
document.writeln("location.port = " + location.port + "<BR>");
document.writeln("location.pathname = " + location.pathname + "<BR>");
document.writeln("location.hash = " + location.hash + "<BR>");
document.writeln("location.search = " + location.search + "<BR> <HR>");
<!-- -->
</SCRIPT>
```

Part
V

Ch
21

continues

Listing 21.4 Continued

```
<FORM NAME="Form1">
    <INPUT TYPE="button" NAME="Button1" VALUE="Goto JOD's Home Page!"
        onClick="gohome()">
</FORM>
</BODY>
</HTML>
```

The *document* Object   Web browsers also expose an object called document; as you might expect, this object exposes useful properties and methods of the active document. The location object refers only to the URL of the active document, but document refers to the document itself. Table 21.5 shows document's properties and methods.

Table 21.5   The *Document* Object Contains Information on the Currently Loaded and Displayed HTML Page

Property	Type	What It Does
title	String	Contains title of the current page, or Untitled if there's no title
URL or Location	String	Contains the document's address (from its Location history stack entry); these two are synonyms
lastModified	String	Contains the page's last-modified date
forms[]	Array	Contains all the FORMS in the current page
forms[].length	Integer	Contains the number of FORMS in the current page
links[]	Array	Contains all HREF anchors in the current page
links[].length	Integer	Contains the number of HREF anchors in the current page
write(x)	Method	Writes HTML to the current document, in the order in which the script occurs on the page

The *history* Object   The Web browser also maintains a list of pages you've visited since running the program; this list is called the *history list*, and can be accessed through the history object. Your JavaScript programs can move through pages in the list using the properties and functions shown in Table 21.6.

Table 21.6 The *history* Object Contains Information on the Browser's History List

Property	Type	What It Does
previous or back	String	Contains the URL of the previous history stack entry (that is, the one before the active page). These properties are synonyms.
next or forward	String	Contains the URL of the next history stack entry (that is, the one after the active page). These properties are synonyms.
go(x)	Method	Goes forward x entries in the history stack if x > 0; else, goes backward x entries. x must be a number.
go(str)	Method	Goes to the newest history entry whose title or URL contains str as a substring; the string case doesn't matter. str must be a string.

The *window* Object The Web browser creates a window object for every document. Think of the window object as an actual window, and the document object as the content that appears in the window. The following are a couple of the methods available for working in the window:

- alert(*string*) puts up an Alert dialog box and displays the message specified in string. Users must dismiss the dialog box by clicking the OK button before Internet Explorer 3 lets them continue.

- confirm(*string*) puts up a Confirmation dialog box with two buttons (OK and Cancel) and displays the message specified in string. Users can dismiss the dialog box by clicking Cancel or OK; the confirm function returns TRUE when users click OK and FALSE if they click Cancel.

The *form* Object There are a series of objects, properties, methods, and events associated with HTML forms when used in a Web page. Some of them you have already seen in the examples presented thus far in this chapter. All of the properties of the form object work the same way in JavaScript as in VBScript.

▶ **See** "The Form Object," **p. 471**
▶ **See** "VBScript Intranet Application," **p. 474**

Example JavaScript Applications

In this section, you'll see a couple of examples of JavaScript applications. A common scripting application generally involves interaction with HTML forms in order to perform

Part

V

Ch

21

client-side validation of the forms data before submission. JavaScript can perform this function very well. If you are interested in seeing an example of using JavaScript in this way, there is a JavaScript version on the CD-ROM that does much the same thing.

In order not to duplicate the forms discussion, the example shown in this chapter shows how JavaScript can be used within a Web browser to interact with browser frames and windows. As usual, the interface between the user and the JavaScript code remains HTML forms elements—the examples also show you how to open, close, and manipulate Web browser windows and frames.

Manipulating Windows

This example shows how it is possible to create an HTML forms-based control panel that uses JavaScript to load and execute other JavaScripts in their own windows. This is done through the use of the window Web browser object and its properties and methods.

Listing 21.5 shows the "main program," the top-level HTML document giving access to the control panel (see Figure 21.6). The JavaScript in this example is very simple, and is included in the onClick attribute of the forms <input> tag. Clicking on the button executes the JavaScript method window open:

```
window.open('cp.htm','ControlPanel','width=300,height=250')
```

This creates a window named "ControlPanel" that is 300 × 250 pixels in size, and loads the HTML document CP.HTM.

On the CD

Listing 21.5   CPMAIN.HTM—A JavaScript Attached to a Forms Button Will Create a New Window when Clicked

```
<HTML>
<HEAD>
<TITLE>JavaScript Window Example</TITLE>
</HEAD>
<BODY BGCOLOR=#FFFFFF>
<CENTER><H3>Activate the control panel by clicking below</H3></CENTER>
<HR>
<FORM>
<CENTER>
<TABLE>
<TR><TD><INPUT TYPE="button" NAME="ControlButton" VALUE="Control Panel"
          onClick="window.open('cp.htm','ControlPanel',
                               'width=300,height=250')"></TD></TR>
</TABLE>
</CENTER>
</FORM>
</BODY>
</HTML>
```

FIGURE 21.6
The Control Panel button calls a JavaScript and creates a new browser window.

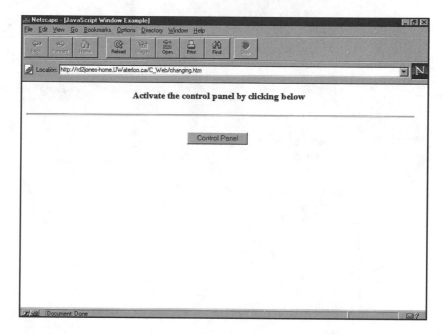

When the button is clicked, CP.HTM is loaded into its own window, as shown in Figure 21.7 (note that in this figure and the next, the windows have been manually rearranged so that they can all be seen). This HTML document uses an interface of an HTML form organized in a table to give access through this control panel to other JavaScript applications, namely a timer and a real-time clock. Listing 21.6 shows CP.HTM. The JavaScript functions `openTimer()`, `openClock()`, `closeTimer()`, and `closeClock()` are used to open and close windows for a JavaScript timer and clock, respectively. These functions are attached to forms buttons that make up the control panel. Note that JavaScript variables `timerw` and `clockw`, because they are defined outside of any of the functions, can be used anywhere in the JavaScript document. They are used to remember whether or not the timer and clock windows are opened.

Listing 21.6 CP.HTM—This HTML Form Calls JavaScripts to Create and Destroy Windows for a Timer or a Real-Time Clock

```
<HTML>
<HEAD>
<SCRIPT LANGUAGE="JavaScript">
<!-- Hide this script from incompatible Web browsers!
var timerw = null;
var clockw = null;
function openTimer() {
   if(!timerw)
      timerw = open("cptimer.htm","TimerWindow","width=300,height=100");
```

continues

Part
V

Ch
21

Listing 21.6 Continued

```
}
function openClock() {
   if(!clockw)
      clockw = open("cpclock.htm","ClockWindow","width=50,height=25");
}
function closeTimer() {
   if(timerw) {
      timerw.close();
      timerw = null;
   }
}
function closeClock() {
   if(clockw) {
      clockw.close();
      clockw = null;
   }
}
<!-- -->
</SCRIPT>
</HEAD>
<BODY BGCOLOR=#EEEEEE>
<FORM>
<CENTER>
<TABLE>
<TR><TD>To Open Timer...</TD>
   <TD ALIGN=CENTER>
      <INPUT TYPE="button" NAME="ControlButton" VALUE="Click Here!"
         onClick="openTimer()"></TD></TR>
<TR><TD>To Close Timer...</TD>
   <TD ALIGN=CENTER>
      <INPUT TYPE="button" NAME="ControlButton" VALUE="Click Here!"
         onClick="closeTimer()"></TD></TR>
<TR><TD>To Open Clock...</TD>
   <TD ALIGN=CENTER>
      <INPUT TYPE="button" NAME="ControlButton" VALUE="Click Here!"
         onClick="openClock()"></TD></TR>
<TR><TD>To Close Clock...</TD>
   <TD ALIGN=CENTER>
      <INPUT TYPE="button" NAME="ControlButton" VALUE="Click Here!"
         onClick="closeClock()"></TD></TR>
<TR><TD>To Open Both...</TD>
   <TD ALIGN=CENTER>
      <INPUT TYPE="button" NAME="ControlButton" VALUE="Click Here!"
         onClick="openTimer();openClock();"></TD></TR>
<TR><TD>To Close Both...</TD>
   <TD ALIGN=CENTER>
      <INPUT TYPE="button" NAME="ControlButton" VALUE="Click Here!"
         onClick="closeTimer();closeClock();"></TD></TR>
<TR><TD></TD></TR>
<TR><TD>To Close Everything...</TD>
   <TD ALIGN=CENTER>
      <INPUT TYPE="button" NAME="ControlButton" VALUE="Click Here!"
         onClick="closeTimer();closeClock();self.close();"></TD></TR>
</TABLE>
```

```
        </CENTER>
        </FORM>
        </BODY>
        </HTML>
```

FIGURE 21.7

JavaScript can create
new Web browser
windows with
definable widths
and heights.

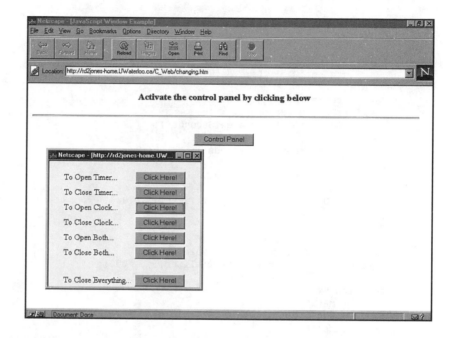

Listing 21.7 and Listing 21.8 show CPTIMER.HTM and CPCLOCK.HTM, the HTML
documents to implement the JavaScript timer and real-time clock. Note that each uses the
properties of the JavaScript *Date* object to access time information. Figure 21.8 shows the
Web page with the control panel, timer, and real-time clock windows all open.

**Listing 21.7   CPTIMER.HTM—The JavaScript *Date* Object Can Be Used to
Keep Track of Relative Time**

```
<HTML>
<HEAD>
<SCRIPT LANGUAGE="JavaScript">
<!-- Hide this script from incompatible Web browsers!
var timerID = 0;
var tStart  = null;
function UpdateTimer() {
   if(timerID) {
      clearTimeout(timerID);
      clockID  = 0;
   }
   if(!tStart)
      tStart  = new Date();
```

Part

V

Ch

21

continues

Listing 21.7   Continued

```
    var tDate = new Date();
    var tDiff = tDate.getTime() - tStart.getTime();
    var str;

    tDate.setTime(tDiff);

    str = ""
    if (tDate.getMinutes() < 10)
        str += "0" + tDate.getMinutes() + ":";
    else
        str += tDate.getMinutes() + ":";
    if (tDate.getSeconds() < 10)
        str += "0" + tDate.getSeconds();
    else
        str += tDate.getSeconds();

    document.theTimer.theTime.value = str;

    timerID = setTimeout("UpdateTimer()", 1000);
}
function Start() {
    tStart = new Date();
    document.theTimer.theTime.value = "00:00";
    timerID = setTimeout("UpdateTimer()", 1000);
}
function Stop() {
    if(timerID) {
        clearTimeout(timerID);
        timerID  = 0;
    }
    tStart = null;
}
function Reset() {
    tStart = null;
    document.theTimer.theTime.value = "00:00";
}
<!-- -->
</SCRIPT>
</HEAD>
<BODY BGCOLOR=#AAAAAA onload="Reset();Start()" onunload="Stop()">
<FORM NAME="theTimer">
<CENTER>
<TABLE>
<TR><TD COLSPAN=3 ALIGN=CENTER>
        <INPUT TYPE=TEXT NAME="theTime" SIZE=5></TD></TR>
<TR><TD></TD></TR>
<TR><TD><INPUT TYPE=BUTTON NAME="start" VALUE="Start"
            onclick="Start()"></TD>
    <TD><INPUT TYPE=BUTTON NAME="stop"  VALUE="Stop"
            onclick="Stop()"></TD>
    <TD><INPUT TYPE=BUTTON NAME="reset" VALUE="Reset"
            onclick="Reset()"></TD>
    </TR>
</TABLE>
```

```
</CENTER>
</FORM>
</BODY>
</HTML>
```

Listing 21.8   CPCLOCK.HTM—The *Date* Object Can Also Be Used to Access the Real-Time Clock of the Client System

```
<HTML>
<HEAD>
<TITLE>Clock</TITLE>
<SCRIPT LANGUAGE="JavaScript">
<!-- Hide this script from incompatible Web browsers!
var clockID = 0;
function UpdateClock() {
   if(clockID) {
      clearTimeout(clockID);
      clockID  = 0;
   }
   var tDate = new Date();
   var str;

   str = "";
   if (tDate.getHours() < 10)
      str += "0" + tDate.getHours() + ":";
   else
      str += tDate.getHours() + ":";
   if (tDate.getMinutes() < 10)
      str += "0" + tDate.getMinutes() + ":";
   else
      str += tDate.getMinutes() + ":";
   if (tDate.getSeconds() < 10)
      str += "0" + tDate.getSeconds();
   else
      str += tDate.getSeconds();

   document.theClock.theTime.value = str;

   clockID = setTimeout("UpdateClock()", 1000);
}

function StartClock() {
   clockID = setTimeout("UpdateClock()", 500);
}
function KillClock() {
   if(clockID) {
      clearTimeout(clockID);
      clockID  = 0;
   }
}
<!-- -->
</SCRIPT>
</HEAD>
```

Part

V

Ch

21

continues

Listing 21.8   Continued

```
<BODY BGCOLOR=#CCCCCC onload="StartClock()" onunload="KillClock()">
<CENTER>
<FORM NAME="theClock">
   <INPUT TYPE=TEXT NAME="theTime" SIZE=8>
</FORM>
</CENTER>
</BODY>
</HTML>
```

FIGURE 21.8
Multiple browser windows can be created by JavaScript, each running its own JavaScripts and performing its functions independently.

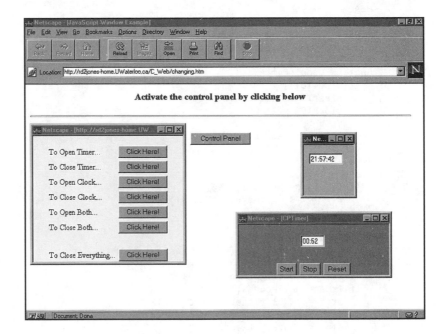

Web Browser Windows and Frames

In this example, you can see further examples of window manipulation using JavaScript—in addition, you will see how different frames can be accessed and manipulated. Listing 21.9 shows WFMAIN.HTM. Like CPMAIN.HTM in Listing 21.5, this is the simple, top-level HTML document for this example. This one is even simpler, in that it doesn't contain any JavaScript at all but simply sets up the frameset and frames for the example and indicates the HTML documents, WFTOP.HTM and WFTEXT.HTM, to be loaded into each frame.

Listing 21.9   WFMAIN.HTM—This Main HTML Document Creates a Frameset and Loads Two Other Documents into the Resulting Frames

```
<HTML>
<TITLE>Windows and Frames</TITLE>
<FRAMESET ROWS="100,*">
   <FRAME SRC="wftop.htm"  NAME="frame1" SCROLLING="no" NORESIZE>
   <FRAME SRC="wftext.htm" NAME="frame2">
</FRAMESET>
<NOFRAMES>
</NOFRAMES>
</HTML>
```

The document that makes up the uppermost frame, shown in Listing 21.10, creates a button bar of functions that can be used to manipulate the frames and windows of this example. The initial contents of the lower frame give some quick instructions on what each button does (see Listing 21.11). The resulting Web page, when this is loaded into a Web browser, is shown in Figure 21.9.

Listing 21.10   WFTOP.HTM—The HTML and JavaScripts in this Web Page Allow the Manipulation of the Windows and Frames in This Example

```
<HTML>
<HEAD>
<TITLE>Windows and Frames</TITLE>
<SCRIPT LANGUAGE="JavaScript">
<!-- Hide this script from incompatible Web browsers!
function bottomColor(newColor) {
   window.parent.frames['frame2'].document.bgColor=newColor;
}
function topColor(newColor) {
   window.parent.frames['frame1'].document.bgColor=newColor;
}
function navi() {
   window.open('wfvisit.htm','Visit',
       'toolbar=no,location=no,directories=no,' +
       'status=no,menubar=no,scrollbars=no,resizable=no,' +
       'copyhistory=yes,width=600,height=200');
}
function Customize() {
var PopWindow=window.open('wfcolor.htm','Main',
       'toolbar=no,location=no,directories=no,status=no,' +
       'menubar=no,scrollbars=no,resizable=no,copyhistory=yes,' +
       'width=400,height=200');

   PopWindow.creator = self;
}
function ConfirmClose() {
   if (confirm("Are you sure you wish to exit Netscape?"))
      window.close()
```

Part
V

Ch
21

continues

Listing 21.10 Continued

```
}
<!-- -->
</SCRIPT>
</HEAD>
<BODY>
<CENTER>
<FONT COLOR=RED>
<H2>Windows and Frames</H2>
<FORM>
<INPUT TYPE="BUTTON" VALUE="Back"
    onClick="parent.frame2.history.back()">
<INPUT TYPE="BUTTON" VALUE="Visit Other Sites"
    onClick="navi()">
<INPUT TYPE="BUTTON" VALUE="Background Colors"
    onClick="Customize()">
<INPUT TYPE="BUTTON" VALUE="Forward"
    onClick="parent.frame2.history.forward()">
<INPUT TYPE="BUTTON" VALUE="Exit"
    onClick="ConfirmClose()">
</CENTER>
</FORM>
</BODY>
</HTML>
```

Listing 21.11 WFTEXT.HTM—This Informational Web Page Also Provides the Jumping-Off Point to Another Site

```
<HTML>
<HEAD>
<TITLE>Windows and Frames Text</TITLE>
</HEAD>
<BODY BGCOLOR=#FFFFFF>
<CENTER>
<H2>Welcome to Windows and Frames Using JavaScript</H2>
</CENTER>
<B>There are 5 control buttons on the control panel:<BR>
<OL><LI>Forward: Takes you to the front of the frame. (This only works
        after you actually choose to go somewhere and come back.)
    <LI>Visit Other Site: This window will let you type a site address and
        you will be able to visit that specific site.
    <LI>Background Color: Lets you choose the top and the bottom frame's
        background color.
    <LI>Back: Takes you back on a frame.
    <LI>Exit: Exits from Netscape.
</OL>
</B>
<CENTER>
Let's check the "back/forward" buttons. Let's<BR>
<FONT SIZE="+2"><A HREF="http://www.microsoft.com">Go Somewhere!!!</A>
</BODY>
</HTML>
```

FIGURE 21.9

JavaScript can use the browser `window` and `frame` objects to create and manipulate the browser and its frames.

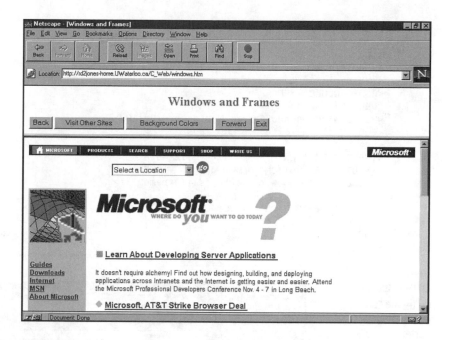

The intent of this example is to use the button bar and attached JavaScript functions of the top frame to manipulate the contents of the lower frame and the appearance of both. If you follow instructions and click the "Go Somewhere!!!" hypertext link in the lower frame, the URL included in the listing for that link (the Microsoft home page) is loaded into the lower frame (see Figure 21.10).

By using a JavaScript function `navi()`, the Visit Other Sites button creates a window and loads in the HTML document WFVISIT.HTM, shown in Listing 21.12. This document uses an HTML form to query the user for an URL (see Figure 21.11) and then makes use of the Web browser frame object to load the Web page referenced by that URL into the lower frame (see Figure 21.12).

Listing 21.12 WFVISIT.HTM—The HTML and JavaScript in This File Allow Other Web Pages to Be Loaded into the Lower Frame

```
<HTML>
<HEAD>
<TITLE>Windows and Frames Navigator</TITLE>
<SCRIPT LANGUAGE="JavaScript">
<!-- Hide this script from incompatible Web browsers!
function visit(frame) {
    if (frame == "frame2")
        open(document.getsite.site.value,frame);
    return 0;
}
```

Part

V

Ch

21

continues

Listing 21.12   Continued

```
<!-- -->
</SCRIPT>
</HEAD>
<BODY BGCOLOR=#FFFFFF>
<CENTER>
<H2><B>Windows and Frames Navigator</B></H2>
<FORM NAME="getsite" METHOD="post">
<hR>
<INPUT TYPE="TEXT" NAME="site" SIZE=50>
<INPUT TYPE="BUTTON" NAME="gobut" VALUE="Go!"
   onclick="window.close();visit('frame2')">
<HR>
<INPUT TYPE="BUTTON" VALUE="Exit" onclick="window.close()">
</FORM>
</BODY>
</HTML>
```

FIGURE 21.10

Clicking the "Go Somewhere!!!" hypertext link loads the Microsoft Web site into the lower frame.

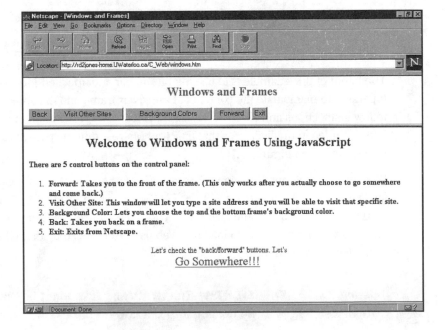

The Back and Forward buttons also call JavaScript functions which use the frame object to move the lower frame backward and forward through its history list.

Another capability given by the upper frame toolbar is the ability to specify the background colors of either the upper or lower frame. Clicking the Background Colors button creates a window and loads the HTML document shown in Listing 21.13. This window uses HTML forms option buttons to allow you to select from five choices of background color for each frame. Note that the creator object and the topColor() and bottomColor()

methods used in Listing 21.13 to change the frame colors are set up in the `Customize()` function of the WFTOP.HTM HTML document (see Listing 21.10). Because this window is created by that function, it inherits those objects and methods, and can use them to change the frame background colors (see Figure 21.13).

FIGURE 21.11
Any valid URL can be typed into this HTML form to be loaded into the lower frame of the main browser window.

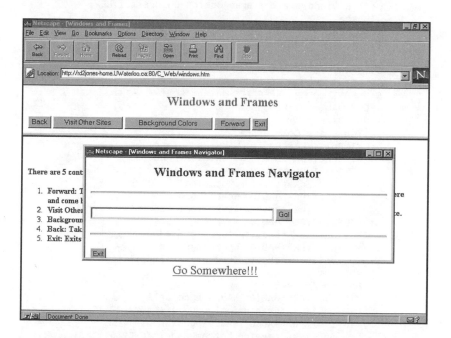

FIGURE 21.12
Once a few documents have been viewed in the lower frame, the Back and Forward buttons in the upper frames can be used.

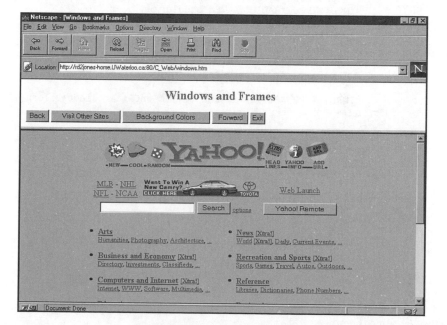

Part
V

Ch
21

Listing 21.13   WFCOLOR.HTM—JavaScript Allows You to Manipulate the Appearance of Windows and Frames That are Being Viewed

```
<HTML>
<HEAD>
<TITLE>Windows and Frames Custom Colors</TITLE>
</HEAD>
<CENTER>
1. <FONT COLOR="#000000">Black</FONT>
2. <FONT COLOR="#FF0235">Red</FONT>
3. <FONT COLOR="#6600BA">Purple</FONT>
4. <FONT COLOR="#3300CC">Blue</FONT>
5. <FONT COLOR="#FFFFFF">White</FONT>
<FORM NAME="background">
<FONT SIZE=4>
    Top Frame Colors<br>
    <INPUT TYPE="RADIO" NAME="bgcolor"
        onClick="creator.topColor('#000000')">1
    <INPUT TYPE="RADIO" NAME="bgcolor"
        onClick="creator.topColor('#FF0235')">2
    <INPUT TYPE="RADIO" NAME="bgcolor"
        onClick="creator.topColor('#6600BA')">3
    <INPUT TYPE="RADIO" NAME="bgcolor"
        onClick="creator.topColor('#3300CC')">4
    <INPUT TYPE="RADIO" NAME="bgcolor"
        onClick="creator.topColor('#ffffff')">5
    <BR>
    Bottom Frame<BR>
    <INPUT TYPE="RADIO" NAME="bgcolor"
        onClick="creator.bottomColor('#000000')">1
    <INPUT TYPE="RADIO" NAME="bgcolor"
        onClick="creator.bottomColor('#FF0235')">2
    <INPUT TYPE="RADIO" NAME="bgcolor"
        onClick="creator.bottomColor('#6600BA')">3
    <INPUT TYPE="RADIO" NAME="bgcolor"
        onClick="creator.bottomColor('#3300CC')">4
    <INPUT TYPE="RADIO" NAME="bgcolor"
        onClick="creator.bottomColor('#FFFFFF')">5
    <p>
    <INPUT TYPE="BUTTON" VALUE="Exit" onClick="window.close()">
</FONT>
</FORM>
</CENTER>
</BODY>
</HTML>
```

FIGURE 21.13

The choices in this box allow you dynamically to change the background color of each frame.

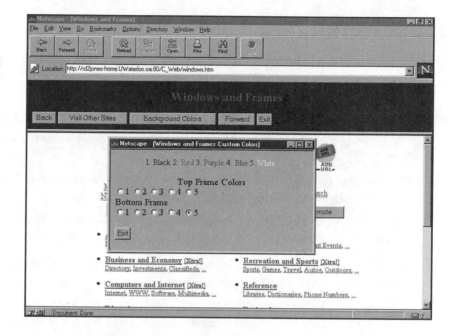

The final button of the upper frame toolbar calls for a JavaScript function which gives the user the ability to exit from the Web browser after first getting confirmation (see Figure 21.14).

FIGURE 21.14

The upper frame's Exit button includes a JavaScript confirmation dialog box.

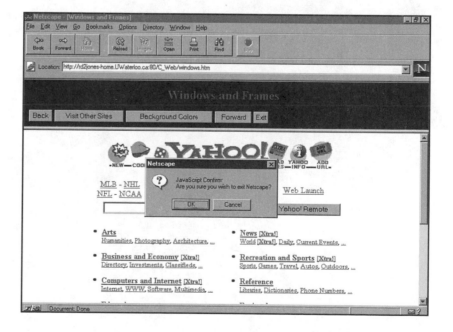

Part

V

Ch

21

From Here . . .

In the last few chapters, we've looked at ActiveX, VBScript, and JavaScript. There are two more ways of getting active content into a page, though, and we'll have a look at these next in the following chapters:

- Chapter 22, "Inserting Java Applets and Browser Plug-Ins," covers MIME media types and Netscape plug-ins, and gives you an overview of the Java programming language.

- Chapter 23, "VRML and Java," provides an introduction to the Virtual Reality Modeling Language and its connections to Java.

Or, if you've had enough active content for a while and would like to do something else, take a look at the chapters in the following parts of this book:

- Part IV, "Creating and Adapting Graphics with Microsoft Image Composer," explores the methods you use to make and modify your own graphics.

- Part VI, "Building and Managing a Web Site," shows you how to integrate the pages you create into a sophisticated, well-organized Web site that will be the envy of your neighbors in cyberspace.

## CHAPTER 22

Inserting Java Applets and Browser Plug-Ins

While HTML is the backbone of any Web page, some effects and functionality can't be added to a page with HTML itself. To get some of these sophisticated features and to provide for browsers that do and don't support them, you'll need two more tools. These are Netscape plug-ins and Java applets. In this chapter, you will learn about these components, and how you use FrontPage Editor to add them to your pages. ■

Understanding Netscape plug-ins

Get acquainted with why Netscape has plug-ins, and how the browser uses them.

About MIME media types

Knowing the media type of your content is essential when setting up a Web page.

Plug-ins on your pages

Learn the tricks of using plug-ins with FrontPage Editor to embed features in your Web page.

Java overview

Take a look at the strengths of Java, and what it means to the World Wide Web and to your Webs.

Basic Java language constructs

Assess the language itself to understand its power.

FrontPage Editor and Java Applets

Learn how to use FrontPage Editor to install Java applets in your pages and configure them.

Understanding Netscape Navigator Plug-Ins

High-end browsers such as Netscape Navigator and Microsoft Internet Explorer handle many different media types, but no browser can handle everything. Both Netscape and Microsoft have put "hooks" in their products to allow programmers to write code, which extends the media types supported by the browser. Netscape Navigator depends on "helpers" and "plug-ins." (Internet Explorer uses ActiveX technology, rather than plug-ins, to achieve similar effects.)

Starting with version 1 of Navigator, Netscape provided ways to enhance its browser with helper applications, which support data formats beyond the built-in graphics and HTML. Then, with Netscape Navigator version 2, Navigator began supporting "plug-ins," another way to extend the range of data types that can be presented on or with a Web page.

To see why plug-ins are useful, go to the desktop of a Macintosh or Windows 95 computer and double-click a few documents. If you choose a document that your system associates with a particular application, that application is launched. But if you double-click a document whose type and creator are unknown, you'll get a dialog box like the one shown in Figure 22.1.

FIGURE 22.1
A Windows 95 user is invited to "associate" a file extension with an application.

On the whole, Apple and Microsoft have developed workable schemes for mapping documents to applications. Even most UNIX vendors provide something of the same sort with the X Windows system.

But today, the user's world goes far beyond her local hard drive. The user may have files on a file server on the local area network. She may access files on a coworker's machine on the other side of the room or, through a company intranet, the other side of the world. She may also use a variety of files from the Internet.

Part

V

Ch

22

When a Netscape Navigator user attempts to open a document that Navigator does not recognize, the user gets the dialog box shown in Figure 22.2. This dialog box allows the user to select an external viewer application through the Pick App button or to save the file.

FIGURE 22.2

A Navigator user attempts to open an unrecognized file type.

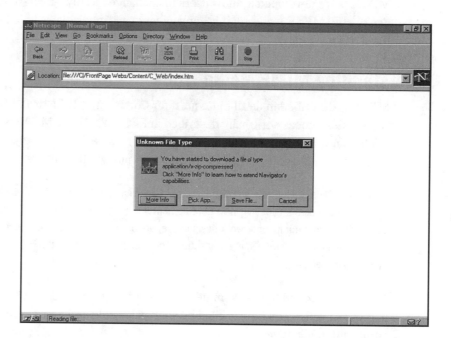

External viewers, also known as *helper applications*, allow the Web user to see a variety of data types that are not built into Netscape Navigator or other popular browsers. The downside of helper applications is that they are, indeed, applications. This means that they are fully separate programs launched outside the browser, while plug-ins work more or less seamlessly within the browser environment. Therefore, to view a file with a helper application, the user's machine must start a whole new program. This fact means the following:

- He has to wait while the new program loads.
- He may run out of memory and not be able to launch the new program.
- If the helper application launches, she sees the document in its own window, out of context from the Web document.
- There's no interaction between the Web document and the external file—for example, if the external file is a movie, there's no provision to allow the user to use buttons on the Web page to control the movie viewer.

Configuring the Server and the Browser

To understand helper applications and plug-ins, you must first understand MIME media types, formerly known as MIME types. Multimedia Internet Message Extensions, or MIME, were developed to allow users to exchange files by e-mail. While the Web does not use the full MIME standard, it is convenient to use media types to tell a Web browser how the file is formatted.

Understanding MIME Media Types

MIME is described in detail in Request for Comments (RFC) 1590. RFC 1590 updates the registration process originally described in RFC 1521. While MIME was originally intended for use in e-mail systems, and RFC 1521 was written with that application in mind, today's user encounters MIME in a variety of multimedia settings.

> **N O T E** RFCs are supervised by the Internet Engineering Task Force (IETF), which is the protocol engineering and development arm of the Internet. The IETF is a large open international community of network designers, operators, vendors, and researchers concerned with the evolution of the Internet architecture. For more information on the IETF and RFCs, go to **http://www.ietf.org/.** ▨

MIME is designed to have a limited number of top-level types, such as `application`, `text`, and `video`, which can be extended by subtypes. Table 22.1 shows some typical MIME-compliant media types.

Table 22.1   MIME Types Consist of a Type and a Subtype

Type	Subtype	Meaning
application	msword	Format of Microsoft Word documents
application	rtf	The "Rich Text Format" for word processors
application	octet-stream	A "catchall" type for a collection of bytes
application	zip	The compressed-file format of PKZIP and its kin
application	pdf	Adobe's Portable Document Format
audio	aiff	An audio interchange format developed by Apple Computer
audio	midi	A music format based on instruments
audio	wav	The RIFF WAVE sound format developed by Microsoft and IBM

Part
V
Ch
22

Type	Subtype	Meaning
image	cgm	Computer Graphics Metafile image format
image	gif	Graphics Interchange Format image format
image	jpeg	File interchange format of the Joint Photographic Experts Group
text	plain	ASCII text
text	html	The Hypertext Markup Language
video	mpeg	Video format of the Motion Picture Experts Group
video	quicktime	Format developed by Apple Computer

When a Web browser requests a document from a server, the server sends several header lines before it sends the document itself. One of the headers is Content-type. That header line contains the MIME type and subtype, separated by a slash. Thus, most Web pages are preceded by the following line:

```
Content-type: text/html
```

N O T E MIME media types are assigned by the Internet Assigned Numbers Authority (IANA) in response to a formal request process. If you plan to develop your own plug-in, check out the list of IANA-approved MIME types at **ftp://ftp.isi.edu/in-notes/iana/assignments/media-types/media-types**.

If you need a private MIME media type for use on an intranet or in a limited-distribution application, use the most appropriate type, then select a subtype that begins with the characters x-. For example, application/x-myType is an acceptable name for a private type.

For information about how to register your own media type and how to program a plug-in, see *Netscape Plug-Ins Developer's Kit* (Que Corp., 1996). ■

Configuring the FrontPage Personal Web Server for MIME Types   Most Web servers have a file that associates file extensions with MIME types. On NCSA, Apache, and similar servers, for example, the file is called mime.types.

FrontPage 97's Personal Web Server, which is a version of the NT Internet Information Server, also has such an arrangement. In a default installation, the file is C:\FrontPage Webs\Server\conf\MIME.TYP, and is a simple text file readable and editable with Notepad. A typical line is as follows:

```
text/html     html htm
```

This line tells the server that if the file has an extension of .html, the server should send text/html and text/htm in the Content-type header.

Configuring Navigator for Plug-Ins   When the Microsoft Windows version of Navigator starts, it looks in the directory that holds the Navigator executable for a directory called Programs. Inside that directory, it looks for a directory named Plug-ins. It examines the files in the plug-ins folder and reads out the MIME type. You can see which plug-ins Navigator found by choosing Help, About Plug-ins.

TIP   On a Windows machine, the names of the plug-in files must begin with the characters np or Navigator will not recognize them as plug-ins.

Later, when Navigator encounters a Content-type header with a type it does not recognize, it looks through the list of MIME types registered by the plug-ins. If it finds a match, it loads that plug-in Dynamic Link Library (DLL) into memory and passes the contents to the plug-in.

If none of the plug-ins on the list match, Navigator looks at the list of helper applications. If none of those match, Navigator starts the plug-in assisted installation process. (Figure 22.2 shows the installation dialog box.)

Using FrontPage Editor to Invoke a Navigator Plug-In

FrontPage Editor's plug-in insertion command generates the <EMBED> tag, which is recognized by both Navigator and Internet Explorer. Essentially, the <EMBED> tag is a type of link; objects specified by it are automatically downloaded and displayed when the document is displayed. To insert a plug-in, do the following:

1. Choose Insert, Other Components, Plug-in. The Plug-in Properties dialog box appears (see Figure 22.3).

2. In the Data Source box, type the path name of the data file to be loaded, or use the Browse button to locate the file. (The Data Source is the file the browser will try to read with its plug-in.)

3. In the Message box, type a message that browsers that don't use plug-ins can display.

4. Specify the size and height of the plug-in region (in pixels) that you want in the browser window. If you don't want any visible evidence of the plug-in region in the browser, mark the Hide Plug-in check box.

FIGURE 22.3
The Plug-in Properties dialog box lets you specify the behavior of the plug-in.

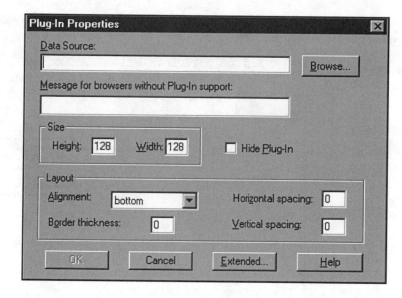

5. Use the Layout section to specify where the plug-in will sit in relation to text, its border thickness, and its spacing away from text.

6. Choose OK. A generic plug-in placeholder appears in the FrontPage Editor workspace.

The workings of such an embedded object can be a little confusing. (For this discussion, we assume a default Netscape 3.0 installation, without any third-party plug-ins.) If you plug in an object whose MIME type is supported directly by Netscape (such as a WAV file) and preview it in Netscape, a WAV audio player loads automatically with the page, and is embedded in the page from which it was called. The user can now play the file with the controls (see Figure 22.4).

This result, which comes from using the <EMBED> tag, is quite different from using a link to access the data source file: In the latter case, the WAV player appears only when the viewer clicks the link, and it is not integrated with the page on which the link resides.

An interesting side effect of making the WAV plug-in hidden is that the sound file plays automatically when the page loads in Netscape. This is a workaround for getting background sound into Netscape without using an applet, though Netscape doesn't enable you to loop the sound for continuous playback.

FIGURE 22.4
You can embed a WAV player in a Netscape-displayed page by using the <EMBED> tag.

As was noted in Chapter 6, "Enhancing Pages with Graphics and Multimedia," Netscape doesn't support inline video with AVI files, as IE 3.0 does. If you simply use the Insert, Video command to put the animation file into the page, Netscape won't display it. However, if you use a plug-in and make the data source the AVI file, Netscape will display the animation quite happily, without the user needing to click a link to go to it. Don't hide the plug-in, though, or you'll get an error message that the window would not be created.

If you use a MIME type for which the user's browser has no plug-in, an icon appears in the browser window at the plug-in location, and when the user clicks the icon she gets the message shown in Figure 22.5. In this case, the MIME type was MPEG, and the Netscape installation being used didn't have an MPEG plug-in. (Using the same page, IE 3.0 provided an MPEG player as soon as the MPEG file was downloaded.) If the user clicks the Get the Plugin button, she's linked directly to Netscape's plug-in resource site.

Browser responses to embedded data sources vary considerably with the MIME types used and the capabilities and configurations of the browsers, so you'll have to do some experimenting to get things just right.

FIGURE 22.5
Netscape asks if the user wants to download a plug-in for an unsupported MIME type.

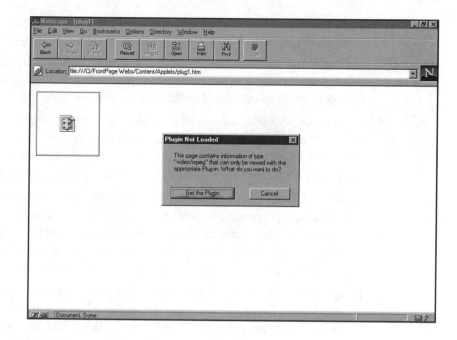

Java: An Overview

"Java," to quote Sun on the subject, "is a simple, robust, object-oriented, platform-independent, multi-threaded, dynamic, general-purpose, programming environment."

Although this rather immodest sentence was meant as a humorous reference to all of the marketing buzzwords and hoopla surrounding Java, the authors quite seriously go on to back up each of their claims. You can read the entire white paper from which this quote was taken at Sun Microsystem's Web site at **http://java.sun.com/java.sun.com/allabout.html**.

What Exactly Is Java?

The term Java can mean any of several completely different things, depending on who you talk to, such as the following:

- JavaScript—JavaScript is an adaptation of Netscape's own scripting language. It consists of Java-like commands embedded directly into your HTML document. Rather than download a precompiled Java executable (more on this later), JavaScript is interpreted on-the-fly, right along with your Web page's HTML, in-line images, and so on. Although many of the concepts and syntax in the Java language are applicable to JavaScript, the two are quite separate entities. Strictly speaking, JavaScript and Java are two separate things. Please refer to Chapter 21, "JavaScript," for a complete discussion of JavaScript.

- Stand-alone Java programs—The Java programming language was originally designed and implemented as a language for programming consumer electronics. Stand-alone Java programs do not need to be run from inside a Web page. In fact, things like URLs and the Internet don't necessarily enter into the picture at all.

  Because of Java's inherent runtime safety and platform independence, stand-alone Java language programs can easily enjoy as much success in areas such as embedded systems software and database access middleware as Java applets are already enjoying among Web developers. Two good examples of stand-alone Java programs are the HotJava Web browser and the Jigsaw HTTPD Web server.

- Java applets—The third and final use of the term Java applies to Java applets. *Applets* are specialized Java programs especially designed for executing within Internet Web pages. To run a Java applet, you need a Java-enabled Web browser such as Netscape Navigator or Microsoft's Internet Explorer. These and other Web browsers are all capable of handling standard HTML, recognizing applet tags within an HTML Web page and downloading and executing the specified Java program (or programs) in the context of a Java virtual machine.

  Java applets are a specialized subset of the overall Java development environment. Although we don't cover writing code for Java applets in this chapter (refer to Que's *Special Edition Using Java, Second Edition*), we do work through the procedure for including Java applets in your pages.

Why Java?

At the time of this writing (late 1996), the Internet is still in its infancy as a medium for dynamic mass communications.

The basic technology that makes up the Internet has been around for many years. But it was the introduction of a simple graphical user interface—the Web browser—that suddenly made it so incredibly popular among millions of users worldwide.

But most Web pages now seen on the Internet have a relatively primitive, static character. Take away all the gaudy flying logos and ticker tapes, and you're usually left with one of the following:

- Static HTML, passively displayed by your Web browser
- Simplistic HTML forms
- Graphical image maps

Although forms and image maps allow a measure of user interaction, all of the main processing is done remotely on the Web server. For any frequently used site (such as **www.netscape.com**), this incurs a considerable load on the server. Moreover, the final result of all of the server's hard work is (you guessed it!) more static HTML, which is downloaded only to be passively displayed by your Web browser.

This kind of interaction is not the style of computing preferred by a generation of users weaned on productivity tools such as VisiCalc, Aldus Pagemaker, Microsoft Word, PowerPoint, Lotus Notes, and, above all, PGA Golf. We are all used to the benefits of running our applications locally on our very own personal computers.

Java promises an alternative model for Web content—a model much closer to the spirit of computer programs people are running on their own PCs. The crucial difference between a Java-based program and a traditional PC application is that Java programs are, by nature, network-aware and truly distributed. As creatures of the Internet, Java programs offer all the benefits of locally executed programs: responsiveness, the capability to take advantage of local computing resources, and so on. Yet at the same time, Java programs break the shackles of being tied to a single PC. They can suddenly take advantage of computing resources from the entire, global Internet. You'll get a taste of this awesome potential as you continue to learn about writing Java applets.

In the context of the Web, Java applets offer the following advantages:

- Java applets are dynamic, whereas native HTML is relatively static.
- Because they run on the client, not on the server, Java applets can make better use of computing resources.
- Java is designed to be "architecture-neutral." This is the software equivalent of "one size fits all." For vendors, it means larger potential markets, fewer inventory headaches, and the elimination of costly software porting efforts. For consumers, it means lower costs, increased choices, and greater interoperability between components.
- Although other languages can be considered architecture-neutral, Java programs can typically execute much faster and more efficiently.

  Because a Java program consists of bytecodes, it tends to be smaller and lends itself better to transferring across the Internet. The bytecode scheme also lends itself to far greater levels of runtime optimization than scripting languages. The *Just In Time* Java compilers built into newer Web browsers can make Java programs run almost as fast as native executables.

Basic Language Constructs

Java syntax is very similar to C and C++. At first glance, this makes the language immediately accessible to the millions of practicing C/C++ programmers. However, though Java and C look very much alike, they are not identical, and sometimes apparent similarities can be misleading.

The following four tables, 22.2 through 22.5, summarize Java's basic language constructs.

Table 22.2   Basic Language Constructs (Java Types)

Type	Example	Notes
boolean	`boolean flag = false;`	A Java `boolean` is just `true` or `false`. It cannot be cast to `char` or `int`
char	`char c[] = {'A','\uu42','C'};`	A Java `char` is a 16-bit Unicode character. You'll usually use the Java class `String` instead
byte	`byte b = 0x7f;`	8-bit signed integer (–127 .. 127)
short	`short s = 32767;`	16-bit signed integer (–32,768 .. 32767)
int	`int i = 2;`	32-bit signed integer
long	`long l = 2L;`	64-bit signed integer. Note the suffix L is be required for a `long` (decimal) literal
float	`float x = 2.0F;`	32-bit IEEE754 number. Note the suffix F is required for a `float` literal
double	`double d = 2.0;`	64-bit IEEE754 number (15 significant digits)

TIP Java is a *strongly typed* language. You must explicitly declare the "type" of every single variable that you use, and you can't arbitrarily mix or interconvert types as easily as you can in C++ or Basic.

Java was deliberately engineered this way. In the long run, the use of strong typing tends to eliminate many common bugs and yield safer, more robust software products. But for novice Java programmers, the compiler's strict typing rules can be a source of frustration.

The easiest way to deal with this problem is to focus on *classes* instead of primitive data types. By thinking at this higher level (at the *class* level), you'll probably need fewer primitive types and they'll be less likely to interact with each other in troublesome ways. By forcing yourself to think in terms of Java classes, you'll save yourself some headaches, and you'll probably end up with simpler, more robust program designs, too!

Table 22.3   Basic Language Constructs (Java Operators)

Operator	Description
.	Member selection
[]	Array subscript
()	Parenthesis/Function call
--, --	Auto-increment/Auto-decrement
*, /, %	Arithmetic: multiply, divide, modulo
+, -,	Arithmetic: add, subtract
<<, >>, >>>	Bitwise: shift left, arithmetic shift right and logical shift right
<=, <, >, >=	Equality: less than or equal to, less than, greater than, greater than or equal to
==, !=	Equality: equal to, not equal to
&, |, ^, ~	Bitwise: AND, OR, Exclusive Or (XOR) and NOT
&&, ||, !	Logical: AND, OR and NOT
? :	Conditional expression
=	Simple assignment
*=,/=, %=, +=, -=, &=,	Complex assignment
|=, ^=, <<=, >>=,>>>=	

TIP   The operators in Table 22.3 are arranged in order of precedence. For example, the compiler will treat the expression 2 + 2 * 2 ^ 2 as 2 + (2 * (2 ^ 2)) by executing 2 X OR 2 first, 2 * the result next, and so on.

In your own Java code, always make liberal use of parentheses to state explicitly the order in which you want the operations in your expression to be carried out. Using parentheses instead of relying on the default precedence hierarchy will help you avoid a common source of bugs.

Table 22.4   Basic Language Constructs (Control Flow)

Construct	Example
if...then...else	if (i >= salesGoal) { ... }
for	for (i = 0; i < maxItems; i++) {...}
while	while (i < salesGoal) { ... }
do...while	do { ... } while (i < salesGoal);
switch (...) case	switch (i) { case 1: ... break; }
break	while (i < salesGoal) { if (I==10) break;...}
continue	while (i < salesGoal) { if (I==10) continue; ... }
labeled break	while (i < salesGoal) { if (I==10) break my_label;...}

Table 22.5   Basic Language Constructs (Java Comments)

Comment style	Format	Notes
C comments	/* ... */	Can span multiple lines
C++ comments	// ...	Comment stops at the end of the line: less prone to error
Javadoc comments	/** ... */	Appropriate for header comments: lets you autogenerate program documentation

ON THE WEB

http://java.sun.com/newdocs.html   This site will give you all the details on Sun's official Java documentation, including reference manuals and language tutorials.

Leveraging Java Classes and Packages

Although operators and data types are obviously very important in Java, classes are where the real action is.

In his book, *Object-Oriented Modeling and Design*, James Rumbaugh defined a "class" as describing "...a group of objects with similar properties (attributes), common behavior (operations), common relationships to other objects, and common semantics." An object, on the other hand, is simply an *instance* of a class, dynamically created by the program during runtime. In other words, *classes* are definitions, *objects* are the real thing.

In Java, everything is a class. Unlike C and C++, Java has no structs and no free subprograms (a "free subprogram" is a subroutine or function that exists independently of a class). Most of the power of C++ stems from the simple notion of extending C's basic struct into the notion of a C++ class, which encapsulates both state (program data) and methods (a program's algorithms) into a single logical entity. Java completes this transition by recognizing that, after you have the power of classes, structs become irrelevant.

Java was designed to be both a simpler and a safer language than C++. Many features of C++ such as multiple inheritance were deliberately left out of Java because Java's authors felt that they could make their new language less complex and make Java programs less prone to common C++ programming and design errors.

Table 22.6 gives a brief overview of Java classes in comparison to C++.

Table 22.6   Java Class versus C++ Class Constructs

Construct	C++	Java
Class	Yes	Yes
Single Inheritance	Yes	Yes
Multiple Inheritance	Yes	No
Constructors	Yes	Yes
Destructors	Yes	No
Templates	Yes	No
Packages	No	Yes
Interfaces	No	Yes

Basically, traditional methods force you to think like the machine and break things down into modules, variables, parameters, and the like. Object-oriented methods allow you to think at a much higher level—in terms of objects, their behavior, and how they relate to each other.

The interesting thing is that Java (unlike, for example, C++) forces you to think in an object-oriented style. When you work with Java, you will probably find yourself spending most of your development time figuring out what objects your program needs, and browsing to see if your library already has existing (canned) classes that you can inherit from, thus reusing existing code with little or no additional effort on your part.

This is a marked contrast from traditional programming styles in languages such as FOR-TRAN, C, or Pascal, where the bulk of your effort goes into "decomposing" a problem into modules, then creating algorithms the modules use to process data. In many subtle (and many not-so-subtle) ways, Java almost forces the programmer to abandon old procedural habits in favor of a more object-oriented perspective.

We'll return to this discussion later. For now, let's get on with the fun stuff—coding and running our very first Java applet.

Where to Get Java Tools

At this writing, Java is so new that there are relatively few decent tools for creating Java applications. Symantec's Cafe Lite, Borland C++ 5.0, and Microsoft Visual J++ come immediately to mind as excellent, GUI-based development tools. If you want to start with the basics, the original Java tools are freely available from the creators of Java, Sun Microsystems. These tools are as follows:

- javac—The Java compiler
- appletviewer—A Java virtual machine for testing and debugging your applet
- javadoc—Automatically generates an online manual documenting your program's classes

You can download a free copy of the Java Developer Kit at **http://www.javasoft.com/**.

 Java requires a 32-bit operating system and support for long, case-sensitive file names. In the PC arena, Java supports only Windows 95 or Windows NT.

Using FrontPage Editor and Java Applets

The above was an overview of Java, to help you decide whether you want to pursue learning the language or not. In the following, we assume you've learned it and have written, compiled, and tested a few Java applets. Now it's time to use FrontPage Editor to add them to your pages. To do this, use the following procedure:

1. Copy the applet file into the same folder as the page that will include the applet. (The applet file likely has the extension .class or .cla; but see the next Caution.) Also, copy into this folder any other files the applet needs to work properly.
2. Choose Insert, Other Components, Java Applet. The Java Applet Properties dialog box appears.
3. Type the name of the source file into the Applet Source box, and the Applet Base URL if the applet isn't stored in the Web site's root folder.

4. In the Message for Browsers without Java Support box, type an appropriate message.

5. Use the Applets Parameters section to add any required parameter values needed by the applet. Because Java does not provide a mechanism for displaying what the parameters and values are for a given applet, you'll have to consult the documentation that comes with the applet (if you didn't write it yourself) to learn the correct parameter names and the legal values for each parameter.

6. Type values for the applet's size and layout into the appropriate boxes, then choose OK. A placeholder for the applet appears.

7. Use the Preview in Browser command to test the applet.

The calculator applet is a simple applet in the sense that it doesn't use any parameters to modify its appearance or behavior. The HTML code to insert the applet into the page is the following example:

```
<applet code="PocketCalc.class" width="395" height="179"></applet>
```

Note that the values for the width and height of the applet, in pixels, must be specified using the Applet Properties dialog box. This is because the screen area needed by an applet isn't detected automatically by FrontPage Editor; you have to get this information from the applet documentation and add it by hand.

> **CAUTION**
>
> When typing the name into the Applet Properties dialog box, you have to preserve the case and spelling exactly as it is given in the applet documentation. Renaming the applet file in FrontPage Explorer and using that name in the page will cause errors. This is especially important to remember if you unzipped a downloaded applet with an unzip utility that doesn't preserve case or long file names. If this happens, you must restore the correct case and file name before using the applet. In the previous example, the correct applet name is PocketCalc.class. Calling the applet with pocketca.cla will not work, even if that's the way the applet's name appears in the Web folder.

The upper applet is military time with white LEDs on a black background; the lower is 24-hour time with red LEDs on a white background. The HTML coding for the upper applet is as follows:

```
<applet code="curtime.class" align="absmiddle"
width="126" height="37">
<param name="LEDColor"value="255,255,255">
<param name="MilitaryTime" value="0">
Clock
</applet>
```

Clock in the code is the text that is displayed by browsers that don't support Java. The HTML for the lower applet is as follows:

```
<applet code="curtime.class" align="absmiddle" width="94"
height="37">
<param name="24HourTime" value="1">
<param name="BackColor" value="255,255,255">
<param name="LEDColor" value="255,0,0">
Clock
</applet>
```

For a third and still more elaborate example, consider the following marquee applet.

The HTML code for the display as shown is the following:

```
<applet code="KzmScroll.class" align="baseline" width="350"
height="40">
<param name="copyright" value="Alex 'Kazuma' Garbagnati, kazuma@energy.it">
<param name="delay" value="50">
<param name="font" value="Arial">
<param name="fontbold" value="1">
<param name="fontsize" value="24">
<param name="message" value="SCROLLING TEXT">
<param name="rect_color" value="0 200 128">
<param name="shift" value="2">
<param name="text_color" value="255 255 255">
</applet>
```

The names of the parameters are defined by the applet code; you have no control over these names. There may be required or out-of-bounds values for some parameters, so check the applet documentation. As is clear from the preceding examples, you don't have to write your own applets to begin experimenting with them. There is a growing number of applets, which you can use in your own pages, available for download from the Web. The following are a few of those applet sites:

Gamelan: **http://www.gamelan.com**

Java Applet Rating Service (JARS): **http://www.jars.com/25.htm**

Cup O'Joe: **http://www.cupojoe.com/applets/**

Café Del Sol (Sun Microsystems): **http://www.xm.com/cafe/**

From Here...

As you can see from the last few chapters, there are now some very powerful tools for integrating active content into Web pages. As the Web develops, such content will become more and more widespread. Active page components do require a lot of bandwidth, though, so remember to use them only when they truly enhance your site. But now it's time to move on, so you can head for the following:

- Chapter 23, "VRML and Java" provides an introduction to the Virtual Reality Modeling Language and its connections to Java.

- Chapter 24, "Building a Web" is where you get down to the business of starting a new Web site using the FrontPage 97 New Web Wizard to help you get up and running quickly and efficiently.

- Chapter 25, "FrontPage's Templates and Wizards," shows you around the creation of specialized Web sites for customer support, projects, and discussion groups.

## CHAPTER 23

VRML and Java

The World Wide Web is about to evolve from a strictly two-dimensional medium into one filled with 3D graphics and multiuser interactivity. The key technology that will enable this evolution to occur is called VRML.

In this chapter you'll learn the basic elements of VRML, as well as how to use it to create some exciting content for the World Wide Web. You'll also see how Java can be used to enhance VRML worlds. ■

What VRML Is All About

Learn where VRML came from and where it's going.

Using VRML with FrontPage

Link your FrontPage documents to VRML worlds.

VRML 2.0 Data Structures and Syntax

Learn how VRML works and take a look at the actual syntax of the language.

Coordinate Systems and Transforms

Transforms are used to position, scale, and rotate objects in a three-dimensional world.

Shapes, Sounds, and Lights

Discover the basic building blocks of every VRML world.

What VRML Is All About

VRML is the standard file format for creating 3D graphics on the World Wide Web. Just as HTML is used for text, JPEG and GIF are used for images, WAV is for sounds, and MPEG is used for moving pictures, VRML is used to store information about 3D scenes. VRML files are stored on ordinary Web servers and are transferred using HTTP.

VRML files have a MIME type of x-world/x-vrml, although this is expected to change to model/vrml in the near future. These files have an extension of .WRL. A three-character extension is used in order to avoid the confusion that might be caused by PC-based servers which truncate extensions at three characters (as happened with HTM versus HTML). It's important that your Web server be configured to serve a file with an extension of .WRL as either x-world/x-vrml or model/vrml; see the section on server configuration elsewhere in this book.

When a user retrieves a VRML file (by clicking on a link in an HTML document, for example), the file is transferred onto the user's machine and a VRML browser is invoked. In most cases, the VRML browser is implemented as a plug-in. Once the scene is loaded, the VRML browser allows the user to travel through it at will, with no further data being transferred from the server.

Starting with version 3.0 of Netscape, VRML support is included as part of the standard distribution. Microsoft recently licensed a VRML browser and will be including it with Internet Explorer. This will put VRML onto a lot of desktops in a very short time.

A Brief History of VRML

The basic idea for VRML originated with Mark Pesce back in 1993. He saw the potential for 3D graphics on the Web, and realized that a standard file format would be needed. He got together with Tony Parisi, and together they created Labyrinth, the first crude 3D Web browser. They demonstrated it at the very first conference on the World Wide Web, and they received an enthusiastic response from everyone they showed it to.

The next step was the creation of an electronic mailing list, which *Wired* magazine offered to host. After several months of discussion, it was decided to base the first version of the VRML file format on an existing language. Several proposals were put forward, and OpenInventor from Silicon Graphics Incorporated (SGI) was selected.

OpenInventor was extremely large and complex, so a subset of the language was used and extensions were added to make it suitable for use on the Web. Gavin Bell of SGI joined

Pesce and Parisi in writing the specifications for VRML 1.0, and people all over the world set about creating VRML browsers.

As time went by, problems began to emerge. By using OpenInventor as its foundation, VRML 1.0 inherited some of that language's weaknesses. The state-accumulation approach that is part and parcel of OpenInventor turned out to be difficult to implement on many platforms. It was also difficult to implement the full lighting model that the spec required. No two VRML browsers would produce exactly the same results for a given scene.

More importantly, VRML 1.0 lacked a lot of features. There was no sound, no interactivity, and no movement of any kind. VRML quickly earned the nickname "Virtual Reality Museum Language," because it was well suited for building museums, and not much else. Clearly, something needed to be done.

Part
V

Ch
23

N O T E The decision to avoid specifying a programming language in VRML 1.0 was a deliberate one. Even in hindsight, it was probably the right choice. Selecting a language would have been a nightmare, because everybody has different ideas about what features such a language should have. Bear in mind that VRML 1.0 was developed before Java had made its presence felt. If it had been available at the time that VRML 1.0 was being formalized, Java would doubtless have been chosen as the behavior language. ■

The limitations and problems of VRML 1.0 were clear enough that work began immediately on the creation of VRML 2.0. It was generally agreed that trying to "fix" VRML 1.0 would be a difficult chore and that a major redesign was required. Half a dozen proposals came in, including some from Microsoft, IBM, Apple, SGI, and Sun. After much discussion and debate, the "Moving Worlds" proposal was selected as the basis for VRML 2.0.

VRML 2.0 resembles VRML 1.0 in syntax, although the semantics are very different.

CAUTION
This chapter deals only with VRML 2.0. I would strongly advise against creating any more VRML 1.0 content at this point, since most VRML browsers will just have to spend time converting your world to 2.0 format before displaying it.

Using VRML with FrontPage

You can link from your Web document to a VRML world as easily as you would link to any other type of document on the Web. Within FrontPage, choose Edit, Hyperlink, or click the Create or Edit Hyperlink button on the toolbar. The Create Link dialog box should appear. When it does, click the World Wide Web tab, and enter the URL of the VRML file into the URL field. Make sure you include the .WRL extension. Finish creating the link as you would normally.

That's all there is to it. When a user clicks on the link you've created, her browser will automatically transfer the VRML world from the server and start up the appropriate plug-in to let the user view the world and navigate through it.

Creating the link is the easy part; building the world itself is much more complex. The rest of this chapter will focus on how to create VRML 2.0 worlds from scratch, using nothing more than a text editor such as Notepad. If you don't want to learn the intricacies of VRML, there are a number of useful VRML authoring tools available; see the VRML Repository **(http://sdsc.edu/vrml)** for a complete list.

Once you've built your world, you can simply put it on your Web site the way you would an HTML document, a GIF or JPEG image, or a WAV file.

An Introduction to VRML 2.0

VRML is a large and powerful scene-description language, so it isn't possible to cover it in any detail in this one chapter. However, this chapter will give you at least a basic understanding of the language. If you need to create more sophisticated VRML worlds (and you will!), you should refer to the upcoming second edition of Que's *Special Edition Using VRML.*

Basic Scene Structure

A VRML file describes a three-dimensional scene. The basic VRML data structure is an inverted tree that is composed of *nodes*, as shown in Figure 23.1.

Notice that there are two basic types of nodes: *leaf* and *grouping*. If you're acquainted with the DOS or UNIX file systems, this will be a familiar concept: Leaf nodes are like files, and grouping nodes are like directories (or folders, if you're on a Macintosh). Each grouping node can contain leaf nodes and additional grouping nodes. The result looks like an inverted tree.

Leaf nodes generally correspond to the sorts of things you'd expect to find in a 3D world: shapes, sounds, lights, and so forth. They have a direct effect on your experience of the virtual world, by being either visible or audible. A table or chair might be represented by a Shape node, the ticking of a clock would be created using a Sound node, and the scene would be made visible using one or more Lighting nodes.

FIGURE 23.1
This diagram shows
the basic VRML scene
structure.

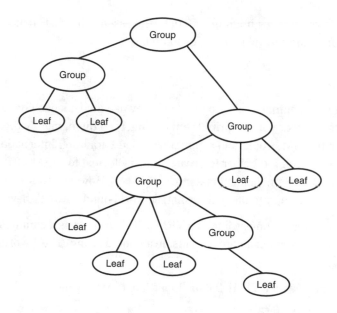

Grouping nodes, on the other hand, are completely invisible. You can't see a grouping node when you view a VRML world, but it's there and it has an effect on the positioning and visibility of the leaf nodes below it in the tree. The most common type of grouping node is a Transform, which is used to position shapes, sounds, and lights in the virtual world.

Nodes that are attached to another node are referred to as the *children* of that node, and that node is the *parent* of each of the children. Occasionally, nodes that share a common parent are referred to as *siblings*. Note that in VRML 2.0, the order of children is generally irrelevant, because sibling nodes don't affect each other the way they did in VRML 1.0. However, the ordering of children is still important in certain types of grouping nodes, such as Switch or LOD, which are beyond the scope of this chapter.

There are also nodes that are not really "in" the tree structure, although they're stored there for the sake of convenience. Among these nodes is the Script node, which will be examined in detail in the second half of this chapter.

There are a number of different types of nodes in VRML 2.0 (54 at last count!), and it's possible to define new nodes using the "prototype" mechanism. Each of these nodes does something specific; fortunately, you don't have to learn very many of them in order to start building simple VRML worlds.

Each type of node has a set of fields that contain values. For example, a Lighting node would have a field that specifies the intensity of the light. If you change the value of that field, the light changes brightness. That's the essence of what "behavior" in VRML is all about—changing the values of fields in nodes.

VRML Syntax

VRML files are human-readable text, and they use the Unicode character set. Because these files are text, you can print them out and read them, modify them with a text editor, and so forth. IBM, Apple, and a company called Paragraph International have announced that they're working together to create a binary format for VRML 2.0, which will make VRML files much smaller and faster to download. However, this format will still be semantically equivalent to the text format, so world-builders won't have to worry about it.

Everything after a # on any line of a VRML file is treated as a comment and ignored. The only exception is when a # appears inside a quoted string. The # works just like / / in a Java program.

The first line of every VRML 2.0 file looks like the following:

```
#VRML V2.0 utf8
```

Notice that this first line begins with a #, so it's a comment. The V2.0 means, "This file conforms to Version 2.0 of the VRML specification." The utf8 refers to the character set encoding.

The rest of the file consists mostly of nodes, as described previously. Each node contains a number of fields that store the node's data, and each field has a specific type. For example, Listing 23.1 shows a typical PointLight node.

Listing 23.1   A *PointLight* Node

```
PointLight
    {
    on TRUE
    intensity 0.75
    location 10 -12 7.5
    color 0.5 0.5 0
    }
```

This node contains four fields. The fact that they're on separate lines is irrelevant; VRML is completely free-format, and anywhere you can have a space, you can also have a tab or a new line. You could just as easily have said:

```
PointLight { on TRUE intensity 0.75 location 10 -12 7.5 color 0.5 0.5 0 }
```

but it would have been harder to read.

The word `PointLight` indicates what type of node this is. The words `on`, `intensity`, `location`, and `color` are field names, and each is followed by a value. Notice that the values are different for each field; the `on` field is a Boolean value (called an `SFBool` in VRML), and in this case, it has the value TRUE. The `intensity` field is a floating-point number (an `SFFloat` in VRML terminology). The `location` is a *vector*—a set of X, Y, and Z values (called an `SFVec3f` in VRML), and the `color` is an SFColor containing the red, green, and blue components of the light.

In other words, the point light source is turned on at 75 percent of its maximum intensity. It's located at 10 meters along the positive X axis (right), 12 meters along the negative Y axis (down), and 7.5 meters along the positive Z axis (toward us). It's a reddish-green color, because the red and green values are each at 50 percent of their maximum value and the blue value is set to zero.

Note that any fields which aren't given values have default values assigned to them, as described in the VRML specification. For example, you could have left out the `on` TRUE because the `on` field has TRUE as its default value.

You can assign a name to a node using the DEF (for "define") syntax. For example:

```
DEF Fizzbin PointLight { intensity 0.5 }
```

would create a `PointLight` and assign it the name `Fizzbin`. You'll see later in this chapter, when we discuss "Instancing," how these names get used.

Types of Fields

VRML supports a number of different types of fields, many of which correspond to data types in Java. Table 23.1 shows the correspondence between Java types and VRML types.

Table 23.1   The Correspondence between Java Types and VRML Types

Java Type	VRML Type
boolean	SFBool
float	SFFloat
int	SFInt32
String	SFString

As mentioned previously, there are also special data types for 3D vectors (`SFVec3f`), colors (`SFColor`), and rotations (`SFRotation`). There are also 2D vectors (`SFVec2f`). A special data type is used for time (`SFTime`) and another for bitmapped images (`SFImage`).

In addition to these single-valued fields (which is what the SF prefix stands for), there are multiple-valued versions of most of the fields (which begin with MF). These multiple-valued fields are arrays of values; for example, an array of vectors would be an MFVec3f. If more than one value is specified for a particular field, the values are surrounded by square brackets, like the following:

```
point [ 0 0 0, 1.3 2.57 -14, 12 17 4.2 ]
```

One other field type that turns out to be very useful is SFNode, which allows fields to have a node as their value. There's also an MFNode, for a field whose value is an array of nodes.

The complete list of VRML 2.0 field types is shown in Table 23.2.

Table 23.2   VRML 2.0 Field Types

VRML Type	Description
SFBool	TRUE or FALSE value
SFInt32	32-bit integer value
SFFloat	Floating-point number
SFString	Character string in double quotes
SFTime	Floating-point number giving the time in seconds
SFVec2f	Two-element vector (used for texture map coordinates)
SFVec3f	Three-element vector (locations, vertices, and more)
SFRotation	Four numbers: a three-element vector plus an angle
SFColor	Three numbers: the red, green, and blue components
SFImage	Bitmapped image
SFNode	A VRML node
MFInt32	Array of 32-bit integers
MFFloat	Array of floating-point numbers
MFString	Array of double-quoted strings
MFVec2f	Array of two-element vectors
MFVec3f	Array of three-element vectors
MFRotation	Array of four-element rotations
MFColor	Array of colors
MFNode	Array of nodes

Coordinate Systems and Transformations

Because VRML describes scenes in three dimensions, you need to understand how 3D coordinate systems work in order to use VRML effectively. Figure 23.2 illustrates the coordinate system used by VRML.

FIGURE 23.2
The coordinate system used by VRML is based on X, Y, and Z axes.

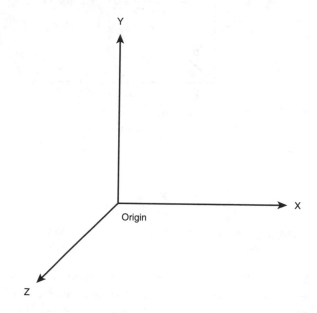

Anyone who's ever looked at an X-Y graph will find this coordinate system familiar. The X axis goes from left to right, and the Y axis goes from bottom to top. What's new is the Z axis, which extends from the X-Y plane toward the viewer. The place where all three axes intersect is called the *origin*.

Translation

Every point in 3D space can be specified using three numbers: the coordinates along the X, Y, and Z axes. In VRML, distances are always represented in meters (a meter is about three feet). If a particular point in a VRML world is at (15.3 27.2 -4.2), then it's 15.3 meters along the X axis, 27.2 meters along the Y axis, and 4.2 meters backwards along the Z axis. This is illustrated in Figure 23.3.

Moving a point in space is referred to as *translation*. This is one of the three basic operations you can perform with a Transform node; the other two are *scaling* and *rotation*.

FIGURE 23.3
The point (15.3 27.2 -4.2) is shown in the VRML coordinate system.

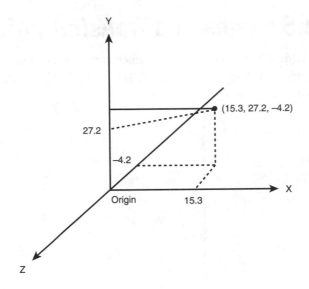

Scaling

Scaling means changing the size of an object. Just as you can translate objects along the X, Y, and Z axes, you can also scale them along each of those axes.

Scaling is always represented by three numbers, which are the amount to stretch the object along the X, Y, and Z axes, respectively. A value greater than 1.0 makes the object larger along that axis, and a value less than 1.0 makes it smaller. If you don't want to stretch or shrink an object along a particular axis at all, use a factor of 1.0 (as was done for the Z axis in the sphere example above).

Rotation

Rotation is more complex than scaling or translation. Rotation always takes place around an axis, but the axis doesn't have to be aligned with one of the axes of the coordinate system. Any arbitrary vector pointing in any direction can be the axis of rotation, and the angle is the amount to rotate the object around that axis. The angle is measured in *radians*. Because there are 3.14159 radians in 180 degrees, you convert degrees to radians by multiplying by 3.14159/180, or about 0.01745.

Transformations

Translation, rotation, and scaling are all *transformations*. VRML stores these transformations in the Transform node that was discussed earlier. A single Transform can store a translation, a rotation, a scaling operation, or any combination of them. That is, a `Transform` node can scale the nodes below it in the tree, rotate them, translate them, or any combination of the above. The sequence of operations is always the same: The objects in the subtree are first scaled, then rotated, and then translated to their final location. For example, Listing 23.2 shows what a typical `Transform` node might look like.

Part

V

Ch

23

Listing 23.2 A Typical *Transform* Node

```
Transform
    {
    scale 1 2 3
    rotation 0 1 0 0.7854
    translation 10 0.5 -72.1
    children
        [
        PointLight { }
        Shape { geometry Sphere { } }
        ]
    }
```

This particular `Transform` node has four fields: `scale`, `rotation`, `translation`, and `children`. The `scale` and `translation` fields are vectors (`SFVec3f`), and the `rotation` is an `SFRotation` (consisting of a three-element vector and a floating-point rotation in radians).

Because `Transform` is a grouping node, it has children that are stored in its `children` field. The children are themselves nodes—in this case, a point light source and a shape whose geometry is a sphere (you'll find out more about these things later in this chapter). Both the light and the shape have their location, orientation, and scale set by the fields of the `Transform`. For example, the sphere is scaled by (1 2 3), then rotated by 0.7854 radians around the Y axis (0 1 0). Finally, it's translated 10 meters along X, half a meter along Y, and negative 72.1 meters along Z.

The full `Transform` node is actually more complex than this, because it can specify a center of rotation and an axis for scaling. Those features are beyond the scope of this chapter. There's also a version of `Transform` called `Group`, which simply groups nodes together without performing any transformations on them.

Transformation Hierarchies

Each `Transform` node defines a new coordinate system or frame of reference. The scaling, rotation, and translation are all relative to the parent coordinate system. For example, consider Figure 23.4.

FIGURE 23.4

Transformations and
coordinate systems
are key ideas in VRML.

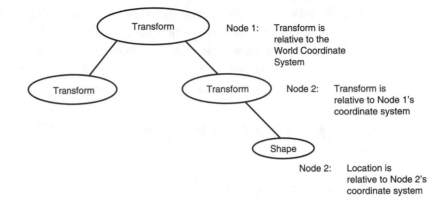

FIGURE 23.5

The transformation
hierarchy for a pool
table.

A typical VRML world has a number of different coordinate systems within it. There's the world coordinate system, of course, but a coordinate system also exists for each Transform node in the world. To understand how all this works, take a look at Figure 23.5.

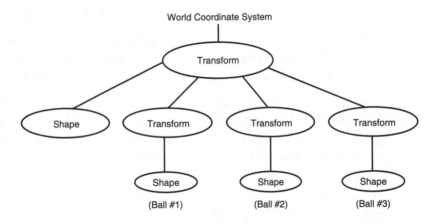

The top-level Transform node is used to position the pool table itself in the world coordinate system; this positioning might involve scaling the table, rotating it to a different orientation, and translating it to a suitable location. Each of the balls on the table has its own Transform node for positioning the ball on the table. Each ball, therefore, has its own little coordinate system that is embedded within the coordinate system of the pool table. As the balls move, they move relative to the table's frame of reference. Similarly, the table's coordinate system is embedded within the coordinate system of the room.

Each of these coordinate systems has its own origin. The coordinate system for each ball might have its origin at the geometric center of the ball itself. The coordinate system of the table might have its origin at the geometric center of the table. The coordinate system of the room might have its origin in the corner near the door. The `Transform` nodes define the relationships between these coordinate systems. Listing 23.3 shows this transformation hierarchy as it would appear in a VRML file.

Listing 23.3   A Pool Table and Balls

```
#VRML V2.0 utf8

DirectionalLight { direction -1 -1 -1 }
DirectionalLight { direction 1 1 1 }

Transform {
    translation 5 1 2    # location of pool table in room
    children [
        Shape {  # Pool table
            appearance Appearance {
                material Material { diffuseColor 0 1 0 }
            }
            geometry Box { size 6 0.1 4 }
        }
        Transform {
            translation 0 0.35 0.75
            children [
                Shape {
                    appearance Appearance {
                        material Material { diffuseColor 1 0 0 }
                    }
                    geometry Sphere { radius 0.3 }
                }
            ]
        }
        Transform {
            translation 1.5 0.35 0
            children [
                Shape {
                    appearance Appearance {
                        material Material { diffuseColor 0 0 1 }
                        }
                    geometry Sphere { radius 0.3 }
                }
            ]
        }
        Transform {
            translation -0.9 0.35 0.45
            children [
                Shape {
                    appearance Appearance {
                        material Material { diffuseColor 1 0 1 }
```

continues

Part

V

Ch

23

Listing 23.3   Continued

```
                }
                geometry Sphere { radius 0.3 }
            }
        ]
    }
  ]
}
```

Notice that there are `Transform` nodes in the `children` field of another `Transform` node; this is how the transformation hierarchy is represented.

Understanding how coordinate systems work in VRML is very, very important. When you start animating your VRML world using Java, you'll often be moving and rotating objects by altering the fields of their `Transform` nodes.

Shapes

Among the most common of the leaf nodes is `Shape`. The `Shape` node is used to create visible objects. Everything you see in a VRML scene is created with a `Shape` node.

The `Shape` node has only two fields: `geometry` and `appearance`. The `geometry` field specifies the geometric description of the object, while the `appearance` field gives its surface properties. Listing 23.4 shows a typical `Shape` node:

Listing 23.4   An Example of a *Shape* Node

```
Shape
    {
    geometry Sphere { radius 2 }
    appearance Appearance { material Material { diffuseColor 1 0 0 } }
    }
```

This example creates a red sphere with a radius of two meters. The `geometry` field has a type of `SFNode`, and in this case it has a `Sphere` node as its value. The `Sphere` has a `radius` field with a value of 2.0 meters.

The `appearance` field can take only one type of node as its value: an `Appearance` node. The `Appearance` node has several fields, one of which is illustrated here: the `material` field. The `material` field can take only a `Material` node as its value. At first these `appearance` `Appearance` and `material` `Material` sequences may seem very odd and redundant, but as you'll see later, these sequences actually turn out to be useful. The other fields of the

Appearance node allow us to specify a texture map to use for the shape and information about how the texture map should be scaled, rotated, and translated. You'll learn more about the Appearance node in a later section, under "Appearance."

The Material node specifies only one field in this example: the diffuseColor of the sphere. In this case, it has a red component of 1.0 and a value of 0.0 for each of the green and blue components. As you'll see later in this chapter, the Material node can also specify the shininess, transparency, and other surface properties of the shape.

Geometry

There are 10 geometric nodes in VRML. Four of them are straightforward: Sphere, Cone, Cylinder, and Box. There's also a Text node that creates large text in a variety of fonts and styles, an ElevationGrid node that's handy for terrain, and an Extrusion node that allows surfaces of extrusion or revolution to be created. Finally, the PointSet, IndexedLineSet, and IndexedFaceSet nodes let you get right down to the point, line, and polygon level.

Sphere, Cone, Cylinder, and Box   The Sphere node has a radius field that gives the size of the sphere in meters. Remember that this is a radius, not a diameter; the default 1.0 value produces a sphere that's two meters across.

A Cone has a bottomRadius field that gives the radius of the base of the cone. It also has a height and a pair of flags (side and bottom) that indicate whether the sides and/or bottom should be visible.

Like the Cone, the Cylinder node has fields that indicate which parts are visible: bottom, side, and top. This node also has a height and a radius.

The Box node is simple: it has only a size field, which is a three-element vector (an SFVec3f) that gives the X, Y, and Z dimensions of the box. In VRML 1.0, Box was called Cube. That name was misleading, though, because the sides are not necessarily all the same length.

ElevationGrid, Extrusion, and Text   The ElevationGrid node is useful for creating terrain; it stores an array of heights (Y values) that are used to generate a polygonal representation of the landscape. This data is sometimes referred to as a heightfield.

The Extrusion node takes a 2D cross-section and extrudes it along a path (open or closed) to form a three-dimensional shape.

The Text node creates flat, 2D text that can be positioned and oriented in the three-dimensional world.

Points, Lines, and Faces   The PointSet node is useful for creating a cloud of individual points, and the IndexedLineSet node is handy for creating geometry that consists entirely of line segments.

However, the most important and widely used geometric node is the IndexedFaceSet. This node allows you to specify any arbitrary shape by listing the vertices of which it's composed and the faces that join the vertices together. Most of the objects you find in a VRML world are IndexedFaceSets, and a large part of any VRML file is made up of long lists of X, Y, and Z coordinates.

Appearance

The Appearance node (which is found only in the appearance field of a Shape node) has three fields. One is used to specify a material for the shape, the second provides a texture map, and the third gives texture transform information.

The example shown in Listing 23.5 will make this clearer.

Listing 23.5   Using the *Appearance* Node

```
#VRML V2.0 utf8

DirectionalLight { direction -1 -1 -1 }
DirectionalLight { direction  1 -1 -1 }
DirectionalLight { direction 0 0 -1 }

Shape {
    geometry Sphere { }
    appearance Appearance {
        material Material {
            diffuseColor 0 0 0.9
            shininess 0.8
            transparency 0.6
        }
        texture ImageTexture {
            url "brick.bmp"
        }
        textureTransform TextureTransform { scale 5 3 }
    }
}
```

This example creates a blue sphere that is shiny and partially transparent. It applies a brick texture, loaded from a BMP file out on the Web, to the surface of the sphere. The texture coordinates are scaled up, which makes the texture itself smaller. This causes it to get repeated, or *tiled*, across the surface as needed.

In addition to the diffuseColor, shininess, and transparency, a Material node can specify the emissiveColor (for objects that appear to glow), the specularColor (for objects that have a metallic highlight), and an ambientIntensity factor (which indicates what fraction of the scene's ambient light should be reflected).

The previous example shows an ImageTexture, which loads the texture from an imagemap (in this case, a Windows BMP file). Another alternative would be to use a MovieTexture node, which would specify an MPEG file that would produce an animated texture on the surface. You could also use a PixelTexture node, in which case you would probably generate the texture map using Java. Generating texture maps is beyond the scope of this chapter.

The TextureTransform node allows you to scale the texture coordinates, shift them, and rotate them. This node is like a two-dimensional version of the Transform node.

Part
V
Ch
23

Instancing

VRML files can be pretty big. That means they take a long time to download, and the nodes can take up a lot of memory. Is there some way to reduce this bloat? It turns out that there is. You can reuse parts of the scene by creating additional instances of nodes or complete subtrees.

Earlier, you saw how it's possible to assign a name to a node using DEF. Once you've done that, you can create another instance of the node by using USE. Listing 23.6 shows an example.

Listing 23.6   An Example of Instancing

```
#VRML V2 0 utf8

DirectionalLight { direction -1 -1 -1 }
DirectionalLight { direction  1 -1 -1 }

DEF Ball Shape {
    appearance Appearance {
        material Material { diffuseColor 1 0 0 }
    }
    geometry Sphere { }
}

Transform {
    translation -8 0 0
    children [
```

continues

Listing 23.6 Continued

```
            USE Ball
    ]
}

Transform {
    translation 8 0 0
    children [
        USE Ball
    ]
}
```

The sphere is created once and then "instanced" twice —once inside a `Transform` that shifts it to the left eight meters, and once inside a `Transform` that shifts it to the right eight meters.

Note that `USE` does not create a copy of a node; it simply reuses the node in memory. `USE` does make a difference; if a behavior came along and altered the color of the ball, it would affect all three instances. Figure 23.6 shows this relationship.

FIGURE 23.6

Instancing of nodes saves memory.

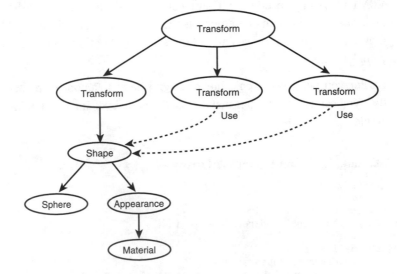

Lights

VRML supports three different types of light sources: `PointLight`, `SpotLight`, and `DirectionalLight`. One important thing to keep in mind is that the more light sources you add to a scene, the more work the computer has to do in order to compute the lighting on each object. You should avoid having more than a few lights turned on at once.

All of the lights have the same basic set of fields: intensity, color, and on (which, not surprisingly, indicates that the light is on). Each light also has an ambientIntensity, which indicates how much light it contributes to the ambient illumination in the scene, as well as some attenuation factors (which are beyond the scope of this chapter).

PointLight

A PointLight has a location field that indicates where the light is placed within its parent's coordinate system. PointLights radiate equally in all directions.

SpotLight

SpotLights are similar to PointLights, except they also have a direction field that indicates which way they're pointing (again, relative to their parent's coordinate system). SpotLights also have some additional information (beamWidth and cutOffAngle) that describes the cone of light that they produce.

DirectionalLight

Unlike PointLight and SpotLight, a DirectionalLight has no location. It appears to come from infinitely far away, and the light it emits travels in a straight line. A DirectionalLight puts less of a burden on the rendering engine, which can result in improved performance.

Sound

One of the most important additions to VRML 2.0 is support for sound. Two nodes are used for this purpose: Sound and AudioClip.

A Sound node is a lot like a SpotLight, except that it emits sound instead of light. It has a location, a direction vector, and an intensity. It also contains an AudioClip node to act as a source for the sound.

An AudioClip node gives the URL of the sound source (a WAV file or MIDI data), a human-readable description of the sound (for users with no sound capabilities), a pitch adjustment, and a flag that indicates whether the sound should loop.

Viewpoint

The Viewpoint node allows the author of a world to specify a location and orientation from which the scene can be viewed. The Viewpoint is part of the transformation hierarchy, and the user is "attached" to it. In other words, you can move the user around the environment at will by altering the values in the Transform nodes above the Viewpoint.

Other VRML Nodes

There are a number of other nodes in VRML that are beyond the scope of this chapter. They are as follows:

- Fog—Creates fog in the environment.
- Background—Allows you to specify a background image as well as give the colors for the sky and ground.
- NavigationInfo—Lets you control the speed and movement style of the user.
- WorldInfo—Lets you embed arbitrary information (the author's name, copyright, and so forth) in the world in a way that won't get eliminated when comments are stripped out.
- Billboard—A type of Transform that always keeps its local Z axis pointing toward the user. It's useful for geometry that must always be seen head-on.
- Anchor—Allows you to make any object or group of objects in your scene work as a link to other VRML worlds or HTML documents.
- Inline—Lets you bring other VRML worlds into yours (much like the include mechanism in the C programming language).
- Collision—Enables or disables collision detection for its subtrees, allowing you to make some of the shapes "solid" to prevent the user from passing through them.

There are grouping nodes for automatically switching the level of detail (LOD) or selecting any of several different subtrees (Switch). For details about these and other nodes, check out the full VRML specification in Appendix E, "VRML Language Reference."

The Sensor Nodes

Interactivity is a key element of the VRML 2.0 specification; therefore, a number of nodes are dedicated to detecting various types of events that take place in the virtual environment. These nodes are referred to as *sensors*.

At the moment, there are seven such sensors, as follows:

- CylinderSensor
- PlaneSensor
- ProximitySensor
- SphereSensor
- TimeSensor
- TouchSensor
- VisibilitySensor

Sensors are able to generate *events*, which should be familiar to anyone who's programmed for Windows, the Macintosh, X-Windows, or other windowing environments. An event contains a timestamp (indicating the time at which the event occurred), an indication of the type of event, and event-specific data. All sensors generate events, and they can generate more than one type of event from a single interaction.

A complete description of all the sensors and how they work is beyond the scope of this chapter. However, two sensors in particular are worth a closer look: TouchSensor and TimeSensor.

TouchSensor

A TouchSensor is a node that detects when the user has touched some geometry in the scene. The definition of *touch* is quite open in order to support immersive environments with 3D pointing devices as well as more conventional desktop metaphors that use a 2D mouse. "Touching" in a desktop environment is usually done by clicking on the object on-screen.

The TouchSensor node enables touch detection for all its siblings. In other words, if the TouchSensor is a child of a Transform, it detects touches on any shapes under that same Transform.

Listing 23.7 shows how a TouchSensor would be used.

Listing 23.7   A *TouchSensor* Example

```
#VRML V2.0 utf8
Transform {
    children [
        TouchSensor { }
        Shape { geometry Sphere { } }
        Shape { geometry Box { } }
    ]
}
```

A `TouchSensor` generates several events, but the two most important ones are `isActive` and `touchTime`. The `isActive` event is an `SFBool` value that is sent when contact is first made; `touchTime` is an `SFTime` value that indicates the time at which contact was made.

A `TouchSensor` can be used for operating a light switch or a door knob, or for triggering any event that is based on user input.

Clicking either the sphere or the box in the example above would cause the `TouchSensor` to send both an `isActive` event and a `touchTime` event, as well as several other events that are beyond the scope of this chapter.

TimeSensor

A `TimeSensor` is unusual in that it's the only sensor that doesn't deal with user input. Instead, it generates events based on the passage of time.

Time is very, very important when doing simulations—especially when it comes to synchronizing events. In VRML, the `TimeSensor` is the basis for all timing; it's a very flexible and powerful node, but a bit difficult to understand.

The best way to visualize a `TimeSensor` is to think of it as a kind of clock. It has a `startTime` and a `stopTime`. When the current time reaches the `startTime`, the `TimeSensor` starts generating events. It continues until it reaches the `stopTime` (assuming the `stopTime` is greater than the `startTime`). You can enable or disable a `TimeSensor` by using its `enabled` field.

Sometimes you want to generate continuous time values. At other times you want to generate discrete events, say once every five seconds. At still other times, you want to know what fraction of the total time has elapsed. A `TimeSensor` is able to do all three of these things simultaneously. It does this by generating four different kinds of events, one for each of these three situations and one that indicates when the `TimeSensor` goes from active to inactive.

The first type of event is simply called `time`. It gives the system time at which the `TimeSensor` generated an event.

N O T E Bear in mind that although time flows continuously in VRML, `TimeSensor` nodes generate events only sporadically. Most VRML browsers will cause `TimeSensors` to send events once per rendered frame, but there's no guarantee that this will always be the case. The time value output by a `TimeSensor` is always correct, but there's no way to be sure you're going to get values at any particular time. ■

The second type of event is called `cycleTime`. The `TimeSensor` has a `cycleInterval` field, and whenever a `cycleInterval` has elapsed, the `TimeSensor` generates a `cycleTime` event.

Again, there are no guarantees that the cycleTime event will be generated at any particular time, only that it will be generated after the cycle has elapsed. The cycleTime is useful for events that have to happen periodically. With loop set to TRUE, the timer will run until it reaches the stopTime, and multiple cycleTime events will be generated. If the stopTime is less than the startTime (it defaults to zero) and loop is TRUE, the timer will run continuously forever and generate a cycleTime event after every cycleInterval.

The third type of event is called fraction_changed. It's a floating-point number between 0.0 and 1.0 that indicates what fraction of the cycleInterval has elapsed. It's generated at the same time as time events.

The final type of event is isActive, which is an SFBool that gets set to TRUE when the TimeSensor starts generating events (such as when the startTime is reached). isActive is set to FALSE when the TimeSensor stops generating events.

Figure 23.7 shows how to conceptualize a TimeSensor node.

Part

V

Ch

23

FIGURE 23.7
The *TimeSensor* node provides a time base.

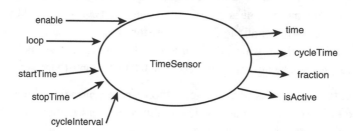

N O T E   The TimeSensor is probably the most complex and potentially confusing node in VRML 2.0, and the details of its operation are extremely subtle. Before making extensive use of it, you should read the description in the VRML 2.0 specification. If you still have problems with it, post a message to the **comp.lang.vrml** newsgroup and someone should be able to help. ■

Routes

Now that you're able to generate events from sensors, you need to be able to do something with those events. This is where the ROUTE statement comes in.

A ROUTE is not a node. It's a special statement that tells the VRML browser to connect a field in one node to a field in another node. For example, you could connect a TimeSensor's fraction_changed event output to a light's intensity field, as shown in Listing 23.8.

Listing 23.8 Using a _ROUTE_

```
#VRML V2.0 utf8

Viewpoint { position 0 -1 5 }

DEF Fizzbin TimeSensor { loop TRUE cycleInterval 5 }

DEF Bulb PointLight { location 2 2 2 }

Shape { geometry Sphere { } }

ROUTE Fizzbin.fraction TO Bulb.intensity
```

This example would cause the light intensity to vary continuously, increasing from 0.0 to 1.0 and then jumping back down to zero again.

Note what's happening in this example. The default value for the `enabled` field of the `TimeSensor` is TRUE, so the timer is ready to run. Because the default value for `startTime` is zero and the current time is greater than that, the `TimeSensor` will be generating events. Because `loop` is TRUE and the default value for `stopTime` is zero (which is less than the `startTime`), the timer will run continuously. The `cycleInterval` is five seconds, so the `fraction_changed` value will ramp up from 0.0 to 1.0 over that interval.

The `ROUTE` statement is what connects the `fraction_changed` value in the `TimeSensor` named `Fizzbin` to the `intensity` field in the `PointLight` named `Bulb`. Note that both `ROUTE` and `TO` should be all uppercase.

N O T E Not all fields can be routed to or routed from; for example, the `radius` field of a `Sphere` node can't be used as the source or destination of a `ROUTE`. However, you can change the size of a sphere by altering the `scale` field of the surrounding `Transform` node. Check the VRML specification for details. ■

The type of values in the fields referenced in a `ROUTE` must match. In other words, it's possible to route the `TimeSensor`'s `fraction_changed` value (an `SFFloat`) to the `PointLight`'s `intensity` field (also an `SFFloat`). However, routing an `SFBool` (like a `TimeSensor`'s `isActive` field) to the `PointLight`'s `intensity` field would have been an error.

Interpolators

There are many times when you want to compute a series of values for some field. For example, you may want to have a flying saucer follow a particular path through space. This is easily accomplished using an *interpolator*.

Every interpolator node in VRML has two arrays: `key` and `keyValue`. Each interpolator also has an input, called `set_fraction`, and an output, called `value_changed`. If you imagine a 2D graph with the keys along the horizontal axis and the key values along the vertical axis, you'll have an idea of how an interpolator works (see Figure 23.8).

FIGURE 23.8
Linear interpolation computes intermediate values.

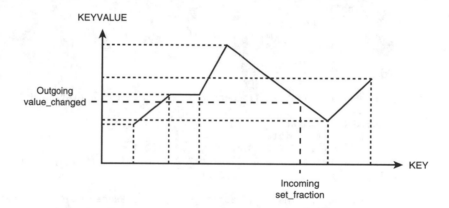

The keys and the key values have a one-to-one relationship. For every `key`, there's a corresponding `keyValue`. When an interpolator receives a `set_fraction` event, the incoming fraction is compared to all of the keys. The two keys on either side of the incoming fraction are found, along with the corresponding key values, and a value is computed that's the same percentage of the way between the key values as the incoming fraction is between the keys. For example, if the incoming fraction value were two-thirds of the way between the 15th and 16th keys, then the output would be two-thirds of the way between the 15th and 16th key values.

There are half a dozen different interpolators in VRML, as follows:

- ColorInterpolator
- CoordinateInterpolator
- NormalInterpolator
- OrientationInterpolator
- PositionInterpolator
- ScalarInterpolator

Each serves a purpose of some kind, but this chapter will use only one: the
PositionInterpolator.

In a PositionInterpolator, the key values (and value_changed) are of type SFVec3f—that
is, they're 3D vectors. Listing 23.9 shows an example of a PositionInterpolator at work.

Listing 23.9   A *PositionInterpolator* at Work

```
#VRML V2.0 utf8

DEF Saucer-Transform Transform {
    scale 1 0.25 1
    children [
        Shape {
            geometry Sphere { }
        }
    ]
}

DEF Saucer-Timebase TimeSensor { loop TRUE cycleInterval 5 }

DEF Saucer-Mover
PositionInterpolator {
    key [ 0.0, 0.2, 0.4, 0.6, 0.8, 1.0 ]
    keyValue [ 0 0 0, 0 2 7, -2 2 0, 5 10 -15, 5 5 5, 0 0 0 ]
}

ROUTE Saucer-Timebase.fraction_changed TO Saucer-Mover.set_fraction
ROUTE Saucer-Mover.value_changed TO Saucer-Transform.set_translation
```

The saucer is just a sphere that's been squashed along the Y axis using a scale in the
surrounding Transform node. The translation field for the Transform isn't given, so it
defaults to (0 0 0). The TimeSensor is just like the one we looked at earlier.

The Saucer-Mover is a PositionInterpolator. It has six keys, going from 0.0 to 1.0 in
steps of 0.2. There's no reason why it had to go in fixed-sized steps; any set of values can
be used, as long as the values steadily increase.

There are six values that correspond to the six keys. Each one is a three-element vector,
giving a particular position value for the saucer.

Once the nodes are defined, you can create the ROUTEs. The first ROUTE connects the
TimeSensor's fractional output to the PositionInterpolator's fractional input. As the
TimeSensor runs, the input to the PositionInterpolator increases steadily from 0.0 to 1.0,
which it reaches after five seconds (the cycleInterval). The second ROUTE connects the
value_changed output of the PositionInterpolator to the translation field of the saucer's

Transform node; this ROUTE is what lets the interpolator move the saucer. Figure 23.9 shows the relationship between these nodes.

FIGURE 23.9
The routes between nodes for the flying saucer example.

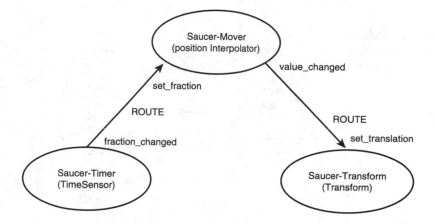

Note that the saucer doesn't "jump" from one value to another; its location is linearly interpolated between entries in the PositionInterpolator's keyValue field.

Scripts and the Interface to Java

So far, you've seen how to create sensors to detect user input or the passage of time, as well as how to create interpolators to compute intermediate values for various quantities. You've also seen how to connect nodes together using ROUTEs. This gives us quite a bit of power, and there are a number of fun things you can do using nothing more than those basic building blocks.

However, you will eventually want to be able to use the power of the Java programming language in building your VRML worlds. The way you do this is through the Script node.

N O T E The remainder of this chapter assumes that you are already familiar with programming in Java. If you don't, then check out Que's *Special Edition Using Java 1.1* for more details. ■

The *Script* Node

The Script node is a kind of nexus. Events flow in and out of the node, just as they do for interpolators or other types of nodes. However, the Script node is special: it allows an actual program written in Java to process the incoming events and generate the outgoing events. Figure 23.10 shows the relationship between the Script node in VRML and the Java code that implements it.

FIGURE 23.10

Java accesses VRML through a Script node.

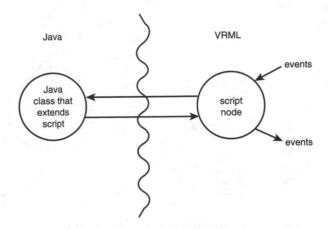

The Script node has only one built-in field that you need to worry about at this stage—url, which gives the URL of a Java bytecode file somewhere on the Internet. There are a couple of other fields, but you don't need to worry about them here.

The Script node can also have a number of declarations for incoming and outgoing events, as well as fields that are accessible only by the script. For example, Listing 23.10 shows a Script node that can receive two incoming events (an SFBool and an SFVec3f), and send three outgoing events. It also has two local fields.

Listing 23.10 A *Script* Node

```
#VRML V2.0 utf8
Script {
    url "bigbrain.class"
    eventIn SFBool recomputeEverything
    eventIn SFVec3f spotToBegin
    eventOut SFBool scriptRan
    eventOut MFVec3f computedPositions
    eventOut SFTime lastRanAt
    field SFFloat rateToRunAt 2.5
    field SFInt32 numberOfTimesRun
}
```

The eventIn, eventOut, and field designators are used to identify incoming events, outgoing events, and fields that are private to the Script node.

The Java bytecode file `bigbrain.class` is loaded in, and the constructor for the class is called. The class should contain a method called `initialize()`, which will be called before any events are sent to the class. As events arrive at the Script node, they're passed to the `processEvent()` method of the class. That method looks like this:

```
public void processEvent(Event ev);
```

where `ev` is an incoming event. An event is defined as follows:

```
class Event {
        public String getName();
        public ConstField getValue();
        public double getTimeStamp();
}
```

The `getName()` method returns the name of the incoming event, which is the name the event was given in the `Script` node in the VRML file. The `getTimeStamp()` method returns the time at which the event was received at the `Script` node. The `getValue()` method returns a `ConstField` which should then be cast to the actual field type (such as `ConstSFBool` or `ConstMFVec3f`).

There are Java classes for each type of VRML field. Each of these classes defines methods for reading (and possibly writing) their values.

A Simple Example

Let's say you want to have a light change to a random intensity whenever the user touches a sphere. VRML itself doesn't have any way to generate random numbers, but Java does (the `java.util.Random` class). Listing 23.11 shows how you would construct your VRML world.

Listing 23.11   A Simple Random Light

```
#VRML V2.0 utf8

Viewpoint { position 0 -1 5 }

NavigationInfo { headlight FALSE }

DEF RandomBulb DirectionalLight { -1 -1 -1 }

Transform {
    children [
            DEF Touch-me TouchSensor { }
            Shape {
                    geometry Sphere { } # something for the light to shine on
```

continues

Part
V

Ch

23

Listing 23.11   Continued

```
          }
      ]
}

DEF Randomizer Script {
       url "RandLight.class"
      eventIn SFBool click
      eventOut SFFloat brightness
}

ROUTE Touch-me.isActive TO Randomizer.click
ROUTE Randomizer.brightness TO RandomBulb.intensity
```

Most of this example should be familiar territory by now. The DirectionalLight is given the name "RandomBulb" using a DEF. A Sphere shape and a TouchSensor are grouped as children of a Transform, which means that touching the Sphere will trigger the TouchSensor.

The Script node is given the name Randomizer, and it has one input (an SFBool called click) and one output (an SFFloat called brightness).

When the RandLight class is first loaded, its constructor is invoked. Next, its initialize() method is called. The initialize() method can do whatever it likes, including send initial events.

Whenever you touch the sphere, the TouchSensor's isActive field is set to TRUE and routed to the script's click eventIn; this in turn causes an event to be sent to the processEvent() method of the RandLight class. The event would have a name of "click," and a value that would be cast to a ConstSFBool. That ConstSFBool would have a value of TRUE, which would be returned by its getValue() method. When you release the button, another event is sent that's identical to the first, but this time with a value of FALSE in the ConstSFBool.

When any of the methods in the RandLight class sets the brightness value (as described later in this chapter), that event gets routed to the intensity field of the PointLight called RandomBulb.

The View from Java Land

Now that you've seen how the VRML end of things works, let's look at it from the Java perspective. We'll return to our random-light project shortly, but first let's take a little detour through the VRML package.

The VRML package is imported as you would expect:

```
import vrml.*;
import vrml.field.*;
import vrml.node.*;
```

These packages define a number of useful classes. There's a class called `Field` (derived from `Object`) that corresponds to a VRML field. From `Field` there are a number of derived classes, one for each of the basic VRML data types, such as `SFBool` and `SFColor`. There are also "read-only" versions of all those classes; they have a `Const` prefix, as in `ConstSFBool`.

The read-only versions of the fields provide a `getValue()` method that returns a Java data type corresponding to the VRML type. For example, the `ConstSFBool` class looks like the following:

```
public class ConstSFBool extends Field {
    public boolean getValue();
}
```

The read-write versions of the fields also provide the `getValue()` method, but in addition they have a `setValue()` method that takes a parameter (such as a Boolean) and sets it as the value of the field. Doing this causes an event to be sent from the corresponding `eventOut` of the `Script` node in the VRML file.

There are, of course, classes that correspond to multiple-valued VRML types such as `MFFloat`. These classes have the `getValue()` and `setValue()` methods, but they also have other methods that let you do things like setting a single element of the array (the `set1Value()` method). Listing 23.12 shows what the `MFVec3f` class looks like.

Listing 23.12   The *MFVec3f* Class from the *vrml.field* Package

```
public class MFVec3f extends MField
{
    public MFVec3f(float vecs[][]);
    public MFVec3f(float vecs[]);
    public MFVec3f(int size, float vecs[]);

    public void getValue(float vecs[][]);
    public void getValue(float vecs[]);

    public void setValue(float vecs[][]);
    public void setValue(int size, float vecs[]);
    public void setValue(ConstMFVec3f vecs);

    public void get1Value(int index, float vec[]);
    public void get1Value(int index, SFVec3f vec);
```

continues

Listing 23.12   Continued

```
    public void set1Value(int index, float x, float y, float z);
    public void set1Value(int index, ConstSFVec3f vec);
    public void set1Value(int index, SFVec3f vec);

    public void addValue(float x, float y, float z);
    public void addValue(ConstSFVec3f vec);
    public void addValue(SFVec3f vec);

    public void insertValue(int index, float x, float y, float z);
    public void insertValue(int index, ConstSFVec3f vec);
    public void insertValue(int index, SFVec3f vec);
}
```

An MFVec3f is an array of three-element vectors (the three elements being the X, Y, and Z components, as you saw earlier). A single entry is a float[], and an MFVec3f is a float[][] type in Java.

Notice that there are three versions of setValue(), one which takes an array of floats, one which takes an array of floats and a count, and one which takes another MFVec3f.

Not only is there a class in the VRML package corresponding to a field in a VRML node, there's also a class for VRML nodes themselves. The Node class provides methods for accessing exposedFields, eventIns, and eventOuts by name. For example, the name of a field in the node is passed to getExposedField(), and it returns a reference to the field. The return value needs to be cast to be of the appropriate type.

There's also a Script class, which is related to Node. When you write Java code to support a Script node, you create a class that's derived from the Script class. The Script class provides a getField() method for accessing a field given its name, and a similar getEventOut() method. It also has an initialize() method, as described earlier, and of course a processEvent() method. There's also a shutdown() method that gets called just before the Script node is discarded, in order to allow the class to clean up after itself.

The Script node also defines two other methods: processEvents() (not to be confused with processEvent()) which is given an array of events and a count so that they may be processed more efficiently than by individual processEvent() calls, and an eventsProcessed() method, which is called after a number of events have been delivered.

And finally, there's a Browser class which provides methods for finding such things as the name and version of the VRML browser that's running, the current frame rate, the URL of the currently loaded world, and so on. You can also add and delete ROUTEs and even load additional VRML code into the world either from a URL or directly from a String.

Back to *RandLight*

Now let's look at some Java code. Listing 23.13 shows the Java source for the RandLight class, which would be stored in a file called RandLight.java.

Listing 23.13   The *RandLight* Class

```
// Code for a VRML Script node to set a light to a random intensity

import vrml.*;
import vrml.field.*;
import vrml.node.*;
import java.util.*;

public class RandLight extends Script {

        Random generator = new Random();

    SFFloat brightness;

        public void initialize() {
                    brightness = (SFFloat) getEventOut("brightness");
                    brightness.setValue(0.0f);
        }

        public void processEvent(Event ev) {
                    if (ev.getName().equals("click")) {
                                ConstSFBool value = (ConstSFBool)
                                ➥ ev.getValue();
                                if ((value.getValue() == false) {   //
                                ➥ touch complete
                            brightness.setValue(generator.nextFloat());
                                }
                    }
        }

}
```

The RandLight.java file defines a single class, called RandLight, which extends the Script class defined in the VRML package as described earlier.

The RandLight class contains a random number generator, and it also has an SFFloat called brightness. As described earlier, the Script class has a method called getEventOut(), which retrieves a reference to an eventOut in the Script node in the VRML file using the name of the field (in this case, brightness). Because the type of eventOut (SFBool, SFVec3f, and so on) is unknown, the getEventOut() method simply returns a

`Field` that is then cast to be a field of the appropriate type using (`SFFloat`). This is then assigned to the variable called `brightness`, which is of type `SFFloat`. The variable didn't have to be called `brightness`, but it's a good idea to keep the field name in the `Script` node consistent with its corresponding variable in the class that supports that `Script` node.

Like all read-write classes that correspond to VRML fields, the `SFFloat` class has a method called `setValue()`. This method takes a float parameter and stores it as the value of that field. This in turn causes the `Script` node in VRML to generate an outgoing event, which may be routed somewhere.

Most of the code is straightforward. The `initialize()` method sets the brightness to zero. The `processEvent()` method, which gets called when an event arrives at the `Script` node in VRML, checks for "`click`" events and sets the brightness to a random value on `false` clicks (that is, releases of the mouse button). That's all there is to it.

The Towers of Hanoi

Now that you have learned how all the pieces work, it's time to put them together. The remainder of this chapter will take one of the oldest puzzles in recorded history and implement it using the latest in cutting-edge technologies.

The Towers of Hanoi is a very simple puzzle, yet it's intriguing and fun to watch. There are three vertical posts that are standing side by side. On one of the posts is a stack of disks. Each disk has a different diameter. The disks are stacked so that the largest disk is on the bottom, the next-largest is on top of it, and so on until the smallest disk is on top.

The goal is to move the entire stack to another post. You can move only one disk at a time, and you are not allowed to place a larger disk on top of a smaller one. Those are the only rules.

If you were moving the stacks by hand, you would start by taking the top-most (smallest) disk from the first post and placing it on the second post. You would then take the next-largest disk and place it on the third post. Then you'd take the disk from the second post and place it on the third one. This process would continue until you'd moved all of the disks.

Even though it's fun to watch the stacks being moved, it's a lot less fun to actually do it. (I could watch people work all day!)

Building a VRML/Java application to move the stacks is a multistage process. The first step is to build the posts and base, along with some lighting and a nice viewpoint. The disks are added next and, finally, the script that animates them. The process of building this simple world will make use of everything you've learned about in this chapter, including TouchSensors, TimeSensors, PositionInterpolators, Scripts, ROUTE statements, and basic VRML nodes.

The Posts and the Base

The three posts are created using Cylinder nodes, and the base is a Box. The base is positioned first, as shown in Listing 23.14.

Listing 23.14   The Base of the Towers of Hanoi

```
#VRML V2.0 utf8

# Base

Transform {
    translation 0 0.0625 0
    children [
        Shape {
            appearance Appearance {
                material Material { diffuseColor 0.50 0.50 0  }
            }
            geometry Box { size 1.5 0.125 0.5 }
        }
    ]
}
```

The box is 1.5 meters wide (X axis), 0.125 meters high (Y axis), and 0.5 meters deep (Z axis). Because you want it resting on the "ground" (the X-Z plane), you need to position its lowest point at Y=0. Because the origin of the box is at its geometric center, you need to shift it vertically by half of its height: half of 0.125 is 0.0625, which is why you have a translation of (0 0.0625 0): no translation in X or Z, and a 0.0625 meter translation in Y.

The next step is to add the first post, as shown in Listing 23.15.

Listing 23.15   The Base and One Post

```
# Posts

Transform {
    translation 0 0.375 0
    children DEF Cyl Shape {
        geometry Cylinder { height 0.5 radius 0.035 }
    }
}
```

The first post is a `Cylinder` that is half a meter high with a radius of 0.035 meters. This shape is assigned the name `Cyl`, because we'll be making "`USE`" of it later. You want the bottom of the post to rest on top of the box. Because the origin of the `Cylinder` is at its geometric center, you need to shift it vertically by half of its height (0.25 meters) plus the height of the base (0.125 meters). Because 0.25 plus 0.125 is 0.375, this shape has a translation of (0 0.375 0). Because there's no X or Z translation, the post will be centered over the middle of the box.

Rather than create two more cylinders, let's make use of instancing. Listing 23.16 shows how this works.

Listing 23.16   Two More Posts, Instances of the First

```
Transform {
     translation -0.5 0.375 0
     children USE Cyl
}

Transform {
     translation 0.5 0.375 0
     children USE Cyl
}
```

The `USE Cyl` creates another instance of the post shape that was created earlier. The first `Transform` moves the post to the left (X = -0.5 meters), the second moves the post to the right (X = 0.5 meters), and they both move the posts to the same Y = 0.375 location as the first post.

A `WorldInfo` node is added to store author information and a title for the world, as well as a `NavigationInfo` node to put the user's VRML browser in `FLY` mode and turn off the headlight. A `TouchSensor` is added to the base to give the user a way to start and stop the movement of the disks. Finally, some lights are thrown in. Listing 23.17 shows our world so far.

Listing 23.17   The Complete Base and Posts

```
#VRML V2.0 utf8

WorldInfo {
     title "Towers of Hanoi"
     info "Created by Bernie Roehl (broehl@ece.uwaterloo.ca), July 1996"
}

NavigationInfo { type "FLY" headlight FALSE }

PointLight { location 0.5 0.25 0.5 intensity 6.0 }
PointLight { location -0.5 0.25 0.5 intensity 6.0 }
```

```
DirectionalLight { direction -1 -1 -1 intensity 6.0 }

Viewpoint { position 0 0.5 2 }

# Base

Transform {
    translation 0 0.0625 0
    children [
        DEF TOUCH_SENSOR TouchSensor { }
        Shape {
            appearance Appearance {
                material Material { diffuseColor 0.50 0.50 0  }
            }
            geometry Box { size 1.5 0.125 0.5 }
        }
    ]
}

# Posts

Transform {
    translation 0 0.375 0
    children DEF Cyl Shape {
        geometry Cylinder { height 0.5 radius 0.035 }
        }
}

Transform {
    translation -0.5 0.375 0
    children USE Cyl
}

Transform {
    translation 0.5 0.375 0
    children USE Cyl
}
```

Part

V

Ch

23

The static part of our world is complete. Now it's time to add the moving parts—the disks themselves.

The Disks

For our example, we'll use five disks. The definition of each disk is pretty simple, as shown in Listing 23.18.

Listing 23.18   A Disk

```
DEF Disk1
Transform {
```

continues

Listing 23.18   Continued

```
    translation -0.5 0.305 0
    children [
        Shape {
            appearance Appearance {
                material Material { diffuseColor 0.5 0 0.5 }
            }
            geometry Cylinder { radius 0.12 height 0.04 }
        }
    ]
}
```

The disks are just cylinders. All of the disks are the same, except for the value of the
`translation` (they're stacked vertically, so the Y component will be different), the value of
the `radius` (each disk is smaller than the one below it), and the `diffuseColor` of the disk.

N O T E   If you're already familiar with VRML 2.0, you're probably wondering why a PROTO
wasn't used for the disks. That is in fact the way it would normally be done.

Unfortunately, this book is being written at a very early stage of VRML 2.0, and no fully compliant
browsers are available. In fact, there are only two VRML 2.0 browsers: Sony's CyberPassage and
SGI's CosmoPlayer. Because CosmoPlayer doesn't have Java support yet, CyberPassage was used
for our examples. CyberPassage has some bugs that are related to the use of prototypes, so it's
necessary to actually replicate the code for each disk. Such is life at the bleeding edge. ■

There'll be some additional nodes for each disk, but for now let's just stop at the
geometry.

Now that all of the geometry is in place, it's time to start dealing with behavior.

Adding the Interpolators and TimeSensors

There's going to be a `PositionInterpolator` for each disk to handle its movement, and it'll
be driven by a `TimeSensor` node. Let's look at the interpolator first. The interpolator for the
first disk is shown in Listing 23.19.

Listing 23.19   The *PositionInterpolator* for a Disk

```
DEF Disk1Inter
PositionInterpolator {
    key [ 0, 0.3, 0.6, 1 ]
}
```

There are four keys, spaced roughly 0.3 units apart. Each disk is going to move from its current location to a point immediately above the post it's on. The disk then moves to a point immediately above the post it's moving to, then finally down into position. Four locations, four keys. Notice that no key values are specified; they'll be filled in later by our Java code.

The timer associated with each disk is a TimeSensor, as shown in Listing 23.20.

Listing 23.20   The *TimeSensor* for a Disk

```
DEF Disk1Timer
TimeSensor {
     loop FALSE
     enabled TRUE
     stopTime 1
}
```

The timer is designed to run once each time it's started (which is why its loop field is FALSE). It starts off being enabled. The startTime is not specified; again, this is because it will be filled in from our Java code.

The next step is to connect the TimeSensor to the PositionInterpolator and the PositionInterpolator to the Transform node for the disk. A pair of ROUTE statements does the trick:

```
ROUTE Disk1Timer.fraction_changed TO Disk1Inter.set_fraction
ROUTE Disk1Inter.value_changed TO Disk1.set_translation
```

Our next step is going to be to add a Script node. It will need to be able to update the keyValue field of the PositionInterpolator and the startTime field of the TimeSensor, so let's add a couple of additional ROUTEs:

```
ROUTE SCRIPT.disk1Start TO Disk1Timer.startTime
ROUTE SCRIPT.disk1Locations TO Disk1Inter.keyValue
```

The Script node called SCRIPT will have a disk1Start field into which it will write the start time for the interpolation. This node will also have a disk1locations field into which it will write the four locations that this disk should move through (current location, above the current post, above the destination post, and final location).

The complete VRML source for a single disk, therefore, looks like Listing 23.21.

Listing 23.21   The Complete VRML Code for a Single Disk

```
DEF Disk1
Transform {
     translation -0.5 0.305 0
     children [
          Shape {
               appearance Appearance {
                    material Material { diffuseColor 0.5 0 0.5 }
               }
               geometry Cylinder { radius 0.12 height 0.04 }
          }
     ]
}
DEF Disk1Inter PositionInterpolator { key [ 0, 0.3, 0.6, 1 ] }
DEF Disk1Timer TimeSensor { loop FALSE enabled TRUE stopTime 1 }
ROUTE SCRIPT.disk1Start TO Disk1Timer.startTime
ROUTE Disk1Timer.fraction TO Disk1Inter.set_fraction
ROUTE Disk1Inter.value_changed TO Disk1.set_translation
ROUTE SCRIPT.disk1Locations TO Disk1Inter.keyValue
```

This complete sequence is replicated for each of the five disks. Of course, `Disk1` is replaced with `Disk2`, `Disk3`, and so on.

Adding the *Script* Node

To keep things simple, there's going to be a single `Script` node to drive the entire simulation. This node has a large number of inputs and outputs, as shown in Listing 23.22.

Listing 23.22   The *Script* Node for the "Towers of Hanoi"

```
DEF SCRIPT Script {
     url    "Hanoi.class"

     eventIn    SFBool clicked
     eventIn SFTime tick

     eventOut MFVec3f disk1Locations
     eventOut SFTime disk1Start

     eventOut MFVec3f disk2Locations
     eventOut SFTime disk2Start

     eventOut MFVec3f disk3Locations
     eventOut SFTime disk3Start

     eventOut MFVec3f disk4Locations
     eventOut SFTime disk4Start
```

```
        eventOut MFVec3f disk5Locations
        eventOut SFTime disk5Start


}
```

The script is loaded from a file called Hanoi.class, which is the result of compiling Hanoi.java. It's described in excruciating detail later. The clicked eventIn is used to let the Script node know when the user has clicked on the base of the posts (to start or stop the simulation). The tick eventIn is used to advance the simulation.

Part
V
Ch
23

For each disk, there's the set of locations that get routed to the PositionInterpolator's keyValue field as described earlier. There is also a start time that gets routed to the disk's TimeSensor's startTime value.

There's also a ROUTE to connect the TouchSensor on the base to the clicked field of the Script:

```
        ROUTE TOUCH_SENSOR.isActive TO SCRIPT.clicked
```

A TimeSensor drives the simulation, as shown in Listing 23.23.

Listing 23.23   The *TimeSensor* which Drives the Simulation

```
DEF TIMEBASE TimeSensor {
        cycleInterval 1.5
        enabled TRUE
        loop TRUE
}
```

This TimeSensor sends a cycleTime event every 1.5 seconds, forever. Each of these cycleTime events triggers the moving of one disk.

And, finally, there's a ROUTE to connect this timer to the Script node's tick field:

```
        ROUTE TIMEBASE.cycleTime TO SCRIPT.tick
```

That's it for the VRML end of things. Figure 23.11 shows an overall diagram of the how the nodes are connected to each other.

The complete source for HANOI.WRL is found on the CD-ROM that accompanies this book.

Now it's time to create our script in Java.

FIGURE 23.11

The routing relation-
ships for the Towers of
Hanoi example.

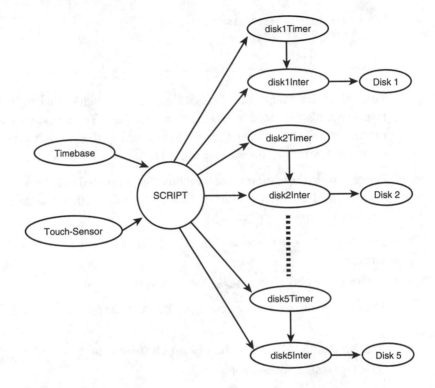

Hanoi.java

The Towers of Hanoi problem is usually given as an example of the power of *recursion*. An explanation of recursive algorithms is beyond the scope of this chapter, but the basic idea is that a function is able to partition a problem and then call itself to handle each of the two (or more) pieces that result.

The `initialize()` method of our `Hanoi` class will be used to generate the complete sequence of moves and store them in an array. Whenever a message arrives from the `TimeSensor`, the next step in the sequence will be carried out. The `click` message will allow the user to turn us on (or off).

The moves themselves will be stored in three arrays: `disks[]`, `startposts[]`, and `endposts[]`. The `disks[]` array stores the number of the disk (0–4, because there are five disks) that's supposed to be moved. The `startposts[]` and `endposts[]` arrays store the starting and ending post numbers (0 through 2, because there are three posts).

There's also a `postdisks[]` array, which keeps track of the number of disks on each post. It'll be used it to compute the height of the top-most disk on each post in order to make the moves.

We'll begin with the standard header and declarations for our data, shown in Listing 23.24.

Listing 23.24   The Beginning of the Hanoi Class

```
import vrml.*;
import vrml.field.*;
import vrml.node.*;

public class Hanoi extends Script {

    // the following three arrays record the moves to be made

    int disks[] = new int[120];      // which disk to move
    int startposts[] = new int[120]; // post to move it from
    int endposts[] = new int[120];   // post to move it to
    int nmoves = 0;          // number of entries used in those three arrays

    int current_move = 0;            // which move you're on now

    boolean forwards = true;         // initially, move from
                                     //  post 0 to post 2

    int postdisks[] = new int[3];    // number of disks on each of the posts
```

Next comes our `initialize()` method. It just calls a recursive routine called `hanoi_r()` to do the actual work, then initializes the number of disks on each post. Because all of the disks are on the first post to begin with, and the entries in `postdisks[]` are all zero initially, this initialization is pretty easy. Listing 23.25 shows how all this works.

Listing 23.25   The *initialize()* Method

```
/***** initialize() builds table of moves *****/

public void initialize() {
            int number_of_disks = 5;
            postdisks[0] = number_of_disks;   // first post has
            ➥ all the disks
            hanoi_r(number_of_disks, 0, 2);   // generate the
            ➥ sequence of moves
    }
```

Next, a flag is defined that indicates whether the routine is running. There's also a `processEvent()` method to handle events coming into the script. These are shown in Listing 23.26.

Listing 23.26   The *processEvent()* Method

```
boolean running = false;  // true if we're running

        /***** clicking on the base starts and stops the action *****/

        public void processEvent(Event ev) {
                        if (ev.getName().equals("click")) {
                                        ConstSFBool value = (ConstSFBool)
                                        ➥ ev.getValue();
                                        if (value.getValue() == false) {
                                                        running = running ?
                                                        ➥ false : true;  // toggle
                                        }
                        else if (ev.getName().equals("tick"))
                                        tick(ev.getTimeStamp());
                        }
        }
```

This code fragment is similar to that from our earlier example. Recall that all readable fields have a getValue() method, which returns a standard Java value. In the case of a ConstSFBool field, the getValue() method returns a Boolean type value. If that value is true, then the user touched the object (by clicking on it with the mouse) and if the value is false, the user "un-touched" the object (for example, by releasing the mouse). In such a case, the running flag is toggled true or false. If the incoming event is a "tick" rather than a "click," then the next move in the sequence is executed.

When we hit the end of the list of moves, all the disks have been moved to their destination post. At that point, we replay the sequence backwards to return to the original configuration. We then play the sequence forwards again, and so on. This is shown in Listing 23.27.

Listing 23.27   The *tick()* Method

```
/***** at each tick (cycleTime), make the
                next move in the sequence *****/

        void tick(double time) {
                        if (running == false)
                                        return;  // do nothing if we're not
                                        ➥ running
                        if (forwards)  // moving from source to destination
                                        {
                                        make_move(disks[current_move],
                                        ➥ startposts[current_move],
```

```
                                      endposts[current_move], time);
                                  if (++current_move >= nmoves) {
                                          current_move = nmoves-1;
                                          forwards = false;
                                  }
          }
          else {  // moving in the other direction
                          make_move(disks[current_move],
                          ➥ endposts[current_move],
                      startposts[current_move], time);
                          if (—current_move < 0) {
                                          current_move = 0;
                                          forwards = true;
                          }
          }
  }
```

The tick() method does nothing if running is false. If the sequence is running forward, the tick() method makes the move and increments the current_move counter. When it hits the last move, it makes the last move into the next one and reverses directions.

If the sequence is running backward, the opposite move is made—from the endposts[current_move] post to the startposts[current_move] post. The current move is decremented. When the first move is reached, it becomes the next one and again the direction is reversed.

The make_move() method is where most of the talking to VRML is done. To start with, some constants are defined for use in array indexing:

```
static final int X = 0, Y = 1, Z = 2;     // elements of an SFVec3f
```

Doing this lets you say (for example) vector[Y] to refer to the Y component of the three-element vector, instead of having to say vector[1].

To make a move, it's necesary to fill in the four-element array of locations, each of which is itself an array of three elements (X, Y, and Z). Listing 23.28 shows how the first position for the disk is computed.

Listing 23.28 Finding the Starting Location

```
/**** Routine to make an actual move *****/

void make_move(int disk, int from, int to, double now) {
    float four_steps[][] = { { 0, 0, 0 }, { 0, 0, 0 },
                             { 0, 0, 0 }, { 0, 0, 0 } };

    // compute starting location for disk
```

continues

Listing 23.28   Continued

```
        // center post is at x=0, left post is x=-0.5 and
        // right post is x=0.5
        four_steps[0][X] = (from - 1) * 0.5f;

        // vertical position is height of disk (0.04) times
        // number of disks on source post, plus height of base
        four_steps[0][Y] = 0.04f * postdisks[from] + 0.145f;

        // disk is centered on post in Z axis
        four_steps[0][Z] = 0f;
```

Since the center post is at X = 0, the left post is at X = -0.5, and the right post is at X = 0.5, the expression `(from-1) * 0.5f` gives the X coordinate of the "from" post. Since each disk is 0.04 meters high, and there are `postdisks[from]` disks on the "from" post, and the base is 0.145 units tall, it's easy to compute the current Y component of the disk's location. The Z component is even easier: it's zero, because the disk is centered on the post along that axis.

Computing the destination location is almost exactly the same, as shown in Listing 23.29.

Listing 23.29   Finding the Ending Location

```
// compute ending location for disk

// center post is at x=0, left post is x=-0.5 and
// right post is x=0.5
four_steps[3][X] = (to - 1) * 0.5f;

// vertical position is height of disk (0.04) times
// number of disks on four_steps[0] post, plus height of base
four_steps[3][Y] = 0.04f * postdisks[to] + 0.145f;

// disk is centered on post in Z axis
four_steps[3][Z] = 0f;
```

The intermediate locations are the same, except that the Y coordinates will be one meter up, as shown in Listing 23.30.

Listing 23.30   Finding the Intermediate Locations

```
// now fill in the missing steps

// one meter above the source post
four_steps[1][X] = four_steps[0][0];
four_steps[1][Y] = 1f;
four_steps[1][Z] = 0f;
```

```
// one meter above the destination post
four_steps[2][X] = four_steps[3][0];
four_steps[2][Y] = 1f;
four_steps[2][Z] = 0f;
```

The next step is to adjust the count of the number of disks on each post:

```
--postdisks[from];  // one less disk on source post
++postdisks[to];    // one more disk on destination post
```

Part

V

Ch

23

Finally, the move is made by updating the eventOuts in the Script (which are routed to the disk's PositionInterpolator and TimeSensor). The code to do this is shown in Listing 23.31.

Listing 23.31 Moving the Disk

```
// now move the disk

MFVec3f locations = (MFVec3f) getEventOut("disk"
                              + (disk+1) + "Locations");
locations.setValue(four_steps);

SFTime timerStart = (SFTime) getEventOut("disk"
                              + (disk+1) + "Start");
timerStart.setValue(now);

}
```

The name of the eventOut is based on the disk number. Notice that 1 is added to the disk; this is because in the VRML file, the disks were counted starting from 1 instead of 0. The eventOut that is found using getEventOut() is routed to the keyValue field of a PositionInterpolator for the disk in question.

The timer is found in a similar fashion. The value now, which is the timestamp of the event that caused this routine to run, is set as the start time for the timer. This starts the timer going, which drives the interpolator, which moves the disk.

So far so good. All that's needed now is the actual recursive routine for generating the moves. This is shown in Listing 23.32.

Listing 23.32 The Recursive Move-Generator

```
/***** hanoi_r() is a recursive routine for
       generating the moves *****/

// freeposts[starting_post][ending_post] gives which post is unused
```

continues

Listing 23.32   Continued

```
static final int[][] freeposts = { { 0, 2, 1 },
                                    { 2, 0, 0 },
                                    { 1, 0, 0 } };

void hanoi_r(int number_of_disks, int starting_post, int goal_post) {
    if (number_of_disks > 0) {  // check for end of recursion
        int free_post = freeposts[starting_post][goal_post];

        hanoi_r(number_of_disks - 1, starting_post, free_post);

        // add this move to the arrays
        disks[nmoves] = number_of_disks - 1;
        startposts[nmoves] = starting_post;
        endposts[nmoves] = goal_post;
        ++nmoves;

        hanoi_r(number_of_disks - 1, free_post, goal_post);
    }
}
```

The `freeposts[]` array is used to determine which post to use to make the move. If the move is from post 0 to post 2, then post 1 is free. This is represented by `freeposts[0][2]` having the value 1. Note that the main diagonal of this little matrix (the [0][0], [1][1], and [2][2] elements) will never be used because the `starting_post` and `goal_post` will never be the same.

And that's it—the complete Towers of Hanoi puzzle, solved using Java and VRML. The complete Hanoi.java source code is included on the CD-ROM that comes with this book.

The Bleeding Edge

All of the examples listed in the text of this chapter should work with any final release (not beta) VRML 2.0 browser that supports scripting in Java.

Just to be on the safe side, I'll be maintaining an "errata" sheet for this chapter on my Web page (**http://ece.uwaterloo.ca/~broehl/bernie.html**).

This chapter has barely scratched the surface of VRML. There's lots more to learn about, such as PROTO and EXTERNPROTO, and there are lots of other nodes that have only been mentioned in passing. VRML promises to be as revolutionary as Java itself, and the combination of the two is very powerful indeed.

Be sure to check the VRML Repository (**http://sdsc.edu/vrml**) for a complete listing of VRML resources, including links to the complete specification and lots of examples and tools.

See you in Cyberspace! ●

Building and Managing a Web Site

## CHAPTER 24

Building a Web

Requirements for Building a Web

What equipment do you need to build a Web, and what software must you put in place?

Starting a New Web Site

How to use FrontPage Explorer to start a new site from scratch.

Using the New Web Wizards

Work through the richest and most complex Web creation wizard in FrontPage to build the essentials of a corporate presence Web site.

In days of yore (say, 18 months ago), building an entire Web from scratch meant planning out in advance exactly what you wanted to include, then writing each page in succession. Once the pages were done, you'd link them all together through a series of internal hyperlinks. If you wanted a graphical unity, you'd have to add the appropriate colors and/or backgrounds to each page.

Advanced planning is still a very good idea, but FrontPage 97 makes it possible to put together a fully functioning Web site, complete with forms programming and graphical themes, by filling in a few dialog boxes. That's because FrontPage 97 offers you, right from the opening screen, a series of wizards for building new Webs. The wizards guide you step by step through some fairly complex designs, and when you've finished you'll have a perfect starting point for developing your Web even further. In other words, the initial drudgery is taken away from you, and as a result you can concentrate your efforts on developing the site exactly as you want it to appear and function.

Of course, you might already have a Web in place. If so, see Chapter 26, "Working with an Existing Web," for details on importing it into the FrontPage Explorer. The present chapter examines the creation of brand new Webs, taking you through the most complex of the various Web creation wizards. ■

Requirements for Building a Web

To create a Web using FrontPage 97, you should be running a Web server. Actually, FP97 gives you the option of creating a Web on your hard drive only, without server software running, but such a Web is limited because the hyperlinks won't function. As a result, we recommend using server software. The server software can reside either on a remote computer accessible over the Internet, or on your local computer through the use of the Microsoft Personal Web Server, which comes included with your FP97 package.

When you create a Web, you must specify where you want that Web to reside. That is, you must tell it which machine you want your Web served from. Usually this is a remote machine, because a fully accessible Web must be served from a machine that is connected to the Internet on a 24-hour basis and (ideally) at high speed. But if you want to build a local Web, which you do primarily for the sake of testing it out, you can specify the address as **localhost** (these addresses are covered later in this chapter). Then, when you begin the Web creation, FrontPage 97 will automatically start the Personal Web Server to make the Web functional.

Of course, you might have a server in place already. Several server packages are popularly available, including O'Reilly & Associates' WebSite and Netscape's FastTrack. To use all of FrontPage 97's features with these servers, you must install the *server extensions* for them. These installations are handled during the initial FP97 installation process, but if you add a server later you must install the extensions for it manually. The server extensions let the server handle FP97's advanced features, such as forms programming and easy incorporation of ActiveX controls (among other features).

▶ **See** "Getting Started," **p. 15**

As shipped, FrontPage supports several popular Web servers, including the Netscape Commerce and Communications servers and O'Reilly's WebSite server. As they become available, extensions for most servers will be made available on Microsoft's Web site, at:

http://www.microsoft.com/frontpage/softlib/fs_fp_extensions.htm

If you're running a Web server that isn't supported by a FrontPage extension, you can still make use of FrontPage. Using a machine other than your Web server machine (always a good idea anyway), connect to the Internet and load the FrontPage Personal Web Server, and then create your Web. Once it's completed, you can export it to the Web server machine using FP97's Publish feature, found in FrontPage Explorer's File menu, or using the WebPost Wizard that ships with FrontPage 97 Bonus Pack.

▶ **See** "Serving Your Web to the World with the Personal Web Server," **p. 707**

 Even if you have a machine with a server supported by FrontPage extensions, you should seriously consider designing, developing, and testing your Webs on a non-public machine, using the FrontPage Personal Web Server that ships with the FrontPage package. This is a much better idea than developing on a live Web server because you can guarantee that nobody will be able to visit it while it's in progress. That way, data is secure, errors and difficulties don't become public, and the final public Web is exactly the one you want people to see.

Starting a New Web Site

To build a Web site, use FrontPage Explorer. Choose File, New Web. The New FrontPage Web dialog box appears, which you can see in Figure 24.1.

This dialog box gives you several choices, ranging from Empty Web to Corporate Presence Wizard. The difference lies in the relative simplicity or complexity of the possibilities. An empty Web is exactly what its name suggests; you get a Web, but there's nothing in it. Selecting the Corporate Presence Web, on the other hand, launches a wizard that takes you step by step through the initiation of a Web site fully populated by page templates designed specifically for establishing a corporate presence. The choice is yours: start with nothing or start with a sophisticated template.

Why would anybody forego the templates and start with an empty Web? The answer lies very much in your confidence and creativity, as well as your experience in Web page design. If you've put together a number of Webs and you know exactly how you want to start and what you want to include, a template might very well be a detriment rather than a benefit. But if you're about to begin your first site or you know very well that you could use a good assistant, by all means start with a template.

The real problem with templates is that they tend to produce Webs that are very similar to other Webs out there. In fact, as FrontPage becomes more and more popular, there's a very real danger that we'll see all kinds of FrontPage-assisted Web designs that offer nothing distinctive whatsoever. Still, the templates in FrontPage are strong enough that even a moderate amount of tinkering produces something at least worth looking at, which is far better than nothing.

If you select Empty Web, you'll have to create all Web pages from scratch. This process is covered throughout the entirety of Part II, "Creating Your Web Pages with FrontPage Editor." For now, adding to an empty Web means choosing Tools, Show FrontPage Editor in Explorer. Once Editor loads, choose File, New Page and proceed from there.

▶ **See** "Introducing FrontPage Editor," **p. 51**

Using the New Web Wizards

FrontPage Explorer offers a choice of wizards for creating new Webs. Two of these are the Corporate Presence Wizard and the Discussion Web Wizard. Both offer an extremely usable system of dialog boxes, and once you've completed them all, you'll have a Web filled with easy-to-alter Web page templates.

To see how these wizards work, we'll step through the Corporate Presence Wizard, creating a site for a company we just created called FrontPagers Corporation. In this hypothetical example, we've applied to the InterNIC registry service (**http://rs.internic.net/ rs-internic.html**) for the domain name **frontpagers.com**, but we haven't yet received confirmation of ownership. As a result, we'll use the *localhost* feature of Explorer to set the Web site for our local machine, in which case we don't even need to be connected to the Web to create the site (see Step 3 later).

N O T E As of this writing (April 1996), the domain name **frontpagers.com** was still unclaimed, as revealed by a WHOIS search at the InterNIC site. But this book's authors didn't actually buy the name (it costs $100 for two years plus the fee charged by the ISP), so it might very well be no longer available by the time this book is published. Then again, Microsoft might object if someone *actually* took it. ■

Step 1: Load FrontPage Explorer   Open the FrontPage Explorer; an empty Explorer window appears.

Step 2: Start the Corporate Presence Wizard   In Explorer, choose File, New Web. The New Web dialog box appears (see Figure 24.1). Click the Corporate Presence Wizard and then click OK. The other choices offered by the dialog box are discussed later in this chapter.

Step 3: Specify an IP address and a Name for Your Web   The New Web from Wizard dialog box in Figure 24.2 is the result of starting the Corporate Presence Wizard or for that matter any other Web with the File, New Web command. In the Web Server text box, you must specify the IP address for your computer, the domain name that has been assigned to that computer, or the computer's network name, as determined in the

Identification area of the Network dialog boxes in Windows 95/NT's Control Panel. Since the frontpagers.com domain name has not yet been assigned to us, we can't use it. In fact, even when it is, we won't be able to use it until frontpagers.com has been associated with the IP address assigned to our machine.

▶ **See** "Serving Your Web to the World with the Personal Web Server," **p. 707**

FIGURE 24.1

The choices shown in the New Web dialog box let you begin a new Web easily.

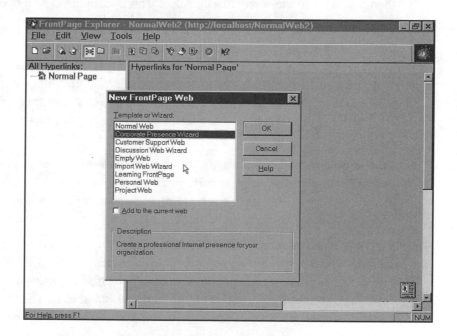

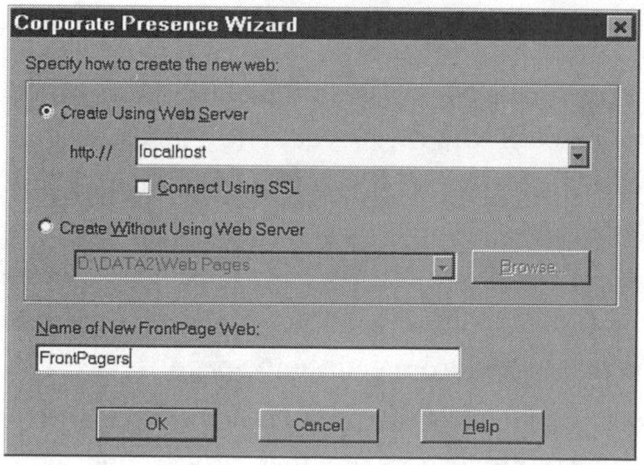

FIGURE 24.2

The New Web from Wizard dialog box lets you set the IP address for your Web server, as well as the name of your Web.

One IP address always available to a Web server, however, is the localhost address of 127.0.0.1 (it's the standard address for a local machine). You may use this IP address to create your Web even if your machine is not currently connected to the Internet. Since FrontPage Explorer lets us copy an entire Web to a different server, the support for localhost means that we can develop the full Web site on an unconnected machine and then transfer it to the server machine later. This is an immensely convenient solution.

Type *127.0.0.1* in the Web Server text box. Then type `FrontPagers` in the Web Name text box. You can actually type anything you want in the Web Name text box, as long as you don't use a space to separate words, because the name doesn't appear anywhere on the Web site itself. It's merely a way to distinguish this Web from other Webs you'll create on your machine. So we'll use FrontPagers to make it easy to remember. Now, click OK to start building your Web. You'll be asked for a username and password as the Web's administrator.

Step 4: Select the Types of Pages You Want in Your Web   Once you've successfully entered the username and password, you'll begin creating the Web's first pages. The Wizard walks you through this procedure, beginning with an opening screen that tells you what you're about to do. From this screen, click the Next button to go to the second stage.

Figure 24.3 shows your first array of choices. You have to create a home page (it's required; thus, the option is grayed out), but you can also include the following types of pages. At this point, you're concerned only with the type of pages you want in your Web. FrontPage creates the pages you decide you need, and they'll all be template pages. After the Web is created, you use FrontPage Editor to change the details on each page, and you use FrontPage Explorer to delete unwanted pages or add new ones.

The page types that you can create from this dialog box are as follows:

■ *What's New*   The What's New page, a standard offering on almost all corporate Web sites, gives readers who revisit your site a quick means of determining whether or not you've added information that might be to their benefit. This page is linked from your home page.

■ *Products/Services*   The Products/Services page, also very common in business sites, allows you to supply information to your readers about what you're actually selling. This page is linked from your home page.

■ *Table of Contents*   Since the Corporate Presence Web is quite extensive, a table of contents page helps your readers find their way around. This page looks like (obviously) a table of contents from a book, with each item linking to the appropriate page.

■ *Feedback Form*   The Wizard can create a form for users to fill in and comment on the site. You can revise this form in any way you like after it's created.

■ *Search Form*   If you have an extensive site, you should provide a search form for users to locate specific information. Note that this isn't a search form for the entire Web (that is, it's not OpenText or Alta Vista) but rather to all the pages within your own Web site.

For this example, you'll create all possible pages from this Wizard. To do so, click the check boxes for all page types that aren't already checked by default. Click Next to continue.

FIGURE 24.3
The more page types you select, the larger your Web site will be.

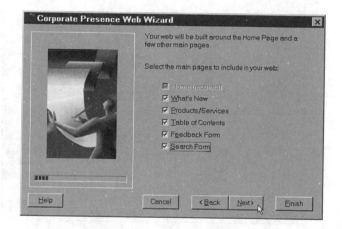

Part
VI

Ch
24

CAUTION
Although this example suggests creating all available pages, in practice you might want to be more selective. Remember that the more pages you create, the more pages you'll need to edit and customize after the Web is in place.

Step 5: Select the Types of Information You Want on Your Home Page   The Wizard creates areas on the home page itself for specific kinds of information. The Introduction offers you a place to tell your users what your home page is about. You can also include a Mission Statement about the company and a full Company Profile outlining what the company is like. Finally, the Wizard creates Contact Information for users to get in touch with you.

Again, you'll create all possible template areas. Click the check boxes for all types. Click Next to continue.

Step 6: Select Elements for the What's New Page   In the "Step 4: Select the Types of Pages You Want in Your Web" section you told the Wizard to create a What's New page. Now, you're asked to select the various elements that appear on that page (see Figure 24.4). Web Changes offers an area to tell users what new pages have been added to the Web since their last visit. If your company issues Press Releases (statements designed for magazines and newspapers about your products, services, and corporate activities), mark the appropriate check box. If your company is well served by Articles and Reviews about your products and services or about further research into your product type, include these as well. In this example, mark all of them for the fullest possible What's New page. Click Next to continue.

FIGURE 24.4
This dialog box lets you tell your reader exactly what's been going on with your company.

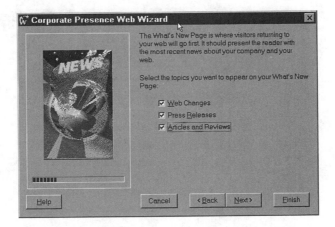

Step 7: Tell the Wizard How Many Products and Services You Want to List   Since you decided in the "Step 4: Select the Types of Pages You Want in Your Web" section to create a Products/Services page, the dialog box lets you determine how many products and services you want to list. The default is three Products and three Services, but let's change it to four products and one service. To do so, enter **5** in the Products text box, and enter **1** in the Services text box. Click Next to continue.

Step 8: Enter Information to Be Displayed About the Products and Services   The dialog box shown in Figure 24.5 lets you set the information you want to offer about the products and services included in the "Step 7: Tell the Wizard How Many Products and Services You Want to List" section. Select Product Image if you have a graphics file with a picture of the product. Pricing Information gives you a place to tell users how much the product costs, while Information Request Form produces a form that potential customers can use to get additional information about the products. For your services, you can offer a list of Capabilities, and you can point to satisfied customers with the Reference Accounts option (but make sure you check with those customers first). A separate Information Request Form lets readers ask for more details about your services.

For this example, check all the items. Click Next to continue.

FIGURE 24.5
Determine in advance how much information you need to provide about each product and service to satisfy your visitors.

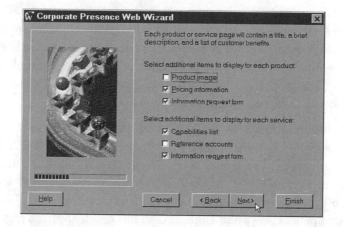

Step 9: Tell the Wizard How to Construct the Feedback Form

In this step, you specify the fields you want to appear on the feedback form you chose in the "Step 4: Select the Types of Pages You Want in Your Web" section (see Figure 24.6). The choices are straightforward, and they include Full Name, Job Title, Company Affiliation, Mailing Address, Telephone Number, FAX Number, and E-Mail Address. Keep in mind that the more information you ask users to produce, the less likely it is they'll fill out the form. But for now, since you're after the most complete site possible, mark all of them. Click Next to continue.

FIGURE 24.6
FrontPage creates a feedback form page with all the options you select.

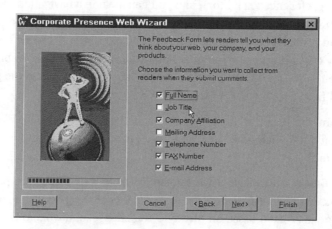

Step 10: Determine Which Format You Want for Forms Information   When users fill in the feedback form, the information is stored in one of two ways. You can have it in Web-page format, which is good if you're going to be taking all the information directly from that page. If you want the information to be fed into a spreadsheet or database, however, you can choose tab-delimited format, which is especially useful if you construct a CGI (Common Gateway Interface) script to place it directly into such a package. As your data needs become more extensive, choosing the tab-delimited method becomes important, but for now, mark Web-Page Format to have the information presented as a Web document. You can change this information once you're inside Editor, where you can add multiple methods for receiving the information. Click Next.

Step 11: Set the Options for the Table of Contents Page   Keep Page List Up-To-Date Automatically does just what it says; FrontPage monitors your Web, adding pages and links to those pages as you create them. Show Pages Not Linked into Web tells Explorer to display, in its viewing area, pages you've created that you haven't actually linked to the main Web (experimental pages or abandoned pages, for example). Use Bullets for Top-Level Pages puts bullets in the Table of Contents beside the main pages, helping your users navigate through your Web. Select all three, and click Next to continue.

Step 12: Tell the Wizard the Information that Should Be Shown on Each Page
Essentially, this dialog box provides a means of adding headers and footers to all the pages in your site (see Figure 24.7). This dialog box lets you specify what elements you want to see on every page in the site, although once the Web is created, you can use Editor to alter or delete these elements on individual pages. If you have a company logo, you might want it to appear on every page, in which case mark Your Company's Logo. The Page Title appears on each page if you want (that is, the HTML title you specify in the document preferences in Editor), and you can include a navigation bar with Links to Your Main Web Pages. At the bottom of the page, you can also offer Links to Your Main Web Pages; you probably don't want this navigation bar both on top and bottom, though, so mark only one. You can also include the E-Mail Address of Your Webmaster (in other words, you), a Copyright Notice that handles the legal thing, and the Date the Page Was Last Modified.

Once again, mark all the boxes, except for the Links to Your Main Web Pages box in the top section of the dialog box (place the navigation bar at the bottom instead). Click Next to continue.

Step 13: Select a Graphics Style for the Pages in Your Site   The principle behind the dialog box shown in Figure 24.8 is to let you choose the global style of your Web site. Every page is created based on the style you choose, and while this offers a corporate theme throughout, if you want some pages to appear different you can alter them by using the document options in Editor. For now, click all the option buttons to see what your choices are, and once you've decided, click Next to continue.

FIGURE 24.7
Several options for presentation style are available for global inclusion across your Web.

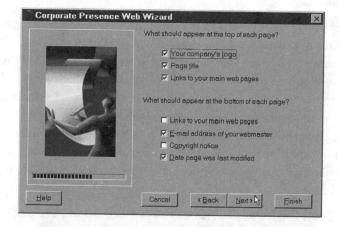

FIGURE 24.8
If you want conservative, be conservative. But cool is still cool.

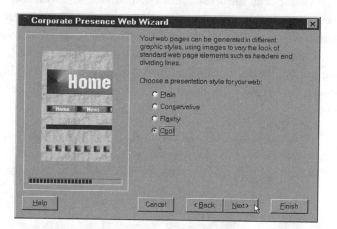

Step 14: Select a Color Scheme for the Pages in Your Site You can select the default color options for all pages in your site. This is a more extensive selection than those found in the preceding section, but it begins with the background you chose in that step. You can alter the background here if you want by choosing a new background color (Solid) or texture (Pattern) in the Pattern drop-down list. You can also specify the colors for Normal Text, Links, Visited Links, and the Active Link. Normal Text refers to the standard text that appears in your document, while Links refer to the normal hyperlinks. Visited Links are those links that the user has already clicked (the change in color reminds the user

Part
VI

Ch
24

that she has done so), and the Active Link is the hyperlink that you are currently clicking; the color changes as you hold down the mouse button. Make your choices and then click Next to continue.

Step 15: Specify Whether or Not You Want Under Construction Signs on Your Unfinished Pages
One of the most common symbols on the Web is the Under Construction sign. The sign tells you that the page has not yet been completed, but at this stage in the Web's history the sign is so overused that it's practically meaningless. This dialog box lets you decide whether or not you want these signs on your pages. Explorer automatically creates a To Do List of uncompleted pages in your Web, which you can update as you complete them (see Chapter 28, "Managing a Web"). As you do so, the Under Construction sign disappears from these pages. However, some people now find the Under Construction sign a bit objectionable, so you should take a few seconds to decide whether or not you want to include it. If so, choose Yes; if not, choose No. Click Next to continue.

Step 16: Enter the Name and Address of Your Company
The next step is to type the full name, abbreviation, and address of your company. This information appears on your Web pages throughout. Figure 24.9 shows the dialog box in which you enter this information. The full name of your company goes in the top text box, and the company's street address in the bottom text box. Type **FrontPagers Corporation** in the first, and any address you want in the bottom. In the middle field goes a one-word version of this name, and the obvious choice is, simply, FrontPagers. When you've completed these entries, click the Next button.

FIGURE 24.9
This information appears throughout the Web, so double-check the spelling.

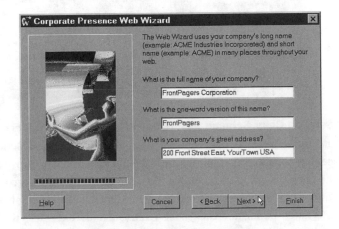

Step 17: Complete Your Company Information   In the dialog box following the name and address dialog box, you can enter the Company's Telephone Number and Fax Number, along with the E-Mail Address of Your Webmaster (that is, the individual responsible for maintaining the Web, probably you), and the E-Mail Address for General Info about the company. Typically, the Webmaster's address is webmaster@yourcompany.com, and the information address is info@yourcompany.com, so for this example type in **webmaster@frontpagers.com** and **info@frontpagers.com**, respectively. Keep in mind, however, that the domain name is still not fully registered, so you can't assign e-mail addresses to it. As a result, you might want to enter your own e-mail address instead. When you're done, click Next.

Step 18: Decide Whether or Not to View the To Do List   The last step in the creation of the Corporate Presence Web is to choose if you want the To Do List to appear whenever the Web is loaded into Explorer. It's always a good idea, so mark the check box. This time, though, click Finish, which has replaced the Next button, because the Wizard has taken you as far as it can go.

Now that you've created the Web, your To Do List appears on-screen, showing the pages you have yet to complete, along with a number of other important details. As explained in detail in Chapter 28, "Managing a Web," you explore how to work with this list, but for now take note of it as an important step in the building of your Web. FrontPage continues to revise this list as you finish some pages and add others. For now, you can hide the list by minimizing it or by clicking FrontPage Explorer, which hides it behind that main window.

▶ **See** "Managing A Web," **p. 689**

When you bring the FrontPage Explorer window to the foreground, you see the Outline View of the Web in the left pane of the window, and the Link view on the right (see Figure 24.10). This is what you've been aiming for: a Web in place and ready for action. If you were connected to the Internet, and if you'd assigned this Web to a real IP number instead of the generic localhost number, your site would now be accessible from any computer in the world connected to the Internet. From this point on, all you need to do is modify and alter your new Web, and once it's finished, you can transfer it to a fully operational, 24-hour Web server machine.

Part
VI

Ch
24

FIGURE 24.10
Presto! Your new Web
is ready for your loving
care.

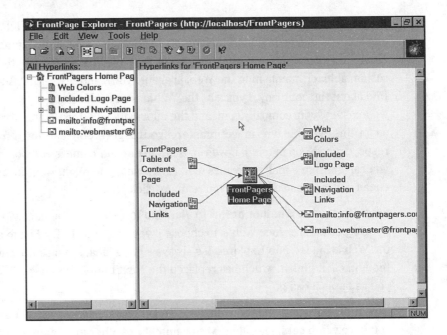

From Here...

In this chapter you've performed the most fundamental task in FrontPage: creating a Web. Since this is the essential purpose of FrontPage, taking it step by step is an important way to get started, hence the approach taken earlier. But there's far more to building the perfect Web than just running through a wizard, no matter how helpful that wizard may be. First, you'll need to consider which wizard or template is the most suited to your needs, and then you'll have to configure the Web and put it into place. To explore all of these issues and to move beyond them, see the following chapters:

■ Chapter 25, "FrontPage's Templates and Wizards," examines each of Explorer's templates and wizards in detail.

■ Chapter 26, "Working with an Existing Web," shows you how to use FrontPage to redevelop a Web you've already put in place.

■ Chapter 27, "Configuring Your Webs," covers the details pertaining to establishing Web permissions and other issues.

FrontPage's Templates and Wizards

In Chapter 24, "Building a Web," you explored the sophistication of FrontPage Explorer's Wizard for creating a Corporate Presence Web, including what to do with it once you've stepped through the process. But FrontPage includes several other templates and wizards for Web building, and this chapter explains how to create each of them and what each of them contains. Since these templates have the potential to form the basis of your Webs—even Webs created for larger organizations—knowing what they hold for you is necessary if you want to use FrontPage to its greatest potential.

The Discussion Web Wizard

Create a full chat site and customize it to your liking by using the Discussion Wizard.

Empty Web and Normal Web

If all you want is a starting point, the Empty and Normal Webs are for you.

Customer Support Web

What does a support Web look like? What should it contain? How should the FrontPage version be altered?

Project Web

How to use Explorer to establish an intranet-like project management site.

Personal Web

Put your resume and your favorite links on the Web with all the necessary trimmings.

Once again, though, there's a downside to all of this. If you let FrontPage create your entire site, and all other FrontPage users decide to do the same, then pretty soon your Web site will look almost identical to lots of other sites out on the Net. To avoid this problem, let the FrontPage wizards work their magic, but then cast a few of your own design spells to make the Web your own. The whole point about the Web wizards is that they give you something to work with, not that they give you a site that needs no further work. To increase your Web's effectiveness, load each page into the FrontPage Editor and change the wording, the appearance, and even the navigation from page to page. In other words, use the Editor to make your site unique. ■

 TIP After creating a Web, the most effective way of seeing what you've done is to load the Web's home page into a Web browser such as Netscape Navigator or Microsoft Internet Explorer. The Webs created by FrontPage's templates and wizards offer links among the various pages to help you discover what's been built. The home page for each Web is the file named INDEX.HTM within that Web's main directory.

The Discussion Web Wizard

The procedure for creating Webs based on one particular FrontPage wizard, the Corporate Presence Wizard, is covered in Chapter 24, but Explorer offers a second wizard, the Discussion Web Wizard, and it deserves a close look as well. Its purpose and its requirements are considerably different from and significantly more advanced than the Corporate Presence Wizard. The Discussion Web creates an area where readers can participate in a forum on a topic of their choice and, as such, demands some special considerations at the time of creation.

Creating a discussion Web from scratch requires an intimate knowledge of the Discussion Bot. This is covered in detail in Chapter 10, "Using WebBots, Wizards, and Interactive Page Templates," but its basics are covered here. Essentially, the Discussion Bot lets discussion groups come into being in the first place by allowing documents created with FrontPage to cooperate with the Web server in a fully interactive way. The Discussion Web, in fact, demonstrates the practical value of FrontPage, because creating such a Web without FrontPage's Bots requires an advanced knowledge of the Common Gateway Interface (CGI). Ultimately, CGI is something you'll want to know, but FrontPage enables you to create interactive Web sites of considerable sophistication without some of the most frequently used programming requirements necessary with CGI.

> **CAUTION**
>
> It's important to keep in mind as you build Webs with FrontPage that its CGI capabilities, although immensely useful and time-saving, are limited. If you want to develop a full Web site with extensive links to databases and other information sources, you'll need to understand CGI programming. What makes FrontPage so welcome in this regard is that it takes care of the most common CGI elements.

The first step in creating a Discussion Web is to launch your Web server (FrontPage's Personal Web Server or another) and then choose File, New Web. Actually, launching Explorer will also launch the FrontPage Personal Web Server, so if that's the server you're using, then this is a one-step process; only if you've chosen to use a different server do you need to start the server first.

From the resulting Create New Web dialog box, choose Discussion Web Wizard. This launches the Wizard, which guides you through the creation of this Web much as the Corporate Presence Web Wizard helps you build a Web of that type from scratch. You will need to name your new Web, and you must inform FrontPage on the initial dialog box whether or not you want to add this Web to the current Web or create an entirely new one.

To keep easy control over access to your Webs and to help you keep track of HTML files you've added, create new Webs rather than adding them to your existing Web. This places your Web files in a new directory and helps compartmentalize your Web designs.

Types of Pages to Include

The first choices you have to make come from the second screen in the wizard. Here you can choose to include the following pages of information:

- Submission Form—The submission form is necessary for readers to compose and post articles. You don't have a choice about including this one, but it's the only required element.

- Table of Contents—This page offers readers an easy-to-navigate area from which to choose whether they want to search or read the discussions, or post a message of their own. If you want, the Discussion Web (on a later dialog box) will replace the current home page of the Web with this table of contents, a recommended procedure if the discussion forum will be a primary focus of your Web. You can just as easily offer a link to the contents page from your existing home page (or any other document for that matter), so at this stage it's probably better to say no to that replacement.

■ Search Form—The Wizard will create a search form with which your readers can find articles in the Web that have the specified text strings or patterns. If you're planning a site with numerous postings, and especially on a variety of topics, be sure to include this form. Without it, the forum will be less useful than it might be.

■ Threaded Replies—Threaded replies are practically a necessity in any kind of discussion forum, especially those with numerous postings. Simply, threads let readers reply to specific articles within a topic, rather than posting only the topic itself. Again, this is a good choice to make, although if your readers don't use threading effectively, you might find that articles tend to be disordered. A well-run discussion forum can make extremely good use of threaded replies, so unless you know why you wouldn't want them, they're always a good idea.

■ Confirmation Page—The confirmation page lets readers know whether or not they've successfully sent their postings to the Web. Without this page, readers' articles are posted without them having any way of knowing it. Like the other possible elements, the confirmation page is a good idea, so there's every reason to include it.

Title and Input Fields

After selecting the pages you want to include, you can give your discussion forum a descriptive title. Don't just call it "Discussion"—instead, give it a name that will make its purpose clear to all your readers. This title appears on the top of all pages in the discussion Web, so giving it a bit of thought is worthwhile.

N O T E   The name you give to your Web is also the name of the subdirectory FrontPage creates in the main document directory for your Web server. This is normally established at the time of naming your Web, not while giving it the descriptive title described here. Still, you can change the name of this folder to something more meaningful as long as you remember to begin the new name with the underscore character. ■

In the subsequent dialog box, you must decide which input fields you want on the submission form for the Web. At the very least, this form will include a subject field and a comments field. In the subject field, the user will enter the topic the posting is about; in the comments field, the user will type the actual message. You can determine the possible topics of discussion by including all possibilities in a pull-down menu; this way, you can ensure that all messages are assigned a meaningful topic.

If you want, you can add either a category field or product field to this list. If you have a discussion about a large topic (let's say types of Internet software), you might want to offer categories in addition to subjects. As with subjects, you can specify the available categories through a pull-down menu on the submission form. The product field replaces the category field on the final grouping of input fields, and if you offer several different products to your customers, or if your subjects are product-based rather than category-based, choose the product field instead.

Registration

The most difficult (and perhaps significant) decision you will make when creating a discussion Web is whether or not to insist that your readers must register in order to read or post articles. If you choose to do so, you will build a *protected* Web, and all who register will have their user names and passwords built into your Web's permissions area. Your other choice is to leave the Web unprotected, meaning that anyone can post messages.

▶ **See** "Configuring Your Webs," **p. 669**

On the surface of it, an unprotected Web might seem the more desirable choice. After all, the World Wide Web is known as a place of freedom and openness, and offering a discussion group in which users must register might seem inappropriate or even offensive. But there are a few things to keep in mind about this issue. First, on a purely nice-to-have basis, articles posted within a registered Web will automatically include the user's registered names.

More importantly, though, you should consider the purpose of the discussion forum. If you want to offer your readers a place all their own in which to post messages, questions, and suggestions to one another, why not give them a protected area in which to do so. Of course, there's nothing stopping anyone on the Web from registering, so even here the discussion can be considered open. To prevent this, you can build in further password protection to your Web, based on product serial numbers. In this latter case, only those who have *Special Edition Using Microsoft FrontPage* in front of them can actually register. This gives the people who bought the book an added value for their purchase. At least, that's our hope.

To participate in the *Special Edition Using Microsoft FrontPage* discussion Web, turn to **http://mariner.uwaterloo.ca**—you'll see a link from there to the discussion area.

Order of Articles and Home Page

After deciding on registration, you can elect to sort the posted articles from oldest to newest or newest to oldest. They will then appear on the Web's Table of Contents in the chosen order. The former gives a chronological feel to the discussions, and as readers scroll the messages they can see how the discussion has developed. On the other hand, this means that extended discussions require scrolling at virtually all times, and that could become a bit annoying. Sorting from newest to oldest places the most recent articles at the top of the page, and frequent readers will know what has come before. Generally, newest to oldest is the preferred order.

After making this decision, you're given the option of having the Table of Contents page become the home page for the discussion Web. If you take the option, the Table of Contents page will replace the current home page. This option takes effect only if you have not chosen to add the discussion Web to the current Web when first creating the Web, because if not, the Table of Contents page automatically becomes the home page for a discussion Web on its own.

Search Details

The next dialog box lets you select the criteria by which the search form will report documents a search has located. There are four choices: Subject; Subject and Size; Subject, Size, and Date; or Subject, Size, Date, and Score. All searches will reveal the subject of the located article. Adding size gives information about the size of the article in kilobytes. Date adds information about when the article was posted. Score shows the reader a measure of how relevant the article is to the search string entered. A score of 1000 is a direct hit, while a score of 100 or less is of lesser relevance.

The choice here has to do with how much information you want your server to compute, as well as how much your feel your readers need. For a large discussion forum, the more information you provide, the more useful the searches will be. Smaller discussion forums, on the other hand, might very well not need this much information about the search.

Page Colors and Frame Styles

As with the Corporate Presence Web shown in Chapter 24, the Wizard for the Discussion Web lets you select the global style for text and link colors and the background graphics or color. After selecting these, however, the Discussion Web Wizard carries the design choice one step further by offering a dialog box for the style of a page displaying frames. This dialog box is shown in Figure 25.1.

The purpose of this dialog box is to let you display your articles on a Web page that contains frames. Frames, or windows inside a main Web window, were first offered with

FIGURE 25.1

The Frames dialog box of the Discussion Web Wizard offers four choices.

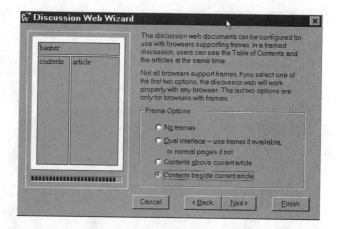

Netscape Navigator 2.0 but have since become an important design component on the Web in general. Microsoft Internet Explorer 3.0 also supports frames, which comes as no surprise given that FrontPage Editor, also from Microsoft, offers a Frame Wizard.

▶ **See** Using WebBots, Wizards, and Interactive Page Templates," **p. 225**

The Discussion Web Wizard offers to divide the discussion articles page into zero, two, or three frames. If you want to guarantee that all Web users will be able to access your articles, choose No Frames. If you want to use frames to their fullest extent, choose either Contents Above Current Article or Contents Beside Current Article (this latter is pictured in Figure 25.1 above). Both choices create three frames, one showing the page's contents, one the actual articles, and the third a banner displaying whatever you want. If you want the best of both worlds—an articles page that offers frames to those with frames-capable browsers and an articles page with no frames for those without—choose Dual Interface. The frames in this last case include one showing the contents and another showing the actual text of the articles; the banner frame is not included.

The Self-Registration Form

After making your decision about frames, you've completed the Wizard. Clicking Finish starts the actual creation of the Web with all your pages in place. Before the Web is formed, however, the Wizard loads FrontPage Editor with the Web self-registration form loaded (see Figure 25.2). Note that this document is created only if you have chosen the registration option discussed above.

Part
VI

Ch
25

FIGURE 25.2

The self-registration form will allow your users to register themselves.

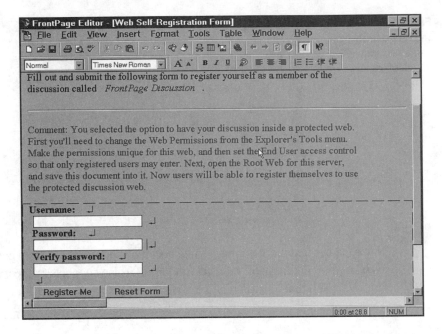

Installing the self-registration form into your Web is a bit complex, and even a bit confusing. Nevertheless, the instructions provided on the template page itself are complete enough to guide you through.

To get the self-registration system working properly, you must first switch from the Editor (don't close it, though) to Explorer, where you'll find the Discussion Web fully created (it's shown in Figure 25.3). Next, you must open the Web Permissions dialog box in Explorer (from the Tools menu), and choose the option Use Unique Permissions for This Web. Click Apply from that dialog box to set these permissions, then click the Users tab to make another change. Here, select the choice Only Registered Users Have Browse Access, and then click Apply once more. Finally, click OK to close the dialog box. You have now set the permissions in your discussion Web to accommodate registered users.

▶ **See** "Configuring Your Webs," **p. 669**

You probably noticed that in the Users dialog box you can set users manually. What makes the self-registration form particularly useful is that you don't have to do so. The information from the self-registration form is passed to Explorer to create the users automatically. Obviously, this saves you both time and trouble.

FIGURE 25.3

The completed discussion Web makes a number of pages available for editing.

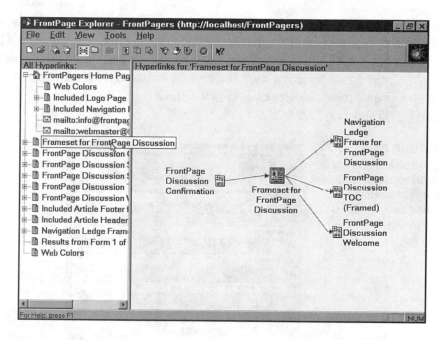

The next step will make the self-registration page available for your readers to add the information necessary to update the Users configuration area. With the Web self-registration form still loaded in FrontPage Editor, return to Explorer and close the Discussion Web. Then open the root Web of the server. Now, switch back to Editor and use the File menu to save the self-registration page into the root Web. Leave the title and file name as suggested by the Save As dialog box.

To assure yourself that the self-registration form is being properly applied to the discussion Web, click any of the form fields (Username will do) to select it. Then right-click in the field and select Form Properties. From the resulting dialog box, click Settings, and you'll see the dialog box shown in Figure 25.4. The form should show the same name in the Web name field as you entered when you began building the Web. This ensures that the registrations will be applied to that Web alone.

At this point, you should test the self-registration form. With your Web server running, launch a Web browser such as Microsoft Internet Explorer or Netscape Navigator and enter the URL for the file WEBREG.HTM (that is, the file containing the self-registration form). If you're running the Personal Web Server from the localhost address, for example, enter in the Location Box of your browser the URL **http://localhost/webreg.htm** or **http://127.0.0.1/webreg.htm** (if you changed the name of the file from

WEBREG.HTM, enter it instead). If you've saved the file to a remote Web server, enter the appropriate IP number or domain name in place of **localhost** or **127.0.0.1**. Because the self-registration form was saved to the root Web, you need not enter a path for the file, merely the file name itself. Later, you'll want to link the self-registration file from your home page, so users can access it without typing the file name. The self-registration form is shown in Figure 25.5.

FIGURE 25.4

Make sure the correct Web name appears in the Forms Settings dialog box.

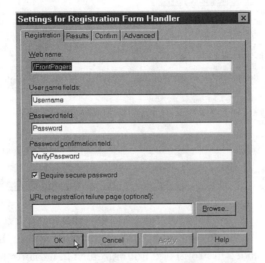

FIGURE 25.5

The self-registration form in Netscape Navigator, ready to accept its first registrant.

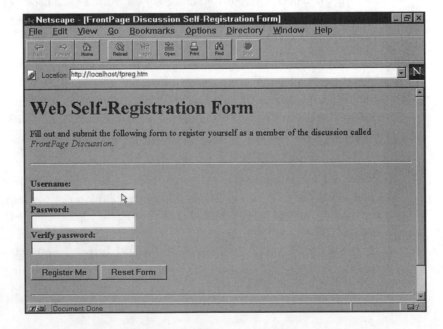

Fill in the username and password fields with whatever names and passwords you want, then click the Register Me button. You'll receive a confirmation page showing that the registration has been successful, unless the username is already in the FrontPage database (this happens if you choose your administrator username as a name here, for instance), if your password is shorter than six characters, or if the password doesn't verify because of mistyping.

To see if the user has been registered, open the discussion Web in Explorer and select the Permissions dialog box from the Tools menu. Click the End Users tab, and you should see that the registered username now appears in the user area. As more and more users register themselves, this listing increases in size. You may close this dialog box.

Returning to the confirmation page, you'll see that it contains a link to the discussion Web itself. When you click that hyperlink, you'll get a dialog box requiring you to enter a username and password. Choose the newly registered name, and you'll be allowed into the Web. At this stage, you may begin posting messages to the discussion forum, and if you establish more than one username, you can experiment by sending and replying to messages, then searching them and checking the contents page for results.

Finishing the Discussion Web

With the discussion Web in place, very little remains to put it into place. You'll probably want to edit the registration form and give it a title that clarifies what Web it belongs to, and you'll definitely want to provide a hyperlink from your main home page to both the registration page—to allow users to register—and to the discussion Web's home page—to let them sign in and participate. Assuming you allowed the Wizard to establish the table of contents page as the discussion Web's home page, the name of that file will be [WebName]/INDEX.HTM (replace [WebName] with the actual name of the Web, of course). The registration file will be in the root Web directory, and will be named whatever you called it when you saved it to that directory after the completion of the Wizard.

Inside the Web, you might want to edit the Contents page and the Welcome page to add some spice to them. Open other pages in Editor and see which you want to edit in addition to these. The last change you might want to make is to set password protection for the posting page itself, in order to restrict further who has access to it. This must be done from your Web server's administrator, however, not from within FrontPage.

Empty Web and Normal Web

Two of FrontPage's Web templates are designed to offer only minimal help to you as Web designer. The Empty Web template creates, as its name suggests, a Web with nothing in it. Its only purpose is to create the directory (which it take from your Web's name) into which all documents will be stored, after which it's your task to develop the Web as you want. The Normal Web adds only one element to this: a home page that gives you a place to start. This home page, however, doesn't actually include any text or graphics; it's simply an empty HTML page, waiting for your design decisions.

Customer Support Web

Creating the customer support Web does not require working through a wizard; in fact, there is no corresponding wizard. To create this Web, select Customer Support Web from the New Web dialog box, and FrontPage will create a Web that looks like that shown in Figure 25.6.

FIGURE 25.6

The customer support Web features all you need to offer top-notch service.

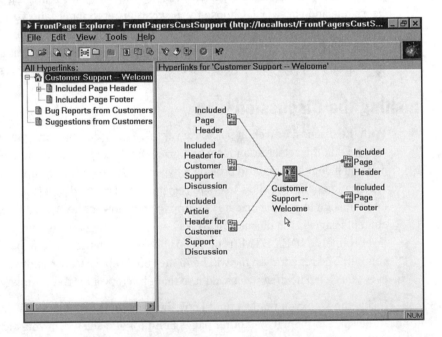

This Web is designed to let you provide a full range of services for your clients. Its design, however, replicates the many computer company sites on the Web, and if you have a different kind of product or service, not all the pages will be of use to you. They can be modified, of course, and certainly two or more of the pages will be useful, but expect to do a significant amount of redesign on this Web. If you plan to offer software or hardware products, on the other hand, the Customer Service Web will get you half-way to your goal.

To make the suggested changes to this Web, you'll need to load each individual page into FrontPage Editor, usually by double-clicking the page's icon from Explorer's Link View. To get an idea of what the page looks like, load it into your Web browser by using the appropriate URL with the path /[Support Web Name]/INDEX.HTM.

Page 1: Welcome

The first page in the Customer Service Web (INDEX.HTM) welcomes your users to your site and provides a set of links to all the other pages on the site. This page provides a general welcome, along with parenthesized "fields" which you are expected to alter to customize the page for your own company. Begin at the top of the file, giving a clear company name and adding a logo if you have one, and be sure to use the Page and Web Properties features to give your site a color and graphical thematic unity. Be sure to change the copyright information at the bottom of the page as well.

▶ **See** "Developing the Basic Page: Text, Lists, and Hyperlinks," **p. 65**

The important thing to realize is that this page provides the entry to the entire Web site. As such, it gives your readers an all-important first impression, and you don't want to let that get away. Work hard on this Welcome page, perhaps even harder than on all the rest.

Page 2: What's New

The purpose of the What's New page is to show your readers what has been added to the site recently. Again, the page needs a great deal of work to make it consistent with your company's image, but more importantly, you must decide precisely how to display the links to the new information, as well as (and this is crucial) how often to update. In a true customer service site, the What's New page is perhaps the single most important component of the site. If you don't intend to keep the page up-to-date regularly, get rid of it and erase all links to it. If you do keep it, make sure that the links point correctly to their corresponding documents. One link is already provided, and this is to a template for a technical document, complete with inline graphic. By all means use this document as a basis, but if you have your own, use it instead.

Page 3: Frequently Asked Questions

One of the main reasons for offering customer support over the Web is to minimize the need for support over the telephone. The most effective way of doing so is to provide answers on the Web site to questions the telephone support staff receive regularly. The FAQ (Frequently Asked Questions) page of the customer support site is designed as a template to help you put these together. This page offers a set of questions early in the page that contains internal links to answers further down the page. This is a good structure by which to get started, but if questions demand more than a paragraph or two of response, it would be better to link to other, longer documents instead.

Page 4: Bug Report

If your business is to sell software, you'll inevitably run into the problem known as "bugs" or imperfections. The purpose of the Bug Report page in the Customer Service Web is to allow your users to report bugs they find in your product. It's not acceptable for software companies to insist that their product does not contain bugs, because all computer users know differently, and generally accept the fact that bugs exist. This page, then, shows that you're up-front about trying to fix them, rather than suggesting that they're not there in the first place.

The Bug Report page offers a form for readers to fill in and submit. This form is shown in Netscape Navigator in Figure 25.7, and it contains two drop-down selection menus and several fill-in fields. Your primary task, aside from introducing the bug report according to your company policies and redesigning the page according to a consistent color and graphic scheme, is to customize the form to invite the information you need. Spend some time considering exactly that question, because an effective bug report form can optimize the usefulness, and thus the salability, of your product.

FIGURE 25.7

The Bug Report form offers several fields for readers to select.

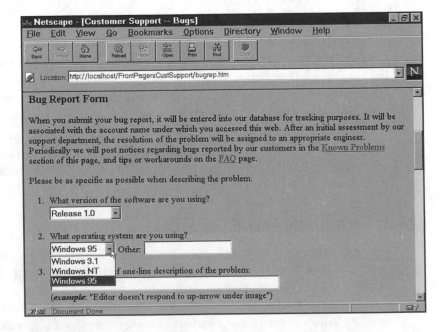

Page 5: Suggestions

If you're genuinely not interested in what your site's visitors think of your Web site or your products, get rid of this page immediately. There's nothing worse than offering a suggestion page that you never pay attention to, because visitors who make suggestions want to feel that they're making a difference. If you are interested in your visitors suggestions, however (and any good service-oriented company should be), customize this page to invite the feedback you need to make your products or services more successful. Of particular importance is customizing the "category" portion of the form, because through this drop-down menu you encourage readers to speak up about specific topics.

Page 6: Download

It's become a given on the Internet that if you want to sell software, you have to let users download at least a demo version so they can try it out. When people purchase your software, you must provide downloadable upgrades from your Web site as well. The Download page lets you provide these services, although to make it work properly you'll have to customize it significantly. The template page provides a simple suggestion of how to deal with different file formats and multiple download items, but visiting any software or hardware company on the Web will give you some much better ideas about how to offer your product.

> **CAUTION**
>
> Failing to test the Download page will cause a negative impression from your readers. If a click does not produce the software, your users will be angry or at least disappointed. Be sure to test—and not just from one machine. Log in to your site through a modem and make sure everything works right.

Part

VI

Ch

25

Page 7: Discussion

The Discussion page on the Customer Service Web offers a place for your readers to discuss your products and services with other users and with company representatives. Note that, while there's no requirement in the Web itself for a company representative to take part, it's extremely important that one be present, to avoid the embarrassing possibility of customers saying incorrect or demeaning things about your products. The discussion area resembles that created with the full discussion Web examined earlier in this chapter, and you can customize it to provide as full a discussion forum as you want, including offering user registration.

> **N O T E** As with the Download page, be absolutely certain the discussion area works well before making it public, and also be sure that you intend to pay attention to the discussion. ■

Page 8: Search

Figure 25.8 shows a portion of the Search page created by the Customer Service Web template. It's simple, but as the description of the query language at the bottom of the page demonstrates, it's not simplistic. You can't possibly know how or even if your readers will make use of this page, but it's a good idea to have one, and it's a good idea also to construct pages that anticipate reader searches, building in common keywords and text strings.

FIGURE 25.8

The Search page contains a description of the query language used by FrontPage.

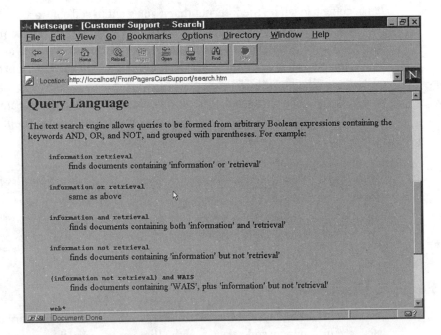

Project Web

The Project Web offers a means for members of a team project to keep in touch with each other, and perhaps more importantly, a place for you to put all information about the project that everyone involved should be able to retrieve. Its primary use will be in an *intranet*, which is a Web site that exists within an organization and which typically does not offer access to users outside the organization. For some organizations, the Project Web will be sufficient to replace more complex software packages such as Lotus Notes, but even within these organizations, a Project Web might suffice for a small working group collaborating on a specific project or portion of a project.

Page 1: Home

The template home page for the Project Web offers a brief description and a What's New area, as well as a series of links to the other pages in the Web. Because a Project Web is meant primarily as an internal site, there's not as much need for extensive editing to appeal to customers. The design decisions made here should reflect your management goals of professionalism and efficiency, and should be less marketing-driven than the customer support site. Members of the Project Web will usually be your coworkers and employees of the same company as yourself, and will expect a certain amount of "cutting through the hype." The efficiency will be displayed in providing ease of access to information, and by constantly updating the What's New information.

Page 2: Members

The Members page of the Project Web offers an alphabetical listing of those involved in the project, and the links from that list lead to the type of generic profile shown in Figure 25.9. By replacing all the names with real names, the pictures with real pictures, and the e-mail addresses and personal URLs with valid ones, you can create a useful, dynamic page of information that members can share. From this page, members can e-mail one another and visit one another's home page, and the page can therefore act as a team bond. Be absolutely certain, however, that all information is correct, or risk anything from embarrassment to downright anger.

Page 3: Schedule

What's a project without a schedule? Nothing, obviously, so the template creates a schedule page for you. On this page are three main sections: a list of goals and activities in the current and following weeks, a showcase of upcoming events pertaining to the project, and a listing of milestones and deliverables.

The function of the schedule, of course, is to keep all project members aware of progress to date and necessary progress to come. To that end, it's imperative that this page be kept updated constantly. Slip here, and you risk losing the very credibility of the Web site. The best bet is to alter this page as soon as you can to fit the project you're running rather than the one the template suggests, then keep returning to it to keep the project team focused.

FIGURE 25.9
From the Members page, team members can interact with one another.

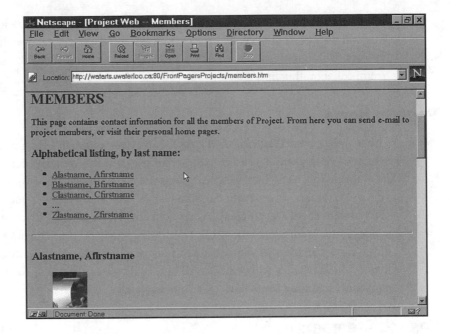

Page 4: Status

Assuming the project is large and long enough, you'll probably be required to file status reports as the work continues. The Status page offers a place to collect those reports and make them available to members of the project team. The titles of the hyperlinks on the template page assume monthly and quarterly reports for the current year, quarterly and annual reports for last year, and annual reports for previous years of the project. The links on the page don't in fact lead anywhere, and it's your job to supply the actual documents. Clearly, this page is only as useful as your status reports allow, and you might not want it as part of your Web if you have no reports to include. But it can be easily modified to allow weekly reports, subteam reports, and so forth.

Page 5: Archive

If your project team has developed a significant number of documents, prototypes, programs, tools, and other demonstrable items, you will want to offer them as a project archive. The Archive page (see Figure 25.10) is designed as a kind of catch-all for this kind of material. Each internal link leads to a description of the item and further links to the documents in a variety of formats. Obviously, it's up to you to provide the materials, and in all likelihood you'll want to completely revamp the presentation of this page. But it's an excellent suggestion for a page within the Web.

FIGURE 25.10
The Archive page offers links to documents in various formats.

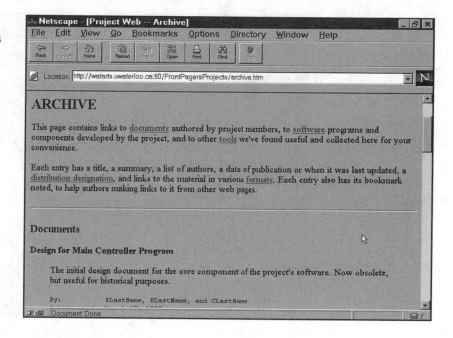

Page 6: Search

The Search page is identical to the one offered in the Customer Support Web discussed above, and requires only a minor degree of tinkering. Otherwise, just leave it as it stands.

Page 7: Discussions

Page 7 of the Customer Support Web was also a discussion area, but the difference here is that the Discussions page of the Project Web contains two discussion groups already built in. The principle is to provide a separate discussion forum for as many topics as your project members require, and the page describes each forum and invites participation from the appropriate parties. You can add as many discussion groups as you want, but starting with two or three seems the best idea, to keep things under control.

Personal Web

The Personal Web is, essentially, a combination resume and special interest Web. Figure 25.11 shows the generic home page information offered by this page, all of which is in need of customization before this Web becomes public.

FIGURE 25.11
The Personal Web is little more than a resume, but a complete one.

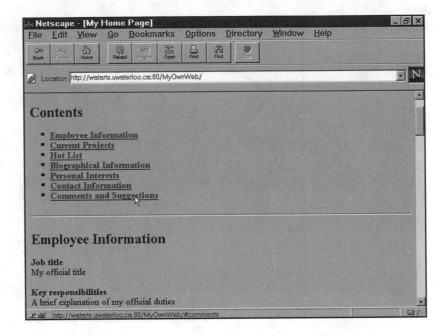

Lower on the page, the template offers a place to insert links to external sites, as well as contact information and even a form for comments from outsiders. There's even an area on this page for links to reports from associates and employees, and obviously you want to make sure these are flattering. In fact, this entire Web template is of questionable value, because a personal site should be handled with very great care depending on its purpose. If you want employers to look at it, be sure to keep that audience in mind. If you want friends or random Web visitors to see it, why include job information? And so on. Consider carefully, and change the site dramatically.

Files Created by FrontPage's New Webs

When you build a Web with the FrontPage New Web feature, several directories and files are created on the machine running the Web server software. Note that these are in addition to the directories and files created by installing the FrontPage server extensions in the first place.

Each Web produces the same directory structure, although individual files differ according to the type of Web (Corporate Presence, Project, and so on) being built. This structure is as follows, and is shown in Figure 25.12 in a Windows 95 Explorer window.

FIGURE 25.12
All FrontPage-created
Webs share this rather
elaborate directory
structure.

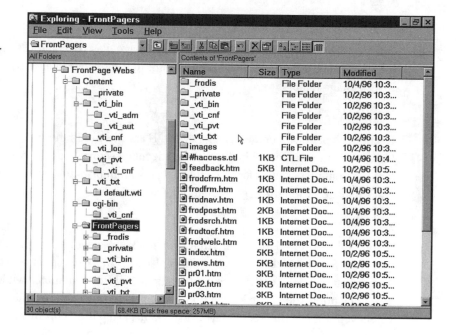

WebName/

The files and directories for the individual Webs you create are stored within a directory that bears the name you gave the Web in the New Web dialog box.

_private/

In general, all directories that begin with the underscore character (_) are hidden from Web visitors. They're also hidden from the view in FrontPage Explorer, unless the option Show Documents in Hidden Directories is toggled on within the Advanced portion of the Web Settings dialog.

The _private/ directory works somewhat differently. It contains files that you want to keep invisible to your Web's visitors, and these files will not show up in a search produced by the Search Bot. But the directory is visible within FrontPage Explorer, because it's one to which you'll want frequent access.

cgi-bin/

The cgi-bin directory is designed to hold any CGI (Common Gateway Interface) scripts you create for the forms you produce in your Web, or CGI programs such as counters to show how many people have visited the site. Note that these CGI scripts have nothing to do with the Form Bots produced by FrontPage itself.

images/

The images directory offers a place to store image files (GIF and JPG, for example). This directory makes it easy for FrontPage Editor to locate your images when you use the Insert Image dialog box.

_vti_cnf/

Every Web page you create, that is, every .HTM file within the Web, has a corresponding file of the same name within the Web's _vti_cnf directory. This private directory holds files that contain name values for the public page, with information such as the last author to edit the page, when the page was edited, and so forth.

_vti_shm/

If you build an HTML document that contains WebBots, one page is kept in the main directory for that Web, while a second is placed in the Web's private _vti_shm directory. The private versions of the page contain the actual Bot definitions, while the Web's main directory holds the expanded version of the page. FrontPage recreates the expanded page whenever you use the Recalculate Links feature from the Tools menu of FrontPage Explorer.

_vti_bin/

The private _vti_bin directory contains three executable programs to be used in conjunction with FrontPage's WebBots and administrative functions. _vti_bin itself contains the file SHTML.EXE, which handles all HTML documents in your Web that control some aspect of the browser's behavior (such as WebBot forms). Within _vti_bin are two subdirectories, _vti_adm and _vti_aut. The first of these contains the ADMIN.EXE file, which handles administrator procedures such as permissions and Web creation. The second contains AUTHOR.EXE, which handles author procedures, including permissions.

_vti_txt/

To make searches possible, each Web contains a _vti_txt directory that contains a text index file. Within each _vti_txt directory in a default.wti/ directory, which contains one set of files for discussion groups created with the Discussion Group Web Wizard (if you've done so for that Web), and another set for all other HTML documents.

TIP If you don't plan to allow searches against your site, consider deleting the _vti_txt directory completely. This will reduce the memory needed for the Recalculate Links command.

_vti_pvt/

The _vti_pvt directory contains several private files, including the Web's parameters, the list of sub-Webs (in the root directory only), the To-Do list, and the To-Do list history.

From Here...

The wizards and templates in FrontPage Explorer's New Web dialog box are immensely useful as a starting point for Web creation. But be careful not just to build a generic Web and then let it drop. Among other reasons, if all FrontPage buyers did the same thing, your site would be utterly indistinctive. More important, though, the Web site is the way potentially millions of people will see you and your company, or how your employees or fellow project members will get a first-hand look at your work. The templates are great to have, but they're just the beginning of the real work. Now it's time to start that work, by moving on to:

- Chapter 26, "Working with an Existing Web," details how to edit and improve a Web already on your server.
- Chapter 27, "Configuring Your Webs," is where you'll learn the techniques behind Web configurations and permissions.
- Part VII, "The FrontPage SDK," is where you'll explore the means by which the package's Software Development Kit lets you fully customize your FrontPage environment.

Part
VI

Ch
25

## CHAPTER 26

Working with an Existing Web

Creating a Web using FrontPage's templates and wizards is all well and good, but once those procedures are complete, your work has merely begun. You'll have to alter each page in the Web by working closely with FrontPage Editor but, just as important, you must change and enhance the existing Web through the powerful features of FrontPage Explorer. This chapter contains a detailed look at the Explorer windows and menu and demonstrates several shortcuts and advanced features for working with your Webs. ■

Loading a FrontPage Web into Explorer

Once you have one or more Webs created with FrontPage 97, you can load them into FrontPage Explorer by choosing File, Open FrontPage Web or by clicking the Open icon on Explorer's toolbar. If you've just loaded FrontPage itself, you can also open a Web by clicking Open Existing FrontPage Web from the Getting Started With Microsoft FrontPage beginning screen. Whichever method you choose, the Open Web dialog box appears (see Figure 26.1).

Note that this command is useful only for loading Webs created with FrontPage itself. If you have a Web created outside FrontPage, use the Import Web feature described later in this chapter.

FIGURE 26.1

At this stage, the Open Web dialog box has no Webs to load.

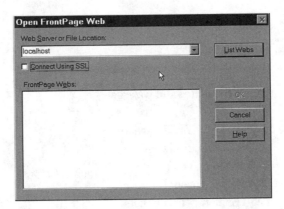

Your first task is to choose the Web server where the Web resides. First, click on the down-arrow beside the Web Server or File Location field to open the drop-down list. This reveals all servers you've worked with so far; if you've dealt only with the localhost IP number, that is the only IP that appears in this field.

▶ **See** "Building a Web," **p. 611**

With the desired Web server showing in the Web Server drop-down list box, determine whether or not you want to connect to the server using Secure Sockets Layer (SSL). This will be the case only if your server supports SSL and if you in fact have the necessary authorization on that server to make this kind of connection. Most full-featured servers do support SSL, but you must establish authentication keys before this feature can be used. Check with your server's documentation to determine how to do this (it's beyond this book's intended scope). If you do wish to establish a secure connection in this manner, click the Connect Using SSL toggle on the Open FrontPage Web dialog box.

Now, click the List Webs button. In the Webs list box, you will see the names of the Webs you have created on the selected Web server (see Figure 26.2). If you're opening a Web from a server on a remote computer, and especially if you're using a modem connection (even 28.8Kbps), getting a list of the Webs can take several minutes. Eventually, however, it appears.

N O T E In most cases, you won't actually click the List Webs button. When the list in the Web Server or File Location field contains more than one entry, and you click the down-arrow to choose an entry different from the entry that appears when the dialog box first opens, the List Webs button is selected automatically by FrontPage Explorer and is thus grayed out. You'll actively select List Webs only if you want to see the Webs on the default entry in the dialog box. ■

FIGURE 26.2
To avoid frustrating yourself with long load times, click the Cancel button to stop the loading process.

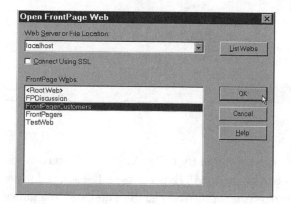

Click the Web you want to work with and then click the OK button. The remainder of this chapter assumes you'll be working with the Web created in Chapter 24, "Building a Web," called FrontPagers, which was built with the help of the Corporate Presence Web Wizard. When you click Open, a dialog box appears and requires a username and password for author permissions, which you established earlier. Once the FrontPagers Web is loaded, you will see the Explorer window shown in Figure 26.3.

Working with Explorer's Views

By default, the Explorer window shows the Hyperlink view. This is the view you'll probably work with most often when you start creating and managing FrontPage Webs, although a second view, Folder view, exists to give you detailed control over all elements of your Web. We'll examine both views here, although Folder view is also treated in Chapter 28, "Managing a Web."

Part
VI

Ch
26

FIGURE 26.3
The FrontPagers Web is
now loaded and ready
to edit.

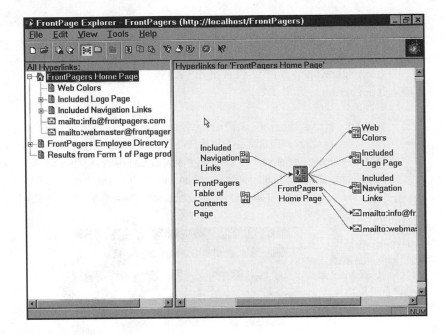

Hyperlink View

For now, let's concentrate on the Hyperlink View, which you can see by referring to Figure 26.3 above. It has two parts: All Hyperlinks on the left, and hyperlinks for the currently selected page on the right. We'll call this latter view the Individual Hyperlinks pane. The purpose of Hyperlink view is to provide both an outline-like perspective and a visual-style perspective of your Web site.

Hyperlink view is accessible through Explorer's View/Hyperlink View command, and also by clicking the Hyperlink view icon in Explorer's toolbar.

All Hyperlinks

Figure 26.4 shows the All Hyperlinks pane expanded by sliding the vertical separator fully to the right edge of the screen. This figure demonstrates how All Hyperlinks functions: It's very similar to the outline feature of word processors or personal information managers, showing the various headings and subheadings distinguished from one another by indentation. In this figure, some of the visible headings are fully expanded, as indicated by the minus signs (-) beside the main topic headings. By contrast, other topic headings remain unexpanded (closed), as indicated by the plus signs (+) beside them.

If you click on the minus sign beside an expanded topic, you also close all the subordinate topics of that topic. Therefore, if you wish to close all topics in the All Hyperlinks pane, close the highest topic in the hierarchy, in this case Customer Support Welcome. If you do, you'll see only one topic, with a plus sign beside it. Again, those familiar with a word processor outliner or with the Windows Explorer interface will find all of this quite apparent.

Actually, the division is not topic and subtopic. Instead, the All Hyperlinks pane shows links among pages. Main links lead to sublinks, sublinks to further sublinks, and so forth.

Note that, as Figure 26.4 also shows, as you move the pointer up and down the All Hyperlinks view, the topic you're currently pointing at is highlighted to show where you are in the view. This helps you orient your way through the hierarchy of topics.

FIGURE 26.4

These are the cascaded headings of Explorer's All Hyperlinks pane.

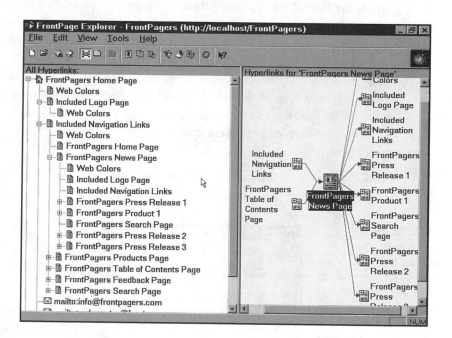

Using the All Hyperlinks Pane By studying the All Hyperlinks pane of your Webs, you can maintain a good sense of how the Web is constructed. Combining this view with the Individual Hyperlinks pane gives you two different perspectives, and together they make a powerful tool.

The main purpose of the All Hyperlinks pane is to help you easily find your way around your Web. You can locate everything in the Individual Hyperlink pane or in Folder view, but it's more cumbersome to do so. Again, there's a similarity here with a word processing outline: A well-outlined word processing document is an extremely easy document in which to locate specific headings and sections. This is exactly the case of the All Hyperlinks pane in FrontPage Explorer.

Part
VI

Ch
26

You can't actually manipulate the Web from the All Hyperlinks pane. Instead, it puts you in the position of being able to do so. Clicking any page in the All Hyperlinks pane immediately shows that page in the center of the Individual Hyperlinks pane, complete with all the links that stem from it. Clicking from subtopic to subtopic changes the display immediately and lets you jump back and forth from one perspective of the Web to the next.

Some icons in Hyperlink View display a plus sign at their top left corner. This indicates that additional documents in the Web are linked to the page represented by the icon. Clicking the plus sign displays the icons for the linked pages, and simultaneously changes the plus sign to a minus sign. Clicking the minus sign hides the icons for the linked pages.

Using the Individual Hyperlinks Pane   Explorer's Individual Hyperlinks pane is, in fact, where you'll do a considerable amount of your work on your Web, except of course for the actual task of constructing HTML pages, for which you'll use FrontPage Editor. The Individual Hyperlinks pane shows the Web from the perspective of the currently selected page in the All Hyperlinks pane, but you can maneuver around the Web by using the Individual Hyperlinks pane alone. Like the All Hyperlinks pane, the Individual Hyperlinks pane shows the Web as a series of pages with or without additional links leading from them, and you can expand or contract the links to see a larger portion of that particular part of the Web.

To show how the Individual Hyperlinks pane changes as you open an increasing number of pages, examine the following series of figures. Figure 26.5 shows the Individual

FIGURE 26.5

In this figure, you can see the basic Individual Hyperlinks pane with hyperlinked images.

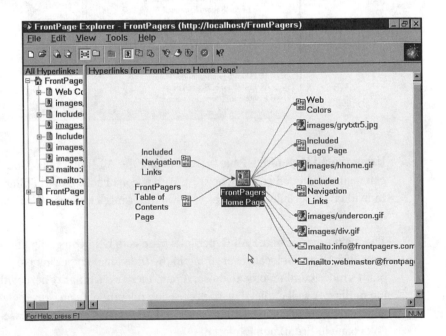

Hyperlinks pane of the FrontPagers Web from the perspective of only the home page and its direct links. In this case, the Hyperlinks to Images toggle in the View menu has been marked, which is why both panes now show the image links in addition to the normal document links. Note the plus signs on several of the pages; as in the All Hyperlinks pane, these pages can be expanded to reveal their links.

In Figure 26.6, the plus sign on the FrontPagers Table of Contents page has been clicked, and the result is the appearance of another closed page icon, called Included Navigation Links, to the far left of the pane. Figure 26.7 shows what happens when that page is expanded: A wide variety of new page icons appears.

FIGURE 26.6
A single new icon appears in the Web after expanding the TOC page.

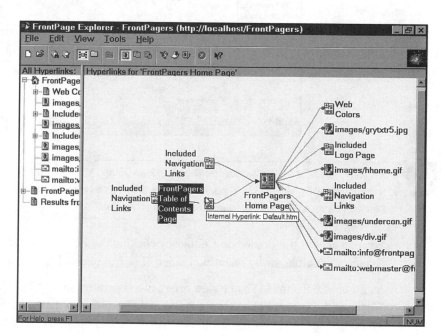

Note also that as you move your mouse pointer over any icon in the Individual Hyperlinks pane (or indeed the All Hyperlinks pane), a small information box appears giving you the URL for that hyperlink. This box is shown in Figures 26.6 and 26.7, and is extremely useful as a Web management tool.

Folder View

While Hyperlink view gives you a designer-oriented perspective on your Web, offering an outline and a visual representation, Folder view provides a more technically oriented perspective. Folder view exists for Webmasters who want to see the Web as a series of individual files in various folders. In other words, it gives you the Web in computerese, which, for many, is more efficient to work with.

FIGURE 26.7

The Individual Hyperlinks pane expands even further to show the navigation links.

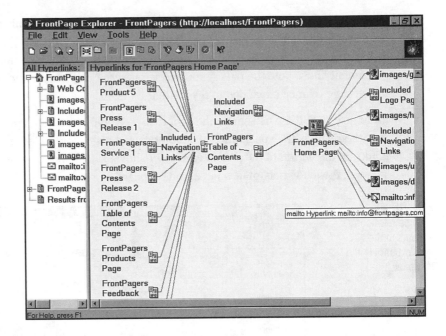

 TIP   The term "folder" is instantly recognizable to Windows 95 and Macintosh users. If you're more familiar with UNIX, MS-DOS, or Windows 3.x, think of folders as "directories" instead. Also, in the Contents frame of Folder view, "Name" really means "file name."

You can access the Folder view either by clicking the Folder View icon on FrontPage Explorer's toolbar, or by selecting Folder View from FrontPage Explorer's View menu.

As Figure 26.8 shows, Folder view offers two separate panes: All Folders and Contents. We'll call the latter "Folder Contents" to make its function more apparent. Essentially, the All Folders pane shows the folders for that Web, and these are the folders that FrontPage created when it built the Web you're working with. The Folder Contents page shows the files and subfolders within the folder selected in the All Folders pane.

In other words, Folder view is very much like the Windows Explorer file viewer found in Windows 95 and Windows NT 4.0. This is immediately apparent when you look at Figure 26.9, which shows the FrontPagers Web as it appears in the c:\wwwroot directory in Windows Explorer.

The only difference between the two views is that Windows Explorer shows all hidden directories, while FrontPage Explorer shows only the _private hidden directory. If you want to see all hidden folders in the FrontPage Explorer Folder view, open the Web Setting dialog from Explorer's Tools menu and select Show Documents in Hidden

FIGURE 26.8

The Folder view for the FrontPagers Web shows the folders on the left and the contents of the folder, including sub-folders, on the right.

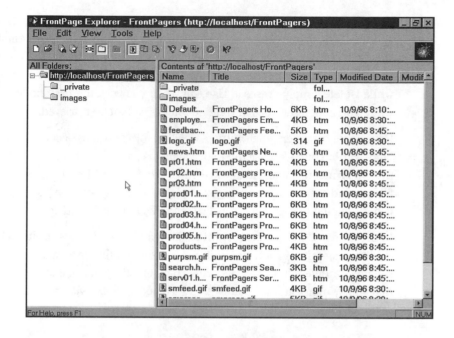

FIGURE 26.9

Windows Explorer's view of the Web is practically identical to FrontPager Explorer's view.

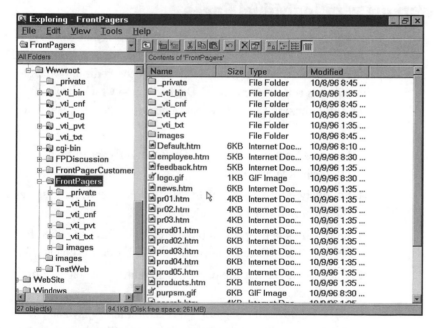

Directories from the Advanced tab. Incidentally, it's clear from the name of this command that Microsoft hasn't quite completed the shift in terminology from "directories" to "folders" either—perhaps next century.

The All Folders pane is primarily a navigation aid. When you click a folder, the subfolders and files contained within that folder will appear in the Folder Contents pane. If you right-click a folder, you can Cut, Copy, Rename, or Delete the folder, or you can view its Properties. The difference between Cut and Delete is that Cut moves the folder to the Clipboard, while Delete simply erases it. Use Cut when you wish to move the folder, and Delete only when you no longer need it. Deleted folders cannot be retrieved.

Be careful, however, when cutting, deleting, or renaming folders. Remember that internal links within your Web use the folder name as part of the hyperlink reference; changing the folder means invalidating those links. Fortunately, FrontPage keeps track of renamed folders and automatically changes the links when you choose Tools/Recalculate Links. Cut or deleted folders appear as broken links in your FrontPage Web.

In the Folder Contents pane, right-clicking a file name offers additional options. You can load the page into FrontPage Editor or another editing program, and you can cut, copy, rename, or delete it, or view its properties. Finally, you can Show Hyperlinks, an action that will switch you immediately to the Hyperlink view with the selected file in the center of the display.

Working with Individual Pages

Once you reach a page you want to work with, in either Explorer view, you can work with it by clicking it. At this point, you have several choices. Double-clicking opens that page in FrontPage Editor, where you can edit it and save it directly back to the Web (even if you're editing it on a remote computer). Depending on which view and which pane you're working in, right-clicking the icon reveals a pop-up menu with some of the following nine options:

- Move to Center—Centers the Individual Hyperlinks pane on that page's icon (Hyperlink view only).

- Show Hyperlinks—Opens the Hyperlink view with the selected page in the center of the display (Folder view only).

- Open—Loads the page into the editor you have specified for that file (see the section "FrontPage Explorer Menus" later in this chapter for more details).

- Open With—Loads the page into an editor you select from the resulting Open With dialog box.

- Cut—Removes the page or folder from the display and places it in the Clipboard, making it available for pasting elsewhere. Simultaneously erases links to other pages, and restores them when you paste. Use Cut to move files or folders.

- ■ <u>D</u>elete—Permanently erases the page from the Web and simultaneously erases links to other pages.

- ■ <u>C</u>opy—Copies the page or folder to the Clipboard and makes it available for pasting to other locations.

- ■ <u>R</u>ename—Lets you change the name of the file or folder, and simultaneously changes names in links to that item.

- ■ <u>P</u>roperties—Opens the Properties dialog box (see the section "FrontPage Explorer Menus" later in this chapter for more details).

Beyond that, any work you do on individual pages occurs through FrontPage Editor, not Explorer. The point of Explorer is to let you see your Web and keep track of it, not to alter or edit individual pages.

FrontPage Explorer Menus

Explorer offers several main menus through which to complete its tasks. Everything you want to do in the program is accessible through these menus. Here we examine all the menu commands. In the following sections, the menu name is shown first, and then the command from that menu.

<u>F</u>ile/<u>N</u>ew/<u>F</u>older

Available only when working in the Folder view, this command lets you create a new folder in the Web.

<u>F</u>ile/<u>N</u>ew/FrontPage <u>W</u>eb

With the <u>N</u>ew FrontPage <u>W</u>eb command, you begin the process of creating brand new Webs. Choosing this command opens the New Web dialog box. Here you can select a wizard or a template to help automate the creation of a Web.

▶ **See** "Building a Web," **p. 611**

Another option is to add the new Web to the current Web. If you have a Web currently loaded, you can create a new Web and insert it directly into the loaded Web. In this case, you are asked if you want to replace or retain files with duplicate names.

Part
VI

Ch
26

File/Open FrontPage Web and File/Close FrontPage Web

If you have already created Webs, you can load them into Explorer through the Open FrontPage Web command. The resulting Open FrontPage Web dialog box lets you choose the Web server on which the Web resides (in the Web Server or File Location drop-down list box), and once you click the List Webs button, the FrontPage Webs list box displays the Webs that exist on that server. By highlighting the one you want and clicking OK, you load that Web into Explorer.

The Close FrontPage Web command from the File menu removes the current Web from Explorer.

File/Publish FrontPage Web

When you complete a Web and you want to store it on another Web server, use the Publish FrontPage Web command from the File menu. When you choose this command, the Publish FrontPage Web dialog box appears. Here you specify the Destination Web Server or File Location, with either the IP address or the domain name for the server. You also specify the Name of Destination FrontPage Web on the destination server (it adopts that name in its new location). You can choose to Connect Using SSL if your server is capable of Secure Sockets Layer authorization, and you can elect to Copy Changed Pages Only or Add This Web to an Existing FrontPage Web on the Server.

In addition, if you are copying the root Web from your current server, you can tell Explorer to copy the child Webs to the destination as well. The root Web is created automatically by Explorer on your server, and the child Webs are all other Webs you create on that server. By copying the root Web and the child Webs, you are, in effect, copying all Webs from your current server.

File/Delete FrontPage Web

If you no longer need a Web, you can delete it by choosing the Delete command. A warning box appears and explains to you that, once deleted, the Web can't be retrieved.

File/Import

If you have files or folders you want to bring into the current Web from your hard drive, choose Import from the File menu. To import a file, click in the All Hyperlinks pane or the Individual Hyperlinks pane where you want your file to appear in the Web. Then choose File, Import. You'll see the Import File to FrontPage Web dialog box, shown in Figure 26.10. Clicking Add File displays the Add File to Import List dialog box, while clicking Add Folder yields the Browse for Folder dialog box, also shown in Figure 26.10. You can add multiple files and folders into the Import File box before clicking OK, and by clicking Edit URL, you can change the hyperlink reference as well.

When you select the appropriate file and click Open, the Add File to Import dialog box disappears and the file name appears in the Import File to Web dialog box. You can add additional files by clicking the Add File button again, and if you change your mind about importing them, you can remove files from the list box by clicking Remove. You can click any file in the list box and click Edit URL to change the URL of the selected page. When you've made the decisions you want, click Import. Now add the file to your Web. As the file is importing, you can click the Stop button, if you change your mind, or simply wait for it to be added.

You can also import files and folders to a Web through drag-and-drop. With a Web open in FrontPage Explorer, simply drag files or folders from Windows Explorer into either pane of the Explorer window and drop them. FrontPage immediately uploads the file to the Web server, even if the server is on a remote machine. Once the files are in place, you can provide links to them or manipulate them as you manipulate other files in your Webs.

If you import files created in Microsoft Office, FrontPage Explorer creates icons for these files that reflect the program of origin. When you double-click these files, instead of loading FrontPage Editor or Image Composer, the two standard editing programs, the file loads into the appropriate Office application instead. But there's one very important point to keep in mind. Unless your visitors are using Microsoft Internet Explorer 3.0 or

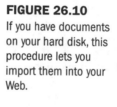

FIGURE 26.10
If you have documents on your hard disk, this procedure lets you import them into your Web.

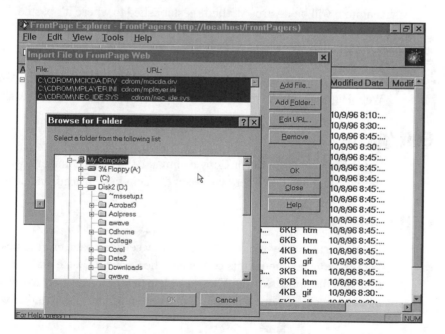

Part
VI

Ch
26

Netscape Navigator (with the appropriate Office viewers plugged in) as their browser, they won't be able to view these Office documents. For this reason, importing Office files directly is best reserved for private intranets, in which the choice of browser can be guaranteed.

FrontPage also provides an Import Wizard, which is available only if no Web is currently loaded into FrontPage Explorer. In such a case, selecting File/Import reveals the Import Web Wizard series of dialogs, in which you can select individual files or entire folders for import. The wizard can also be selected from the Getting Started with Microsoft Front-Page dialog box.

File/Export

Exporting files copies a Web document or graphics file from the current Web to your hard disk for later use with another Web or for later alteration with an editor. To export, click the desired file in one of the views and choose File, Export. The Export Selected As dialog box appears, which is essentially a Save File dialog box. Choose the directory, name the file, and click Save.

Edit/Cut

The Cut command removes the selected file or folder from the Web and places it in the Clipboard. It is now available to be pasted elsewhere on that Web or another Web. Links to that item will be destroyed, then reestablished to where it's pasted.

Edit/Copy

Copy lets you duplicate the selected file or folder elsewhere in the Web or on another Web. Highlight the item, copy it, and then paste it wherever you wish.

Edit/Paste

If you have used the Cut or Copy command, the Paste command will be available. Move to the Web and location where you want the item to be placed, and select Paste.

Edit/Delete

Delete permanently removes the currently selected page or graphics file from the current Web. When you choose this command, the Confirm Delete dialog box appears; if more than one file appears in the Files to Delete field, you can elect to delete the current file or all of them at the same time. Links to the item will be eliminated as well.

Edit/Rename

If you want to change the name of a file or folder, use the Rename command. Links will be changed to reflect the name change.

Edit/Open

When you want to edit the HTML elements of a specific page, click that page in Explorer to select it and then choose Edit, Open. This command loads the selected page into FrontPage Editor, where you can edit it, save it, and manipulate it. Part II, "Creating Your Web Pages with FrontPage Editor," deals with FrontPage Editor in detail.

Edit/Open With

Using the Tools/Options/Configure Editors command, you can specify specific editors for specific types of files. When you select Edit, Open With, the Open with Editor dialog box appears (see Figure 26.11) offering you the choice of editors in which to load the currently selected file. If you use a specific program to edit graphics files, for example, you can choose that particular editor to manipulate the current file, in which case the Open With command loads that editor and the file inside it. You can even choose to establish additional HTML editors to do specific tasks and then open your Web documents into them.

FIGURE 26.11
With the Open With Editor dialog box, you can load specific files into specific editors.

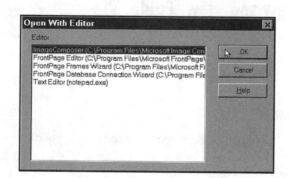

Edit/Add To Do Task

As you work on building your Web, on many occasions you will decide to add elements that you don't currently have time to complete. The Add To Do Task command lets you add these elements to your To Do List.

▶ **See** "Managing a Web," **p. 689**

Edit/Properties

A Properties dialog box is common in Windows programs, but FrontPage's Properties dialog box is unusually powerful. When you select a file and choose E̲dit, P̲roperties, you'll see the Properties dialog box. There are two tabs in this dialog box: Summary and General.

The General tab shows the type of document and the document's URL, and it offers one editable text box, Page URL. You can edit the document's URL in this field. You can simply change the document's name, or you can change its directory as well (the full directory is displayed in the URL text box at the bottom of the General tab). If you change the directory, Explorer automatically moves the document into that directory of your Web. If you specify a directory that does not exist, Explorer creates the directory and then moves the document into it. This procedure can be extremely useful as you maintain your Web.

The Summary tab shows you when the file was created and last modified, and allows you to add comments for your own reference.

View/T̲oolbar and V̲iew/S̲tatus Bar

You can toggle Explorer's toolbar and status bar on and off with these commands. If you want to see more of the Web, toggle them off.

View/H̲yperlink View and V̲iew/F̲older View

These commands let you switch between the two Explorer views covered at the beginning of this chapter.

▶ **See** "Managing a Web," **p. 689**

V̲iew/Hyperlinks to I̲mages

To keep your Web from looking cluttered, the Individual Hyperlinks pane and the All Hyperlinks pane by default don't show links to images (that is, images in your Web pages). If you want a more complete view of your Web, toggle on Links to I̲mages. Images are then displayed with the image icon.

V̲iew/R̲epeated Hyperlinks

Often your pages contain multiple links from one page to another page. There's usually no reason to see these links more than once in the Individual Hyperlinks pane, but for a complete picture you can toggle on R̲epeated Links.

View/Hyperlinks Inside Page

When you create pages, you can include a link to another place within that same page. The purpose behind this is to give your readers strong navigational assistance. By default, however, Explorer's Individual Hyperlinks pane doesn't show these links because they clutter the display. But if you want to see how many of these links you've created, toggle on Links Inside Page to get a more complete view.

View/Refresh

Because several people can be working a Web at the same time, it's entirely possible for new pages and new links to be added without your knowledge. To ensure that you have the most complete Web showing in Explorer, choose View, Refresh. The entire Web is then visible, complete with all current changes.

Tools/Spelling, Find, Replace

This collection of three separate commands are all tasks for Web managers. As such, they are covered in full in Chapter 28, "Managing a Web."

Tools/Verify Hyperlinks and Recalculate Hyperlinks

The Verify Hyperlinks command lets you verify the validity of all hyperlinks in your Web. The Recalculate Hyperlinks command performs several important maintenance functions. Both commands are covered in Chapter 28, "Managing a Web."

Part
VI

Ch
26

Tools/Show FrontPage Editor

Choosing Tools, Show FrontPage Editor opens the FrontPage Editor with no Web documents loaded into it for editing. If FrontPage Editor is already open, this command switches to it. Note that this command does not display a specific page in Editor, even if you've selected that page in Explorer. That task is reserved for the Open command (see Edit menu commands earlier in this chapter).

Tools/Show To Do List

If you want to see the To Do List for the current Web, select this command. The To Do List opens, or if it is already open, the To Do List command switches to it. The menu very helpfully shows how many tasks remain on the To Do list.

Tools/Show Image Editor

This command opens the editor you've assigned to edit graphics files. If you've installed Microsoft Image Composer from the Bonus Pack CD-ROM, it will automatically be established as the program to open with the Show Image Editor command.

Tools/Web Settings, Permissions, Change Password

These three separate commands are all tasks for Web administrators. As such, they are covered in full in Chapter 27, "Configuring Your Webs."

Tools/Options

Three tabs are available from Tools/Options. Proxies is covered in Chapter 27, "Configuring Your Webs." General contains three items. You can elect to have the Getting Started dialog box display whenever you use FrontPage, you can tell FrontPage to warn you when the included WebBot components are out of date because of changes you've made, and you can also specify that you want to be warned when your Text Indexes, which are created by Search Bots, which are out of date. These latter two are covered in Chapter 28, "Managing a Web."

FIGURE 26.12

You can add, modify, or remove the editors that are associated with specific file extensions.

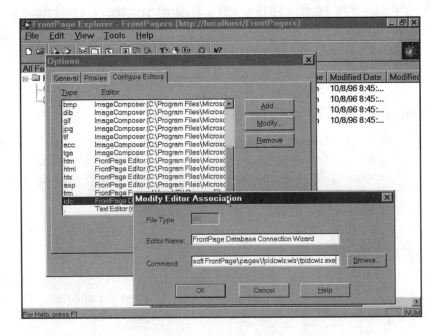

The final tab lets you configure editors to let you edit various types of files. Many of these are already set up for you, but you can change them by using the Modify button or add new ones by clicking the Add button. The principle, as with Windows Explorer, is that specific file types are associated with specific programs. Figure 26.12 shows an example of modifying the editor associated with IDC database files, which are used for interacting with databases. The Modify Editor Association box shows the File Type, the Editor Name, and the Command that opens that editor. You can change the editor and the command so that a different editor handles these files.

From Here...

While you'll certainly use FrontPage Explorer initially to create new Webs, eventually your main task will be to update and edit existing Webs. Explorer makes this relatively easy by giving you full access to and control over your Webs, and the Explorer menu items let you perform all necessary tasks.

- Chapter 27, "Configuring Your Webs," discusses how to set permissions and passwords for your Webs.
- Chapter 28, "Managing A Web," teaches you about the details and issues surrounding managing people and documents with the help of the To Do List.
- Chapter 29, "Serving Your Web to the World with Personal Web Server," teaches you how to deal with the intricacies of server administration.

Part
VI

Ch
26

## CHAPTER 27

Configuring Your Webs

To get your Web working correctly, you need to set its configurations. Furthermore, to make sure the right people are adding and altering material, you need to set permissions. And to establish the appropriate editors and programs for performing various functions that FrontPage doesn't handle, you need to establish when these programs will open. All of these settings and configurations are handled through the Tools menu of FrontPage Explorer, and we'll deal with them in this chapter. ■

Establishing Parameters, Configurations, and Advanced Settings

The intricacies of the various sections of the Web Settings dialog boxes.

Setting Administrator, Author, and User Permissions

How do you guarantee that only authorized persons are changing and accessing your Web site?

Changing Passwords

Passwords can be changed regularly by administrators and authors alike.

Proxy Servers

Setting FrontPage to work from behind your organization's security firewalls.

Configuring Editors

FrontPage will launch the program of your choice to edit documents of various types.

TIP Explorer is not used for the purpose of configuring the Web server and the root web; instead, that's the role of the server administrator.

▶ **See** Chapter 6, "Enhancing Pages with Graphics and Multimedia," **p. 121**.

Establishing Parameters, Configurations, and Advanced Settings

The major settings for the currently loaded web can be set through the Web Settings command in FrontPage Explorer's Tools menu. For the most part, only the Web administrator can change these settings, but since you're probably already that person (having established that during program setup), we'll continue as if that's a given. If not, you'll need to contact your Web administrator if you want to alter any settings.

Choosing Tools, Web Settings opens the Web Settings dialog box (see Figure 27.1).

FIGURE 27.1

The Parameters, Configuration, Advanced, and Language tabs comprise the Web Settings dialog box.

Parameters

Initially, the Parameters tab is probably the most confusing of the three tab choices available from the Web Settings dialog box, mainly because it's not at all obvious what this tab is supposed to accomplish. Clicking the Help button helps a bit, but even here the purpose is a bit obscure. One you go through the procedure of establishing even one parameter on your own, however, it's all crystal clear (well, more or less).

To fully understand what these parameters are all about, you have to know what *Substitution Bots* do. These Bots (automated procedures) are covered in Chapter 10, "Using WebBots, Wizards, and Interactive-Page Templates," which deals with FrontPage Editor. When you create a Web page in Editor, you can create a Bot that tells the Web browser to substitute the text in the Bot for text stored in the parameters, or configuration variables, established through the Parameters dialog box.

In other words, it's like entering a variable time and date stamp in a word processing document; when the file loads into the word processor, the time and date are automatically changed by the software itself, without any action on you part. In your web, you might want to show the reader who developed that page, but the information might change. Or you might want to have the exact current URL for the page, instead of a fixed URL. To do so, you create a Substitution Bot to take care of the substitution, thereby letting FrontPage, instead of yourself, make the changes.

Even though you use FrontPage Editor to program these bots, however, the configuration variables that they rely upon are stored in Explorer, not Editor. They are established primarily in the FrontPage Explorer's Properties dialog box; its two tabs are shown in Figures 27.2 and 27.3. Figure 27.2 shows the page URL and the title of the document (you can change the title in Editor or Explorer), while Figure 27.3 shows the date the page was created and modified, as well as who did the creating and who did the modifying. The Substitution Bot takes the information primarily from these tabs.

TIP To see your new configuration variables in action, load a page from your web into Editor, choose Insert/Bot, then Substitution Bot from the resulting dialog box, and click the arrow to the right of the Substitute With drop-down list box.

FIGURE 27.2
Several information items are available from the General tab of the Properties dialog box.

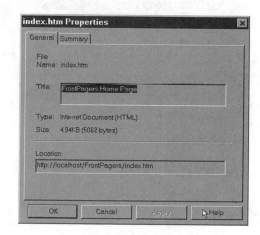

FIGURE 27.3

Only a comments field is accessible from the Summary tab of the Properties dialog box.

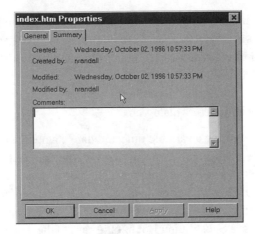

Even though the Substitution Bot is designed to capture information from the configuration variables (Author, Modified By, Description, and Page URL) in these dialog boxes, it's not restricted to that information. The Web Wizards create some of them, as Figure 27.1 (above) demonstrates. Furthermore, you can set additional configuration variables by adding them through the Parameters tab of the Web Settings dialog box. To do so, from the Web Settings dialog box's Parameters tab, click the Add button. The Add Name and Value dialog box appears (see Figure 27.4).

FIGURE 27.4

In this dialog box, you can add the Name and Value of the configuration.

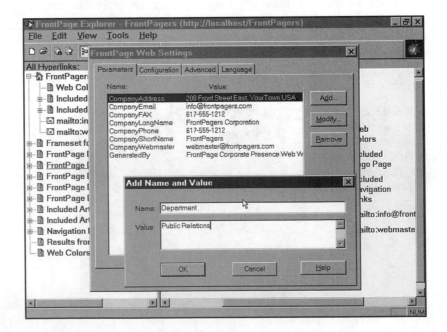

In the Name text box, add the name of the configuration variable you want to be available to the Substitution Bot. This can be any name you want; in Figure 27.4 above, the text box shows Department, but that's only one possibility. The value of the Name text box is whatever you want to appear on the Web page when the Substitution Bot is used; since this is the public display of information, you'll want to make sure it's appropriate. Here the example is Public Relations. What this means is that, when the Web author engages a Substitution Bot, one of the items available will now be Department, and if chosen, the Web page displays Public Relations.

When you've finished specifying the name and value of the name, click OK, and the new configuration variable (which is a combination of the Name and Value fields) appears in the Parameters tab. From here you can click OK or Apply to place it into the Web and thus make it available as a Substitution Bot item. You can also modify or remove it, but when you do so, remember to click OK or Apply to actually place it in the Web.

Configuration

In the Configuration tab (see Figure 27.5) of the Web Settings dialog box, you have the following information:

- Web Name—The name of the Web as it appears in the Open Web dialog box and as it appears as a directory in your Web Server software. You can change that name if you are the authorized administrator of the root web and if your server, such as Personal Web Server, supports the changing of Web names.

- Web Title—By default, the title of the web is the same as the Web Name, but you can change it here. The web title appears in the title bar of the Explorer window, as it is significant for that purpose only.

- Web Server—This is the URL of the Web server. If your server does not have a domain name, this URL is the same as the IP Address information shown in this tab. You can't change the Web Server information; this was set when you created the web.

- Server Version—This gives you information about the version of your Web server. This cannot be altered, unless of course you upgrade your server, in which case the change is automatic.

- IP Address—The IP address of your server, always expressed in numerical format (for example, 129.97.48.53). This is the actual number Web browsers look for; the domain name is simply a more easily remembered alias for the IP address.

- FrontPage Server Extensions Version—FrontPage installs software in your server software to allow the two to work together. These are known as server extensions.

Part
VI

27

This link shows you the version of those extensions and cannot be altered except automatically through software upgrade.

■ Proxy Server—This line shows the URL of the proxy server, the server connected to your internal network that acts as a firewall or buffer between the internal network and the external Internet. You set this information with Explorer's Tools, Proxies.

FIGURE 27.5

The Configuration tab provides several items of important information.

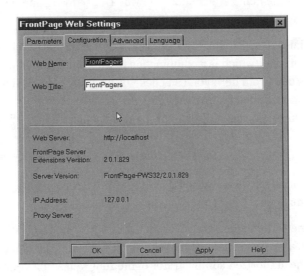

Advanced

The Advanced tab (see Figure 27.6) on the Web Settings dialog box gives you access to four items: imagemaps, validation scripts, hidden directories, and recalculate status.

The Image Maps section lets you configure your web to accept one of several different types of imagemaps. *Imagemaps* are single graphics on your Web page that contain multiple hyperlinks and can be created with FrontPage Editor (see Part II, "Creating Your Web Pages with FrontPage Editor," for details). Imagemaps are of several types, however, and you must tell FrontPage which type you want to use. The Advanced tab of the Web Settings dialog box allows you to set the type (or style) of imagemap you prefer.

The five imagemap types are FrontPage, NCSA, CERN, Netscape, and None. CERN imagemaps were the first type available to Web designers, and NCSA imagemaps came next. Netscape and FrontPage imagemaps are recent additions to the list. Each type handles imagemaps differently.

FIGURE 27.6
The Advanced tab is extremely important if you plan to include imagemaps in your Web.

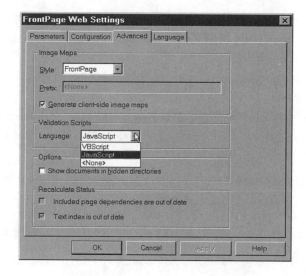

Essentially, the type of imagemap you choose depends on the type of Web server on which you're placing your web. If you're using the Personal Web Server that comes with the FrontPage package, use FrontPage imagemaps. If your server uses NCSA or CERN imagemaps, choose either of those types instead (in which case imagemaps are handled by entirely separate programs on the server). Netscape servers have their own type of map, but they also handle NCSA maps. Choosing None means, in effect, that your server doesn't handle imagemaps, in which case you should probably find a new server because imagemaps are extremely popular.

If you select FrontPage maps, the Prefix text box of the Web Settings dialog box remains grayed out; you can't change it, nor is it necessary because FrontPage handles map directories automatically. If you choose NCSA, CERN, or Netscape maps, you must specify the directory where those maps are found on the Web server. These are given a default directory where the server software typically sets up its maps, but if the server administrator has changed those directories, you must specify them here as well.

The final choice in the Image Maps section of the Advanced tab is whether or not you want FrontPage to generate HTML code for client-side imagemaps. If you do not, FrontPage generates only server-side imagemaps. The difference is that server-side maps have their coordinate information stored on the server, while client-side maps send the coordinate information to the user's Web browser and thus are somewhat faster. In practical terms, the user sees the difference when passing the cursor over the map: The browser's status bar shows x/y coordinates for server-side maps, while for client-side maps, the status bar shows the URLs for the individual links. Not all browsers support

Part
VI

27

client-side maps, but recent ones certainly do. For the most part, client-side imagemaps are far more common today than the server-side versions, because they're faster and more informative to the user.

▶ For more on imagemaps, see Chapter 6, "Enhancing Pages with Graphics and Multimedia," **p. 121**

If you want full compatibility across all browsers and have no interest whatsoever in providing imagemaps, leave the Generate Client-Side Image Maps check box empty. Otherwise, fill in the check box by clicking on it.

> **CAUTION**
>
> Don't simply guess at what kind of imagemap your server uses; check with your server's software manual or with your system administrator. Otherwise, you'll end up with imagemaps that almost certainly will not work.

The Options section of the Advanced tab also contains the option to Show Documents in Hidden Directories. As explained in Chapter 26, "FrontPage's Templates and Wizards," FrontPage 97 installs some directories as hidden directories. If you want to display these in FrontPage Explorer's views, you must specify this on the Web Settings dialog. All hidden directories and files will then be included in the Explorer views, but not in the web itself. Unless you have a specific reason for working with these directories, it's best to leave them hidden. If you want full control over all directories, however, or even if you only want to see every single file that FrontPage generates, by all means unhide them.

When you select to show the hidden directories, FrontPage 97 will recalculate the links. If this recalculation takes place on a remote server, it could take several minutes. If you subsequently uncheck this option in order to remove the hidden directories from view, FrontPage 97 will take a minute or two to refresh the web.

The final section on the Web Settings dialog is to specify the Recalculation Status of the web currently loaded into FrontPage Explorer. As you add links and pages to your web, the text index will need to be regenerated, as will the page dependencies on which these new links rely. The Web Settings dialog tells you that these are out of date by placing a checkmark next to the out-of-date item, in which case you should use the Tools menu to Verify Hyperlinks and Recalculate Hyperlinks. When you do so, reopening the Web Settings dialog will no longer show those checkmarks.

Giving Permission to Administer, Author, and Browse Your Webs

Your webs are important primarily because they show off your company or your personal preferences to the world, or because they offer important information to members of your company or organization. Because of this, you don't want just anybody putting information on your site. In fact, you need strict control over who can make changes, add documents, and alter the web's contents or appearance. If FrontPage didn't offer a system for setting permissions, anyone on the Internet could make changes to your web, and you'd wake up every morning wondering exactly how your public image had been modified. While that would certainly be exciting, it would obviously be unacceptable.

FrontPage lets you set permissions for users to administer, author, and browse your webs. Each of these are explored in detail in this section.

Basically, the differences are as follows:

- *Browse* permissions are given to people who are permitted to visit your web by using a Web browser such as Netscape Navigator. They can read your pages, but they cannot alter them in any way, nor can they add, delete, or otherwise manage your Webs. Their only access to your Web site is through a browser, not through FrontPage Editor or FrontPage Explorer.

- *Author* permissions are given to people who are permitted to create and edit content in the web. But they cannot add or delete webs, nor manage them in any other way. In other words, they can use FrontPage Editor in conjunction with a particular web (and only that web), but they can use FrontPage Explorer only as a viewing tool, or as a means of invoking FrontPage Editor or Image Composer. Those with Author permissions automatically have Browse permissions as well.

- *Administer* permissions are given to people whom you want to have full access to web administration. They can add and delete webs, and they can set web permissions and configurations. Note, however, that only you can restrict administrators to individual webs, with only one administrator having full access to the root web. Those with Administer permissions automatically have Author and Browse permissions as well.

In other words, people with Administer permissions on a web have unlimited access to that particular web, while those with Author permissions have less access, and those with Browse permissions, the least complete access of all.

Part
VI

27

Using the Server Administration dialog boxes (see Chapter 28, "Managing a Web"), you can set the permissions for the root web, which is the web that FrontPage creates as the primary web for your server. If you want, you can have all your webs contain the same permissions. Using the Web Permissions dialog box, however, you can set unique permissions for each web on your server. This allows you maximum flexibility for determining who will work on your webs. This might, in fact, be your most important administrative task as Webmaster.

Establishing the Main Settings

Figure 27.7 shows the Settings tab of the Web Permissions dialog box. You have two choices in this area. You can have the currently loaded web use the same permissions as the root web, or you can establish unique permissions for this web. If you mark the Use Same Permissions as Root Web option button, you can set no other permissions in this dialog box; everything, instead, must be set using the Server Administration dialog boxes. By marking the Use Unique Permissions for This Web option button, you can establish specific permissions for the current web, although this web automatically inherits the root web settings as well.

FIGURE 27.7

For the greatest possible flexibility, establish unique permissions for each web.

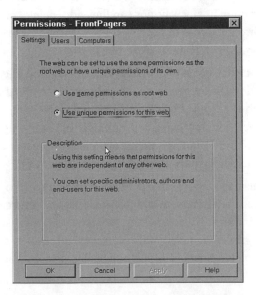

Setting Permissions: People Versus Computers

FrontPage offers two ways of setting browse, author, and administer permissions. You can give these permissions to people via the Users tab, giving each user a name and a password, and this is the most common way (see Figure 27.8). But you can also restrict access by the IP (Internet Protocol) address of computers themselves, through the Computers tab. You can restrict access to individual computers, or to computers who share portions of an IP address.

FIGURE 27.8

Adding Users requires that you specify a name and a password for the person, as well as the level of permissions you're granting.

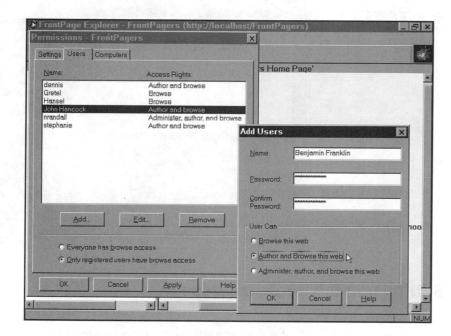

Why would you choose the Computers option? The most obvious choice would be to restrict browse permissions to groups of computers in a single organization. For example, you might be creating a web that contains important company information, and which is designed to be seen only by employees of that company (an intranet, in other words). Each machine in that company will have an IP address such as, for example, 139.205.104.72, and all machines on the company network will likely have IP addresses that are identical for the first 3-6 numbers (139.205). In this case, to prevent outsiders from seeing the information, you can tell FrontPage 97 to restrict browse access to computers with an IP address of 139.205.*.* (the asterisks are called wildcards). This means that when anyone tries to access the web, the server will check the IP address, and if the address is not within that restricted range, the server won't serve any information. This process is called setting an IP *mask*, and is shown in Figure 27.9.

By default, all webs give administer, author, and browse permissions to *all* computers on the Internet (IP *.*.*.*), but to *no* users other than the root web administrator. This means that only the users you set up can get into your web (with whatever level of permissions you grant them), but that they can do so from any computer on the Net. By carefully combining User and Computer restrictions, you can specify exactly who gets to do what on your Web.

Part
VI

27

FIGURE 27.9
To restrict permissions to a group of computers, use the Add Computer dialog to set an IP mask.

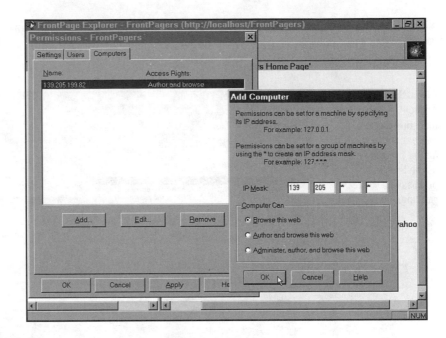

Setting Administer Permissions

Administrators play an important role in creating webs. They have permission to create webs and individual web documents, to delete these pages and webs, and to establish permissions for authors and users. In other words, administrators control exactly who gets to work on the web and, in fact, who gets to see it. Administrators are automatically registered as end users and authors as well.

Through the Users and Computers tabs of the Web Permissions dialog box, the administrator of the root web can give administer permissions on individual webs to users or computers. The process is simple, but it's extremely important.

> **CAUTION**
> When you first create a web, especially if you're not a large company, your first inclination might be to give administer positions to just about anyone. However, give careful thought to this decision; administrators have a lot of power over the web.

When you click the Add button, the Add User dialog box appears. The username and password are entirely up to you, but be sure to remember the password so that the new administrator can access the site. Then select the option User Can Administer, Author, and Browse This Web, and click OK. The new name will appear in the Permissions dialog.

When you have finished adding users, click Apply. If there's a problem, FrontPage 97 will give you with an error message. If there is an error, you can try to edit the entry by clicking the Edit button, but usually it's easier to just Remove it and try adding it without committing the same error.

 Don't let each administrator set her own password. Only one person should be the chief administrator of the web, and that person should establish all access. Set that as a policy as soon as you install FrontPage.

To further assure controlled permissions in your webs, you can click on the Computers tab and restrict administer permissions to specific IP addresses or address masks. IP address masks are ranges of IP addresses; you can specify a full IP address, or you can use the wildcard asterisk character to specify IP addresses within a certain range.

For example, if you want to restrict access so that administrators can access the web only from one specific machine, you can enter the full IP address of that machine. Click Add and then fill in the machine's IP number in the resulting New IP Address dialog box. The IP address looks something like 135.201.123.91—always a four-part number.

More likely, you'll want to restrict access to an IP address range. Because users with dialup connections are usually given a dynamic IP address, that is, one that changes with each new logon—specifying a full IP restriction means that dialup administration is next to impossible. Instead, you can use the wildcard asterisk character in place of some of the IP numbers. In the previous example, the first two numbers (135.201) specify the high level of the domain, so a restriction to that portion of the address means that users have to be logged on to that overall domain, which means a specific organization such as your company, to perform administrative tasks. For this example, you click the Add button and type 135.201.*.* in the New IP Mask dialog box.

TROUBLESHOOTING

I restricted access to a domain mask, but my administrators can still get in from anywhere they like. What happened? All administrators listed in the Administrators tab share the same restrictions. You can't restrict one administrator to access from one IP range and a second from a different IP range. Because of this, if you're going to restrict ranges at all, be sure to remove the default IP address mask (*.*.*.*). This mask allows access from anywhere, which is exactly what you don't want.

When you've set your administrators and IP address masks, click Apply to save them to the web. And remember that they apply to the current web only; you must set individual restrictions for each web you administer.

Part
VI

27

Setting Author Permissions

In addition to establishing administrative authority for each web, you can set authoring authority as well. Authors can create and delete individual web pages from the specific web for which they're authorized. They cannot create or delete the webs themselves, nor can they establish authorial permission for other authors.

Setting author permissions is identical to the process described in the previous "Setting Administer Permissions" section. From the Users tab, click Add, provide a name and password, and then select User Can Author and Browse This Web. Then click Apply. From the Computers tab, you then restrict Author permissions according to IP number or IP mask for added security.

TROUBLESHOOTING

I try to add myself as an author, and it tells me my name already exists with administrator permissions. Does this mean I can't author pages in my own web? Not at all. All administrators automatically have authoring permissions for that web, even though their names do not appear in the Authors tab.

Establishing author permissions is one area in which web management becomes just that, Web management. As chief administrator, you have the sole authority to authorize administrators for each web, but each of those administrators, in turn, can establish as many new authors as she wants. It's extremely important to set firm guidelines about who has permission to author, and this has to be done through frequent communication with your administrators.

Setting Browse Permissions

One of the most important security tasks of web administrators is to establish who may visit your web. Doing so restricts who gets to look at your web, and this can be useful for any number of reasons. When you're first constructing a web, for example, you don't want the world to see it, and once it's established, you might want it to be accessible only to users you choose to register.

Establishing Browse permissions with the User or Computer tabs is identical to establishing Administer and Author permissions, except that, after providing a name and password, you select User Can Browse This Web. If you've set your web so that everyone has browse access (on the Permissions dialog), restricting by IP number or IP mask comes into play if you want to control access anyway. If you've established that everyone has browse access and that all computers have access, then setting user browse permissions effectively does nothing at all.

Restricting user access by name can be valuable if you want to set up a web whereby purchasers of your service or product, for example, are given a common username and password that allows them to access a special web just for them. The only way they can know the username and password is to buy the service or product (perhaps you include it in the packaging), so you can establish all customers as registered users with one username and one password.

Creating User Registration Forms   Obviously, however, this process is tedious if you're attempting to establish a web where all individual users have their own unique usernames and passwords, as is the case in many Web sites on the World Wide Web. To allow users to register themselves and to provide you with valuable information for your database, use FrontPage's Registration Bot. You can initiate this Bot while authoring a page, or from the Discussion Web Wizard.

▶ **See** Chapter 10, "Using WebBots, Wizards, and Interactive Page Templates," **p. 225,** and Chapter 25, "FrontPage's Templates and Wizards," **p. 625**.

With the Registration Bot, you create a registration form that you can specify as belonging to the precise web you want. When users fill in this form and submit it to your server, their usernames and passwords (which they supply) are automatically added to the end user permissions of that web. The following steps describe this process:

1. Specify the current web as being accessible to Registered Users Only; this is accomplished through the End User tab of the Web Permissions dialog box.

2. Open the root web of your server.

3. Open FrontPage Editor and then choose File, New and select User Registration.

4. Edit the page that appears by clicking inside any form field (such as the Make Up a Username field) and choosing Edit, Properties. The Text Box Properties dialog box appears.

5. Select Form from this dialog box; then choose Settings.

6. In the Registration tab, select the name of the web for which you want to register users (that is, the web that you've just established end user permissions for).

7. Either copy the form from the current page onto the home page for the root web, or place a link from the root web's home page to the new page that contains the form. Once that's done, your end users can start registering themselves, and the results appear in the End Users tab of the Web Permissions dialog box. As you'll discover, this is an extremely powerful system.

Part

VI

27

Changing Passwords

As with most network-based programs, you can change your password to prevent unwanted access. In fact, as long as the root web administrator agrees, you should change it frequently. To do so, choose Tools, Change Password. You'll be presented with the Change Password for *username* dialog box, in which you type the current password, the new password, and the new password a second time (to make sure you don't accidentally type something you'll never remember).

Any users with administer or author permissions can change their own passwords. But if you're the main administrator for your organization's webs, you should set policy on password changes, instructing those with administer or author permissions when they can make such changes and even whether or not you're permitting them to do so. This is a significant issue in managing your Web site, because you'll want full control over who gets to access it for the sake of adding, editing, and deleting webs and files, and you should clarify password procedures immediately.

Setting General Options for the Web

Three options are available for each web through the Tools, Options dialog. The first is to show the Getting Started dialog when you load FrontPage 97; this dialog is shown in Chapter 24, "Building a Web." Next, you can have FrontPage 97 warn you when WebBot components included in your web are out-of-date. Similarly, you can be warned if the text index is out of date. If your web depends on up-to-date information, be sure to toggle these warnings on.

Establishing Proxy Servers

If you're using Microsoft FrontPage over a local area network (LAN) in your company or organization, there is a good possibility that you are operating behind a proxy server, which acts as a buffer between your company's LAN and the unruly Internet outside.

Proxies operate from behind *firewalls* on the organization's network; firewalls are software systems designed to prevent machines inside the organization from accessing outside computers directly. Instead, any requests for information on a machine outside the organization are sent to the proxy server, then forwarded out to the server on the Internet.

When the requested information is received, the proxy server decides, based on various criteria, whether or not to pass it through to the internal computer.

Contact your system administrator to get proxy information and then enter this information in the Proxies dialog box (see Figure 27.10), accessible by choosing Tools, Options, and click the Proxies tab.

FIGURE 27.10
Setting proxy server information lets you display your webs to the world.

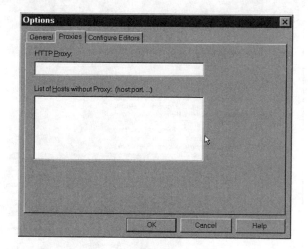

The HTTP Proxy name appears as a full URL, probably with a port assignment added to the end, for example, **http://mycompany.com:2522**. The List of Hosts Without Proxy list box, which accepts anything you type, gives you a place to include servers within your LAN that you know you must connect to. Again, your system administrator provides this information if you don't know it. If you need proxy information but you don't have it, none of your webs will be accessible from the outside Internet.

Configuring Editors

As you work in FrontPage 97, you will realize that the package does a great deal—but not everything. The Bonus Pack includes the Image Composer graphics package, for example, but you might have a favorite image editor you'd like to use as well. Nor does FrontPage have a tool for editing sound or video files. To compensate, FrontPage lets you configure editors to handle specific types of documents.

Part
VI

27

To establish the editors, choose Tools, Options, and click the Configure Editors tab. The Configure Editors dialog appears. Here, the file extension is shown in the Type column, while the editor you want to use for viewing that kind of file is displayed in the Editor column.

FIGURE 27.11

The Add Editor Association dialog box lets you configure additional editors for specific tasks.

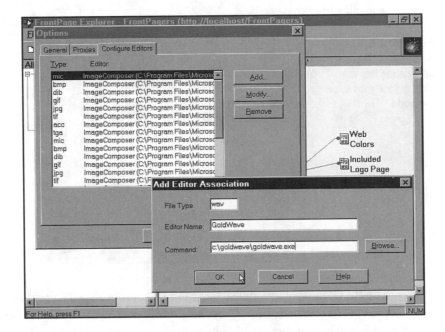

When you click the Add button, the Add Editor Association dialog box appears (see Figure 27.11). This dialog box allows you to specify a file type, the editor name, and the location of that program on your hard disk. In this example, sound files with the .WAV extension will be edited by a sound editing program called GoldWave, which exists on the hard drive in the path C:\Goldwave\GOLDWAVE.EXE. If you don't know the exact path, click the Browse button to locate it.

Once the editors are established, you can invoke them by clicking that file type anywhere in a FrontPage Explorer view and then choosing Edit, Open. The appropriate editor automatically opens with the specified file loaded into it and ready for viewing or editing.

From Here...

In this chapter you've examined the ins and outs of configuring a server created with FrontPage—everything from setting passwords to establishing permissions for administrators, authors, and end users. But even though you're technically ready to show your web to the world, it's nowhere near complete. You have to determine who will develop each web page, and you must set the Web server software itself in place. And then it's on to the much larger task of editing and creating the Web documents themselves.

- Chapter 28, "Managing a Web," examines the management of people, machines, and software, and also the usefulness of FrontPage's To Do List.

- Chapter 29, "Serving Your Web to the World with the Personal Web Server," looks at the requirements for making your work available on the World Wide Web itself.

- Part II, "Creating Your Web Pages with FrontPage Editor," is all about the actual Web pages themselves.

Part
VI

27

## CHAPTER 28

Managing a Web

Creating Web sites is a fascinating exercise, but managing them from initial conception through frequent updates is a challenging task that FrontPage 97 can help you with. Working with the various views of the Web, Explorer's automatic link updating, as well as the mini-project management capabilities of the To Do List, you can have some control over your Web as you work on it. ▪

Managing people, information, and machines

What resources do I need to manage when building a sophisticated Web site?

FrontPage's To Do List

Using the To Do List for your basic project management tasks

To Do columns and buttons

Getting a handle on the inner workings of the To Do List dialog box

Adding and removing tasks

How to note new tasks to be completed, and how to show that tasks are completed

Managing through Explorer's views

How do the three views from Explorer work together to help me manage and manipulate my site?

Web Site Management

One of the primary reasons to work with Microsoft FrontPage 97 lies in its ability to help you not only create Web sites but manage them as well. It's exciting and enjoyable to create a new site from scratch, especially using FrontPage's wizards and templates to get you started. The first several Web documents are even thoroughly enjoyable to design and develop, especially for anyone who's authored Web documents using raw HTML codes. If you've been stumped or simply bored with CGI scripting and developing such advanced items as discussion sites, working with FrontPage is better still.

But creating Webs isn't the greater part of a Webmaster's work. Instead, that dubious honor falls to maintaining and updating Webs. In fact, from start to finish, managing a Web site is every bit as important as creating one, even though the glory clearly goes to the people who make it look like something. Once a Web is in place, however, it remains of interest to users only if it is frequently updated, with new information and new reasons for visiting constantly being built in. Your job as Webmaster is to make sure that everything gets done and that the new and replacement elements are placed in the Web so that they work right from the start.

Managing People

You might be in the position of using FrontPage 97 to create and manage a Web alone. In this case, the only person you'll need to manage is yourself. Assuming that you can be relied on to listen to yourself, FrontPage offers all you need to do the job. But if, like a growing number of Webmasters, you're creating and developing a Web site in conjunction with others, then the management of people becomes quite probably the most difficult task of any you'll face. It's one thing to force a computer to do what you want it to do; it's quite another to get a group of people, no matter how small, to work together on a top-notch creative effort like a Web site. But workgroup dynamics, thankfully, are far beyond the scope of this book.

One of FrontPage 97's greatest strengths is its ease of use. What this means, from a manager's perspective, is that you have a far greater choice when hiring potential Web authors. In the past, you needed to find someone who knew HTML and probably CGI if you wanted to get anything done with reasonable speed, and those skills were hard to find. With a graphical package like FrontPage 97, you can begin to focus your recruitment on people with an eye to design rather than those who can code or program. This isn't to suggest that you no longer need people with programming experience, but FrontPage makes it much easier to share tasks among contributors with differing talents.

Here we'll take a look at the tools within FrontPage that will at least partly ease the assignment of tasks to authors and coadministrators. These tools—the Permissions dialog boxes of the Explorer Configuration menus and the To Do List with its limited but effective tracking mechanism—are by no means extensive, but they're better than nothing by a long shot.

Managing Information

After managing people, the hardest thing about creating a Web site is managing all the information. Information itself changes constantly but, more important, so do the needs and the expectations of its users. If you want your Web site to be effective—which translates into many users visiting many times and finding many rewards for doing so—you have to change the information and its presentation regularly. You also need to change the ways in which your readers interact with that information and, as a result, you'll frequently have to reconsider the interface your Web offers to its users.

With the advent of intranets, a new kind of information has appeared in Webs. This information—which consists of everything from procedures documents, meeting and event schedules, project milestones, and even financial details—is restricted to viewing by members of the organization to which it belongs. As a manager of an intranet site as opposed to an Internet site, your attention to information will be different but at least as important. The organization's information must be complete, readily accessible, and secure. Changes to some intranet information might be less frequent than for an Internet site, but that doesn't make it less demanding.

While information management is an organizational issue and hardly something one person can be responsible for, FrontPage offers a few tools that make such management a bit easier. First, the close link between FrontPage Editor and FrontPage Explorer makes on-the-fly editing and adding of Web pages easier than ever before. Second, Explorer's built-in links management system helps you keep your pages properly connected to one another, solving the problem of hyperlinks that lead nowhere or to the wrong page entirely. Finally, Explorer's multiple views let you see the way the information is presented, thereby negating the need for flow diagrams or such niceties as index cards. Your information is easier to manage because you can visualize it easily.

Managing Computers

At this point in the Web's history, there's still nothing easy about setting up a Web server and making all connected computers work with it happily and without incident. Simply put, managing a Web is still very much about managing computers.

This is one area in which FrontPage does as good a job as anything out there. The fact is that most Web servers exist on UNIX or Windows NT machines. The other fact is that most would-be Web designers work with computers running Windows 3.x or Windows 95. Through its server extensions, and hence its ability to let you work directly with the Webs on your server, FrontPage makes setting up a Web site relatively transparent. Similarly, by incorporating into the authoring software many of the tasks normally given over to the Common Gateway Interface (CGI), FrontPage lets you take command of the server in a way that most nonprogrammers could barely even dream of.

None of this is to suggest that using FrontPage replaces an intimate knowledge of UNIX, networking, or the workings of an HTTP server. What FrontPage does, however, is to render computer management something apart from those highly technical concerns. Suddenly it's up to the technical professionals to try to make the machines do what you want them to do. As long as the server owner cooperates, FrontPage gives you a considerable amount of power when it comes to managing computers.

FrontPage 97's To Do List

The single most useful piece of direct Web management available through FrontPage is the To Do List. Although it's certainly no replacement for sophisticated project management software, it is nevertheless a surprisingly powerful assistant. From the To Do List you can launch and work on every one of the outstanding projects, and you can get an entire history of who did what and when during the building of your site.

FrontPage automatically creates a To Do List for each Web you create. The principle behind the To Do List is this: All pages are incomplete (under construction) on a newly created Web. They will show in the Web as being under construction and will bear the Under Construction icon. As you work on individual pages, you can load them into FrontPage Editor from the To Do List. If you change anything on that page and then save it to the Web, FrontPage will, if you want, automatically mark the task as completed within the To Do List. You can add new tasks in the To Do List from within the To Do List itself, or you can add them from the Explorer and Editor programs as well. To use the To Do List, you must have the Web currently open in FrontPage Explorer.

To Do List Columns

Figure 28.1 shows the To Do List. Along the top of the list are the following column headings: Task, Assigned To, Priority, Completed, Linked To, and Description. Most of these are created through the Task Details or Add To Task dialog boxes, discussed later. The exceptions are Completed and Linked To, and their appearance is also discussed later.

FIGURE 28.1
The To Do List contains enough information to keep track of a Web's planned progress.

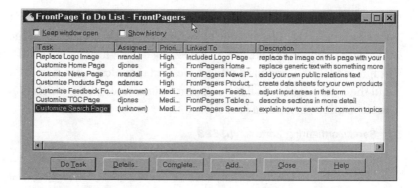

Two check boxes appear at the top of the To Do List: Keep Window Open and Show History. Marking Keep Window Open instructs FrontPage to keep the To Do List open while you are working on a task; otherwise, it will close automatically. Marking Show History shows the Completed column in the To Do List and causes the To Do List to show tasks that have been marked as completed. If Show History is not marked, these tasks disappear from the list as they are completed, but they can be seen by marking Show History at any time.

You can sort the To Do List according to any of the six columns, by clicking the column heading itself. Figure 28.2, for example, shows the same To Do List as seen in Figure 28.1—this time sorted by the Assigned To column. While there might seem little need for this kind of sorting in the pictured To Do List, on a much longer list sorting by priority, by page linked to, or by person assigned to can be of obvious usefulness.

FIGURE 28.2
By sorting the To Do List, you can get a different perspective on the tasks at hand.

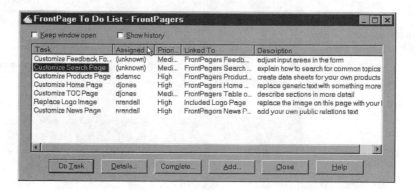

To Do List Buttons

Along the bottom of the To Do List are six buttons. Together, these buttons let you control the items on the To Do List—everything from creating new list items to showing previous items as having been completed.

Do Task   Although simple in concept, this is an extremely powerful tool. When you select a task in the To Do List and click Do Task, the file associated with the task opens into its appropriate editor. HTML files will open by default inside the FrontPage Editor, while graphics files will load inside the associated graphics editor. You establish these editors and their associations in the Configure Editors dialog box, which is available with the Tools, Options command in Explorer.

▶ **See** "Configuring Editors," **p. 685**

Another powerful feature of the To Do List appears after you have edited a file through the Do Task system. When you attempt to save to file to the Web, you will be asked if you want to mark the task as completed as you do so (see Figure 28.3). If you click Yes, the Completed column in the To Do List for that item will be updated with the current date.

FIGURE 28.3

You can have FrontPage Editor automatically update the information on the To Do List.

As an example of this, look at Figure 28.4. Here the Show History toggle has been turned on, and the Task labeled Customize Search Page shows the To Do List with the task now appearing as having been completed on 10/9/96.

FIGURE 28.4

After completing a page, the To Do List shows the date on which it was finished.

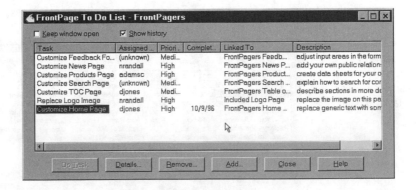

Details   When you select a task and click Details, the Task Details dialog box appears. As Figure 28.5 shows, this dialog box contains several fields; some of these are alterable but four of them are not.

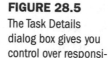

FIGURE 28.5

The Task Details dialog box gives you control over responsibilities and specifications.

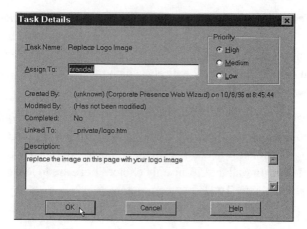

The first item in the dialog box is the Task Name. This name is created either by the FrontPage Wizard that created the Web or by the person who added the task to the To Do List. You can change it from this dialog box.

The Assign To text box lets you specify who should complete the task. This box is wide open, meaning that its contents aren't checked against the list of authors or administrators for the Web (an option to do so would be helpful, in fact). You can enter any name you want in here, but it's a good idea to keep your naming scheme consistent.

To the top right of the dialog box are the Priority option buttons. You can set the selected task as High, Medium, or Low priority, and the choice appears in the Priority column of the To Do List. While it's tempting to set everything at high priority, as a Web manager you'll want to set only the most truly important tasks as such.

The Description list box is another free-form field. Type in anything that might be helpful here, including specific suggestions to the person to whom the task has been assigned. The first few characters of this description appear in the Description column of the To Do List.

The other four fields are determined by FrontPage itself and cannot be altered except by working on the task. Created By shows which author established the task in the first place, including the time and date of its creation. Modified By displays the author responsible for the modification or displays that modifications have not yet been performed. The Completed field is either Yes or No, and simply refers to whether or not the task has been set as Completed in the To Do List. Finally, Linked To displays the file to which the Task item is linked, and this appears in the Linked To column of the To Do List. This can be changed only by altering the link within FrontPage Editor or Explorer.

Part
VI

Ch
28

Complete/Remove   When a task in the To Do List has been finished, click the Complete button to mark it as such. The resulting dialog box gives you two choices. You can either mark the task as completed, in which case it appears in the Completed column of the To Do List, or you can delete the task entirely, which means it will disappear from the To Do List entirely, even if Show History is marked.

When a task has been marked completed and you select that task again, the name of the Complete button changes to Remove. Clicking Remove reveals the same dialog box as initially clicking Complete, except that the first choice, Mark This Task as Completed, is grayed out and thus unavailable. Your only choices here are to leave everything as it is or to delete the task from the To Do List completely.

Add   The Add button lets you enter an entirely new task into the To Do List. The dialog box is identical to the Task Details dialog box shown in Figure 28.5, except that the Task Name and Description text boxes are not filled in, and the Linked To field shows Is not Linked. Because the task hasn't originated from FrontPage Explorer or Editor, the task is not associated with a file in your Web, and thus you cannot open it automatically into an editor. In fact, selecting a task added this way results in the Do Task button being grayed out and thus unavailable.

As a Web manager, you can use this button to add tasks to the list that aren't actually Web creation tasks. For example, you might need several graphics created for a page or series of pages, or you might need pictures or documents scanned for presentation in a document. For that matter, you can use the Add button to schedule meetings, if it helps to get your assistant's attention. But this method of adding tasks is less effective than adding them from FrontPage's main programs because they can't be completed as part of FrontPage activity itself.

Close and Help   The Close button closes the To Do List, while the Help button opens the Help files pertaining to the To Do List. Note that, if you don't mark the Keep Window Open check box at the top of the To Do List, the list automatically closes whenever you click the Do Task button and opens the task for editing in the associated editor.

Adding to the To Do List from FrontPage Editor

Often, when working on a page in FrontPage Editor, you'll realize that something needs to be completed on the page that you don't have time or resources for at that particular time. Instead of jotting down a note to yourself in a text file or a word processor, you can add a task to the To Do List directly from within Editor itself. The following is an example of this extremely useful process.

With the FrontPagers Web open (originally begun in Chapter 24, "Building a Web"), the Webmaster has decided to add a new page showing an employee directory. FrontPage Editor has been opened, and the Employee Directory template has been selected.

At this point, the Webmaster decides that it would be a nice idea to add a photograph of each employee. Knowing that it will take a few days to get these photographs together and to get permission to use them, she decides to add a task to remind her of this, and assigns the task to an assistant, Marty. She chooses Add To Do Task from the Edit menu to start the process.

The first step is a dialog box explaining that, in order to add a To Do task, the current file must be saved. Clicking Yes opens the Save As dialog box, and it is saved with the name Employee Directory. Because an image exists on the page, the next dialog box asks how the image should be saved. After agreeing to save all images, she will see the Add To Do Task dialog box (see Figure 28.6), where she can specify the name of the task, the person assigned the task, the priority of the task, and a description of the task.

FIGURE 28.6
The <u>D</u>escription box will be seen by the Webmaster only.

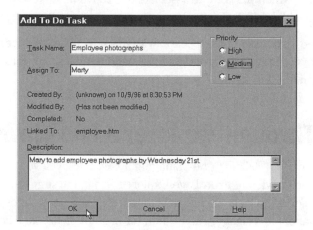

An important element of this dialog box is the Linked To field. The file being edited was saved as EMPLOYEE.HTM, and this now appears in that field. This means that clicking the Do Task button in the To Do List loads the EMPLOYEE.HTM file into FrontPage Editor.

The Task Name is "Employee photographs," and the task is assigned to Marty. This is given medium priority, and the description (which is meant to be seen by the Webmaster, not the assistant), explains what is to be done. Clicking OK sets this task into the To Do List, as the highlighted line of Figure 28.7 demonstrates.

Part
VI

Ch
28

FIGURE 28.7

The new task is ready
for action in the
FrontPage To Do List.

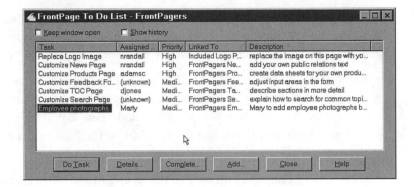

Adding to the To Do List from FrontPage Explorer

If you're working in Explorer and you want to add a task to the To Do List, the procedure
is almost identical to the procedure for adding from Editor. With the Explorer visible,
click the page to which you want to associate the To Do task. Now, with the page highlighted, choose Edit, Add To Do Task.

The Add To Do Task dialog box appears, with the selected page appearing in the Linked
To field. After you fill in the appropriate information, the task appears in the To Do List,
ready for action.

Managing Through Explorer's Two Views

Throughout Part VI, "Building and Managing a Web Site," you've seen examples of the
graphical Hyperlink view in FrontPage Explorer. So far, the suggestion has been that this
view helps you create a Web site and develop all the associated pages. That's true, but if
your role is that of site manager rather than (or in addition to) page creator, the view will
help you here as well. In fact, a second view, Folder view, is especially useful in this
regard.

Figure 28.8 shows a Customer Support Web as created by Explorer. The view here, which
you've seen throughout these chapters, is the Hyperlink view, with a textual hierarchy of
hyperlinks in the left pane and a graphical view of these links in the right.

The All Hyperlinks pane offers one possible assistant for Web management. Using this
pane, you can quickly get a top-level hierarchical look at your Web by keeping all the
headings compressed, or you can look in detail at any particular heading and its components by selectively expanding them. As you expand headings by clicking the plus signs
(+) to the left of the items, you get a sense of the size and scope of your Web, and you can
move quickly to an individual component for editing or assigning.

FIGURE 28.8

The primary Explorer Hyperlink view for a Customer Service Web.

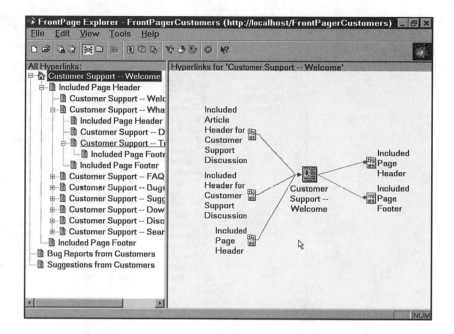

The right pane of the Hyperlink view shows you the Web in a graphical format. With this view you can tell exactly which pages link to which pages, and how the links fit together to form the overall Web. The strength of the Hyperlink view lies in its ability to show you exactly what needs to be added or completed, rather than simply presenting it, like the To Do List, as yet another item in a list. The weakness of the Hyperlink view, however, is that it can show you only a portion of the Web at any one time. Obviously a 21-inch monitor set to ultra-high resolution can display a larger portion than a 14-inch monitor and low resolution, but on such a display the Hyperlink view can become unwieldy. From a management perspective, the graphical Hyperlink view is best as a means of assessing and detailing specific portions of the Web, while the hierarchical All Hyperlinks view gives you a sense of scope and overall shape.

In Figure 28.9, you see the same Web as in Figure 28.8, but this time the Hyperlink view has been replaced by the Folder view, which is similar to the file view of Windows Explorer: folders in the left pane and subfolders and files in the right. Accessing the Folder view is simply a matter of choosing View, Folder View. Obviously, the Folder view is text-based rather than graphical, and as such it doesn't provide the same kind of information the Hyperlink view offers. What it does provide, however, is a short summary of all the details pertaining to the files in your Web site.

FIGURE 28.9

The Folder view shows you exactly which files make up your Web.

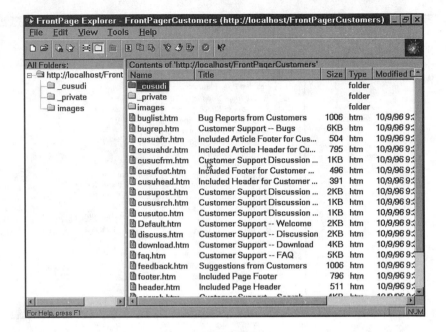

The columns in the Folder view display the following data:

- Name—This is the actual file name of the folder or file. Web documents will almost always end in .HTM or .HTML (note that Windows 95 and Windows NT accept extensions of more than three characters); graphics will end in .JPG or .GIF. You can use the file name information, for example, if you want to edit the file directly by using a different editor or even a text editor such as Windows' Notepad.

- Title—The title of the Web file, as set during the creation of the page. You can change the title using the Page Properties dialog box of FrontPage Editor. In the case of images, the Title column shows the path and file name instead of a title.

- Size—The Size column shows the size of the file in bytes. Files smaller than 1K (1,024 bytes) are shown with their actual byte count, while files greater than 1K are displayed in kilobytes and rounded to the nearest kilobyte. Files larger than 1M (1,024K) are displayed in megabytes, rounded to the nearest megabyte.

 It's entirely possible that files greater than one gigabyte (1,024M) appear in number of gigabytes but, like most people, I didn't have a large enough hard drive to test this. Besides, if you have a file that large in your Web, you should get rid of it if you don't want hordes of angry modem users storming your house.

- Type—The file type simply repeats the extension shown in the file name, unless your operating system doesn't use file extensions in file names, in which case Type is the only place to find the actual file type.
- Modified Date—This column shows the last date and time the file was modified.
- Modified By—This column shows who did the modifications for that page or file.
- Comments—The Comments column shows the comments about the document as entered through the Properties dialog box.

Together, these columns can provide a wealth of information. You can sort the Folder view according to any of these columns by clicking the column heading, and this shows you precise details ordered as you need them. For example, sorting by Modified Date lets you instantly see which pages haven't been updated recently enough to suit the site's needs, as established during planning. With large Webs, it's extremely easy to overlook one or two pages that need updating, especially pages that are less frequently accessed, and this column can help keep your attention focused on that strategy.

The Title, File Name, and Type columns can help you locate specific pages, and here another useful element of the Folder view comes into play. When you find the item you need in the Folder view, you can right-click it and select Show Hyperlinks, which opens the Hyperlink view centered on that file.

Management Tools: Spelling, Find, Verify Hyperlinks, and Recalculate Hyperlinks

FrontPage 97 offers four important tools specifically designed to help Webmasters manage their Webs. These tools tackle four simple but crucial tasks: Global Spell-Checking, Global Find and Replace, and two means of checking a Web's links: Verify Hyperlinks and Recalculate Hyperlinks.

Global Spell-Checking

One of the problems every Webmaster encounters is the difficulty of ensuring accurate spelling across the entire site. Authors can check their work on individual documents in FrontPage Editor, but when all the documents are linked together in a Web, it's essential that spelling be checked for errors and for lack of standardization. Almost nothing can reduce the professional appearance of a site more quickly than a measly little spelling mistake. It simply looks bad.

Part
VI

Ch
28

To invoke global spell-checking, choose Spelling from the Tools menu of FrontPage Explorer. This can be done from either the Hyperlink or the Folder view. You will be asked if you want to check all pages or only the pages you've selected, and whether or not you want to add pages that contain misspellings automatically to the To Do List. Since FrontPage's spelling tool cannot actually correct the spelling (as can a word processor), adding to the To Do List is a good idea. If you want, however, you can choose to Edit pages directly from the results of the spell check, so the To Do List addition might not be necessary, especially in the case of a relatively small Web site.

N O T E   Unfortunately, FrontPage does not offer a global thesaurus to match the global spelling checker. Thesaurus activities are available only within FrontPage Editor and, thus, can be done only one document at a time. ■

Global Find and Replace

Sometimes, several documents in a Web contain a piece of information that needs to be located or changed. The names of products might change or the names of corporate contacts, the prices of services, or any other type of repeated information might need to be found and possibly altered. In a large Web, changing repeated data is extremely tedious, requiring the Webmaster to load each page individually and edit the material. FrontPage 97 makes this considerably more convenient by providing a global Find feature and a separate global Replace feature.

To perform a global Find, select Find from FrontPage Explorer's Tools menu. You will be asked first to save any pages from the current Web that are open in FrontPage Editor. Then you'll type the text string you wish to find, and whether or not you wish to match the whole word or the upper- or lowercase of the word as typed. Finally, you'll be asked if you want to find the string in all pages in the Web or only in the pages you've highlighted.

The results of your search appear in a dialog box almost identical to the Replace dialog box shown in Figure 28.10. This dialog box shows the pages on which the search string has been found. By clicking a page and choosing Edit Page, you can load the selected page into Editor, or by clicking Add Task, you can place the page in the To Do List.

Performing a global Replace is almost identical. Select Replace from the Tools menu of FrontPage Explorer and then type the text strings in the respective Find What and Replace With text boxes on the Replace in FrontPage Web dialog box (shown in Figure 28.10). Here you'll also be asked, as with Find, to specify case and whole word matches, and whether to replace the string across the Web or only in selected pages.

FIGURE 28.10
While not as sophisticated as a word processor's replace function, this dialog box offers some important choices.

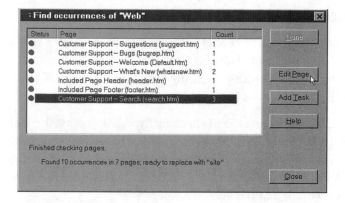

The results of the Replace command appear in the Find Occurrences dialog box shown in Figure 28.11. Here you'll see the titles of the pages on which the string is found, as well as the number of times it occurs on each page. You're also informed, in the information line below the list box, that FrontPage is ready to make the replacements.

FIGURE 28.11
You can add each document to the To Do List to edit later, or you can edit directly from here.

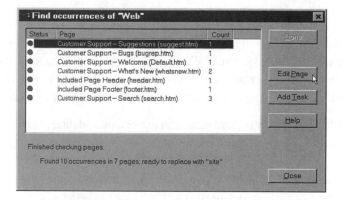

By highlighting a page and clicking Edit Page, you load the document into FrontPage Editor and are immediately presented with the Replace dialog box, complete with the Find and Replace text boxes already filled in. In other words, you haven't actually replaced anything yet, and you have to perform the replacement operations from there.

If you add the document to the To Do List by clicking Add Task instead, you will be presented with the same Replace dialog box when you edit the page from within the To Do List.

Part
VI

Ch
28

Verify and Recalculate Hyperlinks

Another of a Webmaster's crucial but tedious tasks is to check the hyperlinks that point inside and outside a Web. This task is crucial because broken links will frustrate users of the Web, and tedious because a heavily linked site (as most Webs are) contains any number of potential erroneous hyperlinks.

FrontPage 97 offers two ways of checking hyperlinks across the Web, both accessible from the Tools menu. Verify Hyperlinks determines whether or not hyperlinks internal and external to the pages in your site are valid. Recalculate Hyperlinks updates the views of your Webs in FrontPage Explorer and also updates various components of your Webs. Both ways require that you first be online.

Selecting Verify Hyperlinks causes FrontPage to ensure the validity of hyperlinks internal to your Web. It then displays the Verify Hyperlinks dialog box, which displays the URLs it has checked. It displays a green bullet for valid hyperlinks, a yellow bullet for links that have been changed since the last verification or that aren't yet verified, and a red bullet for broken hyperlinks.

From this dialog box you can edit the page or add the page to the To Do List. And you can perform one other essential task as well. By clicking Verify, you tell FrontPage to check the external URLs to which your Web pages point. These take time, which is why they're not checked in the first place, so while the process is going on, the Verify button changes to a Stop button, allowing you to halt the process whenever you wish.

Recalculate Hyperlinks performs several important updating functions. First, it updates the views of the Web in FrontPage Explorer, which is extremely important if you've edited hyperlinks or added or deleted pages. Next, it updates the text indexes that are produced by any Search Bots you have in your Web. Search Bots create indexes of all searchable pages, and as you add or delete pages, these indexes become incomplete. Finally, Recalculate Hyperlinks regenerates all the Include Bots in your Web. These bots are, in a sense, empty containers with pointers to fields in your Webs containing specific information; when a visitor calls up the page, the bots retrieve the most current version of that information. Recalculate Hyperlinks updates all the Web content that depends on these bots.

You should run the Recalculate Hyperlinks and Verify Hyperlinks commands frequently, certainly after any significant changes to your Web.

From Here...

From a Web management perspective, the two Web views and the To Do List are important. When you begin to create Webs, you're almost certain to be captivated by the Hyperlink view and its colorful graphical view of your Web, but from the standpoint of simply getting the work done, you'll quickly find the Folder view and the To Do List your everyday assistants. Outline view, meanwhile, will always be the focus during Web design sessions, and the Hyperlink view offers a convenient way to show people responsible for specific portions of the Web precisely what needs to be changed or added. Even if you're creating a Web purely on your own, the views and the To Do List are helpful, but as soon as you start working with a team of people, they can become indispensable.

You've almost completed your examination of FrontPage Explorer. At this point, you're ready to move on to:

- Chapter 29, "Serving Your Web to the World with the Personal Web Server," provides a detailed look at FrontPage's server administrator and server extensions.

- Chapter 30, "Setting Up an Intranet with FrontPage," takes you through the basics of the important task of building intranets with the FrontPage package.

- Part VII, "The FrontPage SDK," helps you use the Software Development Kit to customize your FrontPage environment even further.

Serving Your Web to the World with the Personal Web Server

Building a Web with FrontPage 97 is enjoyable and sometimes even fascinating. Certainly the program's tools make Web creation as easy as—or easier than—any other products on the market and, unlike many of those other packages, the time you spend with FrontPage almost always translates directly into a more effective, more impressive Web. If you've tried to build a Web from scratch in the past, far too often you spent your time simply trying to get things working. FrontPage doesn't spare you from all such necessities, but certainly from the bulk of them.

A fully constructed Web is, however, of no use whatsoever if nobody can see it. To make it a part of the World Wide Web or a part of your organization's intranet, you have to place your Web on a server. A server is a computer that (ideally) contains Web server software and a full-time, high-speed connection to the Internet. This computer can be on a machine running any flavor of Microsoft Windows (3.x, 95, NT Workstation, or NT Server); a Macintosh; a UNIX machine such as a Sun,

Silicon Graphics, or DEC Alpha (and many others); or any other computer for which Web server software is available.

FrontPage 97 contains not just one, but two pieces of server software. The more basic of the two is the FrontPage Personal Web Server, while the more advanced is the Microsoft Personal Web Server (yes, the similarity of the names is confusing). This chapter deals with both of them, but it focuses on the Microsoft PWS because of its greater capabilities. ■

▶ **See** Part IX, "Using Other Servers with FrontPage" **p. 847**, for information on other Web server software.

How a Web Gets "Served"

To serve your information to the World Wide Web, you need a computer with (ideally) Web server software and a full-time, high-speed connection to the Internet. The hardware and software combination together is called a *Web server*. You can run a server entirely on your own, or you may be assigned it as part of your organization's local area network (LAN).

Increasingly, Web servers are owned by companies who exist precisely to provide such services (they're known as *presence providers*), and it's entirely likely that your Internet service provider (ISP) offers some free Web space for its subscribers. Check the Web page for your ISP and see if they offer this service. If not, and if you need a small Web, switch to another provider.

If such a service exists, you won't need Web server software at all, nor will you need a full-time connection to the Internet. Anyone with an account with the provider, a modem, and a copy of a Web creation tool, such as FrontPage, can develop sophisticated Webs and then transfer them to the server. In such a case, however, be sure that your provider is willing to allow the FrontPage extensions for its server; if not, you will be restricted to using only certain features of the FrontPage package. As this chapter proceeds, you'll see what server extensions allow you to do.

It's not actually necessary to have a full-time, high-speed connection to the Internet to serve a Web. By using FrontPage's Personal Web Server, you can create a Web and run it whenever you log on to your ISP. The problems with doing so are threefold: First, your readers can access your Web only when you're online; second, the connection is slow; third, most ISPs give you a different Internet Protocol (IP) address every time you log on, so you won't be able to provide permanent hyperlinks to your site from anywhere else on the Web. The only way this works is if you have a Web designed for private use by you and a few friends or colleagues, and you can supply them with the IP number every time you're up and running.

On the other hand, your ISP might be willing to provide you (at significant cost) with a 24-hour modem connection and a fixed IP address, in which case you can leave the modem on all the time. This, however, requires a second phone line in your house, and the whole scheme is usually more expensive than renting server space from the same ISP. Several megabytes of server space is typically available for anywhere from $50 to $250 per month.

Web server software is available for practically all types of computers, but the most common serving platforms are UNIX (by far the most prevalent), Windows NT, the Macintosh, and more recently, Windows 95 and Windows 3.x. This software exists solely to serve files; that is, it waits for incoming requests from the Internet and then sends the requested file to the requesting machine. Primarily, this is handled through the protocol known as *HyperText Transport Protocol* (*HTTP*). All requests from Web browser software begin with a protocol statement. This is usually **http://**, but it can also be one of several others. The most common protocols besides http are the following:

- **mailto://**—Sends an e-mail message to the specified address.
- **ftp://**—Requests a document via File Transfer Protocol.
- **gopher://**—Requests a document from a Gopher server (much less common today).

WARNING

In browsers such as Netscape Navigator and Microsoft Internet Explorer, it's no longer necessary for users to type the protocol itself in the Location or Go To field. To reach the Microsoft site, for example, users need only type **www.microsoft.com**, not **http://www.microsoft.com**; and to download from the Netscape FTP site, they need only type **ftp.netscape.com**, not **ftp://ftp.netscape.com**. But be sure to include the full address, complete with protocol, in the links you create in your Web documents, or they won't work.

In effect, the server acts as a communications assistant between the user's machine and the machine on which the Web is stored. When the browser registers a click from the user, the server software initiates the transfer of the HTML file and all its included subfiles, such as graphics, imagemaps, and JavaScripts.

FrontPage 97's Two Personal Web Servers

FrontPage ships with server software called the *FrontPage Personal Web Server*. This is a fully capable piece of server software, but it's called "Personal" because of its built-in limitations. Simply put, if you plan to run a business across the Web, and you're trying for a large number of hits to your server, you'll need a more powerful server—one that can handle more simultaneous accesses and is more configurable—than the FrontPage PWS. In Chapter 31, we'll look at the other server provided with the FrontPage package, *Microsoft Personal Web Server*, which answers some of these limitations.

FrontPage PWS's primary function is to let you build Webs on your local computer, testing them thoroughly before placing then on the main server. When you're developing a Web on a main server, the only way to keep external users out is to protect the Web directory by assigning a username and password to that directory; this is a reasonable solution, but it's safer still to have the developing Web on a different machine entirely. FrontPage PWS lets you do so, and then FrontPage Explorer or the Web Publishing Wizard lets you copy the entire Web over to your main server.

FrontPage PWS installs with the rest of FrontPage 97 when you select the Typical installation option. At that time, it configures itself automatically to run on port 80. The TCP port is the network port that the server uses to listen for incoming requests from Web browsers. As a general rule, ports with numbers lower than 1024 (except for 80 itself, which is the standard HTTP port) are used for Internet services such as FTP, e-mail, and news. Port 80 is the normal port on which servers operate, but if you serve more than one root Web from the same computer, Personal Web Server automatically chooses a second port. By default, it chooses port 8080, which is the standard port for experimental servers.

If you choose the Custom installation option and elect to have the Microsoft Personal Web Server installed instead, then the FrontPage PWS installs but does not automatically assume a port number. In this case, the Microsoft PWS takes port 80, and the best strategy is to give FrontPage PWS a port such as 8080 and use it exclusively as a test server. You assign it a port number by installing the FrontPage extensions for the FrontPage PWS to that port.

Of course, there's a very good chance that you're installing FrontPage 97 on a machine that is already running server software such as Netscape FastTrack or O'Reilly WebSite. If so, FrontPage will recognize the server during installation, and will automatically configure itself—that is, it will install the appropriate server extensions to the correct port—at that time. But if you're not currently running a server, and especially if you're installing to a machine on which you'll build and test your Webs, either PWS will be necessary.

If your server is working properly, there's no reason to change your port number. You can do so, however, by using the Server Administrator, which is described in the section "Server Administration and Server Extensions" below. Note, however, that except for the FrontPage PWS, the port number for the server is set in the server software's configuration system, not through FrontPage itself. A sample process of changing port numbers and uninstalling server extensions is also described in "Server Administration and Server Extensions."

Server Administration and Server Extensions

Even though FrontPage ships with fully functional Web server software, FrontPage's Server Administration tools do not actually control the Personal Web Server; instead, they provide an interface to whatever Web server software you happen to be running. If you're running O'Reilly's WebSite, the Netscape Commerce Server, or the NCSA UNIX server, you can still use Server Administration, although you will do so in conjunction with the Server Administration tools provided by that server.

What does FrontPage Server Administration do? Primarily, it exists as a means of installing FrontPage's server extensions so that FrontPage's features work smoothly with your existing server. All Web servers ship with Server Administration tools, but in all cases these tools let you configure only that particular server. FrontPage Server Administrator, on the other hand, works hand in hand with a wide number of popular servers, with more to be added by Microsoft as the product matures. FrontPage accomplishes this task through the use of *server extensions*, which (as their name suggests) extend FrontPage's capabilities to other Web server software.

The Web servers supported by FrontPage are listed in Table 29.1. Note that these are current as of the end of October 1996. They can be found at **http:// www.microsoft.com/frontpage/softlib/fs_fp_extensions.htm**.

Table 29.1 Web Servers Supported by FrontPage Extensions

Operating System	Web Servers
Microsoft Windows 95	WebSite 1.1 and 2.0 (O'Reilly & Associates), Microsoft Personal Web Server, Netscape FastTrack Server
Microsoft Windows NT Workstation	WebSite 1.1 and 2.0, Microsoft Personal Web Server, Netscape Commerce Server, Netscape Communications Server, Netscape FastTrack Server

continues

Table 29.1 Continued

Operating System	Web Servers
Microsoft Windows NT Server	All for NT Workstation, plus Microsoft Internet Information Server
HP/UX 9.03 (Hewlett Packard)	Apache, NCSA, and CERN servers, Netscape Commerce Server, Netscape Communications Server, Open Market Web Server
IRIX 5.3 (Silicon Graphics)	Same as HP/UX 9.03 (above)
Solaris 2.4 (SPARCstations)	Same as HP/UX 9.03 (above)
SunOS 4.1.3 (SPARCstations)	Same as HP/UX 9.03 (above)
BSD/OS 2.1 (BSDI UNIX on Intel)	Same as HP/UX 9.03 (above)

Note that if you're using FrontPage 1.1, you must disable the SSL (Secure Sockets Layer) security of your Web server before installing the FrontPage extensions, because 1.1 doesn't support SSL. FrontPage 97, however, includes support for SSL.

How Server Extensions Work

As previously mentioned, FrontPage's server extensions are designed to work in conjunction with existing Web servers, such as those available from O'Reilly & Associates, Netscape Communications, the National Center for Supercomputing Applications, and Microsoft. Especially if you have a server for which a FrontPage extension does not currently exist, you will want to know the principles under which the server extensions operate. With this information, you can use FrontPage to develop your Web pages despite having an unsupported server.

Generally, the server extensions communicate with the Web server through the *Common Gateway Interface* (*CGI*). This is the interface mechanism by which servers themselves communicate with databases and other non-Web functions (CGI controls many fill-in forms, for instance), and the server extensions are designed to use CGI exactly as each specific server demands. CGI passes user-configured variables and environment specifics to the server, and CGI returns the requested information in one file format or another, typically HTML. The FrontPage server extensions use this generalized process to communicate with the different servers.

At times, it's necessary for the server extensions to communicate directly with the server. This happens in the instance of setting server configuration and establishing permissions for administrators, users, and authors. Most Web servers have their own idiosyncratic way of managing this information, and the task of the server extension is to interact appropriately with the type of server being run. In addition, newer servers have their own rich interfaces for setting these details (O'Reilly, OpenMarket, and Netscape servers for example), and often the configurations must be set using the server's software before FrontPage's Server Administrator can deal with them.

FrontPage Server Administrator

While the majority of the administration for your individual Webs is handled through the configuration dialog boxes of FrontPage Explorer (see Chapter 27, "Configuring Your Webs"), administration of the Web server itself is through the FrontPage Server Administrator. When you load the Server Administrator, the FrontPage Server Administration dialog box appears (see Figure 29.1).

Note that, unlike FrontPage 1.1, FrontPage 97 has no separate icon for running the Server Administrator. In fact, to get to the Server Administrator you have to go through the thoroughly annoying process of using Windows Explorer to enter the directory where you installed FrontPage 97 (c:\Program Files\Microsoft FrontPage\bin by default) and locate the file FPSRVWIN.EXE, then double-click it. If you prefer, you can use the command line version of the Server Administrator, which is accessible by double-clicking the FPSRVADM.EXE file.

FIGURE 29.1
All major server configurations result from working with this dialog box.

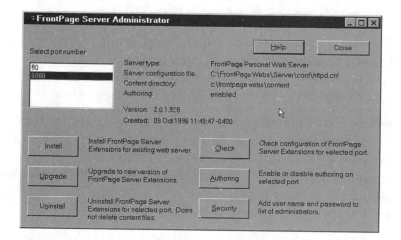

Server Administrator Information Area

In the example shown in Figure 29.1, the port number (8080) is shown in the Select Port Number box, while the text beside the Select Port Number box displays the current server information. This information consists of the following four parts:

■ Server type—The server type reflects the server corresponding to the port number. It also reflects the server extensions you have installed. You can have several server extensions installed simultaneously. In Figure 29.1 above, the Microsoft PWS and the FrontPage PWS are both installed.

■ Server configuration file—Some server software has a corresponding configuration file. The Microsoft PWS does not, but the FrontPage PWS's configuration file is HTTPD.CNF, found in C:\FrontPage\Server\Conf\ This file, shown in the printout under the "Install" section below, can be found in the path C:\FrontPage Webs\Server\Conf, assuming you allowed FrontPage 97 to install into its default directories.

■ Content directory—This item shows the folder in which the Web's actual content files can be located. By default, the FrontPage PWS installs these in the C:\FrontPage Webs\Content folder, while the Microsoft PWS places them in C:\WebShare\wwwroot. O'Reilly WebSite, as another example, places content by default in C:\WebSite\htdocs.

■ Authoring—You can enable or disable authoring permissions on the selected port. By default, authoring is enabled. If you want full security, or if the Web on that port needs no further authoring, you can disable it. This action is explained next, in the section, "Server Administrator Configuration Buttons."

Server Administrator Configuration Buttons

The six configuration buttons in the bottom half of the Server Administration dialog box let you install and configure your server extensions. Clicking some of these buttons results in very simple dialog boxes or even none at all (that is, FrontPage just performs an action instead), but the functions are important nevertheless.

Install: Installing FrontPage Server Extensions   No matter what Web server software you use, you'll need to install the server extensions for that particular server if you want to use all of FrontPage 97's features in conjunction with your server. Table 29.1 lists the servers for which Microsoft has supplied server extensions (which includes the most popular ones), and if yours is not included you should either contact the FrontPage team and request it, or consider changing servers.

Before trying to install the server extensions, keep in mind that the server software itself must be installed and working properly. Moreover, installing server software is rarely easy and automatic, so plan to spend an entire evening, maybe an entire week, putting your server software and Microsoft FrontPage into place. Given the potential importance of a Web server to your organization, this is one area in which speed definitely isn't in order.

TIP The easiest way to set up the extensions for your server is to do so when you install the FrontPage 97 software in the first place. If you have server software on your system, FrontPage will find it and offer to install the extensions. Especially if this is the only server software you'll be using, by all means say yes.

Installing Server Extensions for FrontPage PWS and Microsoft PWS The example here will demonstrate how to install the server extensions for the FrontPage PWS onto port 8080, then the Microsoft PWS onto the default http port 80. That will allow you to use both: FrontPage PWS as a quick and dirty testing server, and Microsoft PWS as the main server.

In all cases, the procedure for installing server extensions begins by clicking the Install button. When you do, you'll see the Configure Server Type dialog box (see Figure 29.2). By default this box displays the FrontPage Personal Web Server, but clicking the down-arrow will reveal others.

FIGURE 29.2
The Configure Server Type dialog box contains existing built-in extensions.

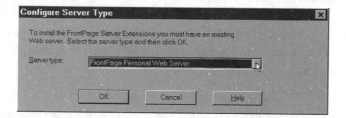

Click OK to continue with the installation of the FrontPage PWS. This yields the Server Configuration dialog box, in which you browse for the name of the file that contains the httpd (http daemon, i.e. server) information for the PWS. By default, this file is a text file called HTTPD.CNF, and is found in the C:\FrontPage\Server\Conf\ directory. But before you select this file, you have to edit it to change the port number to which it is assigned. Remember, you want the FrontPage PWS on port 8080 and the Microsoft PWS on port 80.

Here is a listing showing part of the HTTPD.CNF file as it ships with FrontPage 97:

```
# -FrontPage- version=2.0
# --
#
#   HTTPD.CNF
#
# Main server configuration for the FrontPage Personal Web Server
#
# This is the main server configuration file. It is best to
# leave the directives in this file in the order they are in, or
# things may not go the way you'd like.
#
```

```
# ServerRoot: The directory the server's config, error, and log files
# are kept in. This should be specified on the startup command line.
#
# Format: ServerRoot <path>
#
ServerRoot c:/frontpage\ webs/server/

# Port: The port the standalone listens to. 80 is the network standard.
#
Port 80

# ServerName allows you to set a host name which is sent back to clients for
# your server if it's different than the one the program would get (i.e. use
# "www" instead of the host's real name). Make sure your DNS is set up to
# alias the name to your system!
#
# Format: ServerName <domain name>
#
# no default
```

The important area of concern right now is the Port #, in the middle of this listing. By default, this port number shows as 80, but you should now change it to 8080. So make a copy of the HTTPD.CNF file within the same directory, giving it a different name (in case you want to get it back in its default form), then load HTTPD.CNF into Notepad or another ASCII editor and change the line Port 80 to read Port 8080. Now you're ready to install the server extensions.

Select the HTTPD file (it might show without its .CNF extension, depending on how you have Windows 95 configured). When you do so, you'll see the dialog box in Figure 29.3.

FIGURE 29.3
The Server Configuration dialog box requires the configuration file.

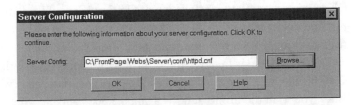

Clicking OK yields an information box letting you see the choices you've just made, and clicking OK again takes you to an Administrator Setup box in which you enter your name and password as administrator for the FrontPage Webs. If you have an administration name and password already established for your server, use these here. Click OK again, and if all goes well you'll see a message saying Install completed successfully. The port number and server information will then appear on the FrontPage Server Administrator dialog.

Now install the Microsoft PWS server extensions. Again, make sure that you've installed the Microsoft PWS from the FrontPage CD-ROM. On the FrontPage Server

Administrator dialog, click Install. From Configure Server Type, choose Microsoft Personal Web Server (it's immediately below the FrontPage Personal Web Server default choice).

Click OK, and you'll receive one of two responses. If you have the Microsoft PWS running, you'll get a Confirmation dialog, in which case click OK and carry on. If you don't have the Microsoft PWS running, you'll be told: In order for FrontPage to work, the WWW Service of the Personal Web Server must be started. Go to the Win95 or WinNT Control Panel, double-click the Personal Web Server icon, click the Startup tab, and click Start. The Web Server State area will read The server is running, and the server's icon will appear in the Taskbar tray. Close Control Panel and return to the FrontPage Server Administrator dialog. Start the Install process again until you see the Confirmation Dialog, then click OK.

Next, enter the account name you'll use when administering and authoring your Webs. This will probably coincide with the username you use for your system. Click OK, and the installation will proceed. A Server Administrator box will tell you that the WWW Service of the Microsoft PWS must be restarted, and clicking Yes lets that happen automatically. Next you'll see: Install completed successfully, and the server will appear on port 80 on the FrontPage Server Administrator dialog.

Now you're ready to roll.

 By this point, if you've been authoring Webs from earlier chapters, you've established several different passwords for your Web. It's a good idea to start a word processing, spreadsheet, or database file to store these usernames and passwords, but be sure to give the file an innocuous name or to password-protect it using your software. Just don't forget this password as well.

Upgrade   Once the server extensions are installed, you can upgrade them easily. When you receive new versions of the server extensions, either directly from the Web server publisher or from the Microsoft Web or FTP site, you can upgrade the relationship between FrontPage and the server by clicking the appropriate port number, then the Upgrade button. The upgrade software must be placed within the Servsupp\ directory of the main FrontPage area on your hard drive.

The only thing that happens when you click Upgrade is that you see a small dialog box saying that FrontPage will perform the upgrade, and then a second dialog box saying that the upgrade has been done successfully.

Uninstall   If you want to remove the server extensions, in the Select Port Number list box highlight the port you no longer want and then click Uninstall.

As the Warning box tells you, only the server extensions for that port will be uninstalled. Nothing will happen to the content files of the Web, so your HTML files, graphics files, and everything else will remain in place. In fact, the uninstall action doesn't actually remove the extension files themselves. All it does, in essence, is to disconnect FrontPage from direct contact with the server. You can no longer perform for that server software all the actions available in FrontPage itself. See the section "Using FrontPage Without Servers Extensions" later in this chapter for the effect this action will have.

So why do you bother uninstalling extensions? For the most part, you don't. But if you upgrade your server software, you might find that the extensions no longer work properly, so uninstalling them and then reinstalling them might be the only solution. Furthermore, you might need to change a port number to which FrontPage links through your server software. In this case, you have to uninstall the server extensions, set the port number through your server's configuration system, and then reinstall the extensions so that FrontPage can read the appropriate port.

TIP Uninstalling extensions is a painless process, and you can reinstall as soon as you've uninstalled them. If you're having difficulty with any aspect of the communication between FrontPage and your server, try uninstalling and then reinstalling as a means of getting past the trouble.

Check Clicking the <u>C</u>heck button causes FrontPage to determine whether or not the server extensions are configured properly for the currently selected port. If anything is wrong, you receive an appropriate error message. Otherwise, you are told that the check was performed okay.

Authoring By default, the authoring option is enabled. To disable it, click the <u>A</u>uthoring button or, if the option is already disabled, click the <u>A</u>uthoring button to enable it again. When authoring is disabled, FrontPage Explorer and FrontPage Editor are not able to access that particular Web. You might want this to happen if there is no more work to be done on the Web, or for any number of other administrative reasons.

Security The final button on the FrontPage Server Administrator dialog box is called <u>S</u>ecurity. Clicking this yields the Administrator Name and Password dialog shown in Figure 29.4.

FIGURE 29.4
This dialog box lets you set administrator permission for any Web on your server.

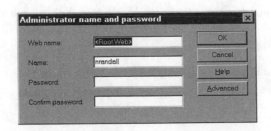

In the Web Name text box, you can type the Web for which you want to change or create administrator information. By default, the root Web is selected, but you can type in whatever Web Name you want to change. Then in the Name and Password text boxes, you can enter an administrator name and password. If the administrator name already exists for your server (that is, you specified that name when you installed the extensions previously), this action replaces the existing password for that name with the password you now enter. If the administrator name is a new one, it is now created and applied to that Web.

Shown in Figure 29.5 is the Internet Address Restriction dialog box. This dialog box results from clicking the Advanced button on the Administrator Name and Password dialog box. Here you specify the exact IP address from which the administrator can access the Web, or a partial address specifying a range of IP addresses. An exact IP address takes a four-part form, such as 129.88.125.37, while a restriction to the first portion of that address (hence, an organization rather than an exact workstation, for example) reads 129.88.*.* (the wildcard asterisk character allows any number, while the first two parts of the address remain fixed). The default address is *.*.*.*, which means that the administrator can access the Web from anywhere on the Internet, as long as the username and password are entered correctly.

FIGURE 29.5
Enter the IP address in the Internet Address Restriction dialog box.

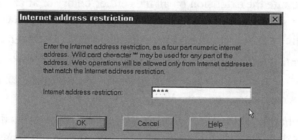

Using FrontPage Without Server Extensions

Server extensions do not exist for all Web server software, but that doesn't mean you can't make use of FrontPage's Web creation and page creation features. You won't be able to use all of them, but it will still be an extremely useful program for building Webs. The following sections provide some items to keep in mind when dealing with a server without FrontPage extensions.

Copying Webs

Copying Webs from your computer to a server without FrontPage extensions requires the following considerations:

■ Don't use the Publish Web feature found in FrontPage Explorer. Instead, transfer files via FTP from your machine to the appropriate directory on the server. Alternatively, use the Web Publishing Wizard that comes with the FrontPage Bonus Pack, and which, when installed, appears in Start/Programs/Accessories/Internet Tools.

■ Don't transfer directories beginning with _vti_. These directories are proprietary to FrontPage's extensions system.

■ Don't transfer files that contain access control information, such as author and administer permissions. These access controls will not work on a server that does not support FrontPage extensions.

Server Differences

Web server software packages differ in the way they treat files and documents. The following points must be considered when building Webs for a server without FrontPage extensions:

■ Web servers vary in what file types they recognize. UNIX servers, for example, typically recognize as Web documents only files with an .HTML extension, while FrontPage for Windows generates these files with an .HTM extension. You might need to change the extension on all files either before or after FTPing them to the destination server. Other file incompatibilities might occur as well, depending on the operating system and the server software on the destination machine.

■ Access control differs from server to server. Even FrontPage's server extensions don't solve all the possible access control problems. In general, try to avoid extensive access restrictions on your Web.

■ Find out what the destination server needs as the name for its default document, that is, the document that appears when users enter your domain name but don't specify an actual document name. Some servers recognize INDEX.HTML as this name, but others use other names (such as WELCOME.HTML). You'll need to know this before transferring your Web to the server.

Bot Interactions

FrontPage's Bots are extremely powerful, but they won't work with a Web server for which FrontPage server extensions do not exist. The following are two points that must be considered if building Webs for such a server:

■ Don't use FrontPage imagemaps. Instead, set them as appropriate for your server when you create them.

■ Some of FrontPage's Bots depend on the existence of server extensions for correct operations. These include the Search Bot, Registration Bot, Discussion Bot, Save Results Bot, and Confirmation Bot. Avoid building these into your documents.

FrontPage TCP/IP Test

A surprisingly useful utility within the FrontPage 97 package is the TCP/IP Test (see Figure 29.6). The TCP/IP Test is found in the FrontPage Explorer's Help menu. Click Help, then choose About Microsoft FrontPage Explorer, then click the Network Test button. This will yield the FrontPage TCP/IP Test box, where you'll see a Start Test button. By clicking this button, you get useful information about the behavior of your TCP/IP network connection.

FIGURE 29.6
FrontPage's TCP/IP Test after clicking Explain Results.

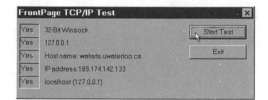

The TCP/IP protocol is the protocol under which the Internet operates. To be on the Internet, in fact, a computer must be running the TCP/IP protocol. Without it, you can be on all kinds of other networks but not on the Internet. Computers connected to LANs sometimes share the TCP/IP stacks necessary to connect to the Internet, but the protocol is still there, even if the individual machine doesn't know it.

NOTE If you are connecting to the Internet through a dynamic IP address system, as is usually the case with modem connections to an Internet Service Provider, you and your readers can access your site only by typing the actual IP number (for example, http:// 129.97.38.164/). This is because your IP address does not actually have a domain name associated with it. Domain names are available through fixed IP addresses only. ■

From Here...

Server administration is simplified considerably through FrontPage's tools, but it still demands constant attention. This is especially true if your Web server resides on a remote machine and uses a different operating system from your own, and if that server software is upgraded at any time. Microsoft promises fast action on creating and upgrading server extensions, so keep visiting the FrontPage Web site at **http://www.microsoft.com/frontpage**, but in the case of upgrades, you can expect a few days or weeks delay.

With your server extensions installed and FrontPage working comfortably in conjunction with it, and with the ins and outs of FrontPage Explorer fully under your control, the creative part of Web design begins. The next several chapters take you directly into FrontPage Editor, the powerful tool for authoring the actual pages that will populate your Webs. You'll learn the ins and outs of Web page creation from start to finish, and when you've finished, you'll have built a complete and functional Web site.

- Chapter 30, "Setting up an Intranet with FrontPage," demonstrates the capabilities of FrontPage in creating and managing private intranets.
- Part VII, "The FrontPage SDK," explains how to make use of the Software Development Kit to customize FrontPage to your needs.

Setting up an Intranet with FrontPage

This chapter covers using FrontPage to develop intranet applications. While the intranet technology may be new to the Web, it's importance is understood to be as great as the Internet itself. The intranet is quickly invading the corporate desktop and becoming seamlessly integrated with existing applications.

The intranet is now in a position to overtake traditional groupware solutions through its ease of use and cost effectiveness. A network environment once dominated by Lotus Notes and Groupwise is now embracing intranet technology.

Imagine that you own a company with fifty employees on the network. Using a client/server application such as Lotus Notes would cost approximately $5000 for the software alone, not to mention time spent developing the content and testing functionality. An intranet solution could quite easily reduce costs while adding additional benefits. The same fifty employees could be using Internet Explorer for the client software and the Microsoft Internet Information Server as the server portion. Total cost? Zero. Zilch. Nothing. Nada. ■

Build an Intranet

Learn how to leverage existing Internet technology into an internal network solution.

Plan out Your Intranet for Optimum Results

Planning your intranet correctly is just as important as the content itself.

Incorporate Office Documents

Utilize existing documents for file-sharing capabilities on the intranet.

Reduce Costs Associated with Networking

Build a cross-platform network application with virtually no associated costs.

Rise of the Intranet

While the buzzword of 1995 may have been "Internet," the buzzword of 1996 has most definitely been "intranet." Simply defined, an intranet is an internal network using TCP/IP technology. Generally, businesses already have networked computers using protocols such as NetBEUI (Microsoft Windows-based networks) and IPX/SPX (Novell NetWare). The idea of another network protocol to monitor and maintain may sound scary, but the cost justification is overwhelming.

One fantastic advantage of using an intranet over existing network products is that employees only have to learn one interface. This amounts to reduced training time, reduced support costs, and easy migration to new client/server technologies. You may be asking yourself: But my employees use Word, Excel, and Access. Why switch? Good question. The truth is, you don't have to stop using your existing tools. Think about using intranet technologies to "embrace and extend" your existing operations base.

With the release of FrontPage 97 and Internet Explorer 3.0, Microsoft has handed over the tools to incorporate many Microsoft Office features into a FrontPage-developed intranet. Through the use of OLE technology, or Active X as we are growing to know it, desktop applications are migrating into Web applications.

Key Advantages of an Intranet

There are quite a number of advantages to building an intranet, most of them leading to a reduction in operating expenses. Typical IS departments are constantly looking for new ways to increase productivity, while reducing costs at the same time. Developing an intranet is clearly the way to take care of both goals simultaneously.

Reduce Publishing Costs

A typical mid-sized company has a Human Resources department that twice a year publishes an employee directory. If the company has 500 employees and prints a directory consisting of 100 pages, the company can expect to pay anywhere from one to three dollars per book, which includes typesetting, printing, and binding. Printing that kind of information twice a year can lead to costs of over $3000 annually. Using an intranet, the same employee directory could be deployed across the network virtually free of charge. If an employee needed to take a portion of the directory home, he could save it to disk or print the pages desired.

Now, imagine all of a company's documents available electronically. Quarterly reports, financial statements, employee memos, and lunchroom menus could all be put into a Web interface, saving the company hundreds or thousands of dollars per year. Of course, you probably wouldn't want all of your employees to see sensitive financial documents. Such access can be limited through security steps described later in this chapter.

Sales Support

Many companies have salesmen traveling constantly. Keeping up with pricing changes, product availability, and contact information can be a headache for a salesperson on the go. An intranet solution is much needed here.

Quite a few companies have dedicated modems and special software for their sales force to dial into remotely. While this can provide up-to-the-minute information for the salesperson, it can hold a tremendous cost weight for the employer. An intranet solution would allow a salesperson to dial into a national Internet Service Provider, log on to the network, and access such mission-critical documents. Of course the site would have to be secure to retain its effectiveness, but this is a small price to pay for reducing costs while making information readily available.

Reduce Training Time

One of the largest costs resulting from a new hire is time spent training the employee on existing systems and software. The employee may have to learn a word processor, a spreadsheet application, and the structure of the internal network all at once. This can be quite overwhelming, both for the new employee and the employer. Integrating an intranet into your existing network structure can help lift the weight off both persons.

Imagine sitting down with the employee on her first day and explaining to her that her main work window will be a Web browser. Furthermore, you explain that all internal company information and documents as well as internal correspondence will be accessed from one interface. You might have to explain what a bookmark file is for, or what a Reload button does, but it's a far cry from trying to show the employee why help in one program is accessed differently from in another. The key to an intranet is consistency. And consistency leads to better productivity.

Reduce Software Costs

Many of today's proprietary client/server software solutions are expensive to keep up with. Most software is now updated on a yearly schedule, resulting in outlandish registration fees for the company trying to keep up with technology. Another problem with proprietary solutions is that they can only be used one way, with one specific client program.

An intranet can be viewed from any Web browser—unless specific tags are used to render the site platform-specific. There are many free Web browsers on the Internet available for downloading, including Microsoft's Internet Explorer, which runs on all Windows platforms, Macintosh, and UNIX in the near future. There are also quite a few Web servers available for free, such as the Internet Information Server by Microsoft, Apache, EMWAC, and Win-HTTPD.

Technical support for network software can also be quite costly, not to mention the time and money spent on long-distance charges while waiting on hold for a technician. Most documentation for intranet-related programs is on the Web already. Forums such as FAQs and discussion groups via Usenet are free to use and can be a real time-saver when you need support quickly.

Creating an Intranet with FrontPage

Though most Web authors like to jump right into development, it's important to remember that a little organization and planning can go a long way. Effective intranets take weeks or months to develop while constantly changing to fit the needs of the company and the promise of technology.

Authoring a functional intranet consists of five main steps:

Planning the Content—good planning leads to good results.

Building a Foundation—the intranet must be structured and organized.

Adding Components—incorporating the pieces that glue the framework together.

Final Touches—adding graphics and other elements.

Deployment—the final phase of Web site development.

Planning the Intranet

The first step to the development cycle of a good intranet is strategic planning. Though you may be able to build a site one page at a time, it's often more useful to create the foundation of a site first and fill in the gaps as you come to them. Begin your development by mapping out by hand the different areas that you plan to incorporate into your site. For our sample Web, we will have five different departments: accounting, human resources, support, announcements, and feedback.

It is recommended that you begin your Web site development by sketching out the rough flow of the pages on paper. Once the ideas are carefully laid out, including additional components like databases and custom scripts, it's time to create a storyboard. The storyboard is a great tool for instant visual feedback. There will be no question about how the site will flow if you can look at its physical form before you design the actual Web pages. The storyboards do not have to be anything complex. In fact, they can be built on one sheet of paper with boxes drawn for each of the Web pages. Don't worry if you're not an artist. Most Web authors are not. The purpose of the storyboard is just to give you an idea of the layout at a quick glance.

Erecting the Framework

Now that the initial site is mapped out, it's time to create the base on which our intranet will be built. You must have a strong foundation on which to develop an intranet application. Many Web authors feel that creating empty pages with text-based links as placeholders help speed up the overall development process. In this section, you will lay out the basis of your intranet, including all of the main sections and pages within. You will also incorporate some existing Microsoft Office documents into your pages to gain an understanding how integrating legacy applications fits into FrontPage.

Begin by opening the FrontPage Explorer and making sure that your Web server is up and running. Take the following steps:

1. In the FrontPage Explorer, create a new Normal Web called Intranet. Double-click the page called INDEX.HTM. x Author: If this is intended to be step-by-step, there are some missing elements here such as selecting a server, entering user name and password, and so on.

2. In the blank page type: Accounting ¦ Human Resources ¦ Support ¦ Announcements ¦ Feedback. Click within the line of text and choose the center button from the toolbar.

3. Create new pages for the first four sections of your intranet by clicking within the individual departments and choosing the Hyperlink button from the toolbar. Choose Normal Page when prompted for each.

4. Click within the word Feedback and choose the Hyperlink button. Create a New Page called FEEDBACK.HTM and choose Feedback Form from the list.

You should now have five hyperlinks on your first page, each leading to a new page within your intranet. Though you may be anxious to enhance your site with graphics and bullets, it's easier to set up the foundation and fill in the rest later, especially if there are going to be multiple authors working on the Web site.

In the FrontPage Explorer, your new intranet Web will look like Figure 30.1.

FIGURE 30.1

A solid foundation to your corporate intranet leads to a reliable final application.

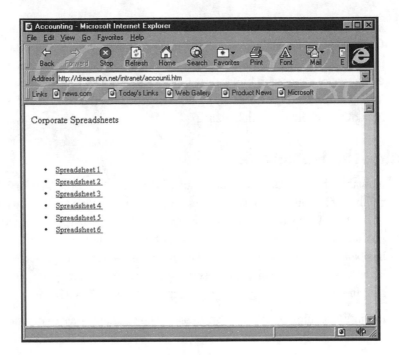

Adding Components

Now that the foundation is laid out, it's time to add content to your intranet. Any existing document can be linked into your intranet, allowing legacy applications to continue to be utilized in the workplace. Adding components is done through building upon the base site, and growing it from there much like a tree sprouts new branches.

The Accounting Page   The Accounting department has asked for six spreadsheets to be made easily accessible to everyone on the network. Your task is to incorporate the Excel files seamlessly into your intranet. Take the following steps:

1. Double-click the Accounting page to open it for editing.

2. Type Accounting Spreadsheets and hit enter. Type Spreadsheet 1, then highlight your text.

3. Click the Hyperlink button on the toolbar and choose World Wide Web. Click a Hyperlink Type of **file://**. This will eventually anchor the Excel file to your hyperlink.

4. Click Browse and choose an Excel file to insert. When you have finished choosing your file, click OK.

5. Repeat the process for spreadsheets 2 to 6.

6. Highlight all six of the spreadsheet links and choose the Bulleted List button from the toolbar. Your list of spreadsheets should look like Figure 30.2.

FIGURE 30.2

Incorporating spreadsheets into an intranet leads to easier document retrieval for end users.

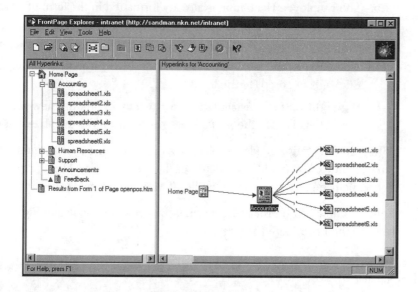

If you open this page in Internet Explorer and click one of the spreadsheet links, Excel will open inside Internet Explorer, allowing the page to be viewed and printed. In other browsers, the user is prompted to save the file to disk or to configure a helper application. By associating Excel with this file type, the program file will launch, allowing instant information at the employee's fingertips.

The Human Resources Page   The Human Resources department has greater needs than that of Accounting. You have been asked to incorporate an Employee Directory, Open Positions, Employee Handbook, and Meeting Schedule into the Human Resources portion of the intranet. Take the following steps:

1. Double-click the Human Resources page in the FrontPage Explorer.

2. Type `Employee Directory ¦ Open Positions ¦ Employee Handbook ¦ Meeting Schedule` into the page. Click within the entire line and center the text on the page.

3. Highlight `Employee Directory` and choose Hyperlink from the toolbar. Create a new page called EMPLOYEE.HTM and choose OK. When prompted, choose `Employee Directory` from the New Page templates listing.

   The Employee Directory page that you've just created will be edited later. For now, we are just setting up the framework.

4. HighlightOpen Positions and choose the Hyperlink button. Create a new page called OPENPOS.HTM and choose OK. When prompted, choose `Employee Opportunities` from the list of templates.

5. The Employee Handbook is already formatted in the form of a Word document. All that is needed is to import the file into FrontPage.

   Highlight `Employee Handbook` and choose Hyperlink from the toolbar. Click the World Wide Web tab and choose **file://**. Click Browse to locate the Word document. Click OK to complete the link.

6. Highlight `Meeting Schedule` and create a hyperlink to a new page called MEETING.HTM. Choose `Meeting Agenda` from the templates menu and click OK.

While the Meeting Agenda template was meant for one specific meeting, it serves our purpose here. You could have just as easily created a new blank page for the Meeting Schedule page and inserted a number of Meeting Agenda pages.

Your addition to the FrontPage intranet project should look like Figure 30.3 when you refer to the FrontPage Explorer.

FIGURE 30.3
Organizing intranet content by a departmental basis leads to easier navigation.

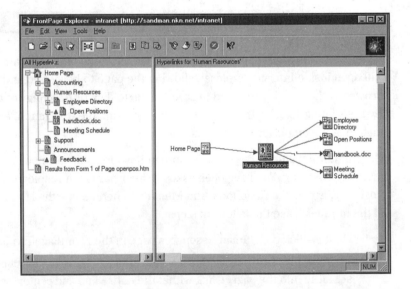

Your intranet is beginning to take shape. You have already created the basis of the Accounting and Human Resources departments, and have only three more sections to go.

The Technical Support Page   The manager of your company's Technical Support department has approached you about putting a detailed list of Frequently Asked Questions into your intranet application. He feels that providing help online for your coworkers will help their department free up time spent on tedious problems. Take the following steps:

1. Double-click the Technical Support page in the FrontPage Explorer.
2. In the body of the page, type `Frequently Asked Questions` and click within the text. Choose Hyperlink from the toolbar and choose New Page. Save the new page as FAQ.HTM and choose Frequently Asked Questions from the template menu. Click OK to continue.

For now, we will leave the new FAQ page as is. It can be completed and then updated at any time.

The Announcements Page   Your company's Executive Secretary has asked that you incorporate an announcements page into your intranet so that employees are kept abreast of new happenings, and she doesn't have to keep stuffing everyone's mailbox with memos every day. The company has announcements often, and she would like people to be able to view the announcements on a monthly basis, with the daily announcement benefiting from a little pizzazz. Take the following steps:

1. Double-click the Announcements page in the FrontPage Explorer. The blank page will open, eagerly awaiting your commands.
2. Choose Insert, Marquee from the menu. Type `Today's Big Announcement` in the Text field. Click OK.
3. Click the new marquee once to highlight it, and choose the Center button on the toolbar.
4. Under the marquee, add the line `Previous Announcements`. This is where you would normally retype the previous day's marquee and date the entry.

At a later time you could add a link on the Announcements page pointing to older announcements. This could be done weekly or monthly, depending on the length of the content.

The Feedback Page   Management wants to know what the employees are thinking about and, more important, how the company can grow to be more profitable. They have requested a Feedback page that will report its comments to a text file that management can review at board meetings. The feedback form is already in working order, though it will need some formatting to reach management's expectations. Take the following steps:

1. Double-click the Feedback page in the FrontPage Explorer.
2. In the FrontPage Editor, highlight all of the form components, beginning with `What kind of comment would you like to send` down to the end of the last text line `Please contact me . . . .` Hit the Delete key to remove this portion of the form.

3. With your cursor at the beginning of the form, choose Insert, Form Field, Scrolling Text Box from the menu. Size the scroll box to the width of the Submit and Clear buttons and about 8 lines tall.

4. Hit Enter to drop down one line. Type Name: then choose Insert, Form Field, One-Line Text Box. Stretch the text box so that it is even with the rest of your form.

5. Right-click within the border of the form and choose Form Properties from the menu. Click settings and pay special attention to the location where your text file will be saved.

The results of the form submission will write to a text file called FEEDBACK.HTM that resides in a directory called _private. This directory is one that FrontPage created when you created your initial intranet Web. Only the Administrator of the Web can read this file. No ordinary employee will be able to access this file from within the intranet.

The last step to completing your feedback page is to format the text that asks the visitor for his or her comments. Anything that management will approve of is fine. When you view the page in a Web browser, it should look like Figure 30.4.

FIGURE 30.4
Forms allow you to gain not only feedback from your employees, but provide a sense of interactivity as well.

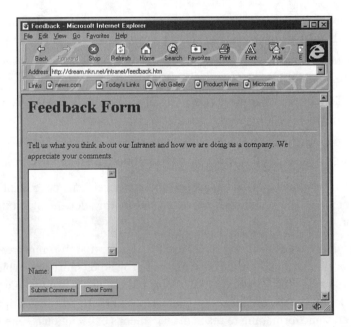

Final Touches

In just a short time, you've seen how to piece together the framework of an intranet. Though it's a simple process, it's far from complete. Graphics can be incorporated into your Web site without much worry about file sizes. The only bandwidth that you are consuming is on your internal network, where speeds are probably much greater than that of your Internet access. You don't have the usual limitations against incorporating huge graphics or other multimedia elements that would normally take a long time to load in a Web browser.

Your intranet might start with only text-based links, but can soon develop into a beautiful site navigated by imagemaps and colorful buttons. Music can be added on the Announcements page to liven things up, or a video excerpt on the main page to provide a true "cutting-edge" feel.

An intranet can also be much more involved than simply linking internal documents and providing feedback forums. In Chapter 19, you learned about incorporating ActiveX controls into your FrontPage Webs. Advanced ActiveX controls will help make your intranet communicate its purpose through multimedia rich elements like Real Audio streamed files and VDO's streamed video segments. Training videos and vocal announcements can be utilized in your intranet for a more personal feel, while still keeping costs down by reducing equipment needs.

Deployment

Actually implementing your intranet is the last step in the creation process. You must decide where your Web will be housed, and what type of server will serve the Web pages. Keep in mind that you also want your intranet secure. Most of the security features for your Web site will be implemented on the server side to restrict access. But many people forget that an unattended Web server is just as open to malicious acts as a Web site published on the Internet with no security at all.

The Personal Web Server by Microsoft is a fine choice for a small company ranging from ten to fifteen people. This Web server is not as robust as other large ones, but it is totally free and it installs with very few modifications. The Personal Web Server can be downloaded from **ftp://ftp.microsoft.com/msdownload/frontpage/enu/pwssetup.exe**.

Windows NT 4.0 incorporates Peer Web Services into the operating system. Peer Web Services is actually a scaled-down version of the Microsoft Internet Information Server found in Windows NT Server. FrontPage extensions can be installed into the Web server just as if it were the complete Internet Information Server. Different departments within your company can actually author and house their own content for the intranet, allowing you to link the content together into navigable form.

The Microsoft Internet Information Server, which currently runs only on Windows NT Server, is a free product that holds robust Web serving capabilities and is easy to install and maintain. The Internet Information Server depends only on your computer's hardware configuration for the amount of simultaneous connections possible. The Internet

Information Server can also utilize the Microsoft Index Server for cross-referencing Web pages and providing detailed search features.

The Web server that you choose to host your intranet can actually be any Web server. But you must find one that works with FrontPage extensions in order to gain the maximum impact from your FrontPage-authored site.

From Here...

The development of the intranet is still in its infancy, though its importance is as great as the Internet itself. The intranet gives System Administrators the freedom to create content once, as if every computer on the network ran the same operating system. The intranet technology itself is easy to understand and far less complicated than a multitude of existing network tools. For more information about protecting your new intranet, refer to the following chapter:

Chapter 32, "Extending and Customizing FrontPage with the SDK," covers the intricacies of installing and administering the new Microsoft Web server created especially for Windows 95.

## CHAPTER 31

The Microsoft Personal Web Server

As Chapter 29, "Serving Your Web to the World with the Personal Web Server," makes clear, FrontPage 97 ships with two servers, one as part of the main product (The FrontPage Web Server) and another with the CD-ROM Bonus Pack. On the CD-ROM is the Microsoft Personal Web Server (MS-PWS), by far the more powerful of the two. This chapter examines the MS-PWS in detail, a necessity given its greater number of features (remote administration, FTP service) and its greater range of configuration choices. ■

Establish Microsoft Personal Web Server as Your Main Web Server

You can have MS-PWS load with Windows itself, so you're ready to serve your Webs online or to test those you're building.

Setting MS-PWS as an FTP Server

Web serving isn't the only thing this server is good for. It also operates as a server for file transfer, including anonymous FTP.

Administering MS-PWS for Web and FTP Services

The server contains a sophisticated administration tool that operates as a set of local Web pages in your favorite browser.

The Server Configuration Files

Configuring your server to serve up new file types and advanced configuration settings.

Getting Started with Microsoft PWS

This chapter assumes that you've already installed the Microsoft Personal Web Server. If you haven't, do so now by following the instructions provided in Chapter 29, "Serving Your Web to the World with the Personal Web Server," or just put the FrontPage 97 CD-ROM in your CD drive, wait for the installation menu to come up, and click the button for the Microsoft PWS.

For this chapter, it will also be assumed that you're running Microsoft PWS as your localhost server. You can test this by doing the following:

- Open your Web browser and in the location box type `http://localhost` and press Enter. If you see a home page that reads `Microsoft FrontPage Personal Web Server`, then you're using the FrontPage PWS and not the Microsoft PWS as your localhost server. If this is the case, go to File/Open in your browser and load the file DEFAULT.HTM in the path C:\webshare\wwwroot\. This will be an exceptionally bland page, but it's the one you want to see when you type `http://localhost`. At the bottom of the page is the phrase: `Brought to you by the Personal Web Server from Microsoft.`

- To make the change in localhost servers, load the FrontPage Server Administrator (see Chapter 29 for instructions), and change the port number for the FrontPage PWS to 8080. Now install the Microsoft PWS server extensions on port 80. Localhost (which is IP 127.0.0.1) requires port 80 to function. x Author: I have not yet seen chapter 30; but based upon the instructions here, I do not see how to change to 8080 in the Server Administrator. –Kyle. - I believe chapter 29 covers this.

- Return to your Web server and try **http://localhost** again. You should get the bland but proper home page. This will also work if you type **http://COMPUTERNAME**, using the name of your computer as you've established it in Windows networking. That's because MS-PWS operates as an intranet server as well as an Internet server.

None of this is necessary if you've already established the MS-PWS as a server on your system under another IP address or domain name. If so, skip ahead to the details about properties and administration.

Setting the Microsoft PWS Properties

After installing MS-PWS, you can set properties or administer it from two different locations. First, you can go into Control Panel and double-click Personal Web Server to open the Properties dialog. Second, if you've restarted Windows 95 or NT, the MS-PWS icon will appear in the taskbar tray at the bottom right of your screen (unless of course you've moved the taskbar). Right-clicking this icon will yield three choices. Administer takes you to the HTML-based administration pages. Home Page opens your browser with the DEFAULT.HTM page showing. Properties opens the same Properties dialog you can get to from Control Panel.

There are four tabs on this dialog: General, Startup, Administration, and Services, as follows:

General—Offers two points of information (see Figure 31.1 above). The first is the location of the default home page for your server (clicking Home Page from the taskbar icon does the same thing). Note that this is the default home page for the root Web of the server, not for any other Webs you create with FrontPage (each contains its own home page). If you wish to change this default home page, you can do so through the Services button (covered below). The second button, More Details, takes you to the documentation for the server that's stored in a set of Web files on your hard drive. The docs will appear in your browser, and they're extremely useful.

Startup—Lets you start or stop the server whenever you wish. Simply click the Start or Stop button to change its current state. From here you can also specify whether or not you want MS-PWS to load whenever you boot Windows (Yes by default), and whether or not you want the server icon to appear in the taskbar tray (Yes by default). If you don't elect to have the icon appear, you must access properties through the Windows Control Panel.

Administer—Offers only one button. Clicking here takes you to the Administration pages in your browser, which we'll cover below. This is the same as what happens when you select Administer from the taskbar icon.

Services—Lets you establish how you want the Web (HTTP) or FTP services to behave. You can change the FTP root directory from here, and you can also specify whether or not the FTP service will start automatically whenever Windows loads. By clicking HTTP Service and selecting Properties, you can change the root Web of the server, and also whether or not the Web service starts automatically. Notice that this is different from the Startup tab, which simply lets you load the Web server when Windows loads. Just because the server is loaded into memory doesn't mean it's actually started and available to serve a Web. It has to be started first.

Administering Microsoft PWS

Clicking the Administer button from the Properties dialog or selecting Administer from the MS-PWS taskbar icon opens the Server Administration pages in your Web browser.

Part
VI

Ch
31

You can also get to these pages by loading your browser and typing `http://localhost/htmla/HTMLA.HTM` in the location box. Either way, you'll see a screen where you can specify how your server will operate as a Web server and as an FTP server, and how you will grant access to local users.

Web Administration

When you click WWW Administration, you'll see a Web page with three tabs and several fields. The tabs offer you the following options:

Service—Here you can specify how long in seconds it will take a connection to time out if nothing happens. Set it low if you want to kick users out quickly, high if you want to give them additional time to connect. You can also restrict the maximum number of simultaneous connections. By default this is set at 300, but if you have a slow connection you'll want to limit this considerably. Also available from the Service tab is the system of password authentication you wish to use. If you're running a public Web, you can allow anonymous connections (the standard). Basic password authentication offers no secure encoding of passwords but is sufficient in many cases. Windows NT Challenge/Response authorization provides fully encrypted password security, but you require at least one Windows NT machine on the network for it to work.

Directories—Takes you to a page that lets you specify the directories on your machine that will be accessible to Web visitors. By default, these are limited to the C:\webshare\wwwroot\ directory and its subdirectories, and as you add FrontPage Webs to this directory these subdirectories will show up here as well. You can, however, add accessible directories directly from this page, and you can edit or delete existing directories. You can also specify the default home page from here, and you can specify whether or not you want to allow your users to browse these directories. By default, this feature is on, but you can turn it off without anything important happening except a bit more security.

Logging—If you want MS-PWS to log its activity, you can do so from the Logging tab. You can also specify how often a new log will be started (a busy server might want a daily log), and where you want the log file to be placed. The log file is called INETSERVER_EVENT.LOG, and can be read with a text editor such as Notepad.

FTP Administration

Often you'll design a Web that allows visitors to download files. This is true, for example, of Webs created with the Customer Support Web Wizard in FrontPage Explorer, which assumes you'll have programs and documents available for download. Or you might simply want FTP access for yourself and your colleagues, to transfer files from your home machine to the machine at work running the MS-PWS. Whatever the reason, you can easily establish MS-PWS as an FTP server as well as a Web server.

First, you'll need to start the FTP service. To do so, go to the MS-PWS Properties dialog, click Services, then FTP Service, and then Start. Now return to your browser and from the Administration contents page click FTP Service.

You'll see four tabs. The fourth, Logging, is identical to the Logging tab for MS-PWS. The third, Directories, is also similar, but far fewer directories will be available. Since the purpose of this FTP server is simply to provide Web visitors with the ability to download files through anonymous FTP (that is, they can click an **ftp://** link and the file downloads automatically), the MS-PWS is not a full-featured FTP server. It's extremely difficult, for example, to restrict certain users to certain directories, as more powerful FTP servers do. For now, the best idea is to establish a directory and/or subdirectories in which you'll place files, and allow FTP logins to those directories alone.

The Service tab lets you specify how quickly the connection times out if nothing happens, and the maximum number of simultaneous connections (16 by default, and it's best to keep it small). You can also specify that you want to allow anonymous connections (the standard for downloading from the Web). Remember: this isn't a full FTP server, it's primarily a server to help you put together a full-featured Web site. The Service tab also lets you see who's currently connected, and by clicking here you can disconnect specific users or indeed all of them. You might want to do this if users have been taking too long, or if you have to stop the FTP service for any reason whatsoever.

From the Messages tab, you can specify a message that will welcome your visitors, another that will display when they exit your server, and a third that will be shown if they attempt an FTP when the maximum number of connections has been reached. These messages aren't really important, but an appropriate message can help your overall image.

Part VI

Ch

31

Administering Local Users

If you're running an intranet, you'll want to establish specific users who can access your files. This is accomplished through the Local User system, also part of the MS-PWS Administration pages.

From the Users tab, you can add new users, remove users, or view the properties of existing users. The Properties dialog holds the username and the user password; you can change the password by typing the new password into the User Password and Confirm

Password fields, then clicking Change Password. If that user belongs to a group, this information will appear at the bottom of the User properties page.

The Groups tab lets you create groups, which are essentially collections of usernames. Simply click on New Group, enter the name of the group, and press OK. Now, by clicking on the User/Group tab, you can add users to groups. Match the username in the User List box with the group name in the Group List box, and press Add User to Group. Now when you return to the Groups tab, the Properties button will show which users are in that group.

The Server Configuration Files

The PWS is descended from the original NCSA httpd web server as are almost all Web servers. The configuration settings for this original server were stored in the httpd.cnf, srm.cnf, access.cnf and mime.typ files and those files still exist with the Personal Web Server. By default, they are stored in the \FrontPage Webs\server\conf \ folder. The in-depth documentation for these files can be found at the NCSA httpd web site, **http:// hoohoo.ncsa.uiuc.edu**. We'll briefly cover each of the files and what they contain, but it is highly recommended that you read all of the NCSA documentation before you change things in these files.

httpd.cnf

This is the main server configuration file. This file contains settings for the following:

- ServerRoot: The directory the server's config, error, and log files are kept in.
- Port: The port the standalone listens to. 80 is the network standard.
- Timeout: The timeout applied to all network operations. It's the maximum time for a network to send or receive, and the maximum time that a CGI script is allowed to take. The default is 20 minutes (1200 seconds).
- ServerAdmin: Your address, where problems with the server should be e-mailed.
- ErrorLog: The location of the error log file. If this does not start with / or a drive spec (recommended!), ServerRoot is prepended to it.
- TransferLog: The location of the transfer log file. If this does not start with / or a drive spec (recommended!), ServerRoot is prepended to it.
- ServerName: Allows you to set a host name which is sent back to clients for your server if it's different than the one the program would get (i.e. use "www" instead of the host's real name).

srm.cnf

This file is responsible for controlling how files are mapped out for users of your web site. It provides for aliasing and redirection, as well as setting default document directories. Some of the information in this file includes:

- DocumentRoot: The directory out of which you will serve your documents. By default, all requests are taken from this directory, but aliases may be used to point to other locations.

- Aliases: You can have up to 20 aliases in the format: Alias fakename realname

- Automatic Directory Indexing: Allows you to specify how the server generates a directory index if there is no file in the directory whose name matches DirectoryIndex.

access.cnf

This file is the global access configuration file. It is not a good idea to mess around with this file.

mime.typ

This file is a little different than the other three. They were all server configuration information dealing with how the server worked. This file has to do with the content the server sends. See, a browser knows how to display a file by means of a MIME type, a piece of information sent by the server indicating the type of file that is being sent. The mime.typ file is where you can add new types and modify existing ones. A MIME type declaration is simple. Here is what a portion of the file looks like:

audio/basic	au snd
audio/x-aiff	aif aiff aifc
audio/wav	wav
image/gif	gif
image/ief	ief
image/jpeg	jpeg jpg jpe
image/tiff	tiff tif

As you can see, there is the MIME type listed on the left (i.e. - audio/wav) and the file extensions that should be designated by that type on the right (i.e. - wav). That is all that needs to be there for a new MIME type to be served up by the PWS.

From Here...

You now know just about everything there is to know about your FrontPage package. From this point on, you'll be embellishing and expanding that knowledge, encountering some detailed technical information in the process. Next comes:

■ Part VII, "The FrontPage SDK," which gives you the details behind creating your own wizards, templates, and other customizations of FrontPage.

■ Part VIII, "Integrating FrontPage and Microsoft Office," demonstrates the ways in which FrontPage works in conjunction with the programs in MS's famous suite of applications.

■ Chapters 35-38, deal with the creativity possible with the Microsoft Internet Assistants for each of the Office apps.

The FrontPage SDK

Extending and Customizing FrontPage with the SDK

For the majority of users, Frontpage provides them with everything they need to create great Web sites. However, there are those of you out there who look at just about any program and think to yourselves, "You know what this thing needs? More power! (insert grunts here)" Well, Microsoft has been kind enough to provide you with a means to tweak FrontPage to your heart's delight, including the capability to use FrontPage as a component in our own applications for you programmers out there. It's the FrontPage SDK (Software Developer's Kit), and it's the focus of this and the next two chapters.

What exactly is a Software Developer's Kit? In a nutshell, an SDK normally consists of documentation of a program's underlying behavior and information on how to modify or add to that behavior. It may also include header files for programmers who would like to add the capabilities of a piece of software to their own programs, and possibly even sample code to show by example how to use the SDK. All of these things are part of the FrontPage SDK. Now, you may be saying to yourself, "Hey, I'm not a computer programmer. When would I ever use the SDK?" The answer to that is: maybe never. Still, even you non-programmers might want to learn about it to Add a menu item to the FrontPage editor that starts up the great new graphics program you just bought to edit your images, create your own custom templates, or even extend the HTML capabilities of FrontPage.

That's right. You are not limited to the templates or menu choices that Microsoft has chosen to give you. You can modify FrontPage to work the way you work, and if you do happen to be a Windows programmer, the SDK will also tell you how to add FrontPage to your application and program it through OLE automation, as well as how to create your own Wizards and WebBots.

The SDK is a powerful part of FrontPage, and it will let you get under the hood and make the program work the way you want it to. ■

Overview of the SDK

The FrontPage SDK consists of a set of files on your FrontPage CD-ROM in the \FrontPg\FPsdk20\ directory. These files include documentation in Word format, templates, wizards, some utility programs, CGI scripts, Designer HTML, and some custom WebBot components. As was mentioned in the introduction to this chapter, these files give you the capability to extend and customize FrontPage.

FrontPage can be extended and customized in many ways by programmers and non-programmers alike. Why is it important to be able to extend FrontPage? Well, the computer world—especially the Internet—changes really fast. New extensions get added to HTML; new programming languages and ways of making your pages interactive and exciting keep popping up. You just might want to keep working with the piece of software you've bought and learned and still be able to do the new stuff. With the SDK, you can. There are other reasons to extend FrontPage. For instance, maybe you are just used to a certain text editor, or you have a special graphics program and you want to make it work with FrontPage. Great! What if you find that the templates included with FrontPage just don't really suit your needs? No problem. The SDK will show you how to create new ones. As you can see, the FrontPage SDK is where you can personalize FrontPage and make it work the way you want (or need) it too.

FrontPage can be extended in all sorts of useful ways with no programming experience whatsoever, and with some HTML knowledge you can do even more. In this chapter, we'll start with the easier stuff and then move on to the more advanced things you can do.

Depending on what you want to do with the SDK, you will need the following:

- A text editor (such as Notepad)
- Some knowledge of HTML
- For custom wizards, a Windows programming language such as Visual C++ or Visual Basic
- For custom WebBots, knowledge of CGI programming using either a Windows development tool like Visual C++ or Visual Basic, and/or programming with another Web language such as Java, PERL, JScript or VBScript. VB Script or J++? -Kyle. - J++ is not a language, it's an environment for Java. Microsoft calls their version of JavaScript, Jscript, so maybe we should use that one.

Customizing FrontPage Menus

Part
VII

Ch
32

The concept of extending and customizing menus is fairly simple. You can add your own menu commands and your own menus to the FrontPage Editor or Explorer. These commands can be used to provide links to other applications you use regularly, to insert the contents of other files into your pages, or even just to insert commonly used text when a menu item is chosen. They work just like the menu items that come with FrontPage. You call the shots, and all it requires is a little planning and the addition of some items to the Windows Registry. In this section, we will walk through the addition of a custom menu and a couple of custom menu items.

How It Works

In Windows 95 and NT there is a database file in Windows called the Registry. This is the place where applications store information about themselves when they are installed and running. FrontPage reads the Registry when it boots up and looks for Registry keys that extend its menus. When you add new items to the Registry, you can extend the menus of FrontPage. This may seem like a lot to do, but the process is actually fairly straightforward. We'll start by talking a little about the Windows Registry and the Registry Editor (REGEDIT.EXE).

The Windows Registry Editor

The Windows Registry is a system database filled with keys and values. If you are at your computer, you can bring up the Windows Registry editor by doing the following:

1. Click the Start Button.

2. Choose Run...

3. Type: regedit.

You should get a window that looks something like Figure 32.1.

FIGURE 32.1

The Windows 95 Registry Editor.

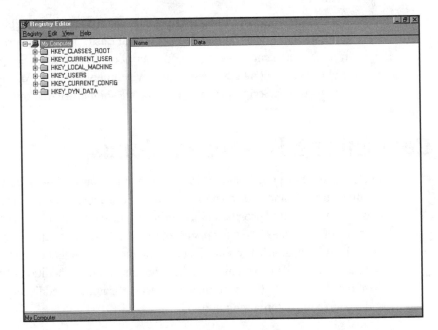

The items on the left are keys, and they define the behavior of various aspects of your system and applications. Clicking on the plus sign to the left of a key will expend that key. Feel free to explore in here, but don't start changing values just for the fun of it. Most of the changes made to the Registry are done by applications themselves. Most Windows 95 books include large sections on the Registry, but here we just want to cover enough to show how to create Registry entries. For more information on the Windows Registry, check out *Special Edition Using the Windows 95 Registry* from Que Publishing.

When you select a key, you might see values set over on the right side. There are two columns, Name and Data. These columns are where the settings for the keys are stored. Each key can have many named values. In order to change a value, do the following (as illustrated in Figure 32.2):

1. Right-click the name of the value you wish to change.
2. Choose Modify from the pop-up menu.
3. Change the value name or data in the box that pops up.
4. Click OK.

FIGURE 32.2

Modifying Registry data.

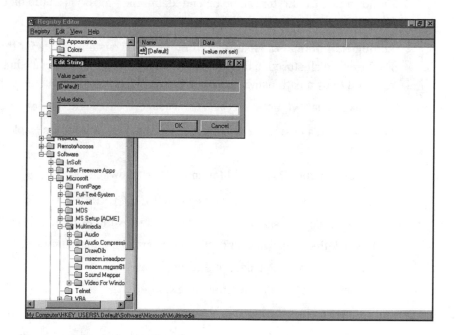

That's all there is to changing a key. To add a new key, do the following:

1. Choose Edit.
2. Select New from the Edit menu.
3. Choose Key.

The Registry Editor will insert a new key value. The name will be highlighted so that you can change it. In order to add a new value to an existing key, do the following:

1. Choose Edit.
2. Select New from the Edit menu.
3. Choose either String value, Binary value, or DWORD value, depending on the type of value you wish to add.

In order to extend the menus of FrontPage, you will be adding only String values.

Part
VII

Ch

32

Adding New Menus

Now that you know how to start up the Registry Editor and are familiar with the basics of working with it, let's do something with it. As I mentioned before, in order to extend the menus for FrontPage, you will be adding values to Registry keys. In FrontPage, both the Explorer and the Editor can be extended, but the process is a little bit different for each. We will start with the Explorer.

Adding New Menus to FrontPage Explorer   The custom menus for the FrontPage Explorer are all stored in the same place in the Registry. This place in the Registry can be referred to by a path name, just like a file on a disk. The path name to this Registry key is:

```
HKEY_CURRENT_USER\Software\Microsoft\FrontPage\Explorer\Init Menus
```

Let's now add a custom menu called MyMenu to the FrontPage Explorer, and then we will look at what we did.

First, start up the Registry Editor and do the following:

1. Click the plus sign next to the key HKEY_CURRENT_USER.
2. Click the plus sign next to the key Software, under HKEY_CURRENT_USER.
3. Click the plus sign next to the key Microsoft, under Software.
4. Click the plus sign next to the key FrontPage.
5. Next click the plus sign next to Explorer.
6. Finally, click the key Init Menus.

This will take you to the place in the Registry mentioned above. When you first install FrontPage, there should be no values on the right side except one named (Default) with a value of (value not set).

Now we need to add a new value by selecting Edit, New, String Value. This command will add a new value named New Value #1 to the list on the right. The text should be highlighted, so change the name to menu1. You can name the values anything you wish, as long as the name is unique. Now, right-click your new menu1, choose Modify from the menu, and type the following into the Value box:

```
2, , 1, M&yMenu, Tools
```

Then click OK and close the Registry Editor. Congratulations! You've just added a menu item to the FrontPage Explorer. The next time FrontPage starts, you will see the menu MyMenu added to the FrontPage Explorer. Take a look at Figure 32.3 to see what it should look like. You will also find that there are no menu items underneath that menu, just the heading. This is where the next section, "Adding Custom Commands," will come in, but for the time being let's look at what we have here. What does the value you typed in mean?

FIGURE 32.3

The FrontPage Explorer shows your new menu.

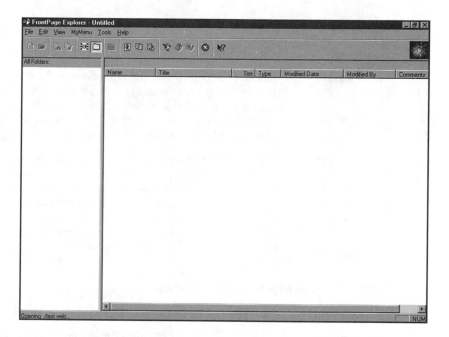

The extended menus in FrontPage are a series of values with the following syntax (pretty much straight from the SDK documentation):

```
first_version, last_version, menu_bar_num, menu_name, menu_position
```

Table 32.1   Custom Menu Arguments

Argument	Description
first_version	The number of the earliest version of FrontPage that should add this new top-level menu command. Values less than 2 are treated as 2 (since that is the first version of FrontPage to support custom menus). Values greater than the current running version of FrontPage tell FrontPage not to create this menu.
last_version	The number of the last version of FrontPage that should add this new top-level menu command. Values less than the current running version of FrontPage tell FrontPage not to create this menu. If omitted, this argument is treated as being higher than the current running version of FrontPage.
menu_bar_num	Number of the built-in menu bar to which you want to add the menu. This field is ignored because there is currently only one set of menus in the Explorer, but the field value should be set to 1 to allow for future expansion.

continues

Table 32.1 Continued	
Argument	Description
menu_name	Name of the new menu. The ampersand is the character that places an underscore in your menu name and works with the ALT key to select your menu from the keyboard. Therefore, M&yMenu will show up as MyMenu and be accessible with ALT+Y. If you wish to include an ampersand in your menu name, simply put two ampersands in a row.
menu_position	Position of the new menu on the menu bar. This may be the name of the menu before which you want to place the new menu, or a number indicating the menu's position from the left end of the menu bar (1-based). If the number or name does not exist, or the argument is omitted, then the new menu is placed to the right of the Tools menu. When comparing this string against menu names, any accelerators present in the menu names are ignored.

So the string you added said the following:

  2—Don't show this menu if the version of FrontPage running is less than 2.

  <no value>—There is no limit on how high the version number can be.

  1—Show this on Menu Bar number 1.

  M&yMenu—The menu should be shown as MyMenu.

  Tools—Show this menu to the left of the Tools menu.

That's it. Any custom menu you need can be created by adding more values to this section in the registry.

Adding New Menus to FrontPage Editor   Adding new menus to the FrontPage Editor is identical to adding them to the Explorer, with exception of the location in the Registry where the commands are added. To add menus to the Editor, simply go to HKEY_CURRENT_USER\Software\Microsoft\FrontPage\Editor\Init Menus in the Registry and follow the same instructions as for the Explorer. There is one more difference. In the Explorer, there is currently only one menu, so the menu_bar_num value will always be 1. In the Editor there are two menu bars, the empty document menu (0) and the active document menu (1), and you will need to specify which one you want your menu to appear on.

Adding Custom Commands

But, you may ask, what good are menus without commands under them? Let's now see how to add commands to new and existing menus. The process is a bit different for the Editor and the Explorer, so we'll start with the Explorer.

Adding Custom Commands to FrontPage Explorer   Now we are going to add a custom command to our MyMenu menu in the FrontPage Explorer. The syntax for adding a new command is a little bit more complicated than the syntax for adding a menu, and we will now go through it by adding a command that starts the Windows Registry Editor from within FrontPage.

As you might expect, the process starts in the Windows Registry again, so open the Windows Registry Editor and this time find the following key:

```
HKEY_CURRENT_USER\Software\Microsoft\FrontPage\Explorer\Init Commands
```

Add a new value to the key by choosing Edit, New, String Value. A new value will be added to the list on the right. You can change the name of the value to anything you wish, as long as it is not the name of an existing custom command. You might just want to name it MyCommand1. Now, right-click your new MyCommand1 and choose Modify. In the Values box, type the following (note that you will need to specify the location of your Windows directory if it is something other than C:\WINDOWS):

```
2,,1,MyMenu, &Registry Editor, C:\WINDOWS\REGEDIT.EXE, , 0, Launches the
Windows Registry Editor.,
```

Now click OK and close the Registry Editor. The next time you start FrontPage you will see something like Figure 32.4.

Part
VII

Ch

32

FIGURE 32.4

The FrontPage Explorer with your new menu command.

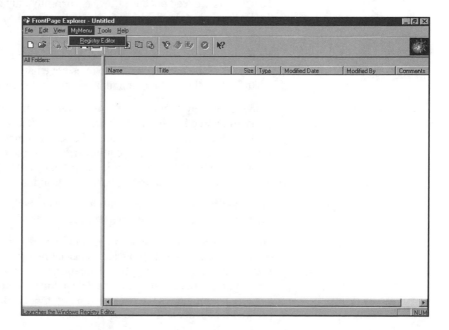

Now, what do all of those values mean? The following is the syntax for custom commands (direct from the SDK documentation):

```
first_version, last_version, menu_bar_num, menu_name, command_name,
command_line, command_position, macro_key, status_text, help_reference
```

Table 32.2 Custom Command Arguments

Argument	Description
first_version	The number of the earliest version of FrontPage that should add this new command to the menus. Values less than 2 are treated as 2. Values greater than the current running version of FrontPage tell FrontPage not to create this command. This is exactly the same as when creating a menu.
last_version	The number of the last version of FrontPage that should add this new command to the menus. Values less than the current running version of FrontPage tell FrontPage not to create this command. If omitted, this argument is treated as being higher than the current running version of FrontPage. Combined with first_version, this argument allows you to create add-ins that are tailored to work only with specific versions of FrontPage. This is also the same as when creating a menu.
menu_bar_num	Number of the built-in menu bar to which you want to add the menu. This field is ignored because there is currently only one set of menus in the Explorer, but the field value should be set to 1 to allow for future expansion.
menu_name	Name or number (1-based) of the menu on which to insert the new command. If the number or name does not exist or the argument is omitted, then the new command is placed on the Tools menu.
command_name	Name of the new command. If a separator is to be added, then the command name is a single dash character "-". If a separator is added, then the only remaining argument after command_name that is significant is the command_position argument; the other arguments are ignored. The menu accelerator is indicated by an ampersand character preceding the accelerator key, e.g., "My &Addin."
command_line	Fully specified file name and path to the executable file that should be run when the user chooses this command in the FrontPage Explorer.
command_position	Position of the command on the menu. This may be the name of the command before which you want to place the new command, or a 1-based number indicating the command's position on the menu, counting from the top of the menu (separators are counted). If the name or position does not exist or the argument is omitted, the command appears at the end of the menu.

Argument	Description
insert_flag	Determines whether to insert the file pointed to by command_line or to execute it. For the Explorer, the command_line is always executed and the value of this field must be 0.
status_text	Message to be displayed in the status bar when the command is selected.
help_reference	File name and topic number for a custom Help topic for the command, separated by an exclamation point.

The string we entered reads as follows:

2—Don't show this if the version of FrontPage is less than 2.0.

<no value>—Any version above 2.0 can show this command.

1—Put this choice on the main menu bar.

MyMenu—Put this command under menu MyMenu.

&Registry Editor—Show command as Registry Editor.

C:\WINDOWS\REGEDIT.EXE—The command line to launch when this command is chosen.

<no value>—Placed at the end of the menu, a number would indicate the menu placement.

0—This number doesn't really mean anything for the Explorer, only for the Editor, but it has to be 0.

Launches the Windows Registry Editor—Displays this message on the status bar when this item is highlighted.

<no value>—There is actually one more parameter that can be specified that we did not do. It is indicated by the comma on the end with no value after it. This one has to do with Windows Help and which help file and help topic should be used to obtain help on this item.

If you would like to add a separator line to the menu for the sake of organization, simply add a menu item with a name "-." This will create a separator line.

That's all there is to adding custom commands to the Explorer. I mentioned previously that the Editor was a little different. We will now discuss this.

Adding Custom Commands to FrontPage Editor   As you may have guessed, the process is the same with a few exceptions, the first of these being the location of the Registry keys for the Editor. You will need to go to HKEY_CURRENT_USER\Software\Microsoft\FrontPage\Editor\Init Commands to add commands to the Editor menus.

Part
VII

Ch
32

The syntax for adding commands to menus in the Editor is identical to adding them to the Explorer, except the Editor will use some settings that are ignored (and required to be a fixed value) by the Explorer. I mentioned one of those when I went through the Explorer menu command we added. It is the `insert_flag`. In Explorer it is meaningless, but in the Editor it allows you to create different types of commands. The other one is the `menu_bar_num`. In Explorer, there is only one menu bar, but in the Editor this can be 0, empty document menu, or 1, active document menu.

The `insert_flag` value demonstrates a very significant difference between custom commands for the Explorer and those for the Editor. This flag can only be used to execute a command-line argument in the Explorer, but it can be used to insert text in the Editor. The flag can mean one of the following:

0—Execute the `command_line` argument as an .EXE program file (this is the only one that is allowed for Explorer).

1—Insert the file pointed to by the `command_line` argument as HTML text. The file will be inserted in the current document with paragraph breaks before and after.

2—Insert the literal text contained in the `command_line` argument as HTML. The actual text of the `command_line` argument will be inserted in-line without paragraph breaks before or after.

We have already seen how option 0 behaves for this parameter. This is the way we added a command to start the Registry Editor. However, what about 1 and 2? The process for creating these commands is exactly the same, but the results are different. In the case of 1, the file listed in the `command_line` parameter is not executed, but inserted with a paragraph break before and after it. This is useful if you have a section of preformatted HTML code that you use regularly, such as a copyright notice or contact information, and that you would like to be able to insert quickly and easily into pages as you work on your Web. Parameter number two also inserts text, but inserts the actual text placed in the `command_line` parameter in-line with no paragraph breaks before or after. How is this useful? One possible use would be to allow for insertion of HTML tags that are not currently available in FrontPage. In order to create a new tag `foo`, you could simply put `<foo></foo>` as your `command_line` parameter.

Custom menus are a very powerful way of customizing the FrontPage working environment and allow you to extend FrontPage to work the way you do.

Designer HTML

This is a powerful feature of FrontPage—and a very important one for a quickly changing Internet world, where there are new things showing up every time you turn around. Designer HTML is what Microsoft calls the extensions added to its WebBot HTML pseudo-tag. Since I have probably already lost you, I'll explain a little about the psuedo-tag and how it's used, and then touch on some possible uses of this nifty little capability.

The WebBot Pseudo-Tag

Basically, the WebBot pseudo-tag is an HTML tag that has been created to work with FrontPage. Why is it a psuedo-tag? This is because the WebBot tag takes place inside an HTML comment, and thus is never seen by a Web browser. It exists for the sole purpose of interacting with FrontPage, either with the development environment at design time or with WebBots and the FrontPage Server Extensions at runtime. The tag looks like the following:

```
<!-WEBBOT bot="HTMLMarkup" ALT= "<Font Size=+3><I>Foobar ISV Feature Place-
holder</I></FONT>" StartSpan ->

[## A bunch of text goes here, maybe preprocessor directives or a new HTML
tag]

<!-WEBBOT bot="HTMLMarkup" EndSpan ->
```

Had this been a normal WebBot—TimeStamp, for example—you would have seen the tag bot="TimeStamp", but in the case of Designer HTML, it will always be "HTMLMarkup". Also note the use of the StartSpan and EndSpan attributes to indicate the start and end of your block of unknown HTML. These always have to be used.

To let the user specify the display characteristics of a block of unknown HTML in the FrontPage Editor, there are two new attributes on the WebBot pseudo-tag. These attributes are as follows:

U-SRC=*filename*—Points to an image file to use to display the unknown HTML block in the FrontPage Editor. If the image is a file: URL on the local machine, it will be automatically included into the web and the URL adjusted to point to the version contained in the web.

Only image files are allowed for the U-SRC tag. Included HTML is not allowed. If text is needed for display, either it should be encoded into the image or the ALT attribute should be used instead of the U-SRC attribute.

ALT=*text* — Limited HTML text to show inside a rectangle in the FrontPage Editor as the display for the unknown HTML block. If both U-SRC and ALT are specified, then U-SRC is used in preference to ALT. Typically, however, only one or the other would be specified.

These attributes allow for an alternate display in the WYSIWYG editor of your Designer HTML, either in the form of text or a graphic. When this tag is inserted into your document, either it will appear as the image, or the text and the standard WebBot cursor will appear whenever you move the mouse over it.

Using Designer HTML

Once you have created your Designer HTML document, you will no doubt want to use it in a document. Well, there are three ways to get this new Designer HTML into your document, as follows:

- Copy and paste the HTML (described in a section below).
- Insert file.
- Drag and drop.

FrontPage applies what Microsoft calls IntelliSense when a user pastes regular text into the Editor. FrontPage will do an autodetection pass through the content before pasting it and will determine if the text is valid HTML. If it is, then it will automatically parse it as HTML and merge the content with the rest of the existing page.

Drag-and-drop operations work just like their copy-and-paste equivalents. FrontPage allows you to drop in text itself, or text and HTML files. Just drop the files you create onto the Web page, and they are automatically handled.

If you combined this capability with a custom menu, you would be able to create a menu command that inserted your own custom HTML that FrontPage didn't even recognize when you bought it, and have that HTML formatted on your WYSIWYG display however you wanted it to display—all without any computer programming. Pretty neat, huh?

Creating Custom Web and Page Templates

Custom menu items allow you to tailor your work environment to fit your needs, but I know they were not the first thing I wanted to do when I first worked with FrontPage. My first thought was the ability to define my own templates, so that I could simplify the creation of the Web pages and site layouts that I used regularly. Fortunately, FrontPage allows you to do just that. We aren't going to discuss this in great detail here, because custom templates are covered in greater depth in Chapter 33, "Creating Templates," but we will just state that you can do it. If you're just dying to do it right now, head on over to Chapter 33 to find out more.

NOTE In addition to custom pages and sites, you also have the ability to create your own custom framesets. We will also cover those in depth in Chapter 33, "Creating Templates." ■

NOTE So far, everything we have covered can be done without any real programming except for a little HTML. Things start to change when you begin to create custom wizards, which require some programming ability. The process of creating wizards, as well as some samples, will be outlined in Chapter 34, "Creating Wizards." ■

Creating Custom WebBots

This is one of the more advanced parts of the SDK and is not going to get coverage in its own chapter. We won't discuss it in gruesome detail here either, since it really goes beyond the scope of this book. However, we will go under the cover on WebBots a little—what they really are, how they work, and how you can go about creating them if you are inclined.

WebBots: What Are They?

WebBots are a concept peculiar to Microsoft FrontPage, and had me puzzled a little at first. They are a way to put interactive content in a page for the average end user without any programming knowledge. For the typical user who bought FrontPage because he didn't want to learn HTML, this is great. No CGI programming, just WebBots. So what exactly are WebBots? Each WebBot has three main parts, as follows:

- A property editing user interface to interact with users in FrontPage
- A presentation to show in the WYSIWYG editor
- A server-side program that delivers the actual interactivity

WebBots are similar to CGI programs, but the additional pieces—the property editor and the WYSIWYG presentation—make them easier for end users to add to their pages. We are not going to cover the actual creation of a custom WebBot in this book, since that requires extensive programming knowledge in a Windows programming language like C++ or Visual Basic. For those of you who are programmers and would like to create your own WebBots, the SDK contains extensive documentation, and I will cover the basics on how they work here.

Part
VII

Ch
32

How Do WebBots Work?

When an end user chooses to insert a WebBot component in his Web page, a dialog box comes up that gets the properties for the component from the end user and then saves that information in the page inside an HTML comment field. When the HTML file is processed, the component information is read, processed, and then expanded into the actual HTML that the end user expects to see in his browser.

A WebBot component becomes active at the following times:

- When a page is saved by the FrontPage editor
- When a page is regenerated by the FrontPage Server Extensions due to a dependency that required updating
- When a page is the target of an HTTP POST request, such as when the browser submits the form
- When a page is fetched through the SmartHTML interpreter by an HTTP GET request

When the component is activated, it can perform whatever actions you would like, based on the current values of its properties, CGI environment variables, or form data that a user may have submitted. The types of things you might have it do include inserting generated HTML into the WebBot component's location in the HTML file, handling a form that was submitted to the page, or even generating a completely new page.

Automating FrontPage Using OLE

For those of you who are developing your own applications with Visual Basic or Visual C++, or any other Windows programming language that allows you to do OLE automation, you can use FrontPage as a component in your application. This gives you the ability to include an HTML editor in a company application or to extend your current client-server applications to include publishing on the Web. This provides a tremendous resource and saves you a lot of work. How might you go about doing this? Let's cover the basic process in Visual Basic.

The FrontPage Objects

FrontPage exposes three main interfaces for OLE automation: the Explorer interface, the Editor interface, and the To Do List interface. Each one of these interfaces can be automated through OLE automation, and they all include a large set of methods that are documented in the SDK. Let's cover the three objects briefly, as follows:

FrontPage Explorer Interface—Just as this is the main interface to the program, it is also the main interface for OLE automation. The Explorer interface operates on web-level objects, and can currently be used to create a web, delete a web, move documents from a local file system to a web server and vice versa, remove documents from a web, set and get web meta-info variables, get page meta-info variables, retrieve a list of files or images in the current web, launch the To Do List, and get the URL and title of the current web.

FrontPage Editor Interface—The FrontPage Editor is the Web page editing part of FrontPage. The FrontPage Editor can open, edit, and save HTML files in the current web being viewed by the FrontPage Explorer, or in the local file system. This can be used to create a new empty page, open a page from the current web or local file system, or determine if a named page is currently being edited. You can also insert files, images, or HTML into the current page at the insertion point.

FrontPage To Do List Interface—The FrontPage To Do List is exactly what it sounds like: a grid object that manages and displays a list of tasks to be performed on the web currently opened by the FrontPage Explorer. These tasks are removed from the To Do List as they are completed. Operations exposed to OLE in this interface include the ability to add, remove, and edit items in the list.

Part
VII

Ch
32

Alright, so there are three OLE interfaces to FrontPage. You might be wondering how you would use them to create your own applications. The basic OLE process works like this. There is an OLE client (your application) and an OLE server (in this case, FrontPage). The server provides the functionality, and the client uses it. The process in codes starts by creating an object variable of the correct type. In VB you would do the following:

```
Dim explorer as Object
Set explorer = CreateObject("FrontPage.Explorer.2.0")
```

or in Visual C++:

```
Iwebber explorer
explorer.CreateDispatch("FrontPage.Explorer.2.0");
```

The preceding code would start up the FrontPage Explorer and allow you to use it in your code just like any other object. Once you have the object, there are quite a few things you can do with it, as the following partial list of the available methods will show you.

Some of the OLE Automation Methods for FrontPage.Explorer.2.0.

- vtiCreateWeb - Creates a new Web
- vtiRefreshWeb - Refreshes current Web

- vtiRemoveWeb - Removes the specified Web from the server

- vtiEditWebPage - Opens a page in the Editor

- vtiGetPageList - Lists pages in current web

Some of the OLE Automation Methods for FrontPage.Editor

- vtiOpenWebPage - Opens an HTML document for editing

- vtiNewWebPage - Starts a new document

- vtiInsertHTML - Inserts HTML in the document

Some of the OLE Automation Methods for FrontPage.ToDoList

- vtiAddTask - Adds a new task to the To-Do list

- vtiGetActiveCount - Gets the number of active tasks in the To-Do List

- vtiCompletedTaskByUrl - Marks a task completed

To put this all together, here is some sample code in Visual Basic and also in Visual C++ that creates a FrontPage Explorer object and refreshes the contents of the web from the server.

Visual Basic:

```
Function btnSomeEvent_Click()
{
Dim explorer as Object

    Set explorer = CreateObject("FrontPage.Explorer.2.0")
    explorer.vtiRefreshWebFromServer
    Set explorer = Nothing
    ' NOTE: it is important to set the OLE object variable
    ' to Nothing so that the OLE connection is released
}
```

Visual C++:

```
#include "webber.h"

void OnSomeEvent()
{
IWebber explorer;
COleException error;

    if(!explorer.CreateDispatch("FrontPage.Explorer.2.0",&error))
    {
        AfxMessageBox("Error connecting to FrontPage Explorer.");
        return;
    }
```

```
        explorer.vtiRefreshWebFromServer();
        explorer.ReleaseDispatch();
    }
```

If you do have an application that can benefit from the capabilities that FrontPage has to offer or you want to customize FrontPage to fit some very specific Web publishing application, all of the power you need is right here.

From here, we are going to cover Creating Templates and Creating Wizards. In these chapters, you will see how to extend the capabilities of FrontPage in other ways by making templates and wizards of your own. ●

Part

VII

Ch

32

## CHAPTER 33

Creating Templates

In the previous chapter we discussed several powerful ways to extend and customize FrontPage ranging in scope from adding a new menu command that didn't previously exist, to extending the HTML that FrontPage displays and even to full-fledged programming of FrontPage through OLE automation. Most of these things have their applications, but the place that most of us will customize FrontPage the most is custom templates. When you create a Web or a page in Frontpage, you likely use templates to get a headstart on your work. After all, often the general layout of all the pages on a site is identical, it is just the content of the pages that changes. ∎

What templates are

Page templates, Web templates. What are they and what can they do for you?

Page templates

Creating your own page templates is easy; we'll show you how.

Automatic Web template creation using Web Template Maker

FrontPage can help you create you own Web templates with this utility.

Manual Web template creation

The Do-It-Yourselfer's guide to creating a Web template.

Frameset templates

Frameset templates let you quickly create great frame layouts using the Frameset wizard.

What Are Templates?

A template is a special directory on a user's local disk that contains prototype Web content (Web pages, text files, images, etc.). This prototype content can be used to start a new Web or page and then edited and managed using FrontPage. There are three kinds of templates in FrontPage:

- Page   Single page templates stored in C:\Program Files\Microsoft FrontPage\pages.
- Web   Templates consisting of several interconnected pages stored in C:\Program Files\Microsoft FrontPage\pages.
- Framesets   A special kind of template that is used only by the Frameset wizard.

The simplest type of template is a Page template. Page templates can be easily created by end-users while in the FrontPage Editor by choosing the "Save As" item on the File menu, and then clicking on the "As Template" button. Fill in the information, press OK, and a complete page template is automatically created. Since these templates are so easy to create, it is likely that you will want to create them frequently for the page styles that you use regularly.

To remove a template once you have created it, you simply need to delete the file you created. In the Windows Explorer, go to C:\Program Files\Microsoft FrontPage\pages and find the directory by the name of your template with the extension .TEM. Delete that directory and your template is gone. If you want to modify an existing template, first start the FrontPage Editor. Then select File, Open and click the Other Location tab in the dialog box that appears. Select From File and click browse. Then go to the C:\Program Files\Microsoft FrontPage\pages directory and find the .TEM directory that contains the template you want to modify. In that directory you should find an HTML file for the template you want to modify. Open it, make the changes you want to make, and save it. Any documents you create from here on out with that template will contain the modifications you made.

If you want to create an entire site in a basic style, what you really need is a Web template, complete with linked documents and images. There are two ways to create these and we will cover them both in the next section.

Creating Web Templates

While the ability to save a Page as a template is a useful feature of FrontPage, if you want to create an entire Web in the style of your choice, you will need to create a Web template.

FrontPage contains a Visual Basic program called Web Template Maker that automates the process of creating a Web template.

N O T E This program requires that you have the Visual Basic 4.0 runtime DLL in your Windows\System directory. This file is called VB40032.DLL, and if you do not have it installed, you can get it from the Microsoft Web site, **http://www.microsoft.com/**. ■

Assuming you have the support DLL installed, to use the Web Template Maker, follow these steps:

1. Launch the Web Templace Maker (WEBTMPL.EXE in the FrontPg\FPSKD20\utility\webtmpl folder on the CD-ROM). You see the dialog box shown in Figure 33.1.

2. Select from the Available Webs list.

3. Enter the New Web Template information.

4. Click the Make Web Template button.

FIGURE 33.1
The Web Template Maker utility.

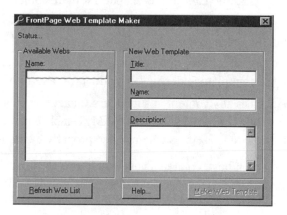

Everything that the Web template maker does can be done by hand. It simply creates a copy of an existing site to use as a building block for a new site. If you cannot get the Web Template Utility to work for you, you will have to create your template by hand. This isn't as hard as you might think. Let's go through the process:

1. First you will need a Web to make your template from, so create a Web using the FrontPage Explorer on your local Web server, or copy a Web from a remote server to a local Web server.

2. Use the Windows Explorer to locate the folder containing the Web's content. By default, this is a folder under C:\FrontPage Webs\Content. For example, if your Web is called Test, then the Web content is located in C:\FrontPage Webs\Content\Test.

3. Using the Windows Explorer, create a folder by the name you wish to refer to your new template by, for example MyTemplate.tem under the Webs folder of where the FrontPage client is installed. By default this is would be the C:\Program Files\Microsoft FrontPage\Webs folder.

4. Copy the Web's images folder into Sample.tem. For example, if the Web is called Test, copy C:\FrontPage Webs\Content\Test\images into your new directory, MyTemplate.tem. If you are using the Windows Explorer, be sure to hold down the CTRL key when doing the copy, or else the folder will be moved, not copied.

5. Copy the Web's pages in the main Web directory (C:\FrontPage Webs\Content\Test) into MyTemplate.tem. Do not copy access control files, such as #haccess.ctl.

6. Using NotePad, create a file called MyTemplate.inf, in the MyTemplate.tem folder. This is the template information file.

7. Create an [info] section in MyTemplate.inf with appropriate title and description keys. For example, set the title to "Sample Web" and the description to "Create a sample Web from a template." Add any tasks or Web meta info variables in their appropriate sections. See later in this chapter for more about the .INF file.

8. If you have any content in Web subfolders (such as _private), repeat the above steps, copying the pages to the same subfolder (_private) in the Web template.

9. If you have any scripts or programs in your Web's cgi-bin folder, create a cgi-bin folder inside your template folder, and copy the programs into it (cgi-bin).

10. If your Web includes any content in subfolders (images, cgi-bin, or _private), you will need to create a [FileList] section in the MyTemplate.inf file as described above, in order to make sure those files get uploaded properly by the FrontPage Explorer.

That's all there is to it. You have created a new template. Now, what about this .INF file and the different sections? Well an .INF file looks something like this:

```
[info]
title=Customer Support Web
description=Create a web to improve your customer support services, particu-
larly for software companies.

[FileList]
bugrep.htm=
cusuaftr.htm=
cusuahdr.htm=
images\scrnshot.gif=images/scrnshot.gif
images\undercon.gif=images/undercon.gif
index.htm=
search.htm=
suggest.htm=
tn-001.htm=
```

```
[MetaInfo]
CompanyName=Microsoft
CompanyAddress=One Microsoft Way, Redmond Washington
```

N O T E It is important to have a meaningful title and description for a page or Web template, since a list of wizards and templates could be quite large. As you can see, this information is kept in an .INF file inside the template directory in the [info] section. The base name of this file must match the base name of the template directory. For example, you would create sample.inf inside the sample.tem directory. ■

The INF file is in the same format as a Windows INI file. The INF file can have several named sections, each surrounded by angle brackets like this: [Section Name]. Underneath each section are name-value pairs, one on each line. An attribute name (also called a key) and its value are separated by an equal sign (=).

The Info Section

FrontPage reads the [info] section of the INF file when it presents a list of wizards and templates to a user. If the INF file is not found, or if the [info] section does not exist, FrontPage displays the base name of the template directory (such as sample), otherwise the dialog boxes display the values of the title and description keys found in the [info] section.

Web templates can also specify three optional sections that are used by the FrontPage Explorer when loading Web templates: [FileList], [MetaInfo], and [TaskList].

The FileList Section

The [FileList] section allows explicit mappings between the file names inside the template directory and the Web-relative URLs where they will be uploaded. It also allows you to upload files from subdirectories of the Web template. Each line has the form filename=URL. In essence, this gives you control over which files in your template go where when a Web is created, and even if certain files should be copied at all.

When you do not provide a [FileList] section, the FrontPage Explorer scans the template directory and uploads all available files except those in subdirectories. All file names are converted to lowercase, and the URLs are set to be the same as the file names. Also, all file names with the image extensions .gif, .jpg, and .jpeg are uploaded to the images directory in the Web.

Part
VII

Ch
33

When you provide a [FileList] however, only the files mentioned in the section are uploaded. FrontPage will not change the case on these URLs either. Your files will contain the exact upper-lower case you specified.

If you look at the sample I've included above, you will notice that many of the files are referred to only by their filename and an equals sign with no further data. When you do this, you simply tell FrontPage to use that file as part of your template, retaining it's current name.

You may refer to files in template subdirectories when creating a [FileList] section, however, only valid Web URL subdirectories can be used. The valid Web subdirectories are images, _private, and cgi-bin. You must use forward-slashes when specifying these directories in URLs. These Web directories, and a few others, are created by the FrontPage Server Extensions when you make a new Web using the FrontPage Explorer.

The MetaInfo Section

What is this section for? Well, meta-info variables. You are probably shaking your head and wondering, what are they? Meta-info variables are a set of name-value pairs stored inside each Web. They allow you to use labels to refer to certain values that might be subject to change, or need to be inserted commonly throughout every site created with your new template. For instance, let's say your template includes company name info throughout the site. If you created a template that just contained this information in every place you wanted to use it, changing it would be difficult. You would have to change the value in every file in which it occured. However, if you use a meta-info variable section such as

```
[MetaInfo]
     CompanyName=Microsoft
     CompanyAddress=One Microsoft Way, Redmond Washington
```

You could then use the meta-info value in order to insert the actual value of the variable. These variables can be used to store configuration information about the Web, or when used in conjunction with the Substitution Bot, to replace instances of certain strings in all your Web pages. You may define a number of these variables in the optional [MetaInfo] section. Keys are case-insensitive. Names beginning with vti_ are reserved for Web administration.

The TaskList Section

You can upload some tasks for the FrontPage To Do List using items in the optional [TaskList] section. A task consists of six attributes:

1. TaskName   A short phrase, typically 3 or 4 words, telling the user what to do.

2. Priority (1 to 3)   An integer, where 1=High, 2=Medium, and 3=Low.

3. CreatedBy   The name of the template creating the task.

4. URL   The page or image the task refers to, such as news.htm or logo.gif.

5. Cookie   An additional identifier for a point within the target URL; currently limited to HTML bookmarks, specified as #bookmark. Basically, this allows you to pinpoint an area that needs work even more specifically than just naming the HTML file. You can point to a specific section within the file.

6. Comment   A short sentence describing in detail what needs to be done; cannot contain any new-line characters.

These attributes are encoded in each line of the [TaskInfo] section as follows:

TaskNum=TaskName|Priority|CreatedBy|URL|Cookie|Comment

TaskNum is a unique key, such as 't01', 't02', and the Task attributes are separated by vertical bar characters ('|').

This is useful if you have things that you want to make sure are consistently done to every new Web created in the style of this template.

Frameset Templates

You might think that since framesets are actually just another type of HTML document that you would be able to create an HTML frames page and use it as a template and be done with it. That is not the case, however. FrontPage has a Frames wizard that is used for creating and editing HTML frameset pages and you will need to create a .FRM file containing the information that the Frames Wizard needs. It is similar to the .INF file you would use to strore information about a Web Template only with different sections and keys. We'll cover creation of framesets in the section.

What Is a Frameset?

A frameset page divides up a page into independent scrollable regions that can each contain a separate Web page. Authors can cause documents to be loaded into individual frames regions by using a special "TARGET" attribute that can be attached to most kinds of links. Whenever you find yourself at a Web page with separate regions of the page that can change independantly of each other, you are looking at frames.

Part

VII

Ch

33

A Frameset is the HTML code that defines how a framed page should look. Some HTML code for a frameset page that created a 65 pixel top frame, a 65 pixel bottom frame and gave the rest of the room to the middle frame would look like this:

```
<HTML>
<FRAMESET ROWS="65, *, 65">
     <FRAME SRC="doc1.html">
     <FRAME SRC="doc2.html">
     <FRAME SRC="doc3.html">
</FRAMESET>
</HTML>
```

As you can see, framesets are just HTML. Why, then you might ask, can I not just create an HTML frameset and make it into a template? This is where the Frames Wizard comes in.

The Frames Wizard

The Frames Wizard automates the creation of not only a Frameset, but also the pages that fill the frames. It offers an option to create an entire frameset, including its component pages, from one of several templates. These templates are stored in the Frames Wizard directory, which is underneath the FrontPage "pages" directory. (c:\Program Files\Microsoft FrontPage\Pages\framewiz.wiz by default.)

Frameset templates are stored differently from the Web and page template structure described above. Each frameset template is kept in its own file, with the extension .FRM. The .FRM files are kept in INI format so they are easily read by the Frames Wizard. Each .FRM file has the following structure:

```
[info]
title=name of frameset as it will appear in the wizard
description=long description of the purpose of the wizard
noframesURL=ignored; alternate page is assigned by wizard
layout=specification of frameset geometry using compact notation


[frame name 1...N]
title=name of frame as it will appear in the page title
description=long description of what the frame should contain
URL=ignored; page URL for frame is assigned dynamically by wizard
marginWidth=width of margin; default is 1
marginHeight=height of margin; default is 1
scrolling=how scrollbars are displayed; default is 'auto'
noresize=turns off scrolling; default is 'False'
target=name of default target frame for this page
```

The first section, [info], describes the main frameset page. Subsequent sections each describe a component frame page. The section names must match the frame names, which are derived from the frameset layout specification in the [info] section. The frameset layout specification is where the frameset geometry is defined. The notation used to define a frameset takes a little getting used to. For example, look at the following sample frameset layout specification:

layout=[R(15%,85%)F("banner",[C(35%,65%)F("contents","main")])]

This layout is describing a frame that looks like Figure 33.2.

FIGURE 33.2

The sample frameset.

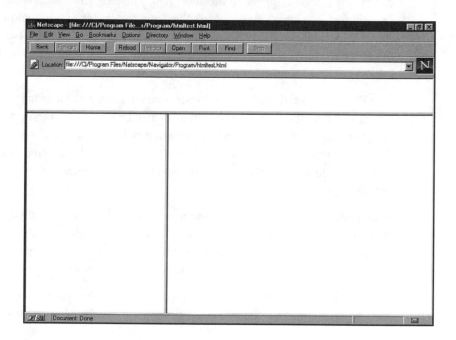

and in standard HTML format, the frameset would be defined like this:

```
<HTML>
<FRAMESET ROWS="15%, 85%">
    <FRAME NAME="banner">
    <FRAMESET COLS="35%,65%"
        <FRAME NAME="contents">
        <FRAME NAME="main">
    </FRAMESET>
</FRAMESET>
</HTML>
```

The condensed notation works like this. Each frameset, including the topmost frameset, is surrounded by square brackets [like these]. Inside the frameset is a row and/or column specification followed by a list of frames. A row specification is an "R" followed by a comma-separated list of row sizes in parentheses (like these), where each entry is expressed as a percentage of the total available height (unlike HTML frameset definitions,

Part

VII

Ch

33

you cannot specify exact pixel measurements). The column specification is the same format as the row specification, but with an initial "C." The frame list is an "F" followed by a comma-separated list, where each item is either a frame name (inside double quotes) or a full frameset specification (inside square brackets).

The sample layout string above can be decoded as follows. The frameset consists of two rows, a short one at 15% of the window height and a long one at 85% of the height. A frame called "banner" is assigned to the short row. The long row contains another frameset, this one divided into two columns of one-third and two-thirds of the window width. This interior frameset is composed of two frames, the first called "contents" (which is assigned to the leftmost third) and the second called "main" (which is assigned to the rightmost two-thirds).

The Frames Wizard reads the frameset information for any files in its directory with the extension .frm. It uses the layout string to display a preview graphic with the frame names alongside the frameset's title and description strings. When a frameset template is chosen, the wizard reads the information for each named frame by looking up a section with the same name in the .frm file. For this reason the section names must match the frame names.

Finally, the wizard generates the frameset page and its component pages and loads them into the current Web or the FrontPage Editor as appropriate. The wizard will place a WebBot Annotation on each page describing its purpose, the frameset it belongs to, what the default target is (if any), and how the page can be edited.

From here, we'll cover creating your own Wizards. If you are a Windows programmer, you can do some great things to take automation of common tasks even further. ●

Creating Wizards

If you have worked with FrontPage for any amount of time, it is likely that you have used a wizard or two to create either a page or a Web or both. Wizards are actually external programs that take you step-by-step through a process, whether that is creating a new Web, page, or frameset. You can write your own wizards in any programming language you want, so long as they behave the way FrontPage expects them to. In this chapter, we are going to talk about how wizards work and show you a wizard written in Visual Basic (VB) to illustrate how wizards need to work. You don't need to write your wizards in VB, any Windows development platform will do. But because of its common usage, we'll use VB in this chapter. ■

Wizards: What They Are and How They Work

First, let's cover what wizards are and how they work. In chapter 33, we discussed using FrontPage's OLE automation interfaces. The Explorer, Editor, and To Do List in FrontPage are all programmable via OLE, and using a third-party development tool, can be automated in just about any way you would like. This is what a wizard is, an independent executable program that usually collects input from a user in a series of dialog boxes, then places OLE automation calls to drive FrontPage by "remote control" to create the new Webs or Web pages.

To get a little bit better feel for how wizards actually work, let's step through the process of what happens in FrontPage when you use a wizard. Let's say we decide to start the Corporate Presence Wizard from the FrontPage Explorer. What happens behind the scenes? FrontPage starts up the executable file VTIPRES.EXE located in the directory [FrontPage Root]\webs\vtipres.wiz. Just like a template, a wizard is contained in a special directory on a user's local disk. A wizard directory must be called *.wiz, and in order to be recognized by FrontPage, this directory must be placed in either the FrontPage Webs or pages directory, depending on what kind of content it holds.

Once the program begins, a series of dialog boxes is presented, prompting the user for all sorts of information about his or her company as well as prompting for information like background and text colors and style of Web design. Most wizards look something like the one shown in Figure 34.1.

FIGURE 34.1

The Corporate Presence Wizard.

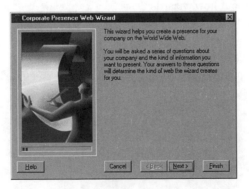

As you can see, the wizard has navigation buttons along the bottom to step through the process, Next, Back, Finish, Cancel, and Help. There is nothing in the world that says that your wizards have to look like the wizards that come with FrontPage, but consistency usually is a good thing for end-users. After having collected all of the information it needs, the wizard uses OLE Automation to make FrontPage create the file or files it needs and then closes, leaving you with FrontPage and your new site or page.

NOTE There really is no enforced difference between a Web wizard and a page wizard other than where they are stored on the disk and from which part of FrontPage they launch. You can write a program that does just about anything, even connecting to a corporate database or getting information from the Internet. It is up to you to logically label your wizards as Web or page wizards, and to make sure that the user interface is easy for your end-users to use. There are some sample VB and VC++ projects in the SDK that can help get you going in the right direction. ■

So now that we have established that wizards are nothing more than external programs that launch from and interact with FrontPage, let's take a deeper look at what your program should do to be a wizard.

Writing Wizards

As we mentioned before, wizards need to live in one of two directories. Either the C:\Program Files\Microsoft FrontPage\webs directory or the C:\Program Files\Microsoft FrontPage\pages directory. When you install your wizard on an end-users machine, one of the first things you will have to do is put your EXE in the right place. You can find out where that might be by checking the settings in the frontpg.ini file installed in a user's Windows directory which will look something like this:

```
[Ports]
Port 80=
[FrontPage 2.0]
FrontPageRoot=C:\Program Files\Microsoft FrontPage
PWSRoot=C:\FrontPage Webs
FrontPageLangID=0x0409
FrontPageLexicon=C:\Microsoft FrontPage\bin\mssp2_en.lex
FrontPageSpellEngine=C:\Microsoft FrontPage\bin\mssp232.dll
CheckedHostName=arbus
[Port 80]
servertype=frontpage
serverconfig=C:\FrontPage Webs\Server\conf\httpd.cnf
authoring=enabled
frontpageroot=C:\Program Files\Microsoft FrontPage
```

NOTE In version 1.0, the INI file was called vermeer.ini. The section was called "FrontPage," and it contained keys for FrontPageRoot, FrontPageBin, WebWizardsDir, and PageWizardsDir. As of version 1.1, the only required key is FrontPageRoot. If you set one of these keys, the change will take effect the next time the FrontPage Explorer or FrontPage Editor is run. ■

Once you have determined where FrontPage is, you will also need to create a WIZ subdirectory for your wizard where the base name of the wizard executable program matches the base name of the wizard directory, for example, sample.wiz\sample.exe. If you want your wizard to be listed as a Web wizard, put it in the Webs subdirectory, and list it in the Pages subdirectory if you wish it to appear as a page wizard. Then create a subdirectory of the same name as your EXE file, but with a WIZ extension. Here's an example.

Let's say I have two wizards I have written and want to install, MyWebWizard.EXE and MyPageWizard.EXE. I would place the first in C:\Program Files\Microsoft FrontPage\webs\MyWebWizard.wiz and the second in C:\Program Files\Microsoft FrontPage\pages\MyPageWizard.wiz.

So you've installed the program in the right place. Is it now a wizard? Not quite. Your wizard needs to tell FrontPage about itself and you will use an INF file to accomplish that task. The INF file is in the exact same format as a Windows INI file and contains an [info] section that contains title and description keys. Place this file in the same directory as your wizard and give it the same name as the EXE file. It can also contain a key called "exename" giving the name of the wizard program, if it does not match the name of the wizard directory as described above. If a page wizard can function as an editor in addition to a generator, the INF file should contain the line "editor=1".

This is the INF file for the Corporate Presence wizard mentioned previously:

```
[info]
title=Corporate Presence Wizard
description=Create a professional Internet presence for your organization.
```

I mentioned previously that Web and page wizards really had no inherent restrictions imposed on them. A page wizard could create a Web and vice versa. However, when looking at your wizard, you will want to categorize it as one or the other. How? Well, generally, a page wizard creates a single page, while a Web wizard creates several interconnected pages. These criteria can help you decide what type of wizard you either have or need. Another thing to keep in mind is the fact that page wizards are always run from the FrontPage Editor, while Web wizards are always run from the FrontPage Explorer. Where you install your wizard can depend as much on where you want users to start it from as what it does.

A Wizard Is Born: How FrontPage Launches Your Wizard

Now you know where to put your program and what it should do in general. Now we'll cover a little more about what FrontPage does when it starts a wizard. All wizards are launched with a single argument: the path to a temporary file in INI format containing name-value pairs. If a wizard is run without any arguments, because the user started it from the Windows File Manager or Windows Explorer, it should behave in a reasonable default manner. It is up to you as the programmer to determine how your wizard will run if started like this, but typically a page wizard should load a page into the FrontPage Editor, and a Web wizard should load pages into the current Web.

The format of the parameter file is as follows:

```
[Input]
arg1=value1
arg2=value2
[Environment]
var1=value1
var2=value2
[Output]
```

The Input section contains all required and optional wizard parameters. The Environment section contains a snapshot of the parent's environment variables. The Output section is initially empty; this is where the wizard can write variables that get sent back to the calling process under certain circumstances.

All wizards receive the following built-in arguments when they are run:

```
Dir=absolute path to wizard directory
Inf=absolute path to wizard's INF file
Blocking=0 or 1 (1 if caller is blocked)
Editing=0 or 1 (1 if wizard is being invoked as an editor)
```

As was mentioned before, a page wizard's INF file should contain the key/value "editor=1" if it can be launched as an editor; otherwise the Editing key will always be set to 0. The Blocking variable has to do with whether or not the wizard will be returning some values to FrontPage in the [Output] section. If that is the case, Blocking will be set to 1 and the launching program will take care of deleting the parameter file when the wizard exits. If your program will not be sending any output back to FrontPage, your program should also delete the temporary parameter file.

A few additional parameters have special meaning to a page wizard:

```
Destination=editor ¦ web ¦ disk
PageURL=web-relative URL where page should be saved
PageTitle=title for new web page
PageFile=path to file being edited (only set if Editing=1)
```

Part
VII

Ch
34

Each page wizard has a notion of its default destination. This is usually the FrontPage Editor; but if a wizard generates content that cannot be edited by the FrontPage Editor, the wizard should load it to the current Web instead. If Destination=editor, the generated file should be loaded directly into the FrontPage Editor via OLE automation. If Destination=web, the generated file should be loaded directly to the current Web via OLE automation. If Destination=disk, the wizard should generate its output into temp files and return a list of filename/URL pairs via the Output section (see below).

`PageURL` is the Web-relative path to the page being created (such as "index.htm"). `PageTitle` is the title of the page being created (such as "My Home Page"). `PageFile` is an absolute path to the file being edited, which has typically just been downloaded by the Explorer.

N O T E For backward compatibilty, the following arguments are still passed to wizards by the FrontPage Explorer when it runs a Web wizard: `WebName`, `ServerName`, `Proxy`, `User`. ■

If `Blocking=1`, then page wizards should return some values via the parameter file's Output section. Those key values that you need to return are:

■ `ExitStatus`   This key should be set to either `error`, `cancel`, or `ok`. If `ExitStatus` is not present, the launching program will assume that an error occurred in the wizard.

■ `FileCount`   If `Destination=disk`, the wizard should write a `FileCount` key and a list of keys from `File1` to `FileN` and `Url1` to `UrlN`. The values of these keys should be set to the absolute paths and target URLs of each file generated by the wizard.

For example, a wizard that generated two files might create an Output section like this:

```
[Output]
ExitStatus=ok
FileCount=2
File1=c:\temp\wiz01.tmp
Url1=index.htm
File2=c:\temp\wiz02.tmp
Url2 = test.htm
```

It is assumed that `File1` will be the main HTML file created by a page wizard.

The FrontPage SDK includes Visual Basic code to do some of these common tasks for you. They have included WIZUTIL.BAS, HTMLGEN.BAS, and BOTGEN.BAS in the FrontPg\FPSDK20\Wizards\VB directory on the CD-ROM. These three files contain many generic utility functions for creating wizards, including generating HTML. There are functions to read the information the FrontPage passes your wizards ready made for you. For example, the following is a `Form_Load` event that executes at the start up of a wizard that simply get's all of the parameter info that the wizard requires:

```
Private Sub Form_Load()

    GetFrontPageInfo
    GetWizardInfo

    Exit Sub

End Sub
```

Of course, you will probably have more happening than this in your start-up event for your wizard, but it illustrates how easy it is for you to get all of these parameters into your program.

Designing Your Wizard

A wizard should look like a dialog box but should have the following buttons to step through the dialog pages: Back, Next/Finish, and Cancel. Most wizards should be self-explanatory, but some may require a Help button. These buttons should always be visible and accessible at the bottom of the wizard's dialog box. If necessary, an image or graphical output area appears to the left of the dialog pages but above the main navigation buttons. The FrontPage SDK contains some sample wizards written in Visual Basic that you can use for templates to get you going. Let's take a look at one of them, the Real Estate Wizard (see Figure 34.2).

FIGURE 34.2
The Real Estate Wizard in the VB development environment.

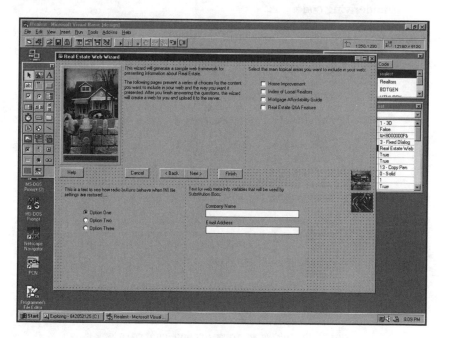

As you can see in Figure 34.2, the wizard has been created using one main Visual Basic form that contains panels for each step in the wizard process and one set of wizard controls of the same style as the ones that come with FrontPage. In the VB code, the panels are simply moved into place as each step in the process is created. This is a good model for creating your wizard in VB.

Part
VII

Ch
34

We have already discussed much of the behavior that your wizard needs to exhibit but there are a few more things you need to know. If you wish to store any settings for your wizard in a permanent state, you will need to use your wizards INI file which is stored in the Data subdirectory of the FrontPage installation directory. The name of each INI file should be the same as the base name of the wizard executable program but with an .INI extension. The INI file is separated from the program so that the wizard directory can be mounted on a read-only disk drive, such as in a local-area network or with a CD-ROM. This is also why all wizards place their generated files into the FrontPage Temp directory.

Putting It All Together: A Sample Wizard

Now that we have covered everything a wizard needs to do, let's see one do it. The FrontPage SDK contains a sample wizard for creation of a Real Estate Web site. Figure 34.2 shows the main form in the development environment, but let's take a look at the underlying code.

When the wizard loads up, it get's the information that it needs to get from FrontPage and then arranges all of the panels on the form so that they will appear in sequence. The following is the Form_Load code that accomplishes this:

```
Private Sub Form_Load()

    Dim titleH As Integer
    Dim i As Integer
    Dim msg As String
    Dim obj As String

    GetFrontPageInfo
    GetWizardInfo

    ' IMPORTANT: have to set the highest page number index manually
    PageMax = 3

    ' fetch any previous settings from INI file
    LoadSettings

    ' set any initial values on pages
    InitPages

    ' shrink-wrap form around controls
    ' (allows form to be much larger in design mode);
    ' this part will vary depending on your control
    ' names and layout
    titleH = Me.Height - Me.ScaleHeight  ' with and without border
    Me.Width = pg(0).Left + pg(0).Width + pnlLeft.Left
    Me.Height = titleH + btnHelp.Top + btnHelp.Height + pnlLeft.Left
```

```
      ' since a wizard is supposed to work like a dialog,
      ' make it centered like a dialog
      CenterFormOnScreen Me

      ' initialize page meter control
      meter.value = 0
      meter.Min = 0
      meter.Max = PageMax

      ' set all pages to be same size and location
      ' (allows them to be spread all over large form in design mode)
      For i = 0 To PageMax
          pg(i).Left = pg(0).Left
          pg(i).Top = pg(0).Top
          pg(i).Width = pg(0).Width
          pg(i).Height = pg(0).Height
      Next i

      ' set initial conditions and show first page
      PageNum = -1
      GoToPage 0

      Exit Sub

  End Sub
```

After this code executes, the wizard displays the first page in a series. The overall operation of the wizard is pretty simple, actually. When the Next or Back button is clicked, the code makes a call to a function called GoToPage, which validates the contents of the current page, hides it, and displays either the next or previous page. It also determines which buttons should be enabled and if the Next button should actually read Finish because of the completion of the wizard. Here is what that looks like:

```
  Private Sub GoToPage(num As Integer)

      If num >= 0 And num <= PageMax Then
          ' validate and then take down previous page (if any)
          If PageNum >= 0 And PageNum <= PageMax Then
              ' check for valid input on the current page
              If Not ValidatePage(PageNum) Then Exit Sub
              pg(PageNum).Visible = False
          End If
          PageNum = num
          ChangePicture PageNum
          pg(PageNum).Visible = True
          If PageNum = 0 Then
              btnBack.Enabled = False
          Else
              btnBack.Enabled = True
          End If
          If PageNum = PageMax Then
              btnNext.Enabled = False
          Else
              btnNext.Enabled = True
```

```
                End If
                meter.value = PageNum
                SetFinishState ' see if Finish button can be enabled
            End If

        End Sub
```

The `ValidatePage` function checks to make sure that all of the controls have been filled out properly and that is going to vary from page to page. This is the basic technique for gathering information throughout the whole wizard. The last thing the wizard needs to do is create the Web (or page) and tell FrontPage what it's been up to. For this wizard, that is done when the Finish button is clicked in the `GenerateWeb` procedure shown here:

```
        Private Sub GenerateWeb()

            ' replace this routine with your own version;
            ' it should generate the HTML pages one-by-one
            ' in the system-dependent temp directory
            ' and upload the files to the web server

            Dim i As Integer
            Dim tempfile As String
            Dim curfile As String
            Dim retval As Long
            Dim wizname As String
            Dim wizversion As String
            Dim tmp As String
            Dim done As Integer
            Dim FileList As String
            Dim URLList As String
            Dim webURL As String

            ' put up the hourglass
            Screen.MousePointer = 11

            Set webber = CreateObject(FrontPageExplorerID)

            webURL = webber.vtiGetWebURL
            If Len(webURL) = 0 Then
                MsgBox "The FrontPage Explorer does not have a web open.",
        ➥vbExclamation
                Set webber = Nothing
                Exit Sub
            End If

            Set todo = CreateObject(FrontPageToDoListID)

            ' set tool name for document upload
            wizname = "Real Estate Web Wizard"
            wizversion = "0.1"

            InitFiles    ' establish a clean slate for upload list
            InitMetaVars ' establish a clean slate for meta-info variables
```

```
' _ _ _ _ _
' construct list of required meta-info vars
' _ _ _ _ _
AddMetaVar "CompanyName", CStr(txtCompanyName.text)
AddMetaVar "EmailAddress", CStr(txtEmailAddress.text)


' _ _ _ _ _
' construct list of files to be uploaded
' _ _ _ _ _
' (AddFile takes name of file as first arg,
'  and whether or not file is generated dynamically
'  as second arg)

' first add any pre-existing files (such as images)
AddFile "masthead.gif", False, "masthead image"
' then add any INCLUDED files (for IncludeBots)
' *BEFORE* the files which will "include" them
AddFile "inc.htm", True, "page footer"
' finally any files that must be generated
AddFile "index.htm", True, "home page"  ' default home page is
➥*REQUIRED*
    If chkImprove.value Then AddFile "improve.htm", True, "home improvement
➥guide"
    If chkRealtors.value Then AddFile "realtors.htm", True, "index of
➥Realtors"
    If chkMortgage.value Then AddFile "mortgage.htm", True, "mortgage guide"
    If chkQuestions.value Then AddFile "question.htm", True, "answers to
➥common questions"

    done = nFiles - 1

    ' _ _ _ _ _
    ' upload any web meta-info variables
    ' _ _ _ _ _

    tmp = PackMetaInfoVars()
    If tmp <> "" Then
        retval = webber.vtiPutWebMetaInfo(tmp)
        If retval <> 1 Then
            ' failure
            Set webber = Nothing
            Set todo = Nothing
            MsgBox "Warning: " & Chr$(10) & "Wizard failed PutWebMetaInfo
➥call."
            Exit Sub
        End If
    End If

    ' _ _ _ _ _
    ' loop through list of files, generating files and creating upload lists
    ' _ _ _ _ _

    FileList = ""
    URLList = ""
```

```
For i = 0 To done

    If Files(i).IsNew Then

        ' create temp file where output will go
        Files(i).path = TempFileName()

        If Not GenerateFile(Files(i).Name, Files(i).path) Then
            MsgBox "Couldn't generate file: '" & Files(i).Name & "'."
            Files(i).path = ""   ' couldn't create file
        End If

    Else

        ' generate full path to file
        Files(i).path = App.path & "\" & Files(i).Name

    End If

    If Files(i).path <> "" Then
        ' TODO: images should go in /images web dir
        FileList = FileList & Files(i).path
        URLList = URLList & Files(i).Name
        ' item separator is newline char
        FileList = FileList & Chr$(10)
        URLList = URLList & Chr$(10)
    End If

Next i

' perform upload

retval = webber.vtiPutDocuments(FileList, URLList)

If retval = 0 Then          ' failed
    MsgBox "Unable to load documents into web."
End If

' _ _ _ _ _
' refresh Explorer's views
' _ _ _ _ _

webber.vtiRefreshWebFromServer

' _ _ _ _ _
' add any items for To Do List
' _ _ _ _ _

todo.vtiAddTask "Customize home page", 1, wizname, "index.htm", "", "Add
➡local content to reinforce unique identity."

' _ _ _ _ _
' remove any temp files
' _ _ _ _ _
```

```
For i = 0 To done
    If Files(i).IsNew And Files(i).path <> "" Then
        Kill Files(i).path
    End If
Next i

'  _ _ _ _ _
' all done
'  _ _ _ _ _

Set webber = Nothing
Set todo = Nothing

' take down the hourglass
Screen.MousePointer = 0

' all done
Unload Me

End Sub
```

Let's look at what this procedure is doing. After declaring some variables, an OLE automation object is created for both the FrontPage Explorer and the To-Do List. The wizard then creates lists of files to be uploaded and meta-info variables to be added to the Web and goes through the lists adding meta-info variables and files to the Web using OLE automation methods. After finishing with this, the wizard refreshes the Web from the server and adds items to the To-Do list, removes it's temp files, set's the OLE objects to "nothing" and quits.

As you can see, wizards are fairly simple programs and the behavior your wizard needs to exhibit is well illustrated by the samples included.

Wizard Creation: A Summary

Go ahead and develop your wizard in any language you like and make it do anything you want; the only rules it has to obey are those for communicating with FrontPage itself and hopefully the overall layout and design as exemplified by the standard FrontPage wizards and the custom projects in the SDK. If you're lucky, your end-users will think you're amazing. ●

Part
VII

Ch
34

Integrating FrontPage and Microsoft Office

## CHAPTER 35

FrontPage and Microsoft Office 97

Word's Web Tools

Word 97 has a new hyperlink capability that functions both in and outside the context of a Web. You can also use hyperlinks as cross-references and save documents in the HTML format.

Excel's Web Tools

Excel 97 has a hyperlink capability similar to Word's, as well as a hyperlink worksheet function. You can save worksheets in HTML format and design forms for user input.

Importing Office Documents into a FrontPage Web

The hyperlinks you establish within an Office document are maintained in a FrontPage Web, and HTML created with FrontPage can link to Office documents in the web.

Since the release of Office 95, Microsoft has gradually moved toward a tighter coupling of its Office applications with Web technology—HTTP, HTML documents, and so on. Internet Assistants, which are add-ins for Office applications, have been available for some time. They enable the user to save, for example, an Excel table in HTML format, to include a mailto in a document, or to insert a hyperlink from a Word document to an HTML file.

With Office 97, many of these capabilities have found their way into the Office application's native code. Word, PowerPoint, and Excel have new Insert Hyperlink commands. Excel even has a HYPERLINK() worksheet function that can be combined with other functions such as IF() to extend the flexibility of a hyperlink.

Even in Office 97, however, not all the Web capabilities are part of the native application code. To use these capabilities you must install add-ins. Excel for Office 97 comes with an Internet Assistant add-in that exports tables to HTML format, and a Web Form Wizard add-in that facilitates building data entry forms for use on a Web.

In FrontPage, you're able to import non-HTML files into a Web. You might create a hyperlink in a standard Web page to an Excel workbook that contains financial information, for example, or to a Word document that contains boilerplate. If the user has access to the document's native application or viewer, invoking the hyperlink causes the document's native application to start up and display the document. Then the user can view or edit the document.

So you're able to go in two directions: from an Office application, create HTML documents; or from FrontPage, open an Office application. The direction you choose depends on what you want to accomplish, and you will often want to do both.

This chapter describes the use of Office 97 web capabilities, and how you can integrate Office documents with FrontPage. If you have not obtained Office 97, you can nevertheless provide much of the same functionality by using Office 95 applications in conjunction with their respective Internet Assistants. These topics are covered in Chapter 36, "Using the Internet Assistant for PowerPoint;" Chapter 37, "Using Internet Assistants for Excel and Word;" and Chapter 38, "Using Internet Assistant for Word, Access, and Schedule+ with FrontPage." ■

Using Word's Web Tools

If you're an experienced user of Microsoft Word, you might find it more convenient to construct web pages using that application than by means of an HTML editor. Word does not give you the degree of control over HTML formatting that you would get with an HTML editor, but it can give you a head start.

Furthermore, if you have Word documents that you would like to convert to HTML format, doing so from Word is surely the most expeditious approach.

Three Web features new to Word 97 are the insertion of hyperlinks, saving a Word document as an HTML file, and the Web Toolbar.

Inserting Hyperlinks

Suppose that you have written a Word document, TRAPS.DOC, that discusses some problems with Excel worksheet functions, and you've saved it on the Windows Desktop. You are at present writing a guide, GUIDE.DOC, to using Office 97 as deployed at your firm. You would like to insert a hyperlink in the GUIDE.DOC that points to TRAPS.DOC. To do so, take the following steps:

1. With GUIDE.DOC open in Word, choose Insert, Hyperlink (or, press Ctrl+k). The Insert Hyperlink dialog box appears (see Figure 35.1).

FIGURE 35.1

The hyperlink in the Word document will operate outside the context of FrontPage.

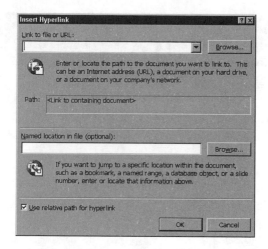

2. Choose <u>B</u>rowse. (Be sure to choose the <u>B</u>rowse button in the upper-right corner of the dialog box.) The Link to File dialog box appears, as shown in Figure 35.2. Navigate to the Desktop, select TRAPS.DOC from the list of available files, and choose OK.

FIGURE 35.2

It's usually easier to browse to a destination file than to type its URL.

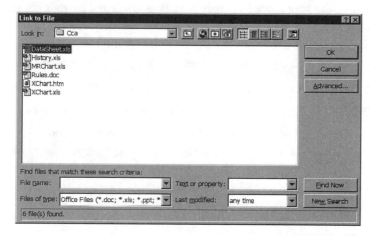

3. You are returned to the Insert Hyperlink dialog box. Choose OK. The hyperlink appears, as shown in Figure 35.3.

You can now save the document as both a Word file and an HTML file. To save the HTML version, choose <u>F</u>ile, Save <u>A</u>s and choose HTML Document from the Save as <u>t</u>ype drop-down dialog box. To save the file in Word format, just choose <u>F</u>ile, <u>S</u>ave.

FIGURE 35.3

You can use a hyperlink to any file, as long as the destination file has an accessible application associated with its extension.

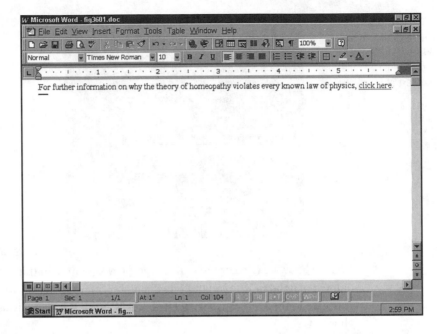

In Word, the appearance of the hyperlink is governed by your choice of hyperlink Style. The default appearance for a hyperlink uses the standard blue underlined font, and a followed hyperlink uses the standard violet underlined font. If consistency of appearance is not an issue, you can change the defaults by taking these steps:

1. Open a document that you have saved in HTML format.

2. Choose Format, Style, and select Hyperlink from the Styles listbox.

3. Choose Modify, and in the Modify Style dialog box choose Format. Choose Font from the shortcut menu. In the Font dialog box, you can choose from different fonts, font styles and sizes, underline types, colors, and effects.

4. Repeat steps 2 and 3 for the Followed Hyperlink style.

After you have resaved the HTML document, your browser displays hyperlinks in the styles you selected.

In Word, hyperlinks are inserted as field codes. You can switch back and forth between viewing the hyperlink itself and viewing it as a field code. Right-click the hyperlink and choose Toggle Field Codes from the shortcut menu.

T I P Before inserting hyperlinks in Office documents, save both the document with the hyperlink and the destination document.

When you create a hyperlink in Word, you have choices as to how you display it, as follows:

- Change the hyperlink text by dragging across it with your mouse pointer and typing some other label—for example, you might type Click here to learn about function traps. (First make sure that the hyperlink text is displayed, not its field code.)
- Display the hyperlink as a graphic, as described in the next section.
- In Word, you can display the hyperlink as a cross-reference (see "Creating Hyperlinked Cross-References in Word," below).

Using the Web Toolbar

When you have arrived at the destination document by clicking the hyperlink, the Office Web toolbar appears in the destination application's window. The toolbar includes a Back and a Forward button, as shown in Figure 35.4, where a hyperlink in an Excel document takes the user to a Word document. Click the Back button to return to the hyperlink; click the Forward button to return to its destination.

FIGURE 35.4
The Web toolbar in Office applications offers much of the same functionality as a browser.

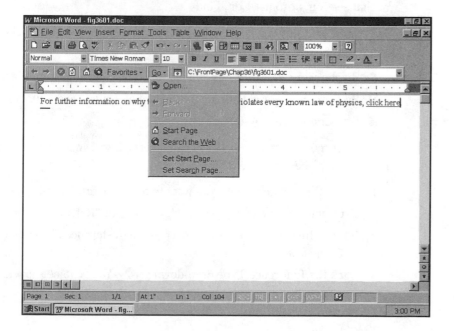

Part
VIII

Ch
35

N O T E   If you're familiar with Office applications, you know about OLE links. For example, you might create an OLE link that connects a cell in an Excel workbook to a cell in another workbook. Or, you might paste-link a Word document into a PowerPoint presentation. This sort of link behaves differently from a hyperlink. When you paste an OLE link from one document into another, changes to the information in the source document are replicated in the target document. Of course, hyperlinks are simply navigation aids. ■

Creating Hyperlinked Cross-References in Word

For some time, Word has enabled the user to insert a cross-reference in a document. A cross-reference draws the reader's attention to another location—usually a page or a heading—in the document.

Word 97 enhances this capability by offering hyperlinked cross-references. Someone reading the document is referred to another location, just as in earlier versions, but by clicking the cross-reference it's possible to jump directly to the destination location.

Suppose that you're writing a lengthy document such as instructions on how to use FrontPage. In the FrontPage Editor section, you want to draw the reader's attention to that part of the document that goes into detail about Bots. You want the cross-reference to read "See Section on Bots." It's convenient for the reader simply to click the cross-reference in order to get there. It's inconvenient to have to page back and forth looking for that section, or to use Edit, Find.

To create a cross reference, you must first outline your document. There are several simple ways to do this in Word, as follows:

- By choosing View, Outline and increasing or decreasing indents.
- By using numbered headings with Format, Bullets and Numbering.
- By using Format, AutoFormat.

Whichever method you choose, you can insert a hyperlinked cross-reference after the outline is in place. Take the following steps:

1. Select the location where you want to place the cross-reference.
2. Type some introductory text, such as "See" or "Refer to."
3. Choose Insert, Cross-reference. The Cross-reference dialog box shown in Figure 35.5 appears.
4. Click the Reference Type drop-down arrow. Your choices appear, as shown in Figure 35.6.

FIGURE 35.5
The For Which list box is blank if your document does not contain any instances of the item in the Reference Type box.

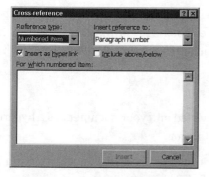

FIGURE 35.6
Your choice of reference type determines what you can insert a reference to.

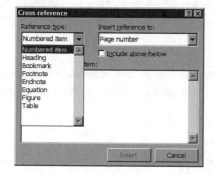

5. Suppose that you chose to number your headings using Format, Bullets and Numbering. You would choose Numbered item in the Reference Type drop-down list. When you do so, the appropriate choices appear in the Insert Reference To drop-down list. See Figure 35.7.

FIGURE 35.7
You can choose to display numbers or text in the cross-reference.

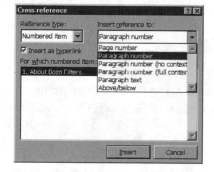

6. Choose an option from the Insert Reference To drop-down list.
7. Fill the Insert as Hyperlink check box.

8. If you want the cross-reference to show either the direction above or below, fill the Include Above/Below check box. This is available only if you have chosen a numbered cross-reference, such as Paragraph Number: The result might be "See 2 above."

9. Choose Insert.

Your cross-reference is now inserted into your document as a hyperlink. Clicking it takes the user to the hyperlink's destination.

The default style for a hyperlink is underlined blue text. However, a hyperlinked cross-reference does not automatically follow that style. To make it more clear to the user that the cross-reference is a clickable hyperlink, select the hyperlink by dragging across it. Then, choose Format, Font, change the cross-reference's font Color to blue, and its Underline to Single.

N O T E Your hyperlinked cross-reference must be to a location in a Word document. If it refers to a location in another Word document, both documents must belong to the same master document. ■

Using Excel's Web Tools

The web tools available to you in Excel are similar to those available in Word. You can save an Excel worksheet in HTML format, insert hyperlinks, and view a web toolbar.

There are also some significant differences between Excel's web capabilities and those in Word. For example, Excel offers a method to build a web form and includes a new HYPERLINK() worksheet function. These differences are discussed in this section.

Saving a Worksheet as HTML

An add-in is required to save an Excel worksheet in HTML format. When you run the Office 97 Setup program, be sure to select the Web Page Authoring component. Then, when you start Excel, look to see whether Save as HTML is an item in the File menu. If not, take the following steps:

1. Choose Tools, Add-Ins.

2. Check to see whether Internet Assistant Wizard appears in the Add-Ins Available list box. If not, click the Browse button and navigate to the location on your working disk that contains the file named HTML.XLA. Normally, this is in the Office\Library subdirectory. Choose HTML.XLA, and choose OK in the Browse dialog box.

3. Ensure that the Internet Assistant Wizard item is checked in the Add-Ins dialog box, and choose OK.

Now when you choose File, Save as HTML, the Internet Assistant Wizard guides you through the process of saving a worksheet in HTML format. For information on using this Wizard, see Chapter 38, "Using Internet Assistant for Word, Access, and Schedule+ with Front Page."

Inserting Hyperlinks in Excel Worksheets

Putting a hyperlink into an Excel worksheet is simply a matter of selecting the cell where you want the hyperlink, and choosing Insert, Hyperlink. The Insert Hyperlink dialog box appears, with the same functionality as Word's Insert Hyperlink dialog box (refer to Figure 35.1 above).

When you have inserted the hyperlink, it appears as shown in Figure 35.8.

FIGURE 35.8
The hyperlink's text appears in Excel's Formula Box; you cannot directly view the URL.

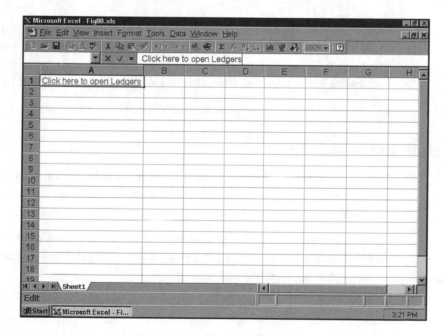

You can change the appearance of the hyperlink in the worksheet cell by selecting the cell—it's best to select the cell using your keyboard arrow keys, because clicking the cell invokes the hyperlink. Then type into the Formula Bar whatever text you want to appear in the hyperlink.

Part VIII
Ch
35

You can also create a hyperlink with Excel 97's new HYPERLINK() function. The syntax of this function is:

```
=HYPERLINK(link location, friendly name)
```

where *link location* is a reference to the destination file (including its path), and *friendly name* is the text that's displayed in the cell containing the function. So, entering this function in cell A1:

```
=HYPERLINK("C:\My Documents\Background.doc","Show Explanation")
```

would appear as Show Explanation in cell A1, and clicking it would open the Word file BACKGROUND.DOC.

You can combine the HYPERLINK() function with other worksheet functions. Suppose that you want to display a hyperlink in cell C1, but only if the user has entered an invalid equation in cell A1—otherwise, you want nothing to appear in C1. Enter this formula in C1:

```
=IF(ISERROR(A1),HYPERLINK("C:\My Documents\HelpUser.doc","Click here for
➥help"),"")
```

Now, if the user enters something like =10/0 in cell A1, which returns the #DIV/0! error value, the IF() function calls the HYPERLINK() function that's nested within it. The HYPERLINK() function then displays the Click here for help message in cell C1, and if the user clicks it, the hyperlink opens the Word file named HELPUSER.DOC.

Otherwise, if there's no error value in A1, the IF() function displays the empty text "".

Building a Web Form

Another Web-related add-in for Excel is the Web Form Wizard. This wizard guides you through setting up a form in your web for users to return information to you. When a user accesses the form from a browser, it appears in an Excel worksheet.

Choose Tools and verify that Wizard is in its menu. If not, take the steps for installing an add-in described above in "Saving a Worksheet as HTML." Ensure that Web Form Wizard is checked in the Add-Ins Available list box.

Now open a new workbook and enter labels for the data that the user will provide: for example, name, address, age, and so on. If you want to include controls such as option buttons and check boxes, choose View, Toolbars, and activate the Forms toolbar.

TIP It's important to use the Forms toolbar rather than the Controls toolbar. Both give you access to controls, but the Web Form Wizard does not recognize controls placed on the worksheet from the Controls toolbar.

To complete the Web Form Wizard, you must have opened the web that will contain the form. Open it using FrontPage Explorer, and switch back to Excel.

Then choose Tools, Wizard, and click Web Form in the cascading menu. Step 1 of the Web Form appears, as shown in Figure 35.9.

FIGURE 35.9
Create the layout of your Excel worksheet as suggested in the Web Form Wizard's first step.

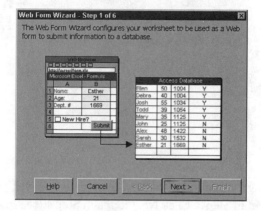

There is no information for you to enter in Step 1. Click Next. Step 2 of the Wizard appears, as in Figure 35.10.

FIGURE 35.10
You can suppress the worksheet's gridlines: Choose Tools, Options, click the View tab, and clear the Gridlines check box.

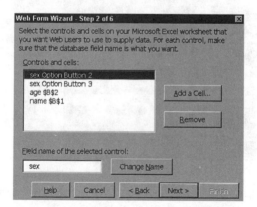

Any controls that you have included in the worksheet with the Controls toolbar are shown in the Controls and Cells list box. You can add to the list box cells where you want the user to supply information. Click Add a Cell, select one of the data entry cells, and click OK in the Add a Cell dialog box. You can associate a name with each cell and each control by selecting them in the Controls and Cells list box, and clicking the Change Name button.

Part
VIII

Ch
35

When you have finished selecting the necessary cells and controls, click Next. Step 3 appears, as in Figure 35.11.

FIGURE 35.11

Choose Common Gateway Interface to supply the form to your FrontPage web.

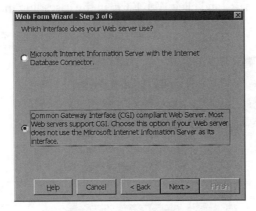

Unless you're also using the Microsoft Internet Information Server, you should choose the CGI interface server in Step 3. Click Next to reach Step 4 (see Figure 35.12).

FIGURE 35.12

You will probably want to save your form both as an Excel file and to your web.

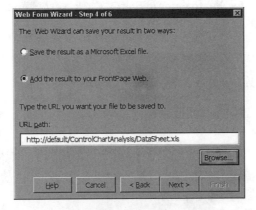

You should save the form as an Excel file if you have not finished designing it. If you're ready to add it to your web, verify the URL and change it if necessary, and then choose Add the Results to Your FrontPage Web. Click Next to display Step 5, shown in Figure 35.13.

In Step 5, you can modify the nature of the message back to the user. When you click Next, the Wizard adds your form, including the Perl script and message data, to your Web. Step 6 appears, and provides you some standard instructions about submitting the files to the web administrator. There is no input for you to supply and there are no options to select; click Finish to end the Wizard.

FIGURE 35.13
The Web Form Wizard automatically generates the requisite Perl script.

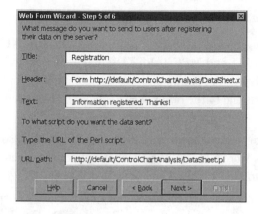

Putting It All Together

The figures in this section illustrate an application jointly supported by FrontPage, Internet Explorer 3.0, Excel 97, and Word 97. The (rudimentary) web described here contains an HTML home page created in FrontPage, with links to Excel workbooks and Word documents. The Office documents use hyperlinks created in Excel and in Word.

Figure 35.14 shows the FrontPage Explorer's view of this web.

FIGURE 35.14
The Links window shows the linkages to the Office documents.

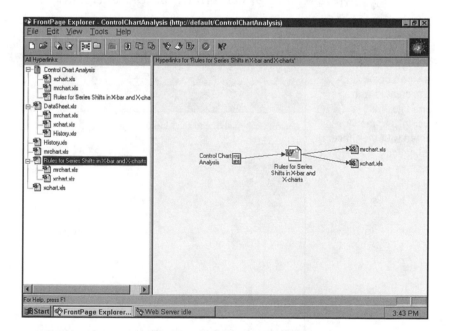

The steps taken to create this Web were the following:

1. Excel was used to create DATASHEET.XLS from HISTORY.XLS. Then it created charts (XCHART.XLS and MRCHART.XLS) that are based on DATASHEET.XLS. Excel's Insert, Hyperlink commmand was used to put hyperlinks from the data sheet to the charts and to the original HISTORY.XLS file. Each of these files was saved in C:\CCA.

2. Word was used to create a document, RULES.DOC, with information pertaining to the Excel charts. Word's Insert, Hyperlink command was used to create hyperlinks in RULES.DOC to XCHART.XLS and MRCHART.XLS.

3. FrontPage Explorer was used to create a new Web named `ControlChartAnalysis`. The Import Wizard imported all the files (Excel charts, Excel data sheets and the Word document) from C:\CCA into the new Web. Unlike earlier versions of FrontPage, it was not necessary explicitly to associate the proper application with the Office documents—FrontPage takes care of that on your behalf.

4. Using FrontPage Editor, the START.HTML document was structured with links to the charts and to the rules document, and placed as a starting point in the `ControlChartAnalysis` web.

5. Once the Office documents were imported, the FrontPage editor was used to insert hyperlinks from START.HTML to the Office documents.

Figure 35.15 shows how the web appears when browsed by Internet Explorer 3.0.

FIGURE 35.15

The web's home page, created with FrontPage, has hyperlinks to the files created with the Office Applications.

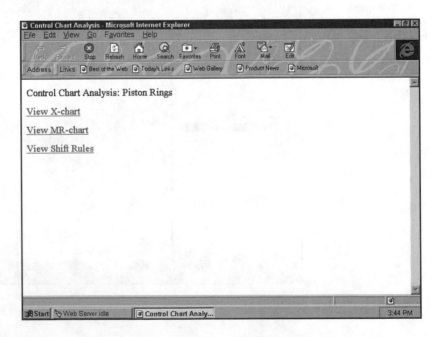

Figure 35.15 shows the Start page. The hyperlinks were created by using FrontPage Editor to type in the text, then selecting each line of text in turn and using Insert, Hyperlink to link the text to the correct file.

Figure 35.16 illustrates what happens when you click the View X Chart link.

FIGURE 35.16
Within Internet Explorer 3.0, Excel's menus are available for the user to modify the document.

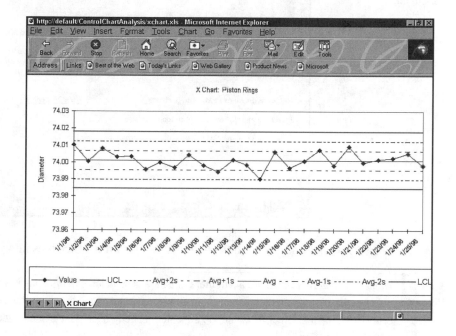

Excel opens in a new window and displays the X chart document. The user can simply view the information in the chart, or can use Excel's menus to modify it: add a trendline, change the properties of the chart axes, modify the title, move or delete the legend—even change the chart type or the values displayed by the chart's markers.

N O T E Notice that the chart shown in Figure 35.16 contains no hyperlinks. At the time that this chapter was written, Excel 97 did not allow the user to insert a hyperlink in a chart that occupies its own page. A workaround is to use File, Save as HTML, and then use FrontPage to insert a hyperlink in the .HTML document. However, the chart in the .HTML document would no longer be linked to its underlying data. ■

Figure 35.17 illustrates what happens when you click the View Rules link on the home page.

Part
VIII
Ch
35

FIGURE 35.17
The hyperlinks in
RULES.DOC were
created using Word's
Insert, Hyperlink
command.

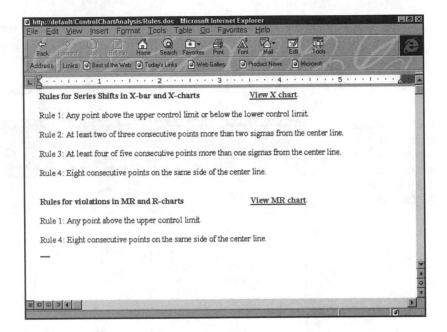

FrontPage maintains these links when you import the Office files into your Web.

 TIP When you create an Office document that will be the destination of a hyperlink in your Web, do not save the destination document with an embedded blank in the file name—for example, *NEW CHART.XLS*. The resulting URL will not be evaluated properly, because it is interpreted as ending with the "w" in "New".

It's always a good procedure in FrontPage to use Tools, Verify Hyperlinks, but it's particularly important when you are employing links that were created by Office applications. If you find a broken hyperlink, and if the hyperlink was created by an Office application, use the application to repair it. Then re-import the file into the FrontPage Web.

From Here . . .

Office 97 applications, including Excel 8 and Word 8, offer useful new capabilities for publishing Office documents on a Web. Because the content found in Excel and Word documents is often confidential, it's more typical to use the new capabilities to put information into an Intranet, rather than on the Web.

PowerPoint, however, is specifically designed to create and manage presentations that you'd like the whole world to see. It is therefore particularly well suited to designing Web pages. Chapter 36 explores the new features in PowerPoint that help you do just that.

Using the Internet Assistant for PowerPoint

The PowerPoint application enables you to design and present slide shows on your computer. It offers a variety of capabilities and special effects that you can use to display any sort of topic, from a sales presentation to a meeting guide to a training session.

The drawback is that the people who view or guide the presentation must have access to the file that contains the slide show. But by using PowerPoint's Internet Assistant (IA), you can convert the presentation's individual slides to files that use HTML and graphic formats. Then, by making the files available to the Web or to an intranet, your presentation becomes accessible to anyone with a browser and the proper connection. ■

Use some of PowerPoint's basic functionality

While this is not a primer on PowerPoint, it discusses several of the capabilities that work differently (or that don't work at all) in the exported version of a PowerPoint slide show. Apply this information to help decide whether to use PowerPoint's IA on a presentation.

Install PowerPoint's IA

Identify and use the necessary files to put the IA functionality into PowerPoint.

Manage the exported files

Understand which files are created when you use the IA on a PowerPoint presentation, what they contain, and how to use them.

Understanding PowerPoint

PowerPoint is a presentation manager. Using PowerPoint, you can:

- Design a series of slides, each of which might contain graphics and text. The graphic and text elements can be created by and linked to other Office applications.
- Apply special effects to elements in the slide. For example, you might use flying text to cause individual bullet points to appear on the slide sequentially, instead of simultaneously.
- Present the slides as a full-screen show, so that PowerPoint's menus and toolbars are hidden from view. Buttons or other objects in a slide enable the user to move through the slides consecutively, or to jump directly to a particular slide.
- Edit various aspects of the slides, such as their order in the presentation.

PowerPoint comes with several templates that contain pre-formatted presentations. These templates have been designed to cover the important aspects of different kinds of presentation.

For example, the template for selling a product or idea provides a slide to describe:

- The objective for the presentation
- The customer's requirements
- How the product meets those requirements
- A cost analysis
- The vendor's strengths
- Key product benefits
- Next steps to take

You might not regard each of these as necessary for a sales or marketing presentation, but it's a good set of bones for you to put some flesh on.

Starting with a template such as this one frees you from initial outline and formatting concerns, so that you can concentrate on content. Figure 36.1 gives an example of one slide from the sales template.

FIGURE 36.1
PowerPoint's templates give you good starting points to develop many different kinds of presentations.

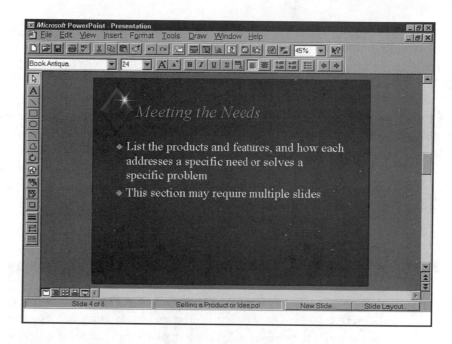

Figure 36.2 shows how you might modify the slide for a particular sales presentation.

FIGURE 36.2
All the contents of this slide are included in the exported graphics image.

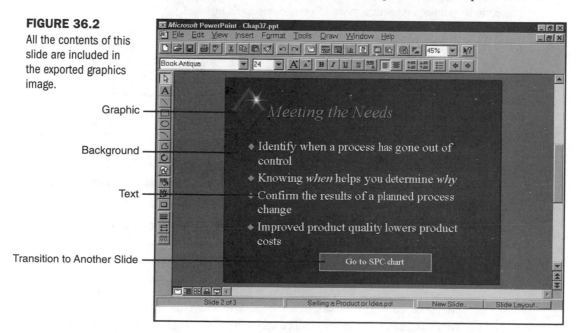

After you have finished designing the presentation and modifying the template's slides to communicate your content, you can display the slides in full-screen mode by choosing View, Slide Show from the PowerPoint menu. Click your mouse button or press Enter to advance manually through the slides.

TIP Another way to move among slides in a slide show is with a Popup button. Choose Tools, Options, select the View tab, and ensure that the Show Popup Menu Button check box is checked. Doing so places buttons in the lower left corner of each slide during the slide show. Clicking the buttons moves you from slide to slide. The buttons become visible when you move the mouse pointer across the slide. This becomes particularly important when you are using the IA: see Running PowerPoint's IA, later in this chapter.

Deciding to Use PowerPoint's Internet Assistant

Suppose that you have created a presentation in PowerPoint that you would like to distribute more broadly. The Web has been used largely as a marketing medium, and you might want to use it to publish a sales presentation, or to distribute descriptive information about your products. You might have developed a training presentation that you want to make available to employees with access to your company's intranet.

N O T E   Some users of PowerPoint's IA put presentations on the Web because they think it's more convenient to view it that way at a client's site. Keep in mind, though, that your client's data communications equipment is unlikely to operate faster than 28,800 bps. On the other hand, you can copy a PowerPoint file from a floppy disk to the client's computer at fractional T1 speeds. PowerPoint comes with a small viewer application that you can take with you. ■

PowerPoint's IA is a convenient way to accomplish this. You just install the IA and run it. Unlike the IAs for other Office applications, nearly the entire process is automated. Other IAs give you more choices about the characteristics of the resulting files.

You can, of course, use a text editor to modify the tags in the .htm files that PowerPoint's IA creates. However, the IA saves your slides' appearance in a series of .jpg or .gif files, one file per slide. These files are static. That is, they do not retain certain special effects that you might have specified for the slide. For example, in PowerPoint:

■ Choose Tools, Slide Transition. In the Slide Transition dialog box, choose Cover Left from the Effect dropdown. This causes the slide to appear from the right side of the screen during the slide show, and to move left to cover the prior slide.

■ Choose Tools, Build Slide Text, and click Fly From Left in the cascading menu. When you view the slide show, any text on the slide is hidden until you press Enter or click the mouse button. Then, bullet points appear from the left side of the screen, one per mouse click. This is a useful way to keep your audience's attention on the current bullet point. (You've probably attended meetings where the presenter emulates this effect by covering up bullet points with a piece of paper, and reveals them one by one.)

These effects can be functionally useful and cosmetically attractive. But you can't retain them in files created by PowerPoint's IA. The absence of such capabilities might not cause you to decide against converting a presentation to HTML, but you shouldn't expect the resulting files to retain all their PowerPoint features.

One feature that you can retain is the ability to jump to a specific slide. Suppose that on the presentation's tenth slide, you want to enable the user quickly to jump back to the fifth slide, which is named *Benefits*. With the tenth slide active, take these steps:

1. Select a shape, such as a rectangle or oval, from PowerPoint's Drawing toolbar. Drag in the slide to establish a new object.

2. With the new object still selected, choose Edit, Edit Text Object. Type an instruction, such as **Go to Benefits**, inside the object.

3. With the new object still selected, choose Tools, Interactive Settings. In the Interactive Settings dialog box, choose the Go to option button, and select Slide from the associated drop-down (see Figure 36.3).

FIGURE 36.3
Including interactive settings makes it easier for a user to navigate among the exported version of your slides.

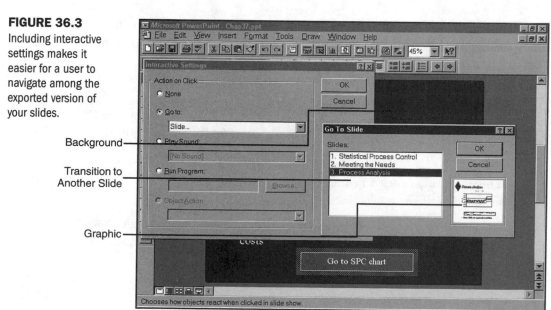

4. In the Go To Slide dialog box, choose the Benefits slide from the Slides list box. Click OK to return to the Interactive Settings dialog box, and click OK again to return to the active slide.

Now, during a slide show, clicking the drawing object displays the Benefits slide.

PowerPoint's IA maintains this functionality. A user who is viewing the exported files with a browser is able to click the object and go to its destination file. (Remember that the IA converts each PowerPoint slide to a different file.)

So, if you are willing to live without PowerPoint's animation effects, you can convert your PowerPoint slide presentation to HTML and graphic format for users to browse. Your presentation maintains any special navigation capabilities that you have built into it.

Installing the Internet Assistant for PowerPoint

All the IAs for Office applications are available via download from the Web at **www.microsoft.com/msdownload/**. You can also obtain them from other sources, such as Microsoft Technet. PowerPoint's IA is included on this book's companion CD. PowerPoint's IA is likely to be compressed into an executable file named Pptia.exe. From the Windows Explorer, double-click Pptia.exe to extract its contents.

N O T E You must be running PowerPoint for Windows 95 to use the IA. PowerPoint versions 4.0 and earlier are incompatible with the IA. ■

Among those contents is another executable file, which at the time of this writing was named ia4ppt95.exe. This file installs the IA in PowerPoint. To perform the installation, follow these steps:

1. If you have PowerPoint running, exit the application.
2. From the Windows Explorer, double-click ia4ppt95.exe.
3. Respond Yes to the *Install Internet Assistant for PowerPoint?* query.
4. Click OK in response to the Successful Installation message.

If the installation does not complete successfully, try first moving ia4ppt95.exe into the same folder where you have stored the PowerPoint application file.

The installation process places a new menu item, Export as HTML, in PowerPoint's File menu. The menu item is visible only if you have opened a presentation.

To uninstall PowerPoint's IA, remove these files from PowerPoint's folder:

- Ppt2html.ppa
- Ppt2html.dll
- Slidedmp.exe
- Pp2hintl.dll
- Image.tpl
- Text.tpl

Another file that you find when the initial extraction process is complete is Ia4ppt95.doc. This is a Word document that contains additional documentation and recent changes to information about running PowerPoint's IA.

Running PowerPoint's IA

To convert a PowerPoint presentation to HTML and graphic files, just open the presentation in PowerPoint and choose File, Export as HTML. The dialog box shown in Figure 36.4 appears.

FIGURE 36.4
Compared to the GIF format, JPEG bitmaps can save file space, but very small JPEG files tend to have poor image quality.

Use the HTML Export Options dialog box to specify:

- Whether the graphics files should be saved in black-and-white (Grayscale) or Color.
- Whether you want the graphics files saved in the JPEG or GIF format.
- If you select JPEG, the size and image quality that the .jpg file is to maintain.
- The location to store the converted files on your working disk. Type the path in the Folder for HTML Export edit box, or use the Browse button to navigate to your preferred location.

PowerPoint's IA automatically creates a new folder at the end of the path. The new folder is where the IA stores the converted files. The folder's default name is the same as that of the presentation. That is, if the active presentation is named *Training.ppt*, the default folder is named *Training*.

When you are satisfied with your choices in the HTML Export Options dialog box, choose OK. The IA converts your slides to HTML and graphic format.

During the conversion process, you may see a window with the contents of any folders that you have open, or with another active application, appear on top of the PowerPoint window. This is normal behavior.

You will then see a window appear in the upper left quadrant of your screen. This window displays your slide show, slide by slide. PowerPoint's IA takes pictures of the show and saves them in either .jpg or .gif format.

Because of the way that the IA captures your slides in this slide show window, there are a few steps you should take prior to beginning the export process:

- Close any floating toolbars that may occupy the upper left quadrant of the PowerPoint screen. (For this reason, you might want to close any applications other than PowerPoint.)

- Close any dialog boxes or Help files whose "Always on Top" property has been set and that appear in the upper left quadrant.

- Choose Tools, Options and select the View tab; then, clear the Show Popup Menu Button check box. If you leave it checked and if you move your mouse pointer during the export process, the pop-up menu buttons might appear and be captured in the exported graphic files.

Of course, you need sufficient space on your working disk to store the exported files. Typically, you should budget for around 20K for each graphic file. However, the export process itself requires considerably more space. Try to have at least 5 M free on your working disk before beginning the export.

TIP If you have text in any grouped objects in a PowerPoint slide, ungroup them via Draw, Ungroup prior to the export process. Grouped text is not added to the text-only versions of your slides.

Understanding the Converted Files

When PowerPoint's IA has completed its export of your slides, you will find several types of files in the destination folder:

■ An Index.htm file, containing the presentation's name, your name, your company name and hyperlinks to each slide in the presentation.

■ Files with the .gif extension that contain Next, Previous, First Page, and Text View buttons. These are displayed on each slide when viewed with a browser.

■ Files with the .jpg or .gif extension, depending on which format you selected in the HTML Export Options dialog box. These files contain the graphic representation of each slide.

■ Files with the .htm extension, and that begin with Sld001, Sld002, and so on. These contain the conventional HTML tags for each slide.

■ Files with the .htm extension, and that begin with Tsld001, Tsld002, and so on. These are text-only versions of your slides, for users who still have an antediluvian browser that can't handle graphics—or, for quicker browsing.

It's time to take a look at these files. Figure 36.5 shows a slide as it's displayed by PowerPoint.

FIGURE 36.5
PowerPoint is a useful way to provide commentary about a chart created in Excel.

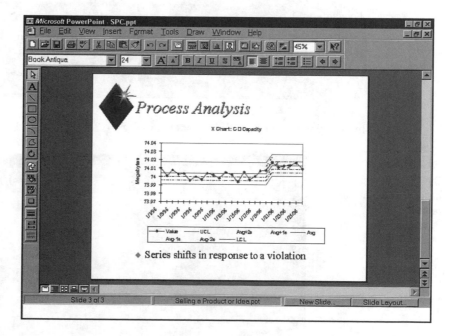

 TIP It's easy to put an object from another Office application into a PowerPoint slide. Select the object, such as an Excel chart, within its native application. Choose Edit, Copy. Switch to PowerPoint and choose Edit, Paste. More options are available if you choose Edit, Paste Special.

Figure 36.6 shows graphic version of the same slide after it's been exported. Notice the navigation buttons that PowerPoint's IA has added. There's a Back shortcut, a Forward shortcut, a shortcut that takes the user to Index.htm, and a shortcut that switches to the text-only version.

FIGURE 36.6

The graphic version of the slide is identical to that displayed by the PowerPoint slide show.

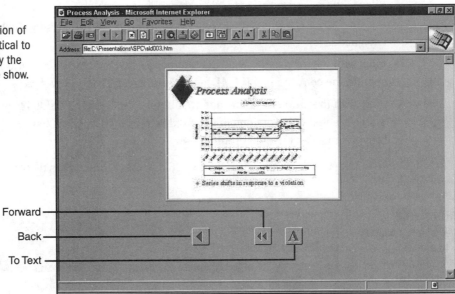

Forward
Back
To Text

The text-only version of the slide is shown in Figure 36.7.

FIGURE 36.7

The graphic version's navigation buttons are replaced by hyperlinked text in the text-only version.

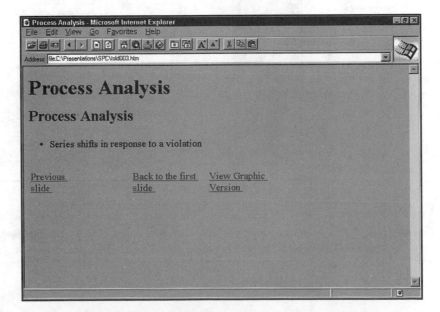

Part
VIII

Ch
36

Notice that, compared to the graphic version of the slide, the text-only version is uninformative. If you anticipate that many users will choose to view the text-only version, if only to accelerate their browsing, you should probably add enough textual material to each slide that users will be able to infer their current location in the show.

N O T E PowerPoint's IA treats any hidden slides in your presentation as normal slides—that is, it converts them to HTML and graphic files. (To hide a slide in PowerPoint, choose Tools, Hide Slide. This prevents its display during a slide show.) If you don't want the browser to display these slides, save the presentation with a new name and delete the hidden slides. ■

PowerPoint offers a way for you to keep speaker's notes for each slide. These notes are text material that's associated with each slide. As you are developing a presentation, you can make notes to yourself: These might be reminders to bring up a topic that's not shown in the slides, or information about your audience, or the name and location of another document that you want to display temporarily—virtually anything that you, as the presenter, would want to see and that you might not want the audience to see.

To attach speaker's notes to a slide while you're running PowerPoint, choose View, Notes Pages. The slide changes to appear as shown in Figure 36.8.

FIGURE 36.8

Speaker notes are visible only via View, Notes Pages—they do not appear in a slide show.

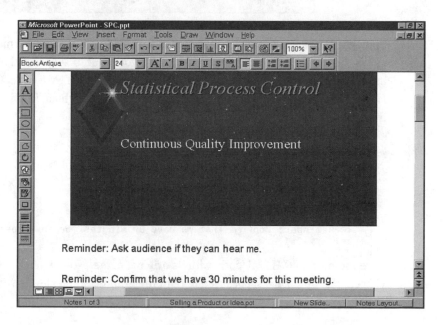

Type whatever notes you wish in the Notes window. When you have finished designing your presentation, choose File, Print. In the Print dialog box, choose Notes Pages from the Print what drop-down. You then have a copy of your notes to refer to as you're delivering the presentation.

PowerPoint's IA exports these notes to the HTML version, as shown in Figure 36.9.

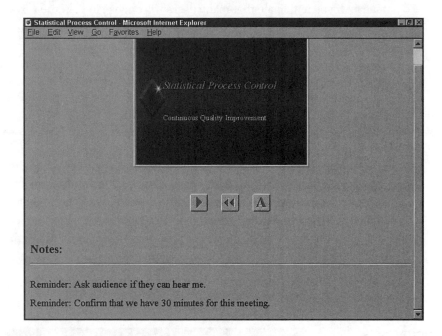

You can, of course, construct these notes to provide additional information to a user who views the presentation with a browser. But if you want to suppress the notes without deleting them from the PowerPoint presentation, modify the HTML code. Open the associated HTML file with your text editor, and delete these lines (which, in this case, correspond to the notes shown in Figure 36.9):

```
<Font size=4> <STRONG> Notes:</FONT></STRONG>
<HR  SIZE=3>
<P> </P>
<P>Reminder: Ask audience if they can hear me.</P>
<P></P>
<P></P>
<P></P>
<P>Reminder: Confirm that we have 30 minutes for this meeting.</P>
<P> </P>
```

Save the modified HTML code with its original name. Now, when the presentation is viewed, the notes are suppressed in both the graphic and text-only versions.

## CHAPTER 37

Using Internet Assistants for Excel and Word

The Internet Assistants for Excel and Word do not resemble one another. In Excel, the Internet Assistant (IA) is a wizard—a sequential series of dialog boxes where you select among various options. Excel's IA provides you with an abbreviated set of HTML formatting elements, limited to data tables, horizontal rules, headers, footers, and e-mail addressing.

In contrast, Word's IA provides a reasonably rich set of formatting options. You create an HTML document in Word by means of different menu items and toolbars. Most permissible HTML elements are supported.

However, the Word and Excel applications combine beautifully by means of object linking and embedding (OLE). By using them and their associated IAs judiciously, you can create some very sophisticated HTML documents. ■

Install and Operate the Word and Excel IAs

Make the IAs available to their respective applications, and invoke them to create HTML documents.

Integrate Excel Data with Word Documents

Bring Excel worksheet ranges into Word documents for subsequent HTML formatting, and link the information so as to keep it current in both locations.

Create Pivot Tables in Excel

Use the special capabilities of pivot tables to extend your presentation options and make data summaries more flexible.

Installing and Running the Internet Assistants

Both the IA for Excel and the IA for Word are add-ins. Add-ins are programs that modify the way Excel and Word work: for example, they typically add capabilities via new options in the applications' menus. Add-ins must be made available to the application that uses them, and you make them available by an installation process. Both the Word and the Excel IA can be installed and uninstalled whenever you wish.

Installing Excel's Internet Assistant

To install Excel's IA, use the Windows Explorer if necessary to determine where you stored it. (Excel's IA is named HTML.XLA.) Then, take the following steps:

1. Start Excel, and choose Tools, Add-Ins. The dialog box shown in Figure 37.1 appears.

2. If you stored HTML.XLA somewhere other than Excel's Library folder, use the Browse button to navigate to its location. When you reach the correct folder, select HTML.XLA and click OK. A new item, Internet Assistant Wizard, appears in the Add-Ins list box.

3. Fill the Internet Assistant Wizard check box, and choose OK.

FIGURE 37.1

It's easiest to locate Excel add-ins if you put them all in the Excel Library folder.

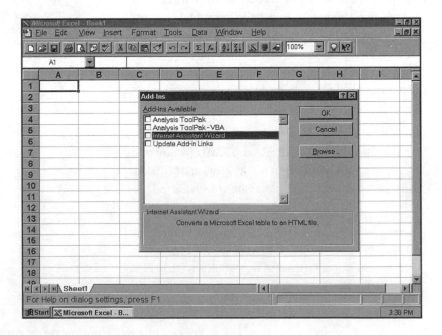

When the Assistant is installed, you will find an Internet Assistant Wizard item in the Tools menu. Selecting this menu item starts the Wizard.

To uninstall the IA, choose Tools, Add-Ins and clear the Assistant's check box.

Installing the Internet Assistant for Word

Word's IA is also an add-in. When you obtain the Word IA, it's usually in an executable file. Double-clicking the file from the Windows Explorer causes several new files to be extracted. The extraction routine stores one of these files, WIAHTM32.WLL, in Word's Startup folder.

When you next start Word, you should see the Glasses button in Word's toolbar area. Clicking the button changes the view to Web Browse, and the button changes to depict a pencil. Click the Pencil button to return to Edit view. See Figure 37.2.

FIGURE 37.2

Word's menus and toolbars change, depending on whether you are in Edit view or Web view.

Glasses button ─

Pencil button ─

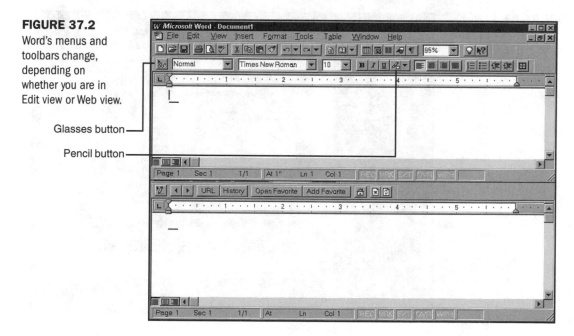

If you see neither of these buttons, choose File, Templates. In the Global Templates and Add-ins box, make sure that WIAHTM32.WLL is checked, and then choose OK.

To uninstall Word's IA, clear the WIAHTM32.WLL check box.

Using the Internet Assistants in Excel and Word

There is very little to using Excel's IA. It is a five-step Wizard, and the choices it offers are quite restricted. Word's IA is more complex, and it's necessary to become familiar with its different menu items and toolbars to use it to best advantage.

Running the Internet Assistant Wizard in Excel

To use Excel's IA, begin by highlighting with your mouse the range of data that you want to convert to HTML format. Then follow these steps:

1. Choose Tools, Internet Assistant Wizard. Step 1 of the Wizard appears, as shown in Figure 37.3. Use this step to adjust the selected range, if necessary. Then, click Next.

FIGURE 37.3
Use the Reference Edit box in Step 1 if you want to extend or reduce your worksheet selection.

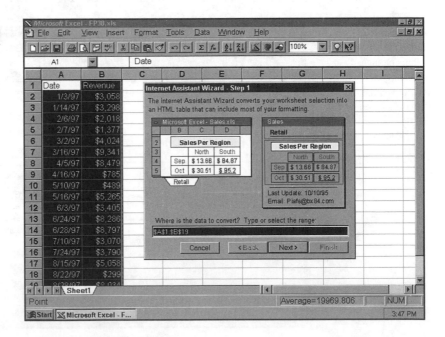

2. In Step 2 of the Wizard, shown in Figure 37.4, you can choose either to create an HTML page with header, table, and footer or to insert the table into an existing HTML document. Because inserting the table requires that you first open and edit a target document, it's recommended that you choose to create a full HTML document. Click Next.

3. Step 3 appears, as in Figure 37.5. Provide whatever title, header, description, update, and name you choose, and insert an e-mail address if you wish. Then click Next.

FIGURE 37.4

Choosing to create an HTML page results in an HTML document that can be viewed with a browser.

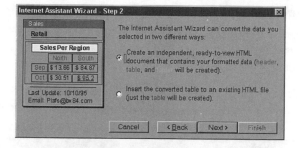

FIGURE 37.5

An e-mail address in the HTML document has functionality only if an e-mail application is available.

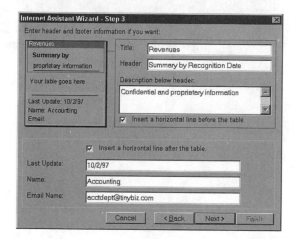

Part VIII

Ch

37

4. In Step 4, choose to convert as much formatting as possible to HTML, or choose to convert the data only. Click Next.

5. In Step 5, indicate a document path and name for the HTML document. Click Finish.

You now have a ready-to-view HTML document saved in the path you specified.

Using the Internet Assistant in Word

Word's IA gives you considerably more control over HTML formatting than does Excel's IA. It is more than just a matter of running a simple wizard: there are menu choices, toolbars, and formatting styles to deal with.

To see the menu items and toolbars that are available with Word's IA, click the Glasses button to switch to Web Browse view. Doing so also gives you access to Help files that are specific to Word's IA.

The typical tasks that you might need to accomplish are discussed in the following sections.

Creating an HTML Document   From Word's File menu, choose New, and click the HTML.DOT document template. In the new document, enter whatever information you wish, including text, graphics, tables, and hyperlinks. Of course, you could also begin by opening an existing Word or text document.

To apply a particular style to an element in the document, select the element and click the Style box drop-down arrow to see the available styles. See Figure 37.6.

FIGURE 37.6
You can select an HTML style from the Style box as shown, or by choosing Format, Style.

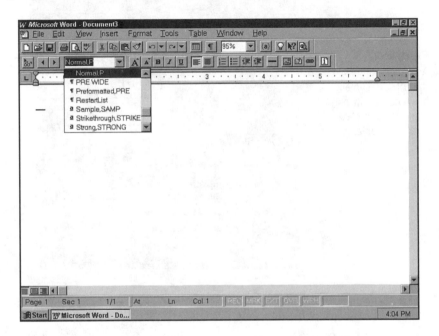

Apply a style in the Style box drop-down list by clicking it. When you have applied the HTML formats to the elements in your document, choose File, Save As. In the Save As dialog box, choose HTML Document from the Save File As Type listbox.

Establishing a Hyperlink to a Local File or to a URL   Type the text or insert the graphic that you want to display as the hyperlink's hotspot. Then, save the active document.

Select the text or graphic, and choose Insert, HyperLink. The Hyperlink dialog box appears, as shown in Figure 37.7.

If you began by selecting text, you can change the displayed text in the Text to Display edit box. Either type the path and name of the destination file in the File or URL box, or use the Browse button to navigate to the file on your computer or your LAN; you can also enter a Web URL.

FIGURE 37.7
If you began by selecting a graphic, the Text to Display edit box is unavailable.

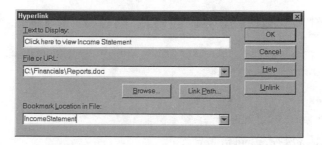

Part
VIII

Ch
37

Convert a relative link path to a fixed file location, or a fixed location to a relative path, by clicking Link Path.

You can also specify a target location in the destination file with the Bookmark Location in the File drop-down list. If the destination file is a Word document, you could specify a bookmark that it contains.

Inserting a Form   Word's IA supports forms with text edit boxes, drop-down lists and check boxes. To insert these form fields into your document, choose Insert, Form Field. The dialog box shown in Figure 37.8 appears.

FIGURE 37.8
Including a Reset button enables the user to abandon the current entries and begin again.

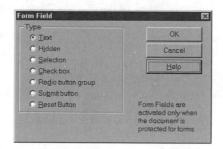

It's easiest to insert these fields into your document by using the Forms toolbar. Click one of the toolbar's buttons to insert a form field, and then drag in your document to establish a location and size for the form field.

When you have finished inserting fields, supply a Submit button in the document for the user to click when the fields have been completed. Finally, click the Protect Form button on the toolbar to prepare it for data entry by its user.

NOTE The IA does not support scripting: that is, you cannot use the IA to write a script that enables the retrieval and storage of information that users supply to your form. Use VBScript or JavaScript for this purpose (see Chapters 20 and 21), or use FrontPage's scripting capabilities. Otherwise, you should check with your system administrator to find out how you can enable data retrieval. ∎

Integrating Excel's IA with Word's IA

The options provided in Excel's IA are quite limited. As you have seen, you can use it to do the following:

- Display cell values in a table
- Insert horizontal rules
- Include a header and footer
- Include an e-mail field

But in addition to tables, rules, headers, and footers, you can use Word's IA to format elements as the following, among many others:

- Hyperlinks and cross-references
- Form fields
- Marquees
- Directory lists

Integrating Excel with Word gives you the best of both applications: Excel's ease of creating tables of values, and the extra capabilities of Word's IA. The next section tells you how.

Embedding Excel Data into Word

Once you have established a range of data in an Excel worksheet, you're in a position to copy the data from the worksheet into a Word document. Follow these steps:

1. Start Word. If you have already created a Word document that will contain the Excel data, open it.

2. Start Excel, and open the workbook that contains the data that you want to convert to HTML format.

3. Select the range of worksheet cells that you want to convert by dragging across them with the mouse pointer.

4. Choose Copy from Excel's Edit menu.

5. Switch to Word. Click in the Word document where you want the Excel data to appear.

6. Choose Paste Special from Word's Edit menu. The dialog box shown in Figure 37.9 appears.

FIGURE 37.9
Paste Special gives you greater control over the way Word treats the pasted object.

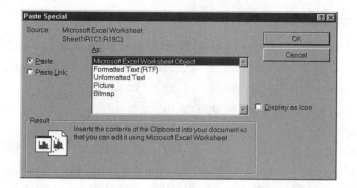

The Paste Special dialog box gives you several options for the format of the data that you paste. In most cases, you will want to choose Microsoft Excel Worksheet Object. If you choose this option, you will later be able to edit the data with Excel's tools by double-clicking the worksheet object.

Another option is Formatted Text. This option means that the object appears in your target document with most of the formatting (fonts, borders, and so on) from the source document. This option is different from the Unformatted Text option, in which the text takes on the default format of the target document.

Once you have pasted the Excel data into the Word document, you can use the capabilities of Word's IA to add the HTML formatting elements that you want.

Linking Excel Data into Word

Another option to consider when you paste Excel data into a Word document is the Paste Link option in the Paste Special dialog box (refer to Figure 37.9). This option is particularly useful if you expect the Excel data to change.

For example, you might be placing an income statement in HTML format on your intranet. So long as the company is profitable, its income statement's numbers change from time to time. You would want any changes to Excel's income statement to be reflected in the Word document.

You can arrange for this direct, live linkage between the Word and Excel documents by choosing the Paste Link option. But HTML documents created by an IA are not live—they're static. You will need to update the HTML document manually, but at least by linking the files you can save the effort of moving data from Excel to Word.

To create the linkage, follow these steps:

1. Choose Paste Link instead of Paste in the Paste Special dialog box. Choose OK.
2. Choose Tools, Options and select the General tab. Ensure that the Update Automatic Links at Open check box is checked.
3. While you still have the Options dialog box open, select the Print tab and make sure the Update Links check box is checked. Choose OK.
4. Choose Edit, Links, select the Automatic option, and choose OK.

Now, whenever you open the Word document, its links to the Excel workbook automatically update to show the most recent information. You need only resave the Word document as an HTML file to ensure that those who view it will see current data.

Creating Pivot Tables in Excel

The principal function of Excel's IA is to convert a range of data in an Excel worksheet to HTML format. If you're not yet familiar with Excel pivot tables, you're missing out on one of Excel's most powerful and flexible capabilities—and, therefore, the HTML representation of the data will not be as useful as it might.

A pivot table is a way to summarize long, detailed lists of data. Figure 37.10 contains an example of a pivot table and its underlying data.

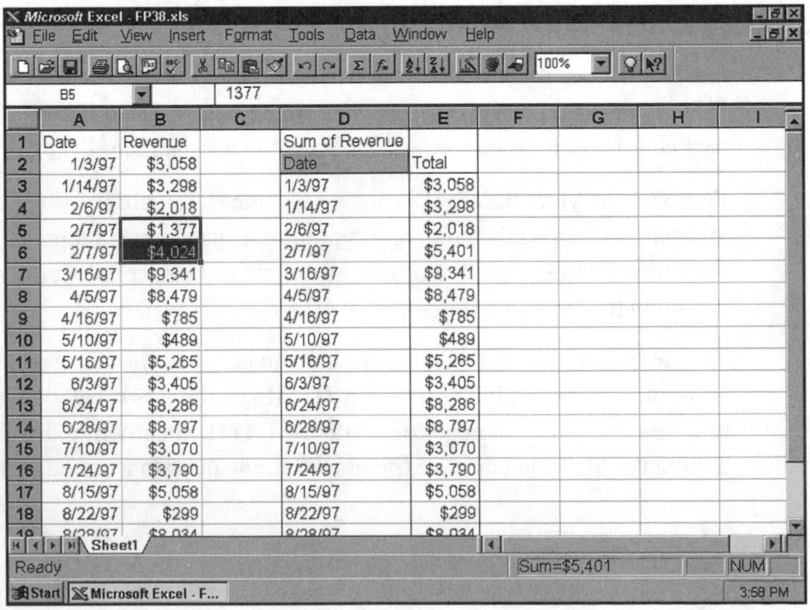

	A	B	C	D	E
1	Date	Revenue		Sum of Revenue	
2	1/3/97	$3,058		Date	Total
3	1/14/97	$3,298		1/3/97	$3,058
4	2/6/97	$2,018		1/14/97	$3,298
5	2/7/97	$1,377		2/6/97	$2,018
6	2/7/97	$4,024		2/7/97	$5,401
7	3/16/97	$9,341		3/16/97	$9,341
8	4/5/97	$8,479		4/5/97	$8,479
9	4/16/97	$785		4/16/97	$785
10	5/10/97	$489		5/10/97	$489
11	5/16/97	$5,265		5/16/97	$5,265
12	6/3/97	$3,405		6/3/97	$3,405
13	6/24/97	$8,286		6/24/97	$8,286
14	6/28/97	$8,797		6/28/97	$8,797
15	7/10/97	$3,070		7/10/97	$3,070
16	7/24/97	$3,790		7/24/97	$3,790
17	8/15/97	$5,058		8/15/97	$5,058
18	8/22/97	$299		8/22/97	$299

FIGURE 37.10
Identical values in the Date column are combined in the pivot table.

Notice in Figure 37.10 that the list, in columns A and B, contains the dates on which a company earned its revenue. In the pivot table, the revenue is totalled for each month. Also notice that multiple entries in the list are combined into one entry in the pivot table: for example, the entries for 2/7/97. To create this pivot table, follow these steps:

1. Select any cell in the list.

2. Select Data, PivotTable. The PivotTable Wizard starts.

3. In Step 1, confirm that the data source is a Microsoft Excel list or database. Click Next.

4. In Step 2, confirm or edit the address of the worksheet range that contains the list. Click Next.

5. In Step 3, drag the Date button into the Row area, and drag the Revenue button into the Data area.

6. While you are still in Step 3, double-click the Revenue button in the Data area. In the PivotTable Field dialog box, click Number. Choose a currency format, and choose OK. Click OK to exit the PivotTable field dialog box, and click Next.

7. In Step 4, enter the address of the cell where you want the pivot table to begin in the PivotTable Starting Cell edit box. Click Finish.

The pivot table appears, as shown in Figure 37.10 above.

Once you have created a pivot table, you can modify its characteristics very easily. For example, if you decided that you wanted the different dates to occupy columns instead of rows, you would click and drag the Date button on the pivot table to the right. When you release the mouse button, you find that the pivot table has been reoriented.

Another very useful aspect of pivot tables is the ability to group their control variable (in this example, the control variable is Date). Suppose that you wanted to show total revenue for each month rather than each day in the underlying list. Follow these steps:

1. Select any cell containing a date in the pivot table's Date column.

2. Choose Data, Group and Outline. Select Group from the cascading menu. The dialog box shown in Figure 37.11 appears.

3. Choose Month in the By list box, and choose OK.

The pivot table's Date field changes to show the revenue total for each month, rather than for each day. You could also choose, say, Month *and* Quarter in the By list box. So doing would cause the pivot table to employ two control variables: Quarter, and Month within Quarter.

FIGURE 37.11

In HTML documents, brief summaries are usually more informative than lengthy, detailed lists.

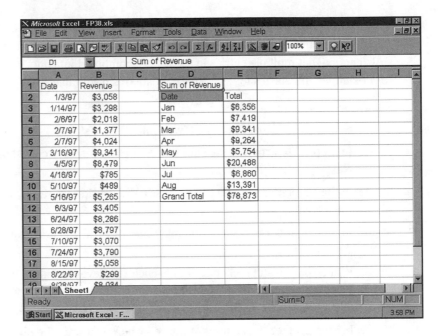

To convert the pivot table to HTML format, just select the table by dragging across it with the mouse pointer, and choose Tools, Internet Assistant Wizard. Or select and copy the pivot table, and then paste it into a Word document to use Word's IA.

As noted at the beginning of this section, pivot tables are extremely powerful. Therefore, there are many choices involved in structuring them—too many to describe here. To become more familiar with the capabilities of pivot tables, you'll need to experiment with them. A few possibilities you might consider include the following:

- Add another control variable as a pivot table column. Extending the present example, you might include Region to show total revenue by both region and date.

- Show the data field (here, Revenue) as a percent of total. In the PivotTable Field dialog box, click Options. Then select Percent of Total in the Show Data As drop-down list.

- Show the data field with some other subtotal function, such as Count or Average. Or drag the data field's button into the Data area twice—then you can show the data two different ways in the same pivot table.

## CHAPTER 38

Using Internet Assistant for Word, Access, and Schedule+ with FrontPage

Schedule+ enables you to set different permission levels as to the availability of your Schedule+ files. You can, for example, enable an assistant to maintain your schedule on your behalf, or a colleague to view your schedule without the ability to modify it. While convenient, Schedule+ permissions assume that these co-workers have the necessary connectivity to the location of your Schedule+ files. By exporting your Appointment Book in HTML format, and posting it to a Web server, you can broaden the availability of your schedule.

Similarly, Access supports different permission levels for different users. But Access databases, particularly in a corporation, are likely to contain sensitive, proprietary information that must be kept inaccessible to prying eyes, both inside and outside the company. By using the Access IA, you can publish on a Web server any information—product lists, for example, or the

Installation procedures

You learn how to install the IAs for Schedule+ and Access, and to identify and understand the purpose of files that accompany the IAs.

Running the Schedule+ IA

The Schedule+ IA enables you to create HTML files that display your Schedule+ Appointment Book. Maintaining your privacy is important when you publish your appointments on a Web server, and you learn the privacy implications of different choices you make when you run the Schedule+ IA.

Running the Access IA

You can convert Access tables, queries, forms and reports to HTML format with the Access IA. It's useful to understand how to use the different HTML templates that accompany the Access IA, and important to know how to avoid problems when you create the HTML versions of Access Forms.

current standings in sales contests—that is fit for public consumption, and yet keep safe in the Access database the information that must stay hidden. ■

Installing the Access and Schedule+ Internet Assistants

The IAs for Access and Schedule+ are available via download from the Web at www.microsoft.com/msdownload/. You can also obtain them from other sources such as Microsoft Technet.

At the time of this writing, the most recent IA for Schedule+ was still termed a beta version: Internet Assistant Beta 2 for Schedule+. If you have obtained a more recent version, you might encounter discrepancies between the information in this chapter and your version of the Schedule+ IA.

Installing the Schedule+ IA

The Schedule+ IA is packaged in a file named Schia.exe. To install the IA, have the Schedule+ application installed on your computer, but close Schedule+ if it is running. From the Explorer, double-click the Schia.exe file. There are no questions for you to answer or options for you to choose. When Schia.exe has finished, the IA for Schedule+ is installed.

A text file, Schpost.txt, is placed in your Windows folder. This file, which you can read with any text editor or word processor, contains recent information about the IA. The Beta 2 IA does not offer complete functionality. In particular, there is a Post to Web function that's intended to enable you to post the output HTML file (called "schedule.htm") to a Web server. Although the installation process places the associated menu item in the Schedule+ menu, the capability is not implemented in Beta 2.

To uninstall the Schedule+ IA, use Add/Remove Programs in the Control Panel. Click the Windows Taskbar Start button, choose Settings, and select Control Panel from the cascading menu. In the Control Panel window, double-click Add/Remove Programs. Select Microsoft Schedule+ Internet Assistant (Remove Only) from the list box, and choose Add/Remove.

Installing the Access IA

Installing the Access IA is only slightly more complicated than installing the Schedule+ IA. Have Access installed, but not running, when you double-click the Access IA's installation program (named IA95.exe).

The installation process starts the familiar Setup routine. You will be asked to confirm that you want to install the Access IA, and that you accept the terms and conditions of the end user license agreement. Then, a Setup message box appears with an Install button. After you click the button, the required files are made available to Access. All that's necessary now is to start Access.

To uninstall the Access IA, follow the same Add/Remove Programs procedure as for the Schedule+ IA (see the prior section, Installing the Schedule+ IA).

Running the Schedule+ IA

FIGURE 38.1

When you choose to publish *times and descriptions*, the Include Private appointments checkbox becomes enabled.

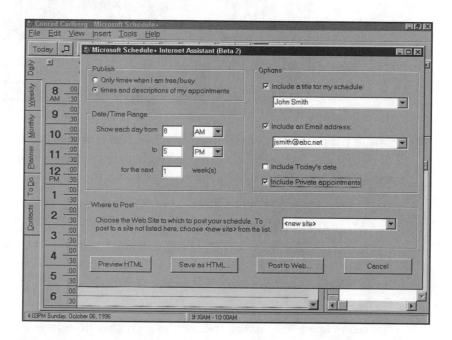

After you have installed the Schedule+ IA, a new item, Internet Assistant, appears in the Schedule+ File menu. When you choose File, Internet Assistant, the dialog box shown in Figure 38.1 appears.

The dialog box, as shown in Figure 38.1, includes all the options that are available to you in the Schedule+ IA. These options have the effects that are described below.

Publishing Schedule+ Items

In the Schedule+ IA dialog box, you choose between displaying whether you are free or busy at each date and time, or displaying the appointment descriptions for each date and

FIGURE 38.2
Choosing to publish
times only suppresses
details that you might
want to keep private in
the HTML output.

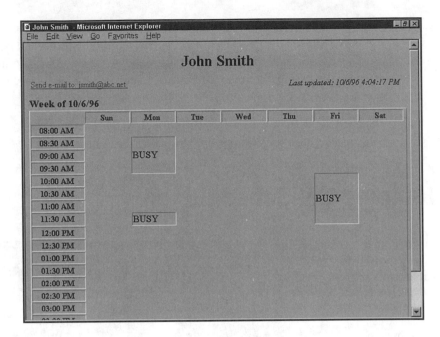

time. If you choose Only times when I am free/busy, the resulting HTML shows the word "Busy" for any day and time that you have scheduled an appointment. Otherwise, that day and time is blank in the HTML. Figure 38.2 displays the result of choosing this option.

You would, of course, choose the times-only option if you wanted to keep information about what you're up to from appearing in the HTML file—all it shows is that you're busy.

If you choose times and descriptions of my appointments, the HTML shows the appointment description. The description shown is the one that's entered in the Appointment Book, not the description that's in the associated To-Do entry. Figure 38.3 illustrates this distinction.

Notice in Figure 38.3 that the To-Do list's description for October 11 shows an appointment with a doctor. The Appointment Book merely indicates that the user will be off-site from 10:00 a.m. until noon, and it is this description that appears in the HTML file.

Specifying a Date/Time Range

Use the Date/Time group box in the Schedule+ IA's dialog box (refer to Figure 38.1) to specify which hours of each day are displayed in the HTML file, and how many weeks ahead to display. The more hours you choose, the longer the file—there is one table row for each hour. And, of course, the more weeks you specify, the longer the file.

VIII

Ch

38

FIGURE 38.3

The HTML will show "Off-site," not "Doctor's appointment".

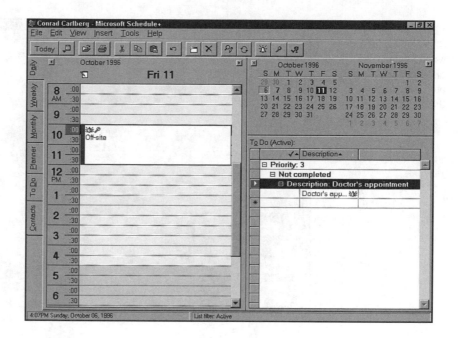

 TIP On occasion, you might see this error message: `Error updating file C:\Windows\Schedule.htm! You may need to reinstall.` If you do, before you reinstall the IA make sure that you have entered a valid range of times of day. In Beta 2, you would receive this message if you specify, say, 8 a.m. as both a from time and as a to time.

Figure 38.4 shows how the HTML file appears if you display 8:00 a.m. to 10:00 a.m., and how it appears if you display 8:00 a.m. to 12:00 p.m.

 TIP Keep in mind that Schedule+ and its IA both treat 12:00 p.m. as noon, and 12:00 a.m. as midnight.

Setting Other Options

Fill the Include a title for my schedule checkbox if you want the HTML file to have a title. This is a convenient way to display your name in the file, so users who are browsing it can easily determine whose schedule they are looking at.

If your email address makes your identity self-evident, you could save a small amount of file space and a useful amount of screen space by omitting the title. Fill the Include an Email address checkbox to put a mailto tag in the HTML file.

FIGURE 38.4
Choosing 10:00 a.m.
as an ending time
displays appointments
beginning through
9:30 a.m.

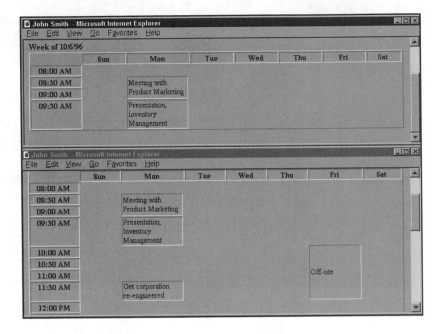

The Beta 2 version of the Schedule+ IA associates no functionality with the Include Today's date checkbox.

Clearing the Include Private appointments checkbox is a useful way to suppress the details of any appointments that you might have flagged as Private. To make an appointment Private, select the appointment and choose Edit, Private—or, press Ctrl+Shift+P.

If you have cleared the Include Private appointments checkbox, any private appointments are displayed as "Busy" in the HTML file. This is a good way to arrange to display the appointment description for most appointments.

Recall that you can choose to show either the times that you are busy, or a description of a given appointment (refer to Figure 38.3). If you show busy times only, no appointment descriptions are given. But if you choose to show appointment descriptions, you can still clear the Include Private appointments checkbox to suppress the descriptions of private appointments.

Completing the Schedule+ IA Dialog Box

When you have made your choices in the IA dialog box, choose either Preview HTML or Save as HTML. As noted at the beginning of this chapter, Beta 2 of the IA does not enable you automatically to post a schedule directly to a Web server. Rather than using the Post to Web button, it's necessary to post the schedule manually.

Choose the Preview HTML button to save the HTML in a file named schedule.htm. Beta 2 of the IA saves the file in your Windows folder. The IA then invokes your Web Browser so that you can view the output file. This means, of course, that you must have a Web browser installed on your computer.

After previewing the output, make any changes you want to the options you have chosen. Then, choose the Save as HTML button to save the output HTML file. A standard Save As dialog box appears, enabling you to name the file and navigate to the folder where you want to save it. After saving the file, provide it to your Web administrator so that it can be posted to the appropriate Web server.

Running the Access IA

After you have installed the IA for Access, invoke it by choosing Tools, Add Ins, and choose Internet Assistant from the cascading menu. You need to have a database open before the Add Ins menu item is available. This section demonstrates the use of the IA by means of the Northwind Traders sample database that accompanies Access.

The Access IA works by means of a four-step wizard—a sequence of dialog boxes where you specify your options. The steps you take to complete the wizard are the same regardless of the type of information that you want to output.

When you choose Tools, Add Ins, Internet Assistant, a welcome screen identifying the IA appears. There is no user input for you to enter; choose Next. The next step appears as shown in Figure 38.5.

FIGURE 38.5
The Next and Finish buttons become available when you have chosen at least one Object Name.

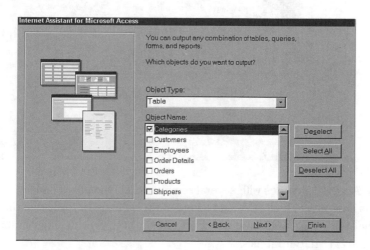

The step shown in Figure 38.5 is how you specify the information that you want to output to HTML format. It is a complex step, and this chapter covers it in greater detail in the next section, "Specifying the Access Output." For now, notice two aspects of the dialog box:

■ The Object Type drop-down list box. Table is the currently selected object type, but the drop-down list box enables you also to select Query, Form, Report, and All. These are not mutually exclusive choices: for example, you can decide to output both queries and forms during the same instance of the IA.

■ The Object Name list box. Because Table is the currently selected object type, the names of the tables defined for the database appear in the list box. If *Query* were the selected object type, the names of all defined queries would appear in the Object Name list box.

Any tables, queries, forms or reports that you have created in the database are accessible by means of the combination of the Object Type drop-down list box and the Object Name list box.

When you have selected an object name, click Next. (You could also click Finish to accept the defaults for remaining options and complete the wizard.) The next step appears as shown in Figure 38.6.

FIGURE 38.6
In this step you can choose an existing template or elect to use no template.

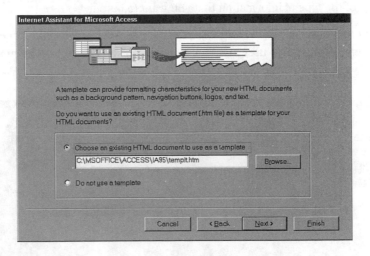

The Access IA comes with several templates. The default template, named templt.htm, adds little more than a title and a logo to the database information that the IA outputs. Other templates, such as stones.htm and sky.htm, provide different background patterns for the HTML output files.

Each template that accompanies the Access IA has another version, identified by an underscore and the letter "r" (for *report*): an example is templt_r.htm. These report templates provide linked hypertext to enable the user to go to the Next, Previous, First, and Final pages.

Each template also places the Access logo (named msaccess.jpg, and supplied with the IA) at the bottom of each HTML page. If you want to display a different logo on the HTML output, change the reference to msaccess.jpg in the templates to the name of some other graphic file. Then, store that graphic file in the same folder that contains the templates.

If, in the wizard's second step, you choose the Report Object Type, the IA automatically uses a report template, with the linked hypertext. Suppose that you decide to output both a table and a report, and specify templt.htm as the template. The IA uses templt.htm for the table output, and templt_r.htm for the report output. When a report template is used, the HTML file includes the linked hypertext to navigate from page to page even if the IA creates only one page.

When you have made your template choice in this step, click Next. The final step, shown in Figure 38.7, appears.

FIGURE 38.7
All you need do in this step is specify a location for the output HTML files.

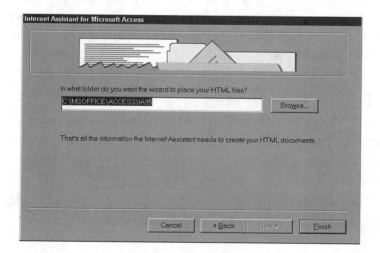

If you click the Browse button, a dialog box named *HTML documents folder* enables you to navigate to the site where you want to store the output. Once you have identified a site for the HTML files, click Finish.

T I P If you decide to save the HTML files in a different location than is proposed by the IA, be sure to put a JPEG-format file named msaccess.jpg in the destination folder. Otherwise, the HTML output displays a missing file placeholder instead of the logo.

When you click Finish, a message box appears and keeps you posted on the IA's progress if your output contains multiple pages. A counter shows which output page is being built. This is a convenient way to tell how many pages each HTML file contains. There is at least one file for each object type that you selected, and an object type that contains page breaks results in multiple files—one per page.

N O T E If you create, in the same folder, more than one file based on the same object name, the Access IA gives the files an incremental index. For example, three HTML files based on the Employees table would be named Employees.htm, Employees1.htm and Employees2.htm. ■

Specifying the Access Output

Here's a closer look at how the Access IA wizard's second step works. In the second step, you choose the type of database object—table, query, form, or report—as the basis for the HTML files. The resulting HTML files differ according to the choice you made in the wizard's second step.

Selecting a Table for Output

Suppose that you choose to output the contents of a database table, and the table you want is the Northwind database's Customers table. In the second step, you would select Table from the Object Type drop-down list box, and you would fill the Customers checkbox in the Object Name list box. Figure 38.8 shows a portion of the resulting HTML file.

Because the default template, templt.htm, was used in Figure 38.8, the HTML file contains no hyperlinks: just the table itself and the Access logo.

FIGURE 38.8
The Access IA presents the information from an Access table in a simple table format.

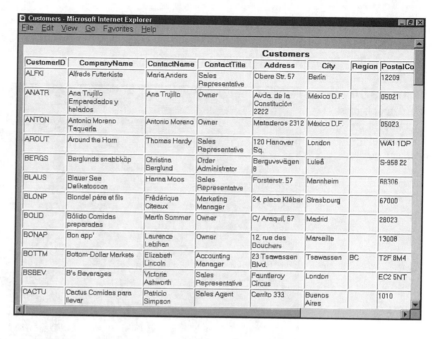

Selecting a Query for Output

Now, suppose that after you filled the checkbox for the Customers table, you then selected Query from the Object Type drop-down list box and Quarterly Orders by Product from the Object Name list box, as shown in Figure 38.9.

FIGURE 38.9
Choosing to output a Query often invokes the relational database's table linking capability.

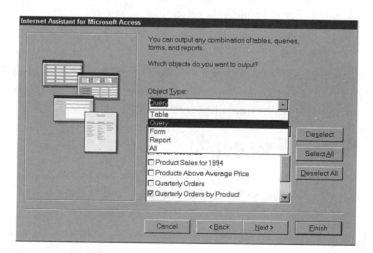

When you click Finish, the Access IA outputs the two files that you specified: one for the Customers table, and one for the crosstab query Quarterly Orders by Product. A portion of the Query output is shown in Figure 38.10.

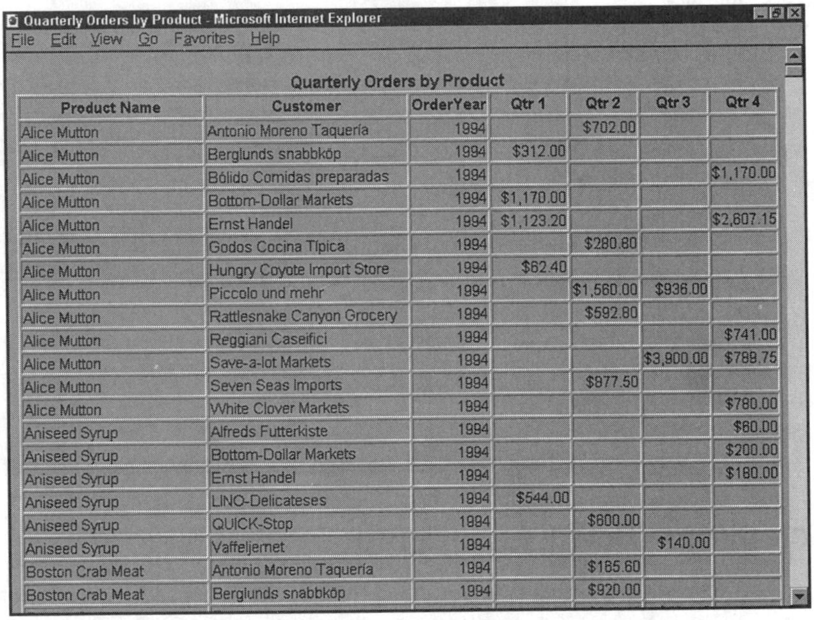

FIGURE 38.10

HTML output is most useful when it provides summaries of the underlying details.

Quarterly Orders by Product

Product Name	Customer	OrderYear	Qtr 1	Qtr 2	Qtr 3	Qtr 4
Alice Mutton	Antonio Moreno Taqueria	1994		$702.00		
Alice Mutton	Berglunds snabbköp	1994	$312.00			
Alice Mutton	Bólido Comidas preparadas	1994				$1,170.00
Alice Mutton	Bottom-Dollar Markets	1994	$1,170.00			
Alice Mutton	Ernst Handel	1994	$1,123.20			$2,607.15
Alice Mutton	Godos Cocina Típica	1994		$280.80		
Alice Mutton	Hungry Coyote Import Store	1994	$62.40			
Alice Mutton	Piccolo und mehr	1994		$1,560.00	$936.00	
Alice Mutton	Rattlesnake Canyon Grocery	1994		$592.80		
Alice Mutton	Reggiani Caseifici	1994				$741.00
Alice Mutton	Save-a-lot Markets	1994			$3,900.00	$789.75
Alice Mutton	Seven Seas Imports	1994		$877.50		
Alice Mutton	White Clover Markets	1994				$780.00
Aniseed Syrup	Alfreds Futterkiste	1994				$60.00
Aniseed Syrup	Bottom-Dollar Markets	1994				$200.00
Aniseed Syrup	Ernst Handel	1994				$180.00
Aniseed Syrup	LINO-Delicateses	1994	$544.00			
Aniseed Syrup	QUICK-Stop	1994		$600.00		
Aniseed Syrup	Vaffeljernet	1994			$140.00	
Boston Crab Meat	Antonio Moreno Taqueria	1994		$185.60		
Boston Crab Meat	Berglunds snabbköp	1994		$920.00		

Notice in Figure 38.10 that the conditions set up by the query are maintained in the HTML output. For example, this domain aggregate function:

```
ProductAmount: Sum(CCur([Order Details].[UnitPrice]*[Quantity]*
(1-[Discount])/100)*100)
```

is used in the Quarterly Orders by Product query to calculate the order value of each record in the Order Details table. The resulting values are then summarized, in crosstab fashion, by Product, by Customer, by Year and by Quarter.

Selecting a Report for Output

If you were to choose Report in the Object Type drop-down list box, and Employee Sales by Country in the Object Name list box, you would observe two differences in the IA's behavior:

- When the output process begins, you see two input boxes: one for you to enter a beginning date, and one to enter an ending date. These are in response to the requirements of the Employee Sales by Country report's design. This report uses a dialog form to request that the user specify the date criteria that the report should use to select the desired records.

■ The report design calls for page headers and footers. When the report generates a new page, the IA closes the current HTML file and begins another. You will see a progress report on your screen as each new file is created. Because the Object Type is a report, the IA uses a report template. Report templates add hyperlink text to the HTML files so that the user can navigate through the pages. See Figure 38.11.

FIGURE 38.11

Consider replacing the Microsoft Access logo with one that represents your own firm.

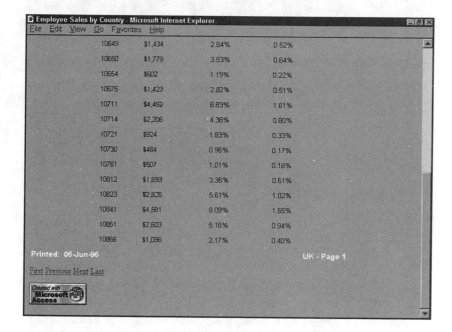

Employee Sales by Country - Microsoft Internet Explorer			
File Edit View Go Favorites Help			
10649	$1,434	2.84%	0.52%
10650	$1,779	3.53%	0.64%
10654	$602	1.19%	0.22%
10675	$1,423	2.82%	0.51%
10711	$4,452	8.83%	1.61%
10714	$2,206	4.38%	0.80%
10721	$924	1.83%	0.33%
10730	$484	0.96%	0.17%
10761	$507	1.01%	0.18%
10812	$1,693	3.36%	0.61%
10823	$2,826	5.61%	1.02%
10841	$4,581	9.09%	1.65%
10851	$2,603	5.16%	0.94%
10866	$1,096	2.17%	0.40%

Printed: 06-Jun-96   UK - Page 1

First Previous Next Last

TIP

If you find it inconvenient to move back and forth between the Object Type drop-down list box and the Object Name list box, begin by choosing All from the Object Type drop-down list box. Then, the Object Name list box will include each of the tables, queries, forms and reports available in the database. Just fill the checkboxes associated with each object that you want to export to an HTML file.

The most visually complex HTML output usually results from exporting a report object type. Notice the special formatting in Figure 38.12, which illustrates the output of the Invoice report in the Northwind sample database. The HTML file employs the fonts and patterns that the designer used to create the report.

VIII

Ch

38

FIGURE 38.12

Use Access reports to create visually interesting formats, such as italics and reverse font colors.

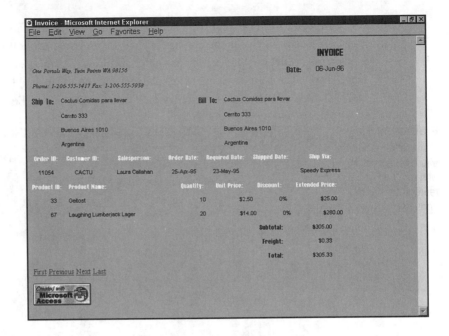

Although the Access IA can handle a report's fonts and patterns, it does not output certain special elements—lines and control borders, for example, or charts and pivot tables created in Excel—that you might have included in your database design and contents.

For example, the Northwind database includes bitmap pictures of the company employees. Although HTML output based on a database element that includes the picture field contains a placeholder for the picture, the pictures themselves are not output. You can, however, modify the resulting HTML to reference the associated bitmap files.

Selecting a Form for Output

Some care is needed when you decide to convert an Access Form to HTML format. Some of the forms contain no information, and the resulting HTML files therefore include nothing of value.

The Northwind sample database includes, among others, forms named Customer Labels Dialog, Sales by Year Dialog, and Sales Reports Dialog. If you choose to convert any of these to HTML format, the IA will report successful completion. But when you open the HTML file, you find nothing of interest. This is because these forms are used by other elements in the database that *do* contain information.

For example, to use the Sales by Year Dialog you must be previewing or printing the Sales by Year Report. You are alerted to this if you run the Sales by Year Dialog in Access—but not if you are attempting to output the Sales by Year Dialog with the Access IA.

Similarly, if you attempt to output the Sales Analysis form, you obtain an HTML page with nothing but the logo shown. The Sales Analysis form is an Excel pivot table, and, as noted above, the Access IA cannot output pivot tables. (In this case, you would use the Excel IA to obtain HTML output of the pivot table.)

If you try to create HTML files from Access forms, then, be sure that you know what's in the form. Using the Access IA to create HTML output willy-nilly is liable to create meaningless files.

VIII

Ch

38

Using Other Servers with FrontPage

## CHAPTER 39

Using FrontPage with Microsoft Internet Information Server

While the number of Web servers on the market has gone from just a few less than two years ago to over a hundred now, Microsoft has gone to great lengths to become a leader in the field of Web servers.

While the FrontPage Personal Web Server as well as the Microsoft Personal Web Server will work well for a number of Webs, Microsoft Internet Information Server is for you heavier-weights out there.

Internet Information Server is an inexpensive, yet very powerful alternative to expensive Web servers. By bundling the Internet Information Server with NT 4.0 Server and Workstation, Microsoft has raised the level on which Web server expectations are created. They have put a complete Web-serving solution in the hands of anyone who can author one line of HTML. ■

The Microsoft Internet Information Server

The Microsoft Internet Information Server is compatible with FrontPage through server-side extensions.

Download the Internet Information Server

Download the right version for your machine.

Install the FrontPage Extensions

Server extensions extend the ability of your FrontPage Webs to utilize Web bots on a robust server.

Administer the Internet Information Server

Configure IIS to work the way you need it to.

Control IIS remotely via the WWW

Adjust Web settings and monitor activity in the Internet Service Manager across the Internet.

Up and Running with the Internet Information Server

The Personal Web Server included with FrontPage is great for sending out a few documents a day to the world or your friends. But what if you needed to serve hundreds of thousands of requests a day while still retaining all of your FrontPage specific features like the Web bots? Enter the Microsoft Internet Information Server.

In early 1996, Microsoft announced the release of the Internet Information Sever 1.0. What caught the world by surprise was the fact that the new Web server would be absolutely free and available for downloading from the Internet. The Internet Information Server promised ease of use, advanced security features, and scalability between multiple servers and across a network. While the server software only runs in Windows NT Server, it provides a cheaper alternative to other Web server software ranging from $500.00 to $5000.00 in price.

Some of the highlights of the Internet Information Server are as follows:

> Tight integration with NT's security model and directory system
>
> Configurable TCP/IP Port
>
> Integration with SNMP administration tools
>
> Programming deployment with ISAPI
>
> Database integration with IDC / HTX
>
> System monitoring capabilities with the Performance Monitor
>
> Capable of SSL security

The release of IIS 2.0 for Windows NT 4.0 adds the following features:

> HTML-based administration from any browser
>
> 40% gain in speed over version 1.0
>
> The Microsoft Index Server for indexing your Web content easily
>
> The installation is integrated into the NT 4.0 installation routine
>
> FrontPage and the FrontPage extensions are included in Windows NT Server 4.0

Microsoft has gone to great lengths to become a leader in the field of Web servers. By providing an alternative to expensive Web servers, Microsoft has raised the level on which Web server expectations are created. Bundling the Internet Information Server with NT 4.0 Sever and Workstation puts a complete Web serving solution in the hands of everyone who can author one line of HTML.

Obtaining and Installing the Server

The Internet Information Server is available in 1.0 form for Windows NT Server 3.51 at **http://www.microsoft.com/Infoserv/IISInfo.htm**. The Web server can be downloaded at no cost, other than accrued time spent online. You must also download the latest service pack (currently Service Pack 5) from **ftp://ftp.microsoft.com/bussys/winnt/ winnt-public/fixes/usa/nt351/ussp5/**. IIS and the newest service pack can easily be a 10M download. But the cost associated with downloading such a product far outweighs the cost of buying an off-the-shelf Web server (see Figure 39.1).

FIGURE 39.1

Downloading Microsoft's Internet Information Server is much more cost effective than purchasing an alternative Web server.

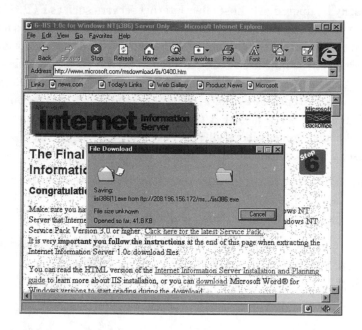

Internet Information Server 2.0, like FrontPage, is built into the Windows NT Server 4.0 operating system. You will find the option to install the server software when you install Windows NT onto your system, or by adding the component under Network in Control Panel.

Once the installation process begins, you will be asked for the directories where you want your Web and Gopher files kept. When the program is finished installing, you will have a new group set up called Internet Information Server where you can access the Internet Service Manager and product documentation.

A special note to Windows NT Workstation 4.0 users. The Internet Information Server is also integrated into NT Workstation. Microsoft refers to the server as Peer Web Services and gears the product towards corporate Intranets, or anywhere that information needs to

Part
IX

Ch

39

be served from in a small-scale environment. All of the functionality of the Internet Information Server is included with Peer Web Services, though it is not as optimized for file throughput as machines running NT Server. In fact, even advanced features such as Web-based administration and remote use of the Internet Service Manager through Windows 95 are included.

Installing the FrontPage Extensions

Microsoft created the Internet Information Server with extensibility in mind. The server can easily be upgraded to host other Internet servers such as FTP, Gopher, and the new suite of Normandy Internet servers. One of the first add-on releases for the Internet Information Server was the FrontPage Web bot extensions. These extensions allow for all of FrontPage's Web bots to be scaled to a robust Web server, and retain all of their functionality. FrontPage's extensions also allow for remote uploading of Web content to a secure NT Server. A FrontPage author must have Administrator permissions on the NT Server before the files can be uploaded. Once the user submits his username and password, the authentication process checks the user's identity against the User Manager and will reject any user that does not have an existing account.

You must have FrontPage installed onto your desired Web server, as well as the FrontPage extensions to use with the Internet Information Server. To install the FrontPage extensions for IIS:

1. Run the file "setup.exe" from the FrontPage CD-ROM or diskettes.
2. Choose Custom Setup from the Setup Types dialogue box.
3. Place a check in the box next to Server Extensions.
4. Click OK to install the Server Extensions.

If you are only installing the FrontPage extensions, the installation process will be very brief. Once installed, the Server Administrator will start, displaying the installed ports that the FrontPage extensions reside in, as well as giving you options for setting up security for authoring and adding extensions to new FrontPage Webs (see Figure 39.2).

FIGURE 39.2

The FrontPage Administrator allows you to control the FrontPage extensions on your Web server and set security permissions.

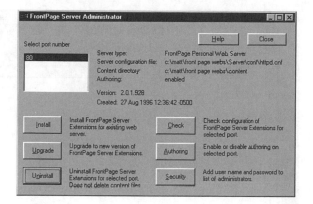

The Server Administrator will always show Port 80 as your default Web address. This essentially means that the base IP address for your machine has the FrontPage extensions loaded on the Web server found at Port 80. If the machine has multiple IP addresses assigned to the Network card, you will see additional addresses below Port 80. Additional IP addresses can be added to your server in Network found in Control Panel. By default, Windows NT can hold up to five separate IP addresses and bind them to one card. In actuality, hundreds of IP addresses can be bound to the network card through editing of the System Registry. Documentation for adding IP addresses to the System Registry can be found at Microsoft's Knowledge Base at http://www.microsoft.com/kb/bussys/winnt/q149426.htm. Do not change any System Registry settings unless you know exactly what you are doing. One minor change to the Registry can cause a system to fail to start when rebooted.

When the server extensions are installed, FrontPage adds the folders "_private", "_vti_bin", "_vti_log", "_vti_pvt", and "cgi-bin" under the root folder of your Web. It is recommended that you do not modify this directory structure, or any of the files contained within. These directories and their respective files are used for the FrontPage extensions and for security settings. If any of these files or directories are modified, it can lead to server instability.

Configuring the Internet Information Server

The Internet Information Server is configured through the Internet Service Manager. The Internet Service Manager holds all of the Microsoft Internet server components, including WWW, FTP, and Gopher (see Figure 39.3). This centralized way of containing the different servers provides a uniform way of running services, monitoring servers, and configuring the different options.

Part IX
Ch
39

FIGURE 39.3
The Internet Service Manager controls every aspect of the Internet servers installed on your local machine and across the network.

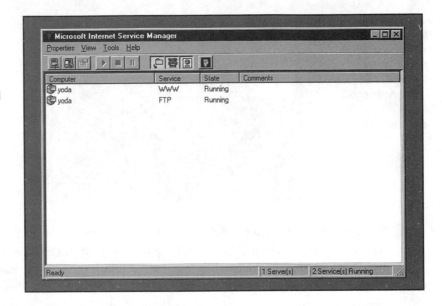

All of your Internet services should be currently running. If not, highlight the server that you wish to start and click the Start Service button on the toolbar at the top of the Internet Service Manager.

To administer the WWW server component, begin by double-clicking the WWW Service. The WWW Service Properties for your machine will open, allowing you to administer changes on your Web server (see Figure 39.4).

FIGURE 39.4
The WWW Service Properties allow you to modify default settings in IIS to fit your Web-serving needs.

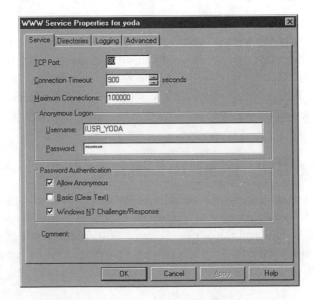

The Service Properties window contains tabs for each of the configuration screens, Service, Directories, Login, and Advanced. Examining each of these screens in more detail will help you gain a better understanding of the customizable functions.

The Service Window

The Service window is made up of two main components, connection settings and access authentication. The connection settings determine which port the Web server is running on, as well as limits for connection times and maximum connections. The access authentication settings allow you to specify which system account will be used for anonymous access, and which type of authentication schemes to use.

Connection Settings   The TCP Port is normally set to Port 80, the standard Port for HTTP. You can change the port number, though standard settings arc generally fine. You will have to restart your server after modifying port changes.

Connection Timeout refers to the amount of time that the server will wait until it disconnects a connected user with no activity. Though the HTTP protocol generally closes the TCP/IP connection after the requested document is served, the connection timeout ensures that all clients will be disconnected if the protocol fails to close properly.

Maximum connections place a limit on the number of connections that the Web server will try to serve simultaneously. If you have a high-volume Web site, placing limits on maximum connections can help to stabilize the server in case it encounters too many requests for information. Monitoring the memory and processor usage with the Performance Monitor will help you judge the number of simultaneous users your Web server can handle.

Access Authentication   By default, the Anonymous user uses an account set up in the User Manager called IUSR_computername. This account was generated a random password upon installation and must be changed in the User Manager as well as in the Internet Service Manager. If you choose to restrict access to your Web server, you do so by adding a different account into the Anonymous Logon region. Note that if you restrict access, it restricts users globally, and only those users who know the Username and Password of the WWW account will be allowed access. Restricting access to only a portion of your Web site is obtained through the FrontPage Explorer's Security features, or by changing the access rights for a directory in Explorer or File Manager.

Choose the correct authentication process under Password Authentication. It you allow anonymous users, there will be no authentication. Basic authentication can be used by most browsers, and should be implemented when you wish to restrict access other than by NT's built in security mechanisms. Windows NT Challenge / Response should be used when directories of files from the Web site have been restricted to accounts in the NT Domain. All NT Challenge / Response logons are encrypted and therefore kept protected from hackers. You must choose at least one type of Authentication to allow users to log onto your Web site.

The Comments line allows you to enter a description of your Web server that will appear next to the service's name within the Internet Service Manager.

The Directories Window

The Directories Window contains settings for mapping directories to the Web, setting directory permissions, and general Web server properties (see Figure 39.5).

FIGURE 39.5
The Directories Window maps out file system directories that will be accessed by Internet visitors.

The Directory Listing Box   In the Directory listing box, a mapped directory is shown next to its Web alias. For example, if you had an area on your Web called Technical Support, you could map a directory called c:\techsup to an alias called "/techsup". This would make it possible for a user to type in the name of your Web server followed by the Web alias and reach the Technical Support area (ex. **http://www.yourserver/techsup/**).

To install a new Web alias, begin by clicking the Add button.

1. Choose the Browse button to search your file system for the correct directory that you wish to alias. Click OK to make your selection.

2. Choose Virtual Directory to enter an alias.

3. Determine whether the directory needs executable access for CGI scripts and make the appropriate choice.

4. Choose OK to complete the aliasing process.

It is also possible to map a directory to a virtual IP address. This is useful when you wish to host multiple domains on your Web server, instead of a dedicated server for each Web site. If you have more than one IP address bound to your network card, choosing Home directory will allow you to map the alias of an IP address by specifying it within the Directory Properties. This allows you to give the IP address a name in your DNS server such as http://Web2.domain.com and have it answer as if it were a stand alone server.

To remove a mapped Web directory, simply highlight the specific directory and choose the Remove button. All traces of the original alias are gone and cannot be restored unless you enter all of the information again.

Default Documents and Directory Browsing   The Default Document refers to the document name that the Web site needs to contain to open up to a Web page correctly when the machine's address is entered into a Web browser. The default document name is "default.htm". This means that if your URL is http://www.domain.com you must have a document titled "default.htm" in your root Web directory or the user will be returned HTTP 404 error message stating that the document is not found.

Directory browsing is useful when providing lists of downloadable files from the Web. Placing a check mark in the box will allow anyone to view the contents of a directory that does not contain a document with the default document name. For safety sake, it's best to leave Directory browsing unchecked unless you are sure that you want a user to see all of the contents of your directories.

The Logging Window

The Logging window allows the Web site administrator access to the advanced logging features built into the Internet Information Server. Logfiles are important for spotting trends in Web site access, calculating the number of visitors, and effectiveness of different Web site areas (see Figure 39.6). A straight logfile is written in a comma-delimited format which can be easily imported into your favorite database.

There are two major ways of logging activity. You can configure the server to write to a text-based logfile, or directly to an SQL / ODBC compliant database.

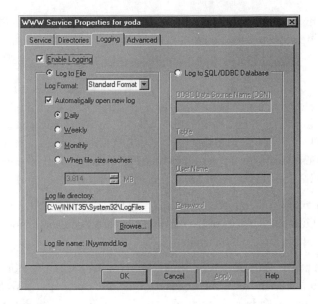

Logging to a File   Logfiles can be written in two different formats, NCSA and Standard.
The NCSA logfile is considered to be the standard among Web servers around the world.
Many programs have been written to interpret NCSA logfile results, providing detailed
statistics and graphs. The Standard logfile format is Microsoft's standard way of writing
logfiles in Windows NT. Both types of logfiles are easily imported into databases or
interpreted by simple parsing tools.

The Internet Information Server can log files daily, weekly, monthly, or to a specific file
size. For a high-traffic site, these files can easily be 10M a day. When setting up file logging, it's important to remember that parsing programs and databases can choke on very
large files. It's probably best to generate logfiles on a daily or weekly basis for the best
performance.

The default location that Windows NT uses for all of its logfiles is
C:\WINNT\System32\LogFiles. Grouping all system logfiles together ensures that you will
not have to hunt around the entire Web server to find the information you are looking for.
The WWW logfiles are identified by the prefix INyymmww, where yy is years, mm is
months, and ww is weeks. If you choose daily reports, the file will begin with the prefix
Inmmwwdd where dd is the day of the week.

Logging to a Database   If you choose to log directly to an SQL / ODBC database, you'll
be happy to know that you can use any ODBC compliant database you wish. Databases
ranging in scale from Access to SQL Server can all be used easily. The database must be
registered with the ODBC component in the Control Panel.

To begin logging Web site access directly to a database:

1. Enter the ODBC Data Source Name (DSN). This must be the DSN that is registered to the database you wish to use in the ODBC section of the Control Panel.

2. Enter the name of the table you wish to log to under Table. This must be the exact name of the database table. For integrity sake, use a case-sensitive format.

3. Enter the Username and Password of the account set up to access the database. The WWW logfile will not be allowed to write to the database table unless it is granted permission through authentication.

Once the logfile is captured to a database, the raw data can be easily formatted into Queries for information retrieval.

The Advanced Window

The Advanced Window gives you the option of restricting access to specific IP addresses on the Internet. This is useful for blocking suspicious Web addresses from the Web server completely, or publishing an Intranet on the Internet and keeping visitors out (see Figure 39.7).

FIGURE 39.7
Blocking access through IP address will secure your site from unwanted visitors.

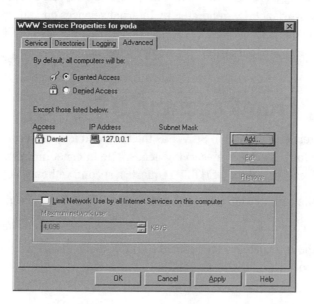

Part

IX

Ch

39

To block users from accessing your site:

1. Click the Add button to access the security controls.
2. Enter the IP address of the machine that you wish to deny access to.
3. Click OK to deny access.

For blocking access to a range of machines:

1. Enter the block of IP addresses that you wish to block in the following format:

   `127.0.0.*`

2. Enter the Subnet Mask of the range of IP addresses like the following:

   `255.255.255.0`

3. Click OK to finish the restricting process.

If you want the default Web server function to deny access to all computers except those that you specify, click the Deny Access button. By choosing this feature, you will have to manually enter individual or groups of IP addresses that can access the Web site. This would be useful in an Intranet situation where you might want remote salespersons to have the ability to reach online company resources.

Finally, by placing a check in the Limit Network Use box, you can place a limit on the amount of Network activity generated by Internet services on your machine. This is best utilized when your Internal network will route for the Internet server and you wish to reduce the overall amount of Internet network traffic.

Integrating FrontPage and IIS

Using the Internet Information Server as the back end for your FrontPage Webs is a robust solution for scaleable Web-serving needs. The Internet Information Server has the ability to address thousands of HTTP requests a second without keeping clients waiting.

To create a site using FrontPage on the Internet Information Server, follow these steps:

1. Create a directory on your server where you want the Web site housed.
2. Open the Internet Service Manager, double-click the server you wish to modify, and choose the Directories Tab.
3. Click Add to access the Directory Properties.
4. Click the Browse button and locate the desired directory. Choose OK.
5. Enter the name of the Virtual Directory. Click OK to finish.

If you wish to create a virtual Web server:

1. Open Network in Control Panel and assign a new IP address to your server. You will have to know the Subnet Mast to complete the addressing successfully.

2. Restart the server for the new IP address to be bound to your server.

3. Once the server is restarted, Directory Properties within the Internet Service Manager for the machine you wish to modify.

4. Click Add to access the Directory Properties.

5. Click the Browse button and locate the desired directory. Choose OK.

6. Click the Home Directory radio box to create a mapped root directory to your new Web site.

7. Place a check in Virtual Server and enter the new IP address for the Web site. Click OK to close the Directory Properties. Choose OK again to close the Internet Service Manager Properties.

8. Open the FrontPage Server Administrator. Choose the Install button to install the FrontPage extensions on the new IP address.

9. Choose Microsoft Internet Information Server from the drop-down menu. Click OK.

10. Enter the new IP address in the Multi-Homed section. Click OK. When the confirmation window appears, verify the information and choose Install.

The FrontPage Server Administrator will take a few minutes to install the extensions for your new Web site. Once completed, you will be able to log in to the new virtual server as you would any other.

HTML Administration

Both of the 4.0 versions of NT Server and NT Workstation come with a feature for remote Web server administration from a Web browser. The browser does not have to be Internet Explorer or Netscape Navigator. Any HTML compliant Web browser with the ability to authenticate users can be used for administration.

The default URL for administering the Internet Information Server is **http://www.domain.com/iisadmin/default.htm**.

To administer to Web server, simply click the button called WWW and enter your Username and Password. Note that you must log on with an account that has Administrator privileges. Any other account will not grant you access (see Figure 39.8).

FIGURE 39.8
Every aspect of your server can be administered through a Web browser without stopping services.

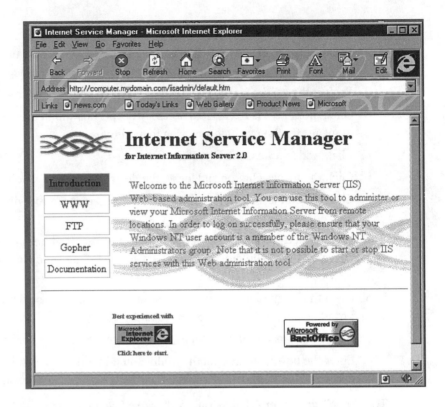

All of the functionality of administering your Web server is contained within these Web pages, with the exception of starting and stopping Internet services. You now have the ability to remotely alias Web directories and create new Web sites, without laying a finger on the keyboard of the server.

From Here...

In this chapter, you learned how to utilize Microsoft's Internet Information Server for robust serving of your FrontPage Webs. Microsoft's IIS, in conjunction with the FrontPage Server extensions, creates a powerful Web-serving environment with advanced security functions and logging capabilities. To learn more about advanced serving environments and added database functions read the following:

Chapter 40, "Using Non-Microsoft Servers," describes how to use FrontPage Server extensions with other popular Web servers such as Website by O'Reilly and the Fast Track series by Netscape.

Chapter 42, "Database Tools," examines further database integration within FrontPage and the move from static content to dynamic content.

Using Non-Microsoft Servers

As you're well aware by now, Microsoft includes two servers with the FrontPage 97 package, and FrontPage 97 is designed expressly to work well with the company's major Web server, the Internet Information Server (covered in Chapter 39). But you don't have to use a server that Microsoft provides. A wide variety of additional servers is available for use, and some are extremely popular among Webmasters. Here we'll cover a number of them. ■

Server Basics

Web server software is a software package that, when installed on a computer (the host system), lets the computer operate as a World Wide Web site or Intranet web server. What this means is that the computer will now support **HTTP**, officially known as the HyperText Transport Protocol. This protocol effects the connection between the client software (usually called a browser) and the server software, allowing a connection, request, response, and close. Server software and the network on which it operates can handle only a limited number of requests, so large companies will have several machines operating as Web servers simultaneously.

Like all software, Web server packages come in many shapes and sizes. The most recent ones boast speed of response, support for security such as Secure Sockets Layer (SSL) and Secure HTTP, and the ability to handle Java, ActiveX, advanced database connectivity, and many other features. Server software is advancing as quickly as browser software, albeit much more quietly since very few people realize it even exists.

Any computer on the Internet that contains TCP/IP networking software and has its own Internet Protocol (IP) address, even temporarily, can act as a Web server: dedicated machines with an ultra-fast T3 connection, right down to a lowly 386 PC running on a 9600 bps modem. But to be efficient, a Web server should be connected to the Internet on a 24-hour basis at a speed high enough to enable file transfers that won't bore and frustrate users unduly. That means, practically, an ISDN connection at the very least (even a 28.8 kbps modem won't cut it), and preferably something even faster, such as an Ethernet connection through a company local area network (LAN) that is sharing a T1 or T3 line with the rest of the organization's computers. The server will ideally possess its own Internet domain name as well, because then it can easily be assigned memorable addresses. This last suggestion, however, isn't really necessary, since virtual domain names (i.e., aliases) are possible.

There are may different servers packages available, and some support Web features that others don't, such as server-side scripting, security, and Java. Some come bundled with HTML tools and browsers; others leave the choice of editing and viewing tools up to you. They can offer varying security levels, which are sometimes dependent on the host machine's operating system; for example, Microsoft's new Internet Information Server runs under Windows NT and uses the NT security features. In short, to run a Web site, you have to have a Web server installed on the computer.

Servers exist for all the major operating systems, including UNIX (all flavors), Windows (all flavors), Macintosh (all versions), VMS, OS/2, and so on. All support the CGI standard, and many support Perl, a scripting language used for creating simple Web applications such as forms. Increasingly, servers are differentiated according to whether or not they support such advanced features as digital signature security, various key-level security, and the newest in programmability.

Installing Servers

Often the installation of server software is as simple as slipping a CD-ROM or a few floppies into the host machine, running the setup program, and responding to a series of prompts about passwords and defaults. This is what you did when you installed FrontPage; you may have hardly noticed that you were installing a Web server. However, the Personal Web Server is just that, a personal Web server. Heavy-duty Web server software, intended to run large or multiple Webs and deal with large numbers of access requests at the same time, are considerably more complex, though their installation may be almost as simple.

What's All This About the FrontPage Server Extensions?

When you installed FrontPage 97, you installed not only the Personal Web Server software, but software "extensions" that run in complement with the Personal Web Server itself. The extensions are intended to:

- Add to the server some specialized functions that are needed by the "FrontPage client." This client is simply the package comprised of FrontPage Explorer, FrontPage Editor, and the To Do List.

- Make it possible for different types of servers to operate properly with the functions that FrontPage offers. This is necessary because different servers handle some common tools, such as image maps, in different ways.

- Make it possible for FrontPage-generated Webs to be fully interactive with their visitors, providing facilities for registrations, searches, and forms submission.

FrontPage has built-in extensions for Windows 95 and Windows NT. This means that you don't have to worry about extensions at all, if you create and operate your Web site on a Windows-based PC with FrontPage installed on it. However, if you decide to base your Web on your ISP's site, the ISP administrator will have to install FrontPage extensions that have been designed for whatever server software is running on the ISP host machine. At the time of writing, FrontPage came with extensions for O'Reilly Web Site 1.1 for

Part
IX

Ch
40

Windows 95 and for Netscape FastTrack Windows NT. Other extensions can be downloaded free from the Microsoft site at **http://www.microsoft.com/frontpage/**. The FrontPage 97 extensions currently available are for Apache, CERN, NCSA, and Netscape (Commerce, Communications, Enterprise, and FastTrack). More will doubtless be added as the demand for FrontPage-based Web sites grows.

The Major Servers

These are the servers most commonly in use at the moment, though there are plenty of others. You'll find an excellent site for server information at Paul Hoffman's **http://www.proper.com**. The authors want to acknowledge the use of some of that information in the following descriptions of Web servers.

O'Reilly WebSite and WebSite Pro (O'Reilly)

Website is a 32-bit multithreaded World Wide Web server for Windows NT and Windows 95. The server supports access control, desktop directory indexing, multi-homing, and server-side includes. You can also do custom CGI programming to process data from spreadsheet, database, and word-processing applications. Site management is handled with a graphical display of documents and links on the server. The software also provides for searching and indexing (it has an integrated search engine). Setup and maintenance are GUI-based and remote maintenance is permitted. Website supports the Windows CGI interface. WebSite Pro supports advanced security mechanisms, plus Java and all the latest goodies, and includes a package that allows for relatively easy but powerful database connectivity.

The package comes with several bundled applications, notably the Spyglass Mosaic browser, Sausage Software's HotDog Standard HTML editor, and WebView printing, which lets users print out a view of what's in their Web.

Commerce Builder (Internet Factory)

Running under Windows NT or Windows 95, this server from the Internet Factory offers Secure Sockets Layer (SSL) 2 technology and Public Key encryption technology. In the security area, you can prohibit access by both domain name and IP address, and parts of documents can be hidden according to security rules. One useful feature is that you can change the user access control list without a server restart. Setup and maintenance are GUI-based, and remote maintenance is permitted. There is no search engine included, but the server does support chat and a newsgroup system. It can be used as an HTTP proxy server, and as a proxy server it will do caching. One interesting feature is its online store software.

Netscape FastTrack Server (Netscape)

This Windows NT or UNIX server is designed for lower-end World Wide Web or intranet sites that do not have extremely heavy traffic. It comes with an installation wizard to automatically detect system configuration and uses Netscape Navigator as its administrative interface. Also with the package is Netscape Navigator Gold, a WYSIWYG Web page editor that supports forms. Remote management of the server is supported, and it provides statistics like total site hits, unique users hitting the site, and most frequently served documents. For security, document access can be granted to user name/password pairs, groups, IP addresses, host names, or domain names. The security layer itself is Secure Sockets Layer 3.0.

For development work and CGI interfacing, the server supports Java and JavaScript, as well as C and Perl. In addition, developers using Visual Basic can communicate with the server through Windows CGI support. An optional add-on, LiveWire, converts popular image file formats such as .BMP and .WMF, provides conversion for document file formats like Microsoft Word, and provides a compiler to compile applications that include JavaScript, images, and HTML. LiveWire also does external link checking and carries out automatic link reorganization when part of a site is changed.

Netscape Enterprise Server (Netscape)

This UNIX and Windows NT package is a high-end server designed for sites with large amounts of traffic. It has or extends all the features of the Netscape Fastrack Server and adds integrated full-text search (the Verity search engine), multiple version control (the MKS Integrity Engine), and server-parsed HTML, which allows system administrators to replace HTML tags with dynamic content. Security is also upgraded, with read/write access control for individual files and directories and authentication based on public-key certificates. The LiveWire package is included with the server, instead of being an option, as with FastTrack.

WebSTAR for Windows 95/NT (Quarterdeck Corporation)

WebSTAR runs under Windows 95 and Windows NT and is targeted to small-business Internet connections and to corporate intranets. It runs on low-end hardware, including 486-based machines, and installation and maintenance are simplified by its GUI interfaces. It has directory-level security and supports multiple virtual servers on a single, non-dedicated PC. It supports some additional security in the area of document access, allowing the system administrator to prohibit access by domain name and IP address. You can configure user groups and change the access control list without restarting the server. WebSTAR supports the Windows CGI interface, has Mosaic image map support, and comes with a built-in scripting language.

Purveyor (Process Software Corporation)

This server runs under Windows NT and Windows 95 and is compatible with Novell Netware. It includes a data wizard to create HTML forms that allow users to execute database queries. There is also a special API, intended as an alternative to CGI scripting. There are proxy services to screen http, gopher, and ftp functions, in support of firewalls. Further security is provided by SSL 2 and user names/passwords can reside in external databases. Search engines (Verity and WAIS) are provided, and a link viewer helps with the location and correction of broken links. Maintenance and setup are GUI-based, and the server can be remotely maintained.

SPRY Web Server (Spry)

This is a Windows NT server that lets you publish Web documents over an internal network and on the World Wide Web. Typical applications, according to Spry, might include sales force updates, customer database access, and online policy and procedure manuals. It has a built-in scripting language called BGI and built-in image map handling, but it doesn't support the Windows CGI interface. There is password support and access prohibition by domain name or IP address but no support for SSL security. You can configure user groups, but to change the access control list you must restart the server. GUI-based setup and maintenance is provided, as well as remote maintenance. It can act as a proxy server, and in this mode provides caching.

SPRY Safety Web Server (Spry)

This is the secure version of the Spry Web Server (above), with the additional security provided by SSL 2 technology. GUI-based installation and maintenance is provided, as well as remote maintenance. Included is a Web search engine and the HoTMetaL Pro HTML editor. The server is targeted to organizations with financial security needs, for conducting transactions over the Internet or over an intranet. Suggested applications are subscription-based access to financial records and electronic retailing through online order forms.

NCSA HTTP (NCSA)

Running under UNIX, this is among the longest-lived servers around and has the virtue of being small, fast, and free. It lets users create HTML directory indexes and allows them to access publishing tools on the Web. ISP administrators can customize CGI scripts for searches and form handling, and the server also supports image map files without requiring an external CGI application. There is no built-in scripting language, however. Security is provided by password and by access prohibition by domain name or IP address, but SSL is not supported. However, Kerberos and MD5 provide extra security tools. It has an internal search engine and WAIS support. Installation is GUI-based, but maintenance is not. Additionally, remote maintenance is not allowed.

Apache (Apache Group)

Apache is based on the NCSA server and runs under UNIX only. It's the most common Web server around because it's happy with most UNIX variants and is fast and efficient. It doesn't have GUI-based installation or maintenance, but it does allow remote maintenance. There is no built-in scripting language. Image map support has been improved in version 1.1 with better handling of default, base, and relative URLs and with support for creating non-graphical menus. Access protection is based on passwords, domain name, and IP address prohibition and, most recently, by URL-based security. Version 1.1 can be used as a proxy server, with caching. Filetype-based script actions permit the running of CGI scripts whenever a particular type of file is requested. Anonymous HTTP logons are now supported.

Open Market Secure WebServer (Open Market)

This high-performance server runs under UNIX. With its multiprocessor capabilities, it can (in an appropriate configuration) support up to 5,000 simultaneous connections, according to the vendor. It supports FastCGI, a new open-architecture programming interface that reduces the performance penalty of standard CGI. In addition to FastCGI, it offers the scripting language Tcl (Tool Control Language). It also provides tools for interfacing existing code from the user's choice of programming languages.

Security is extensive, with support for Secure HyperText Transfer Protocol (S-HTTP), SSL 2, and Microsoft's new Private Communications Technology (PCT). This flexibility lets developers write applications that work with all secure browsers.

It has elaborate methods of logging user access. In combination with Open Market's WebReporter utility, system administrators can track individual users' movements through a site, log the most frequent browsers and machine types, report the most frequent referring URLs, and determine the most-used entry and exit points for a site. The WebReporter output, which has several preconfigured report formats, can be in HTML, postscript, or text documents. Installation and setup are GUI-based, and remote maintenance is permitted.

From Here...

Only two place left to go: learning about database connectivity and browsing through the appendices. So now it's off to:

- Chapter 41, "Custom Database Query Scripts," which covers the task of querying your databases to produce suitable results in your site.

- Chapter 42, "Database Tools," which provides information on utilities for managing databases from which your FrontPage webs take information.

- The Appendices, which offer reference guides to everything from Java to Virtual Reality Programming Language.

Advanced Database Connectivity

## CHAPTER 41

Custom Database Query Scripts

Using the World Wide Web to access databases can save your organization tremendous amounts of time. The task may seem daunting at first, but any effort on your part to integrate your existing database with the Web is well worth the effort.

No matter how much information the Web site for your organization might contain, a great deal more information is undoubtedly available on the computer databases the organization has been building over the years. These databases will contain everything from employee information through detailed customer profiles, product and service information, prices, items in inventory, and any number of other important details. If you're creating a company intranet, you'll find yourself face to face with the problem of allowing access to some of the information stored in these databases, and if you're creating an Internet Web site where users are asked to provide or request information, you'll need to access these databases as well.

Connecting your Web to your databases

Scenarios for when you'd want to make a database connection, and how FrontPage goes about completing the task.

Using the Database Connector Wizard

The database connectivity wizard is one of FrontPage 97's most powerful features, and here you'll learn how to make it sing.

Special Considerations for database connections

The things you can and can't do with FrontPage's connectivity features.

Database Design

Using Databases in conjunction with the World Wide Web takes a lot ot thought and planning. In this chapter we'll discuss some of those concerns.

FrontPage 97 offers sophisticated database connectivity. In fact, it's one of the leading additions to the upgraded FrontPage package. Furthermore, FrontPage offers a database connector wizard to make this difficult process as user-friendly as possible. Connecting your Web site with your databases is still anything but a walk in the park, and it helps a great deal to know how it's done before starting to use the wizard, but FrontPage eases the burden to a considerable degree. ■

Database Connectivity

Connecting an organization's Web to its databases has become one of the most important considerations of all for Webmasters. So much information already resides on databases that it makes no sense whatsoever reproducing it so that Web visitors—whether intranet or Internet users—can make use of it. Whether that data has to do with internal company information such as policies, procedures, employee statistics, sales figures, client profiles, or contact details, or with externally important data such as products, services, programs, and pricing, the point is that if it already exists in a form that's being regularly updated, why not make use of it?

Let's say, in a very simple example, that you're using your Web site to market a line of shirts. You have T-shirts and sweatshirts in various sizes and colors, and each with a picture of one (of five) dangerous snakes (hey, it's an example, okay?). You're not allowing them to actually buy the shirts over the Web, but you want them to be able to fill in a form that will show them a picture of the particular shirt they want. You also want to use the form to collect information about the visitors to your site, and you'll invite them to subscribe to a mailing list and to get a product brochure via snail-mail. So you use FrontPage 97 to design a form that lets them request information about precisely the shirt they want, and which also gives you the information you need for your business.

Here's what you need on your form:

- Customer's Name
- Customer's E-mail
- Customer's Street Address
- Customer's City
- Customer's State or Province
- Customer's Country
- Customer's Zip or Postal Code
- Type of Shirt (choice: T-shirt, Sweatshirt)

- Size of Shirt (choice: Small, Medium, Large)
- Color of Shirt (choice: White, Black, Red, Green)
- Dangerous Snake (choice: Python, Anaconda, Cobra, Viper, Rattler)
- Get information by e-mail? (choice: yes or no)
- Receive product brochure by mail? (choice: yes or no)

You finish the form, and it looks great. Drop-down lists, radio buttons, whatever. The only problem is: What exactly is it supposed to do? Where will it get the information about the shirts, and where will it store the information about the customers and their choices?

To make this form work properly, you'll need to build a database of information (or tap into one you already have). Your database should have fields for type of shirt, color of shirt, and type of snake, and a means of querying those items so that a request returns a picture of that particular shirt and a price for that shirt. You might even need data on shipping costs to various locations. And it doesn't stop there. Your database (or another related database) must be able to accept data from the Web form, collecting the customer's name and address information into the appropriate fields.

Obviously, this is way beyond basic HTML. In fact, it requires database programming knowledge. Fortunately, FrontPage 97 ships with tools to help you do some of this programming, although certainly nothing that takes programming away from you completely. FrontPage's database connectivity features, which come to life in the Database Connector Wizard, help your data make the transition from your databases to your Web pages, and from your Web forms into your databases. In effect, it lets you use your Web to query your databases and to add records to them as well.

The Database Connector Wizard helps you with the process of producing an Internet Database Connector or IDC file. This file includes the information necessary to interact with a database that is compliant with the ODBC (Open Database Connectivity) standards and that is currently running on a Web server. It interacts by allowing requests that conform to the Structured Query Language (SQL) for data retrieval, data additions, and data changes.

Part
X

Ch
41

The information contained in the IDC file tells the database connector how to connect with the database and what queries and operations to conduct. In addition, the wizard lets you point to a file known as a query results file, which will have an HTX extension in the file name and which will co-operate with the IDC file. This results file, which in effect is a different type of Web document, holds information such as database record values, parameters for a variety of operations, if-then programming choices, and so on. The Edit menu of FrontPage Editor lets you add and modify the information in this HTX file.

The whole point of creating these files is to let your Web forms make use of them. You do so by calling up the Form Properties dialog from within FrontPage Editor, then choosing Database Connector in the Form Handler field. If the form shares field names with the IDC file, then the HTX file can run the queries and return the results right in the Web browser, where the user can see them.

Using the Database Connectivity Wizard

Once you've created your form which will allow the visitor to place an order, you will want to use the FrontPage Database Connectivity Wizard to create the IDC file which will process the visitor's order.

If you haven't already done so, at the top of the FrontPage Editor, click View, and then click Advanced Toolbar. This will display a toolbar that contains an icon for the Database Connector Wizard.

Once the Advanced Toolbar appears on your screen, click the Database Connector Wizard. The wizard will open and allow you to specify an ODBC data source. This field is required as it tells the Wizard (and your IDC file) which database, it will retrieve or store your visitor's information in. The ODBC (Open Database Connectivity) data source should be a data source already specified through the use of the ODBC32 icon on your system's Control Panel.

Next set the username and password required to access your database if required (not all databases require the use of a username and password, most SQL servers do though).

Then specify the name of the HTX file (required) which will be used to display information that the user entered, and information collected from the database (if any). If you haven't created the HTX file already, you will have to do so before allowing visitors to your site to fill out your form.

Last, you will notice a button called Advanced Options. This button will allow you to set options for your ODBC driver, including information on how, or if, the database is supposed to cache information retrieved, set timeouts, translations, and additional information.

Once you have finished entering the ODBC data source, the HTX filename, and additional information for your ODBC driver, click Next. The wizard will provide you with another dialog box that will allow you to enter one or more database queries, which will be placed in the IDC file required to process the information entered in your form. In our example, we're taking information from the visitor and placing that information into the database, which can be later retrieved by the appropriate personnel, who will then process the customer's order.

The wizard only makes entering a query a little easier. You will still have to know how to query the database, deciding what information you want to store, and how that information will be stored.

The Insert Parameter button helps you enter information into the query by allowing you to enter the name of a field from the form, and insert that information into the actual query in the proper format. For example, if you clicked Insert Parameter, a dialog box will appear asking for the name of the field from the form. If you were to enter name, the dialog box would place the string, %name% into the query box.

Since our query will simply enter the information provided by the visitor, I have placed the following query into the Query Dialog Box:

```
INSERT name,e-mail,street,city,state,country,zip,
type,size,color,snake,list,brochure
INTO orderinfo
VALUES ('%name%', '%e-mail%', '%street%', '%city%', '%state%', '%country%',
'%zip%',
'%type%', '%size%', '%color%', '%snake%', '%list%', '%brochure%')
```

Once you are finished entering your query, click Next. The Wizard will then allow you to enter additional parameters.

Along with the Datasource, Template, and SQLStatement directives, which are placed in the IDC file by the Database Connector Wizard, additional directives are available. These directives are not required, but add a bit of flexibility when dealing with the database connector. The rest of this section examines each of these directives and explains how you can use them.

The *DefaultParameters* Directive

You can use the DefaultParameters directive to specify the default parameters to use if the visitor doesn't fill out the form completely. For example, you can set the following default in case a visitor fails to enter a name:

```
DefaultParameters: name=%John Doe%
```

You can specify more than one parameter, but you must separate each with a comma.

The *RequiredParameters* Directive

The RequiredParameters directive enables you to specify which items the visitor must fill. If you want to ensure that the visitor enters a name and address, for example, you specify the following:

```
RequiredParameters: name, street, city, state, zip
```

Part
X

Ch
41

The *MaxFieldSize* Directive

With the MaxFieldSize directive, you can specify a record's maximum length. If you don't specify the MaxFieldSize, the default value is 8,192 bytes.

The *MaxRecords* Directive

You can use the MaxRecords directive to set the maximum amount of records that a query returns. If you don't set the MaxRecords directive, the IDC allows the return of all records that match the query. This default setting isn't a problem with smaller databases, but can be with larger ones. Set this directive to a reasonable number of records, based on the kind of information that you are retrieving.

The *Expires* Directive

If you don't set the Expires directive, the database is accessed each time for information. If you do set this directive, the query returns to the user from a cache instead of accessing the database again. This can help reduce the system's load and return information to the visitor more quickly. Using the Expires directive, you specify the amount of seconds before the cache is refreshed.

For our example, we don't require any additional parameters, so we will then click **Finish**. The Wizard will disappear, and the IDC file is then created, storing the information we entered. Listing 41.1 shows you what our IDC file looks like.

Listing 41.1   order.idc—The IDC File Specifies Which Data Source to Use, and the Query Information Which Will Process the Information Entered by the Visitor.

```
Datasource: Order
Template: order.htx
SQLStatement: INSERT name,e-mail,street,city,state,country,zip,
+type,size,color,snake,list,brochure
+INTO orderinfo
+VALUES ('%name%', '%e-mail%', '%street%', '%city%', '%state%',
+'%country%', '%zip%', '%type%', '%size%', '%color%', '%snake%',
+'%list%', '%brochure%');
```

HTML Extensions

Now all you need to do is create an .HTX file that creates the HTML document that you return to the visitor. The Database Connector Wizard can help you with HTX file. Using the FrontPage Editor, click on Edit, and then click on Database. A list of options will then be shown. These options are:

- Database Column Value
- IDC Parameter Value
- Detail Section
- If-Then Conditional Statement
- Else Conditional Statement
- Remove Database Directive

As with the IDC file, the .HTX file uses special directives that help format the HTML document. Here we will introduce you to each of these directives, and then we'll create a .HTX file which will process some of the information entered by the visitor when they ordered one of our very special snake t-shirts.

Database Column Values

This item allows you to insert a value from the database into your .HTX file. If you have the columns, name, e-mail, and phone in the database, you can enter these into the dialog box (one at a time please), and they will be placed in your .HTC file as:

`<%name%>`, `<%e-mail%>`, and `<%phone%>` respectively.

These tags will be replaced by the actual information stored in each column when the database has been queried.

IDC Parameter Values

After a visitor enters fields within an HTML form, you can pass them directly to the .HTX file by adding the *idc.* prefix. For example, if you want to return information to the visitor that entered it, you could use the following code line:

```
Hello %idc.name%. How is the weather in %idc.city%,
➥ %idc.state%?<BR>
```

The Detail directives

If a visitor to your site wants to query the database, the `<%begindetail%>` and `<%enddetail%>` directives store the returned information. For example, suppose that a visitor perusing your company product catalog enters a query to search for shirts, and that your database includes a field called `shirt`. You can format the .HTX file to report each instance that matches the field:

Part
X

Ch
41

```
<table>
<%begindetail%>
<tr><td><%shirt%><td><%price%></td></tr>
<%enddetail%>
</table>
```

This code opens the <TABLE> tag. For each instance of a match, the file creates a row with the shirt (which could simply be a name) and the price. The <%enddetail%> directive specifies the end of a section. You then use the <\TABLE> tag to close the table. If no records are found, this section is skipped.

An option not provided by the menu, but used often is the CurrentRecord directive. The CurrentRecord directive counts the number of times that records are processed. You can use this directive to check whether the query generated any results and then inform the visitor of any results.

Soon you'll see how to use the CurrentRecord directive, but first let's examine another directive that enables you to check information and return results based on conditions.

Conditional Operators IF-Then and Else

Within the .HTX file, you can use the following simple conditional operators: <%if%>, <%else%>, and <%endif%>. Using these operator directives, you can check whether certain conditions are met. For example, you can check whether any records were returned, and if not, you can inform the visitor.

```
<table>
<%begindetail%>
<tr><td><%shirt%><td><%price%></td></tr>
<%enddetail%>
</table>
<%if CurrentRecord EQ 0 %>
I'm sorry, but there isn't anything in the database
➥ that matches your query.
<center>
<a href="tshirt.htm">[Product Database]</a>
</center>
```

The <%if%> directive uses four conditional words that you can use to check information.

EQ checks whether a value is equal to the test, as in the following example:

```
<%if snake EQ "Viper" %>
Viper T-Shirt
<%endif%>
```

GT enables you to check whether one value is greater than another, as in the following example:

```
<%if price GT 500 %>
```

LT checks whether a value is less than another value, as in the following example:

```
<%elseif price LT 10 %>
<%endif%>
```

CONTAIN enables you to check whether a value is anywhere within another value, as in the following example:

```
<%if snake CONTAINS "Cobra" %>
Cobra
<%endif%>
```

The MaxRecords variable contains the value of the MaxRecords directive that the IDC file specifies, as in the following example:

```
<%if CurrentRecord EQ MaxRecords %>
Results have been abridged
<%endif%>
```

You can also use HTTP variables within .HTX files. To do so, select HTTP variable. The variable will be displayed in the .HTX file within the <% %> delimiters, as in the following example:

```
You are using, <%HTTP_USER_AGENT%>
```

Continuing with our Example

To continue with the order-entry example, we will simply thank the visitor for entering the order and let the visitor know that you have processed his or her order, storing it in the database.

```
<!DOCTYPE HTML PUBLIC "-//IETF//DTD HTML//EN">
<html>

<head>
<meta http-equiv="Content-Type"
content="text/html; charset=iso-8859-1">
<meta name="GENERATOR" content="Microsoft FrontPage 2.0">
<title>Thank you!</title>
</head>

<body bgcolor="#FFFFFF">
<div align="center"><center>

<table border="0" width="580">
    <tr>
        <td><img src="cobra5.jpg" width="320" height="240"></td>
        <td align="center"><h1>Thank you for your order!</h1>
        </td>
    </tr>
</table>
</center></div>
<p> </p>
```

Part

X

Ch

41

```
<hr>
<h2>Thank you, <%idc.name%>.</h2>
<p>You ordered:<br>
Type of shirt: <%idc.type%><br>
Size: <%idc.size%><br>
Color: <%idc.color%><br>
Type of snake: %idc.snake% <%if% idc.list EQ "No">
<%else%></p>
<p>You have been placed on our mailing list <%if% idc.brochure EQ
"No">
<%else%> </p>

<p>Also a brochure will be send to you at the following address:</p>

<pre>
<%idc.name%>
<%idc.street%>
<%idc.city%>
<%idc.state%>
<%idc.country%>
<%idc.zip%>
<hr></pre>
</body>
</html>
```

Understanding Database Design

How you go about designing your database depends on the tools you currently have, what type of information you need to store, and what you're willing to purchase. The nice thing is that there are different methods to save and retrieve information, no matter what your budget.

The most difficult and daunting task is how to go about designing your database to store information and to retrieve that information. What would happen if you wanted to upgrade your database, or if you needed to add on to your database?

Figure 41.1 shows you how information flows from the point in which someone on the Web requests a page that needs information from your database. When requesting information that derives from a database, quite a few steps are involved to complete that request. Your Web server receives the request from the visitor to your site, then sends that information on to your CGI script. The CGI script acts as the main gateway tying two very different systems together. The CGI script performs the actual query, receives the results from the database, formulates a proper reply, and sends it off to the Web server, which in turn sends it to the person visiting your site.

As you can see there's quite a few steps involved in this process. Your goal is to tie all this together in such a way that it is totally transparent to the person visiting your site.

FIGURE 41.1
This diagram shows the information flow between those on the Web and your database.

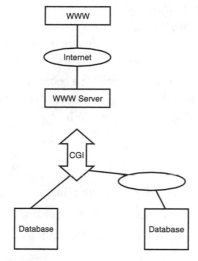

Why Access a Database?

Most likely your organization already has an existing database in which they have stored information about their products, their customers, and other aspects of business life. Some of this information you might want to allow your customers to see, or you might even want to make the information in the database available to your workers stationed away from the office. If so, you would have to create HTML documents that contain all this information all over again, which, if you're part of a large organization, can be a tedious task. Integrating the Web with your databases can save you tremendous amounts of time in the long run, especially when it comes to maintaining that information. As the database changes, your Web pages change.

Another good reason to use the World Wide Web to access your database is that any Web browser that supports forms can access information from the database—no matter which platform is being used.

Database Access Limitations

Although the limitations in accessing databases have decreased in the last few months as database companies have scrambled to ensure that their product easily integrates with existing Web applications, there are still a few left you will want to look out for.

There is a lack of an official standard which you can use to connect to a database. If you were to create a script to access one type of database, there is no guarantee that the same script would work on a different database—even if the query used was the same. (People are working on this though.) Because of this you will be required to learn a good deal about each database application that you come across.

Also, the browser and the server are stateless in relation to each other. The browser makes a request, the server processes the query, sends the result back to the browser, and the connection is closed. This creates a problem with databases, because a connection to a database is usually constant. Someone, through a normal method, could access the database, which keeps a connection open, locking a record if any editing is performed, and closes the connection only when the person is finished. Accessing a database doesn't work exactly the same way when doing so from the Web.

Consider the following events:

1. Person one accesses the database for editing.

2. Next person two comes along and does the same thing.

3. Person one makes his changes, and saves that information to the database.

4. Person two saves his information as well, possibly writing over what person one just saved.

5. A short time later, person one is wondering where his data went.

There are two ways to go about handling this. The first method involves keeping track of all entries with a timestamp. This will allow both entries to be maintained by the database, without the possibility of either person's entries being overwritten.

Another way is to only provide information from the database, and not allow someone on the Web to edit, remove, or insert information to the database. While this limits some of the possibilities for having the database on the Web, it also alleviates some of the security problems as well.

Security Issues

The major problem with having those on the Web accessing your database is that your CGI script is trusted by your database program. That is to say, your database has to accept commands from your CGI script, and your CGI script needs to perform queries based upon what you wish to provide to those on the Web. This can lead to problems if someone with ill intentions gains access to a script that has the ability to edit your database.

Also, most databases require the use of a password. Since your CGI script stores user information to the database, as well as retrieving information from the database, your script is going to need to have to have the password to access your database. You need to ensure that your script cannot be read by others both within your organization and outside your organization.

In this chapter, you take a look at two different kinds of databases: flatfile and DBM databases, building a phonebook for each one so that you can see the differences between the three methods to store information.

Creating and Using Flatfile Databases

Flatfile databases are just about the easiest database you can create. Although flatfile databases aren't incorporated into FrontPage, they can provide you with a method in which to store information. Other than the necessity to have a language with which to program, there is nothing else needed to create a small ASCII text database.

A flatfile database mainly consists of lines of text where each line is its own entry. There is no special technique to index the database. Because of this, flatfile databases usually are relatively small. The larger the database, the longer it takes to perform queries to the database.

The first thing that you need is an HTML page, which will allow someone to enter information into the database. You must first decide what you want the visitor to enter.

Your HTML document consists of three forms which can be created using FrontPage. The first form will allow the visitor to enter information into the phonebook database. The second form will allow the visitor to display the contents of the database, and the third form will allow the visitor to perform a keyword search on the database.

You can expand on this later, but right now I simply want the visitor to be able to enter a first name, a last name, and a telephone number, all of which will be stored in your flatfile database.

The first form assigns the input from the visitor into three names: fname, lname, and phone. A hidden input type (see Listing 41.2), named act (for action), is created that tells your script which action it is expected to perform. Once he or she fills out the form, they can click Add to Phonebook (see Figure 41.2 to get an idea of what this would look like).

On the CD

Listing 41.2 Pbook.html—HTML Code That Will Allow Visitors to Query a Phonebook Database.

```
<HTML>
<HEAD><TITLE>Flatfile Phonebook</TITLE></HEAD>
<BODY>
<H1>Your Flatfile Phonebook</H1>
<HR>
<H2>Insert Information</H2>
<FORM ACTION="/cgi-bin/pbook.bat" METHOD="POST">
<PRE>
  First Name: <INPUT TYPE="text" NAME="fname">
   Last Name: <INPUT TYPE="text" NAME="lname">
Phone Number: <INPUT TYPE="text" NAME="phone">
</PRE>
<INPUT TYPE="hidden" NAME="act" VALUE="add">
<INPUT TYPE="submit" value="Add to Phonebook">
</FORM>
<HR><P>
```

FIGURE 41.2
This form allows
a visitor to enter
information into a
flatfile phonebook
database.

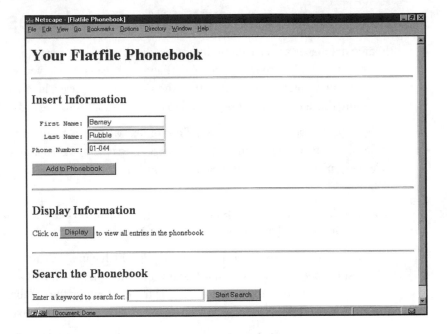

The second form consists of a line in which the visitor can click Display to get a listing of everyone who has been entered into the database. Notice the use of the hidden input type; this time, the name act will have the value of display.

```
<H2>Display Information</H2>
<FORM ACTION="/cgi-bin/pbook.bat" METHOD="POST">
<INPUT TYPE="hidden" NAME="act" VALUE="display">
Click on <INPUT TYPE="submit" value="Display">
to view all entries in the phonebook
</FORM>
<HR><P>
```

The last form on the Web page will allow the visitor to enter a keyword, which is used to search through the database. We have assigned a string entered by the user to the name keyword. We have also given the value, search, to the hidden input type named act.

```
<H2>Search the Phonebook</H2>
<FORM ACTION="/cgi-bin/pbook.bat" METHOD="POST">
Enter a keyword to search for: <INPUT TYPE="text" NAME="keyword">
<INPUT TYPE="hidden" NAME="act" VALUE="search">
<INPUT TYPE="submit" VALUE="Start Search">
</FORM>
</BODY>
</HTML>
```

Now that you have finished with the HTML document, it's time to write the script that handles the information provided by the visitor.

Writing to a Flatfile Database

If you take a look at Listing 41.3, the first part of your script needs to be able to read STDIN and separate the contents, assigning each value to the array contents.

Listing 41.3   Pbook.pl—The Script Reads *STDIN* and Separates Its Contents.

```
if ($ENV{'REQUEST_METHOD'} eq 'POST')
{
    read(STDIN, $buffer, $ENV{'CONTENT_LENGTH'});
    @pairs = split(/&/, $buffer);
    foreach $pair (@pairs)
    {
        ($name, $value) = split(/=/, $pair);
        $value =~ tr/+/ /;
        $value =~ s/%([a-fA-F0-9][a-fA-F0-9])/pack("C", hex($1))/eg;
        $contents{$name} = $value;

    }
}
```

Next you need to declare the content type to the server, and provide the path to the file that will store your names and phone numbers.

```
print "Content-type: text/html\n\n";
$phonebook = "c:\\website\\cgi-shl\\phonebk.txt";
```

Now your script checks to see what value the name act contains. Here it checks to see if the value of act is equal to the string, add. If so, then it will open up the database, or it will go to the subroutine no_open, if for some reason your script cannot open the database. If the script successfully opened the database, then it appends the information entered by the visitor, and then creates a Web page (see Figure 41.3) stating that the information entered by the visitor was added to the database. Last, use the exit; command to end the script because no other functions are possible.

Listing 41.4   Pbook.bat—The First Form Checks to See if the Visitor Wanted to Enter Information.

```
if ($contents{'act'} eq "add") {
open(BOOK, ">>$phonebook") || do {&no_open;};
print BOOK "$contents{'fname'}:$contents{'lname'}:$contents{'phone'}\n";
close(BOOK);
print <<"HTML";
<HTML>
<HEAD><TITLE>Information added</TITLE></HEAD>
<BODY>
<H1>Information added</H1>
```

continues

Listing 41.4 Continued

```
The information entered has been added to the phonebook.
<HR>
<CENTER>
<A HREF="/pbook.html">[Return to the Phonebook]</A>
</CENTER>
</BODY>
</HTML>
HTML
exit;
}
```

FIGURE 41.3

A Web page is created on-the-fly, letting the visitor know that his or her entry was placed in the database.

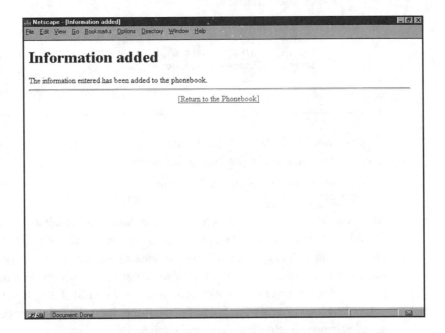

If you recall from just a bit ago, you told your script to go the subroutine no_open if the script wasn't able to access the database for some reason. Listing 41.5 shows you what happens if an error does occur. A Web page is generated (see Figure 41.4) informing the visitor that the database couldn't be accessed.

FIGURE 41.4

If the database could not be opened you need to inform the visitor of this.

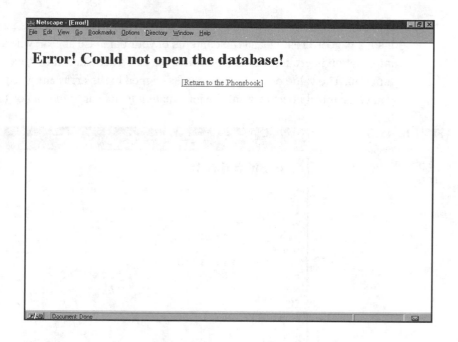

Listing 41.5   Pbook.bat—An Error Page Is Created Informing the Visitor of a Problem.

```
sub no_open {

print <<"HTML";
<HTML>
<HEAD><TITLE>Error!</TITLE></HEAD>
<BODY>
<H1> Error! Could not open the database!</H1>
<CENTER>
<A HREF="/pbook.htm">[Return to the Phonebook]</A>
</CENTER>
</BODY>
</HTML>
HTML

exit;
}
```

Part

X

Ch

41

Reading from a Flatfile Database

If the visitor clicked Display, the information from the database is retrieved and simply appears to the visitor in a table. By using a table, the contents of the phonebook could be easily formatted into something that is easy to view.

As you can see in Listing 41.6, you check to see if the value of act is equal to display; if so, a page is created, and the contents of your database appear, where each line of information is broken into its respective parts. To accomplish this, use Perl's split function. The value of $line is split and assigned to the array entry. By splitting each line, you can control how you want the information to appear to the visitor (see Figure 41.5).

FIGURE 41.5
The script displays the phonebook in its entirety.

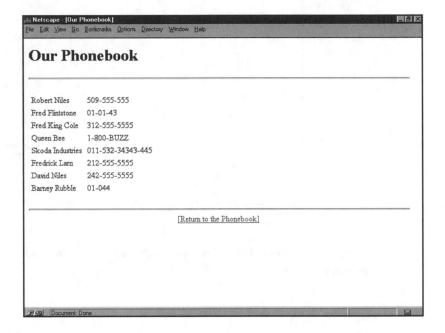

Listing 41.6   Pbook.bat—The Contents of the Database Are Read, and Displayed to the User in HTML.

```
if ($contents{'act'} eq "display") {

...

open (BOOK, $phonebook) || do {&no_open;};
until (eof(BOOK))
{
  $line = <BOOK>;
  @entry = split(/:/, $line);
  print "<TR><TD>$entry[0] $entry[1]</TD><TD> $entry[2]</TD></TR>";
}

close(BOOK);

...
```

Once the information from the database is displayed, you finish the HTML document and exit the script.

Searching a Flatfile Database

Last, you need to check to see if the visitor requested to perform a keyword search (see Listing 41.7). If so, you need to open the database and check each line against the keyword entered by the visitor.

First, the database is opened and the top portion of the results page is created. Next, you have a counter, which is initially set to zero (more on this in a moment). Now each line is read and checked against the value contained in the variable $contents{'keyword'}. If so, then the count is incremented and the result printed as part of the created Web page (see Figure 41.6). Use the same technique here as earlier by splitting each line that is to be printed into an array.

FIGURE 41.6

A Web page is created in which all entries are displayed that match the keyword entered by the visitor.

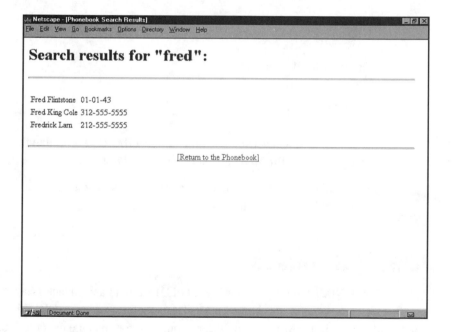

> # Search results for "fred":
>
> Fred Flintstone 01-01-43
> Fred King Cole 312-555-5555
> Fredrick Larn   212-555-5555
>
> [Return to the Phonebook]

Once you exit the loop, you check the count. If the count is equal to zero, then you know that there were no entries in the database that matched the keyword search, and you inform the visitor that his or her search produced no results.

Listing 41.7   Pbook.bat—The Script Checks to See if Anything Matches the Keyword.

```
if ($contents{'act'} eq "search") {

open (BOOK, "$phonebook") || do {&no_open;};

$count=0;

 until (eof (BOOK))
  {
    $line = <BOOK>;
    chop($line);
    if ($line =~ /$contents{'keyword'}/gi)
      {
        $count++;
        @entry = split(/:/, $line);
        print "<TR><TD>$entry[0] $entry[1]</TD><TD> $entry[2]</TD></TR>";
      }

 }

if ($count==0)
  {
    print "No Matches";
  }

close(BOOK);
```

Once the script has checked each line against the keyword, then the database is closed; the script finishes the Web page and exits the script.

To get a better feel of how the script works, take a look at the script, which is an enhanced version of this script, located on the CD-ROM.

DBM Databases

Most UNIX systems have some sort of DBM database; in fact, I have yet to find a system that runs without one, but even MS-DOS platforms can use DBM databases to store information. DBM is a set of library routines that manage data files consisting of key and value pairs. The DBM routines control how users enter and retrieve information from the database. Although not the most powerful mechanism for storing information, using DBM is a faster method of retrieving information than using a flat file.

On UNIX systems, DBM databases are commonly used. This isn't so for MS Windows–based systems. Even so, ports have been made available. SDBM is one dbm library that comes with the Perl archive, which has been ported to many platforms. Therefore, you can use DBM databases as long as there is a version of Perl for your computer. SDBM was written to match the functions provided with NDBM, so portability of code shouldn't be a problem since Perl is available for most of the popular platforms, including the Amiga, MacIntosh, MS-DOS, and UNIX.

ON THE WEB

http://www.perl.com/perl/   For more information on SDBM and Perl, visit the Perl home page.

Writing to a DBM database

First, you create a Web page which will allow us to enter information into the database. You can use FrontPage to create the Web page, but Listing 41.8 will give you an example of what we need. In this chapter's example, you ask the visitor to enter a name, e-mail address, and phone number.

Listing 41.8   dbbook.html—The Web Page Allows Visitors to Enter Information into the Database.

```
<HTML>
<HEAD><TITLE>DB Phonebook</TITLE></HEAD>
<BODY>
<H1>DB Phonebook</H1>
<FORM ACTION="/cgi-bin/dbbookadd.bat" METHOD="POST">
<pre>
Name:<INPUT NAME="name">
Email:<INPUT NAME="e-mail">
Phone:<INPUT NAME="phone"><P>
</pre>
<INPUT TYPE="SUBMIT">
</FORM>
</BODY>
</HTML>
```

The script shown in Listing 41.9 uses the SDBM library to store information. Again, you're constructing a phonebook which can be used via the Web. This is done so that you can see how each database works in relation to the other.

First, the information that the script receives from STDIN is split and stored in an environmental variable. Then the database name is stored in the variable file. Next, you open the database using the dbmopen() function, which allows us to specify how the database will be opened.

Next, you check to see if the name entered by the visitor has been already entered earlier. To do this, all you need to do is code a line that reports an error if the key is used, which is the name entered by the visitor, already exists in the database. If the key does exist, then the script goes to the subroutine `error`.

Next,

```
$db{$form{'name'}}=join(":",$form{'e-mail'},$form{'phone'});
```

is the heart of the whole script. This line takes the information that the user entered and places that information into the database. The name entered by the visitor becomes the key, and the e-mail address and the phone number are joined together using a colon to form the value. Without all the coding the previous line looks something like the following:

```
Robert Niles=rniles@selah.net:555-5555
```

On the CD

Listing 41.9   Dbbookadd.bat—A Small Script That Adds Information to a DBM Database.

```
...$file="addresses";
$database=dbmopen(%db, $file, 0770);

&error if $db{"$form{name}"};

$db{$form{'name'}}=join(":",$form{'e-mail'},$form{'phone'});

dbmclose(%db);
...


print "Location: /cgi-bin/dbbook.bat\n\n";
```

Lastly, since a script should always return something to the visitor, you redirect the visitor to another script, which displays the information in the phonebook.

Reading from a DBM Database

To retrieve information from a database all you have to do is create a loop that reads the contents of the database and separates the value of each key at the colon. In your script,

```
while (($key,$value)= each(%db)) {
```

starts the loop that accomplishes this task (see Listing 41.10). Within the loop the value of each key is split and assigned to the array `part`. Once that is done, you can format the result in any manner you choose. In this example, I have placed the name to be printed as part of a `mailto:` anchor, using each entry's e-mail address if it was entered.

On the CD

Listing 41.10 dbbook.bat—This Script Reads the Information From the Database.

```perl
use AnyDBM_File;


print "Content-type: text/html\n\n";

$file="c:\\website\\cgi-shl\\addresses";
$database=dbmopen(%db, $file, 0660) || die "can't";
...
while (($key,$value)= each(%db)) {
 @part = split(/:/,$value);
 if ($part[0]) {
   print "<TR><TD><A HREF=\"mailto:$part[0]\">$key</A></TD>";
   }
 else {
   print "<TR><TD>$key</TD>";
   }
 print "<TD>$part[0]</TD><TD>$part[1]</TD></TR>\n";
}
...


exit;
```

The script produces a Web page that would look like that in Figure 41.7.

FIGURE 41.7
The phonebook script produces a Web page in which the names entered are hyper-linked with their corresponding e-mail addresses.

Netscape - [Simple dbm address book]		
File Edit View Go Bookmarks Options Directory Window Help		

A Simple Address Book

Robert Niles	rniles@selah.net	509-555-5555
Mary Little Lamb	mary@porkchop.com	1-800-NO-BEEF
Rambo	rambo@firstblood.part1.com	304-555-5555
Nandor Felson	nandor@golden.com	404-555-5555
Todd Laventure	todd@sergeant.com	212-555-5555

[Add to address book]

Document Done

Part
X

Ch
41

Searching a DBM Database

If your database starts to get large, it's convenient when you can provide a means by which visitors to your site can search for a specific keyword. The Web page needed to perform this search needs to have the following tags included (see Listing 41.11).

Listing 41.11   Dbbooksearch.html—This Form Allows a Visitor to Enter a Keyword to Perform a Search.

```
<FORM ACTION="/cgi-bin/dbbooksearch.bat" METHOD="POST">
Name:<INPUT NAME="name"><BR>
<INPUT TYPE="SUBMIT">
</FORM>
```

Performing a search works much in the same manner as when you simply display the whole database. Except that this time, instead of immediately displaying each entry, you check it first to see if it matches the keyword entered by the visitor. If the keyword matches the key, then you print the line; otherwise, you simply skip ahead and check the next entry.

On the CD

Listing 41.12   dbbooksearch.bat—By Matching Each Field Against a Query, You Can Limit What Information Is Returned to the Visitor.

```
...$file="c:\\website\\cgi-shl\\addresses";
$database=dbmopen(%db, $file, 0660) ¦¦ die "can't";

...while (($key,$value)= each(%db)) {
if ($key =~ /$form{'name'}/i) {
 @part = split(/:/,$value);
 if ($part[0]) {
   print "<TR><TD><A HREF=\"mailto:$part[0]\">$key</A></TD>";
   }
 else {
   print "<TR><TD>$key</TD>";
   }
 print "<TD>$part[0]</TD><TD>$part[1]</TD></TR>\n";
 }
}
...
```

Now that you have seen how DBM databases work, you can take the same concepts from these scripts and apply them to something different. For example, a hotlinks script in which you can store information on all your favorite Web sites. Or maybe a proper address book that stores the names, addresses, and phone numbers of all your customers. You can also create a database that stores names and e-mail addresses which you can use as a mailing list, providing friends and customers news about you or your organization—or your products.

Relational Databases

Most relational database servers consist of a set of programs which manage large amounts of data, offering a rich set of query commands that help manage the power behind the database server. These programs control the storage, retrieval, and organization of the information within the database. This information within the database can be changed, updated, or removed, once the support programs or scripts are in place.

Unlike DBM databases, relational databases don't link records together physically like the DBM database does using a key/value pair. Instead, they provide a field in which information can be matched and the results of which can be sent back to the person performing the query as if the database was organized that way.

Relational databases store information in tables. Tables are similar to a smaller database which sits inside the main database. Each table usually can be linked with the information in other tables to provide a result to a query. Take a look at Figure 41.8 which shows how this information could be tied together.

Figure 41.8 depicts a query in which it requests employee information from a database.

FIGURE 41.8
A relational database stores certain information in various parts of the database which can later be called with one query.

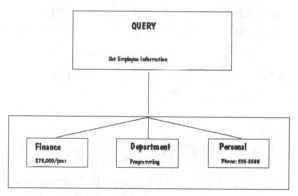

To get a complete response, information is retrieved from three different tables, each of which stores only parts of the information requested. In the figure, information about the person's pay rate is retrieved, while Departmental information and Personal information are retrieved from other tables. Working together, this can produce a complete query response, producing an abundant amount of information on an individual.

Each table consists of columns and rows. The columns identify the data by a name, while the rows store information relevant to that name. Take a look at the following example:

Part
X

Ch
41

Name	Number	E-Mail
Fred Flinstone	01–43	ff@bedrock.com
Barney Rubble	01–44	br@bedrock.com

The column heads give a name to each item below it. Information within a table is stored in much the same way.

Now if you add more tables to the database, you could have something that looks like the following:

Name	PayRate
Fred Flintstone	$34/month
Barney Rubble	$29/month

And you could have department information as well.

Name	Department	Tardy Record
Fred Flintstone	Dino-Digger	17
Barney Rubble	Pebble Pusher	3

With this information, you can perform a query to get a complete look on an individual.

```
Select * from personal,department,finance where Name="Fred Flintstone
```

This would pull up all information on Fred Flintstone, from all three records. You could even be more specific, pulling only certain parts from each table:

```
select Name.finance,Name.finance where Tardy > 5
```

With this information, I think Fred would be in serious trouble—but you should have an idea of how relational databases work.

Introduction to Structured Query Language

Structured Query Language (*SQL*) is a language which provides a user interface to relational database management systems (RDBMS). Originally developed by IBM in the 1970s, SQL is the de facto standard for storing and retrieving information for relational databases, as well as being an ISO and ANSI standard. The current standard is SQL2 with SQL3 being planned for release in 1998.

The purpose of SQL is to provide a language, easily understandable by humans, which interfaces with relational databases. ●

## CHAPTER 42

Database Tools

It is an appealing idea to take information that is stored in your database and allow its access to those visiting your site (for either Internet or *intranet* purposes). Not only can it save you the time of reentering all that data to create an HTML document but also allows you to use your database to create Web pages that change the moment the information in your database changes.

Not too long ago, it was quite difficult to create Web pages based on information from a database. Now, though, there is so much support, that trying to figure out which way to go can be an intimidating task. Because of this, we'll briefly cover the most favorite databases available and the gateways used to access and place that information on the Web. ■

Using existing databases

Most organizations are using one type of database or another to store information. Can your database be used with your CGI scripts? This chapter will talk about those databases currently used to enhance Web-based applications.

Gateways used to interact with databases

This chapter will cover what programs or gateways exist which will help you get your information out to your Web-based customers.

Databases Available

In this section, we'll take a quick look at the most commonly used databases on the Web and where you can look for further information and support.

Oracle

Oracle is the largest database developer in the world. Microsoft exceeds them only in the software arena. Oracle provides databases for Windows NT and various UNIX flavors. Oracle has created their own set of tools (mainly PL/SQL) which, coupled with the Oracle Webserver, allows you to create Web pages with little effort from information in the database. PL/SQL allows you to form stored procedures which help speed up the database query. The Oracle database engine is a good choice for large businesses that handle large amounts of information, but of course, you're going to pay for that. Today's price range for Oracle 7 and the Oracle Webserver together is over $5,000.00.

ON THE WEB

http://dozer.us.oracle.com/   For more information on Oracle and how you can use Oracle with the World Wide Web, visit their Web page online!

Sybase

Sybase System 11 is an SQL database product that has many tools that can be used to produce dynamic Web pages from the information data in your database. A new product by Powersoft, the NetImpact Studio, integrates with Sybase providing a rich set of tools to help anyone create dynamic HTML documents. The NetImpact Studio consists of an HTML Browser/Editor accompanied by a Personal Web server. These allow you to create pages using a WYSIWYG or "What You See Is What You Get" interface. The Studio also comes with a Web database, support for JavaScript (which they see as the future of CGI scripting), and support for connecting to application servers.

NetImpact can be used in conjunction with PowerBuilder, an application which is used to create plug-ins and ActiveX components. It also can be used to compliment Optima++, which creates plug-ins and supports the creation of Java applets.

Sybase also can be used with web.sql to create CGI and NSAPI (Netscape Server Application Programming Interface) applications that access the Sybase database server using Perl.

Sybase is available for Windows NT, and UNIX.

ON THE WEB

http://www.sybase.com/   For more information on Sybase, web.sql, and other Sybase-related
API's visit the Sybase home page.

mSQL

As introduced in Chapter 41, "Custom Database Query Scripts," mSQL is a middle-sized
SQL database server for UNIX which has been ported to Windows95/NT as well as OS/2.
Written by David Hughes, it was created to allow users to experiment with SQL and SQL
databases. It is free for non-commercial use (non-profit, schools, and research organizations)—although for individual and commercial use, the price is quite fair, at about $170.

ON THE WEB

http://Hughes.com.au/product/msql/   This site provides additional information on mSQL,
along with documentation, and a vast array of user contributed software.

Informix Workgroup/WorkStation Server

Informix provides two solutions in which you can use their database solutions with the
World Wide Web. The Informix Workgroup Server allows your organization to allow those
on the Web to access your company's database. Useful for both Internet and intranet applications. The Informix Workstation is available for single users, allowing an individual to
access his or her database via the Web—no matter where he or she are located. Using
DSA, or Dynamic Scalable Architecture, queries from either server are returned at amazing speeds. The servers use a GUI which helps with setting up a database, making it more
intuitive.

ON THE WEB

http://www.informix.com/   This site contains detailed information the Informix Workgroup
Server along with additional information on how you can use the Workgroup server with your web
based applications.

Microsoft SQL

Microsoft released their own SQL database server as a part of their BackOffice suite.
Microsoft is trying heavily to compete with Oracle and Sybase. They have released the
server for $999, but you also must buy the SQL Server Internet Connector which costs
$2,995. These two products allow you to provide unlimited access to the server from
the Web.

ON THE WEB

http://www.microsoft.com/sql/   This site will provide additional information on Microsoft's SQL server and how you can use Microsoft's SQL server in conjunction with the World Wide Web.

Ingres

Ingres (Interactive Graphics Retrieval System) comes in both a commercial and public domain version. The University of California at Berkeley originally developed this retrieval system, but Berkeley no longer supports the public domain version. You can still find it on the University's Web site.

Ingres uses the QUEL query language as well as SQL. QUEL is a superset of the original SQL language, making Ingres more powerful. Ingres was developed to work with graphics in a database environment. The public domain version is available for UNIX systems.

ON THE WEB

ftp://s2k-ftp.cs.berkeley.edu/pub/ingres/   Visit this site to download the public domain version of Ingres.

Computer Associates owns the commercial version of Ingres. This version is quite robust and capable of managing virtually any database application. The commercial version is available for UNIX, VMS, and Windows NT.

ON THE WEB

http://www.cai.com/products/ingr.htm   Visit this site to find out more information on the commercial version of Ingres.

ON THE WEB

http://www.naiua.org/   For information about both the commercial and public domain versions of Ingres, visit the North American Ingres Users Association.

FoxPro

Microsoft's Visual FoxPro has been a favorite for Web programmers, mostly because of its long-time standing in the database community as well as its third-party support. FoxPro is an Xbase database system that is widely used for smaller business and personal database applications.

ON THE WEB

http://www.microsoft.com/catalog/products/visfoxp/   Visit the FoxPro home page on
Microsoft's Web site for more information on FoxPro and visit Neil's Foxpro database page at

http://adams.patriot.net/~johnson/html/neil/fox/foxaol.htm

Microsoft Access

Microsoft Access is a relational database management system that is part of the Microsoft
Office suite. Microsoft Access can be used to create HTML documents based on the
information stored in the Access database with the help of Microsoft's Internet Assistant.
Microsoft's Internet Assistant is an add-on that is available free of charge for Access users.
Microsoft Access can also support ActiveX controls which makes Access even more pow-
erful when used with the Microsoft Internet explorer.

ON THE WEB

http://www.microsoft.com/accessdev/DefOff.htm   This site will provide you with details on
Microsoft Access and how you can use Access with your web based applications. Additionally, you
can test the Job Forum as well as look at the code used to create this application.

Database Tools

Now that you have taken a look at the various databases available, it's time to take a look
at the third-party tools which help you create applications that tie your databases together
with the Web.

Cold Fusion

Allaire created Cold Fusion as a system that enables you to write scripts within HTML.
Cold Fusion, a database interface, processes the scripts and then returns the information
within the HTML written in the script. Although Cold Fusion currently costs $495, the
product is definitely worth the price. Allaire wrote Cold Fusion to work with just about
every Web server available for Windows NT and integrates with just about every SQL
engine—including those database servers available on UNIX machines (if a 32-bit ODBC
driver exists).

Cold Fusion works by processing a form, created by you, that sends a request to the Web
server. The server starts Cold Fusion and sends the information to Cold Fusion which is
used to call a template file. After reading the information that the visitor entered, Cold
Fusion processes that information according to the template's instructions. It then returns

an automatically generated HTML document to the server and then returns the document to the visitor.

For example, the following form asks the visitor to enter their name and telephone number. Once the visitor clicks Submit, the form is processed by Cold Fusion which calls the template enter.dbm.

```
<HTML>
<HEAD><TITLE>Phonebook</TITLE></HEAD>
<BODY>
<FORM ACTION="/cgi-bin/dbml.exe?Template=/phone/entry/enter.dbm"
➥ METHOD="POST">
Enter your full name:<INPUT TYPE="text" NAME="name"><BR>
Enter your phone number:<INPUT TYPE="text" NAME="phone"><P>
<INPUT TYPE="submit">
</FORM>
</BODY>
</HTML>
```

The template contains a small script that inserts the information into the database and then displays an HTML document to the visitor. This document thanks them for taking the time to enter their name and telephone number into the database.

```
<DBINSERT DATASOURCE="Visitors" TABLENAME="Phone">
<HTML>
<HEAD><TITLE>Thank you!</TITLE></HEAD>
<BODY>
<H1>Thank your for your submission!<H1>
Your name and phone number has been entered into our database.
➥ Thank you for taking the time to fill it out.
<P>
<A HREF="main.html">[Return to the main page]</A>
</BODY>
</HTML>
```

Although Cold Fusion is a lot more complex than this, you can get an idea of how easy it is to handle information and place that information into the database.

ON THE WEB

http://www.allaire.com/   Visit this site for the complete details on Cold Fusion.

Gorta

Gorta is an ODBC driver which is used to allow CGI scripts, developed using the ODBC interface, to access a MINI-SQL (mSQL) database running on a UNIX or NT server.

ON THE WEB

ftp://Bond.edu.au/pub/Minerva/msql/Contrib/ODBC/   Visit the ODSC directory on the mSQL ftp server to download Gorta, and even read the Gorta FAQ.

Microsoft's dbWeb

Microsoft's dbWeb allows you to create Web pages on-the-fly with the use of an interactive Schema Wizard. The Schema Wizard is a GUI interface that specifies what is searched for within the database and which fields appear within the Web page.

dbWeb allows you to publish information from a database in HTML format without having to know any HTML programming or make you learn how to use the ISAPI interface. dbWeb can be used with the Microsoft Internet Information Server and supports the Oracle database server, the Microsoft SQL server, Access, Visual FoxPro, and any other databases which support the 32-bit ODBC driver.

ON THE WEB

http://www.microsoft.com/intdev/dbweb/   Visit this site for the latest information on dbWeb and how it can be used to integrate your database with the World Wide Web.

WDB

On the CD

WDB is a suite of Perl scripts that help you create applications that allow you to integrate SQL databases with the World Wide Web. WDB provides support for Sybase, Informix, and mSQL databases but has been used with other database products as well.

WDB uses what its author, Bo Frese Rasmussen, calls "form definition files" which describe how the information retrieved from the database should display to the visitor. WDL automatically creates forms on-the-fly that allow the visitor to query the database. This saves you a lot of the work to prepare a script to query a database. The user submits the query and WDB then performs a set of conversions, or links, so the visitor can perform additional queries by clicking one of the links.

ON THE WEB

http://arch-http.hq.eso.org/wdb/html/wdb.html   Visit the WDB home page for further information on WDB.

Part
X

Ch
42

DBGateway

On the CD

DBGateway is a 32-bit Visual Basic WinCGI application which runs on a Windows NT machine as a service that provides World Wide Web access to Microsoft Access and FoxPro databases. It is being developed as part of the Flexible Computer Integrated Manufacturing (FCIM) project. DBGateway is a gateway between your CGI applications and the Database servers. Because your CGI scripts only "talk" with the Database Gateway, you only need to be concerned with programming for the gateway instead of each individual database server. This performs two functions—programming a query is much easier because the gateway handles the communication with the database and scripts can be easily ported to different database systems.

The gateway allows a visitor to your site to submit a form which is sent to the server. The server hands the request to the gateway which decodes the information and builds a query forming the result based on a template, or it can send the result of the query raw.

ON THE WEB

http://fcim1.csdc.com/   Visit this site to view the DBGateway's user manual, view the online FAQ, and see how DBGateway has been used.

Additional Resources on the Web

Additional information on Web database gateways are found at the Web-Database Gateways page at

> **http://gdbdoc.gdb.org/letovsky/genera/dbgw.html**

and also on Yahoo at

> **http://www.yahoo.com/Computers_and_Internet/World_Wide_Web/ Databases_and_Searching**

Appendixes

HTML 2.0 and 3.2 Quick Reference

HTML is made up of a lot of different elements. Each element or *tag* behaves differently from all the other HTML tags. The effects of some of them are so elementary that you only need to invoke them and they'll be used. Others require beginning and ending markers, so that the element's behavior is applied to the enclosed text.

For those tags that do have attributes, most of them are optional. To use a specific attribute, you must include the attribute name, the equal sign (=), and the value to set it to. Invalid values are automatically ignored by most Web browsers. The assignment of attributes is done inside the starting marker of the particular HTML element that you want to use.

Every HTML document must be enclosed within the <HTML> starting marker and the </HTML> ending marker. Between these two markers is the actual code that produces the Web page. The content of a particular HTML document is made up of head and body portions. The information for the head portion is enclosed within the <HEAD> and </HEAD> markers. The information for the body portion is enclosed within the <BODY> and </BODY> markers.

The following list covers the most commonly used HTML elements and their most commonly used attributes. The appropriate FrontPage Editor menu command and toolbar button name accompany each element, if applicable. ■

Elements in the HEAD

■ <BASE>—This is used to indicate the default location of relative URL links. Common attributes:

HREF—Baseline URL for relative links.

TARGET—Indicates which window to display the destination hypertext link.
FrontPage command: None
Button/Toolbar: None

■ <ISINDEX>—This is used to indicate that the entire Web page can be searched by keywords. There are no commonly used attributes.
FrontPage command: None
Button/Toolbar: None

■ <LINK>—This is used to specify relationships to other HTML documents. Commonly used attributes:

HREF—Destination URL to establish a relationship with.

REL—Indicates relationship with destination document.

REV—Used to verify a reversed relationship with destination document.

TITLE—The title for the destination URL.
FrontPage command: None
Button/Toolbar: None

■ <SCRIPT></SCRIPT>—This is used to specify a program script to be embedded in the page.
FrontPage command: Insert, Script
Button/Toolbar: Insert Script Button/Advanced Toolbar

■ <TITLE></TITLE>—You can specify the document's title with this element. The <TITLE> element is a mandatory element in every HTML document.
FrontPage command: File, Page Properties, Title
Button/Toolbar: None

Elements in the BODY

The majority of tags are specified in within the BODY elements. Typically, anything contained inside the start and end markers will be displayed. The following sets of related elements are all available:

Text Elements

This group of tags is used to apply general attributes to a group of text. Typically, these elements are word wrapped by the browser.

■ <BLOCKQUOTE>[Text]</BLOCKQUOTE>—This will cause [Text] to be displayed as quoted text.
FrontPage command: None
Button/Toolbar: Increase Indent Button/Format Toolbar
- <P>[Text]</P>—The [Text] is treated as if it were an entire paragraph by itself. The [Text] will be word wrapped.
FrontPage command: Format, Paragraph, Normal
Button/Toolbar: Change Style Box, Normal/Format Toolbar
- <PRE>[Text]</PRE>—The [Text] will be displayed with embedded tabs, strings of spaces, and carriage returns/linefeeds, by default in a monospaced font like Courier.
FrontPage command: None
Button/Toolbar: Change Style Box, Formatted/Format Toolbar

Hypertext Links

Hyperlinks are the underlying component of the Web.

■ <A>[Text]</A>—This defines that [Text] is a hypertext link. If the <IMG> element is used in place of [Text], the image will be hyperlinked. Common attributes:

HREF—URL to link to.

NAME—Defines the current line as a named anchor. Named anchors are addressed by specifying the pound sign (#) followed by the desired NAME.

TARGET—This indicates the name of the window to display the destination URL.

TITLE—The title of the destination URL.
FrontPage command: Edit, Hyperlink
Button/Toolbar: Create or Edit Hyperlink Button/Standard Toolbar

Headers

Header elements are used to provide a consistent organization for your document. There are no commonly used attributes for these elements.

- <H1>[Text]</H1>—[Text] is displayed in the most prominent header.
  FrontPage command: Format, Paragraph, Heading 1
  Button/Toolbar: Change Style Box, Heading 1/Format Toolbar

- <H2>[Text]</H2>—[Text] is displayed in the second most prominent header.
  FrontPage command: Format, Paragraph, Heading 2
  Button/Toolbar: Change Style Box, Heading 2/Format Toolbar

- <H3>[Text]</H3>—[Text] is displayed in the third most prominent header.
  FrontPage command: Format, Paragraph, Heading 3
  Button/Toolbar: Change Style Box, Heading 3/Format Toolbar

- <H4>[Text]</H4>—[Text] is displayed in the fourth most prominent header.
  FrontPage command: Format, Paragraph, Heading 4
  Button/Toolbar: Change Style Box, Heading 4/Format Toolbar

- <H5>[Text]</H5>—[Text] is displayed in the fifth most prominent header.
  FrontPage command: Format, Paragraph, Heading 5
  Button/Toolbar: Change Style Box, Heading 5/Format Toolbar

- <H6>[Text]</H6>—[Text] is displayed in the smallest header.
  FrontPage command: Format, Paragraph, Heading 6
  Button/Toolbar: Change Style Box, Heading 6/Format Toolbar

Logical Text

Logical style elements define attributes for a group of text. The text is automatically word wrapped by the browser.

- <CITE>[Text]</CITE>—This tag is used to indicate that the [Text] is a citation. There are no commonly used attributes.
  FrontPage command: Format, Font, Special Styles, Citation
  Button/Toolbar: None
  - <CODE>[Text]</CODE>—The [Text] is displayed as being computer source code. There are no commonly used attributes.
  FrontPage command: Format, Font, Special Styles, Code
  Button/Toolbar: None
- <DFN>[Text]</DFN>—[Text] will be displayed as if it were a definition. There are no commonly used attributes.
  FrontPage command: Format, Font, Special Styles, Definition
  Button/Toolbar: Change Style Box, Definition/Format Toolbar

- <EM>[Text]</EM>—The [Text] is emphasized in some way. There are no commonly used attributes.
  FrontPage command: None
  Button/Toolbar: Italic Button/Format Toolbar

- <KBD>[Text]</KBD>—This tag is used to display [Text] as something to be typed on the keyboard. There are no commonly used attributes.
  FrontPage command: Format, Font, Special Styles, KeyBoard
  Button/Toolbar: None

- <SAMP>[Text]</SAMP>—To display [Text] as a sampling of something, such as from an article, use this element. There are no commonly used attributes.
  FrontPage command: Format, Font, Special Styles, Sample
  Button/Toolbar: None

- <STRONG>[Text]</STRONG>—This element displays the [Text] as more emphasized than <EM>. There are no commonly used attributes.
  FrontPage command: None
  Button/Toolbar: Bold Button/Format Toolbar

- <VAR>[Text]</VAR>—This displays [Text] as some sort of variable, such as for formulas. There are no commonly used attributes.
  FrontPage command: Format, Font, Special Styles, Variable
  Button/Toolbar: None

Physical Styles

This group of HTML elements is used to affect the visual display of text. There are no commonly used attributes for these elements.

- <B>[Text]</B>—[Text] will be made boldface.
  FrontPage command: Format, Font, Special Styles, Bold
  Button/Toolbar: None

- <I>[Text]</I>—[Text] will be set in italics.
  FrontPage command: Format, Font, Special Styles, Italic
  Button/Toolbar: None

- <TT>[Text]</TT>—[Text] will be made to look as though it came from a teletype.
  FrontPage command: Format, Font, Typewriter
  Button/Toolbar: None

- <U>[Text]</U>—[Text] will be underlined.
  FrontPage command: Format, Font, Underline
  Button/Toolbar: Underline Button/Format Toolbar

Definition List

This list type allows you to present a dictionary-type presentation of a definition. The left hand side has the word, <DD>, and the right hand side has the definition, <DT>.

■ <DL>[Definitions]</DL>—This is the main container for a definition list. It has the following commonly used attributes.
FrontPage command: None
Button/Toolbar: Change Style Box, Definition/Format Toolbar

■ <DD>[Text]</DD>—This element is used to specify that [Text] is the definition portion of the definition list. There are no commonly used attributes.
FrontPage command: None
Button/Toolbar: None

■ <DT>[Text]</DT>—This element is used to specify that [Text] is the term portion of the definition list. There are no commonly used attributes.
FrontPage command: None
Button/Toolbar: Change Style Box, Defined Term/Format Toolbar

Unordered (Bulleted) List

You can create a list with a bullet in front of each item.

■ <UL>[List of items]</UL>—This presents [List of items] as an unordered (bulleted) list.
FrontPage command: None
Button/Toolbar: Bulleted List Button/Format Toolbar; or Change Style Box, Bulleted List/Format Toolbar

■ <LI>[Text]</LI>—[Text] will be an item in the list. There are no commonly used attributes.
FrontPage command: None
Button/Toolbar: None

Ordered (Numbered) List

You can create a list with a number in front of each item. The number is automatically added.

■ <OL>[List of items]</OL>—This presents [List of items] as an ordered (numbered) list.
FrontPage command: None

Button/Toolbar: Numbered List Button/Format Toolbar; or Change Style Box, Numbered List/Format Toolbar

- <LI>[Text]</LI>—[Text] will be an item in the list. There are no commonly used attributes.
  FrontPage command: None
  Button/Toolbar: None

Directory List

You can create a list so that each item appears to be a list of files from a directory.

- <DIR>[List of items]</DIR>—This presents [List of items] that appears to be a list of files from a directory.
  FrontPage command: None
  Button/Toolbar: Change Style Box, Directory list/Format Toolbar

- <LI>[Text]</LI>.1—[Text] will be an item in the list. There are no commonly used attributes.
  FrontPage command: None
  Button/Toolbar: None

Graphics

Graphics can be inserted into your page very easily.

- <IMG>—This element is used to put a GIF or JPEG graphic into your page. It has the following commonly used attributes:

  ALIGN—This attribute indicates how the picture will be aligned. It has a number of acceptable values: LEFT, RIGHT, TOP, BOTTOM, and MIDDLE.

  ALT—This string will be shown if the user doesn't have a graphical browser.

  HEIGHT—This value indicates the height of the image in pixels.

  ISMAP—This tells the Web browser that this graphic is an image map.

  SRC—This points to a URL that contains the graphic to use.

  WIDTH—This value indicates the width of the image in pixels.
  FrontPage command: Insert, Image
  Button/Toolbar: Insert Image Button/Standard Toolbar

Miscellaneous Tags

There are several unclassifiable, commonly used HTML tags.

- <!— [Text] —>—This element is completely ignored by the Web browser. The [Text] is treated as comments from the HTML author.
  FrontPage command: None
  Button/Toolbar: None
  - <ADDRESS>[Text]</ADDRESS>—This tag shows [Text] as an address of some sort. There are no commonly used attributes.
  FrontPage command: None
  Button/Toolbar: Change Style Box, Address/Format Toolbar For the most recent information on HTML standards, refer to the Web Design Group page for this subject, at:

http://www.htmlhelp.com/

VB Script and JScript Command Reference

To quote Microsoft, VB Script is a lightweight subset of Visual Basic. Don't confuse lightweight with wimpy, however. VB Script is not wimpy. You can create remarkably complex, dynamic Web pages with VB Script, and instantly distribute those Web pages to millions of users around the World. Try that with Visual Basic.

Although VB Script is a subset of Visual Basic, you'll find a lot of differences between the two. That won't keep Visual Basic programmers from quickly getting up to speed, as long as they understand these differences. This section does exactly that. If you're a Visual Basic programmer, you'll find an overview of the differences in this appendix, as well as a list of Visual Basic keywords available in VB Script and a list of Visual Basic keywords omitted from VB Script. ■

Key Differences Between VB and VB Script

You didn't run out to the computer store and buy a copy of VB Script. You didn't install a VB Script diskette on your computer, either. All you did was install a browser that supports VB Script, such as Internet Explorer, on your computer—just like millions of other folks. Everyone of them has the VB Script engine on their computer, and everyone of them has the ability to create Web pages with VB Script.

So where's the integrated development environment that you're used to using in Visual Basic? Keep looking, because there isn't one. All you have is your favorite text editor, the ActiveX Control Pad and a Web browser. That in itself is the single largest difference between Visual Basic and VB Script. It leads to some specific differences, too. Here's what they are:

- **Debugging**. VB Script doesn't have a debugger like Visual Basic. You'll resort to using lots of message boxes, instead.

- **Event-handlers**. You don't have an editor in which you select an object and event to edit an event-procedure. You have to name event-procedures in your scripts so that the scripting engine can find the appropriate handler when an object fires an event.

- **Forms**. VB Script doesn't have a forms editor. It doesn't need one, because you can't display forms anyway. You put forms and controls on the Web page, instead. You can use the ActiveX Control Pad to insert all those nasty <OBJECT> tags in your Web page, however.

You don't compile a VB Script program into an EXE file like you do with a Visual Basic program. You distribute your scripts as plain old text embedded in HTML files. Everyone and their uncle can read your scripts. The script engine interprets this text into intermediate code when it loads the Web page. It also creates a symbol table so that it can quickly look up things such as event-procedures and variable names. The scripting engine uses the ActiveX Scripting technology to interact with the browser.

N O T E   You'll find a plethora of nit-picky differences between Visual Basic and VB Script, too. You have to use the value property to query an objects value, for example. Thus, instead of reading a text box's value using form.text, you have to read it using form.text. value. These subtle differences are too numerous to document in this appendix. Go to Microsoft's Web site (www.microsoft.com) and their knowledge base for further explanation of these differences. ■

Another significant difference between Visual Basic and VB Script is the keywords that Microsoft omitted from VB Script. You'll learn more about the keywords included in VB Script in the next section. You'll learn about the keywords that Microsoft omitted from VB Script in "Visual Basic Keywords Omitted from VB Script," later in this chapter.

Visual Basic Keywords Included in VB Script

VB Script includes all the keywords and features that you need to activate a Web page. You can't read or write files, as you'll learn later in this chapter, but you can handle any event that an object fires. You can also handle just about any type of data that you'll find on a Web page and manipulate the Web page in anyway you want.

Table B.1 describes each keyword or feature available in VB Script. I've divided this table into broad categories, with each entry under a category describing a single feature. I've used the same categories that Microsoft uses so that you can keep this information straight as you bounce back and forth between Microsoft's Web site and this book. If you don't find a feature that you expect to see, check out table B.2 to see if that feature is in the list of Visual Basic features omitted from VB Script.

ON THE WEB

You can find more information about VB Script's features at Microsoft's VB Script Web site: **http://www.microsoft.com/vbscript.**

Table B.1   VB Script Keywords

Keyword/Feature	Description
	Array handling
Dim	Declare an array
ReDim	Redimension an array
Private	Declare an array at script level
Public	Declare a public array at script level
IsArray	Returns True if a variable is an array
Erase	Reinitializes a fixed-size array
LBound	Returns the lower bound of an array
UBound	Returns the upper bound of an array
	Assignments
=	Assigns a value to a variable
Let	Assigns a value to a variable
Set	Assigns an object to a variable

continues

Table B.1 Continued

Keyword/Feature	Description
	Comments
'	Include inline comments in your script
Rem	Include comments in your script
	Constants/Literals
Empty	Indicates an uninitialized variable
Nothing	Disassociate a variable with an object
Null	Indicates a variable with no data
True	Boolean True
False	Boolean False
	Control flow
Do . . . Loop	Repeats a block of statements
For . . . Next	Repeats a block of statements
For Each . . . Next	Repeats a block of statements
If . . . Then . . . Else	Conditionally executes statements
Select Case	Conditionally executes statements
While . . . Wend	Repeats a block of statements
	Conversions
Abs	Returns absolute value of a number
Asc	Returns the ASCII code of a character
AscB	Returns the ASCII code of a character
AscW	Returns the ASCII code of a character
Chr	Returns a character from an ASCII code
ChrB	Returns a character from an ASCII code
ChrW	Returns a character from an ASCII code
CBool	Converts a variant to a boolean
CByte	Converts a variant to a byte
CDate	Converts a variant to a date
CDbl	Converts a variant to a double

Keyword/Feature	Description
	Conversions
Cint	Converts a variant to an integer
CLng	Converts a variant to a long
CSng	Converts a variant to a single
CStr	Converts a variant to a string
DateSerial	Converts a variant to a date
DateValue	Converts a variant to a date
Hex	Converts a variant to a hex string
Oct	Converts a variant to a octal string
Fix	Converts a variant to a fixed string
Int	Converts a variant to a integer string
Sgn	Converts a variant to a single string
TimeSerial	Converts a variant to a time
TimeValue	Converts a variant to a time
	Dates/Times
Date	Returns the current date
Time	Returns the current time
DateSerial	Returns a date from its parts
DateValue	Returns a date from its value
Day	Returns day from a date
Month	Returns month from a date
Weekday	Returns weekday from a date
Year	Returns year from a date
Hour	Returns hour from a time
Minute	Returns minute from a time
Second	Returns second from a time
Now	Returns current date and time
TimeSerial	Returns a time from its parts
TimeValue	Returns a time from its value

Part
XI

App
B

continues

Table B.1   Continued

Keyword/Feature	Description
	Declarations
Dim	Declares a variable
Private	Declares script-level private variable
Public	Declares public-level public variable
ReDim	Reallocate an array
Function	Declares a function
Sub	Declares a sub-procedure
	Error Handling
On Error	Enables error handling
Err	Contains information about last error
	Input/Output
InputBox	Prompt the user for input
MsgBox	Display a message to the user
	Math
Atn	Returns the Arctangent of a number
Cos	Returns the cosine of a number
Sin	Returns the sine of a number
Tan	Returns the tangent of a number
Exp	Returns the exponent of a number
Log	Returns the logarithm of a number
Sqr	Returns the square root of a number
Randomize	Reseeds the randomizer
Rnd	Returns a random number
	Operators
+	Addition
-	Subtraction
^	Exponentiation
Mod	Modulus arithmetic
*	Multiplication

Keyword/Feature	Description
	Operators
/	Division
\	Integer Division
-	Negation
&	String concatenation
=	Equality
<>	Inequality
<	Less Than
<=	Less Than or Equal To
>	Greater Than
>=	Greater Than or Equal To
Is	Compare expressions
And	Compare expressions
Or	Compare expressions
Xor	Compare expressions
Eqv	Compare expressions
Imp	Compare expressions
	Objects
CreateObject	Creates reference to an OLE object
IsObject	Returns True if object is valid
	Options
Option Explicit	Forces explicit variable declaration
	Procedures
Call	Invokes a sub-procedure
Function	Declares a function
Sub	Declares a sub-procedure
	Strings
Asc	Returns ASCII code of a character
AscB	Returns ASCII code of a character

continues

Table B.1 Continued	
Keyword/Feature	**Description**
	Strings
AscW	Returns ASCII code of a character
Chr	Returns character from an ASCII code
ChrB	Returns character from an ASCII code
ChrW	Returns character from an ASCII code
Instr	Returns index of a string in another
InStrB	Returns index of a string in another
Len	Returns the length of a string
LenB	Returns the length of a string
Lcase	Converts a string to lower case
Ucase	Converts a string to upper case
Left	Returns the left portion of a string
LeftB	Returns the left portion of a string
Mid	Returns the mid portion of a string
MidB	Returns the mid portion of a string
Right	Returns the right portion of a string
RightB	Returns the right portion of a string
Space	Pads a string with spaces
StrComp	Compares two strings
String	Pads a string with a character
Ltrim	Removes leading spaces from a string
Rtrim	Removes trailing spaces from a string
Trim	Removes leading and trailing spaces
	Variants
IsArray	Returns True if variable is an array
IsDate	Returns True if variable is an date
IsEmpty	Returns True if variable is empty
IsNull	Returns True if variable is null
IsNumeric	Returns True if variable is a number
IsObject	Returns True if variable is an object
VarType	Indicates a variable's type

Visual Basic Keywords Omitted from VB Script

VB Script leaves out a bunch of Visual Basic keywords such as `DoEvents`, `Print`, and `Shell`. You can't read or write files, either, and you can't do much graphical programming. This won't stop you from creating great Web pages with VB Script, though, because VB Script provides every feature you need to do just about anything you want on the Web page. For example, you can dynamically change the contents of the Web page itself and you can interact with every object on the Web page.

Don't look at the list of omitted keywords and features yet. You need to understand why Microsoft didn't include them so that you'll understand why each feature is on this list. Take a look:

- **Portability.** Microsoft intends to make VB Script available on a variety of platforms including Windows, Mac, Unix, and so on. They've wisely removed keywords and features that make VB Script less portable to these platforms.

- **Performance.** You've heard it before: speed or features—pick one. Microsoft removed many non-essential features from VB Script to allow scripts load and run faster.

- **Safety.** You should be concerned with security on the Internet. You don't want to open a Web page and discover that it contains a script which crashes your drive, do you? Microsoft removed any Visual Basic feature that might cause a security problem with scripts such as file I/O. You can still get access to these features, however, if you create an ActiveX object which you control with VB Script.

Table B.1 describes each keyword or feature available in Visual Basic but omitted from VB Script. I've divided this table into broad categories, with each entry under a category describing a single feature. I've used Microsoft's categories so that you can keep the list on Microsoft's Web site in sync with this list.

N O T E The Internet Explorer Script Error dialog box tells you that it found a statement in your script which it couldn't interpret. I'm sure that you've seen error messages such as `Expected while` or `until` or `nested comment` that just don't make any sense. When VB Script encounters a keyword it doesn't recognize, it spews out all sorts of garbage like the previous example. It usually points to the offending keyword, however, by placing a caret (^) directly underneath it. The next time you get one of these unexplained errors, look up the keyword in table B.2 to see if Microsoft omitted it from VB Script. ∎

Part

XI

App

B

Table B.2   Visual Basic Keywords Not in VB Script

Keyword/Feature	Description
	Array Handling
Option Base	Declare default lower bound
Arrays with lower bound <> 0	All arrays must have 0 lower bound
	Clipboard
Clipboard object	Provides access to the clipboard
Clear	Clears the contents of the clipboard
GetFormat	Determines format of clipboard object
GetData	Returns data from the clipboard
SetData	Stores data in the clipboard
GetText	Returns text from the clipboard
SetText	Stores text in the clipboard
	Collection
Add	Adds an item to a collection
Count	Returns number of items in a collection
Item	Returns an item from a collection
Remove	Removes an item from a collection
Access collections using ! character	Accessing a collection with !
	Conditional Compilation
#Const	Defines a compiler constant
#If ... Then ... #Else	Conditional compilation
	Constants/Literals
Const	Define a constant
All intrinsic constants	Predefined constants such as vbOK
exponent-based real number	Real numbers using exponents
Trailing data type characters	Define data types implicitly

Keyword/Feature	Description
	Control Flow
DoEvents	Yields execution to Windows
GoSub ... Return	Branches to a label in a procedure
GoTo	Goes to a label in a procedure
On Error GoTo	Goes to a label on an error
On ... GoSub	Branches to a label on an index
On ... GoTo	Goes to a label on an index
Line numbers	Line numbers
Line labels	Labels define GoTo/GoSub targets
With ... End With	Provides easy access to an object
	Conversion
Chr$	Returns a character from an ASCII code
Hex$	Returns string hex from a number
Oct$	Returns string octal from a number
Ccur	Converts expression to currency
Cvar	Converts expression to a variant
CVDate	Converts an expression to a date
Format	Formats a string
Format$	Formats a string
Str	Returns string form of a number
Str$	Returns string form of a number
Val	Returns a number from a string
	Data Types
All intrinsic data types except variant	Data types such as Date
Type ... End Type	Defines user-defined data type
	Date/Time
Date statement	Returns the current date
Time statement	Returns the current time
Date$	Returns the current date

Part

XI

App

B

continues

Table B.2   Continued

Keyword/Feature	Description
	Date/Time
Time$	Returns the current time
Timer	Returns seconds elapsed since midnight
	DDE
LinkExecute	Sends command during DDE conversation
LinkPoke	Sends data during a DDE conversation
LinkRequest	Receives data during DDE conversation
LinkSend	Sends data during a DDE conversation
	Debugging
Debug.Print	Print to the debugging window
End	Shut down the application
Stop	Stop the application
	Declaration
Declare	Declare a DLL
Property Get	Define a user-defined class
Property Let	Define a user-defined class
Property Set	Define a user-defined class
Public	Declare a public variable
Private	Declare a private variable
ParamArray	Accept a variable number of arguments
Optional	Specifies an optional argument
New	Creates a new object
	Error Handling
Erl	Returns the line number of an error
Error	Returns an error message
Error$	Returns an error message
On Error ... Resume	Enables error handling
Resume	Resumes after an error
Resume Next	Resumes after an error

Keyword/Feature	Description
	File Input/Output
All	Open, read, write, and close files
	Financial
All financial functions	Financial function such as Rate
	Graphics
Cls	Clear the screen
Circle	Draw a circle
Line	Draw a line
Point	Draw a point
Pset	Change a points color
Scale	Defines the coordinate system
Print	Print to a file
Spc	Position output using Print
Tab	Insert a tab character
TextHeight	Returns height of a text string
TextWidth	Returns width of a text string
LoadPicture	Load a picture from disk
SavePicture	Save a picture to disk
QBColor	Returns a RGB color code
RGB	Combines RGB color codes
	Manipulating objects
Arrange	Arranges windows
Zorder	Changes z-order of windows
SetFocus	Sets focus to a window
InputBox$	Prompts the user for a string
Drag	Begins a drag-and-drop operation
Hide	Hides a form
Show	Shows a form

Part
XI

App
B

continues

Table B.2   Continued

Keyword/Feature	Description
	Manipulating Objects
Load	Loads a form
Unload	Unloads a form
Move	Moves a form
PrintForm	Prints a form
Refresh	Repaints a form
AddItem	Adds item to listbox
RemoveItem	Removes item from a listbox
	Miscellaneous
Environ	Returns the user's environment
Environ$	Returns the user's environment
SendKeys	Sends keystrokes to a window
Command	Returns the command line parameters
Command$	Returns the command line parameters
AppActivate	Actives an application's window
Shell	Launches another program
Beep	Beeps the speaker
	Object Manipulation
GetObject	Returns an OLE object from a file
TypeOf	Returns the type of an object
	Operators
Like	Compares to strings
	Options
def *type*	Sets default data type for variables
Option Base	Sets default lower bound for arrays
Option Compare	Defines default comparison method
Option Private Module	Defines default scope

Keyword/Feature	Description
	Printing
TextHeight	Returns height of a text string
TextWidth	Returns width of a text string
EndDoc	Terminates a print operation
NewPage	Ejects the current page
PrintForm	Prints a form
	Strings
All fixed-length strings	Strings with a fixed length
LCase$	Converts a string to lower case
UCase$	Converts a string to upper case
Lset	Left aligns a string
Rset	Right aligns a string
Space$	Pads a string with spaces
String$	Pads a string with a character
Format	Formats a string
Format$	Formats a string
Left$	Returns left portion of a string
Mid$	Returns mid portion of a string
Right$	Returns right portion of a string
Mid Statement	Replaces a portion of a string
Trim$	Removes leading and trailing spaces
LTrim$	Removes leading spaces from a string
RTrim$	Removes trailing spaces from a string
StrConv	Performs various conversions
	Using classes
TypeName	Define a user-defined class
	Optional arguments
IsMissing	Indicates missing optional argument

Part
XI

App
B

JavaScript Command Reference

If you've read chapter 21, you've already learned a great deal about JavaScript—the scripting language developed by Netscape for HTML documents. In addition to a text editor and compatible browser, this appendix will give you a quick, yet comprehensive reference as you create JavaScript Web docuents.

In addition to objects and keywords, the general terms used when studying JavaScript and its implementation are included, making this appendix a practical aid to your understanding of JavaScript and how it works.

Terms

Cookie   A special object containing state/status information about the client that can be accessed by the server. Included in that `state` object is a description of the range of URLs for which that state is valid. Future HTTP requests from the client falling within a range of URLs described within the state object will include transmission of the current value of the state object from the client back to the server.

This simple form of data storage allows the server to provide "personalized" service to the client. Online merchants can store information about items currently in an "electronic shopping basket," services can post registration information and automate functions such as typing a user-id, and user preferences can be saved on the client and retrieved by the server when the site is contacted. For limited-use information, such as shopping services, it is also possible to set a time-limit on the life of the cookie information.

CGI scripts are typically used to set and retrieve cookie values. To generate the cookie requires sending an HTTP header in the following format:

```
Set-Cookie: NAME=Value; [EXPIRES=date;] [PATH=pathname;]
➥[DOMAIN=domainname;] [SECURE]
```

When a request for cookie information is made, the list of cookie information is searched for all URLs which match the current URL. Any matches are returned in this format:

```
cookie: NAME1=string1; NAME2=string2; ...
```

Cookie was an arbitrarily assigned name. For more information about the cookie and its function, see **http://home.netscape.com/newsref/std/cookie_spec.html**.

Event Handler   Attributes of HTML tags embedded in documents. The attribute assigns a JavaScript command or function to execute when the event happens.

Function   A user-defined or built-in set of statements that perform a task. It can also return a value when used with the `return` statement.

Hierarchy   Navigator objects exist in a set relation to each other that reflects the structure of an HTML page. This is referred to as *instance hierarchy* because it only works with specific instances of objects, rather than general classes.

The `window` object is the parent of all other Navigator objects. Underneath `window`, `location`, `history`, and `document` all share precedence. `Document` includes forms, links, and anchors.

Each object is a descendant of the higher object. A form called `orderForm` is an object, but it is also a property of `document`. As such, it is referred to as `document.orderForm`.

Java   An object-oriented, platform-independent programming language developed by Sun Microsystems and used to add additional functionality to Web pages. Programming in Java requires a Java Development Kit with compiler and core classes.

JavaScript   A scripting language developed by Netscape for HTML documents. Scripts are performed after specific user-triggered events. Creating JavaScript Web documents requires a text editor and compatible browser.

Literal   An absolute value not assigned to a variable. Examples include 1, 3.1415927, "Bob," `true`.

Method   A function assigned to an object. For example, `bigString.toUpperCase()` returns an uppercase version of the string contained in `bigString`.

Object   A construct with properties that are JavaScript variables or other objects. Functions associated with an object are known as the *object's methods.* You access the properties of an object with a simple notation:

```
objectName.propertyName
```

Both object and property names are case-sensitive.

Operator   Performs a function on one or more operands or variables. Operators are divided into two classes: binary and unary. Binary operators need two operands, and unary operands can operate on a single operand.

For example, addition is a binary operand:

```
sum = 1 + 1
```

Unary operands are often used to update counters. The following example increases the variable by 1:

```
counter++
```

See Appendix D, "JavaScript Commands and Grammar," for a list of operators and their precedence.

Property   Used to describe an object. A property is defined by assigning it a value. There are several properties in JavaScript that contain *constants:* Values that never change.

Script   One or more JavaScript commands enclosed with a `<script>` tag.

Part

XI

App

C

Objects

JavaScript is an object-oriented language, so at its heart is a pre-defined set of objects which relate to the various components of an HTML page and their relation to each other. To view or manipulate the state of an object requires the use of properties and methods, which are also covered in this appendix. If an object is also used as a property of another object, that relationship is listed following the definition. Related properties, methods, and event handlers for each object are listed following the definition.

anchors   A piece of text that can be the target of a hypertext link. This is a read-only object which is set in HTML with `<A>` tags. To determine how many anchors are included in a document, use the `length` property.

    document.anchors.length

Unless the anchor name is an integer, the value of `document.anchor[index]` will return null.

Property of `document`. See `link` OBJECT; see `anchor` METHOD.

button   An object that is a form element and must be defined within a `<form>` tag and can be used to perform an action.

Property of `form`.

See OBJECTS `reset` and `submit`; see PROPERTIES `name` and `value`; see `click` METHOD; see `onClick` EVENT HANDLER.

checkbox   A form element that the user sets to *on* or *off* by clicking and that must be defined in a `<form>` tag. Using the `checkbox` object, you can see if the box is checked and review the name and value.

Property of `form`. See `radio` OBJECT; see PROPERTIES `checked`, `defaultChecked`, `name`, `value`; see `click` METHOD; see `onClick` EVENT HANDLER.

Date   Replaces a normal date type. Although it does not have any properties, it is equipped with a wide range of methods. In its current release, `Date` does not work with dates prior to 1/1/70.

Methods for getting and setting time and date information are divided into four classes: `set`, `get`, `to`, and `parse`/`UTC`.

Except for the date, all numerical representation of date components begin with zero. This should not present a problem except with months, which are represented by zero (January) through 11 (December).

The standard date syntax is `"Thu, 11 Jan 1996 06:20:00 GMT."` US time zone abbreviations are also understood, but for universal use, specify the time zone offset. For example, `"Thu, 11 Jan 1996 06:20:00 GMT+0530"` is a place five hours and 30 minutes west of the Greenwich meridian.

See METHODS `getDate`, `getDay`, `getHours`, `getMinutes`, `getMonth`, `getSeconds`, `getTime`, `getTimezoneOffset`, `getYear`, `parse`, `setDate`, `setHours`, `setMinutes`, `setMonth`, `setSeconds`, `setTime`, `setYear`, `toGMTString`, `toLocaleString`, `toString`.

document An object created by Navigator when a page is loaded, containing information on the current document, such as title, background color, and forms. These properties are defined within `<body>` tags. It also provides methods for displaying HTML text to the user.

You can reference the anchors, forms, and links of a document by using the `anchors`, `forms`, and `links` arrays of the `document` object. These arrays contain an entry for each `anchor`, `form`, or `link` in a document.

Property of window. See frame OBJECT; see PROPERTIES `alinkColor`, `anchors`, `bgColor`, `cookie`, `fgColor`, `forms`, `lastModified`, `linkColor`, `links`, `location`, `referrer`, `title`, `vlinkColor`; see METHODS `clear`, `close`, `open`, `write`, `writeln`; see `onLoad` and `onUnload` event handlers.

elements An array of `form` elements in source order, including buttons, checkboxes, radio buttons, text and text area objects. The elements can be referred to by their index:

```
formName.elements[index]
```

Elements can also be referenced by the element name. For example, a password element called newPassword is the second form element on an HTML page. It's value is accessed in three ways:

```
formName.elements[1].value
formName.elements["newPassword"].value
formName.newPassword.value
```

Values cannot be set or changed using the read-only `elements` array.

Property of `form`. See `length` PROPERTY.

form A property of the `document` object. Each form in a document is a separate and distinct object that can be referenced using the `form` object. The `form` object is an array created as forms are defined through HTML tags. If the first `form` in a document is named `orderForm`, then it could be referenced as `document.orderForm` or `document.forms[0]`.

Property of `document`. See hidden OBJECT; see PROPERTIES `action`, `elements`, `encoding`, `forms`, `method`, `name`, `target`; see `submit` METHOD; see `onSubmit` EVENT HANDLER.

frame A window that contains HTML sub-documents that are independently, though not necessarily, scrollable. Frames can point to different URLs and be targeted by other frames—all in the same window. Each frame is a window object defined using the <frameset> tag to define the layout that makes up the page. The page is defined from a parent HTML document. All sub-documents are children of the parent.

If a frame contains definitions for SRC and NAME attributes, then the frame can be identified from a sibling by using the parent object as parent.frameName or parent.frames[index].

Property of window. See document and window OBJECTS; see PROPERTIES defaultStatus, frames, parent, self, status, top, window; see METHODS setTimeout and clearTimeout.

hidden A text object suppressed from appearing on an HTML form. Hidden objects can be used in addition to cookies to pass name/value pairs for client/server communication.

Property of form. See PROPERTIES cookie, defaultValue, name, value.

history This object is derived from the Go menu and contains URL link information for previously visited pages.

Property of document. See location OBJECT; see length PROPERTY; see METHODS back, forward, go.

link A location object. In addition to providing information about existing hypertext links, the link object can also be used to define new links.

Property of document. See anchor OBJECT; see PROPERTIES hash, host, hostname, href, length, pathname, port, protocol, search, target; see link METHOD; see onClick and onMouseOver EVENT HANDLERS.

location Contains complete URL information for the current document, while each property of location contains a different portion of the URL.

Property of document. See history OBJECT; see PROPERTIES hash, host, hostname, href, location, pathname, port, protocol, search, target.

Math Includes properties for mathematical constants and methods for functions. For example, to access the value of pi in an equation, use:

```
Math.PI
```

Standard trigonometric, logarithmic, and exponential functions are also included. All arguments in trigonometric functions use radians.

See PROPERTIES E, LN10, LN2, PI, SQRT1_2, SQRT2; see METHODS abs, acos, asin, atan, ceil, cos, exp, floor, log, max, min, pow, random, round, sin, sqrt, tan.

navigator   Contains information on the current version of Navigator used by the client.

See OBJECTS link and anchors; see PROPERTIES appName, appCodeName, appVersion, userAgent.

password   Created by HTML password text fields, and are masked when entered by the user. It must be defined with an HTML <form> tag.

Property of form. See text OBJECT; see PROPERTIES defaultValue, name, value; see METHODS focus, blur, select.

radio   Objects created within HTML <form> tags and represent radio buttons. A set of radio buttons enables the user to select one item from a list. When it is created, it takes the form of document.formName.radioName[index], where the index is a number representing each button beginning with zero.

Property of form. See OBJECTS checkbox, select; see PROPERTIES checked, defaultChecked, index, length, name, value; see click METHOD; see onClick EVENT HANDLER.

reset   Correlates with an HTML reset button, which resets all form objects to their default values. A reset object must be created within a <form> tag.

Property of form. See OBJECTS button and submit; see PROPERTIES name and value; see click METHOD; see onClick EVENT HANDLER.

select   A selection list or scrolling list on an HTML form. A selection list enables the user to choose one item from a list, while a scrolling list enables the choice of one or more items from a list.

Property of form. See radio OBJECT; see PROPERTIES length, name, options, selectedIndex; see METHODS blur and focus; see EVENT HANDLERS onBlur, onChange, onFocus.

For the options PROPERTY of select, see defaultSelected, index, selected, text, value.

string   A series of characters defined by double or single quotes. For example:

```
myDog = "Brittany Spaniel"
```

returns a string object called myDog with the value "Brittany Spaniel." Quotation marks are not a part of the string's value—they are only used to delimit the string. The object's value is manipulated using methods that return a variation on the string, for example myDog.toUpperCase() returns "BRITTANY SPANIEL". It also includes methods that return HTML versions of the string, such as bold and italics.

Part XI App C

See `text` and `text area` OBJECTS; see `length` PROPERTY; see METHODS `anchor`, `big`, `blink`, `bold`, `charAt`, `fixed`, `fontcolor`, `fontsize`, `indexOf`, `italics`, `lastIndexOf`, `link`, `small`, `strike`, `sub`, `substring`, `sup`, `toLowerCase`, `toUpperCase`.

submit Causes the form to be submitted to the program specified by the `action` property. It is created within an HTML `<form>` tag. It always loads a new page, which may be the same as the current page if an action isn't specified.

Property of `form`. See OBJECTS `button` and `reset`; see PROPERTIES `name` and `value`; see METHOD `click`; see EVENT HANDLER `onClick`.

text A one-line input field on an HTML form that accepts characters or numbers. `Text` objects can be updated by assigning new contents to its value.

Property of `form`. See OBJECTS `password`, `string`, `textarea`; see PROPERTIES `defaultValue`, `name`, `value`; see METHODS `focus`, `blur`, `select`; see EVENT HANDLERS `onBlur`, `onChange`, `onFocus`, `onSelect`.

textarea Similar to a `text` object, with the addition of multiple lines. A `textarea` object can also be updated by assigning new contents to its value.

Property of `form`. See OBJECTS `password`, `string`, `text`; see PROPERTIES `defaultValue`, `name`, `value`; see METHODS `focus`, `blur`, `select`; see EVENT HANDLERS `onBlur`, `onChange`, `onFocus`, `onSelect`.

window Created by Navigator when a page is loaded containing properties that apply to the whole window. It is the top-level object for each `document`, `location`, and `history` object. Because its existence is assumed, you do not have to reference the name of the window when referring to its objects, properties, or methods. For example, the following two lines have the same result (printing a message to the status line):

```
status("Go away from here.")
window.status("Go away from here.")
```

A new window is created using the `open` method:

```
aNewWindow = window.open("URL","Window_Name",["windowFeatures"])
```

The variable name is used to refer to the window's properties and methods. The window name is used in the target argument of a form or `anchor` tag.

See OBJECTS `document` and `frame`; see PROPERTIES `defaultStatus`, `frames`, `parent`, `self`, `status`, `top`, `window`; see METHODS `alert`, `close`, `confirm`, `open`, `prompt`, `setTimeout`, `clearTimeout`; see EVENT HANDLERS `onLoad` and `onUnload`.

Properties

Properties are used to view or set the values of objects. An object is simply a vague generality until a property is used to define the values which make it specific.

action The action property is a reflection of the action attribute in an HTML <form> tag, consisting of a destination URL for the submitted data. This value can be set or changed before or after the document has been loaded and formatted.

In this example, the action for a form called outlineForm is set to the URL contained in the variable outlineURL.

```
outlineForm.action=outlineURL
```

Property of form. See PROPERTIES encoding, method, target.

alinkColor The color of a link after the mouse button is depressed—but before it's released—and expressed as a hexadecimal RGB triplet or string literal. It cannot be changed after the HTML source is processed. Both of these examples set the color to alice blue.

```
document.alinkColor="aliceblue"
document.alinkColor="F0F8FF"
```

Property of document. See PROPERTIES bgColor, fgColor, linkColor, vlinkColor.

anchors An array of all defined anchors in the current document. If the length of an anchor array in a document is 5, then the anchors array is represented as document.anchors[0] through document.anchors[4].

Property of document. See anchor OBJECT; see PROPERTIES length and links.

appCodeName Returns a read-only string with the code name of the browser.

```
document.write("The code name of your browser is " + navigator.appCodeName)
```

For most Netscape Navigator 2.0s, this returns:

```
The code name of your browser is Mozilla
```

Property of navigator. See PROPERTIES appName, appVersion, userAgent.

appName Returns a read-only string with the name of the browser.

Property of navigator. See PROPERTIES appCodeName, appVersion, userAgent.

appVersion Returns a string with the version information of the browser in the format "releaseNumber (platform; country)." For a release of Netscape 2.0:

```
document.write(navigator.appVersion)
```

returns

```
2.0 (Win95; I)
```

Part
XI

App

C

This specifies Navigator 2.0 running on Windows 95 with an international release. The U country code specifies a US release, while an I indicates an international release.

Property of `navigator`. See PROPERTIES `appName`, `appCodeName`, `userAgent`.

bgColor   The document background color expressed as a hexadecimal RGB triplet or string literal. It can be reset at any time. Both of these examples set the background to alice blue.

```
document.bgColor = "aliceblue"
document.bgColor = "F0F8FF"
```

Property of `document`. See PROPERTIES `alinkColor`, `fgColor`, `linkColor`, `vlinkColor`.

checked   A Boolean value (`true` or `false`), indicating whether a checkbox or radio button is selected. The value is updated immediately when an item is checked. It's used in the following form:

```
formName.checkboxName.checked
formName.radioButtonName[index].checked
```

Property of `checkbox` and `radio`. See `defaultChecked` PROPERTY.

cookie   String value of a small piece of information stored by Navigator in a client-side cookies.txt file. The value stored in the `cookie` is found using substring `charAt`, `IndexOf`, and `lastIndexOf`.

For more information, see the discussion under TERMS.

Property of `document`. See `hidden` OBJECT.

defaultChecked   A Boolean value (`true` or `false`) indicating whether a checkbox or radio button is checked by default. Setting a value to `defaultChecked` can override the checked attribute of a form element. The following section of code will reset a group of radio buttons to its original state by finding and setting the default button:

```
for (var i in menuForm.choices) {
    if (menuForm.choices[i].defaultChecked) {
        menuForm.choice[i].defaultChecked = true
    }
}
```

Property of `checkbox` and `radio`. See `form` OBJECT; see `checked` PROPERTY.

defaultSelected   A Boolean value (`true` or `false`) representing the default state of an item in a form select element. Setting a value with this property can override the selected attribute of an `<option>` tag. The syntax is identical to `defaultChecked`.

Property of `options`. See PROPERTIES `index`, `selected`, `selectedIndex`.

defaultStatus The default message displayed in the status bar at the bottom of a Navigator window when nothing else is displayed. This is preempted by a priority or transient message, such as a mouseOver event with an anchor. For example:

```
window.defaultStatus = "Welcome to my home page"
```

displays the welcome message while the mouse is not over a link, or Netscape is not performing an action that it needs to notify the user about.

Property of window. See status PROPERTY.

defaultValue The initial contents of hidden, password, text, textarea, and string form elements. For password elements, it is initially set to null for security reasons, regardless of any set value.

Property of hidden, password, text, textarea. See value PROPERTY.

E The base of natural logarithms, also known as Euler's constant. The value is approximately 2.7182818285...

Property of Math. See PROPERTIES LN2, LN10, LOG2E, LOG10E, PI, SQRT1_2, SQRT2.

elements An array of objects containing form elements in HTML source order. The array index begins with zero and ends with the number of form elements -1.

Property of form. See elements OBJECT.

encoding Returns a string reflecting the Mime encoding type, which is set in the enctype attribute of an HTML <form> tag.

Property of form. See PROPERTIES action, method, target.

fgColor The color of foreground text represented as a hexadecimal RGB triplet or a string literal. This value cannot be changed after a document is processed. It can take two forms:

```
document.fgColor="aliceblue"
document.fgColor="F0F8FF"
```

Property of document. See PROPERTIES alinkColor, bgColor, linkColor, vlinkColor; see fontcolor METHODS.

forms An array of objects corresponding to named forms in HTML source order and containing an entry for each form object in a document.

Property of document. See form object; see length property.

frames An array of objects corresponding to child frame windows created using the <frameset> tag. To obtain the number of child frames in a window, use the length property.

Property of window. See frame object; see length property.

hash   Returns a string with the portion of an URL beginning with a hash mark (#), which denotes an `anchor` name fragment. It can be used to set a `hash` property, although it is safest to set the entire URL as a `href` property. An error is returned if the `hash` isn't found in the current location.

Property of `link` and `location`. See `anchor` OBJECT; see PROPERTIES `host`, `hostname`, `href`, `pathname`, `port`, `protocol`, `search` properties.

host   Returns a string formed by combining the `hostname` and `port` properties of an URL, and provides a method for changing it.

```
location.host = "www.montna.com:80"
```

Property of `link` and `location`. See PROPERTIES `hash`, `hostname`, `href`, `pathname`, `port`, `protocol`, `search`.

hostname   Returns or changes a string with the domain name or IP address of an URL.

Property of `link` and `location`. See PROPERTIES `hash`, `host`, `href`, `pathname`, `port`, `protocol`, `search`.

href   Returns a string with the entire URL. All other `location` and `link` properties are substrings of `href`, which can be changed at any time.

Property of `link` and `location`. See PROPERTIES `hash`, `host`, `hostname`, `pathname`, `port`, `protocol`, `search`.

index   Returns the index of an option in a select element with zero being the first item.

Property of `options`. See PROPERTIES `defaultSelected`, `selected`, `selectedIndex`.

lastModified   A read-only string containing the date that the current document was last changed, based on the file attributes. The string is formatted in the standard form used by JavaScript (see `Date` object). A common usage is:

```
document.write("This page last modified on " + document.lastModified)
```

Property of `document`.

length   An integer reflecting a length- or size-related property of an object.

Object	Property Measured
history	Length of the history list
string	Integer length of the string; zero for a null string
radio	Number of radio buttons

anchors, forms,	Number of elements
frames, links,	in the array
options	

Property of `anchors`, `elements`, `forms`, `frame`, `frames`, `history`, `links`, `options`, `radio`, `string`, `window`.

linkColor The hyperlink color displayed in the document, expressed as a hexadecimal RGB triplet or as a string literal. It corresponds to the `link` attribute in the HTML `<body>` tag, and cannot be changed after the document is processed.

Property of `document`. See PROPERTIES `alinkColor`, `bgColor`, `fgColor`, `vlinkColor`.

links An array representing `link` objects defined in HTML using `<a href=URL>` tags with the first `link` identified as `document.links[0]`.

See `link` object. See PROPERTIES `anchors` and `length`.

LN2 A constant representing the natural logarithm of 2 (approximately 0.693).

Property of `Math`. See PROPERTIES `E`, `LN10`, `LOG2E`, `LOG10E`, `PI`, `SQRT1_2`, `SQRT2`.

LN10 A constant representing the natural logarithm of 10 (approximately 2.302).

Property of `Math`. See PROPERTIES `E`, `LN2`, `LOG2E`, `LOG10E`, `PI`, `SQRT1_2`, `SQRT2`.

location Returns a string with the URL of the current document. This read-only property (`document.location`) is different from the location `objects` properties (`window.location.propertyName`), which can be changed.

Property of `document`. See `location` OBJECT.

LOG2E A constant representing the base 2 logarithm of `e` (approximately 1.442).

Property of `Math`. See PROPERTIES `E`, `LN2`, `LN10`, `LOG10E`, `PI`, `SQRT1_2`, `SQRT2`.

LOG10E A constant representing the base 10 logarithm of `e` (approximately .434).

Property of `Math`. See PROPERTIES `E`, `LN2`, `LN10`, `LOG2E`, `SQRT1_2`, `SQRT2`.

method Reflects the method attribute of an HTML `<form>` tag: either `<GET>` or `<POST>`. It can be set at any time. The first function returns the current value of the form object, while the second function sets the method to the contents of `newMethod`.

```
function getMethod(formObj) {
   return formObj.method
}
function setMethod(formObj,newMethod) {
   formObj.method = newMethod
}
```

Property of `form`. See PROPERTIES `action`, `encoding`, `target`.

Part
XI

App

C

name   Returns a string with the `name` attribute of the object. This is the internal name for `button`, `reset`, and `submit` objects, not the on-screen label.

For example, after opening a new window with `indexOutline = window.open("http://www.wossamatta.com/outline.html","MenuPage")` and issuing the command `document.write(indexOutline.name)`, JavaScript returns "MenuPage," which was specified as the name attribute.

Property of `button`, `checkbox`, `frame`, `password`, `radio`, `reset`, `select`, `submit`, `text`, `textarea`, `window`. See `value` PROPERTY.

options   An array of `option` objects created by a `select` form element. The first option's index is zero, the second is 1, and so on.

See `select` OBJECT.

parent   Refers to the calling document in the current frame created by a `<frameset>` tag. Using `parent` allows access to other frames created by the same `<FRAMESET>` tag. For example, two frames invoked are called "index" and "contents." The "index" frame can write to the "contents" frame using the syntax:

```
parent.contents.document.write("Kilroy was here.")
```

Property of `frame` and `window`.

pathname   Returns the path portion from an URL. Although the `pathname` can be changed at any time, it is always safer to change the entire URL at once using the `href` property.

Property of `link` and `location`. See PROPERTIES `hash`, `host`, `hostname`, `href`, `port`, `protocol`, `search`.

PI   Returns the value of pi (approximately 3.1415927). This is the ratio of the circumference of a circle to its diameter.

Property of `Math`. See PROPERTIES `E`, `LN2`, `LN10`, `LOG2E`, `LOG10E`, `SQRT1_2`, `SQRT2`.

port   Returns the port number of an URL address, which is a substring of the `host` property in `href`.

Property of `link` and `location`. See PROPERTIES `hash`, `host`, `hostname`, `href`, `pathname`, `protocol`, `search`.

protocol   Returns a string with the initial portion of the URL, up to and including the colon, which indicates the access method (`http`, `ftp`, `mailto`, etc.).

Property of `link` and `location`.

See PROPERTIES `hash`, `host`, `hostname`, `href`, `pathname`, `port`, `search`.

referrer   Returns a read-only URL of the document that called the current document. In conjunction with a CGI script, it can be used to keep track of how users are linked to a page.

```
document.write("You came here from a page at " + document.referrer)
```

Property of `document`.

search   Returns a string containing any query information appended to an URL.

Property of `link` and `location`. See PROPERTIES `hash`, `host`, `hostname`, `href`, `pathname`, `port`, `protocol`.

selected   Returns a Boolean value (`true` or `false`) indicating the current state of an option in a `select` object. The selected property can be changed at any time, and the display will immediately update to reflect the new value. The selected property is useful for `select` elements that are created using the `multiple` attribute. Using this property, you can view or change the value of any element in an `options` array without changing the value of any other element in the array.

Property of `options`. See PROPERTIES `defaultSelected`, `index`, `selectedIndex`.

selectedIndex   Returns an integer specifying the index of a selected item. The `selectedIndex` property is useful for `select` elements that are created without using the `multiple` attribute. If `selectedIndex` is evaluated when the `multiple` option is selected, the property returns the index of the first option only. Setting the property clears any other options that are selected in the element.

Property of `select`, `options`. See PROPERTIES `defaultSelected`, `index`, `selected`.

self   Refers to the current window or form, and is useful for removing ambiguity when dealing with `window` and `form` properties with the same name.

Property of `frame` and `window`. See `window` PROPERTY.

SQRT1_2   The square root of 1/2, also expressed as the inverse of the square root of 2 (approximately 0.707).

Property of `Math`. See PROPERTIES `E`, `LN2`, `LN10`, `LOG2E`, `LOG10E`, `PI`, `SQRT2`.

SQRT2   The square root of 2 (approximately 1.414).

Property of `Math`. See properties `E`, `LN2`, `LN10`, `LOG2E`, `LOG10E`, `PI`, `SQRT1_2`.

status   Specifies a priority or transient message to display in the status bar at the bottom of the window, usually triggered by a `mouseOver` event from an `anchor`. To display when the mouse pointer is placed over a link, the usage is:

```
<A anchor definition onMouseOver="window.dstatus='Your message.'; return
➥true">link</A>
```

Part

XI

App

C

Note the use of nested quotes and the required `return true` required for operation.

Property of `window`. See `defaultStatus` PROPERTY.

target   A string specifying the name of a window for responses to be posted to after a form is submitted. For a link, `target` returns a string specifying the name of the window that displays the content of a selected hypertext link.

```
homePage.target = "http://www.wossamatta.com/"
```

A literal must be used to set the `target` property. JavaScript expressions and variables are invalid entries.

Property of `form`, `link`, `location`. See PROPERTIES `action`, `encoding`, `method`.

text   Returns the value of text following the `<option>` tag in a `select` object. It can also be used to change the value of the option, with an important limitation, while the value is changed, its appearance on-screen is not.

Property of `options`.

title   Returns the read-only value set within HTML `<title>` tags. If a document doesn't include a title, the value is `null`.

Property of `document`.

top   The top-most window, called an ancestor or Web browser window, that contains `frames` or nested `framesets`.

Property of `window`.

userAgent   Header sent as part of HTTP protocol from client to server to identify the type of client. The syntax of the returned value is the same as `appVersion`.

Property of `navigator`. See PROPERTIES `appName`, `appVersion`, `appCodeName`.

value   The value of an object depends on the type of object it is applied to.

Object	Value Attribute
`button`, `reset`, `submit`	Value attribute that appears on-screen, not the button name
`checkbox`	*On* if item is selected, `off` if not
`radio`	String reflection of value
`hidden`, `text`, `textarea`	Contents of the field

| select | Reflection of option value |
| password | Return a valid default value, but an encrypted version if modified by the user |

Changing the value of a text or textarea object results in an immediate update to the screen. All other form objects are not graphically updated when changed.

Property of button, checkbox, hidden, options, password, radio, reset, submit, text, textarea.

For password, text, and textarea, see defaultValue PROPERTY.

For button, reset, and submit, see name PROPERTY.

For options, see PROPERTIES defaultSelected, selected, selectedIndex, text.

For checkbox and radio, see PROPERTIES checked and defaultChecked.

vlinkColor Returns or sets the color of visited links using hexadecimal RGB triplets or a string literal. The property cannot be set after the document has been formatted. To override the browser defaults, color settings are used with the onLoad event handler in the <BODY> tag:

```
<BODY onLoad="document.vlinkColor='aliceblue'">
```

Property of document. See PROPERTIES alinkColor, bgColor, fgColor, linkColor.

window A synonym for the current window to remove ambiguity between a window and form object of the same name. While it also applies to the current frame, it is less ambiguous to use the self property.

Property of frame and window. See self PROPERTY.

Methods

Methods are functions and procedures used to perform an operation on an object, variable, or constant. With the exception of built-in functions, methods must be used with an object:

```
object.method()
```

Even if the method does not require any arguments, the parentheses are still required.

The object which utilizes the method is listed after the definition as "Method of *object*," followed by any cross-references to other methods. Stand-alone functions that are not used with objects are indicated with an asterisk (*).

abs Returns the absolute (unsigned) value of its argument.

```
document.write(Math.abs(-10));
document.write(Math.abs(12))
```

The above examples return 10 and 12, respectively.

Method of Math.

acos Returns the arc cosine (from zero to pi radians) of its argument. The argument should be a number between -1 and 1. If the value is outside the valid range, a zero is returned.

Method of Math. See METHODS asin, atan, cos, sin, tan.

alert Displays a JavaScript Alert dialog box with an OK button and a user-defined message. Before the user can continue, they must press the OK button.

Method of window. See METHODS confirm and prompt.

anchor Used with write or writeln methods, anchor creates and displays an HTML hypertext target. The syntax is:

```
textString.anchor(anchorName)
```

where textString is what the user sees, and anchorName is equivalent to the name attribute of an HTML <anchor> tag.

Method of string. See link METHOD.

asin Returns the arc sine (between -pi/2 and pi/2 radians) of a number between -1 and 1. If the number is outside the range, a zero is returned.

Method of Math. See METHODS acos, atan, cos, sin, tan.

atan Returns the arc tangent (between -pi/2 and pi/2 radians) of a number between -1 and 1. If the number is outside the range, a zero is returned.

Method of Math. See METHODS acos, asin, cos, sin, tan.

back Recalls the previous URL from the history list. This method is the same as history.go(-1).

Method of history. See METHODS forward and go.

big Formats a string object as a big font by encasing it with HTML <big> tags. Both of the following examples result in the same output—displaying the message "Welcome to my home page" in a big font:

```
var welcomeMessage = "Welcome to my home page."
document.write(welcomeMessage.big())
```

```
<BIG> Welcome to my home page.</BIG>
```

Method of `string`. See METHODS `fontsize`, `small`.

blink Formats a `string` object as a blinking line by encasing it with HTML `<blink>` tags. Both of the following examples produce a flashing line that says "Notice:"

```
var attentionMessage = "Notice"
document.write(attentionMessage.blink())

<BLINK>Notice</BLINK>
```

Method of `string`. See METHODS `bold`, `italics`, `strike`.

blur Removes focus from the specified `form` element. For example, the following line removes focus from `feedback`:

```
feedback.blur()
```

assuming that `feedback` is defined as:

```
<input type="text" name="feedback">
```

Method of `password`, `select`, `text`, `textarea`. See METHODS `focus` and `select`.

bold Formats a `string` object in bold text by encasing it with HTML `<b>` tags.

Method of `string`. See METHODS `blink`, `italics`, `strike`.

ceil Returns the smallest integer greater than, or equal to, its argument. For example:

```
Math.ceil(1.01)
```

returns a 2.

Method of `Math`. See `floor` METHOD.

charAt Returns the character from a string at the specified index. The first character is at position zero and the last at length -1.

```
var userName = "Bobba Louie"
document.write(userName.charAt(4)
```

returns an "a."

Method of `string`. See METHODS `indexOf` and `lastIndexOf`.

clear Clears the contents of a window, regardless of how the window was filled.

Method of `document`. See METHODS `close`, `open`, `write`, `writeln`.

clearTimeout Cancels a `timeout` set with the `setTimeout` method. A timeout is set using a unique timeout ID, which must be used to clear it:

```
clearTimeout(waitTime)
```

Method of `frame` and `window`. See `setTimeout` METHOD.

click Simulates a mouse click on the calling `form` element with the effect dependent on the type of element.

Form Element	Action
`Button`, `Reset`, and `submit`	Same as clicking button.
`Radio`	Selects radio button.
`Checkbox`	Marks checkbox and sets value to *on*.

Method of `button`, `checkbox`, `radio`, `reset`, `submit`.

close For a `document` object, closes the current stream of output and forces its display. It also stops the browser winsock animation and displays "Document: Done" in the status bar.

For a `window` object, closes the current window. As with all window commands, the `window` object is assumed. For example:

```
window.close()
close()
self.close()
```

all close the current window.

Method of `document` and `window`. See METHODS `clear`, `open`, `write`, `writeln`.

confirm Displays a JavaScript confirmation dialog box with a message and buttons for OK and Cancel. Confirm returns a `true` if the user selects OK and `false` for Cancel. The following example closes and loads a new window if the user presses O.K.

```
if (confirm("Are you sure you want to enter.") {
    tourWindow = window.open("http:\\www.haunted.com\","hauntedhouse")
}
```

Method of `window`. See METHODS `alert` and `prompt`.

cos Returns the cosine of the argument. The angle's size must be expressed in radians.

Method of `Math`. See METHODS `acos`, `asin`, `atan`, `sin`, `tan`.

escape* Returns ASCII code of its argument based on the ISO Latin-1 character set in the form %xx, where xx is the ASCII code. It is not associated with any other object, but is actually part of the JavaScript language.

See `unescape` METHOD.

eval* This built-in function takes a string or numeric expression as its argument. If a string, it attempts to convert it to a numeric expression. `Eval` then evaluates the expression and returns the value.

```
var x = 10
var y = 20
document.write(eval("x + y"))
```

This method can also be used to perform JavaScript commands included as part of a string.

```
var doThis = "if (x==10) { alert("Your maximum has been reached") }
function checkMax () {
    x++;
    eval(doThis)
}
```

This can be useful when converting a date from a form (always a string) into a numerical expression or number.

exp Returns e (Euler's constant) to the power of the argument to compute a natural logarithm.

Method of Math. See METHODS log and pow.

Formats the calling string into a fixed-pitch font by encasing it in HTML <tt> tags.

Method of string.

floor Returns the integer less than, or equal to, its argument. For example:

```
Math.floor(2.99)
```

returns a 2.

Method of Math. See ceil METHOD.

focus Navigates to a specific form element and gives it focus. From that point, a value can be entered by JavaScript commands or the user can complete the entry.

Method of password, select, text, textarea. See METHODS blur and select.

fontcolor Formats the string object to a specific color expressed as a hexadecimal RGB triplet or a string literal, similar to using <font color=color>.

Method of string.

fontsize Formats the string object to a specific font size: one of the seven defined sizes using an integer through the <fontsize=size> tag. If a string is passed, then the size is changed relative to the value set in the <basefont> tag.

Method of string. See METHODS big and small.

forward Loads the next document on the URL history list. This method is the same as history.go(1).

Method of history. See methods back and go.

getDate Returns the day of the month as an integer between 1 and 31.

Method of Date.

See setDate method.

getDay Returns the day of the week as an integer from zero (Sunday) to six (Saturday). There is not a corresponding setDay command because the day is automatically computed when the date value is assigned.

Method of Date.

getHours Returns the hour of the day in 24-hour format, from zero (midnight) to 23 (11 PM).

Method of Date. See setHours METHOD.

getMinutes Returns the minutes with an integer from zero to 59.

Method of Date. See setMinutes METHOD.

getMonth Returns the month of the year as an integer between zero (January) and 11 (December).

Method of Date. See setMonth METHOD.

getSeconds Returns the seconds in an integer from zero to 59.

Method of Date. See setSeconds METHOD.

getTime Returns an integer representing the current value of the date object. The value is the number of milliseconds since midnight, January 1, 1970. This value can be used to compare the length of time between two date values.

For functions involving computation of dates, it is useful to define variables defining the minutes, hours, and days in milliseconds:

```
var dayMillisec = 1000 * 60 * 60 * 24 //1,000 milliseconds x 60 sec x 60 min
➥ x 24 hrs
var hourMillisec = 1000 * 60 * 60 //1,000 milliseconds x 60 sec x 60 min
var minuteMillisec = 1000 * 60 //1,000 milliseconds x 60 sec
```

Method of Date. See setTime METHOD.

getTimezoneOffset Returns the difference in minutes between the client machine and Greenwich mean time. This value is a constant except for daylight savings time.

Method of Date.

getYear   Returns the year of the date object minus 1900. For example, 1996 is returned as 96.

Method of Date. See setYear METHOD.

go   Loads a document specified in the history list by its URL or relative to the current position on the list. If the URL is incomplete, then the closest match is used. The search is not case-sensitive.

Method of history. See METHODS back and forward.

indexOf   Returns the location of a specific character or string, starting the search from a specific location. The first character of the string is specified as zero and the last is the string's length-1. The syntax is:

```
stringName.indexOf([character¦string], [startingPoint])
```

The startingPoint is zero by default.

Method of string. See METHODS charAt and lastIndexof.

isNaN*   For UNIX platforms only, this stand-alone function returns true if the argument is not a number. On all platforms except Windows, the parseFloat and parseInt return NaN when the argument is not a number.

See METHODS parseFloat and parseInt.

italics   Formats a string object into italics by encasing it in an HTML <I> tag.

Method of string. See METHODS blink, bold, strike.

lastIndexOf   Returns the index of a character or string in a string object by looking backwards from the end of the string or a user-specified index.

Method of string. See METHODS charAt and indexOf.

link   Creates a hypertext link to another URL by defining the <href> attribute and the text representing the link to the user.

Method of string. See anchor METHOD.

log   Returns the natural logarithm (base e) of a positive numeric expression greater than zero. An out-of-range number always returns -1.797693134862316e+308.

Method of Math. See METHODS exp and pow.

max   Returns the greater of its two arguments. For example:

```
Math.max(1,100)
```

returns 100.

Method of Math. See min METHOD.

min Returns the lesser of its two arguments.

Method of `Math`. See `max` METHOD.

open For a document, opens a stream to collect the output of `write` or `writeln` methods. If a document already exists in the target window, then the open method clears it. The stream is ended by using the `document.close()` method.

For a window, it opens a new browser window in a similar fashion to choosing File, New Web Browser from the Netscape menu. Using the URL argument, it loads a document into the new window; otherwise, the new window is blank. When used as part of an event handler, the form must include the window object; otherwise, the document is assumed. Window features are defined by a comma-separated list of options with `=1` or `=yes` to enable and `=0` or `=no` to disable. Window features include toolbar, location, directories, status, menubar, scrollbars, resizable, copyhistory, width, and height.

Method of `document` and `window`. See METHODS `clear`, `close`, `write`, `writeln`.

parse Takes a date string, such as `"Jan 11, 1996,"` and returns the number of milliseconds since midnight, Jan. 1, 1970. This function can be used to set date values based on string values. When passed a string with a time, it returns the time value.

Because `parse` is a static function of Date, it is always used as `Date.parse()` rather than as a method of a created `date` object.

Method of `Date`. See `UTC` METHOD.

parseFloat* Parses a string argument and returns a floating-point number if the first character is a plus sign, minus sign, decimal point, exponent, or a numeral. If it encounters a character other than one of the valid choices after that point, it returns the value up to that location and ignores all succeeding characters. If the first character is not a valid character, `parseFloat` returns one of two values based on the platform:

Windows   0
Non-Windows   NaN

See `isNaN` METHOD.

parseInt* Parses a string argument and returns an integer based on a specified radix or base. A radix of 10 converts the value to a decimal, while eight converts to octal, and 16 to hexadecimal. Values greater than 10 for bases above 10 are represented with letters (A through F) in place of numbers.

Floating-point values are converted to integers. The rules for evaluating the string are identical to `parseFloat`.

See `isNaN` and `parseFloat` METHODS.

pow Returns a base raised to an exponent.

Method of Math. See exp and log METHODS.

prompt Displays a prompt dialog box that accepts user input. If an initial value is not specified for inputDefault, the dialog box displays the value <undefined>.

Method of window. See alert and confirm METHODS.

random On UNIX machines only, returns a pseudo-random number between zero and 1.

Method of Math.

round Returns the value of a floating-point argument rounded to the next highest integer if the decimal portion is greater than, or equal to, .5, or the next lowest integer if less than .5.

Method of Math.

select Selects the input area of a specified form element. Used in conjunction with the focus method, JavaScript can highlight a field and position the cursor for user input.

Method of password, text, textarea. See METHODS blur and focus.

setDate Sets the day of the month.

Method of Date. See getDate METHOD.

setHours Sets the hour for the current time.

Method of Date. See getHours METHOD.

setMinutes Sets the minutes for the current time.

Method of Date. See getMinutes METHOD.

setMonth Sets the month with an integer from zero (January) to 11 (December).

Method of Date. See getMonth METHOD.

setSeconds Sets the seconds for the current time.

Method of Date. See getSeconds METHOD.

setTime Sets the value of a date object.

Method of Date. See getTime METHOD.

setTimeout Evaluates an expression after a specified amount of time, expressed in milliseconds. This is not repeated indefinitely. For example, setting a timeout to three seconds will evaluate the expression once after three seconds—not every three seconds.

Part
XI

App
C

To call `setTimeout` recursively, reset the timeout as part of the function invoked by the method. Calling the function `startclock` in the following example sets a loop in motion that clears the timeout, displays the current time, and sets the timeout to redisplay the time in one second.

```
var timerID = null;
var timerRunning = false;
function stopclock () {
  if(timerRunning) cleartimeout(timerID);
  timerRunning=false;
}
function startclock () {
  stopclock();
  showtime();
}
function showtime () {
  var now = new Date();
  ...
  document.clock.face.value =   timeValue;
  timerID = setTimeout("showtime()",1000);
  timerRunning = true;
}
```

Method of `window`. See `clearTimeout` METHOD.

setYear Sets the year in the current date using an integer representing the year minus 1900.

Method of `Date`. See `getYear` METHOD.

sin Returns the sine of an argument. The argument is the size of an angle expressed in radians, and the returned value is from -1 to 1.

Method of `Math`. See METHODS `acos`, `asin`, `atan`, `cos`, `tan`.

small Formats a `string` object into a small font using the HTML `<small>` tags.

Method of `string`. See METHODS `big` and `fontsize`.

sqrt Returns the square root of a positive numeric expression. If the argument's value is outside the range, the returned value is zero.

strike Formats a string object as strikeout text using the HTML `<strike>` tags.

Method of `string`. See METHODS `blink`, `bold`, `italics`.

sub Formats a string object into subscript text using the HTML `<sub>` tags.

Method of `string`. See `sup` METHOD.

submit Performs the same action as clicking a submit button.

Method of `form`. See `submit` OBJECT; see `onSubmit` EVENT HANDLER.

substring   Returns a subset of a string object based on two indexes. If the indexes are equal, an empty string is returned. Regardless of order, the substring is built from the smallest index to the largest.

Method of string.

sup   Formats a string object into superscript text using the HTML <sup> tags.

Method of string. See sub METHOD.

tan   Returns the tangent of an argument. The argument is the size of an angle expressed in radians.

Method of Math. See METHODS acos, asin, atan, cos, sin.

toGMTString   Converts a date object to a string using Internet Greenwich mean time (GMT) conventions. For example, if today is a date object:

```
today.toGMTString()
```

then the string "Mon, 18 Dec 1995 17:28:35 GMT" is returned. Actual formatting may vary from platform to platform. The time and date is based on the client machine.

Method of Date. See toLocaleString METHOD.

toLocaleString   Converts a date object to a string using the local conventions, such as *mm/ dd/yy hh:mm:ss*.

Method of Date. See toGMTString METHOD.

toLowerCase   Converts all characters in a string to lowercase.

Method of string. See toUpperCase METHOD.

toString   Converts a date or location object to a string.

Method of Date, location.

toUpperCase   Converts all characters in a string to uppercase.

Method of string.

See toLowerCase method.

unEscape*   Returns a character based on its ASCII value expressed as a string in the format %xxx where xxx is a decimal number between zero and 255, or 0x0 to 0xFF in hex.

See escape METHOD.

UTC   Returns the number of milliseconds for a date in Universal Coordinated Time (UTC) since midnight, January 1, 1970.

UTC is a constant, and is always used as `Date.UTC()`, not with a created date object.

Method of `Date`. See `parse` METHOD.

write   Writes one or more lines to a document window, and can include HTML tags and JavaScript expressions, including numeric, string, and logical values. The `write` method does not add a new line (`<br>` or `/n`) character to the end of the output. If called from an event handler, the current document is cleared if a new window is not created for the output.

Method of `document`. See METHODS `close`, `clear`, `open`, `writeln`.

writeln   Writes one or more lines to a document window followed by a new line character, and can include HTML tags and JavaScript expressions, including numeric, string, and logical values. If called from an event handler, the current document is cleared if a new window is not created for the output.

Method of `document`. See methods `close`, `clear`, `open`, `write`.

Event Handlers

Event handlers are where JavaScript gets its power. By looking for specific user actions, JavaScript can confirm or act on input immediately, without waiting for server introduction, since user activity within an HTML page is limited to mouse movement and input on form elements.

onBlur   Blurs occur when a `select`, `text` or `textarea` field on a form loses focus.

Event handler of `select`, `text`, `textarea`. See EVENT HANDLERS `onChange` and `onFocus`.

onChange   A change event happens when a `select`, `text` or `textarea` element on a form is modified before losing focus.

Event handler of `select`, `text`, `textarea`. See EVENT HANDLERS `onBlur`, `onFocus`.

onClick   Occurs when an object, such as a button or checkbox, is clicked.

Event handler of `button`, `checkbox`, `radio`, `link`, `reset`, `submit`.

onFocus   A form element receives focus by tabbing to or clicking the input area with the mouse. Selecting within a field results in a `select` event.

Event handler of `select`, `text`, `textarea`. See EVENT HANDLERS `onBlur` and `onChange`.

onLoad   A load event is created when Navigator finishes loading a window or all frames within a `<frameset>` tag.

Event handler of `window`. See `onUnload` EVENT HANDLER.

onMouseOver Occurs when the mouse pointer is placed over a `link` object. To function with the `status` or `defaultStatus` properties, the event handler must return `true`.

Event handler of `link`.

onSelect A select event is triggered by selecting some or all of the text in a `text` or `textarea` field.

Event handler of `text`, `textarea`.

onSubmit Triggered by the user submitting a form. The event handler must return `true` to allow the form to be submitted to the server. Conversely, it returns `false` to block the form's submission.

Event handler of `form`. See `submit` OBJECT and METHOD.

onUnload Occurs when exiting a document. For proper operation, place the `onUnload` handler in the `<body>` or `<frameset>` tags.

Event handler of `window`. See `onLoad` EVENT HANDLER.

Part
XI

App
C

Index

S

Check out Que® Books on the World Wide Web
http://www.mcp.com/que

As the biggest software release in computer history, Windows 95 continues to redefine the computer industry. Click here for the latest info on our Windows 95 books

Make computing quick and easy with these products designed exclusively for new and casual users

Examine the latest releases in word processing, spreadsheets, operating systems, and suites

The Internet, The World Wide Web, CompuServe®, America Online®, Prodigy® —it's a world of ever-changing information. Don't get left behind!

Find out about new additions to our site, new bestsellers and hot topics

In-depth information on high-end topics: find the best reference books for databases, programming, networking, and client/server technologies

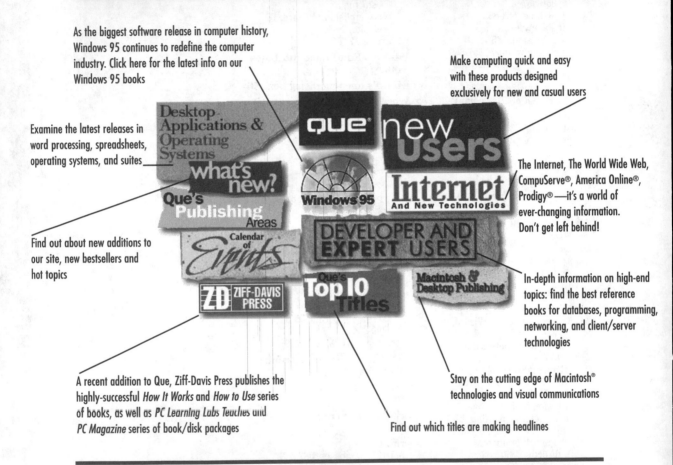

A recent addition to Que, Ziff-Davis Press publishes the highly-successful *How It Works* and *How to Use* series of books, as well as *PC Learning Labs Teaches* and *PC Magazine* series of book/disk packages

Find out which titles are making headlines

Stay on the cutting edge of Macintosh® technologies and visual communications

With 6 separate publishing groups, Que develops products for many specific market segments and areas of computer technology. Explore our Web Site and you'll find information on best-selling titles, newly published titles, upcoming products, authors, and much more.

- Stay informed on the latest industry trends and products available
- Visit our online bookstore for the latest information and editions
- Download software from Que's library of the best shareware and freeware

Complete and Return this Card
for a *FREE* Computer Book Catalog

Thank you for purchasing this book! You have purchased a superior computer book written expressly for your needs. To continue to provide the kind of up-to-date, pertinent coverage you've come to expect from us, we need to hear from you. Please take a minute to complete and return this self-addressed, postage-paid form. In return, we'll send you a free catalog of all our computer books on topics ranging from word processing to programming and the internet.

Mr. ☐   Mrs. ☐   Ms. ☐   Dr. ☐

Name (first) ☐☐☐☐☐☐☐☐☐☐☐   (M.I.) ☐   (last) ☐☐☐☐☐☐☐☐☐☐☐☐☐☐☐☐☐

Address ☐☐☐☐☐☐☐☐☐☐☐☐☐☐☐☐☐☐☐☐☐☐☐☐☐☐☐☐☐☐☐☐☐

City ☐☐☐☐☐☐☐☐☐☐☐☐☐☐☐☐☐   State ☐☐   Zip ☐☐☐☐☐   ☐☐☐☐

Phone ☐☐☐   ☐☐☐   ☐☐☐☐   Fax ☐☐☐   ☐☐☐   ☐☐☐☐

Company Name ☐☐☐☐☐☐☐☐☐☐☐☐☐☐☐☐☐☐☐☐☐☐☐☐☐☐☐☐

E-mail address ☐☐☐☐☐☐☐☐☐☐☐☐☐☐☐☐☐☐☐☐☐☐☐☐☐☐☐☐

1. Please check at least (3) influencing factors for purchasing this book.

Front or back cover information on book ☐
Special approach to the content ☐
Completeness of content ☐
Author's reputation ☐
Publisher's reputation ☐
Book cover design or layout ☐
Index or table of contents of book ☐
Price of book ☐
Special effects, graphics, illustrations ☐
Other (Please specify): _____ ☐

2. How did you first learn about this book?

Saw in Macmillan Computer Publishing catalog ☐
Recommended by store personnel ☐
Saw the book on bookshelf at store ☐
Recommended by a friend ☐
Received advertisement in the mail ☐
Saw an advertisement in: _____ ☐
Read book review in: _____ ☐
Other (Please specify): _____ ☐

3. How many computer books have you purchased in the last six months?

This book only ☐   3 to 5 books ☐
2 books ☐   More than 5 ☐

4. Where did you purchase this book?

Bookstore ☐
Computer Store ☐
Consumer Electronics Store ☐
Department Store ☐
Office Club ☐
Warehouse Club ☐
Mail Order ☐
Direct from Publisher ☐
Internet site ☐
Other (Please specify): _____ ☐

5. How long have you been using a computer?

☐ Less than 6 months   ☐ 6 months to a year
☐ 1 to 3 years   ☐ More than 3 years

6. What is your level of experience with personal computers and with the subject of this book?

	With PCs	With subject of book
New	☐	☐
Casual	☐	☐
Accomplished	☐	☐
Expert	☐	☐

Source Code ISBN: 0-7897-1036-6

7. Which of the following best describes your job title?

Administrative Assistant .... ☐
Coordinator .... ☐
Manager/Supervisor .... ☐
Director .... ☐
Vice President .... ☐
President/CEO/COO .... ☐
Lawyer/Doctor/Medical Professional .... ☐
Teacher/Educator/Trainer .... ☐
Engineer/Technician .... ☐
Consultant .... ☐
Not employed/Student/Retired .... ☐
Other (Please specify): _____ ☐

8. Which of the following best describes the area of the company your job title falls under?

Accounting .... ☐
Engineering .... ☐
Manufacturing .... ☐
Operations .... ☐
Marketing .... ☐
Sales .... ☐
Other (Please specify): _____ ☐

9. What is your age?

Under 20 .... ☐
21-29 .... ☐
30-39 .... ☐
40-49 .... ☐
50-59 .... ☐
60-over .... ☐

10. Are you:

Male .... ☐
Female .... ☐

11. Which computer publications do you read regularly? (Please list)

_____
_____
_____
_____
_____
_____
_____
_____
_____

Comments: _____
_____
_____

Fold here and scotch-tape to mail.

WinNET
COMMUNICATIONS, INC.

Instant FrontPage Server!

Special Offer available only on the enclosed CD-ROM — run D:\WINNET\SETUP.EXE to get started

Host your FrontPage World Wide Web site on WinNET for only $29.95 a month. You'll get 100 Mb of space on your own remote World Wide Web server with the Microsoft® FrontPage® extensions for only $29.95 a month. There are no setup charges and no hidden fees. You'll be able to use FrontPage on a live site within minutes. This is a risk-free offer and your satisfaction is guaranteed.*

Here's what you get for only $29.95 a month:

➤ Internet access through one of America's leading ISP's – WinNET Communications

➤ A FrontPage enabled World Wide Web site

➤ An FTP site

➤ 100 Mb of live storage space for your sites

➤ Your own unique World Wide Web address

➤ Internet Email and USENET News access

➤ and much much more.

Visit our web site at www.win.net/que.html for more details of this fantastic offer!

Satisfaction Guarantee – If you are not completely satisfied with WinNET's Internet service for any reason you can cancel your account within the first 30 days and we will completely refund 100% of your money without exception.

There's absolutely no risk and nothing to lose!

NOTE: This special offer is valid until 1/1/98, and is subject to change at that time.

http://www.win.net
info@win.net

Before using any of the software on this disc, you need to install the software you plan to use. If you have problems with *Special Edition Using Microsoft FrontPage 97*, please contact Macmillan Technical Support at (317) 581-3833. We can be reached by e-mail at **support@mcp.com** or by CompuServe at GO QUEBOOKS.

Read this Before Opening Software